Autobiographical Writings on Mexico

An Annotated Bibliography of Primary Sources

RICHARD D. WOODS

McFarland & Company, Inc., Publishers
Jefferson, North Carolina, and London

Library of Congress Cataloguing-in-Publication Data

Woods, Richard Donovan.
Autobiographical writings on Mexico : an annotated bibliography
of primary sources / Richard D. Woods.
p.   cm.
Includes bibliographical references and indexes.

ISBN 0-7864-2245-9 (softcover : 50# alkaline paper)

1. Autobiographies — Mexico — Bibliography.
2. Mexico — Biography — Bibliography.   I. Title.
Z5305.M6W655   2005
[CT553]   016.92072 — dc22   2005014054

British Library cataloguing data are available

Cover photograph ©2005 Clipart.com

Manufactured in the United States of America

*McFarland & Company, Inc., Publishers
Box 611, Jefferson, North Carolina 28640
www.mcfarlandpub.com*

Again for Mary Soderberg

Acknowledgments

In fifteen years of research on this bibliography, I have incurred many favors.

The dispersed nature of Mexican autobiography meant reliance on a variety of libraries. First, of course, is the Elizabeth Huth Coates Library at Trinity University. Maria McWilliams and her co-workers, Amalia Garza and Erlinda Barrientos, located titles in all parts of the English-speaking world and also in Mexico. Another major source was the University of Texas at Austin's Nettie Lee Benson Latin American Collection with its bonanza of books on Mexico and a staff to match its resources. Third, Laurie Gruenbeck shared with me her knowledge of food writers through personal advice and her unique collection now housed in the John Peace Library, the University of Texas at San Antonio.

The generosity of the National Endowment for the Humanities gave me use of Latin American collections outside of Texas. A grant from the Texas Committee for the Humanities under Dr. Robert O'Connor coincided with my research needs at that moment. The Institute of Latin American Studies of the University of Texas at Austin allowed a summer at the Benson Collection with a Mellon Grant. My own institution, Trinity University, provided both sabbaticals and stipends. Twice the Department of Modern Languages and Literatures funded my attendance at the Guadalajara Book Fair, a mecca for recent Mexican autobiography.

My final thanks go to Mary, who not only endured the inconvenience of my absences but also played an active role in proofing the manuscript. Lynn Foster, Babette Guajardo, and Nelda Cortés, support staff for the Department of Modern Languages and Literatures, availed themselves for any technical crisis. And I give special thanks to Information Technology Services for implementing computer format.

I thank individuals and institutions for my years of fun with a delightful topic.

Table of Contents

Introduction

The autobiographies enumerated here are important. Primary sources generated by witnesses to an event or time period, these are useful documents in almost any field of study relating to Mexico in the humanities, the social sciences, and, to some extent, the sciences. Although the testimonies may be inaccurate, biased, self-serving, or susceptible to contradiction, they provide multiple perspectives on the nineteenth century, the Mexican Revolution, the 1930s, Tlateloco, Vera Cruz, and a multitude of other topics. At the very least, they are portraits of individuals, whether ordinary or illustrious.

Taken together, these works tell us what Mexicans opt to include in their life stories, and, just as significantly, what they opt to omit. Mexican autobiographies and the forms they take may be an overlooked key in the analysis of national character. The dominance of the memoir, almost 70 percent of the total number of works listed here, leads one to speculate how the Mexicans perceive life. The constant tendency to present life at its crescent, a characteristic of the memoir, as opposed to the painful recall of childhood and growing up, a

characteristic of autobiography proper, is a study in itself.

In 1988, Greenwood Press published my *Mexican Autobiography: An Annotated Bibliography*. A modest effort with more than 300 annotated entries, it was nevertheless the first book-length treatment of the subject in bibliography for a Spanish-speaking country. This new edition has more than 1,900 entries and owes its size to various factors. For instance, the Internet allows much more rapid and sophisticated searching of databases; scholars, softening the boundaries of autobiography, now include examples that once belonged to other genres; and Mexicans themselves have written many autobiographies since 1988 (for evidence, see Appendix A). Ultimately, too, the contribution to autobiography by foreigners living in Mexico was too great to be excluded. British and Americans make up the largest component of these outsiders, but almost every European nation is represented in the Mexican-based autobiographies.

This bibliography uses *autobiography* in a broad sense, referring equally to auto-biography proper; memoirs; oral autobiographies; interviews; autobiographical novels; autobiographical essays; collections of letters; diaries or journals; and hybrid forms that incorporate elements of two or more genres. In this bibliography, each work by a native-born Mexican is classified among these types, which may be defined as follows.

Autobiography proper refers to an effort by the subject to present his or her entire life, usually from the perspective of mature age. Rather than focusing on one triumphant moment—a characteristic of the memoir—autobiography proper includes all of life's stages: childhood, adolescence, middle age, maturity, and old age. The key term in this difficult form is *entire*. Relatively few entries merit the label of autobiography proper. Yet quality makes up for quantity as some of Mexico's best writers exercise this form in expressing their lives. If a work is multi-volume, the volume covering the early years is often the best of the series. Three authors display this characteristic: José Vasconcelos in *Ulises criollo* (1936), Jaime Torres Bodet in *Tiempo de arena* (1955), and Nemesio García Naranjo in *Panoramas de la infancia* (1963?).

Memoirs record a fragment of years from a life. Usually they will be the author's significant years as a participant in an historical event or proximity to a celebrity; frequently, Mexican memoirs represent a justification for the author's actions and a refutation of his or her enemies. They lack both the formality and completeness of autobiography proper. Most of all, the memoir has characteristics that harmonize with the Mexican personality. As a type of autobiography, the memoir is ego-satisfying in that it allows the subject "to set the record straight" or even strive for immortality. At the same time, this form, with its focus on external circumstances, respects a national taboo against exposing one's family to public scrutiny. A superb example is *Memorias de Victoriano Salado Alvarez*

(1946), in which the author not only sketches leading personalities of the Porfiriato but also cogently outlines the intellectual formation of the upper classes during the dictatorship. The epoch is manifest as much as the author, who tells us little of family or personal life.

An interest in ordinary lives, probably the first domain of historians and anthropologists, has generated a type of autobiography unique to the twentieth and twenty-first centuries. Called in the present work *oral autobiography*, it could just as easily be labeled *as-told-to autobiography* or even *case history* or *life story*. It is the collaborative effort of author and subject, resulting in a document that records the life of one individual as prompted and edited by another. It is an obvious avenue for an unlettered but intelligent subject from a preliterate culture whose life merits recording, or for celebrities too busy to write their own autobiographies, or just for ordinary individuals amenable to the recording of their lives.

And who are the subjects? As can be guessed, the disinherited can find their voice in this often abused form. Consequently, peasants, women, Indians, juvenile delinquents, domestic servants, revolutionaries, and Cristeros present their lives to a broader public, but always through an amanuensis. Martín Luis Guzman's *Las memorias de Pancho Villa* (1936) is an early oral autobiography that has become a classic. Yet at the other extreme, the celebrity just as often exploits this form. Painters, writers, journalists, and singers lend themselves and their lives to oral autobiography. Diego Rivera has done so twice; painter colleagues Juan O'Gorman and David Alfaro Siqueiros contented themselves with one attempt. Other stars comprise this constellation of oral autobiographies: Julián Carrillo, Pedro Infante, Lydia Mendoza, El Indio Fernández, Pedro Vargas, and Amparo Montes. Probably no other subgenre has enriched Mexican autobiography as much as the oral exchange. Its chronological contours suggest that the cultivation of this species predominates in the last quarter of the twentieth century. Although the genre has richly contributed to Mexican autobiography, its practitioners sometimes present their subject without attention to methodology. The best manual for this form is Calixta Guiteras Holmes's *Los peligros del alma* (1972). The author pays attention to the entire process of achieving oral autobiography from the selection of a subject to the promptings of information and to its final arrangement in book form. She alerts the reader to the pitfalls in a hazardous and contradictory undertaking: the composing of an autobiography not of the self but of the other.

Autobiographies result from *interviews*. Journalists who engage in dialogue with celebrities and mix biography and autobiography create this type of document. In comparison with oral autobiography (its closest kin), the interview has an aura of snobbishness. The little known appear here rarely, if at all. These hybrids stray from the purer form, the case history, by the obvious presence of the interviewers, who clearly direct both subject and reader by inserting their questions. In giving context to these questions, the inquirer is forced to resort to some of the techniques of biography. The interview, like the oral autobiography, has enjoyed its popularity mainly since 1975. However, pioneers in this form are scholars James Wilkie and Edna Monzón de Wilkie, who in the 1960s began interviewing prominent politicians. In 1969, they published their first volume of interviews. Since that early date, they have three additional volumes (1995, 2001, 2002) in which they incorporate the 1969 interviews plus thirteen more. Another volume came out in 2004, and, moreover, other interviews await publication. Without the Wilkies, no autobiographies would be ex-

tant for Luis Chávez Orozco, Manuel Gómez Morín, Germán List Arzubide, Vicente Lombardo Toledano, and Miguel Palomar y Vizcarra.

The *novel* also has influenced Mexican autobiography. Mexicans themselves have never recognized life writing. Furthermore, critics cavalierly categorized these under the label *novel of the Mexican Revolution*. This misclassification, for whatever reason, removed from the field of Mexican autobiography some of its most stunning successes. Yet a small group of participants in autobiography admit to the influence of the novel in labeling their life writings *autobiographical novels* or novelized autobiographies. It is as though they anticipated later critics who claim that all autobiography is fiction or that the individual must resort to the techniques of fiction in order to create the self. Two of the most famous of this group are Rosario Castellanos's *Balún Canán* (1957) and the much earlier *Tomochic* (1893) by Heriberto Frías.

Autobiographical essays, few in number, have their genesis in a publishing house that commissions established younger writers to cover their lives in a sixty-page essay. The result is self-portrayal in language sufficiently sophisticated to call these authors writers. Had professionals other than writers composed these examples, their success, especially in the realm of style, would have been limited. The few titles, all originating in the second half of the twentieth century, prove this genre to be the domain of the professional writer.

Collections of letters naturally comprise part of autobiography for Mexico as for any other Western culture. This form, because of its spontaneity and lack of overall program, almost belongs to the field of inadvertent autobiography. It is unlikely that the writer had a broader public in mind beyond the correspondent. In this sense the *letter* relates to the diary or the journal because of limited perspective. This much-cultivated genre, so abundant in the English-speaking world, is a relative newcomer to Mexico. Almost all of the collections noted in this bibliography have a publication date of the last quarter of the twentieth century. Mexico is blessed with the presence of don Alfonso Reyes, author of over twenty collections of letters and the doyen of Spanish American literature. Yet two other cultivators merit notice. Marte R. Gómez's two-volume *Vida política contemporánea* (1978) verifies the vast cultural life of its author. It also proves that an office holder can express himself beyond the mere formulaic. So far the richest collection of letters ever composed by a Mexican woman is Rosario Castellanos's *Cartas a Ricardo* (1994). Mapping the poet's wanderings as a student and professor, these letters to her husband reveal much of their author.

A close kin of the letter is the *diary or journal*. Like the letter, these two do not attempt to relate a full life or tell a premeditated life story; they merely record a day-by-day account. English speakers may say either "diary" or "journal." The former is an accumulation of data taken on successive days; the latter is the same but with an added level that allows emotion to intervene. In Spanish, however, there is only one word: *diario*. Consequently, because of lack of differentiation, the two words are synonymous here. Not many examples exist within the corpus of Mexican autobiography. Lázaro Cárdenas's *Apuntes* (1974–1975) hints at the politician who shares his daily routine but not the personal self. A delightful diary is *Viajando con Vasconcelos* (1938) by Alfonso Taracena, a sort of Mexican Boswell.

Finally, one last category includes materials too recalcitrant to fit into any of the above classifications. The best word for these amorphous creations is *hybrid*, a catchall phrase used when autobiography shares space with other genres and formats. For example, Felipe Angeles's *Documentos rel-* *ativos al general Felipe Angeles* (1982) is self-explanatory about the presentation of Pancho Villa's general.

In the search for appropriate items for this bibliography, I was attentive to the above definitions and to various other criteria. The author or at least the subject had to be a native-born Mexican or someone who arrived in Mexico very young, such as the children of Spanish exiles. These entries, 74 percent of the text, are privileged with the most complete data: full bibliographical information, life years of author, genre, chronological period covered, translations, and an annotation.

To another rather large body of entries, approximately 26 percent of the total, I gave more casual treatment. These life writings are the works of foreigners. I incorporated them here with author, title, date of publication, and a summary of their contents. They do not include life dates of author, type of genre, and period covered. It would be tempting and even logical to exclude foreigners from this bibliography. However, such an omission would fail to call attention to Fanny Calderón de la Barca's *Life in Mexico* (1843) as well as Charles Flandrau's *Viva Mexico!* (1908) for their autobiographical content and their outsiders' view of this country. Also I note such celebrities as John Steinbeck, Graham Greene, Lawrence Ferlinghetti, Katherine Anne Porter, Tina Modotti, and Edward Weston.

Geographically, most of the autobiographies come from Mexico as determined by the boundaries set by the Treaty of Guadalupe Hidalgo in 1848. However, a period rich in autobiography, at least for foreigners, was the Mexican-American War. Many works that incorporate the years 1846–1847 are annotated here. This allowed for the inclusion of the life writing of transitional Mexicans, the Tejanos and Californianos, i.e., those Mexicans inhabiting territory annexed to the U.S. by this treaty.

Yet I also placed two other types of writers among the foreigners: the Mexican who leaves his country to live in the U.S. either as an immigrant or as a less permanent type of resident, and the Mexican-American born in the United States but with very tangible ties to the mother country. José A. Cárdenas for his *My Spanish Speaking Left Foot* (1997) and Ramón Ruiz for his *Memories of a Hyphenated Man* (2003) find place in this bibliography.

At the end of the book, Appendix A lists all the works chronologically. Seeing the works grouped by year of publication allows the reader to resituate the authors in a different context.

A few generalizations about the works may be of interest. First, unsurprisingly, more men write autobiographies than women, who contribute one of every six of the entries. Time slowly rectifies this deficiency. Worth restating is the predominance of the memoir over other autobiographical forms. Few life writers come from the colonial period; the nineteenth century, with its Mexican-American War and the French Intervention, was not a prolific period for the genre; the twentieth century, especially after 1950, saw an increase in the presence of autobiography, with each decade incrementally greater in its number of examples. In quality, however, the years 1928 to 1940, which saw the publication of the Vasconcelos suite, are so far unequaled for quality of life writing. Politics dominates as the major single theme in over 300 years of autobiography.

Other less important characteristics describe the history of this genre in Mexico. Protestants, never numbering more than 5 percent of the Mexican population, need better representation, at least through natives. Missionaries from the U.S. do most of the life writing. But the natives they Christianize and often educate rarely respond with autobiography. The Mexican-American War generated an entire bibliography of writings of American soldiers in this controversial engagement. In contrast, few Mexican participants penned memoirs about these difficult times. Guillermo Prieto's *Mi guerra del 47* proves the exception.

Success in business is as notable in Mexico as in other countries. Yet Mexican entrepreneurs contribute little to autobiography. Mexico is not a leader in science, a fact reflected by the absence of autobiographies by scientists. Labor finds little space here. Although peons, railway workers, and household domestics occasionally find their way into print, the whole gamut of Mexican labor lacks representation in life writing. Seamstresses have as yet to tell their stories in autobiography. Nor has a garment maker even collaborated with an enterprising anthropologist or feminist to create an oral autobiography. Thus unnoticed are the accomplishments of Evangelina Corona, seamstress and for fifteen years the secretary general of the Nineteenth of September National Garment Workers Union, born from the 1985 earthquake that highlighted the plight of the seamstresses.

With a twenty-year work record on Mexican autobiography, I would be delinquent not to mention what I consider the outstanding examples and their themes within this emerging genre. Two criteria, content and readability, directed my selection of the fifty items listed in Appendix B. Their listing alerts the reader to the best Mexico has to offer in both Spanish and English.

The following entries prove that autobiography, native and foreign, is of sufficient number for a bibliography useful in many fields. Autobiographical writing, though not yet of the stature of the novel, the short story, the drama or poetry, merits its own forum.

Format of the Entries

I accord special treatment to native-born Mexicans, who contribute approximately 1,389 of the 1,932 autobiographies listed in this book. The format of an entry for a work by a native-born Mexican is shown in the following example:

> Rosales Alcaraz, José. (1928–) *La huella de mis pasos.* COL: Archivo Histórico del Municipio de Colima, 2000. 56pp. Memoirs. Period covered: 1900–1987.
>
> Honest and uncomplicated life retold with short chapters and direct syntax. He introduces us to four grandparents, parents, and then himself in setting where he spent most of his life, the Coquitmatlán-Colima area of Nayarit. Appraisals, generally more favorable to women than men, note of womanizers in family. Preparation for teaching, rural schools, and retirement after thirty-seven years occupy much of memoirs. Earthquakes and Cristero rebellion interrupt tranquil and successful life.

This example contains the following information:

Basic bibliographical data: author, title, place of publication, publisher, date of publication, and number of pages.

Genre: In very few words I attempt to note the type of autobiographical scaffolding employed by the author: *autobiography proper, memoirs, oral autobiographies, interviews, autobiographical novels, autobiographical essays, collections of letters, diaries* or *journals,* and *hybrid.* (See Introduction for an explanation of these terms.)

Author's dates: Whenever possible, I give the complete life dates of each native-born author. If the life dates cannot be determined, the entry notes their absence as follows: (Dates?)

Narrative dates: In each case I make an effort to note the years that provide the chronological structure for the subject's narrative. This permits the retrieval of material without a specific time focus.

Translation into English: If an English translation of the Spanish is extant, I note it in the entry.

Annotation: Comments that enable the user to judge the potential value of the contents for his or her own purposes. These summaries are intended to alert the user to the cultural and informational potential of the work.

The next example shows a standard

entry for a foreign author. Charles Macomb Flandrau, an American, has written an autobiographical book incorporating Mexico. Data are limited to author, title, publisher, year of publication, and pagination.

Flandrau, Charles Macomb. *Viva Mexico!* NY: Appleton, 1908. 293pp.

Harvard-educated Charles Flandrau travels in Porfirian Mexico and recounts impressions. Unlike contemporary travelers, has persistent sense of humor and pays no homage to Diaz. Author describes his coffee plantation, mixes with Mexicans, and tempers negative remarks with comparisons to U.S. He berates ignorance of Gringos. Each nationality thinks it sets standard for honesty. Supports solitude but derides thieves' appeal to honor. What other author has mastered baroque course of Mexican conversation? Classic reissued 21 times since 1908 and in Spanish in 1994.

The Bibliography

1. Abarca Cancino, Marianela (Dates?). *Anécdotas en la escuela.* La Paz, BC: Imprenta Juárez, 1996. 82pp. Memoirs. Period Covered: 1969–1995.

Working twenty-six years in la Escuela Normal Urbana and also another school in La Paz, Baja, author wrote anecdotes relevant to period. Brief stories suggest both career and personality of dedicated teacher.

2. Abascal, Salvador (1905–?). Entrevista en James W. Wilke y Edna Monzón Wilke's *Frente a la Revolución mexicana: 17 protagonistas de la etapa constructiva v.3.* México: Universidad Autónoma Metropolitana, 2002. Pp.5–132. Interview. Period Covered: 1910–1973.

Document reveals more of Abascal than own autobiography. The Wilkes elicit major facets of the fanatical Catholic: childhood and religiosity of father; persecution under Calles; founding of *Sinarquismo* in 1937 with colony in Baja California in 1943 and Abascal as head of movement in 1946. Advocates Catholic household with mother at home versus career. Echoes Ramiro de Maeztu and José Vasconcelos in affirming Catholic and Hispanic values. Interviewed in 1964 and 1973. In latter, talks of Cuernavaca, Sergio Méndez, and Iván Illich.

3. Abascal, Salvador (1905?–?). *Mis recuerdos, sinarquismo y Colonia María Auxiliadora* (1935–1944). México: Tradición, 1980. 791pp. Memoirs. Period Covered: 1905–1972.

Abascal rose through ranks to become head of UNS (Unión Nacional del Sinarquismo) in 1940. For him, Revolution has malignant influence on Catholic Church. About 1940, he and followers set up María Auxiliadora, *Sinarquista* colony in Baja that failed. Lengthy memoirs detail movement in various parts of Mexico. Text has structural weaknesses common to works of many politicians, i.e., insertion of documents and quotes that inhibit momentum of story. Wilkies' interview, see preceding entry, essences Abascal more efficiently.

4. Abert, J.W., John R. Galvin. *Western America in 1846–1847.* San Francisco: Howell Books, 1966. 116pp.

West Point graduate in 1846 reported for duty with "Army of the West" and headed for Mexico's New Mexico and California. Not in combat, he recorded geography, Indians and Mexicans. "And surely it has value as a revelation of character … resolute, courageous, conscientious, resourceful…"(p.1). He mapped New Mexico.

5. Abreu Gómez, Ermilo (1894–1971). *Andanzas y extravíos: memorias.* México: Ediciones Botas, 1965. 169pp. Memoirs. Period Covered: 1947?

1

In third volume of memoirs (*La del alba sería... y Duelos y quebrantos*), Abreu Gómez travels. Contacts as professor or some official capacity limited to the U.S., Central America, Caribbean, Southern Cone, and Andean countries. Travel and autobiography combine when author reveals self through leadership positions.

6. Abreu Gómez, Ermilo (1894–1971). *Duelos y quebrantos.* México: Ediciones Botas, 1959. 162pp. Memoirs. Period Covered: 1919?–1937?

Yucatecan novelist and journalist episodically recounts activities and personalities: other authors, self-instruction, journalism, and theater. Man of books, libraries, archives, research, and intellectuals, Abreu Gómez describes Ramón del Valle Inclán and Artemio de Valle Arizpe among others.

7. Abreu Gómez, Ermilo (1894–1971). *La del alba sería....* México: Ediciones Botas, 1954. 263pp. Autobiography Proper. Period Covered: 1894–1920?

Recounts childhood focusing on educational system, family, and turn of century ambience that nurtured him in diverse geographical locations such as Mérida, Campeche, and Puebla. Describes love of writing.

8. Acevedo Escobedo, Antonio (1909–1985). *Los días de Aguascalientes.* México: Editorial Stylo, 1952. 89pp. Memoirs. Period Covered: 1922–1951.

Fragmented memories of idealized childhood in province. Sensitive recorder of rural atmosphere, he alternates chapters from environment to narrator. Former, almost Azorine in mood; latter, active adolescent eager for book learning.

9. Acevedo y de La Llata, Concepción (1891–1979). *Obregón: memorias inéditas de la Madre Conchita.* México: Libro-Mex, 1957. 230pp. Memoirs. Period Covered: 1914–1931.

Confessions of nun accused of complicity with Luis de León Toral in assassination of president-elect Alvaro Obregón. Imprisoned in las Islas Marías, former abbess sensitively records surroundings and reflects on condition as ex-cloistered nun. Proclaiming

innocence in death of Obregón, la Madre Conchita far better stylist than many of her male contemporaries.

10. Acevedo y de la Llata, Concepción (1891–1979). *Yo, la madre Conchita.* México: Oceáno, 1985. 139pp. Memoirs. Period Covered: 1926–1940.

Nun implicated in assassination of President Alvaro Obregón emotionally recounts tempestuous years of life: persecution of church in 1926, meeting with Luis Toral and his trial and death, imprisonment in las Islas Marías, and marriage.

11. Aceves Montijo, Aurelio (1910–?). *Rostro vivo del pasado: Mexicali-Calexico, 70 años de vida.* Mexicali: F. Lizárraga Ochoa, 1990. 143pp. Oral Autobiography. Period Covered: 1911–1930.

Lizárraga Ochoa collected forty-seven anecdotes from Aceves Montijo, who lived on Mexicali-Caléxico border and knew incidents and personalities: bootleggers, politicians, actors, and artists.

12. Acosta, Adalberto Joel (1909–?). *Chicanos Can Make It.* New York: Vantage, 1971. 340pp. Autobiography Proper. Period Covered: 1914–1960?

Problems with Villa force Acosta to emigrate from Durango to U.S. and spend youth in New Mexico and Arizona and adult years in California. Immigrant success story: minimal conflict with Anglo environment, exemplary father, foundry work and prosperity, and college-educated wife and children. Acosta laments some habits of Mexicans and advocates hard work and education for success.

13. Acosta, Helia d' (1906 Birth of Indiana Nájera)(Dates? of Concha Villarreal). *Indiana y Concha: dos brillantes periodistas, dos trágicos destinos.* México: Editorial Regina de los Angeles, 1979. 52pp. Memoirs. Period Covered: 1930–1956?

Journalist Acosta interacted with Indiana Nájera and Concha de Villarreal, both victims of patriarchal system in personal lives and careers. Indirectly Acosta hints at own professional life and that of all women journalists in Mexico.

14. Acosta, Oscar Zeta (1935–). *The Autobiography of a Brown Buffalo*. San Francisco: Straight Arrow Books, 1972. 199pp.

Writing in Kerouac style of Beat Generation, lawyer Acosta attempts to find self in either spatial or psychological journey. Moves through California and Southwest and into Mexico searching for roots. Mexican-born parents suggest strong ties to that country. Yet end is contradictory: in Mexico he is told to learn his father's language; at immigration he is questioned because he looks too Mexican.

15. Adalpe, Eliseo Castro (1939–). "Entrevista con Eliseo Castro Adalpe." Waco, TX: Institute for Oral History, Baylor, 1979. 23pp. Memoirs. Period Covered: 1939–1979.

Leobardo Estrada interviewed various Mexican-American Baptists in late 1970s. From Crystal City, Texas, Adalpe with ties to Mexico from where parents emigrated in 1926. Early life, history of Baptists in Crystal City, baptism, and call to ministry. Former president of Mexican Baptists Convention of Texas, Adalpe laments new generation of pastors unable to function in Spanish.

16. Adams, Alice. *Mexico: Some Travels and Some Travelers There*. New York: Prentice Hall, 1990. 216pp.

Sojourns in Zihuateanejo, Baja, San Miguel de Allende, Oaxaca, Cuernavaca, Mérida, Guadalajara, and Mexico City. Differs from standard guidebook in that she returns year after year to same place. Another distinction is concentration on self rather than on environment, e.g., description of hotel room not meant for potential tourist but rather setting conducive to writing. Never alone, she finds other Gringos who sympathize with her interests. Experience with Mexico makes her neutral in comments, often negative, and rarely laudatory. Natives not colorful, but skulking and conniving. Autobiography distinguishes *Mexico* from other travel books.

17. Agueda Sánchez, Jorge (1922–). *Generación 40*. México: Impresores Michoacana, 1972–1975. 257pp. Memoirs. Period Covered: 1940–1945.

Neither autobiography nor history of generation nor novel but "a mosaic formed by memory" confides author (p.7). From Michoacán, recalls experiences of his generation in university in downtown Mexico City. Noting courses and professors, he feels impingement of WWII on his generation.

18. Aguila, Olga Eugenia (1952–). *Por ti viviré*. Edición Original, 2002. 227pp. Memoirs. Period Covered: 1951–2002.

First person narration by mother of son with cystic fibrosis, disease that attacks lungs. Narrative of detection and treatment both in Mexico and United States. Happy ending with final chapter of victim receiving a successful organ transplant in California.

19. Aguilar, Enrique (1900–1993 Dates of Elías Nandino). *Una vida no/velada*. México: Editorial Grijalbo, 1986. 172pp. Oral Autobiography. Period Covered: 1900–1986.

Interviews with Aguilar plus letters and archives of Nandino. From Cocola, Jalisco, he attended preparatory in Guadalajara and finished medical school in Mexico City. Surgeon and poet became friends of *los Contemporáneos*, two profiled: Xavier Villaurrutia and Salvador Novo. Combines medicine, poetry, and description of practice among prisoners. Honest and explicit about homosexuality.

20. Aguilar Belden de Garza, Sara (1914–). *Una cuidad y dos familias*. México: Editorial Jus, 1970. 411pp. Memoirs. Period Covered: 1909–1917?

Member of Monterrey aristocracy and relative of Maderos reminisces about family's role in Revolution. Imagined dialogs with parents and grandparents evoke happiness of Porfiriato. More value as *costumbrismo* than character study.

21. Aguilar Castro, Salvador (Dates?). *Veinte años de medicina rural*. Oaxaca: Instituto Oaxaqueño de las Culturas, 1994. 280pp. Memoirs. Period Covered: 1968–1993?

Combines personal experiences with sociological and economic data of Indian Oaxaca in negatively assessing medicine. Doctor specifies conditions of childbirth that exemplify entire health milieu. Sociology, anthropology, and folklore create primer on status of medicine among rural Indians.

22. Aguilar García, Leopoldo (1914–).
Memorias de un médico en el Barrio de Santa Julia, D.F. México: Editorial Hombre, 1984. 277pp. Memoirs. Period Covered: 1914–1983.

Native of Otumba, Mexico, from humble background is medical doctor. In self-narration, profiles health system from training of doctors to care of patients. Sociology competes with and often dominates portrayal of personality in account of dedication to profession.

23. Aguilar Gómez, Delfina (Dates?).
Rosa Caralampia, la historia de una mujer tojolabal. México: Instituto Veracruzano de Cultura, 1998. 71pp. Oral Autobiography. Period Covered: ?–1998.

Life dates and narrative dates impossible to locate. Father sold motherless Rosa to villager in Chiapas. Slave destiny changed little when she worked for another *amo*. Illegitimate child and later marriage did not alter life of Tojolabal Indian.

24. Aguirre, Amado (1863–1949). *Mis memorias de campaña: apuntes para historia.* México, 1953. 430pp. Memoirs. Period Covered: 1910–1929.

Carrancista fought Villa and upon success of constitutionalists became military chief of Guadalajara. Interim governor of Jalisco, he held other important government positions under Carranza. Details battles and incorporates documents and quotations. "I publish this book guided only by the interest that historical truth be not lost…" (p.1).

25. Aguirre, Eugenio (1944–). *De cuerpo entero: Eugenio Aguirre.* México: Ediciones Corunda, 1991. 63pp. Autobiographical Essay. Period Covered: 1950–1991.

Aesthetic view of life from food to travel and love to painting. Second half on writing of journalist and creative writer with various novels including chivalric *El caballero de las espadas.* Maternal grandfather was writer Jacobo Dalevuelta.

26. Aguirre Beltrán, Gonzalo
(1908–1996). "Entrevista a Gonzalo Aguirre Beltrán por Fernando Salmerón." En *Caminos de la antropología: entrevistas a cinco antropólogos/* compiladores, Jorge Durand y

Luis Vázquez. México: Instituto Nacional Indigenista, 1990. Pp.201–237. Interview. Period Covered: 1931–1984.

Trained to write *La población negra de México, 1519–1810* (1946) under Melville J. Herskovits. Outlines major contours of twentieth century Mexican anthropology.

27. Aguirre Benavides, Luis (1890?–?). *De Francisco I. Madero a Francisco Villa: memorias de un revolucionario.* México: Tallares A. del Bosque, 1966. 273pp. Memoirs. Period Covered: 1910–1914.

Personal secretary of Gustavo Madero and Francisco Villa also knew Francisco Madero, Venustiano Carranza, and Francisco Escudero. Partisan memoir with too many documents. Value in defense of Gustavo Madero and anecdotes of Villa.

28. Agundis, Teódulo Manuel (1905?–?).
Sala de espera: páginas médicas. México, 1954. 261pp. Memoirs. Period Covered: 1934–1954.

Medical doctor has talent as writer. Like a short story, each medical incident enclosed in well-constructed chapter. Collectively reads as memoir with focus on author and relationship to medicine.

29. Agustín, José (1944–). *Confrontaciones.* Azcapotzalco, DF: Universidad Autónoma Metropolitana, 1984. 51pp. Memoirs. Period Covered: 1960–1984.

In keeping with format of series, author responds to questions. Unlike other autobiographers, he concentrates on *Onda*, 1960's literary movement incorporating adolescents and their coded language. Related to Vietnam period, *Onda* concerned with drugs, rock music, and violence.

30. Agustín, José (1944–). *José Agustín.* México: Empresas Editoriales, 1966. 61pp. Autobiographical Essay. Period Covered: 1955–1966.

Reveals significant formative moments: schooling, literary environment, and writing. Absorbed contemporary cultural period and manifests it in essay. Proves that he is writer.

31. Agustín, José (1944–). *El rock de la cárcel.* México: Editores Mexicanos Unidos,

1986. 132pp. Memoirs. Period Covered: 1964–1971.

Chronologically complements earlier *¿Quién soy?* Action focuses on two women in Agustín's life (Margarita and Angélica), writing, and work with films. *El Rock* translates frenetic sixties and drugs. Title refers to his imprisonment for alleged drug abuse. *Contra la corriente* (1991) continues theme of rock music with several autobiographical chapters, "Carlos Castañeda" and "Grandes bolas de fuego."

32. Alamillo Flores, Luis (1908?–?). *Memorias: luchadores ignorados al lado de los grandes jefes de la Revolución mexicana.* México: Extemporáneos, 1976. 617pp. Memoirs. Period Covered: 1914–1940?

Career officer started as volunteer in Revolution and rose to rank of general. Attended military academy and served as military attaché both in France and in U.S.

33. Alatorre, Antonio (1922–). "Antonio Alatorre." En *Egohistorias: El Amor a Clío* coordinated by Jean Meyer. México: Centro D'Etudes Mexicanes et Centraméricaines, 1993. Pp.13–55. Memoirs. Period Covered: 1928–1992.

Educator, philologist, and essayist, author of *Los 1001 años de la lengua española* (1979), and editor of *Nueva Revista de Filología Hispánica* pens intense memoir. Concentrating on intellectual development, he notes favorite elementary teachers, family, books and libraries, study for priesthood, and mentors Juan José Arreola, Agustín Yáñez, Raimundo Lida, and Daniel Cosío Villegas. Frank and hostile, he castigates boring professors and censors literary nationalism.

34. Alba, Pedro de (1887–1960). *Niñez y juventud provincianas.* Instituto Cultural de Aguascalientes, 1996. 209pp. Memoirs. Period Covered: 1887?–1910.

Though one of best memoirists is relatively unknown. Present document testifies to writing and is an evocation of Porfiriato in San Juan de Los Lagos, Jalisco, and Aguascalientes. In former, he attended primary school; in latter, high school and preparatory at Institute of Science. Family and environment come alive in Jalisco; culture and personality dominate in Aguascalientes. Fond of Ramón López Velarde.

35. Alba, Pedro de (1887–1960). *Viaje al pasado: memorias.* Guadalajara, 1958. 286pp. Memoirs. Period Covered: 1894–1909?

San Juan de los Lagos, Jalisco revealed with much nostalgia and sentiment by doctor and historian. Church, home, family, and neighbors recalled from distance and in harmless anecdote. More clarity and precision of style than most memoirists.

36. Alba, Víctor. *Sísifo y su tiempo: memorias de un cabreado, 1916–1996.* Barcelona: Laertes, 1996. 460pp.

Over third of book devoted to Mexico, where Spaniard Alba arrived in 1945. Collaborated on journals and newspapers, *Economía, Fianzas,* and *Excelsior.* Notes association with other exiles, contacts with Mexican literati, and comments on culture such as local Spanish. Third-person narration and quotes from diary.

37. Alcántara Gómez, Francisco (Dates?). *Reminiscencias de un viaje.* México: Editorial E.C.L.A.L., 1960. 157pp. Memoirs. Period Covered: 1957.

Poetry and prose in account of three-month trip to Europe by 155 Mexicans called *Peregrinación Mariana.* Visited traditional European sites but devotes large chapter to Rome.

38. Alec-Tweedie, Mrs. *Mexico as I Saw It.* London: Nelson, 1901. 480pp.

World-traveler Mrs. Alec-Tweedie in memoirs/travelogue references other exotic places that Mexico calls to mind. Entered Mexico with access to highest society and even chummed with President Díaz and Carmelita. Indefatigably covered much of Mexico undaunted by terrain or tribes. Always interests even though obsessed with Diaz's abilities, distrustful of socialism, and dependent on stereotypes about Mexico's masses. In spite of class consciousness, good raconteur.

39. Alemán Valdés, Miguel (1905–1983). *Remembranzas y testimonios.* México: Editorial Grijalbo, 1987. 437pp. Memoirs. Period Covered: 1905–1961.

President from 1946 to 1952 covers political life with few references to self. Childhood, school, marriage, and death of father receive cursory treatment. Shows successful political career but little on functioning of political system or presidency.

40. Alessio Robles, Miguel (1884–1951). *A medio camino.* México: Editorial Stylo, 1949. 273pp. Memoirs. Period Covered: 1917–1928?

Although well known to author, *los siete sabios* do not emerge in sharp portraits: Manuel Gómez Morín, Alberto Vázquez del Mercado, Teófilo Olea y Leyva, Vicente Lombardo Toledano, Alfonso Caso, Antonio Castro Leal, and Jesús Moreno Baca. Author either lauds contemporaries or ignores them if in his disfavor. Bland presentation of Mexico in 1920s. Culture and love for Spain but with few insights. Parts of book read as travelogue.

41. Alessio Robles, Miguel (1884–1951). *Contemplando el pasado.* México: Editorial Stylo, 1950. 318pp. Memoirs. Period Covered: 1921–1923.

In third volume, writer, historian, and diplomat recounts travels in Spain and Italy as well as relations with President Obregón and other famous literary and political personalities, e.g., Azorín and Limantour.

42. Alessio Robles, Miguel (1884–1951). *Mi generación y mi época.* México: Editorial Stylo, 1949. 276pp. Memoirs. Period Covered: 1909–1917.

Remembers final years of Porfiriato and youths that surrounded him in law school. Portrayals of major personalities he met in Revolution. Final chapters on trip to Europe.

43. Alessio Robles, Vito (1879–1957). *Mis andanzas con nuestro Ulises.* México: Ediciones Botas, 1938. 387pp. Memoirs. Period Covered: 1911–1930.

Military, historian, and journalist despises José Vasconcelos. Satirizes, castigates, and vilifies Mexican Ulysses. Passion that attracted Bustillo Oro and Mauricio Magdaleno repelled this writer. Chapters serialized in *Jueves de Excelsior* in 1938.

44. Aline (1975–). *Mi despertar: después de la gloria por el infierno.* México: Editorial Grijalbo, 1999. 227pp. Memoirs. Period Covered: 1991–1998?

Young woman's revelation like a soap opera. Apparent sequel to *Aline, la gloria por el infierno,* above accuses two celebrities, Gloria Trevi and Sergio Andrade, of inveigling adolescent girls into white slavery through ruse of career in entertainment world. Both autobiography and denunciation.

45. Allende, Fernando (1952–). *Mis memorias hasta hoy.* Bogotá: Plaza y Janés, 1993. 318pp. Memoirs. Period Covered: 1952–1991.

Film, television, and nightclub star covers youth and moves into career. Film of Jorge Isaacs's *María* brought early success. Notes other media work, travels, marriage, and family.

46. Almada, Bartolomé Eligio (1817–1872). *Almada of Alamos: The Diary of Don Bartolomé.* Translated and with a narrative by Carlota Miles. Tucson: Arizona Silhouettes, 1962. 197pp. Diary. Period Covered: 1859–1863.

Liberal senator from Sonora, Juarista, and businessman wrote diary during French Intervention. Travels within Mexico, political life and personalities, family, mining, and details of daily existence. Portrays life of aristocrat during tumultuous years of Intervention.

47. Almada, Pedro J. (1883–1960). *Con mi cobija al hombro por el general de división Pedro J. Almada.* México: Editorial Alrededor de América, 193–? 338pp. Memoirs. Period Covered: 1900?–1935.

Held military posts under various Revolutionary presidents: Obregón, Calles, and Cárdenas. Yet inner workings of government and military not revealed. Unselectively narrates without interpreting. An adolescent escaping from home, he follows picaresque structure more than autobiographical one. Childhood, military life, and politics major topics.

48. Almada, Pedro J. (1883–1960). *Mis memorias de revolucionario.* México, 1928. 61pp. Memoirs. Period Covered: 1913–1927.

Sonorense fought in infantry on side of Alvaro Obregón in Sonora, Guadalajara, and Oaxaca. Promoted to general, he was colonel and then inspector general of police in Mexico City. Writes with verve always with appropriate anecdote.

49. Almada, Pedro J. (1883–1960). *...99 días en con el presidente Cárdenas.* México: Ediciones Botas, 1943. 249pp. Memoirs. Period Covered: 1939.

Inspector general of army and personal friend of Cárdenas. Invited to accompany president on train journey through northern Mexico and Pacific Coast. Since Cárdenas totally depersonalizes political life in both *Apuntes* and *Epistolario*, Almada's work lends human element to itinerary.

50. Almaguer, Gilberto (Dates?). "El maestro rural en la década de los años 30." En *Los maestro y la cultura nacional, v.1, Norte.* México: Museo Nacional de Culturalas Populares, 1987. Pp.89–123. Memoirs. Period Covered: 1927–1950?

Teacher in rural areas of native Coahuila emphasizes charges placed upon teachers to improve community beyond school. Involved in labor movement and in land redistribution.

51. Almazán, Juan Andreu (1891–1965). *Memorias: informe y documentos sobre la campaña política de 1940.* México: Quintanar, 1941. 206pp. Memoirs. Period Covered: 1940.

Fought against Madero, joined Zapatistas, and became Huertista. Unsuccessful campaign as independent presidential candidate in 1940 most significant moment. Incumbent Lázaro Cárdenas preferred Avila Camacho. Memoirs and documents tell of struggle.

52. Alonso, Enrique (1924–). *Confrontaciones: Enrique Alonso.* Azcapotzalco, DF: Universidad Autónoma Metropolitana, 1987. 37pp. Interview. Period Covered: 1932?–1986?

Promoter of children's theater and creator of Cachirulo in *La princesita encantada* talks about career. Children's theater is major theme; notes María Conesa's influence as well as that of other Spanish actors. Praises María Tereza Montoya's efforts to attract students to theater.

53. Alonso, Enrique (1923–). *Conocencias.* México: Escenología, 1998. 862pp. Memoirs. Period Covered: 1923–1997.

Related to popular theater mainly in second half of twentieth century: vaudeville, children's theater where he acquired nickname "Chachirulo" and managed *el Teatro Fantástico* on television. Author gives more history of popular theater than autobiography. Anecdotal about Tereza Montoya, María Conesa, Esperanza Iris, Virginia Fábregas, and other greats of this genre. Much on *género chico* and *zarzuela.*

54. Altamira G., Armando (Dates?). *Alpinismo mexicano.* México: Editorial Ecial, 1972. 207pp. Memoirs. Period Covered: 1954–1965.

Introductory pages on history of mountain climbing in Mexico. Describes adventures mainly in central Mexico.

55. Alvarez, Augusto H. (1914–). *Historia oral de la Ciudad de México: testimonios de sus arquitectos (1940–1990).* México: Instituto de Investigaciones Dr. José María Luis Mora, 1994. 74pp. Oral Autobiography. Period Covered: 1940–1990.

Member of Yucatecan *hacendado* family recalls introduction to architecture and some of favorite projects: Cuauhtémoc apartments, Sierra Vertientes apartments, Conjunto Urbano Palmas (Palmas Complex), Colegio Oxford, and la University Iberoamericana. Gives philosophy of architectural space and comments on Mexico City's monuments.

56. Alvarez, Concha (1892–1961). *Así pasó mi vida.* México: Editorial Porrúa, 1962. 214pp. Autobiography Proper. Period Covered: 1892–1912.

Writer and teacher details life as student or until graduation from Escuela Nacional de Maestras. Outside of protector, don Vicente, her environment is feminine. Describes classmates and professors including favorite, Antonio Caso. She taught over thirty years but dismisses career in one sentence.

57. Alvarez, Donanciano (1895–?). "La autobiografía de don Chano de Agustín Bustamante." En *Revista Mexicana de Sociología.* V.33, No.2, abril–junio, 1971. Pp.333–363.

Oral Autobiography. Period Covered: 1895–1953.

From peasant background in León, Guanajuato. With no schooling, worked as traveling salesman and also in oil fields. He and family illegally entered U.S. Interviewer notes selection process and methodology.

58. Alvarez, Griselda (1918–). *Cuesta arriba: memorias de la primera gobernadora.* México: Universidad de Colima, 1992. 190pp. Memoirs. Period Covered: 1918–1992.

Poet, journalist, literary critic, politician, and one of first female governors of Mexico. First woman to write political memoirs. Career in public service: archivist at general hospital, IMSS (Instituto Mexicano del Seguro Social), chamber of deputies, and governor. Advocate for women in politics, she differs little from male counterparts in not revealing political process.

59. Alvarez Bravo Martínez de Anda, Lola (1907–1993). *Lola Alvarez Bravo, fotografías selectas 1934–1985: [exposición] 29 de octubre de 1992–31 de enero de 1993.* México: Fundación Cultural Televisa, 1992. 449pp. Interview. Period Covered: 1907–1991.

Sixty pages dedicated to interviews with Rosa Castro, Manuel Fernández Perera, Luis Zapata, and José Joaquín Blanco. Some of same material as in *Recuento.* Speaks of childhood, family, marriage to Manuel Alvarez Bravo, apprenticeship and success in photography, and the famous she has known in art world. Frank and generous in appraisals of others, she is always engaging.

60. Alvarez Bravo Martínez de Anda, Lola (1907–1993). *Recuento fotográfico.* México: Editorial Penélope, 1982. 222pp. Memoirs. Period Covered: 1914?–1980?

Unique memoirs as few women in arts disclose selves through autobiography. Explains ideas on photography including over 100 b/w photos which accompany text and in visual terms express her theories. Each of four autobiographical components done in collaboration with another author. An early feminist and ex-spouse of Manuel Alvarez Bravo, LAB was self-taught in photography. Childhood, marriage, divorce, and friendships comprise life story. Knew artists including Tina Modotti, María Izquierdo, and Frida Kahlo.

61. Alvarez Del Castillo, Graciana (Dates?). *Rincón de recuerdos.* México: Impresora Juan Pablos, 1962. 254pp. Memoirs. Period Covered: 1908–1927.

Placed in context of Mexico City and Tulancingo, Hidalgo, memoirs have little of author's personality. Life story eroded by *costumbristic* Mexico and nostalgia. Friendship with Belisario Domínguez.

62. Alvarez Del Castillo, Juan Manuel (1894–1966). *Memorias.* Guadalajara, 1960. 635pp. Memoirs. Period Covered: 1894–1955.

Soldier, journalist, diplomat, personal secretary of President Adolfo de la Huerta, ambassador to U.S., Peru, Dominican Republic, Norway, Portugal, Colombia, Argentina, Canada, and Brazil. Totally descriptive.

63. Alvarez del Toro, Miguel (1917–1996). *¡Así era Chiapas! 42 años de andanzas por montañas, selvas, y caminos en el estado.* Tuxtla Gutiérrez, CHP: Instituto de Historia Natural, 1990. 551pp. Memoirs. Period Covered: 1942–1985.

Zoologist, naturalist, conservationist, author, and director of Instituto de Historia Natural del Estado de Chiapas designed and built similar institutions in adopted state. Adventures of Colima-born Alvarez in wilds of Chiapas searching for animals.

64. Amezcua, José Luis (Dates?). *Memorias de una campaña.* México: Tallares Gráficas de la Nación, 1924. 74pp. Memoirs. Period Covered: 1923–1924.

Treats military revolt of Adolfo de la Huerta and campaigns to subdue him. Little of author present nor much of Mexican character or customs revealed. Praise for men on his side. Photographs of military life.

65. Amor, Guadalupe (1920–). *Yo soy mi casa.* México: Fondo de Cultura Económica, 1957. 350pp. Autobiographical Novel. Period Covered: 1920–1929?

Autobiography and creativity. First person narrator, also named Pita, reflects life of author from upper class family with normal experiences of girlhood: religion, family relationships, and surroundings. Details and recall of conversations, techniques more common to novel than to life story, raise this above standard autobiography. Imagination allows for more satisfying reading than comparable works susceptible to verification.

66. Amor, Inés (1912–1980). *Una mujer en el arte mexicano: memorias de Inés Amor, Jorge Alberto Manrique, Teresa Del Conde.* México: UNAM, 1987. 271pp. Oral Autobiography. Period Covered: 1936?–1976?

Gallery owner, discoverer of Mexican painters, and general patroness of art both at home and abroad, speaks freely. Prominent artists in biographies filtered through Amor. Interviewers discuss purpose, techniques, and their own interventions in the document.

67. Amor Poniatowska, Paula (1908–?). *Nomeolvides.* Traducción y prólogo de Elena Poniatowska. México: Plaza y Janés, 1996. 305pp. Memoirs. Period Covered: 1908–1994?

Elena Poniatowska stimulates, edits, and translates mother's memoirs. Paula Amor Poniatowska's life merits involvement of writer daughter: born of rich Mexican family but at home in Europe, Paula Amor married Polish nobleman, Jean Poniatowska. Family, children, participation in WWII, and remaining years in Mexico part of exciting life. Amor Poniatowska automatically interacted with celebrities on both continents.

68. Anaya, José Homobono (1836–1906). *Epistolario del Sr. Cura y obispo Dr. José Homobono Anaya a la familia Agraz.* Tecolotlán, JAL, 1975. 88pp. Letters. Period Covered: 1869–1884.

Priest and finally bishop of Sinaloa corresponded with ten members of Agraz family. Postmarked Mascota (Jalisco), Tecolotlán (Jalisco), and Chilapa (Guerrero), letters attest to gratitude and affection for family plus personal events in life of Anaya: building of church, protecting statue of Saint Anthony, death, and illness. Illustrated collection with photographs and biographies of Agraz family.

69. Anderle, Ádám; Monika Kozári; Tibor Berta. *Un húngaro en El México rev-*olucionario: correspondencia [sic] de Kálmán Kánya....* México: EDAMEX, 1999. 220pp.

Comprised of letters, 1914–1917, on Mexico's tumultuous years with Carranza. Information not new. Of interest is Kánya's hatred of U.S. Possibly only Hungarian to experience Revolution.

70. Anderson, Elizabeth; Gerald R. Kelly. *Miss Elizabeth: A Memoir.* Boston: Little, Brown, 1969. 315pp.

Elizabeth Anderson, one of Sherwood Anderson's ex-wives, found compatible home in Taxco in 1930s. Reconnected with old friend of New Orleans days, William Spratling, and the memoir focuses on him. Anderson became couture and did for sewing and embroidery what Spratling did for silver, i.e., organized and saved dying forms of native art. Anecdotes on Taxco's number one citizen, Spratling, and also American colony in haven near Cuernavaca.

71. Anderson, Robert; Eba Anderson. *An Artillery Officer in the Mexican War, 1846–7: Letters of Robert Anderson....* New York: Putnam, 1911. 339pp.

Enters Mexican-American War at Vera Cruz and proceeds to Perote, Puebla, and Mexico City. Sounds routine but Anderson's memoir one of best of period for its proportions: he is concerned about wife, his correspondent; he knows both officers and men; he is interested in Mexicans and their reactions to war; he wants to learn Spanish; he notes landscape but never lets it dominate; and finally, he freely expresses emotions.

72. Anderson, William Marshall; Ramón Eduardo Ruiz. *An American in Maximilian's Mexico, 1865–1866....* San Marino, CA: Huntington Library, 1959. 132pp.

Another source for Mexico under empire. Private citizen and surveyor for Maximilian has positive comments in diaries about country as potential home for southern Confederates.

73. Andrews, Lynn V. *Jaguar Woman and the Wisdom of the Butterfly Tree.* San Francisco: Harper & Row, 1985. 194pp.

An insight into shamanism. "All at once

I shot upward out of my body and was flying over the tops of trees. Then I was on the ground, running amazingly fast through the jungle…. I realized I was a jaguar spirit…" (p.58). Words epitomize apprenticeship in efforts to become shaman. Appeals for help of shamans from North American Hemisphere but especially Agnes and Zoila, two priestesses of Yucatan who tutor neophyte.

74. Angeles, Felipe (1869–1919). *Documentos relativos al General Felipe Angeles*. México: Editorial Domés, 1982. 368pp. Hybrid. Period Covered: 1914?–1919.

Career military officer graduated and taught at military academy and fought for Madero and Villa in Revolution. Documents mosaic personality of brilliant tactician: biography of Genovevo de la O, *diario de la Batalla de Zacatecas*, and twenty-eight letters to Gen. José María Maytorena. In 1998, *La batalla de Zacatecas* published under separate cover.

75. Anguiano, Hildelisa (1910–?). *Querer es poder: Hildelisa Anguiano platica con Agustín Vaca*. Zapopan: Colegio de Jalisco, 2000. 278pp. Oral Autobiography. Period Covered: 1910–1997.

Taught elementary school for fifty years in Jalisco. "Both [her longevity and the Revolution] combine to allow her to witness the series of social changes that have taken place in Jalisco during the twentieth century" (p.9). In colloquial manner speaks of own education, dominating mother, teaching, labor unions, and opportunities for women, patriotism, and negative view of government. Intrigue and pettiness in education. Vaca notes forty ninety-minute interviews and assures that Anguiano organized materials.

76. Anguiano, Raúl (1913–). *Expedición a Bonampak: diario de un viaje*. México: UNAM, 1955. 73pp. Memoirs. Period Covered: 1949.

Artist in Bonampak, Chiapas, records impressions in words and drawings. Always involves self with companions, climate, and flora. Intimacy contrasts with objectivity and distancing that frequently characterize travel genre. In diary form, arduous three-week sojourn shares much with memoir.

77. Anguiano, Raúl (1913–). *Raúl Anguiano, remembranzas*. Toluca: Universidad Autónoma del Estado de México, 1995. 132pp. Memoirs. Period Covered: 1915–1993.

Established painter reveals self in thematic fragments: childhood, relations with other painters (Rivera, Orozco, Tamayo, Cuevas, Kahlo, etc.), writers (García Márquez, Rulfo, Arreola, Neruda, Pellicer, etc.), and commentaries on most famous paintings. Informal and anecdotal, author illuminates twentieth century Mexican art and forms most cohesive autobiography.

78. Anonymous (1968–?). "La neta, estuviera chido que no hubiera ley." En *¿Qué transa con las bandas?* de Jorge García-Robles. México: Editorial Posada, 1985. Pp.205–239. Oral Autobiography. Period Covered: 1968–1985.

Narrator anonymous for use of drugs, crimes, and inter-gang warfare. Valuable for jargon.

79. Anonymous. *A Young English Man's Account of His Imprisonment and Sufferings in Mexico during Part of the Years 1855 & 1856*. London: Simpkins, Marshall, 1857. 30pp.

In 1855, Englishman volunteers in Mexico to help Santa Anna's opponent, Comonfort. Foreigner receives ambivalent treatment from Mexicans: chain gangs and warm hospitality.

80. Anzaldúa, Gloria (1942–2004). *Borderlands=frontera: The New Mestiza*. San Francisco: Spinsters/Aunt Lute, 1987. 98pp.

Born in Rio Grande Valley of south Texas to migrant labor family, she exposes some autobiographical facts but stresses condition of Hispanic women. Claims Indian heritage and advocates Chicano-feminist-lesbian politics. Chicano ties with Mexico appear blatant in title: borderlands, *frontera*, and *mestiza*. Most hybrid of Mexican-American autobiographies, *Borderlands* aggressively speaks to women in both countries.

81. Aragón, Alfredo (1885–1936). *Escenas de la Revolución mexicana….* París: Soc. an. Des imprimeries Wellhoff et Roche, 1916. 127pp. Memoirs. Period Covered: 1913.

Lieutenant colonel in Constitutionalist

Army, journalist, and diplomat mixes memoirs with other documents. Twenty-eight-year-old soldier, imprisoned by Porfirista officer, Blanquet escaped north to join Carranza's forces and later became general's chief assistant. Adventures including interview with Carranza. Mirrored translation in Spanish and French.

82. Aramburo Salas, Francisco (Dates?). *La Europa que yo vi: cartas de un viajero sudcaliforniano.* México, 1962. 278pp. Memoirs. Period Covered: 1960.

Young author from Baja tours Europe: England, France, Spain, Italy, Austria, and Germany. Confesses motive for memoirs: promise of impressions to many friends made publication necessary. Interaction with other tour members and reactions to sites comprise autobiography.

83. *The Architecture of Ricardo Legorreta* (1931 Birth of Legorreta). London: Thames and Hudson, 1997. 240pp. Memoirs. Period Covered: 1967–1989?

Few Mexican architects with autobiographies. Defines professional self in poetry and prose. Topics of design, buildings created (hotels, houses, and factories), commissions in Mexico and U.S., restorations, color, and fascination with walls and their mastery prevail in illustrated work.

84. Arellano Rocha, Gloria (1922?–). "Relatos, testimonios y Experiencias." En *1920–1952, v.1, Norte.* México: Museo Nacional de Culturas Populares, 1987. Pp.55–76. Memoirs. Period Covered: 1940–1973.

Worked in education for thirty years. Began as primary teacher in Santa Barbara, Chihuahua; later taught high school in Parral; in 1947, named principal of high school in Ensenada, Baja, and ended career in Delicias, Chihuahua. Enthusiasm, dedication, and professionalism pervade.

85. Arenal, Angélica (1909–1989). *Páginas sueltas con Siqueiros.* México: Editorial Grijalbo, 1980. 279pp. Memoirs. Period Covered: 1896–1979.

First forty pages give life of Siqueiros and remaining intertwine his life with adulating spouse Arenal. Born in Tabasco, she met Siqueiros through her brother, artist Luis Arenal. Widow mentions travel, family, paintings, communism, and struggles against Trotsky. Constant use of *tú* which personalizes events as *tú* mixes with *yo* and *nosotros*.

86. Arenas, Francisco Javier (1917–). *La flota: cuadernos universitarios.* México: AUM, 1963. 223pp. Memoirs. Period Covered: 1940s.

Traces life as student in Mexico City before school moved to Ciudad Universitaria. In study for law degree, portrays professors and close companions. Notes favorite rendezvousing place of students. Of more interest are university student political factions.

87. Arenas, Rebecca (1914 Birth of Muñoz). *Marco Antonio Muñoz: testimonios.* Veracruz: Gobierno del Estado Libre y Soberano de Veracruz-Llave, 1992. 184pp. Interview. Period Covered: 1914–1992.

In seven interviews, Muñoz answers queries and remembers: family, education, Revolution, lawyer, politics, Vera Cruz, governorship, and politics.

88. Arenas Betancourt, Rodrigo. *Crónicas de la errancia del amor y de la muerte....* Bogotá: Instituto Colombiano de Cultura, 1976. 117pp.

Colombian-born sculptor and gifted writer enhances Mexican autobiography with his techniques: he ignores chronology and has imaginary dialogs with friends and family. Colombia, Mexico, and Italy are geographical locales for monologues. "La experienca de México amalgamó todo y lo puso en su sitio" (p.70). He sculpts, meets other artists, and participates in Communist Party.

89. Argudín, Raúl S. (1900?–?). *De la vida y aventuras de un médico de provincia.* México: Editorial Citlatepetl, 1964. 326pp. Memoirs. Period Covered: 1926–1960.

For most of life practicing doctor in San Andrés Tuxtla, Veracruz, where he combated snakes and yellow fever. Medical school dominates more than childhood.

90. Aridjis, Homero (1940–). *El poeta niño.* México: Fondo de Cultura Económica, 1971. 178pp. Memoirs. Period Covered: 1944?

Poet rather than prose writer emerges in evocative recall of childhood in Michoacán: relationship with parents, unusual perspective on adult family members, competition with brothers, and illness. Description rather than action carries reader.

91. Armienta Calderón, Gilberto

(1931–?). *Caminando por el Tiempo....* Culiacán: Archivo Histórico General del Estado de Sinaloa, 2001. 142pp. Memoirs. Period Covered: 1936?–1950?

A subgenre in Mexican autobiography is nostalgia of time and space which overwhelms narrator's personality. Loves Culiacán, Sinaloa, and remembers places, customs, and personalities. Reader's knowledge of author through topics and their development in an idealized past.

92. Arnold, Channing; Frederick J. Tabor. *The American Egypt, A Record of Travel in Yucatan.* Garden City, NY: Doubleday, 1909. 391pp.

Archaeologists aware of contributions of previous Mayanists but note selves as first Englishmen to publish book on Yucatan. Archaeology may be quaint but authors never lose vitriolic attitude of British traveler toward Mexico: "The Mexicans are polite all the time but beneath the veneer of this nauseating oleaginous manner...they are possessed of the most unpleasant characteristics" (pp.32–33). Authors have no illusions about dictator Diaz exposed as tyrant.

93. Arreguín Vélez, Enrique (1907–?). *Páginas autobiográficas.* Morelia: Nicolás de Hidalgo, 1982. 178pp. Memoirs. Period Covered: 1907–1970.

Medical doctor from Michoacán spent career in education: student at University of Michoacán and graduate of department of medicine; professor here, at UNAM, and Instituto Politécnico Nacional; secretary of education; and other positions. Speeches and ideas dominate memoir.

94. Arreola, Juan José (1918–2001). *Memoria y olvido: vida de Juan José Arreola, 1920–1947.* México: Consejo Nacional para la Cultura y las Artes, 1994. 179pp. Oral Autobiography. Period Covered: 1920–1947.

Short story writer of *La feria* and *Confabulario personal* recounts pre-publication days to novelist comrade, Fernando del Paso. Studying acting in Paris with Louis Jouvet alternates with scenes of childhood, family, reading, religion, journalism, and Zapotlán, village in Guadalajara. Young Arreola reveals self more in theme than in chronological progression. Paso notes forty meetings with Arreola.

95. Arreola, Orso (1918–2001 Dates of Juan José Arreola). *El último juglar: memorias de Juan José Arreola.* México: Editorial Diana, 1998. 422pp. Oral Autobiography. Period Covered: 1937–1968.

Orso Arreola provocateur in telling of life of writer-father. Four sections encompass stages in writer's life: (1) Mexico City, theater, and Rodolfo Usigli; (2) Manzanillo, Pablo Neruda, Revista *Eros*, wife Sara, Paris, and Louis Jouvet; (3) Universities, Carlos Pellicer, Agustín Yáñez, editorship, and La Casa del Lago; (4) Cuba, la revista *Mester*, and return to Zapotlán (Jalisco). Orso's voice dominates but Juan José Arreola speaks for self in diary and letters. Illustrated with photos.

96. Arruza, Carlos; Barnaby Conrad (1920–1966 Dates of Arruza). *My Life as a Matador: The Autobiography of Carlos Arruza with Barnaby Conrad.* Boston: Houghton Mifflin, 1959. 246pp. Autobiography Proper. Period Covered: 1930?–1951?

Ghost-written autobiography of matador tells of training and successes in Spain, Portugal, and Mexico. Career typifies bullfighter: apprenticeship, trials, and triumphs in ring; capriciousness of aficionados; and his contribution to spectacle.

97. Artaud, Antonin. *The Peyote Dance.* New York: Farrar, Straus and Giroux, 1975. 63pp.

Another aspect of this culture broached in Artaud's title. In Mexico in 1936, he lived with Tarahumara and experimented with peyote. To paraphrase French author, he visited Tarahumara not as tourist but in search for something that Europe doesn't have: a means of expanding preconsciousness.

98. Asencio Navarrete, José (Dates?). *Por qué fui un perseguido político de Borge Martín.* México, 1995. 24pp. Memoirs. Period Covered: 1955–1989.

Few memoirs on politics at local level and even fewer from Quintana Roo. He worked with various agencies within home state: delegate of industry and commerce, general manager of *chiclero* cooperative, delegate of CONASUPO, national basic commodity cooperation, and finally mayor of Othón P. Blanco in 1989. In final position, incurred wrath of Miguel Borge Martín, governor of Quintana Roo. Author defends self.

99. Atala, Alejandra (Dates?). *Señor mío y dios mío Ricardo Garibay: la fiera inteligente.* México: Océano, 2003. 250pp. Diary. Period Covered: 1999.

Daughter-in-law, both student and admirer of Garibay, writes diary entries relating to the last months of author. With spinal cancer, he evokes sympathy of diarist, who gives us Garibay's biography but also much of herself.

100. Atl, Dr. (Gerardo Murillo) (1875–1964). *Gentes profanas en el convento.* México: Ediciones Botas, 1950. 279pp. Hybrid. Period Covered: 1914–1930.

Journalist, miner, politician, military man, and painter hints at each profession in hybrid document. Essay, short story, poetry, and autobiography vie for attention as well as confuse fact and fiction. Following topics verifiable: Revolution, Carranza, writing(s), art and landscape painting, volcanoes, and Liga de Escritores de América.

101. Aub, Max; Manuel Aznar Soler. *Diarios, 1939–1972.* Barcelona: Alba Editorial, 1998. 556pp.

Differs much from typical Spaniard exiled in Mexico. Constant introversion creates mood rather than knowable environment of adopted country. Many epigrammatic sentences approach proverbs. Art (literature) more than politics occupies thoughts. Aub worked on behalf of theater in Mexico as well as editor and contributor to several literary periodicals. In *Diarios*, covers Mexican years, 1942–1952.

102. Aubertin, J.J. *A Flight to Mexico.* London: K. Paul, Trench, 1882. 325pp.

British scholar and translator of *The Lusiads,* J.J. Aubertin recounts trip in late nineteenth century. Enters through Vera Cruz and travels to Mexico City via Puebla and Cholula. Like all travelers, wants reader to know Mexico. Best chapters on mining in Pachuca, Hidalgo, haciendas, and sixty-one-page account of Querétaro and Maximilian.

103. Audirac, Augusto (1898–?). *Historia de un colegio.* México: Secretaría de Educación Pública, 1949. 67pp. Memoirs. Period Covered: 1895?

Nostalgic recovery of adolescence in Teziutlán, Xalapa. In tribute to father, Audirac incorporates much of self. Scenery, excursions, and classmates comprise idyll of youth. Earlier and shorter *El fiel recuerdo* (1945) also recalls youth in Tezuitlán.

104. Audubon, John Woodhouse; Maria Rebecca. *Audubon's Western Journal, 1849–1850....* Glorieta, NM: Rio Grande, 1969, (1906). 249pp.

Some Americans, drawn to California because of the discovery of gold in 1848, opted to go through Mexico. Thus Audubon's itinerary included Roma, Monterrey, Saltillo, Buena Vista, Parras, Mampimi, Parral, and Sonora. Cholera, grasshoppers, climate, and landscape through eyes of naturalist.

105. Aurioles, Eric (1983?–). *Los sabores de mi vida: recetas, reflexiones, anécdotas y confesiones antes y después de Big Brother.* México: Promexa, 2003. 292pp. Memoirs. Period Covered: 1989–2002.

Author is chef and musician. Food and/or music in all of autobiographical sections that introduce recipes. From school through *prepa*, he notes various stages of childhood and relates to food that he has prepared or even created. He worked at all levels of food preparation. In final chapter, successful in both careers.

106. Aveleyra-Sadowska, Teresa (1920–). *Cartas de Polonia.* México: Editorial Porrúa, 1982. 217pp. Letters. Period Covered: 1975–1976.

Professional writer acquired Polish name

through marriage during year's visit to teach Mexican literature. Expresses emotions about love, marriage, and premature widowhood. Profiles fragments of Polish culture, mood, and personality.

107. Avendaño Martínez, Roberta

(Dates?). *De la libertad y el encierro*. México: La Idea Dorada, 1998. 153pp. Memoirs. Period Covered: 1969–1971.

Part of student movement in 1968, she spent two years in prison at Cárcel de Mujeres de Santa Martha Acatitla. Describes arrest, mistreatment, and other experiences while incarcerated. Anecdotal format divulges much about fellow prisoners as well as her survival techniques.

108. Aviles Fabila, René (1940–). *Memorias de un comunista: maquinuscrito encontrado en un basurero de Perisur*. México: Gernika, 1991. 167pp. Memoirs. Period Covered: 1958?–1988?

Professor, novelist, essayist, and short story writer humorously recounts years as communist. Anecdotes expose party's contradictions.

109. Avilés Fabila, René (1940–). *Recordanzas*. México: Editorial Aldus, 1996. 471pp. Memoirs. Period Covered: 1945?–1995.

Prolific writer of novels and short stories and editor of *El Buho*, cultural section of newspaper *Excelsior*, collected articles relating to writers, artists, and his family. (Political articles found in *Memorias de un comunista*.) *Recordanzas* relates to books read, written, or reviewed or authors known. Life in letters in context of second half of twentieth century. Boldly expresses opinions.

110. Aviña, Rubén (1975 Birth of Aline). *Aline, la gloria por el infierno*. México: Editorial Grijalbo, 1998. 284pp. Oral Autobiography. Period Covered: 1960–1998.

Author interviews Aline and family to provide prequel to *Mi despertar*. Early dates relate to courtship and marriage of Aline's parents. Soap opera text on perils for young women trapped and abused by lure of stardom.

111. Azar, Héctor (1930–). *Confrontaciones*. Azcapotzalco, DF: Universidad

Autónoma Metropolitana, 1984. 43pp. Interview. Period Covered: 1937?–1984.

Playwright expounds theories of theater: debt of radio, film, and television to genre; world theater; theatricality; ethical theater; and difference between actor and persona. Speaks specifically of CADAC (Centro de Arte Dramático, A.C.). One of best in series of interviews.

112. Azar, Héctor (1930–). *De cuerpo entero: Héctor Azar*. México: Ediciones Corunda, 1991. 49pp. Memoirs. Period Covered: 1935–1967.

Poet and dramatist focuses on early years in Atilixco, Puebla, where Lebanese mother had clothing store which she later moved to Mexico City. Noting education, including Carlos Pellicer as teacher, and attempts at theater and poetry, he creates a prose style that interests as much as content.

113. Azcárate, Juan E. (1890?–?). *Esencia de la Revolución*. México: Costa-Amic, 1966. 277pp. Memoirs. Period Covered: 1910–1946.

Maderista soldier in Revolution emphasizes military activities in northern and central Mexico. Final pages concern Vasco de Quiroga.

114. Azcárate Sánchez S., Sergio

(1935–). *La duda del maestro y otros relatos de mi vida médica*. Guadalajara: Editorial Conexión Gráfica, 1988. 214pp. Memoirs. Period Covered: 1909?–1985?

Fragments medical experiences through eight independent stories. Each reflects doctor during *servicio social* (internship) in village or as established M.D. involved in personal lives of patients. Autobiography subordinated to plot.

115. Aziri Pavón, Ramón (1937 Birth of Carretero). *Revelaciones de un soldado: del capitán Gilberto Carretero*. Monterrey: Ediciones Castillo, 1994. 226pp. Oral Autobiography. Period Covered: 1937–1979.

Twenty-seven-year career in military, Carretero presents self through writer Azpiri Pavón. From 1952 to 1979, subject had various assignments and adventures in Mexico including search for gold from wrecked plane and also hijacked plane. Subject's relationship to Adolfo Ruiz Cortines and his exoneration of military in Tlateloco in 1968 arouse most interest.

116. Azuela, Arturo (1938–). *La mar de utopías.* Madrid: Ediciones de Cultura Hispánica, 1991. 197pp. Memoirs. Period Covered: 1962–1989.

Professor of math and history of science and author of essays and novels travels and covers travels, literary themes, and search for self. Envelopes ideas and personalities but always as they relate to him, e.g., Juan Rulfo, Julio Cortázar, Ernesto Sábato, Vargas Llosa, Pablo Neruda, and Salvador Allende. Most valuable autobiographical piece, "En la Sociedad de Escritores." Like Salvador Novo, he divulges personality in intellectual form of travel writing.

117. Azuela, Arturo (1938–). *Prisma de Mariano Azuela.* México: Plaza y Valdés, 2002. 346pp. Memoirs. Period Covered: 1945?–1952.

Thirty-five pages of relationship between famous grandfather and grandson: travels, bookbinding, writing, family conflicts and celebrations, elder's opinion of other celebrities, unanswered questions, and awareness of don Mariano's imperfections.

118. Azuela, Mariano (1873–1952). *Epistolario y archivo.* Recopilación y apéndices de Beatrice Berler. México: UNAM, 1969. 324pp. Letters. Period Covered: 1898–1943.

Like *Páginas autobiográficas,* this is casual autobiography. Letters reveal man of honor, generous with friends and impatient with enemies. Alfonso Reyes, Waldo Frank, Manuel Pedro González, José María González de Mendoza, John Englekirk, Lawrence B. Kiddle, Enrique Munguía, and Anita Brenner most important correspondents.

119. Azuela, Mariano (1873–1952). *Páginas autobiográficas.* México: Fondo de Cultura Económica, 1974. 276pp. Memoirs? Period Covered: 1873–195?

Selection of writings posthumously. Fragmented and with little editing, pieces leave no unifying thread other than Azuela. Confessions on how he writes and history surrounding seven of novels including *Los de*

abajo. In chapter "Autobiografía del otro," dialogs with creative self. Mentions revolutionary period and Lagos de Moreno, but persons and geographical places secondary.

120. Azuela, Salvador (1902–1984). *La aventura vasconcelista, 1929.* México: Editorial Diana, 1980. 173pp. Memoirs. Period Covered: 1915–1934.

La aventura forms part of suite of autobiographies whose authors focus on Vasconcelos. Although present in moments of memoirs, such as in praise, "Caminar con Vasconcelos…es una fiesta" (p.105), Azuela too often becomes historian, i.e., he writes about unobserved events. 1929, year of Vasconcelos's debacle, centers narration for young idealistic author then student activist.

121. Badú, Antonio (1914–1993). *Sortilegio de vivir: la vida de Antonio Badú en conversaciones con Jorge Mejía Prieto.* México: Editorial Diana, 1993. 159pp. Interviews. Period Covered: 1914–1993?

Born in Real del Monte, Hidalgo, to Lebanese parents, Badú started career in early days of radio, silent film, and television. Singer, actor, and film producer decants popular culture of entertainment world. Films, songs, events, personalities, opinions, and photos combine into oral history by producer and eyewitness of culture.

122. Bailey, Mari Vawn. *Marita — Missing in Mexico.* Murray, UT: Aspen Books, 1996. 278pp.

Young Morman goes to Mexico on church mission in 1970s and marries native Mexican. Mutual religion does not save marriage with violent husband. Memoir revolves around mother's efforts to retrieve daughter, illegally held by family in Puebla. Divulges familial culture of Mexico, machismo, and physical and emotional closeness of Mormon community in U.S. or abroad.

123. Baker, Frank Collins. *A Naturalist in Mexico: Being a Visit to Cuba, Northern Yucatan and Mexico.* Chicago: Oliphant, 1894. 145pp.

Academy of Natural Sciences of Philadelphia sponsored expedition whose "…object was to collect data and specimens

illusrating the fauna, flora and geology of
Yucatan and southern Mexico..." (p.xii).
Gives some autobiography and much of
nature: birds, insects, mollusks, mountains,
volcanos, vultures, etc. Mentions archaeolog-
ical sites and agriculture. Tour also to Vera
Cruz, Orizaba, Mexico City, Amecameca,
Pátzcuaro, and Cuautla.

124. Balbas, Manuel (Dates?). *Recuerdos
del yaqui: principales episodios durante la
campaña de 1899 a 1901.* México: Sociedad de
Edición y Librería Franco-Americano, 1927.
117pp. Memoirs. Period Covered: 1899–1901.

Member of forces sent to subdue Yaquis
of Sonora during Porfiriato performs dual
role of observer and participant. Sympathizes
with Yaquis but is ever partisan of dictator.
Assumes role of historian by commenting on
unobserved events and drawing conclusions
possible only with perspective.

125. Balboa (Gojón), Práxedis (1900–
1980). *Apuntes de mi vida.* México, 1975.
196pp. Memoirs. Period Covered: 1905–1973.

From Ciudad Victoria, Tamaulipas, and
with active political life: federal deputy from
Tamaulipas, 1928–1932 and 1934–1937; governor of Tamaulipas, 1963–1969; PNR federal
conciliator for railroads, head of legal department for PEMEX, and active in formulation
of federal labor law and agrarian reform law.
Totally political and in defense of self with
little of private life.

126. Balbontín, Manuel (1824–1894). *Un
día del mes de enero a los 40 grados de latitud
norte.* México: Imprenta de Vicente García
Torres, 1873. 70pp. Memoirs. Period Covered: 1873.

Delightful account by soldier and writer
of one day spent in New York City. In
impressions may be described as innocent
traveler. Clear unpretentious style.

127. Balbontín, Manuel (1824–1894). *La
invasión americana 1846 a 1848....* México:
Tip. de G.A. Esteva, 1883. 137pp. Memoirs.
Period Covered: 1846–1848.

Both historian and soldier fought
against U.S. in 1847 invasion. Focuses on
Angostura, Valley of Mexico, Churubusco,
and Chapultepec. Witness-participant details

battles, climate, recruitment, food, officers,
etc. in clear, succinct style. One of few Mexican memoirs on this war.

128. Balbontín, Manuel (1824–1894).
Memorias del coronel.... San Luis Potosí, SLP:
Tip. de la Escuela I. Militar, 1896. 546pp.
Memoirs. Period Covered: 1845–1876.

Military man and historian participated
in many nineteenth century battles: war with
U.S.; on liberal side against conservatives in
Michoacán, Jalisco, and Puebla; and French
Intervention in 1863. Memoirs totally on military life: number of soldiers, personnel, supplies, strategy, etc. Personal touches,
landscape, and views of self missing.

129. Ballentine, George B. *Autobiography
of an English Soldier in the United States
Army....* New York: Stringer & Townsend,
1853. 288pp.

Valuable perspective of double outsider,
Scotsman in U.S. Army and member of
Winfield Scott's army that entered Mexico
from Vera Cruz. Journey starts in New York,
proceeds to Florida, then to Tampico, Vera
Cruz, Cerro Gordo, Jalapa, Puebla, and Mexico City. Like Bernal Díaz del Castillo in *True
History of the Conquest of Mexico*, Ballentine
goes beyond military campaigns. Insects, vegetation, natives, *aguardiente*, and Mexican
caste system fill pages.

130. Bancroft, Griffing. *Lower California:
A Cruise; The Flight of the Least Petrel.* New
York: Putnam, 1932. 403pp.

Ornithologist author, partner, and minimal crew go "Down one side of the Peninsula
and up the other and the islands in the fabled
Sea of Cortez!"(p.5). Geographical sites,
Ensenada, Todos Santos Island, Vizcaino
Desert, La Paz, and Mexicali, chapter divisions. Thoughtful and subjective view.
Accepts natives and reacts to pristine environment.

**131. Bandelier, Adolph Francis Al-
phonse; George Peter Hammond.** *A Scientist on the Trail: Travel Letters of A.F.
Bandelier, 1880–1881.* Berkeley, CA: Quivira
Society, 1949. 142pp.

American Bandelier studied Indians of
Cholula and Mitla. Does more than record

data; includes problems of logistics plus landscape and firm opinions on topics like beauty. Bandelier's experience in Mexico helped him to put into perspective indigenous culture of Southwest.

132. Barbosa, Paulina (1941–). *Entre el amor y la angustia.* México: EDAMEX, 2001. 125pp. Memoirs. Period Covered: 1955–1999.

Four generations of family here. Author's father, unjustly imprisoned in Lecumberri, became main focus of her life. Marries and has three daughters. Victim of her family managed to rear daughters with love. Much religious sentiment.

133. Barbour, Philip Norbourne; Martha Isabella Hopkins Barbour; Rhoda van Bibber Tanner Doubleday. *Journals of the Late Brevet Major Philip Norbourne Barbour…and His Wife, Martha Isabella Hopkins Barbour.* New York: Putnam, 1936. 187pp.

Journals of patriotic and naïve Philip in juxtaposition with simultaneous journal of wife make different type of reading. Participates in battles of Palo Alto and Resaca de la Palma. With family in Galveston, she keeps home front journal of family, household tasks, and longings for absent husband.

134. Baroni, Aldo; Enrique Gonzáles Aparicio. *Yucatán.* México: Ediciones Botas, 1937. 211pp.

Italian-born journalist from Havana in 1937 accompanied President Cárdenas on tour of Yucatan. Climate, environment, railways, ruins, Yucatecans, politics, and Cárdenas comprise vivid memoir. Aldo Baroni's presence felt in each paragraph.

135. Barragán, José Miguel (1835–1864). *Pequeño diario portátil, 1864: (memorias de un guerrillero durante la intervención francesa).* San Luis Potosí, SLP: Academia de la Historia Potosina, 1972. 29pp. Diary. Period Covered: 1864.

Fought on side of Juárez in War of French Intervention in San Luis Potosí and Tamaulipas. Part of diary for years 1862 and 1863 missing. Present work: impressions until death by firing squad, August 2, 1864. Maneuvers more important than emotions.

136. Barraza, María Haydée (1918–1998). *María Haydée, 1918- 1998.* Culiacán: Universidad Autónoma de Sinaloa, 1998. 139pp. Memoirs. Period Covered: 1918–1998.

Born in Sinaloa, she lived in Culiacán and Los Mochis before marriage and move to Mexico City. Husband Alfonso G. Calderón, labor leader and politician, governor of Sinaloa. Brother Alfonso Barraza worked for Communist Party. Contented wife and mother.

137. Barrera, Aida (1940–). *Looking for Carrascolendas: From a Child's World to Award-Winning Television.* Austin: University of Texas Press, 2001. 224pp. Memoirs. Period Covered: 193?–1976.

Lived on border in Brownsville and Edinburgh, Texas, and visited family in Monterrey. Bilingual, bicultural background enabled her to create and to produce *Carrascolendas*, Spanish English TV program for Hispanic children from 1970 to 1976. Program is centerpiece of autobiography; much on growing up in Catholic-Mexican-Anglo culture.

138. Barrientos Velasco, Herlinda (Dates?). "El compadre don Emiliano." En *Con Zapata y Villa: tres relatos testimoniales.* México: Instituto Nacional de Estudios Históricos de la Revolución Mexicana, 1991. Unpaged. Memoirs. Period Covered: 1907–1976?

Author's father and Zapata were *compadres.* After death of father, Zapata helped her and other survivors. Anecdotal and close-up view of hero from perspective of young narrator as well as details of life on hacienda.

139. Barrios, Elías (Dates?). *El escuadrón de hierro.* México: Ediciones de Cultura Popular, 1978. 182pp. Memoirs. Period Covered: 1920–1930.

Self-confessed, humble man of working class views labor movement in Mexican railways of 1920s.

140. Barrios de Márquez, Guadalupe (1933–). *Amor a la vida.* N.p., 1990. 106pp. Memoirs. Period Covered: 1933–1990?

Success story of naturalized Mexican-American born in Sombrete, Zacatecas. Death of mother and loss of father's fortune meant poverty and lack of education for family. Removal from Zacatecas to Ciudad Juárez and then to El Paso ended in happy marriage and family for author. Notes survival skills with family and hostile environment.

141. Barton, Mary. *Impressions of Mexico with Pen and Brush.* London: Methuen, 1911. 163pp.

Publication date of 1911 suggests that artist Mary Barton enjoyed Mexico before 1910 Revolution. Irish painter, she in eclectic travels had no interest in social protest. From Victorian period, she traveled alone in search of scenes to paint in Mexico City, Orizaba, Cuernavaca, Pátzcuaro, Cuatla, and Puebla. Landscape, vegetation, and occasional Mexican describe writing agenda. One of few writers capable of illustrating own work.

142. Basch, Samuel. *Memories of Mexico: A History of the Last Ten Months of the Empire.* San Antonio: Trinity University Press, 1973. 253pp.

Dr. Basch, sent from Europe to Mexico, became Emperor Maximilian's personal physician. Thus Austrian archduke is center of sympathetic narrative. Basch's knowledge of German made him invaluable in aiding harassed emperor in composing diary that runs from September 1866 to June 17, 1867. Very detailed on Maximilian's last days. Generals Leonardo Márquez, Tomás Mejía, and Miguel Miramón along with Father Fischer frequently mentioned.

143. Bassi, Sofía (1913–1998). *Bassi...prohibido pronunciar su nombre: anécdotas de Sofía Bassi.* México: Tallares de la Imper. Venecia, 1978. 329pp. Memoirs. Period Covered: 1968–1977.

Self-taught painter, scenery designer, and illustrator of books was accused of homicide in 1968 and spent four years in Acapulco jail. Incarceration and continued interest in painting main topics. Also covers relations with family and successful career as artist.

144. Bassols, Narcisso (1897–1959). *Cartas.* México: UNAM, Instituto Politécnico Nacional, 1986. 439pp. Letters. Period Covered: 1933–1959.

Law professor and government official held many offices: secretary of public education, government, and treasury; ambassador to Great Britain, France, Russia; and adviser to Adolfo Ruiz Cortines. Topically organized, letters fall into nine categories: personal, national politics, economic and social problems, nationalization of petroleum, democratic rights, educational and cultural affairs, world politics, Spain (Civil War and refugees), and anti–Facisim. Detailed table of contents indicates scope of contacts of brilliant lawyer.

145. Bastian, Jean-Pierre; Carlos Mondragón (1899–1983 Dates of Báez Camargo). *Una vida en la vida del protestantismo mexicano: diálogos con Gonzalo Báez-Camargo.* México: Centro de Estudios del Protestantismo Mexicano, 1999. 103pp. Interview. Period Covered: 1920–1960.

Purpose of 1978 dialogs was "...conseguir información; . . de unos de los actores más conocidos del protestantismo mexicano..."(p.16). Thus subject often speaks of self when he broaches following topics: outstanding Mexican Protestants (Andrés Osuna, Pascual Orozco, Aarón Sáenz, etc.); Revolution and Protestants; divisions within Protestant churches; and future of movement within Mexico and Latin America.

146. Bataille, Léon. *México, 1931–1946: memorias de un forastero que pronto dejó de serlo.* México: Sociedad Cooperativa Publicaciones Mexicanas, 1987. 210pp.

Records life of journalist and communist. French speaking and sixteen years of age, Bataille immigrated to Mexico in 1931. Attended school, learned language, and wrote for periodicals. Belonged to Federación de Jóvenes Comunistas and las Juventudes Socialistas Unificadas de México. Participation in these two groups and love for Mexico comprise much of memoirs.

147. Batalla, Paula (1904–?). *Donde quiera que me paro, soy yo.* Entrevista y edición Carola Carbajal Ríos y Ana Victoria Jiménez A. México: Editorial Libros de México, 1988. 141pp. Oral Autobiography. Period Covered: 1910?–1987?

Creates idiomatic life story in "unedited" words. From state of Mexico, she could serve as model for Poniatowska's Jesusa Polancares in *Hasta no verte jamás, Jesús mío*. Survival skills and spunkiness permeate life. Agrarian leader Rubén Jaramillo, assassinated in 1962, pivotal to story. Little on methodology of interviewer.

148. Batchelder, Roger. *Watching and Waiting on the Border*. Boston: Houghton Mifflin, 1917. 220pp.

Villa's threat changed lives of many Americans. From Massachusetts National Guard, Private Roger Batchelder called up for duty because of Mexican hero/bandit. More than hardships, such as bad food, poor equipment, and hot climate, young soldier manifests typical American bias against Mexicans. He notes war fever as troop train with its "To Hell with Mexico" lettering passes through idyllic American communities that agreed with sentiment.

149. Batis, Huberto (1934–). *Lo que "Cuadernos del viento" nos dejó*. México: Consejo Nacional para la Cultura y las Artes, 1994, (1984). 227pp. Memoirs. Period Covered: 1960–1984.

Excellent for focus on life of literary journal, *Cuadernos del viento*. Batis and Carlos Valdés godfathered enterprise in 1960. Inside details of functions of one important vehicle for *Generación del medio siglo*.

150. Bátiz, Enrique (1942–). *Confrontaciones*. Azcapotzalco, DF: Universidad Autónoma Metropolitana, 1984. 26pp. Interview. Period Covered: 1980s.

Musical conductor, graduate of Juilliard School of Music in New York and founder of Symphony of State of Mexico, comments on field: purpose of conductor, importance of information of new generation of musicians, significance of vocation, and desire to bring music to masses.

151. Bayardo Gómez, Patricio (1941–). *De tierra mojada al viento norte: memorias*. Guadalajara: Secretaría de Cultura, 1998. 70pp. Memoirs. Period Covered: 1951–1993.

Journalist born in Etzatlán, Guadalajara, records years here and moves in 1959 to Tijuana. In Baja, exercised profession in both Tijuana and Mexicali. Ardent Vasconcelista

and Panista reveals self and journalism at regional level.

152. Bazán, Nellie (1898–?). *Enviados de Dios*. Miami: Editorial Vida, 1987. 158pp. Memoirs. Period Covered: 1898–1987.

Nellie and Demetrio Bazán dedicated lives to Assembly of God Church in Texas, New Mexico, and Colorado and in mission to Latin America. From Helotes, Texas, Nellie tells of courtship and marriage to Mexican-born Demetrio, her family, and devotion to religion. Mentions H.C. Ball and Josué Sánchez, two leaders of Mexican-American Assembly of God Church.

153. Bazant de Saldaña, Milada; Jan Jakub Bazant. *El diario de un soldado: Josef Mucha en México, 1864–1867*. México: Miguel Ángel Porrúa, 2004. 147pp.

Mucha, a Moravian in Austrian Army, was in Mexico from June 1965 to February 1967. Never in battle, semi-literate soldier describes customs and Indians. His sympathy evolves to favor Juárez. Most European autobiographical documents on French Intervention written by upper classes.

154. Beach, Rex. *Oh, Shoot! Confessions of an Agitated Sportsman*. New York: Harper, 1921. 280pp.

Sportsman and humanist journeys to Sonora through Guaymas. Here he meets and comments on Yaquis. Next destination, Baja California, allows hunting and comments on Seris. Comprises last chapter of book including the above and carries title, "Messing Around in Mexico."

155. Beals, Carleton. *Brimstone and Chili: A Book of Personal Experiences in the Southwest and in Mexico*. New York: Knopf, 1927. 333pp.

Twenty-seven years old and sick of capitalism, he picks up brother Ralph and sets out for Sonora in search of gold in 1916. Penniless men must live by their wits through journey that takes Carleton from Sonora to Sinaloa and Durango, to Zacatecas, and finally to Mexico City, where he teaches. Finds American colony insipid. Adventures, worthy of picaresque hero, have salutary effect on him. "My experience had been like a sweeping fire that burnt away the clutter of dead growth...Fear disappeared..." (p.318).

156. Beals, Carleton. *Glass Houses: Ten Years of Free-Lancing.* Philadelphia: Lippincott, 1938. 413pp.

About 1918, congenial socialistic journalist arrived in Mexico penniless and survived. Knew many of native politicos and literati but specialized in commenting on Americans, e.g., variegated collection of diplomats, intellectuals, entrepreneurs, and frauds. Deflates Henry Lane Wilson and Dwight Morrow. Nasty to natives as in sketch of father of art patroness, Antonieta Rivas Mercado: "He was a huge man, well along in years, who rose up like a vast pyramid from short and stubby legs and the most enormous paunch I have seen..." (pp.73–74).

157. Beals, Carleton. *The Great Circle: Further Adventures in Free-Lancing.* Philiadelphia: Lippincott, 1940. 358pp.

About half of book devoted to Mexico in late 1920s: Toral and Madre Conchita episode, assassination of Cuban Julio Antonio Mella, Vasconcelos's failure as a politician, and, most important, Beals's imprisonment because of his antagonism to President Pascual Ortiz Rubio. A jaunt through Indian Oaxaca and a revisit to capital ends book.

158. Beals, Carleton. *House in Mexico.* New York: Hastings House, 1958. 214pp.

Beals travels slowly to Acapulco through state of Guerrero. Passes nights in many villages comprised of anti-foreigners, thieves, and filth.

159. Beauregard, G.T. *With Beauregard in Mexico: The Mexican War....* Baton Rouge: Lousiana State University Press, 1956. 115pp.

Some autobiographies of Mexican-American War stick strictly to campaign operations as does this one. Such is the above title. Feeling slighted in reports of superior officers, engineer defends self: work at Tampico, siege of Vera Cruz, battle of Cerro Gordo, and entrance to Mexico City. With Robert E. Lee, engineer emphasizes deeds and notes nothing of Mexico except terrain.

160. Becerra Acosta, Manuel (1932–). *Las primeras aventuras.* México: Editorial Nueva Imagen, 1983. 310pp. Memoirs. Period Covered: 1944?–1954?

Prose of *Primeras aventuras* shows talented writer. Captures feelings of 1930s-born generation that grew to adolescence during Alemán years. Mexico City, Puebla, and Paris venues for young man in love, companions, and relationship to father Fiodor.

161. Becerril, Leticia Román de (Dates?). *Comitán — un lugar para soñar: calendario gastronómico.* México: Gernika, 1995. 149pp. Memoirs. Period Covered: 1920?–1994?

Cookbook combined with memoirs arranged by twelve months and feast days. Family, place (Comitán, Chiapas), and customs in gentle autobiography interspersed with recipes.

162. Bedford, Sybille. *The Sudden View: A Mexican Journey.* New York: Harper, 1953. 288pp.

Curious change of title from Sybille Bedford's *The Sudden View* to *A Traveller's Tale from Mexico* suggests that British and Americans are two different reading clientele. Results of semi-fictional work positive. Hybrid work here: abstract travel information, short story involving Don Otavio, small buried essays on Mexican history, and author's irascibility. Moving throughout Mexico, Bedford at Lake Chapala creates character of don Otavio, caballero who incarnates peccadilloes and virtues of fallen Diaz aristocracy. Knowing history and some literature, author enhances with both.

163. Beebe, William. *Two Bird-Lovers in Mexico.* Boston: Houghton, Mifflin, 1905. 407pp.

Beebes cared only about wildlife and nature in 1903–1904 journey from port of Vera Cruz to Jalisco and Colima. Birds, mice, flowers, ants, swamps, and volcanoes occupied them and are captured on ubiquitous camera. "There is one joy of reading, another of painting, and another of writing, but none to compare with the thrill which comes to one who, loving Nature, in all her moods, is about to start on a voyage of discovery to a land familiar to him in dreams along" (p.1).

164. Behar, Ruth (1930? Birth of Esperanza). *Translated Woman: Crossing the Border with Esperanza's Story*. Boston: Beacon Press, 1993. 372pp. Oral Autobiography. Period Covered: 1930?–1989.

Esperanza Hernández, pseudonym of Mexquitic protagonist and "de-Indianized" woman of lower class, narrates three generations of females in family. Daughter, mother, and street vendor, she dialogs with Behar in quasi-novelistic life of survival and oppression. Behar examines process of capturing life of another and "translating" it for foreign consumption: "One problem with the genre [life history] has always been its use of the Western form of the autobiography to encase the self-narrative of a person marginalized by the West, a person usually lacking access to the means of production and often the ideological constructs necessary to turn talk into an autobiography in the first place, let alone into pages in a book" (p.272).

165. Bell de Aguilar, Sylvia (1895–?). *Bell.* México: El Autor, 1984. 219pp. Memoirs. Period Covered: 1858?–1910.

Daughter and granddaughter of circus performers and owners grew up in Porfirian Mexico, where her father Richard Bell, celebrated clown in Circo Orrín, opened circus. She narrates unique aspect of popular culture with family in Mexico, Cuba, and U.S.

166. Bello Hidalgo, Luis (1896–?). *Antropología de la Revolución de Porfirio Díaz a Gustavo Díaz Ordaz*. México: Costa Amic, 1966. 410pp. Memoirs. Period Covered: 1896–1965.

Author from Teziutlán, Puebla, and observer in Revolution utilizes memoir as vehicle for history he lived under eleven presidents: Díaz, Madero, Huerta, Carranza, Calles, Cárdenas, Avila Camacho, Alemán, Ruiz Cortines, López Mateos, and Díaz Ordaz. Partial to his contemporary Manuel Avila Camacho, also born in Teziutlán.

167. Beloff, Angelina. *Memorias.* México: Coordinación de Difusión Cultural, 1986. 98pp.

Russian-born Angelina Beloff met Diego Rivera in Belgium and was his companion from 1911 to 1921. Paris, birth and death of child, painting, and abandonment by Rivera describe years. Arrived in Mexico City in 1932. Survived through teaching, painting, and illustrating books. Died there in 1969.

168. Beltrán, Enrique (1903–1994). *Medio siglo de recuerdos de un biólogo mexicano.* México: Sociedad Mexicana de Historia Natural, 1977. 493pp. Memoirs. Period Covered: 1903?–1976.

Biologist in self-portrayal writes history of field in Mexico in twentieth century. Graduate of Columbia, founder of marine biology station, president of forestry commissions, Beltrán authored at least fifteen books and many articles. Sixteen species bear his name.

169. Benavides González, Javier (1948–). *Contra la corriente.* Chihuahua, CHH: Doble Hélice, 2002. 142pp. Memoirs. Period Covered: 1979–2002.

Valuable for two major themes. Author, active in Chihuahua PAN (Partido de Acción Nacional), reveals constant electoral fraud by PRI (Partido de la Revolución Institucional). Engaged in police work, Benavides, assistant director of City of Chihuahua police force, belonged to SEV (Servicios Especiales de Vigilancia) and served as coordinator of Instituto Nacional de Combate a las Drogas. PAN and police work rarely touched in Mexican autobiography.

170. Benítez, Fernando (1912 Birth of Espiridión Altamirano Lucas). *Historia de un chamán coro.* México: Ediciones Era, 1973. 142pp. Oral Autobiography. Period Covered: 1912?–?

Visits Cora settlement in Nayarit in Jesús María del Nayar. Journalist and anthropologist establishes context for oral autobiography of shaman, Espiridión Altamirano Lucas. Pilo (nickname) focuses upon role as intermediary for his people. Mixes witchcraft and hallucinatory drugs with biographical data. Benítez interrupts narration with explanatory paragraphs.

171. Benítez, José R. (1882–1957). *Cómo me lo contaron te lo cuento: por la calle de*

Juárez. Guadalajara: Ediciones del Banco Industrial de Jalisco, 1963. 147pp. Memoirs. Period Covered: 1882–1947.

Guadalajara engineer and author of books on history composed twenty-eight sketches of city before renewal. Subtlety and humor reminiscent of José Rubén Romero. In descriptive scenes of nineteenth century Guadalajara, he centers self, recording houses and inhabitants.

172. Benítez Valle, Manuel (1896–?). *Dichas y desdichas de un músico zacatecano.* Zacatecas, 1969. 90pp. Memoirs. Period Covered: 1897–1941.

Working-class flute player. Life as musician and of Villa-Murguía struggle in Zacatecas during Revolution. History of music at provincial level.

173. Berg, Richard L. (1940 Birth of Shwan). *Shwan: A Highland Zapotec Woman.* New York: Vantage, ca.1976. 149pp. Oral Autobiography. Period Covered: 1940–1960.

Another autobiography with intervention of second party, Shwan chronologically details life of typical Zapotec woman of Oaxaca from age six to twenty: child rearing practices, work patterns, religion, superstitions, intergroup relations, marriage, and death. Berg gives context for subject's life.

174. Berger, Bruce. *Almost an Island: Travels in Baja California.* Tucson: University of Arizona Press, 1998. 211pp.

Contrastive view of more sophisticated Baja. He knows Baja intimately through trips there starting in 1968. In best chapter, "Port of Illusion," he anatomizes Baja's capital, La Paz. Personality, history, values, and environment emerge. Dominant themes are nostalgia for earlier time and alarm at erosion of values and environment.

175. Bernal, Ignacio (1860–1929 Dates of Nicolás León) (1825–1894 Dates of García Izcazbalceta). *Correspondencia de Nicolas León con Joaquin García Izcazbalceta.* México: UNAM, 1982. 314pp. Letters. Period Covered: 1883–1894.

A young M.D., León wrote to venerable García Icazbalceta until latter's death in 1894. Exchange involves two scholars of antiquar-

ian books or pre–Columbian subjects of sixteenth century Mexico: their authors, condition of item, location, acquisition, and enjoyment. Ethnologist León wrote 344 works. García Icazbalceta was historian and bibliographer. Occasional note about family.

176. Bernal, María. *Raúl Salinas y yo: desventuras de una pasión.* México: Océano, 2000. 203pp.

Title fills in personal touches in Salinas de Gotari family. Brother Raúl met María Bernal in Spain and promised her marriage in Mexico. Disappointed when he married Mexican for political reasons, Bernal exposes intrigues of family. Information on death of José Francisco Ruiz Massieu, married to Raúl's sister.

177. Bernal, María Cristina Macouzet de (1922–). *Media vuelta al corazón: diario de una mujer.* México: Treyma Ediciones, 1989. 359pp. Memoirs. Period Covered: 1937–1956.

In 1939, married Miguel Bernal Jiménez, composer from Morelia, Michoacán. Life in two parts: love, children, and life with Miguel including trip to Spain and other parts of Europe, and Bernal Jiménez's tenure at Loyola in New Orleans, 1954–1956. Sudden death in 1956 initiates second part of life: widowhood, eleven children, and poverty. María Cristina endures by teaching table manners and by opening boarding house in Michoacán. Marital and maternal love and devout Catholicism predominate as themes. Paean to traditional values.

178. Bernal, Nicolás T. (1892–1973). *Memorias.* México: Centro de Estudios Históricos del Movimiento Obrero Mexicano, 1982. 158pp. Memoirs. Period Covered: 1892–1973.

In close contact with Ricardo Flores Magón and other anarchist sympathizers who attacked dictatorship from abroad, Bernal writes of political activities on both sides of border. Knew anarchist personalities from first decades of century: Flores Magón brothers and families, Alexander Berkman, Emma Goldman, Ethel Duffy Turner, Ramón Delgado, Librado Rivera, etc. Highly readable.

179. Bernal Jiménez, Miguel (1910–1956). *Páginas de un diario íntimo*. Morelia: Fimax Publicistas, 1982. 96pp. Diary. Period Covered: 1928.

Prolific author and composer from Michoacán in Rome to perfect self as organist. Stayed from 1928 to 1933 to gain expertise in Gregorian music. Devout Catholic comments on music lessons, performances, and churches.

180. Berrones, Guillermo (1948 Birth of Luna Franco). *Ingratos ojos míos: Miguel Luna y la historia de El Palomo y El Gorrión*. Monterrey: Centro de Información de Historia Regional, Universidad Autónoma de Nuevo León, 1995. 159pp. Oral Autobiography. Period Covered: 1952–1993.

Luna Franco of duet El Palomo and El Gorrión speaks freely of difficult childhood in Nuevo León. Regional musical group that reached national popularity with original songs accompanied by accordion and bass viol. Radio and recordings help spread fame. "Ingratos ojos míos" one of popular recordings.

181. Berrueto Ramón, Federico (1900–1980). *Obras completas, v.1. Memorias*. Saltillo, COA, 1984. 451pp. Memoirs. Period Covered: 1915?–1979.

High school teacher, college professor and administrator, and founding member of Federation of Teachers' Union in Coahuila, PRI member Berrueto Ramón also served in Congress. Recounts professional and political life. Personal self submerged under details of active career.

182. Besserer, Federico; Moisés Cruz (1959 Birth of Cruz) *Moisés Cruz: historia de un transmigrante*. Culiacán Rosales: Universidad Autónoma de Sinaloa, 1999. 307pp. Oral Autobiography. Period Covered: 1959–1987.

Of many oral autobiographies in present bibliography, *Moisés Cruz* is distinct in its enhancements: presentation of subject, discussion of theory, methodology, historical background of colony, and eight narrative chapters with sociological explanation. Subject, from San Juan Mixtepec, Oaxaca, immigrated to U.S., worked as bracero in California, was jailed, and returned home.

183. Betancourt Villaseñor, Amadeo (1907–?). *Entrevista con Amadeo Betancourt V.* Jiquilpan, MIC: Centro de Estudios de la Revolución Mexicana Lázaro Cárdenas, 1982. 103pp. Oral Autobiography. Period Covered: 1860?–1980?

From Jilquilpan in central Mexico, Betancourt Villaseñor seems representative of ordinary Mexicans. His family stretches back to nineteenth-century Michoacán. Son of medical doctor and *hacendado* family occupies lower status than forebears. Scattered questions relate to Revolution, life on hacienda, education, results of agrarian reform, and influences of television.

184. Beteta, José Luis (1933–?). *Viajes al México inexplorado*. México: Editorial Contenido, 1976. 185pp. Memoirs. Period Covered: 1930–1974.

Reared in sheltered environment, Beteta became enthusiastic outdoorsman and one of founders of Guía de Alpinismo and Grupo de Búsqueda y Salvamento. Each chapter refers to new adventure: Barranca del Cobre, Usumacinta, Sótano de las Golondrinas, Pedregal de San Angel, México Mágico, las grutas de Cacahuamilpa, and mountain climbing.

185. Beteta, Ramón (1901–1965). *Camino a Talxcalantongo*. México: Fondo de Cultura Económica, 1961. 126pp. Autobiography Proper. Period Covered: 1920.

Youth details life as Carrancista reconstructing year he and older brother fought in battles in state of Puebla. Building incidents to climax, autobiography approaches novel. Closure with death of Carranza. Beteta returns home and cycle of life begins. Reminiscent of Stephen Crane's *The Red Badge of Courage* for naïve youth and initiation into battle.

186. Beteta, Ramón (1901–1965). Entrevista en James W. Wilke y Edna Monzón de Wilkie's *México visto en el siglo XX*. México: Instituto Mexicano de Investigaciones Económicas, 1969. 58pp. Interview. Period Covered: 1901–1958.

Diplomat and politician shares childhood, role in Revolution, parents and family, education, presence at death of Carranza, and studies on poverty in Mexico. Talks about politics, economics, and social questions.

187. Beteta, Ramón (1901–1965). *Jarano.* México: Fondo de Cultura Económica, 1966 (1961). 207pp. Trans: *Jarano.* Translated from Spanish by John Upton. Austin: University of Texas Press, 1970. Memoirs. Period Covered: 1890?–1940?

Beteta fragments period by describing parents, their deaths, other family relationships, schooling, middle-class poverty, and Revolution. No coherent unity in memoirs. Yet book of great interest. Honest depiction of father (Jarano), who at times overshadows narrator son. Jarano created with love, fear, and finally understanding. One of best autobiographies of childhood.

188. Bigler, Henry William; Erwin Gustav Gudde. *Bigler's Chronicle of the West....* Berkeley: University of California Press, 1962. 145pp.

Bigler one of Mormon Battalion that went from Illinois to California in 1846 via Gila River in Arizona to San Diego and to Los Angeles. Calfornia landscape, Stephen Kearny, methods of travel, and Mormons comprise pertinent chapters.

189. Bingham de Urquidi, Mary. *Misericordia en Madrid.* México: Costa-Amic, 1975. 497pp.

British nurse married to Mexican ambassador to Spain. Exercising her profession on behalf of Republicans from 1936 to 1938, she treats the following: Mexican embassy in Madrid and its treatment of its own nationals; period of time in Valencia; President Cárdenas and his handling of embassy; intrigue from Mexico against Urquidi; effects of war on foreigners; and her meeting and rapport with Dolores Ibarruri (La Pasionara).

190. Blanco, Miguel (1816–1900). *Exposición que hace al pueblo mexicano el ciudadano Miguel Blanco....* México: J.S. Ponce de León, 1870. 84pp. Memoirs. Period Covered: 1863–1867.

Lawyer and military man from Coahuila fought in war against U.S. and on Constitutional side in War of Reform. Returned to hacienda during French Intervention. In disharmony with government following intervention; discredited and bankrupt Blanco presents his case.

191. Blanco Moheno, Roberto (1920–?). *A manera de justificación.* México: Editorial Diana, 1973. 79pp. Autobiography Proper. Period Covered: 1920–1973?

Makes jumps in autobiography. Describes Vera Cruz, where parents met and married, their large family, and poverty. Concentrates on early and unsuccessful experiences with school system, selling newspapers, and eventual career as journalist. Mentions marriage and family. Lived in Jicaltepec when sixteen years old. Second section, thirteen autobiographical short stories with author as protagonist, tells more about village than earlier part.

192. Blanco Moheno, Roberto (1920–?). *Memorias de un reportero.* México: Editorial V. Siglos, 1975. 303pp. Memoirs. Period Covered: 1956?–1964.

Reveals self only in comments about others. No background on early days nor what formed him as journalist. Comments on news but not in relation to self. Persistent vitriol wearisome to read. Strong likes and dislikes and treats subjects accordingly. Table of contents indicates topics: "Los reporteros de cantina," "Cuando cayó Ubico en Guatemala," "Adolfo Ruíz Cortinas," etc. More reportage than autobiography. Mexicans sketched without finesse.

193. Blanco Moheno, Roberto (1920–?). *La noticia detrás de la noticia.* México: Editorial V Siglos, 1975. 320pp. Memoirs. Period Covered: 1956?–1964?

Sequel to *Memorias de un reportero, La noticia* mixes autobiography and interpretive essays of Mexican history. In usual polemical form, he battles politicians and journalists. Communism, agrarian reform, and Central America major themes.

194. Blanco Moheno, Roberto (1920–?). *Ya con ésta me despido: mi vida, pero la de los demás.* México: Editorial Grijalbo, 1986. 351pp. Memoirs. Period Covered: 1920–1985.

More than two earlier works reporter

gives trajectory of life from birth to current moment. *Ya con ésta* reflects memoirs for concentration on external events. Subtitle suggests diffusion of narration. Opinionated and scandalous, he portrays alcoholic father, suffering mother, and poverty-burdened siblings in Coatepec (Guerrero) and in Mexico City. Discursive flow of brief essays and autobiographical fact.

195. Blanco Ribera, Carlos (1898–1983). *Mi contribución a la epopeya cristera....* Guadalajara: Asociación Pro-Cultura Occidental, 2002. 345pp. Memoirs. Period Covered: 1913–1924.

Wants to prove that *Cristero* movement was "acción de varones muy varones" (p.13). Gives chronological approach for indicated dates and notes own participation mainly in Jalisco. Yet differs from other *Cristero* memoirists: alludes to history and literature, notes universal context for movement, serves as soldier and diplomat for *Cristeros*; and shows awareness of inner conflicts of body of fanatics. Autobiographical thread sometimes lost in information pertinent to movement but peripheral to author's life.

196. Blancornelas, Jesús (1936–). *Conversaciones privadas.* México: Ediciones B. México, 2001. 179pp. Memoirs. Period Covered: 1943?–2001.

Begins with story of drug lords who attempted author's assassination in 1997. Born and reared in San Luis Potosí, he spent most of career in Tijuana exercising combative journalism against government: PRI, the presidency, and cavalier treatment of the press. One of better autobiographies of journalist with focus on career, some mention of personal life, and exposé of press censorship and reprisals.

197. Blasio, José Luis (1842–1923). *Maximiliano íntimo, el emperado Maximiliano y su corte....* París: Vda. de C. Bouret, 1905. 478pp. Trans: *Maximilian, Emperor of Mexico: Memoirs of His Private Secretary.* Translated from the original Spanish and edited by Robert Hammond Murray. New Haven: Yale University Press, 1934. Memoirs. Period Covered: 1863–1867.

Makes known romantic French Intervention. Young Blasio, Maximilian's private secretary, writes well and perceptively even though at times obsessed with Emperor's sex life. Sympathizes with Emperor perceived as liberal. Book in three parts: Court, from Miramar to Rome, and Querétaro. Insights and interpretations of period.

198. Blichfeldt, Emil Harry. *A Mexican Journey.* New York: Crowell, 1912. 280pp.

Follows normal itinerary. Unusual chapters include "Henequin," "The Government," "Higher than the Alps," etc. Published in 1912, *A Mexican Journey* researched under Porfirio Díaz. Talks of deportation of Yaquis from Sonora to Yucatan and deduces that Yaquis are slaves. Hurries on with "We believe these natives are generally and for the most part better off with some one both to command them and to provide for them" (p.54) Defends Protestantism in Mexico.

199. Blom, Frans Ferdinand. *En lugar de los grandes bosques: epistolario, 1919–1922, y diarios de dos expediciones.* Tuxtla Gutiérrez, CHP: Consejo Estatal de Fomento, 1990. 232pp.

Documents translated from Danish to Spanish of archaeologist's first contacts with Mexico. Held various jobs in petroleum, and frequently mentioned Coatzacoalcos and Minatitlán, centers for this industry. Diary covers expedition into Tabasco, Chiapas, and Veracruz where he looked for oil seepage and guided geological parties; here he introduces self to Mayan culture and specifically Lacandón Indians.

200. Blue Demon (1922–?). *Blue Demon.* México: Clío, 1999. 89pp. Memoirs. Period Covered: 1922–1988.

Successful wrestler with proletarian roots narrates career from village to railway worker and eventually to success in ring and retirement in 1988. He even starred in several movies. Insider's view of spectator sport including development of persona through wearing of mask. Excellent for popular culture.

201. Blue, Paty (Dates?). *La casa, la calle and otras debilidades: de tour con Paty Blue.*

Universidad de Guadalajara, 1994. 272pp. Memoirs. Period Covered: 1970?–1994.

Collection of newspaper columns from weekly *Paréntesis* that Blue began in 1988. Reacts to daily and boring aspects of life suggested by categories of titles. Much humor.

202. Bly, Nellie. *Six Months in Mexico.* New York: American, 1888. 205pp.

Few female visitors in Mexico had fame of Bly. Critical but praised Mexicans in Porfiriato. Detailed bullfight, noted presence of tobacco, and talked about her profession. Dismayed by low quality of Mexico's twenty-five newspapers and need of self-censorship for survival.

203. Boetticher, Budd. *When in Disgrace.* Santa Barbara, CA: Neville, 1989. 391pp.

Author incorporates much of Mexico and documents Arruza's life in 1960s. Boetticher, bullfighter himself and as master of B westerns, was natural choice for Arruza documentary. In disfavor with Mexican authorities, author imprisoned.

204. Boinas (1967?–?). "Aquí no hay ganchudos." En *¿Qué transa con las bandas?* de Jorge García-Robles. México: Editorial Posada, 1985. Pp.13–60. Oral Autobiography. Period Covered: 1970?–1984?

Sociologist interviewed members of gangs. Resulting forty-page monologue consists of inventory of juvenile crimes. Personality of narrator "Boinas" does not emerge in recounting.

205. Bojórquez, Juan de Dios (1892–1967). Entrevista en James W. Wilkie y Edna Monzón Wilkie's *Frente a la Revolución Mexicana: 17 protagonistas de la etapa constructiva,* v.2. México: Universidad Autónoma Metropolitana, 2001. Pp.304–362. Interview. Period Covered: 1892–1940.

Secretary of Ministry of Interior under both Presidents Abelardo Rodríguez and Lázaro Cárdenas, subject also had close connections with Calles. He addresses political and military career: Revolution in 1912 as Carrancista and member from Sonora of Congreso Constituyente. Invaluable informant for opinions on political leaders from 1913 to 1940. High praise for brilliance of

Obregón. Some personal life: birth, family, education in Sonora and in Mexico City.

206. Bojórquez, Juan de Dios (1892–1967). *Pasando por París.* México: Imprenta Mundial, 1929. 215pp. Memoirs. Period Covered: 1927.

Senator from Sonora, man of public service, engineer, author, and director of three newspapers. In 1927, traveled to France, Egypt, Italy, and Spain. Focus is Paris. Personalizes experience at each site.

207. Bonifaz, Evaristo (1920?–?). *Así son las gentes, iguales y diferentes: imágenes inolvidables.* Ensenada, BC, 1975. 95pp. Memoirs. Period Covered: 1914?–?

Lawyer selects three locations for eleven memoir-like stories: San Cristóbal de Las Casas, Chiapas (his native places), Mexico City, and Ensenada, Baja. In each *relato* interacts with neighbors, godfather, family, and acquaintances.

208. Bonifaz, Evaristo (1920?–). *La política: experiencias de un político bisoño.* México, 1982. 150pp. Memoirs. Period Covered: 1924–1952.

Chiapas lawyer enjoyed some regional political success during Calles years. Changing venue, he was in Baja when it achieved statehood in 1951. Valuable for political intrigues at state level.

209. Bose, Johanne Caroline Wehmeyer; Robert W. Blew. *Farewell to Durango: A German Lady's Diary in Mexico, 1910–1911.* Lake Oswege, OR: Smith, Smith, and Smith, 1978. 93pp.

From Bremen, Germany, Johanne Bose first lived in Durango from 1900 to 1904. She and husband returned to Germany and in 1909 once again in Durango to rescue family business. With two children and husband, she witnesses Revolution from 1910 to 1911. Like most foreigners, Boses support dictator. Records confusion and chaos of city of Durango.

210. Bosques Saldívar, Gilberto (1892–1995). *Historial oral de la diplomacia mexicana.* México: Archivo Histórico Diplomático

Mexicano, 1988. 165pp. Memoirs. Period Covered: 1892–1962.

Born in Villa de Chiahutla, Puebla, Bosques Saldívar, schoolteacher and senator, focuses on years in diplomatic corps in France, Portugal, Sweden, Finland, and Cuba. 1938–1964 service spanned WWII through Cuban Revolution. Attention to concrete incidents: Spanish refugees, prisoner of Germans, Cold War, and mounting of Mexican art exhibit. Aids in interpretation of relations with Cuba from Batista's final years to Revolution. No details on methodology or editing.

211. Bourne, John. *Recollections of My Early Travels in Chiapas.* Santa Fe, NM: Cloudbridge, 2001. 46pp.

Autobiographical account of discovery of ruins of Bonampak in 1946 by disenchanted author who belatedly was credited with find. Meeting with Giles Healy, one of discoverers; primitive conditions in Chiapas; visits to Mexico City; interaction with Lacandon; description of ruins; and efforts to share part of fame.

212. Bowden, Charles; Jack W. Dykinga. *The Secret Forest.* Albuquerque: University of New Mexico Press, 1993. 141pp.

Sonora and Chihuahua sites for above title. Seeks botanical secrets of Sierra and on way visits Mayos and other Mexicans. Literate author mentions other texts, Hernán Cortez, Martín Luis Guzmán, J. Frank Dobie, and John W. Hilton. "We live many different forms of consciousness" (p.49) suggests his mystical apprehension of forest. Indispensable photos by Jack Dykinga.

213. Bowles, Paul. *Without Stopping: An Autobiography.* New York: Putnam. 1972. 379pp.

Composer and communist reserves few pages for Mexico. Both labels give status as minor celebrity that moves about: Mexico City, Tehuántepec, Jajalpa (Toluca), Acapulco, and Taxco. Mingles with other celebrities; composes music; refuses to accept Trotsky but suspect member of Communist Party. Ends in 1941.

214. Bowman, Health; Stirling Dickinson. *Mexican Odyssey.* Chicago: Willett Clark, 1935. 292pp.

Two travelers, writer Heath Bowman and illustrator Stirling Dickinson and personified Ford car Daisy, make ideal trio as they travel Pan-American Highway from Laredo to Mexico City with unscheduled stops inbetween. Belong to years of Gringo adoration of Mexico. Stops, halting dialog with natives, forays into local markets, and verbal sketches of landscape that Daisy must master entertain as well as instruct.

215. Boyce, Marguerite Payne. *I Heard the Donkeys Bray: Thirty Years in the Mission Field.* Franklin, TN: Providence House, 1992. 192pp.

Presbyterianism has various aspects in Mexico. In 1940, author and spouse appointed evangelistic and educational missionaries to Mexico. James Boyce received medical degree from University of Mexico and opted to do *servicio social* by researching malaria in primitive site of Ometepec, Guerrero. Only medical clinic within a 100-mile radius of Ometepec. Survival, Mexican culture, and humor combined in narrative.

216. Brambila, David S.J. (1910–?). *De la tierra herida.* México: Buena Prensa, 1964. 40pp. Memoirs. Period Covered: 1930s.

Too short to qualify as monograph, *De la tierra herida* serves as companion piece to *Hojas de un diario*, which recounts Jesuit's experience among Tarahumara. Present work contrasts by almost poetic concision and accompanying b/w photographs.

217. Brambila, David S.J. (1910–?). *Hojas de un diario.* México: Editorial Jus, 1950, 125pp. Memoirs. Period Covered: 1930s.

Impressions fit more into category of memoirs than diary. Structure independent of chronological form and much external to writer. Jesuit, doing missionary work among Tarahumara Indians of Chihuahua, deplores their pagan character and laments failure of Christianity to change their nature. Yet more optimistic as he describes devout Indian or successful priest. Twentieth century scenes could be from colonial period. Feeling for landscape and Indian character in clear and sparse prose (illustrated with b/w photographs) present in *De la tierra herida*. Author's presence not as notable.

218. Bravo, Ramón (1925–1998). *Bajo las aguas del Mar Rojo.* México, 1962. 125pp. Memoirs. Period Covered: 1960.

Deep-sea diver travels to Arabian Peninsula to search underwater in Red Sea. He and companion dialog revealing emotion and events. In 1975, author published two works combining adventure and autobiography, *Holbox, isla de tiburoneros* and *Isla Mujeres*.

219. Bravo, Roberto (1947–). *De cuerpo entero: Roberto Bravo.* México: Ediciones Corunda, 1991. 49pp. Autobiographical Essay. Period Covered: 1965?

Veracruzano and author of several books, Bravo brings alive years as student at Xalapa. In second half of autobiography, he shares hell created through drugs.

220. Bravo Baquero, Jesús (1909–?). *Memorias universitarias: algunas cuestiones académicas importantes....* Morelia: Michoacana de San Nicolás de Hidalgo, 1985. 256pp. Memoirs. Period Covered: 1920–1980.

From 1920–1980, he attended or served as professor at la Universidad Michoacana. Arranged into eleven chapters corresponding to various phases of university life, memoir places him in academic environment.

221. Bravo Izquierdo, Donato (1890–1971). *Lealtad militar: campaña en el estado de Chiapas e Istmo de Tehuantepec, 1923–1924.* México, 1948. 144pp. Memoirs. Period Covered: 1923–1924.

Army general and loyal to Alvaro Obregón fought against Adolfo de la Huerta. Frustrated in bid for presidency, the latter rebelled against Obregón along with thirty-six other generals in Vera Cruz. Title's precision of time indicates autobiographical character of memoir. Eyewitness/participant moments of suppressing revolt diluted with historical commentary. Author usurps role of historian by incorporating unobserved events.

222. Bravo Izquierdo, Donato (1890–1971). *Un soldado del pueblo.* Editorial Periodística e Impresora de Puebla, 1964. 23pp. Memoirs. Period Covered: 1911–1925?

Gives no background on life, no motivations for activities, no curiosity as to outcome. Autobiography more akin to chronicle. Military experiences catalogued chronologically with little effort at chapter division or thematic organization. Over attention to details and inclusion of lists of names indicate book's major problem. No interpretation or analysis.

223. Breceda Mercado, Alfredo (1886–1966). "El verdadero camino de la Revolución mexicana: del campo de batalla a la iniciativa privada." En *Los revolucionarios* by Daniel Cazes. México: Editorial Grijalbo, 1973. Pp.261–350. Oral Autobiography. Period Covered: 1910–1917.

Coahuilense early joined forces of Madero and witnessed all of events of Revolution during indicated period. Villa, Carranza, Obregón, Zapata, and North American invasion structure memoirs.

224. Bremauntz, Alberto (1897–1978). *Setenta años de mi vida: memorias y anécdotas.* México: Ediciones Jurídico Sociales, 1968. 234pp. Memoirs. Period Covered: 1897–1967.

Lawyer, professor of economics, high school teacher, president of University of Michoacán, mayor of Morelia, federal deputy, and founding member of Socialist Party. Emphasis on career instead of personal life. Much on education in Michoacán: Nicolaita in Morelia, director of San Nicolás, and rector of la University Michoacana.

225. Brenton, Thaddeus Reamy T. *Bahía: Ensenada and Its Bay....* Los Angeles: Westernlore, 1961. 156pp.

Author identifies own work: "This expression [*olla podrida*] has broadened in its meaning to signify a miscellaneous collection, a medley, a hodgepodge" (p.xiii). Essays relate to history, day in own life, celebration of Revolution, Catholicism, etc. With little criticism and some autobiography, he promotes own part of Baja.

226. Brett, Dorothy. *Lawrence and Brett: A Friendship.* Philadelphia: Lippincott, 1933. 300pp.

One third of autobiography relates to Mexico. Threesome, author, Lawrence, and Frieda, together in Oaxaca in 1925. Brett always refers to Lawrence in second person and establishes a rapport between the two of them. Jealous Frieda ends this platonic affair in Indian Oaxaca.

227. Bright, John. *Worms in the Winecup: A Memoir.* Lanham, MD: Scarecrow, 2002. 260pp.

Bright has two chapters devoted to Mexico, a haven for former communists. Harassed by House Un-American Activities Committee, Bright and family settled in Mexico in 1950. Screenwriter, he was contracted to help in production of B. Traven's *Rebellion of the Hanged.* Interesting anecdotes on film adventures. Less happy is persecution from U.S. government and Bright's brusque deportation to U.S. after seven years in Mexico.

228. Brimmer, Gaby (1947–). *Cartas de Gaby.* México: Editorial Grijalbo, 1982. 136pp. Letters. Period Covered: 1973–1981.

Collection forms three separate components: letters to Elena Poniatowska, to family, and to friends. As intimate of Poniatowska, Brimmer reveals self-surviving and achieving with physical handicap. Frankness about family relationships, excitement over adopted daughter, and frequent comments on current events or human condition comprise other themes.

229. Brimmer, Gaby and Elena Poniatowska (1947 Birth of Brimmer). *Gaby Brimmer.* México: Editorial Grijalbo, 1979. 200pp. Oral Autobiography. Period Covered: 1947–1979.

Born with cerebral palsy, she narrates life with confessions dominating; nurse and companion, Florencia and her mother Sari, intervene with their perceptions of her life. Gaby refuses to surrender to illness, determines to live normally, and attends university. Frustrations and disappointments in personal relationships. Gaby occasionally amplifies with poems. Many of themes in present work and in *Gaby, un año después* and also in *Cartas de Gaby.*

230. Briseño, Romo (Dates?). *Confidencialmente: México social y burocrático al descubierto.* México: Costa-Amic, 1967. 200pp. Memoirs. Period Covered: 1965–1966.

Although exposes problems of bureaucracy and society, only first part is autobiography. Efforts to publish novel, *Sueños, ilusiones y realidades* (1965), unifies work. Insider's view on publishing, carnal love, incompetent medical services, and shoddy contractors. Disparate subjects filtered through own experiences.

231. Brito Sansores, William (1913–). "¡Adiós maestro rural." En *Los maestros y la cultura nacional, 1920–1952, v.5, Sureste.* México: Museo Nacional de Cultural Populares, 1987. Pp.39–72. Memoirs. Period Covered: 1919–1951.

Different from others in series, he prefaces autobiography with brief history of education in Yucatan. Called to right injustice, became rural schoolteacher in Kikil and in Tizimin and professor in Escuela Normal of Mérida.

232. Brizuela Virgen, Enrique (1928–). *Historia de la familia Brizuela.* Archivo Histórico del Municipio de Colima, 1998. 114pp. Memoirs. Period Covered: 1928–1997.

Only twenty-nine pages comprise autobiography: childhood in Colima, father's death, education, medical degree, marriage, experiences as doctor, and political life. Remaining pages trace family's lineage from sixteenth century to birth in 1928.

233. Brondo Whitt, Encarnación (1877?–1956). *La campaña sobre Zacatecas.* Gobierno del Estado de Zacatecas, 1990. 94pp. Diary. Period Covered: 1914.

Writer and M.D. leaves diary dating from June 9 to 29, month of battle of Zacatecas. Villa destroyed army that defended Victoriano Huerta. Brondo Whitt records "insignificant" details: supplies on train, human urine tinted by prickly pear, lice-infested soldiers, horses, men of North, etc. Battles never overwhelm incidental or subordinate parts. Telegraphic style.

234. Brondo Whitt, Encarnación (1887–1956). *Chihuahuenses y tapatios (De Cuidad Guerrero a Guadalajara).* México: Editorial Lumen, 1939. 165pp. Memoirs. Period Covered: 1938.

Journey through Chihuahua with anecdotes on hunting, folklore, and regional personalities. Subdued second part on ten-day visit with family in Guadalajara. Inferior to war experiences related in *La Division del norte*.

235. Brondo Whitt, Encarnación (1877–1956). *La división del norte (1914) por un testigo presencial*. México: Editorial Lumen, 1940. 363pp. Memoirs. Period Covered: 1914–1915.

Writer and M.D. practiced both professions for Villa in military train in Chihuahua and other parts of northern Mexico. Superior to most memoirists of Revolution, author relates self directly both to environment and action and creates personalized document of period. Registers supposedly insignificant details.

236. Brondo Whitt, Encarnación (1887–1956). *Nuevo León: novela de costumbres, 1896–1903*. Chihuahua, CHH: Editorial Lumen, 1935. 364pp. Memoirs. Period Covered: 1896–1903.

Relates to doctor's youth and medical experience. Focusing on contemporaries, memoirs *costumbrista* with profiles of regional personalities introduced in anecdotes. *La división del norte* superior in unity, style, and mood.

237. Brooke, George. *With the First City Troops on the Mexican Border, Being the Diary of a Trooper*. Philadelphia: Winston, 1917. 166pp.

Almost 100 troops, ninety-five men and four officers including George Brooke, relocated from Mt. Gretna, Pennsylvania, to El Paso, Texas. The book details expedition from July 6, 1916, to January 16, 1917. Burdensome process of training and caring for horses in cavalry. Food, sickness, animals, passes for leave, guard duty, maneuvers, boxing, and daily routine comprise diary of young and patriotic recruit.

238. Brown, James Stephens. *Giant of the Lord: Life of a Pioneer*. Salt Lake City: Bookcraft, 1960. 542pp.

Persecuted Mormons in Iowa raise battalion for Mexican-American War. "I am not writing a history of the Mormon Battalion,

but relating my individual experiences in that detachment of the United States army..." (p.38). Incredible suffering on trip from Leavenworth to Santa Fe to San Diego. New Mexico to California in 1,800 miles. Terms of enlistment expired and returned home in July of 1847. Remembered for march, not combat.

239. Bruccoli, Matthew Joseph. *Reconquest of Mexico: An Amiable Journey in Pursuit of Cortés*. New York: Vanguard, 1974. 252pp.

Bernal Díaz del Castillo and William H. Prescott wrote about original trek of Spaniards from Vera Cruz to Tenochtitlan. Most recent effort of recount of venture is above title. Through various modes of transportation he stops at fifteen places and comments on hotels, environment, natives, food, and landscape in amiable style. Arrives in Mexico City with jocular recall of historic march. Irreverent Bruccoli notes forerunner Prescott.

240. Bruell, James D. *Sea Memories or, Personal Experiences in the U.S. Navy in Peace and War*. Biddeford Pool: The Author, 1886. 67pp.

Few books on Mexican-American War from perspective of a sailor. Author's ship plied Atlantic coast from Rio Grande de Norte to Vera Cruz, Tampico, Lobos, and San Juan de Ulloa. Major action was blockade of Tampico and Vera Cruz. Transported men from island of Lobos to Vera Cruz for invasion. Items about crew, provisioning of food, and anecdote of pretending to be British to buy supplies from Mexicans.

241. Brunell Meneses, Alberto (1945–). **Nancy Peniche de Zubieta.** *Ríos de vida: anecdotario*. Monterrey: Ediciones, 1991. 404pp. Hybrid. Period Covered: 1928–1991.

Memoir and oral autobiography of Mexican Jewish family and youngest son Alberto. Monterrey and U.S. venues for ambitious subject who fought in Vietnam War. Businessman, head of National Radio and Television, and state and national politician, Brunell Meneses co-authors book with Peniche de Zubieta.

242. Bruschetta, Angelina (1898?–?).
Agustín Lara y yo. Xalapa: Gobierno de Veracruz, 1979. 285pp. Memoirs. Period Covered: 1920–1938?

Boon for popular culture buffs, book emotionally reveals tempestuous life with singer and songwriter. Love, betrayal, and passion, themes of Lara's compositions, repeat themselves in relationship between humble woman and musical celebrity. News clippings, letters, photographs, and song lyrics accompany text.

243. Bryant Edwin. *What I Saw in California....* Minneapolis: Ross & Haines, 1967. 468pp.

Newspaperman begins journey from Kentucky to California in 1846. Much on flora and fauna, description of natives, and details of journey. In 1847, marched under command of Col. John Charles Frémont. He also met Gen. Vallejo. Curious penultimate chapter with sentence, "Wherever the Anglo-Saxon race plant themselves, progress is certain to be displayed in some form or other" (p.427).

244. Buck, Robert N. *Battling the Elements.* New York: Putnam, 1934. 192pp.

Another pioneer, American Bob Buck, flew plane to Mexico. Knew almost no Spanish and even less about plane repair. Gives aerial view of Mexico including capital and Yucatan and extols adventure: "Flying in Mexico never becomes uninteresting, the country is always changing.... Therefore, it was impossible to get the feeling of monotony that is experienced in flying long hours in the states" (p.88). Routine invariable: searches for landing strip, lands, registers plane, interacts with Mexicans, describes meals, and then leaves. In Mexico City met Ambassador Josephus Daniels.

245. Bufill, José Angel (1889–1959 Dates of Alfonso Reyes). "Los amigos cubanos de Alfonso Reyes: un diálogo ennoblecido por la cultura." Ph.D. dissertation, George Washington University, 1986. 2 v. Letters. Period Covered: 1914–1956.

First volume is biography of Reyes and twenty-two Cuban correspondents, especially Jorge Mañach, José María Chacón and Felix Lizaso. Fewer letters between Reyes and José Varona, Francisco José Castellanos, Mariano Brull, Juan Marinello, Eugenio Florit, etc. In forty-two years of letters from Cuba, Reyes's personality emerges: intellectual liveliness, loyalty, and warmth.

246. Buick, Harry Arthur. *The Gringoes* [sic] *of Tepehuanes.* London: Longmans, 1967. 197pp.

Boy growing up on American frontier could not have more exciting youth than Buick in Durango. As fourteen year old, he landed in Mexico with family and left there at outbreak of WWI. Oil and mining absorbed him and brother. Skirmished with Mexican Revolution.

247. Buitimea Romero, Cipriano (1945–). *Como una huella pintada: (testimonio).* Hermosillo: El Colegio de Sonora, 1994. 85pp. Memoirs. Period Covered: 1945–1990.

Gives no suggestion of oral autobiography but follows independent format of Yaqui born in Guamuchil, Sonora. Given Yaqui conflict with invaders, Buitimea concentrates on struggle for land. Individual voice submerged in collective experience, norm in Indian autobiography.

248. Bullock, W. *Six Months Residence and Travels in Mexico.* Port Washington, NY: Kennikat, 1971 (1824). 532pp.

Britisher Bullock passed six months in Mexico in 1822 and 1823. Much more travel than autobiography, *Six Months* is trove of information on Mexico. He notes such things as buildings, landscapes, races, vegetation, farm animals, liquor, and tobacco and always in an interesting fashion. Bullock had neither time nor connections of his successor Fanny Calderón de la Barca; but as a stylist and observer, he is not much inferior to venerable Scottish aristocrat who wrote *Life in Mexico* in 1843.

249. Buñuel, Luis; José de la Colina; Tomás Pérez Turrent. *Luis Buñuel, prohibido asomarse al interior.* México: Mortiz/Planeta, 1986. 216pp.

In 1975 and 1976, two film critics interviewed Buñuel, who lived in Mexico from 1946 to 1962 and directed twenty-one pictures. He talks in detail about nineteen of these including *Los olvidados, Subida al cielo, Nazarín, Viridiana, El angel extermidor* y *Simón del desierto.* Buñuel's 1983 memoirs, *Mi último suspiro,* has chapter on years in Mexico (1946–1961). Here he made ten films. Jeanne Rucar de Buñuel's *Memorias de una mujer sin piano* (1990) illuminates Buñuel's domestic life during Mexican years, 1946–1961.

250. Burciaga, José Antonio (1940–). *Drink cultura: Chicanismo.* Santa Barbara, CA: Capra, 1993 (1979). 145pp.

Preceding *Spilling the Beans, Drink cultura* includes previously published autobiographical essays. Rarely with self-revealing intent, essays capture personality of painter/writer. Language, food, regionalism, schooling, Mexico and Mexican-Americans, childhood, art, Jews, Chicano heroes, and Ernesto Galarza relate directly to Burciaga.

251. Burciaga, José Antonio (1940–). *Spilling the Beans.* Santa Barbara, CA: Joshua Odell Editions, 1995. 215pp.

Chicano muralist, journalist, and humorist mosaics self in twenty-three essays relevant to Mexican-American/Mexican culture. Born in El Paso, Texas, he incorporates childhood, family, language, painting, and protest.

252. Burgoa Orihuela, Ignacio (1918–). *Memorias: epítome autobiográfico.* México: Editorial Porrúa, 1987. 590pp. Memoirs. Period Covered: 1918–1987.

Doctor of law from UNAM was professor, university administrator, and judge in Federal District. Author of over fifteen books on law, his *Las garantías individuales* and *El juicio de amparo* popular. In addition to law, he focuses on youth, family, and travels.

253. Burns, Archibaldo (1914–?). *En presencia de nadie.* México: Ortiz, 1964. 252pp. Autobiography Proper. Period Covered: ?–1939?

En presencia de nadie captures ennui of upper classes. Narrator, *un niño bien,* begins life in Mexico, travels to Europe for education, and returns under Cárdenas and expropriation of family properties. Author

involved in each moment and has style of professional writer.

254. Burstein, John (Dates?). *En sus propias palabras: cuatro vidas Tzotziles*/una compilación de John Burstein, Amber Past, y Robert Wasserstrom. Chiapas: Fray Bartolomé de las Casas, ca.1979. 217pp. Oral Autobiography. Period Covered: ?

Three anthropologists from Columbia University recorded lives of four Indians: Juan Santis Velio, Salvador López Pérez, Margarita Vázquez Gómez, and one labeled "una mujer de Magdalena." Bilingual autobiographies, Tzotzil and Spanish, collect either episodes or summarized lives of twentieth century Indians living in poverty.

255. Bush, Ira Jefferson. *Gringo Doctor.* Caldwell, ID: Caxton, 1939. 261pp.

Some books are dull; others, sporadically exciting. *Gringo Doctor* (1939) like *La División del Norte* never flags in making reader want more. Dr. Ira Bush's career climaxes in El Paso in 1910–1911, when he organized hospital to help wounded Maderistas fighting Porfirio Díaz. Author exercises profession and comments on personalities: Pancho Villa, members of Madero family, and two Creel brothers from Chihuahua.

256. Bush Romero, Pablo (Dates?). *México y África: desde la mira de mi rifle.* México: Gráfica Panamericana, 1958. 326pp. Trans: *Mexico and Africa from the Sight of My Rifle.* Mexico City: Gráfica Panamericana, 1960. Memoirs. Period Covered: 1954.

Hunted large game in Mexico and in Africa. Many photos of trophy animals: jaguars, elephants, pumas, grizzlies, tapirs, kudus, and bison.

257. Bush Romero, Pablo (Dates?). *My Adventures with Tigers and Lions.* México: Gráfica Panamericana, 1957. 234pp. Memoirs. Period Covered: 1950s.

Similar to *Mexico and Africa.* Persistent hunter records exploits in journeys to Japan, Hong Kong, Macao, Kenya, Rhodesia, France, Greece, Istanbul, Beirut, Jordan, Syria, Egypt, and Tanganyika. Travel and slaughter compete for attention.

258. Bush Romero, Pablo (Dates?). *Under the Waters of Mexico.* New York: Carlton, 1964. 184pp. Memoirs. Period Covered: 1959–1961.

Professional diver and founding member of CEDAM (Club de Exploraciones y Deportes Acuáticos de México) relates adventure in search for lost treasure off coasts of Yucatan and Quintana Roo. Also search for buccaneer Jean Lafitte.

259. Bustamante Martínez, José (1903–?). *El gran lente/fotografía de José Antonio Bustamante.* México: SEP, INAH, 1992. 112pp. Memoirs. Period Covered: 1930–1973.

Self-taught photographer exercised profession in Fresnillo, Zacatecas, and Mexico City. Chronologically reconstructs life and evolution of photography in twentieth century Mexico. In photography, art is touch up as exemplified by Indian woman who became a Spaniard through his magic. Exudes lower and middle-class values.

260. Bustillo Oro, Juan (1904–1989). *México de mi infancia.* México: Colección Metropolitana, 1975. 176pp. Memoirs. Period Covered: 1908?–1914?

Writer and film director witnessed much of Revolution as child in besieged capital. Work focuses on daily problems of non-combative and neutral civilians who tried to survive. Memoirs result more from perspective on Revolution than organized attempt at depicting growth of personality. Final chapters thematically alien to book.

261. Bustillo Oro, Juan (1904–1989). *Vida cinematográfica.* México: Cineteca Nacional, 1984. 350pp. Memoirs. Period Covered: 1909–1965.

In two previous volumes, writer and film director concentrated on childhood and infatuation with Vasconcelos movement. In present, notes childhood only as it relates to theater. Personal involvement with production of sixty-two films basis of book.

262. Bustillo Oro, Juan (1904–1989). *Vientos de los veintes.* México: Sep Setentas, 1973. 183pp. Memoirs. Period Covered: 1920s.

José Vasconcelos rather than author main figure. Young Bustillo Oro swept up by idealism of Vasconcelos movement in 1920s. Little on writer and more on young men surrounding Vasconcelos and sharing ideas. *Vientos* relates more to political system than single life.

263. Butler, Helen. *Doctor Gringo, as Told to Helen Butler.* Chicago: Rand McNally, 1967. 241pp.

Another M.D. with ties to U.S., young American completed medical training in Mexico and prepared for *servicio social,* six months of free medical service in some neglected village. Anonymous narrator assigned Lagos in southern Mexico, where he meets poor and middle-class Mexicans. Service primitive and pays $80.00 per month. Meets gamut of eccentrics with determined folk beliefs. Political and economic life manifested in microcosm.

264. Butler, Karl Douglas. *The Family of John Topham and Susan Elizabeth Redd Butler.* Provo, UT: Bringham Young University, 1990. 294pp.

Autobiographies of Mormons in Mexico can be one chapter of larger study as in above title. Latter born in Utah to polygamous family that fled to Colonia Juárez in Chihuahua in 1891. Schooled in Júarez, married and lived in Morelos, Sonora. Mentions Oaxaca, Sonora, destroyed by flood in 1905, year family returned to U.S. to live in Douglas, Arizona. Morelos and Oaxaca, Sonora, unnoted among Mexican Mormons, receive attention. Butler refers to Douglas and exodus of Mormons to U.S. in 1912 because of Revolution. Notes little interaction with natives.

265. Bynner, Witter. *Journey with Genius: Recollections and Reflections Concerning the D.H. Lawrences.* New York: Day, 1951. 361pp.

In 1922, poet Witter Bynner met D.H. Lawrences in Mexico. The capital, Cuernavaca, and Cholula prelude party's stay at Lake Chapala from May to June. Bynner, in constant contact with Lawrence, likes Frieda; and although he admires Lawrence, he notes constant nastiness to others of group and to natives. Bynner also exposes incidents that go into plot of *The Plumed Serpent. Journey with Genius; Recollections and Reflections Concern-*

ing the D.H. Lawrences (1951) shows Bynner scrutinizing an eccentric set of foreigners in Mexico.

266. Caba Bazán, Tito (Dates?). *Yo fui guardaespaldas de Rigo Tovar.* México: Editores Asociados Mexicanos, 1982. 120pp. Memoirs. Period Covered: 1979.

Rigo Tovar, singer who founded *Afroantillana* musical group Costa Azul, also composed popular songs. Life as celebrity seen through experiences of ex-policeman bodyguard.

267. Cabada, Juan de la (1903–1986). *Confrontaciones.* Azcapotzalco, DF: Universidad Autónoma Metropolitana, 1987. 37pp. Interview. Period Covered: 1937?–1986?

Short storywriter, raconteur, and scriptwriter describes collaboration with Luis Buñuel; estrangement from Octavio Paz, Hermilo Abreu, and Siqueiros; and travels. Presents self well through anecdote.

268. Cabada, Juan de la (1903–1986). *Memorial del aventurero: vida contada de Juan de la Cabada.* México: Conaculta, 2001. 198pp. Oral Autobiography. Period Covered: 1913?–1959?

Sophisticated and seamless autobiography produced in 1979 for TV and retold by Fierros. Migratory figure Cabada relates life with energy and style of published writer. From hacendado family of Campeche, he ignored privilege, left school, worked as roustabout in Cuba and oil worker in Tampico, and joined Communist Party in Mexico City. Journalist for *El Machete* and scriptwriter for film.

269. Caballero Sosa, Guillermo (1908–?). *Memorias de un bajacaliforniano.* Tijuana: Centro de Investigaciones Históricas, 1984. 40pp. Memoirs. Period Covered: 1908–?

Native of Baja was educator, lawyer, and politician. Held high state government positions and interacted with prominent politicians: Antonio I. Villarreal, Juan Sánchez Azcona, Abelardo Rodríguez, and Sánchez Taboada. Author helped found University of Baja and worked with desalinization. Successful regional politician.

270. Cabrera Barroso, Enrique (1953?–1971). *Cárcel municipal.* México: Ediciones de Cultura Popular, 1973. 81pp. Memoirs. Period Covered: 1961–1962.

One of founders of communist student group traveled to Cuba for Revolution. In 1961, jailed for political activities in la Cárcel de San Juan de Dios. Detention generates document of prison life, work, love, and other relationships. Introduction and first chapter most autobiographical. In remaining pages, records impressions without active involvement.

271. Cabrera de Tablada, Nina (1871–1945 Dates of José Juan Tablada) *José Juan Tablada en la Intimidad.* México: Imprenta Universitaria, 1954. 113pp. Memoirs. Period Covered: 1917–1945.

Cuban widow's memoirs deserve forum. Touches on life with Tablada and notes his creative moods and inspirations. They traveled to Cuba, Mexico, South America, and U.S. Memoirs should be read in conjunction with Tablada's *La fería de la vida.*

272. Cabrera Ypiña de Corsi, Matilde (1906–?). *La Lonja de San Luis Potosí: un siglo de tradición.* San Luis Potosí?, 1957. 417pp. Diary. Period Covered: 1874–1915.

Author María Asunción belonged to one of San Luis Potosi's prestigious families during Porfiriato. Diary ends with Revolution and exile in San Antonio, Texas. Invalid author, trying to lead normal life, comments on society of upper class as it relates to locus of their activities, La Lonja, exclusive type of country club. Social calendar with its proper participants. Visits of dignitaries such as Porfirio Díaz, William Jennings Bryan, and Sarah Bernhardt. Young author notes scientific progress. Superb first-person account of lives untouched by economic needs.

273. Cabrera Ypiña de Corsi, Matilde (1906–?). *Mis viajes: memorias de ayer y de hoy.* México: Editografía Guadalajara, 1985. 187pp. Memoirs. Period Covered: 1928–1945.

From wealthy San Luis Potosí family and married to diplomat, author visited all European capitals plus Constantinople, Holy Land, and Egypt. Noting nobility and palaces, she suggests attitude of Revolution's lingering Porfirian aristocracy.

274. Cadwallader, Sharon. *Savoring Mexico: A Travel Cookbook.* New York: McGraw-Hill, 1980. 207pp.

Cadwallader combines cooking, travel, and autobiography. Arranged geographically, Mexico's diverse regions offer both travel and culinary challenge to author. Gives history, visits restaurants, orders specialties, finds recipes, and moves on.

275. Calderón, Miguel G. (1885–?). *Aventuras: versión abreviada de las memorias....* editadas por Y.C. de Carter. Austin, TX: Amistad, ca.1975. 85pp. Memoirs. Period Covered: 1885–1920?

Fought in Revolution and became lawyer, judge, and Mexican Consul in Denver. Recreates Huck-Finn type childhood in Oaxaca.

276. Calderón de la Barca, Madame. *Life in Mexico during a Residence of Two Years in That Country.* London: Chapman and Hall, 1843. 437pp.

No other book by outside observer achieved status or permanence of popularity of Calderón de la Barca's *Life in Mexico* (1843), trove of letters to friends from 1839 to 1842. Much information through eyes of well-placed Scottish woman. Landscape, customs and manners, industry, civil wars, presidents, servants, modes of travel, food, church, and much regionalism abound in unequalled pages of Mexico.

277. Calixto, Héctor Manuel (1920?–). *La carpa y yo.* Instituto de Cultura del Estado de Durango, 2000. 175pp. Memoirs. Period Covered: 1930?–1987.

Writes of apprenticeship in theater and career in road shows in home state, San Luis Potosí, Aguascalientes, and Sinaloa. Started in declamation, performed in over a hundred plays, and was heard on radio.

278. Calles, Plutarco Elías (1877–1945). *Correspondencia personal, 1919–1945. Introducción, selección y notas de Carlos Macías.* México: Fondo de Cultura Económica, 1991. 535pp. Letters. Period Covered: 1919–1945.

Governor of Sonora from 1917 to 1919 and president of Mexico, 1924–1928, spent much of career in government service. First volume, revealing little of self, incorporates exchange of correspondence between him and other government officials. Self-revelation most keen in family correspondence, pp.407–476.

279. Camacho, Ramiro (Dates?). *Mi madre y yo: estampas históricas de provincia, 1855–1937.* Guadalajara: Editorial El Estudiante, 1943. 483pp. Memoirs. Period Covered: 1855–1937.

Combined autobiography of mother and son. Secundina Ruiz de Camacho (1855–1936) left unpublished autobiography from which son Ramiro Camacho excerpted paragraphs and complemented them with fragments of own life plus historical context. Fanatical Catholics from Guadalajara, mother and son oppose reform of 1857 and anticlericalism that prompted *Cristero* revolt of 1920s.

280. Camacho Solís, Manuel (1946–). *Yo Manuel, memorias apócrifas? de un comisionado.* México: Rayuela Editores, 1995. 125pp. Memoirs. Period Covered: 1988–1994.

Insider memoirs attributed to Camacho Solís, highly educated member of PRI and holder of various prestigious government positions. Focus on government and condemnation of its activities and processes in *sexenio*.

281. Camacho y García, Rafael Sabás (1826–1908). *Itinerario de Roma a Jerusalén. Escrito en el año 1862.* México: Lugo, 1885. 290pp. Memoirs. Period Covered: 1862.

Camacho y García, exiled by government in 1861, went to San Francisco (Calif.) and then to Rome and Palestine. Enough of self present to qualify as memoirs, e.g., notes error of placing Mary at foot of Cross. In 1885, elevated to bishop of Querétaro.

282. Cámara y Zavala, Felipe de la (1815–1878). *Memorias de....* México: Editorial Yucalpétén, 1975. 78pp. Memoirs. Period Covered: 1836–1840.

Outstanding document for nineteenth century. As federalist fought against centralizing efforts of Santa Anna. Author intersperses clearly written political/military memoirs with autobiographical data and anecdotes.

283. Camarillo de Pereyra, María Enriqueta (1872–1968). *Del tapiz de mi vida.* Madrid: Espasa-Calpe, 1931. 258pp. Meditations. Period Covered: 1890–1929.

Poet spent much of life in Europe. Meditations relate to thoughtful, innocent, and mature child. Series of thirty-one moments of childhood rather than unified book. First-person perspective and each chapter with gemlike quality. No violence mars tranquility of ideal childhood. European origin of passages permits little of Mexico. Qualifies as autobiography only in limited way.

284. Cameron, Charlotte. *Mexico in Revolution: An Account of an English Woman's Experiences....* London: Seeley, Service, 1925. 278pp.

British writer differs little from Americans who write on Mexico. Views dictatorship in positive light: "During the Diaz dynasty the watchword was Progress" (p.113). Contribution is description of years prior to 1925 when de la Huerta gave provisional presidency to Alvaro Obregón. In 1923, with collusion of Gen. Guadalupe Sánchez, Huerta proclaimed self president. Exile to Los Angeles proved his failure.

285. Camp, Roderic Ai (1905 Birth of Antonio Gutiérrez). *Memoirs of a Mexican Politician.* Albuquerque: University of New Mexico Press, 1988. 230pp. Memoirs. Period Covered: 1905–1970.

Compiler of biographies of Mexican politicians creates Gutiérrez, "...a composite of politicians who grew up during the last decade of the Porfiriato..." (p.ix). Michoacán protagonist, rising from poverty through education and political connections, becomes senator. Generic memoirs focus on political life and achievements rather than personal life. Differ from authentic memoirs for too much detail on early years, absence of documents, and little flattery for cohorts. Narrator here tells only what he observed and avoids role of historian. Three other collective autobiographies in present bibliography: Herrera-Sobek, Máximo Peón, and Vaca del Corral.

286. Campa S. Valentín (1904–?). *Memorias de Valentín Campa: 50 años con el movimiento obrero y revolucionario.* Monterrey: Facultad de Filosofía y Letras, 1978. 73pp. Memoirs. Period Covered: 1920–1968.

Notes initiation into labor movement at age sixteen. Gives personal and communistic interpretation: 1926–1927 and 1958–1959 railway strikes, Cárdenas and Calles, nationalization of oil, Cedillo's rebellion, and Leon Trotsky.

287. Campa S. Valentín (1904–?). *Mi testimonio: Experiencias de un comunista mexicano.* México: Ediciones de Cultura Popular, 1978. 361pp. Memoirs. Period Covered: 1911–1977.

Militant communist spent almost fourteen years in prison. Historicizes communism and labor movement rather than focusing on self.

288. Campbell, Federico (1941–). *De cuerpo entero: Federico Campbell.* México: Ediciones Corunda, 1990. 59pp. Memoirs. Period Covered: 1941–1960.

Finds beginnings through lives of parents in dialog with sister. Railroad-telegrapher father and primary school-teacher mother emerge more delineated in personality than author. Action in Navojoa, Sonora, and Tijuana.

289. Campbell, Henry Murray. *Mexican Cavalcade.* Mexico: Editorial Cultura, 1952. 324pp.

English citizen and writer of memoir cum history recalls Mexico from Porfirio Díaz to Adolfo Ruiz Cortines. Revolution and aftermath, church strike, and oil expropriation dominate. Comments on American, English, and German colonies in Mexico. Alert to Nazi activities among German colony. Sympathetic to Mexico.

290. Campbell, Howard. *Mexican Memoir: A Personal Account of Anthropology and Radical Politics in Oaxaca.* Westport, CT: Bergin & Garvey, 2001. 149pp.

Campbell shows intense integration by foreigner. Anthropology and autobiography mix as author, centered in Juchitán, studies Zapotecs. Married Zapotec woman and adopted Zapotec child. Debunks stereotype of Tehuántepec matriarchy. Criticizes training of anthropologists.

291. Campo Venegas, Oscar del (1929–?). *De niño de la calle a periodista: novela autobiográfica.* Tijuana: Tallares Color Graph, 1999. 133pp. Autobiographical Novel. Period Covered: 1929–1999.

Early type of street gamin survived various odd jobs including army. Arrived in Tijuana in 1956, where he is now journalist. Curious third-person narrative about self.

292. Campobello, Nellie (1909–1968). *Cartucho: relatos de la lucha en el norte de México.* México: Compañia General de Ediciones, 1960 (1931). 143pp. Trans: *Cartucho*; and *My Mother's Hands.* Translated by Doris Meyer and Irene Matthews. Austin: University of Texas, 1988. Memoirs. Period Covered: 1911?–1971?

Series of staccato portraits of military men and civilians in Revolution of northern Mexico. Place, naïve perspective, and violence unite autonomous images into whole of cruelty and irony. Titled *Cartridges* for individual nature of each episode and its explosive quickness. Villistas portrayed from author's memory.

293. Campobello, Nellie (1909–1968). *Las manos de mi mamá.* México: Compañiá General de Ediciones, 1960 (1937). 75pp. Trans: *Cartucho*; and, *My Mother's Hands.* Translated by Doris Meyer and Irene Matthews. Austin: University of Texas Press, 1988. Memoirs. Period Covered: 1911?–1971?

Lyrical memoirs of Revolution centered on mother. Incidents joined by her presence in northern Mexico. Widow must fend for children. As in *Cartuchos*, events and persons filtered through naïve perspective of child. Although labeled a novel, *Las manos*'s evocation of revolutionary past and incorporation of actual places and personalities make it more akin to memoir.

294. Canby, Peter. *The Heart of the Sky: Travels among the Maya.* New York: Harper Collins, 1992. 368pp.

Canby moves freely in the Mayan lands of Guatemala, Honduras, and Mexico. Mayan site of pre–Columbian culture covered. Autobiography, archaeology, ethnology, history, and current events mix in incisive study of Maya and their subdivisions and their confronting late twentieth century European culture. Dialogs with Mayan and lives in their environment.

295. Cano Manilla, Ramón (1888–1974). *Prisonero de Valle Nacional: bello capítulo de mi vida.* Ciudad Victoria: Instituto Tamaulipeco de Cultura, 1985. 299pp. Memoirs. Period Covered: 1905.

Tamaulipan painter left typewritten manuscript. Unusual document condemns Porfiriato. Hacienda peon escaped to Vera Cruz for better life. Inveigled to go to Valle Nacional, enforced prison camp, he worsens life. Ends happily with escape and return to Vera Cruz. Accompanied by autobiographical painting.

296. Cantrell, Florine. *Mexican Odyssey: The Diary of a Missionary's Lifetime of Service in Mexico.* United States: Rust Engineering, 1977. 81pp.

Cantrell records thirty-seven years as Protestant missionary/nurse in Los Nogales and Los Haro, Zacatecas. Member of Christian Church, Cantrell went to Mexico in 1928. Recounts cures, conversions to Protestantism, Catholic antipathy to Protestant intruders, furloughs to U.S., and anecdotes of Mexican patients and converts. Sums up problem: "In leaving an established traditional religion to become part of a Protestant movement, Mexicans have created a minority group. In so doing they have sacrificed certain privileges which they would otherwise enjoy" (p.29).

297. Cantú, Juan Luis (1894–?). *Memorias de un modesto e ignorado revolucionario: años de 1908–1912.* Monterrey: 1948. 118pp. Memoirs. Period Covered: 1908–1912.

Pro-Madero revolutionary from Monterrey, fifteen years old in 1909, eager to be in conflict. Because of age he becomes aid to Col. Justiniano Gómez but never sees action. More than reportage of military events, valuable for images of two leaders, Bernardo Reyes and Venustiano Carranza. Middle-aged Cantú captures war fever of younger self.

298. Capetillo Villaseñor, Manuel
(1920–?). *Manuel Capetillo: más allá de la leyenda.* México: Pearson Educación, 2002. 192pp. Memoirs. Period Covered: 1947–1979?
Bullfighter, actor, and singer recalls life mainly in bullring. Started fighting bulls in 1947 and has retired several times. Different from other *toreros*, he notes rivalry between Mexico and Spain in spectacle. More candid about marriages and personal life.

299. Capistrán Garza, René (1898–1974). *Andanzas de un periodista y otros ensayos.* México? 195–? 224pp. Memoirs. Period Covered: 1919.
Describes single experience of harassment of journalists under Carranza. Kidnapped and taken to Chihuahua, he later escaped. Combative personality writes exciting narrative.

300. Caraveo Estrada, Baudilio B.
(1874–1968). *Historia de mi odisea revolucionaria....* Chihuahua, CHH: Doble Hélice Ediciones, 1996. 428pp. Memoirs. Period Covered: 1910–1916?
Guzmán's *Memorias de Pancho Villa* outstanding memoir of Revolution in Chihuahua. Middle-class Caraveo Estrada from Moris gives different perspective. Maderista, he was in Batoplias, Yoquivo, Rocheáchic, and Norogáchic (all in Chihuahua) but was in Mexico City and other parts of republic. Posthumous document with concentration on author as observer/participant.

301. Caraveo Frías, Marcelo (1886–1955). *Crónica de la revolución (1910–1919).* México: Editorial Trillas, 1992, 207pp. Memoirs. Period Covered: 1886–1929.
From Chihuahua and revolutionary since 1910, he rose to general with active military career: Orozquista fought in siege of Ciudad Guerrero; participated in surrender of Ciudad Juárez, decisive in defeat of Díaz in 1911; battled against Huerta until 1913; fought against Villistas; joined Zapata, enemy of Carrancistas in la Huasteca (Vera Cruz and Tamaulipas); and fought against Delahuertistas. In 1929, governor of Chihuahua.

302. Carbajal, Francisco (1812?–?). *Vindicación de D. Francisco Carbajal.* México:

Imprenta de Vicente García Torres, 1845. 53pp. Memoirs. Period Covered: 1812–1845.
Printer, archivist, military man, and holder of positions in Department of State and national treasury defends self. Attacked by journalist Carlos Bustamante, author compelled to write defense. Idea of political life for indicated period.

303. Carballido, Emilio (1925–). *Confrontaciones: Emilio Carballido.* Azcapotzalco, DF: Universidad Autónoma Metropolitana, 1987. 46pp. Interview. Period Covered: 1945?–1986?
Short story and script writer, novelist, and dramatist discourses on preferred topic: theater. Noting its status in Spanish America but especially Colombia and Mexico, he pays tribute to teacher and master, Rodolfo Usigli. Two of Carballido's plays noted: *Yo también hablo de la rosa* and *Fotografía en la playa.* Touches on process of creation.

304. Carballo, Emmanuel (1929–). *De cuerpo entero: Emmanuel Carballo.* México: Ediciones Corunda, 1991. 65pp. Memoirs. Period Covered: 1912?–1990.
Short story writer and critic in lineal account reveals basics of childhood in Guadalajara in honest portrait of parents and growing up with widowed mother. Captures Tapatío atmosphere. Pages on education from primary through university some of best in autobiography.

305. Carballo, Emmanuel (1929–). *Ya nada es igual: memorias, 1929–1953.* México: Editorial Diana, 1994. 382pp. Memoirs. Period Covered: 1929–1953.
Author and literary critic composes autobiography/ memoir of first twenty-four years in Guadalajara. Since books comprise life, he focuses on reading, writing, interacting with other authors, education, editing, *tertulias*, and bookstores. Youth serves as literary history of Guadalajara. Superbly captures teachers, colleagues, and girl friends. So far no sequel to cover second half of twentieth century.

306. Carballo, Isaías (1966?–). *Gay.* México: Selector, 1993. 180pp. Memoirs. Period Covered: 1971–1993?

From large and poor Vera Cruz family, he discovered sexual orientation at early age. Tells of action in Mexico City, where Carballo introduced to sex. Shares homosexual encounters and efforts to achieve stable relationship. Themes of AIDS and outing.

307. Carballo, Marco Aurelio (1942–). *De cuerpo entero: Marco Aurelio Carballo.* México: Ediciones Corunda, 1990. 58pp. Autobiographical Essay. Period Covered: 1945?–1991.

Novelist and short story writer spent first eighteen years in Tapachula, Chiapas. Shows family relationships, love of reading, journalist in Mexico City, and other efforts at writing.

308. Cardenal, Ernesto. *Vida perdida.* México: Fondo de Cultura Económica, 2003. 447pp.

Nicaraguan poet attended University of Mexico from 1943 to 1947 and returned in 1959 for spiritual reasons. On advice of Trappist Thomas Merton, he pilgrimaged to Cuernavaca to combine psychoanalysis and spirituality under guidance of Gregorio Lemercier, prior of Benadictine Monastery. Here Erich Fromm influenced him. Cardenal also published two books of poetry under tutelage of fellow Nicaraguan poet, Ernest Mejía Sánchez. Only one chapter, thirty-four pages, relates to Mexico.

309. Cárdenas, Emilia (1900?–). *Emilia, una mujer de Jiquilpan/Griselda Villegas Muñoz.* Jiquilpan, MIC: Centro de Estudios de la Revolución Mexicana Lázaro Cárdenas, 1984. 208pp. Oral Autobiography. Period Covered: 1906–1983?

Interviewing Cárdenas in 1982 and 1983, Villegas Muñoz claims she recorded words as spoken. Mentions nothing of interventions in organizing document of woman typical for one born early in century. If women's lives comprised of ordinary happenings, then Emilia's in Michoacan town exemplifies that of many Mexican women. Presents self in midst of folkloric culture of masses: work, marriage, parents, stories, riddles, songs, funerals, etc. History impinges in Revolution and *Cristero* Wars.

310. Cárdenas, José A. (1930–). *My Spanish Speaking Left Foot.* San Antonio: Intercultural Development Research Association, 1997. 135pp. Memoirs. Period Covered: 1934–1997.

Bilingual-bicultural San Antonio educator grew up on Laredo border and in Monterrey. Family, customs, schools, language, and cultural traditions pervade in mix of autobiography and sociology. His contact with both nations clearly places him in two cultures. Choice of left foot for marching as well as choice of Spanish language for speaking.

311. Cárdenas, Lázaro (1895–1970). *Apuntes, 1913–1940, 1941- 1956, 1957–1966, 1967–1970, 1974–1975.* México: Siglo Veintiuno Editores, 1974–1975. 4 v. Journal. Period Covered: 1913–1975.

Memoirs in diary form: eighteen year old in Revolution, lieutenant colonel and general of division in 1928, in same year governor of Michoacán, secretary of gobernación under President Ortiz, president of PRI, secretary of war, and president from 1934 to 1940. Entries perfunctory. Rarely reveal emotion or insight into government operations. Neither this nor other volumes show surprises. Follows same formula: comments on political and economic situation with emphasis on agrarian, succinct itineraries noting only place and time, and occasional references to family members. Bland neutrality interrupted only by death of close friends. Shows politician at work but does not reveal personality. Portrayed more fully in Fernando Benítez's *Entrevistas con un solo tema: Lázaro Cárdenas* (1979), where six intimates record impressions.

312. Cárdenas, Lázaro (1895–1970). *Epistolario de Lázaro Cárdenas* México: Siglo Veintiuno, 1974, 2 v. Letters. Period Covered: 1925–1970?

Division into two parts, internal and external affairs, indicates direction in giving image. Almost totally public persona or liberal president who worried about U.S. machinations towards weaker neighbor, fulfillment of agrarian reform, program of education, etc. Formality of statesman revealed. Inner Cárdenas never escapes to expose character. Did Cárdenas or competent secretary write letters? Valuable for political affairs and history. Second volume on international themes.

313. Cárdenas Aréchiga, María Dolores
(Dates?). "¡Esta noche te vas conmigo"! En *Con Zapata y Villa: tres relatos testimoniales.* México: Instituto Nacional de Estudios Históricos de la Revolución Mexicana, 1991. Pp.49–76. Memoirs. Period Covered: 1915–1962?

Wife, schoolteacher, and artist. Nayarita married soldier and fulfilled duties of *soldadera* with army of Rafael Buelna (one of Villa's officers) in North. For forty-seven years plucky survivor taught school. In later years became painter.

314. Cárdenas D. Hipólito (1900?–?). *Mi padre y yo.* México: Editorial Stylo, 1962. 198pp. Memoirs. Period Covered: 1913–1924.

Focus on father as much as self suggests precision of title. Child/adolescent growing up in undiscovered Acapulco, he experiences early Revolution. Father, type of *caudillo,* mysteriously imprisoned and freed and protected by Maderistas, raised cattle in Guerrero. Coupled with skirmishes with enemy and survival of family is desire for education, achieved by migration to Mexico City in 1924.

315. Cárdenas Hernández, Gregorio
(Dates?). *Adiós.* México: Editorial Diana, 1981. 391pp. Memoirs. Period Covered: 1942–?

As in earlier work *Celda 16,* he vacillates between sociology and autobiography. More observer and recorder than emotional sentient being. Brief history of prisons preludes sociological nature of work. Life in prison rather than life of prisoner.

316. Cárdenas Hernández, Gregorio
(Dates?). *Celda 16.* México: Editorial Diana, 1970. 236pp. Memoirs. Period Covered: 1954.

Headliner criminal apprehended and jailed. Story of infrastructure of prison life. Catalogs penal life but fails reader at emotional level. More sociologist-observer than suffering human being.

317. Cárdenas Hernández, Gregorio
(Dates?). *Pabellón de locos de la Cárcel Preventiva del Distrito Federal....* México: Editorial Diana, 1973. 351pp. Memoirs. Period Covered: ?

Author of two other prison autobiographies in this novelized memoir focuses on inmates in *Pabellón de locos de la Cárcel Preventiva del Distrito Federal.* Direct experiences in nightmarish world lend reality to presentation.

318. Cárdenas Rodríguez, Antonio
(1906–1969). *Alas sobre América.* México: Artis, 1943. 343pp. Memoirs. Period Covered: 1939.

Pilot in 1939 began Panamerican flight from Oakland, California, to almost every Latin American country. Details of origin and plans for odyssey plus initial paragraphs of each chapter connect book to memoir. Reflects concern with reporting political, economic, and social development of each country to Mexicans.

319. Cárdenas Rodríguez, Antonio
(1906–1969). *Mis dos misiones: monografía aérea.* México: Tallares Gráficos de la Nación, 1949. 252pp. Memoirs. Period Covered: 1943–1945.

Mexico's participation in WWII rarely recorded in autobiography. Lt. Col. Cárdenas Rodríguez served as pilot in two missions: one to Africa and Mediterranean and one to Pacific. Memoirs, more of place and military action than personality, verify his country's presence in war. Little of personal or anecdotal survives.

320. Cárdenas Solórzano, Cuauhtémoc
(1929–?). *Cuauhtémoc Cárdenas: un perfil humano.* México: Editorial Grijalbo, 1997. 247pp. Interview. Period Covered: 1934–1997.

Subject talks freely with interviewer: relationship with father; governorship of Michoacán; presidents from Avila Camacho to López Portillo; Tlateloco; candidature for presidency; and marriage and family.

321. Cardona Peña, Alfredo (1886–1957 Dates of Diego Rivera). *El monstruo en su laberinto.* México: Editorial Diana, 1980.

202pp. Oral Autobiography. Period Covered: 1948–1950.

Realized by questions and responses. Sixty-three-year-old Rivera reflects on topics: primitive, folk, pre–Hispanic, and Mexican paintings and art critics. Invariably anecdotes from childhood grace earlier pages.

322. Careaga, Gabriel (1951 Birth of Omar Martínez). *Biografía de un joven de la clase media*. México: Océano, 1977. 177pp. Oral Autobiography. Period Covered: 1965–1976.

Careaga based manuscript on tape recordings, dictations, and observations of Omar Martínez. Pessimistic oral autobiography with desperate air and tone more fitting to 1950s than 1970s. Omar, son of middle-class couple, passes through experiences of adolescence: school, family, women, and liquor. Devoid of values and relating to no one, he is patterned after existentialist anti-hero. Autobiography contrasts with image of youth in most memoirs.

323. Careaga Soriano, Teresa María (1915?–?). *Mi México de los veinte*. Toluca: Universidad Autónoma del Estado de México, 1994. 129pp. Memoirs. Period Covered: 1920s.

From well-to-do family, she evokes with humor and nostalgia Mexico of 1920s. Holidays, *posadas*, seamstresses, theater, film, radio, home, sweethearts, birthdays, *tertulias* and mourning summarize chapters. Something of autobiography but more of Mexico.

324. Carey, Robin. *Baja Journey: Reveries of a Sea-Kayaker*. College Station: Texas A&M University Press, 1989. 175pp.

Shakespeare professor writes *Baja Journey* but ignores traditional information. Houses, towns, and natives do not attract him. Title word *reveries* best enables reader to categorize author who guides to mysticism of location. Worries about environment; returns to pristine time when man and surroundings coalesced. Psychological and chronological time disappears.

325. Carmony, Neil B.; David E. Brown. *Mexican Game Trails: Americans Afield in Old Mexico, 1866–1940*. Norman: University of Oklahoma Press, 1991. 270pp.

Carmony and Brown edited *Mexican Game Trails*. Among sixteen selections appear famous contributors: Lew Wallace, Frederic Remington, Kermit Roosevelt, Aldo Leopold, and John Steinbeck. Nature predominates in hunting, exploring, bird watching, and interaction with Indians. Nature more mportant than Mexico.

326. Caro, Jesús C. (1912–?). *Caro amigo: The Autobiography of Jesús C. Corral*. Tucson: Westernlore, 1984. 238pp. Memoirs. Period Covered: 1860–1971?

Sonora and Arizona backdrops for Mexican-American sculptor, engineer, and restaurant owner. Jesús Corral emigrated from Cananea, Sonora, to Scottsdale, Arizona. Mexican-American at ease in both cultures and without bitterness towards Anglo.

327. Caro Baroja, Pío. *El gachupín*. México: Alianza Editorial, 1992. 257pp.

Nephew of Spanish novelist Pío Baroja immigrated to Mexico City. Focuses on talents as writer, film critic, producer of documentary films, and cultivator of other Spanish exiles such as León Felipe and Luis Buñuel. Covering years 1950 to 1956, he highlights culture of fellow exiles as much as own life. In early 1990s, Caro Baroja leaves Spain and returns to Mexico on a trip of nostalgia. He visits familiar sites and tries to locate what is left of exile community he once knew. He and daughter Carmen travel to Yucatan and to Guanajuato. "¡Adiós México! ¡Adiós juventud perdida!" (p.318) echoes second part of *Gachupín; seguido de En busca de la juventud perdido* (1995).

328. Carpenter, Frank G. *…Mexico*. Garden City, NY: Doubleday, Page, 1924. 287pp.

Professional travel writer visited Mexico and Toluca. As voyager through many countries, he might have written predictable book on eighth destination, Mexico. Yet some chapters stand out. How business functions in Mexico verges on insider's view of profit motive at work here. "Old Popo" focuses on commercial possibilities and failure of Mexico's most famous volcano. Toluca merits chapter. "Slicing Up the Big Estates" reveals accomplishments of one of Revolution's main goals and simultaneous legal technicalities that frustrate actual redistribution.

329. Carpenter, William W. *Travels and Adventures in Mexico….* New York: Harper, 1851. 300pp.

Unique memoirs of Mexican War. He entered Mexico at Brazos in 1846 and exited at Mazatlán in 1848. Carpenter fought at Monterrey. Later taken prisoner, he spent remainder of time trying to escape. As an American, he pretended to be Irish. His journey took him from León to Sayula to Guadalajara and Tepic. Much autobiography in adventures; much on Mexico.

330. Carr, Harry. *Old Mother Mexico.* Boston: Houghton Mifflin, 1931. 270pp.

Carr takes eastern side of Mexico to Yaquis, San Blas, Tepic, Guadalajara, Morelia, and Mexico City. Meeting with governor of Michoacán, Gen. Lázaro Cárdenas, and praise for military predict future of most popular twentieth century president. Always present and filtering exotic Mexico through self, he notes both Mexico and his own life here.

331. Carrasco, Aledo (1875–1945). *Mis recuerdos.* Edición, introducción, notas críticas y catálogo de Lucero Enríquez. México: UNAM, 1996. 640pp. Memoirs. Period Covered: 1875–1941.

Organist of cathedral of Guadalajara and teacher of music composed religious music. He appealed to more secular public with salon music. Posthumous memoirs detail semi-orphanhood and beginnings of career. Excellent for state of music during sweep of career.

332. Carreño, Alberto María (1865–1938 Dates of González Obregón). *El cronista Luis González Obregón.* México: Ediciones Botas, 1938. 215pp. Memoirs. Period Covered: 1833–1938.

Suggests symbiotic nature of relationship between biographer and subject. Dying González Obregón, historian and author of *Las calles de México* (1922), collaborated with Carreño on memoirs. Although in third person, writings betray influence of subject who describes childhood, education, professors, books, and research.

333. Carrillo, Julián (1875–1965). *Testimonio de una vida.* Prólogo y relato de Dolores Carrillo. San Luis Potosí, SLP: Comité Organizador "San Luis 400," 1992. 304pp. Oral Autobiography. Period Covered: 1879–1975.

Daughter Dolores Carrillo confesses role in realization of work on Don Julián. Favorite child and companion of father, she heard stories, took dictation, and added chapter concerning her mother. Fascinating read about poor Indian violinist from San Luis Potosí discovered and sponsored by Porfirio Díaz. Rags-to-riches story with study in Europe, directorship of conservatory, exile in U.S., musical compositions, several books, and *el sonido 13*, theory and realization of microtones.

334. Carrillo Marcor, Alejandro (1908–1998). *Apuntes y testimonios.* México: El Nacional, l989. 432pp. Memoirs. Period Covered: 1904–1979?

Lawyer, educator, editor of periodicals, politician, and diplomat presents self in fragments in hybrid memoir of documents and quotations. Born in Hermosillo, Sonora, was educated both in U.S. and Mexico. Interesting life does translate to interesting autobiography.

335. Carson, Kit; Blanche C. Grant. *Kit Carson's Own Story of His Life.* Taos, NM, 1926. 138pp.

In 1832, followed Spanish trail from Taos to California. In non-Mexican lands for long period, he tells of Taos again when he married Josepha Jaramillo in 1847. Both guide and courier in contact with Frémont, he set out for Monterey, California. Mentioning San Diego and Los Angeles, he was in California when war broke out with Mexico.

336. Carson, William English. *Mexico: The Wonderland of the South.* New York: Macmillian, 1914. 449pp.

Reflects attitude toward subject pervasive in U.S. Anti-Indian and anti–Mexican sentiment: "When contrasted with the present decadence of the Indian races in Mexico, …"(p.109) or "Mexicans being naturally averse to all business enterprise or energetic action…" (p.170). Chapter in praise of Díaz mandatory. Carson witnessed scenes similar to those recorded a year later in Turner's *Barbarous Mexico*: "Prisons were full to choking, and those criminals caught red-handed were transported to the host lands in southern Mexico as plantation slaves. The result has been more than good"(pp.213–214). Carson seems blind to injustices but complains about government's extermination of Yaquis.

337. Casasús de Sierra, Margarita (1892–1972). *Las llaves perdidas.* México: UNAM, 1961. 281pp. Memoirs. Period Covered: 1918–?

Far more spiritual autobiography than *33 de la U.F.F.* Although she occasionally details fragments of concrete reality, writings tend to self analysis and goal, "Mi deseo de penetrar el significado de las almas, es más agudo cada dia..." (p.139), is no less true for herself than for others. Comparison to Simone Weil and Albert Schweitzer evidences mysticism and love for humanity.

338. Casasús de Sierra, Margarita (1892–1972). *33 de La U.F.F.* México: Editorial Cultura, 1930. 188pp. Memoirs. Period Covered: 1922?–1930?

As nurse/postulant, young author finds meaning in sufferings of others. Working in hospital, she observes and succors the deformed and ailing. Abandoning more worldly existence, she validates Christianity by serving others.

339. Caso, Antonio (1883–1946). *Ramos y yo: un ensayo de valoración personal.* México: Editorial Cultura, 1927. 30pp. Essay. Period Covered: 1927?

Philosopher and educator divulges portions of intellectual life in defending self against Samuel Ramos, former student who attacked the *maestro's* philosophical work in journal *Ulises*.

340. Cassel, Jonathon F. *Lacandon Adventure: Last of the Mayas.* San Antonio: Naylor, 1974. 219pp.

Not every researcher is a professional anthropologist. In this book three Cassels, spouses and son, venture to San Cristóbal de las Casas with goal of researching Lacandones. Cautionary remarks of Gertrude Duby

Blom, doyenne of Lacandon studies, do not deter them from spending an unspecified time amid Mayas near village of Ocosingo. Filled with anecdote of Lacandon customs and Cassel family's dual efforts to study Indians and to ameliorate their conditions.

341. Cassel, Jonathon F. *Tarahumara Indians.* San Antonio: Naylor, 1969. 160pp.

Author, wife, and fifteen-year-old son in 1960s challenge selves by hiking to Tarahumara in Chihuahua. Gringo family lives with this tribe near towns of Sisoguichic and Tehuerichic. Autobiography here and also amateur anthropology as author studies and records environment and customs of Tarahumara: birth, death, health, alcoholism, etc.

342. Castaneda, Carlos. *Journey to Ixtlan: The Lessons of Don Juan.* New York: Simon and Schuster, 1972. 315pp.

Apprentice sorcerer learns from Don Juan, a Yaqui Indian. Goal appears to make world stop, state that carries bearer beyond present reality. Ixtlan is locus of Nirvana. Journey-type autobiography in quest for other reality. Spirit world of Yaquis.

343. Castañeda, Salvador (1946–). *Los diques del tiempo: diario desde la cárcel.* México: UNAM, 1991. 141pp. Memoirs. Period Covered: 1971–1977.

Writer and political agitator fought on side of guerrilla group Movimiento Armado Revolucionario and as punishment spent six years in three prisons: Lecumberri, el Reclusorio Norte, and Santa Martha. Details of horrors of prison life vivid in illicitly composed document. Better writer among prison authors.

344. Castaños, Carlos Manuel (1932–?). *Testimonios de un agrónomo.* México: Editorial Futura, 1981. 378pp. Memoirs. Period Covered: 1970–1977.

Agronomist from la Escuela Nacional de Agricultura de Chapingo involves self in two experiments: sunflower and *chahuixtle* of wheat. Sunflower introduced to Durango. Sonora locale to experiment on wheat disease.

345. Castaños, Salvador (1929?–). *Memorias de un médico rural.* Durango,

DUR: Smythe Impresores, 1996. (1961).
229pp. Memoirs. Period Covered: 1955?
   Novelistically records apprenticeship to
medicine in Durango. Saves victim with health
problem. Venue changes from village to village; doctor practices under primitive conditions. Child birthing most popular medical
challenge. Like Rubén Marín, Castaños has
greater sense of style than most doctors.

346. Castellanos, Rosario (1925–1974).
Balún Canán. México: Fondo de Cultura
Económica, 1961 (1957). 291pp. Trans: *The
Nine Guardians, a Novel*. Translated by Irene
Nicholson. New York: Vanguard, 1960. Autobiographical Novel. Period Covered:
1934–1936?
   Letters to Ricardo Guerra comprise
most tangible autobiography of poet Castellanos. 1957 novel *Balún Canán* delineates
early years at family hacienda in Comitán,
Chiapas. City along with other names and
historical events corresponds to reality of
Cárdenas years in southern Mexico. Death of
preferred child, brother Mario, and trauma
of land expropriation harmonize with Castellanos's childhood. Nine-year-old narrator
gives more of context then of self.

347. Castellanos, Rosario (1925–1974).
Cartas a Ricardo. México: Consejo Nacional
para la Cultura y las Artes, 1994. 336pp.
Letters. Period Covered: 1950–1967.
   Richest collection of letters ever published by Mexican woman. Postmarked Chiapas, *S.S. Argentina*, Madrid, Naples, Rome,
Vienna, Tuxtla, Chapatenga, Madison (Wisconsin), Bloomington (Indiana), Boulder
(Colorado), and Mexico, D.F., letters map
wanderings as student and professor. Love for
Ricardo dominates; self-revelation, almost
unknown in Mexican autobiography, pervades; parenting small son Gabriel and teaching in U.S. main subjects. Source for most
important twentieth century woman poet. In
2000, poet Oscar Bonifaz Caballero published
Una lámpara llamada Rosario. He briefly
biographizes Castellanos, who wrote four letters to him between 1952 and 1957. Poetry
dominates as theme.

348. Castellanos Everardo, Milton
(1920–?). *Del Grijalva al Colorado: recuerdos y*

vivencias de un político. Mexicali: Universidad
Autónoma de Baja California, 1999. 435pp.
Memoirs. Period Covered: 1925?–1977?
   From Tuxtla Gutiérrez, he notes political
life: senator from Chiapas, alternate senator
from Baja, governor of Baja, active in PRI,
and director of campaigns of Adolfo Ruiz
Cortinas, Braulio Maldonado Sánchez, and
Eligio Esquiel Méndez. Something of child-
hood but mainly political career.

349. Castellanos Everardo, Milton
(1920–?). *Testimonio de un hombre: Entrevistas de Humberto Hernández....* Tijuana:
Litografía Limón, 1983. 253pp. Interview.
Period Covered: 1971–1974.
   Former governor of Baja answers questions relating to regime. Little on personal
life. Federal senator and head of campaign for
Adolfo Ruiz Cortines in Baja. Book centers
on campaigning and government, drinking
water, civic center, public finance, etc.

350. Castellar Rosa, Marquesa de
(Dates?). *My Stove Is My Castle*. México: Editorial Intercontinental, 1956. 166pp.
   Catalan adds to autobiography through
culinary memoir. Creative divorcee converts
Cuernavaca mansion and kitchen into source
of income. Original recipes enlivened by
anecdotes.

**351. Castelló Carreras, Salvador; José
N. Iturriaga de la Fuente.** *Diario de viaje
por el Río Balsas y Costa Grande de Guerrero
(1910)*. México: Fondo de Cultura
Económica, 1990. 175pp.
   Spanish uncle of Carmen Romero Rubio
on Canadian expedition of Río Balsas from
Cuernavaca to Pacific Coast. One month
Southwest trip took author through Morelos,
Michoacán, and Guerrero to Acapulco.
Involved in both river and land expeditions,
author in subjective style inventories land-
scape, climate, food, and Indians and notes
his own moods.

352. Castillo, Eric del (1934–). *¿Por qué
me hice actor?* México: Océano, 2000. 408pp.
Autobiography Proper. Period Covered:
1934–1954?
   Story to point where he becomes actor.
Maybe next volume with professional life.

Present is autobiography for intense view of youth. Celaya sporadically focuses on troubled youth with divorced parents, no interest in school, and several years in reform school. Strong emotional attachments to mother and brother; despised stepfather.

353. Castillo, Guillermo J. (1894–?). *Chapingo: evocaciones de un profesor de zoología*. México, 1943. 101pp. Memoirs. Period Covered: 1911–1923?

National School of Agriculture established during Porfiriato well covered in humorous accounts of students, faculty, and events.

354. Castillo, Heberto (1928–). *Si te agarran, te van a matar*. México: Océano, 1983. 150pp. Memoirs. Period Covered: 1961–1975?

Engineer and author but mainly polemical journalist founded Movimiento de Liberacion Nacional, anti-imperialistic organization. In 1968 revolt, he spent over two years in prison. Tells of capture; of more value, delves into psychological problems such as meaning of time for prisoner.

355. Castillo, Porfirio del (1884–1957). *Puebla y Tlaxcala en los días de la Revolución*. México, 1953. 321pp. Memoirs. Period Covered: 1910–1925?

Constitutionalist colonel in army of Gen. Pablo González and Inspector General of Police in Puebla in 1920 writes typical memoirs for Revolution. Maderista in contact with Serdáns and other revolutionaries from Puebla and Tlaxcala. Usually observer/participant rather than historian. Photographs and other documentation support text.

356. Castillo Nájera, Oralba (1897–1986 Dates of Renato Leduc). *Renato y sus amigos*. México: Editorial Domés, 1987. 431pp. Interviews. Period Covered: 1910?–1986.

Nájera generated dispersed autobiography by arranging meetings between Renato Leduc and close friends: Aurora Reyes, Alejandro Gómez Arias, Raquel Díaz de León, Andrés Iduarte, Alejandro Eleguézabal, Alejandro Gómez Maganda, Andrés Henestrosa, Francisco Liguori, Vicente Colunga, Federico Cantú, Juan de la Cabada, Sonia Amelio, Luis

Castro, Silverio Pérez, and Juan Bustillo Oro. Personalities and lives of Leduc and companions illuminated in conversations with Nájera.

357. Castillo y Piña, José (1884–1964). *Las oasis del camino*. México: Imprenta Efrén Rebollar, 1936. 486pp. Memoirs. Period Covered: 1911–1936.

Traveling in interior of Mexico and communicating with nature, priest at times is pantheist. Incidents of travel and companions merit mention, but generally he records emotions about landscape. Monterrey, Guadalajara, Pátzcuaro, and Popocatépetl noted on itinerary.

358. Castillo y Piña, José (1888–1964). *Mis recuerdos*. México: Rebollar, 1941. 507pp. Memoirs. Period Covered: 1900–1941?

Writer and priest educated in Colegio de Infantes and selected to study in Rome for ordination. Describes religious persecution before Calles era. Travelogue and personality profiles mainly of literary figures comprise much of memoirs.

359. Castro, Carlos Antonio (1901 Birth of Che NDU). "Che NDU, ejidatario chinateco." En *Siluetas mexicanas*. Jalapa, VER: Editorial Amate, 1980. 107pp. Oral Autobiography. Period Covered: 1909–1949.

Anthropologist recorded life of Che NDU, Indian from Papaloapan, Vera Cruz. Subject describes parents, family, education, marriage, children, and work. Like *Juan La Chamula, Che NDU* focuses more on culture than personality. No methodology mentioned.

360. Castro, Carlos Antonio (Dates?). "Lupe, la de Altotonga." En *Siluetas mexicanas*. Jalapa, VER: Editorial Amate, 1980. 107pp. Oral Autobiography. Period Covered: ?

Companion piece to oral testimony of Che NDU, document involves life of Vera Cruz Indian woman: growing up and family, literacy, marriage customs, children and *padrinos*, relations between sexes, and menarche. Emphasizes lack of status of females.

361. Castro, Simón Hipólito (1942–). *De albañil a preso político*. México: Editorial

Posada, 1978. 133pp. Memoirs. Period Covered: 1976.

Leftist journalist of humble family from Atoyac de Alvarez de Guerrero. Previously lived as bricklayer. Imprisoned, he denounces penal system for unjust incarcerations.

362. Castro Solórzano, Antonio
(Dates?). *Las haciendas de Mazaquiahuac, El Rosario y El Moral, 1912–1913: catálogo de la correspondencia....* Ma. Eugenia Ponce Alcocer. México: Centro de Información Académica, Iberoamericana, 1990. 215pp. Letters. Period Covered: 1912–1913.

Administrator of three Tlaxcalan haciendas wrote forty letters to cousin José Solórzano "El Chepe" then residing in various European capitals. Mentions hacienda affairs and Revolution in early years. Letters from El Chepe present.

363. Castro Valle, Alfonso (1914–1989).
Alfonso Castro Valle. México: Secretaría de Relaciones Exteriores, 1987. Pp.45–88. Oral Autobiography. Period Covered: 1959–1974.

Served country in diplomatic corps from 1933 to ambassadorship to Sweden in 1982. Focuses on years in Japan, Holland, Germany, Czechoslovakia, and Turkey. Secretary of Foreign Relations sponsored autobiography.

364. Castro y Castro, Fernando (1925–?).
El acontecer de un funcionario público: etapas previas 1947–1981 y efemérides 1981–1988. México: Editorial Diana, 1992. 600pp. Memoirs. Period Covered: 1981–1988.

Has public service career of forty-one years (1947–1988): legal advisor for Federal district, sub-director of National Bank for Small Business, secretary of National Advisory Commission of Fishing, director in chief of Secretariat of Foreign Relations, director general of International Affairs, etc. In routines of public service he mixes information about family and personal life: films, books, friends, illnesses, holidays, and grandchildren.

365. Castro y Castro, Fernando (1925–).
Pensamiento, personas y circunstancias en 30 años de servicios. México: Bufete de Ediciones, 1979. 560pp. Memoirs. Period Covered: 1948?–1978?

More autobiographical data on public servant. Lawyer, diplomat, and politician held many government positions. Presents self in eighty-page memoir. More revealed in second part, "People and Circumstances." Autobiographical material in short biographies of acquaintances and friends from Ramón Alatorre to Roberto Valdes Ramón. Type of who's who in Mexico.

366. Cazals, Felipe (1937–). *Felipe Cazals habla de su cine.* Universidad de Guadalajara, 1994. 300pp. Interview. Period Covered: 1961?–1992?

Film director delays little on childhood and background. Twenty titles in filmography including *Familiaridades, Emiliano Zapata, El jardín de tía Isabel, Canoa, Los poquianchis,* etc. Spanish-born Cazals brought to Mexico by Republican parents. Title, *Gabriel Veyre, representante de Lumiere: Cartas a su madre* (1996), explains filming and exhibiting of Frenchman Veyre from 1896 to 1900. Made thirty-five films during brief stay in Mexico.

367. Cazneau, Jane Maria McManus.
Eagle Pass: or, Life on the Border. Austin, TX: Pemberton, 1966 (1855). 194pp.

After Mexican-American War author lived here from 1850 to 1852. Sojourn allows accumulation of negative impressions of border and specifically of Mexicans: lack of legal system on American side, peonage or caste system of Mexico, fear of invasion of lawless Mexicans, and corrupt Mexican officials.

368. Ceballos Silva, Carlos (1912–?). *De lejos y a mi alrededor.* Universidad de Colima, 1996. 293pp. Memoirs. Period Covered: 1916–1992.

Journalist, businessman, farmer, politician, and family man compiled memoirs from *Diario de Colima.* Columns arranged by theme: ancestors, early age, hotelier, farmer, businessman, preaching, and friendship. Entrepreneurial, vigorous, and *picante*, he displays fragmented life in Cuyutlán and Tecomán, Colima.

369. Cedillo, Luciano (1909–?). *¡Vaaamonos! Luchas, anécdotas y problemas de los ferrocarrileros.* México: Ediciones de Cultura

Popular, 1979. 146pp. Memoirs. Period Covered: 1933–1978?

Brakeman and assistant to chief of railway yards records work and labor struggles in train unions. Much time in railway yards of Monterrey. Appropriate anecdotes liven narration.

370. Cejudo, Roberto F. (1890–?). *Del Diario de Campaña del General de Brigada Roberto F. Cejudo.* Mazatlán: León, 1935. 42pp. Memoirs. Period Covered: 1904–1935.

Few military autobiographies with sincerity and honesty of author, who began career in 1904. Roughness and humiliation in recruit's life but always with good humor. Moralistic tone and patriotism characterize period. Pages of tribute to *soldaderas*.

371. Céliz, Francisco. *Diary of the Alarcón Expedition into Texas, 1718–1719.* Los Angeles: Quivira Society, 1935. 124pp.

Diary entries from April 19, 1718, to February 10, 1719, relate to efforts to thwart French encroachments on Spain's northern territories. One of results was establishment of San Antonio and reconnaissance of New Braunfels, Seguin, and San Marcos areas. Diarist present but not individualized as he comments on landscape, food, illness, distance, religious ceremonies, and Indians.

372. Cerda, Rubén (Dates?). *Mis vivencias en las Mañanitas: My Life in Las Mañanitas.* México: EDAMEX, 1990. 161pp. Memoirs. Period Covered: 1955–1990?

American Robert Krause opened small restaurant-hotel Las Mañanitas in Cuernavaca in 1955. Cerda, one of first employees, grew with business. From handyman, he rose to chef and studied in Europe. Life of grateful employee who idolizes innovative boss and shows inside of business.

373. Cervantes, Federico (1885–?). "El ejército porfirista, el pundonor del soldado y la pasión por Angeles y Villa…." En *Los Revolucionarios* de Daniel Cazes. México: Editorial Grijalbo, 1973. Pp.127–199. Oral Autobiography. Period Covered: 1885–1918.

Product of military college fought on side of Felipe Angeles, his instructor. Angeles, Villa, Madero, Carrancistas, and Zapatistas

populate memoir. One of first to train in aviation.

374. Cervera Espejo, Alberto (Dates?). *Un yucateco en Cuba socialista: morrocutuda historia de un viaje.* Mérida: Maldonado Editores, 1985. 77pp. Memoirs. Period Covered: 1976?

Journalist and daughter travel to Castro's Cuba. In brief light-hearted chapters he talks about Revolution. Highly literate author, interested in Cuban culture, lauds literacy and book programs. Notes similarities between Cuba and Yucatan.

375. Cevallos, Miguel Angel (1887–?). *Un hombre perdido en el universo.* México: Editorial Cultura, 1954. 489pp. Autobiography Proper. Period Covered: 1891–1947.

Work tries to recapture psychologically an entire life in various stages: infancy, adolescence, youth, and maturity. Pseudonymously renamed, he then distances himself in third-person narration and exteriorizes inner life presenting autobiography of emotional life. External world for philosopher-author limited to teaching, marriage, and contact with Antonio Caso.

376. Chacón, Joaquín-Armando (1944–). *De cuerpo entero: Joaquín-Armando Chacón.* México: Ediciones Corunda, 1992. 73pp. Memoirs. Period Covered: 1969?–1988?

From Chihuahua, novelist spent much of life in Mexico City and Cuernavaca. Both linear and temporal space limited as he describes struggles to write and interaction with Nilda and family. Focus on intellectual, creative, and writing Chacón.

377. Chacón, Rafael (1833–1925). *Legacy of Honor: The Life of Rafael Chacón, a Nineteenth-Century New Mexican.* Ed. by Jacqueline Dorgan Maketa. Albuquerque: University of New Mexico Press, 1986. 439pp. Memoirs. Period Covered: 1833–1912?

Meketa, translator and editor of manuscript of New Mexican soldier, enriches nineteenth century through life of Hispano who incarnates much of history of state: cadet in Chihuahua, Indian fighter and trader in decade of 1850s, head of New Mexico unit of Union Army in 1861, and fighter in war against Navajos. In 1870s, moved to Trinidad, Colorado, to ranch. Significant document for Mexican-Americans and for Mexicans.

378. Chadourne, Marc. *Anahuac: Tale of a Mexican Journey.* London: Elek Books, 1954. 196pp.

Frenchman speaks for Pre-Columbian Mexico and region of Quezalcoatl's return. He values life of Indian: "When the choice lies between these two Americas, who would not, like Stewart Chase, choose Tepozotlán"[over Middletown] (p.73)?

379. Chamberlain, Samuel E. *My Confession.* New York: Harper, 1956. 301pp.

Interesting but unreliable. Many anecdotes, relating to conflict and amorous conquests, prove him master of every situation. Also adventurer and liar. With Taylor in northern Mexico, likeable Chamberlain mixes memoir with novel. Illustrated own work with primitive drawings and paintings. Later editions of autobiography rightly subtitled *Recollections of a Rogue.*

380. Chambon, Ludovic. *Un gascón en México.* México: Dirección de Publicaciones del Consejo Nacional para la Cultura y las Artes, 1994. 214pp.

Delightful travel adventure of Frenchman. Yucatan, Tabasco, Chiapas, Vera Cruz, and Mexico comprise author's itinerary. Cultured Chambon betrays no European superiority complex as he observes customs, visits ruins, or converses with natives. Credited with discovering ruins of Piedras Negras.

381. Chanteau, Miguel. *Las andanzas de Miguel: la autobiografía del Padre expulsado de Chenalhó.* San Cristóbal de Las Casas, CHP: Editorial Fray Bartolomé de las Casas, 1999. 123pp.

Catholic priest Miguel Chanteau in *Las andanzas de Miguel: la autobiografía del padre expulsado de Chenahló* (1999) suffered accusations. Ordained in France, Chanteau missionized in Chenalhó, near San Cristóbal de Las Casas. Accused of subversive activities against government, priest expelled and returned to France in 1998.

382. Chapa Martínez, Roberto. (1876–1965 Dates of Chapa Campos) *Realidades de una vida: Dr. Hermenegildo Chapa Campos.* Zuazua: Universidad Autónoma de Nuevo León, 1991. 58pp. Memoirs. Period Covered: 1876–1951.

Horatio Alger story of poor boy from Nuevo León destined to be goatherd until discovered as student worthy of education. Attends school in Monterrey and becomes medical doctor. Value of hard work, strict parents, and supportive family.

383. Chapman, Frank M. *Autobiography of a Bird-Lover.* New York: Appleton-Century, 1933. 420pp.

Mexico is one of locales of exploration in title. In Yucatan in 1896 he enjoyed ruins, vegetation, and bird life. Although he notes several species, he emphasizes ocellated turkey and *chachalacas.* In 1897, he similarly explores Vera Cruz: temperatures, Mt. Orizaba, vegetation, and birds. Author instrumental in ornithology in U.S.

384. Charlot, Jean (1898–1979). *Charlot Murals in Georgia.* Athens: University of Georgia Press, 1945. 178pp. Memoirs. Period Covered: 1941.

Of French ancestry, he has roots in Mexico: both grandfather and great grandfather (officer in Maximilian's retinue) lived in Mexico; artist himself arrived in Mexico and participated in art movement until 1929. In brief and illustrated book recounts painting murals at University of Georgia.

385. Charlot, Zohmah. *Mexican Memories (1931).* N.p. 1989 (1931). 69 leaves.

Zohmah [Dorothy] Day arrived in Mexico City in 1931 to visit artist friend Ione Robinson. Most of memoir relates to meeting and romance with Jean Charlot. Unknown Day in touch with foreign and native celebrities such as Eduardo Villaseñor, Carleton Beals, Adolf Best-Maugard, Sergei Eisenstein, Pablo O'Higgins, Emily Edwards, Siqueiros, and Manuel Alvarez Bravo.

386. Charnay, Désiré. *Viaje a Yucatán a fines de 1886....* Mérida: Tallares Gráficos Guerra, 1933. 64pp.

Between 1857 and 1888, he explored

archaeological sites. In this work, however, confined self to Yucatan: Izamal, Kobá, Valladolid, Ek-Balam, and Campeche. Much on artifacts and ruins of Maya, but some personality emerges in contact with priests and other natives. He expresses typical lament: "Mis trabajos marchaban con lentitud y los hallazgos eran raros… " (p.50).

387. Chaves, Fernando (1902–?). *Crónicas de mi viaje a México: 1934–1935.* Quito: Banco Central del Ecuador, 1992. 349pp.

Ecuadorian author, in exile from hostile land and sponsored in Mexico by Moisés Sáenz, traipsed republic and wrote 128 *crónicas* (editorials) about host country. Geographical regions, cities, churches, prisons, and customs come under personalized scrutiny. Sketching personalities such as Diego Rivera, Vicente Lombardo Toledano, Antonio Caso, and Celerino Cano, Chaves also pauses to capture a mulatto washwoman singing lyrics of Agustín Lara. Ecuadorian lover but not idolater of Mexico.

388. Chávez, Carlos (1899–1978). *Epistolario selecto de Carlos Chávez. Selección, introducción, notas y bibliografía de Gloria Carmona.* México: Fondo de Cultura Económica, 1989. 1107pp. Letters. Period Covered: 1919–1978.

According to *New Grove Dictionary of Music and Musicians* (1980), [Chávez was a] "Mexican composer, conductor, teacher, writer on music and government official. His role in musical and cultural life of Mexico was decisive during the second quarter of the twentieth century" (V.4, p.185). Some of more voluminous correspondents: Aaron Copland, Henry Cowell, Lincoln Kirstein, Claire R. Reis, Moisés Sáenz, Leopoldo Stokowski, and Paul Strand. Letters suggest public man more than private individual.

389. Chávez, Carlos (1899–1978). *Mis amigos poetas: López Velarde, Pellicer y Novo.* México: El Colegio Nacional, 1977. 43pp. Memoirs. Period Covered: 1915–1925.

One of major musicians of twentieth century intersected lives of three poets. Personalizes relationship with poets during indicated decade in 1973 lectures. Use with letters.

390. Chávez, César (1927–1993). *César Chávez: una entrevista.* México: Instituto Matías Romero de Estudios Diplomáticos, 1993. 36pp. Interview. Period Covered: 1927–1993.

One of last interviews with Chávez includes origins and struggles for justice through organizing farm workers. Document tied to Mexico in Chávez's incorporation of Mexicans into union and in origins of interview. Jacques E. Levy's *Cesar Chavez: Autobiography of La Causa* (1975) deserves mention. Latter title concerns Chavez's efforts to organize agricultural workers in California but no ties to Mexico.

391. Chávez, Ezequiel Adeodato (1868–1949). *¿De dónde venimos y a dónde vamos?* México: El Colegio Nacional, 1946. 268pp. Memoirs. Period Covered: 1872–1942.

Lawyer, educator, and philosopher held positions during career: undersecretary of public instruction and Bellas Artes, head of preparatory school, and university rector. Taught in U.S. Combines autobiographical data and educational and philosophical theory. Chávez, with universal culture, one of better writers of memoirs.

392. Chávez, Ezequiel Adeodato (1868–1946). *En respuesta.* México, 1941. 49pp. Memoirs. Period Covered: 1882–1941.

In two eloquent speeches in response to homage, educator and politician synthesizes life mainly in education. Significant information: Ignacio Altamirano was his professor; Chávez taught at University of California.

393. Chávez, Ignacio (1897–1979). *Epistolario selecto: 1929–1979.* México: El Colegio Nacional, 1997. 443pp. Letters. Period Covered: 1929–1979.

Collection of letters of famous physician. Variety of sixty individuals including Diego Rivera, Jaime Torres Bodet, and Francisco Vega Díaz among most frequent. These three provide a sampling of letters that Chávez wrote to politicians, poets, artists, and other cardiologists. Present bibliography has many doctors; however, Chávez best shows range of activities: cardiology; medical buildings; patients; conferences; honors; students; administrative difficulties; and Cuban,

American, French, and Spanish correspondents.

394. Chávez, José Carlos (?–1939 Death of Francisco Castro). *Peleando en Tomochi.* 3 ed. Chihuahua, CHH: Centro Librero La Prensa, 1979. (1943) 158pp. Oral Autobiography. Period Covered: 1891–1892.

Gen. Francisco Castro, second lieutenant in 11th Battalion that helped "subdue" Indians of Tomichic, narrated memoirs to José Carlos Chávez. Sympathy for Indians abused by government. Mention of Teresa Urrea, Santa of Cabora.

395. Chávez, Julio (1920–). *Vestidas y desvestidas: 50 años en la farándula de México.* México: Raul Juárez Carro Editorial, 1991. 286pp. Memoirs. Period Covered: 1920–1985.

Successful couturier quickly abandons story of humble beginnings and leaps into film and vaudeville world. Livelihood derived from entertainment personalities for whom he created costumes. Women stars were friends or acquaintances. From 1949 to 1968, designed costumes for 216 films. Source for popular culture, he exposes demimonde in escapades of transvestite friend.

396. Chávez, Leticia (1864–1949 Dates of Ezequiel Chávez). *Recordando a mi padre.* México: Asociación Civil: Ezequiel A. Chávez, 1967, 4 v. Memoirs. Period Covered: 1875–1946?

Adoring daughter of educator, Ezequiel A. Chávez, subjectively incorporates her life with father's autobiography and letters. In mentioning relationships, she creates collective autobiography with father as center. Much of material from his two volumes, *¿De dónde venimos...?* and *Apuntes autobiográficas*: I. 1868–1891. Genealogy, early schooling, and *preparatoria*. II. 1891–1910. Courtship and marriage, involvement with education, writings, and California. III. 1911–1915. Revolution, defense of education, la *Decena Trágica*, director of higher education, and rector of University. IV. 1916–1917. Exile to New York, life in Cincinnati, and return to Mexico. V. 1917–1925. Problems of secularism in private schools and religion in public schools, thoughts on reform of Department of Education, need for civic edu-

cation, named director of *preparatoria*, and rector again of University. VI. 1926–1929. Leticia's professional exam, Chávez's indirect influence on future teachers, reasons that made him opt for good, conflict of devout Catholic who is also government official, trip to Europe, conference at Sorbonne, and return to Mexico. VIII. 1929–1949. Retirement yet concern for university, prep school, displeasure with third article of 1917 Constitution, and crisis in Mexican education. IX. Pinnacle of success, family life, readings, 70th birthday, WWII, and 50th anniversary in public life. X. 1942–1946. Letters, premonition of death, teaching, Chávez's final book, old age, and death.

397. Chávez, Oscar O. (1935–). *Confrontaciones.* Azcapotzalco, DF: Universidad Autónoma Metropolitana, 1985. 36pp. Interview. Period Covered: 1980s.

Actor, singer, songwriter, folklorist, and poet mentions biographical data: role in film, *Los caifanes*, musical creations, ideas on popular music, and artist's role in social change.

398. Chávez Orozco, Luis (1901–1966). Entrevista en James W. Wilkie y Edna Monzón Wilkie's *Frente a la Revolución mexicana: 17 protagonista de la etapa constructiva, v.1.* México: Universidad Autónoma Metropolitana, 1995. 113pp. Interview. Period Covered: 1901–1966.

Journalist, politician, diplomat, and self-taught historian reveals some of personal life and more of career: family from León, Guanajuato; his arrival in Mexico City in 1917; secretary of public education, 1933–1939; head of department of Indian Affairs, 1939–1940; advisor to President Cárdenas; and ambassador to Honduras. Unique views as historian most autobiographical: Iturbide's persuasiveness in letters; substratum of democracy among pre–Columbian Indians; necessity of military background in caudillos such as Rosas and Díaz; and grasp of past to interpret actions of current politicians. Also had contacts with Wm. Cameron Townsend.

399. Chávez Padrón, Martha (1925–). *Testimonio de una familia petrolera.* México: Petroleos Mexicanos, 1988. 149pp. Memoirs. Period Covered: 1898–1987.

Lawyer presents self occasionally in biography of parents, Pemex employee, and registered nurse. Locales of Tampico and Mexico City background for parents and four children. Notes growth of Tampico and history of petroleum.

400. Cházaro Pous, Gabriel (1888–?). *Pluviosilla, reminiscencias.* México: Imprenta Gama, 1941. 49pp. Memoirs. Period Covered: 1880?–1900?

Biographer and essayist born in Tlacotalpam, Vera Cruz. Self-revelations scattered among nostalgic scenes of school, servants, women, medical doctors, family, etc. Past reviewed with humor and contentment.

401. Claraval, Bernardo (1909?–?). *Cuando fui comunista.* México: Ediciones Polis, 1944. 232pp. Memoirs. Period Covered: 1928–1940?

Disillusioned ex-communist joined Mexican party and Comité Central de la Juventud. Concentrating on years 1928 to 1932, notes government persecution of communists and disenchantment with Russia. Mentions various foreign personalities in party including Cuban, Julio Antonio Mella, assassinated in Mexico City in 1929.

402. Clark, Leonard. *A Wanderer Till I Die.* New York: Funk & Wagnalls, 1937. 246pp.

Last chapter relates to Mexico. Adventurer visits Cholula and pyramid; main goal is el Pico de Orizaba in state of Veracruz. Succeeds in climbing mountain but with suffering and illness.

403. Clark, Leonard. *Yucatan Adventure.* London: Hutchinson, 1959. 256pp.

Author and companion in 1950 trek through bush of Quintana Roo in *Yucatan Adventure* (1959). Explore ruins and deal with jungle and frenzied animal life. *Yucatan* mainly autobiography, for author places self in jungle milieu and reacts. Story often first-person account of survival in non–twentieth-century world.

404. Clarke, Asa Bement; Anne Perry. *Travels in Mexico and California....* College Station: Texas A&M University Press, 1988. 143pp.

Discovery of gold in California in 1848 sent Americans flocking to that state. One route was through Mexico and hence motive for this journal for 1849. Author started from New York on January 29 and entered Tucson in June. His west and northwestern route through Mexico carried him to Camargo, Mier, Cerralvo, Saltillo, Mapimi, Janos, and finally into Tucson. Clarke describes each place, notes Mexicans, Indians, customs, and condition of road. Bad knee mandated riding in wagon.

405. Cocom Pech, Jorge Miguel (1947–). *Mukult'an in nool= Secretos del abuelo.* México: UNAM, 2001. 158pp. Memoirs. Period Covered: 1961–?

Bilingual Spanish and Maya document on author's relationship with maternal grandfather, Gregorio Pech. Cocom Pech recalls teaching of shaman grandfather. Each chapter draws on Maya folklore/history as recited by young author in close contact with grandfather. Nature themes predominate.

406. Cohan, Tony. *On Mexican Time: A New Life in San Miguel.* New York: Broadway Books, 2000. 289pp.

San Miguel, Guanajuato has tranquility. Tony Cohan's autobiographical work entails buying and refurbishing house. He and spouse love Mexico and do not let home ownership with its bureaucracy turn book into exotic scenario of eccentric Mexicans. Problems solvable and natives civilized. Private world here as opposed to potential public world in supreme city of tourism.

407. Coit, Daniel Wadsworth. *Digging for Gold without a Shovel....* Denver: Old West, 1967. 116pp.

Letters from February 10, 1848, to March 15, 1849. With Mexican-American War over, American firm, Howland and Aspinwall, is eager to resume business and sends author to Mexico City. His residency is during occupation of capital by U.S. troops. "The letters preserved by his family reflect an educated, experienced traveler, knowledgeable in the ways of life in a Latin country. He was a keen observer and ... gives a dramatic insight into the conditions of the peoples..." (pp.6–7). He moved in highest circles of Anglo and Mexican society. Comments on quarrel between Gen. Gideon J. Pillow and Gen. Scott. Coit visited churches and illustrates book with his sketches.

408. Cole, Merl Burke. *Romantic Trage-dies of Mexico.* Boston: Christopher, 1956. 311pp.

Extended Madero family both of Coahuila and Mexico City figures in this title. From 1876 to 1928, Cole family had ties to ruling elite. Richard Hood Cole, spouse of author, special envoy to Mexico during Madero and Carranza years of Revolution. He influenced Washington for recognition of Carranza's regime. Picturing social scene in both Washington and Mexico City, Merl Cole leaves snippets of Mexican history.

409. Cole, Merl Burke. *Six Days on a Mule in Mexico.* Boston: Chapple, 1928. 80pp.

The Coles, with concession to exploit magnesite on Santa Margarita Island on Magdalena Bay, plan trip on steamer in 1910. Adventures, including lack of funds, await naïve spouses who plan to rough it. Storm, insects, and lack of food make venture unpleasant. Six days like survival camp.

410. Colina Riquelme, Rafael de la (1898–1995). *Rafael de la Colina: una vida de hechos.* México: Secretaría de Relaciones Exteriores, 1985. 142pp. Memoirs. Period Covered: 1898–1982.

Enjoyed long career in service of government: member of Consulate in Philadelphia, St. Louis, Eagle Pass (Texas), Boston, New Orleans, Los Angeles, San Antonio, and New York; ambassador to U.S., United Nations, Canada, and Japan, and OAS. Concentrates on these positions with one chapter on family and youth. Because of postings, talks of Mexican-Americans. Minimal personal life.

411. Collins, Francis; Maria Clinton. *Journal of Francis Collins: An Artillery Officer in the Mexican War.* Cincinnati: Abingdon, 1915. 109pp.

Another West Pointer served in Mexico starting on east coast: Tampico, Vera Cruz, Jalapa, Cerro Gordo, Puebla, Cholula, Mex-ico City, and Toluca. Notes number of *léperos* or discarded class and corruption of Catholic Church. Withdrawal from Toluca to Vera Cruz to New Orleans in 1847.

412. Colorado, Belisario, Jr. (Dates?). *Epistolario de viaje: un vivido relato de la Alemania actual....* México: Editorial Divulgación, 1966. 142pp. Memoirs. Period Covered: 1965.

Author attended seminar in Berlin organized by German Foundation for Developing Countries. Personal involvement, i.e., subjective impressions of events, personalities, and customs, differentiates work from general objective travel account. *Epistolario* has status of memoirs.

413. Conde, Teresa del (1939–) (1936 Birth of Manrique). *Cartas absurdas: correspondencia entre Teresa del Conde y Jorge Alberto Manrique.* México: Grupo Azabache, 1993. 307pp. Letters. Period Covered: 1989–1992.

Art historians/critics, personal friends, and prolific publishers exchange letters that form dialog on art of Mexico and Western world. Letters serve as vehicle for lecture/essays rather than notes of personal well-being or gossip.

414. Conover, Ted. *Coyotes: A Journey through the Secret World of America's Illegal Aliens.* New York: Vintage Books, 1987. 264pp.

This is Conover's experience with illegals from homes in Mexico to parts of U.S. Like Pérez's *Diary, Coyotes* meets humanistic goal: "What *La Migra* does not know — what it perhaps cannot afford to know — is the human side of the men and women it arrests, the drama of their lives" (p.xviii).

415. Conrad, Jim. *On the Road to Tetlama: Mexican Adventures of a Wandering Naturalist.* New York: Walker, 1991. 196pp.

Author hovers in Tamazunchale (San Luis Potosí) region of Mexico. Watches habits and comments on observations of Nahuatl-speaking natives. Occasionally records birds and plant life. Negative profiling of natives makes greater impression than notes as naturalist.

416. Contreras, Gloria (1938–). *Diario de una bailarina*. México: UNAM, 1997. 183pp. Memoirs. Period Covered: 1958–1959.

Choreographer and ballerina covers two years as member of New York City Ballet. Constantly present, George Balanchine is both tutor and equal. Her diary, unusual in Mexican letters for genre, style and frankness, makes dance as art form intelligible as well as revealing sensitive, articulate human being.

417. Contreras, Tino (1926–?). *Mi amor, el jazz*. México: Ediciones del gobierno del Estado de Chihuahua, 1986. 72pp. Memoirs. Period Covered: 1920–1926.

Inspired by Gene Krupa and Buddy Rich, Chihuahuense tailor apprentice found career as jazz drummer. Possibly only Mexican jazz musician with autobiography. Brief chronological chapters follow improvisational style covering author's meanderings in Mexico, U.S., Europe, Turkey, and Argentina.

418. Contreras Humarán, Gloria (1941–). *Recuerdos: memorias, poemas, pensamientos y acrósticos*. México: Instituto Nacional de Antropología e Historia, 2000. 345pp. Memoirs. Period Covered: 1953–1993.

One predicts bland autobiography with adoring parents, confirmation, marriage, and children, supposed ideals of middle-class Mexican woman. Contreras Humarán shatters comfortable stereotypes. Illegitimate and unwed mother herself, secretary of insurance company, and involved with extended family, she details life. One of most informative autobiographies of women. Arranged confusingly into thematic and then chronological topics, *Recuerdos* deserves more attention.

419. Cooke, Philip St. George. "Cooke's Journal of the March of the Mormon Battalion, 1846–1847." In *Exploring Southwestern Trails, 1846–1854*. Glendale, CA: Clark, 1938. Pp.64–240.

Professional soldier Cooke was appointed by Kearny to lead Mormon Battalion from Santa Fe, New Mexico, to California from 1846 to 1847. Much on landscape and vegetation, illnesses, Indians, mules, food, and news on Mexican-American War.

420. Cordan, Wolfgang. *Secret of the Forest: On the Track of Maya Temples*. Garden City, NY: Doubleday, 1964. 225pp.

Germans studied Maya as evidenced in above title. Book dated with recent decipherment of Maya hieroglyphics. Details drudgery of everyday life in search for ruins. Exposes rivalry among scholars who seek Maya ruins for knowledge and natives who seek same sites for quick profits.

421. Cordero, Joaquín (1926–). *Anécdotas de un actor*. México: Editorial Diana, 1990. 347pp. Memoirs. Period Covered: 1947–1988?

Actor in more than 150 films and pioneer in television presents self chronologically under sub-chapters bearing names of films in which he performed. Behind-the-scenes view of film industry.

422. Córdova Ruiz de Velasco, Ana M. (1973 Birth of Elisa). *Elisa: un alma libre en un cuerpo limitado*. México: Panorama, 1992. 102pp. Memoirs. Period Covered: 1973–1991.

Mother of child with cerebral palsy distills eighteen years with handicapped daughter. Poignant incidents such as teaching daughter not to be frightened of rain.

423. Corella Yslas, Emiliano (1848–1925). *Apuntes para la narración de mi vida*. Sonora: Gobierno del Estado, 1991, 97pp. Memoirs. Period Covered: 1848–1921.

Prologue notes absence of Sonoran memoirs and contributions of present work. Covers childhood and capture by highwaymen, escape to Michoacán, death and funeral of uncle Gen. Diodoro Corella, entrance into military school, and career as topographical engineer. Of influential Sonoran family, he fought envious colleagues eager to sabotage his military career.

424. Corona del Rosal, Alfonso (1906–?). *Mis memorias políticas*. México: Editorial Grijalbo, 1995. 296pp. Memoirs. Period Covered: 1906–1992.

Hidalguense achieved military and political success: senator, governor of Hidalgo, campaign committees for Avila Camacho and Adolfo Ruiz Cortines, key positions in PRI, and head of Department of Federal District during student strike in 1968. Justifies government's role in Tlateloco.

425. Corona Ochoa, José (Dates?). *Pepito: Cocula, la vida alegre de un pueblo triste.* México: Costa-Amic, ca.1972. 420pp. Memoirs. Period Covered: 1900–1972?

Portrays arcadian village in Jalisco about 1900. Author rarely reveals self in picaresque escapades in which he is usually victor. Absence of bitterness about small town life expressed in North American novel. Older man repossessing past by selectively remembering only happy events. Occasional chapters, "La institutriz" and "Mujeres de mi tierra," illuminate facets of Mexican life.

426. Corral Romero, Octavio (Dates?). *Memorias de un regidor.* Chihuahua, CHH: Tallares Gráficos del Gobierno del Estado de Chihuahua, 1992. 145pp. Memoirs. Period Covered: 1989–1992.

Political experiences of disenchanted Panista frustrated by Priistas. Reveals how he became alderman for city of Chihuahua and some of duties: finance, security, public works, sanitation, ecology, city property, pensions, participation in city council, and public relations. Unique for workings of political system at lower level.

427. *Correspondencia: Alfonso Reyes, Octavio Paz [1939–1959]* (1889–1959 Dates of Reyes) (1915–1998 Dates of Paz). México: Fondo de Cultura Económica, 1998. 261pp. Letters. Period Covered: 1939–1959.

Thirty-eight pages of introduction verify solid editing of Anthony Stanton, who arranged eighty-four letters into four chronological periods: 1939–1943, 1949–1951, 1952–1953, and 1953–1959. Editor emphasizes twenty-year period, last two decades of Reyes's life and first two of Paz's literary career. Reyes is mentor. Exchange is sixteenth collection of his correspondence. First published collection of Paz's letters. Subject index.

428. Cortés Leyva, Carlos Roberto. *De El Salvador a Baja California (apuntes autobiográficos).* N.p.: Patronato del Estudiante Sudacaliforniano, 1978. 51pp.

Salvadorian and wife leave native country and immigrate to Mexico City. In capital, he furthers pedagogical education. From 1928 to 1955, taught in Baja, mainly in Loreto, where he built new high school. Influential in raising money for hospital and in receiving flood control aid from President Adolfo López Mateos.

429. Cortina, Leonor (Dates?). *Lucia.* México: Editorial Libros México, 1988. 224pp. Oral Autobiography. Period Covered: 1930?–1960?

Author employed Lucia Rodríguez as maid and requested her story. Cortina shares no methodology with reader. Contributions of heroine and editor blur. From poor family with ten children in Arandas, Jalisco, Lucia spends life in Mexico City. Virtuous, hardworking, and intelligent, she endures multiple unskilled jobs, but usually as maid. Married and abandoned with illegitimate child, she endures. Cunning, honesty, and perseverance endear her to reader. Life follows picaresque mode: multiple adventures and adversities but always at same level of society, undeveloped character during course of story, continual portrayal of marginal classes, and her code of morality. Lucia similar to Elena Poniatowska's Jesusa Polancares.

430. Corzo, Miguel Angel (1890–1948 Dates of Ranulfo Penagos) *Mis 2501 dias en el colegio military.* México: Universidad de Ciencias y Artes del estado de Chiapas, 1999. 118pp. Memoirs. Period Covered: 1901–1907.

Semi-verse text unusual contribution to military autobiography. Entered Normal Militar in Tuxtla Gutiérrez. Laudatory view of idyllic period in life: classes, military exercises, teachers, courtship, and classmates. Penagos, not career military, became full time schoolteacher in 1912.

431. Cosío Villegas, Daniel (1900–1976). Entrevista en James W. Wilkie y Edna Monzón Wilkie's *Frente a la Revolución Mexicana: 17 protagonista de la etapa constructiva, v.1.* México: Universidad Autónoma Metropolitana, 1995. 102pp. Interview. Period Covered: 1900–1964.

Historian talks about Revolution, historiography, family in Latin America, intellectuals in society, politics, etc.

Autobiographical sections include childhood and youth, personal data (education in Mexico and U.S. and professorship), and family.

432. Cosío Villegas, Daniel (1900–1976). *Memorias*. México: Mortiz, 1977. 320pp. Memoirs. Period Covered: 1900–1968.

Exemplifies multifaceted scholar unique to Latin America. Diplomat, journalist, professor, and scholar of philosophy, sociology, law, economics, history, and political science, he was also founder of Casa de España, Colegio de México, and various journals under auspices of Colegio. Details of early years but concentrates on active diplomatic and intellectual life. Shows relationship to other leaders and functioning of political system. Final chapters deteriorate in vindication of quarrel with President Echeverría Alvarez.

433. Costa, César (1942–). *Llegar a ser: mi autobiografía*. México: Grupo Editorial Sayrols, 1985. 167pp. Memoirs. Period Covered: 1942–1985.

Born to affluent family, Costa had advantages of cosmopolitan background with Chicago-born mother, who cultivated music of Vivaldi. Told to Elisa Robledo, life concerns adolescent pranks plus desire and achievement of fame as music star (singer with rock group Blue Jeans and later soloist in style of Paul Anka) and movie actor. More thoughtful finale as he reflects on life without celebrity. Valuable for adolescent culture of late 1950s.

434. Cota Sández, Fernando Inés (1918–?). *Autobiografía*. La Paz: Gobierno de Baja California Sur, 1984. 39pp. Memoirs. Period Covered: 1918–1974.

Teacher from Baja taught mainly in Tamaulipas. Elected national delegate from territory of Baja and successful PRI candidate for senator in 1974. After years of teaching, ends with miscellaneous items: Cabo San Lucas, fishing, marriage and family, and travel.

435. Coulter, Richard; Thomas Barclay; Allan Peskin. *Volunteers: The Mexican War Journals of Private Richard Coulter and Sergeant Thomas Barclay....* Kent, OH: Kent State University Press, 1991. 342pp.

Two enlisted men from Westmoreland Guards of Greensburg, PA, present selves in parallel texts in day-by-day account of Mexican-American War from December 30, 1846, to July 10, 1848. Personal accounts follow battles from Vera Cruz, Cerro Gordo, Jalapa, Perote, Puebla, and Mexico City. Detailed view of war from below by educated soldiers. Friends but of different temperaments, the two complement one another in their variations of reports of same day. Many references to Scott; a few to Taylor.

436. Covarrubias, Miguel (1940–). *Junto a una taza de café: (conversaciones)*. Monterrey: Ediciones, 1994. 222pp. Oral Autobiography. Period Covered: 1940–1993.

Essayist, poet, playwright, and critic presents self in original way: in twenty-three intellectual encounters he interviews other writers or they interview him. Vaguely chaotic results yield portrait of individual reared in literary environment to which he now contributes and scrutinizes in native Nuevo León.

437. Cox, Patricia (Bustamante) (1911–?). *Amanecer*. México: Editorial Anthony, 1946. 230pp. Autobiography Proper. Period Covered: 1912?–1918?

Focus on early years conforms more to autobiography proper than other subgenres of life writing. Life is sad: early happiness ends with death of Irish mother, loving father generally absent, several school teachers who either love or despise Cox, and evil Indian maid who torments her young subjects. Cox is a writer. No other woman autobiographer so concentrates on formative years.

438. Cravioto Muñoz, Rafael (1915–?). *Memorias de un adolescente*. México: Pachuca de Soto, 1955 (1938). 135pp. Memoirs. Period Covered: 1927-.

With nostalgia past recovered: loss of one hacienda and removal to new one, El Zoquital, both near Pachuca, Hidalgo. Separate chapters refer to education, devoutly Catholic maiden aunts, early films, peddlers, hotels, and railway stations. *Costumbrismo* dominates in unintegrated document.

439. Crosby, Harry. *The King's Highway in Baja California....* La Jolla, CA: Copley Books, 1974. 182pp.

Photographer-writer along with student of Jesuit history attempts to rediscover Camino Real or old mission roads. Photographs landscapes, meets natives, enjoys small adventures, and incorporates information of earlier scholars. Jesuit and Dominican missionaries revitalized by Crosby's words and those of earlier explorers.

440. Cruz, Pablo (1930–). *Pablo Cruz and the American Dream: The Experiences of an Undocumented Immigrant from Mexico.* Compiled by Eugene Nelson. Salt Lake City: Peregrine Smith, 1975. 171pp. Oral Autobiography. Period Covered: 1934–1959.

Nelson met Cruz in 1964 in Fresno, California, and recorded story. Born in Jalisco, Cruz had few opportunities. Migrated to Mexicali and became illegal alien. Life story about job conditions, problems with immigration, and efforts to become citizen. Nelson, creating generic bracero, forgets Cruz the human being. Occasionally seen in relation to mother, wife, and brother, he is one-dimensional.

441. Cruz, Roberto (1888–1990). *Roberto Cruz en la Revolución mexicana.* México: Editorial Diana, 1976. 191pp. Memoirs. Period Covered: 1910–1946.

Career of Maderista soldier and supporter of Obregón and Calles. Cruz knew many revolutionaries. Clarity, brevity, and personal perspective make work superior to most memoirs of Revolution.

442. Cuéllar, Alfredo B. (Dates?). *Impresiones y anécdotas de mi viaje al Brasil en 1922.* México: La Helvetia-Cipsa, 1947. 32pp. Memoirs. Period Covered: 1922.

In 1922, centennial year of independence, Brazil invited Mexican athletes to attend ceremonies. Cuéllar paid own way. Comments on ceremonies and travels with Dominican Pedro Henríquez Ureña. National Library Director José Vasconcelos's mistaken impression that Cuéllar's *charro* attire disgraced Mexico lends humor to memoir.

443. Cuero, Delfina (1900?–?). *The Autobiography of Delfina Cuero, A Diegüeño Indian,*
as Told to Florence C. Shipek. Los Angeles: Dawson's Book Shop, 1968. 67pp. Oral Autobiography. Period Covered: 1900–1967.

Born in California, she and parents migrated to northern Baja, area of Diegüeño Indians. Brief narrative mainly *costumbrista*: labor, games, food, dance, taboos, puberty rites, birth rituals, religion, and marital customs. Life delineates more culture of entire ethnic group rather than one individual.

444. Cuero, Delfina; Florence Connolly Shipek. *Delfina Cuero: Her Autobiography, An Account of Her Last Years, and Her Ethno Botanic Contributions.* Menlo Park, CA: Ballena, 1991. 98pp.

Shipek, author of *The Autobiography of Delfina Cuero, a Diegüeño Indian,* published above title in 1991. Fifteen pages on folk herbs in Delfina'a language supplement 1968 oral autobiography.

445. Cueva, Eusebio de la (1893–1943). *Por tierras de Quevedo y Cervantes.* Monterrey: Mireles y Estrada, 1917. 239pp. Memoirs. Period Covered: 1914?

Young journalist leaves country to travel to Spain. Detailed account of voyage, arrival in Vigo, and trip to Madrid. Focuses more upon own feelings and experiences than Spanish culture. Description of routine life as he loses financial resources and looks for other means of support. Narrator's survival absorbs attention. Self assumes more importance than Spanish environment.

446. Cuevas, José Luis (1934–). *Cartas a Bertha: historia de un amor loco.* México: Aguilar, 2001. 467pp. Letters. Period Covered: 1953–2001.

Tenth volume of autobiography and second comprised of letters directed to Bertha Riestra, fiancée, spouse, estranged wife, and finally dying ex. One-sided dialogue with occasional interruptions by Cuevas, who with perspective, summarizes and interprets. Love story, marriage, children, and disintegration of union with Bertha's family as main culprits.

447. Cuevas, José Luis (1934–). *Confrontaciones/José Luis Cuevas.* Azcapotzalco, DF: Universidad Autónoma Metropolitana,

1984. 40pp. Interview. Period Covered: 1950–
1984.

Iconoclastic in touching upon variety of
themes: leaving Mexico in 1976, art imposed
by U.S., Marta Traba as friend and supporter,
Kafka, erotic art, docile younger generation
of artists, stupidity of critics, and obsessive
self-photography each day.

448. Cuevas, José Luis (1934–). *Cuevario.*
México: Editorial Grijalbo, 1973. 215pp.
Hybrid. Period Covered: 1962?–1973.

Continues other autobiographical works
and reveals frank, polemical, and iconoclastic
nature. Letters, essays on art, autobiographical pieces, and illustrations comprise work.
Uninhibited in expressing personal feelings,
he can write as well as paint. Difficult to categorize as to autobiographical genre.

449. Cuevas, José Luis (1934–). *Cuevas
antes de Cuevas.* México: Bruguera Mexicana,
1990? 228pp. Memoirs. Period Covered:
1936?–1955?

In fourth volume of *cuevario*, continues
life story in fragmented form. Yet volumes
overlap chronologically. Each "memoria" encapsulates incident of artist's struggle for success: drawing, travel, family, encounters with
celebrities, and love affairs. Monsters that populate drawings occasionally incarnate in life.

450. Cuevas, José Luis (1934–). *Cuevas
por Cuevas: notas autobiográficas.* México:
Ediciones ERA, 1967 (1965). 223pp. Trans:
Cuevas by Cuevas (bilingual edition). Memoirs. Period Covered: 1934–1954?

Hybrid document, including memoirs,
biography of fictional artist, and vindication
of Cuevas and his art, book always entertaining. Little on autobiography but more on
attacking canons of art and artists who represent these, Rivera and Tamayo. Caustic and
succinct, Cuevas attacks whatever inhibits his
success. Bilingual edition with illustrations.
In 1983, *José Luis Cuevas, Self Portrait with
Model* was published. Resulted from challenge to fill notebook with unrepeated drawings and letters. Self-portrait varied in 105
drawings with interpretation.

451. Cuevas, José Luis (1934–). *El gato
macho.* México: Fondo de Cultura Econó-

mica, 1994. 728pp. Memoirs. Period Covered:
1934–1994.

May repeat some of items already listed
in bibliography. First fifty years covered in
129 pages; from 1985 to 1994 events under
appropriate year. Egotist writes as well as
paints; and pages rarely bore as he introduces
celebrities, art, love(s), family, illnesses, and
travels.

452. Cuevas, José Luis (1934–). *Historias
del viajero.* México: Premia, 1987. 78pp.
Memoirs. Period Covered: 1961?–1985?

Twenty-one independent selections
from daily *Excélsior.* Encapsulated incidents
of travel expose enormous ego. Each cluster
of memories bears structure suggesting short
story. Themes of painting, sexual encounters,
prizes, and conflict with editors involve outrageous Cuevas.

453. Cuevas, José Luis (1934–). *Historias
para una exposición.* México: Premia, 1988.
95pp. Memoirs. Period Covered: 1940–1986.

Twenty-one autobiographical essays
similar to above entry. He easily triumphs
over enemies. Childhood, painting, sexual
encounters, and travel comprise contents. Art
relationship with Argentine critic Marta
Traba. Style, ego, and theme vary little in
series of autobiographies.

454. Cuevas, José Luis (1934–). *José Luis
Cuevas Letters....* Letters and text translated
by Beth M. Sundheim. La Jolla, CA: Tasende
Gallery, 1982. 82pp. letters. Period Covered:
1978–1981.

Thirty-one letters written to José María
Tasende, gallery owner, friend, and
confidante. Original in handwritten Spanish
but of more value than translation because of
Cuevas's drawings. Topics of friendship,
travel, art shows, works in progress, competition, Bertha, and fear of assault in Mexico
expose more human and vulnerable Cuevas
than one presented in other autobiographies.
1981 edition, *Cartas para una exposición,* has
seventy-one letters written to José María
Tasende. Well-illustrated letters but original
text indecipherable.

455. Cuevas, José Luis (1934–). *José Luis
Cuevas, el ojo perdido de Dios.* Toluca: Uni-

versidad Autónoma del Estado de México, 1997. 180pp. Memoirs. Period Covered: 1957–1997.

Presents self in interaction with thirty-five other famous Mexicans from art, literature, film, and journalism. Noting when they met, he recalls them in biography and anecdote. Much of author emerges from collective reading.

456. Cumplido, Ignacio (1811–1887). *Correspondencia del Ignacio Cumplido a León Ortigosa....* Editada por Sylvia Cárdenas. Monterrey, 1969. 63pp. Letters. Period Covered: 1848–1860.

Publisher, editor, and politician edited most important newspaper of nineteenth century Mexico, *El siglo XIX*. Ortigosa, businessman interested in politics, close friend of Cumplido. Letters suggest friendship, *El siglo XIX*, health, death of friend, cholera, and politics.

457. Curiel, Fernando (1902–1974 Dates of Torres Bodet) (1889–1959 Dates of Reyes). *Casi oficios: cartas cruzadas entre Jaime Torres Bodet y Alfonso Reyes, 1922–1959.* México: El Colegio de México, 1994. 298pp. Letters. Period Covered: 1922–1959.

Collection of 176 letters, 111 from Torres Bodet to Reyes; sixty-five from Reyes to Torres Bodet. Spanning major political and literary career of Torres Bodet, editorship of *La Falange* in 1922 to French ambassadorship in France in 1958, collection suggests relationship with mutual admiration on publications. Title indicates diplomatic posts of authors and informality from friendship.

458. Curiel, Fernando (1942–). *De cuerpo entero: Fernando Curiel.* México: Ediciones Corunda, 1991. 59pp. Memoirs. Period Covered: 1942–1991.

Cubistic memoirs of writer. No normal chronology but chunks of information characterized by self-dialog or probing of unknown, relentless, and accusing questioner. Topics of family, Nicaragua, Paris, New York City, London, reading interests, and literary acquaintants.

459. Curtis, Samuel Ryan. *Mexico under Fire....* Fort Worth: Texas Christian University Press, 1994. 307pp.

West Point graduate and engineer organized regiment which stayed in Matamoros, Camargo, Monterrey, and Saltillo. Lack of great movement and relative permanence of occupation gave Curtis opportunity to create different type of war diary. He can record local customs and even participate in them. He met Scott and Taylor. Notable is effort to restrain troops from harassing natives and his cooperation with *alcaldes*. Issue of regular troops versus volunteers. "Wood and water are the matters most important to our encampments" (p.115). Good read.

460. Cusi, Ezio (1879–?). *Memorias de un colón.* México: Editorial Jus, 1969. 335pp. Memoirs. Period Covered: 1884–1938.

Born in Italy, he immigrated to Mexico with family in 1887. Father Dante Cusi, acquiring and developing thousands of acres in Michoacán, became rich *hacendado*. No dilettantish *hacendado* but agricultural entrepreneur of irrigation systems and rice fields. Laments expropriation of 64,000 hectares transformed into cooperative *ejidal* in 1938.

461. Cutler, Lance. *Tequila Lover's Guide to Mexico.* Sonoma, CA: Wine Patrol, 1998. 230pp.

In first seventy-one pages Cutler introduces self and speaks autobiographically of relationship since boyhood with tequila. He leads reader through Mexico *tequilado* or process of growing, harvesting, brewing, and marketing tequila. Jalisco figures prominently here.

462. Dale, John T.; Jean Rumbaugh. *Messenger of the Cross: Memoirs of the Life and Ministry of Dr. John T. Dale.* Edinburg, TX: Rio Grande Bible Institute Print Shop, 2001. 141pp.

Protestant who spent life working for church in Mexico. As child, he witnessed parents and missionary work in Tamazunchale. After college graduation in U.S., Dale returned to Mexico and was involved in evangelism from 1940s to 1975: studied Aztec dialects, helped found new churches, established Casa Hogar (medical work), directed Indian mission, and participated in national conventions. His wife contributed to efforts.

463. Dalquest, Walter Woelber. *The Tehuantepec Jungle: A Memoir.* Wichita Falls, TX: Midwestern State University Press, 1996. 175pp.

Naturalist and college professor from U.S. in mid–1940s ransacked Tehuantepec jungle for animals: jaguars, tapirs, curassows, peccaries, and rats. Slaughter to increase knowledge of biology. Excellent jungle descriptions.

464. Dame, Lawrence. *Yucatan.* New York: Random House, 1941. 374pp.

Maya ruins receive no more space than incidents of travel; donkeys and armadillos fascinate as much as talking cross supposedly unseen by white man. Dame belongs to type of Gringo traveler using Mexico as testing ground for stamina. Shows lingering 1930's attitude that primitive life is superior to civilization.

465. Dana, Napoleon Jackson Tecumeseh. *Monterrey Is Ours! The Mexican War Letters of Lieutenant Dana, 1845–1847.* Lexington: University Press of Kentucky, 1990. 218pp.

Document of regular soldier who was at Rio Grande in 1846 when war started. Matamoros, Reynosa, Camargo, Monterrey, Tampico, Vera Cruz, and Cerro Gordo indicate that Dana followed path of war. He writes well and personally to his wife. In correspondence, he escapes camp life.

466. Daniel, Karen (1971–). *A unos pasos de lograr el reto.* México: Editorial Letras Vivas, 2001. 112pp. Memoirs. Period Covered: 1971–2000?

Born with cerebral palsy, she tells of supportive Jewish family and therapists in native country and in U.S. Now owner of computer business.

467. Daniels, Josephus. *Shirt-Sleeve Diplomat.* Chapel Hill: University of North Carolina Press, 1947. 547pp.

Incorporates ambassador's years in Mexico during Roosevelt administration, 1933 to 1942. Poorly integrated life story abounds in sincerity and suggests journalistic background of owner of Southern newspaper. Climax of well-intentioned ambassador and

consort is photograph dressed as *charro* and as *china poblana*. Other photographs reinforce spirit of Roosevelt's Good Neighbor Policy personified by Daniels and wife.

468. Dauvin, Daniel; Mary Dauvin. *Walking on the Water: Family Pilgrimage to Guadalupe in the Spirit of Saint Francis.* Eganville, ON: Perfect Joy Productions, 1994. 155pp.

Entails experience of Canadian family on pilgrimage to Virgin of Guadalupe. Climax is blessing by priest at shrine.

469. Davidson, John. *The Long Road North.* Garden City, NY: Doubleday, 1979. 189pp.

In 1970s, Davidson convinced two Mexicans to take him along in entering U.S. illegally. Two abortive attempts and third try successful. Trio lands in San Antonio and two function in confusing Anglo environment. Sensitively told.

470. Davis, George Trunbull Moore. *Autobiography of the Late Col. Geo. T.M. Davis….* New York: Jenkins and McCowan, 1891. 395pp.

One of highest-ranking officers in Mexican-American War to write long memoirs on this event. Laredo, Vera Cruz, Cerro Gordo, Jalapa, Perote, Puebla, and Mexico City comprise his war journey. Davis notable as aide-de-camp to Gen. James Shields and insider of administration of war: mission to Washington to see President Polk and witness to military trials, to traitorous Irish brigade, and to negotiations for peace.

471. Davis, William Brownlee. *Experiences and Observations of an American Consular Officer during the Recent Mexican Revolutions….* Chula Vista, CA: Davis, 1920. 248pp.

Author received permission (exequatur) to act as vice-consul in Guadalajara from November 1915 to July 1916: "I decided to serve…my government and the fifteen hundred or more Americans in that District…"(pp.2–3). Duties became overwhelming with Guadalajara as pawn between Carranza and Villa. Manuel Diéguez Lara, named military commander of Jalisco by

Carranza, most frequently mentioned. Gives details of Davis's interventions with Mexican government on behalf of Americans.

472. Dawson, Armon. *Dry Ground into Watersprings.* Huntington Beach, CA: Wycliffe Bible Translators, 1978. 132pp.

Another Wycliffe missionary tells story. Armon Dawson and wife went to Mexico in 1950s. Caught up with Wycliffe movement, they adopted Otomi of Mezquital Valley of Hidalgo. Indiana farm couple convinced of need to translate Bible into Otomi and to evangelize. Document reflects effort and zeal to involve other Americans as missionaries in Mexico and Guatemala.

473. Degollado Guízar, Jesús (Dates?). *Memorias de Jesús Degollado Guízar, último general en jefe del ejército cristero.* México: Editorial Jus, 1957. 319pp. Memoirs. Period Covered: 1920–1928.

Author's subtitle suggests both political and religious posture during *Cristero* rebellion in Michoacán and Jalisco against government, mainly President Calles in guerrilla crusade. Valuable for *Cristero* perspective of moral righteousness.

474. Dehesa, Germán (1944–). *No basta ser padre.* México: Planeta, 2001. 227pp. Memoirs. Period Covered: 1984–2001.

Journalist dispenses autobiography through 125 articles published in periodicals. Collective reading serves as memoir and apprenticeship but never mastery of parenting three children. Shows humor, Mexican culture, and subject's personality. His caution could apply to all autobiographical writing: "Nada es… rigurosamente verdadero; nada es… enteramente falso" (p.128).

475. Delaflor y Casanova, Noé (1904?–?). *Autobiográficas y escritos: fragmentos, virutas y astillas.* México: Costa-Amic, 1983. 241pp. Memoirs. Period Covered: 1907–1983.

Born in Teapa, Tabasco, writer was governor and judge of Superior Tribunal of Justice for Federal District. Mixes autobiography with history and aphorisms; concentrates on education and politics. Many tributes to social reformer.

476. De La Fuente, Mario (1909–?). *I Like You, Gringo…but!* By Mario De La Fuente with Boye De Mente. Phoenix: Phoenix Books, 1972. 176pp. Hybrid. Period Covered: 1914–1969.

Coahuilense immigrated to Texas in 1914 because of Revolution. Experienced prejudice in new environment but managed to graduate from University of Texas as baseball star. Rest centers on businessman living in Nogales, Sonora. Much of book, comprised of anecdotes, focuses on author as macho and as mediator for Anglo friends on Arizona border. Later autobiography, *The Impresario of the Bullrings: Godfather to Men and Bulls* (1989) adds details to youth. De la Fuente indulges in life of bullring. Only bullfight autobiography from point of view of impresario.

477. De La Peña, Rafael Angel (1837–1906). *Epistolario de Miguel Antonio Caro y Rufino José Cuervo con Rafael Angel De La Peña y otros mexicanos.* Bogotá: Instituto Caro y Cuervo, 1983. 473pp. Letters. Period Covered: 1878–1902.

De La Peña, scholar of linguistics and member of Mexican Academy, sustained correspondence with Caro and Cuervo, two Colombian scholars of Spanish language. Mainly philological themes; exchange lacks intimacy and familiarity of Pedro Henríquez Ureña/Alfonso Reyes correspondence.

478. Delgado de León, Bartolomé (1927–1974). *Y dígalo que yo lo dije —: memorias de amor y vida en el Valle del Yaqui.* Hermosillo: Gobierno del Estado de Sonora, 1994. 338pp. Memoirs. Period Covered: 1927–1972?

Son of deceased Sonorense journalist collects autobiographical articles of father, which form personality of writer from Ciudad Obregón, Sonora, and La Chona, Jalisco. Schooling, teachers, cemeteries, environment, priests, and other regional personalities combine in autobiography cum social protest. High quality of regional journalism.

479. Delgado Martínez, César (1929–1992 Dates of Flores Canelo). *Raúl Flores Canelo: arrieros somos.* México: Instituto Nacional de Bellas Artes, 1996. 223pp. Hybrid. Period Covered: 1929–1992.

Posthumously constructed through interviews with Flores Canelo, professional dancer and choreographer. Entering dancing as career late in life, he associated with major names in ballet and founded own troupe in 1979. Opinions of family, friends, and collaborators enhance interview.

480. Del Plaine, Carlos Werter (1893–?). *Son of Orizaba: Memories of Childhood in Mexico*. New York: Exposition, 1954. 62pp. Memoirs. Period Covered: 1893–1902.

Author's Nova Scotian parents lived in Orizaba, Vera Cruz. Father inspector for Mexican Cable and Telegraph Company. Mexican-born author recalls happy Victorian childhood with excursions, servants, and instruction in private schools and at home. Yellow fever forced family back to Canada in 1912.

481. Del Villar, Mary. *Where the Strange Roads Go Down*. New York: Macmillan, 1953. 244pp.

Two New York journalists on walking tour of Mexico in Michoacán. Finished, they exult: "But we had made it, over 700 miles of walking: deserts, rivers, mountains, beaches, towns, villages and lonely ranches, in spite of fatigue, hunger, insects, heat and cold" (p.242). Tour proves that Mexico is beautiful, country folk hospitable, and two out-of-shape New Yorkers equal to physical challenge of walk.

482. Denegri, Carlos (1910–1970). *Luces rojas en el canal: un reportaje*. México: Tallares Gráficos de Excelsior, 1944. 246pp. Memoirs. Period Covered: 1943.

Born in Argentina to a Mexican father, Denegri exercised profession of journalist. In 1943, in midst of WWII, he traveled to England via New York. In England he not only reported on war but also interviewed several celebrities: H.G. Wells, Salvador de Madariaga, and Nancy Cunard.

483. De Ribeaux, Mary Beth. *The Martin Chronicles: A True Story of Adoption and Love in Mexico*. San Jose: Writer's Club Press, 2000. 209pp.

Infertile couple adopts Mexican infant. Years 1997–2000 suggest process of Mexico's legal system to accomplish adoption. Prospective parents residing in Puerto Vallarta with access to Guadalajara, focus of negotiations. Culture and congeniality of Mexican emerges in story of infant Martin. First autobiography from Mexico based on electronic mail.

484. De Vries, Lini M. *Up from the Cellar*. Minneapolis: Vanilla Press, 1979. 420pp.

Lini M. DeVries is trained nurse frustrated with F.B.I. harassment because of her involvement in Spanish Civil War. Refuged in Mexico in 1949, she exercised nursing skills and developed new talent and training methods. Teaching health to native Oaxacans required use of puppets. President Adolfo López Mateos granted her citizenship in 1962. Only Mexican years from the above title in *Please, God, Take Care of the Mule* (1969).

485. Diamant, Gertrude; John O'Hara Cosgrove. *The Days of Ofelia*. Boston: Houghton Mifflin, 1942. 226pp.

Author goes to Mexico on mission to determine I.Q.'s of Otomi Indians. She lives in Mexico City on Atoyac. Here she meets the Escotos and daughter Ofelia. Poor but ambitious Ofelia becomes maid to Gringa giving Diamant subject for book.

486. Díaz, Porfirio (1830–1915). *Memorias íntimas del general Porfirio Díaz....* San Antonio: Casa Editora Whitt, 1929. 433pp. Memoirs. Period Covered: 1830–1867.

Start with Diaz's birth in Oaxaca and incorporate role in Guerra de los Tres Años with emphasis on military exploits.

487. Díaz Barreiro, Francisco (Dates?). *Un periodista mexicano en los frentes franceses....* México: Imprenta Francesa, 1919. 178pp. Memoirs. Period Covered: 1916.

In political disfavor in Mexico, he covers WWI France for Venezuelan and Puerto Rican newspapers. Subtitle, "Trenches and Hospitales; Scenes of the frightful World Tragedy, Described Truly and Impartially," sets both theme and tone. Travels from Lourdes in southwest France to Compeigne in north.

488. Díaz Covarrubias, Francisco
(1833–1889). *Viaje de la Comisión Astronómica Mexicana al Japón....* México: Ramiro y Ponce de León, 1876. 448pp. Memoirs. Period Covered: 1874.

Engineer, mapmaker, and professor of astronomy headed Mexican Astronomical Commission to Japan in 1874. Describes arrival in Japan and concentrates on information about country. Autobiography mixes with Japanese culture in illustrated book. Mexican travel writers on Japan rare in nineteenth century; almost forty-five years later, José Juan Tablada published *En el país del sol.*

489. Díaz de León, Francisco (1897–?).
Zodíaco provinciano: memorias escritas en la pizarra de un escolar. Instituto Cultural de Aguascalientes, 1992. 65pp. Memoirs. Period Covered: 1905?–1910?

Engraver and illustrator of own autobiography recaptures provincial religiosity in *Zodíaco.* Twelve chapters, corresponding to zodiac signs, combine in type of generic autobiography for youth of period. School, seasons and church dominate in recollections. Mood reminiscent of introductory pages of Yáñez's *Al filo del agua.*

490. Díaz Du-Pond, Carlos (1911–?). *Cincuenta años de ópera en México: testimonio operístico.* México: UNAM, 1978. 326pp. Memoirs. Period Covered: 1924–1974.

Performer, director, and fanatic opera buff writes of personal experiences. As in later work, he mixes accounts of own life with fifty opera seasons.

491. Díaz Du-Pond, Carlos (1911–?).
Opera en Monterrey, 1953–1987. Monterrey: Secretaría de Educación y Cultura, 1990. 125pp. Memoirs. Period Covered: 1953–1980.

Expert of opera once again involves self with musical genre but in Monterrey setting. Knowing operas and their stars, he writes year-by-year account.

492. Díaz Du-Pond, Carlos (1911–?). *15 temporadas de ópera en Guadalajara: testimonios operísticos.* Guadalajara: Departamento de Bellas Artes, 1987. 63pp. Memoirs. Period Covered: 1954–1986.

Director of operas biographizes each year of season in Guadalajara. Interweaves operas with impressions and own life.

493. Díaz Infante, S.J. Carlos (Dates?).
100,000 [i.e.] cien mil kilómetros misioneros en la nueva tarahumara. Siseguichi, Chihuahua, 1967. 103pp. Memoirs. Period Covered: 1955.

Jesuit priest converts Tarahumara Indians of Chihuahua. As in colonial times, Christianization of Indians involves cognate activities like literacy and health. Glimpses of personality of dedicated missionary in contact with daily lives of Tarahumara and their environment.

494. Díaz Olvera, José (1904?–?). *En la otra orilla: estampas médicas del Tepeji del Río.* Pachuca, HID: Instituto Hidalguense de Cultura, 1992. 572pp. Memoirs. Period Covered: 1910–1991?

Unable to attend school because of Revolution, he accelerated education to become doctor. Practicing in Tepeji del Río near Pachuca in state of Hidalgo, he regales reader with anecdotes of fifty years in medicine. Experiences made provincial M.D. equal and even superior to any in Mexico City.

495. Díaz Ramírez, María Eugenia
(1907–?). *Memorias de una niña queretana.* Querétaro, QUE: Dirección de Patrimonio Cultura, 1989. 92pp. Memoirs. Period Covered: 1907–1930.

Idealized view of childhood in Querétaro: family, hacienda, Revolution, social life, and marriage. Although still alive in 1983, she abruptly ended memoirs with admission: "I got married, had eight children, traveled, lived in a world, but this is another story that I don't feel like writing" (p.92).

496. Díaz Serrano, Jorge (1921–?). *Yo, Jorge Díaz Serrano.* México: Planeta, 1989. 262pp. Memoirs. Period Covered: 1921–1988.

Mechanical and electrical engineer was head of Pemex, ambassador to Soviet Union, senator from Sonora, and finally prison inmate due to accusation of corruption in Pemex. Readable memoirs focus on public life rather than personal. Much Pemex history in *Yo Jorge Díaz Serrano....* Self-made individual outspoken in attitude towards Mexico's political system.

497. Díez de Urdanivia, Fernando
(Dates?). *Mi historia secreta de la música.*
México: Luzam, 1991. 147pp. Memoirs.
Period Covered: 1950?–1970?

Promotor of music justifies purpose of
book: "Artículos donde se relatan las
peripecias que rodean el espectáculo musical;
los hechos ocultos que el público nunca se
entera y que salpimentan los conciertos,
aunque a veces los pongan en riesgo" (p.9).
Witty, brief pieces cluster about central
themes of great musicians, jazz, maestro
Vásquez, symphonies, etc. Reveals self in
multiple anecdotes on twentieth century
Mexican music.

498. Dilworth, Rankin. *The March to
Monterrey....* El Paso: Texas Western, 1996.
119pp.

Another intimate view of war. Dates,
April 28, 1846, to September 19, 1846, enclose
diary of Ohio-born graduate of West Point
who entered Mexico at Matamoros under
Gen. Taylor. Microscopic approach to war:
weather, food, battles, and death, landscape,
native Mexicans, thoughts of home, other
soldiers, and camp life. Dilworth is eyewitness, participant, and victim in war.

499. Dimitroff, Stephen Pope. *Apprentice
to Diego Rivera in Detroit and Fresco Work-
shops Manual.* Gualala, CA: The Author,
1986. 55pp.

Narrates plight as dropout from Chicago
Art Institute in 1932 and successful efforts to
learn fresco technique from Rivera in
Detroit. Willing apprentice, ingratiating self
with both artist and Frida Kahlo, rewarded
with increasingly more difficult jobs relating
to murals.

500. Dodge, David. *How Green Was My
Father, A Sort of Travel Diary by David
Dodge.* New York: Simon and Schuster, 1947.
217pp.

Book takes unusual title from movie
¡Qué verde era mi padre! or *How Horny Was
My Father!* Thus reader led into humorous
excursion south of border with author,
spouse, and two children. Plan to motor
from San Francisco to Central America
fraught with problems of food, illness, car
permits, insects, and language. Mexico of

1940s ceased as haven for materialistically
ridden Gringos and simply became stage for
comical and non-threatening incidents.

501. Domecq, Brianda (1942–). *De
cuerpo entero: Brianda Domecq.* México: Ediciones Corunda, 1991. 60pp. Memoirs. Period
Covered: 1942–1991.

Born in U.S., she has lived in adopted
country Mexico since 1951. Novelist, short
story writer, and essayist profiles major
influences on writing: understanding grandmother who enjoyed child's fantasies, college
literature courses which stimulated her, and
love of Mexico with will to master language.
Original sense of humor.

502. Domecq, Brianda (1942–). *Mujer
que publica...mujer pública. Ensayos sobre literatura feminina.* México: Editorial Diana,
1994. 296pp. Essays. Period Covered:
1972?–1993?

Novelist, journalist, and feminist
expresses opinions. Eleven or half of selections autobiographical: act of writing,
women and writing, marginality of Latin
American literature, women authors with
whom she interacted (Alaíde Foppa, Adela
Fernández, and Margarita Dalton), house-
wife-mother-writer, and novelized history of
Teresa Urrea (1873–1906), preaching social
reform, and achieving fame as Santa de Cabora. Present anthology and *Cuerpo entero*
profile growing celebrity.

503. Domecq, Brianda (1942–). *Once
días...y algo más.* Xalapa, México: UV Editorial, 1979. 323pp. Trans: *Eleven days.* Translated by Kay S. Garcia. Albuquerque: University of New Mexico Press, 1995. Diary. Period
Covered: 1978.

Journalist and member of wine family
(Domecq sherry, brandy, cordials, etc.) kidnapped for eleven days in 1978 and describes
episode day by day. Dialogs with captors and
with self. Thoughts of family and escape narrated with humor.

504. Domenech, Emmanuel. *Missionary
Adventures in Texas and Mexico....* London:
Longmans, Brown, Green, 1858. 366pp.

French Catholic priest assigned to Texas
in 1846, author in 1851 and 1852 visited Texas

and Mexico, Tamaulipas, Coahuila, and Nuevo León, and spent time on border. Comments on Protestant missionaries. Much on landscape and general culture. Interesting tale of trying to save Mexicans refuged in church.

505. Domingo, Plácido (1941–). *Mis primeros cuarenta años*. traducción del inglés por Juan Antonio Gutiérrez-Layrraya. Barcelona: Planeta, 1984. 185pp. Trans: *My First Forty Years*. Barcelona: Planeta, 1984. Memoirs. Period Covered: 1941–1981.

Born in Madrid, youth moved with parents to Mexico in 1949. Attended high school at Instituto México and studied music at National Conservatory of Music. Focuses on operatic career in Americas, Europe, and Israel. Few words on family or personal life.

506. Domínguez, Rafael (1883?–?). *Añoranzas del Instituto Juárez*. México: Editorial Cultura, 1940. 201pp. Memoirs. Period Covered: 1897.

Nostalgic for *colegio* years in Tabasco. Friendly account evokes personalities of professors and classmates. School curricula and events typical of author's generation under Porfiriato.

507. Domínguez, Rafael (1888–1959). *Veracruz en el ensueño y el recuerdo: apuntes de la vida jarocha*. México: Editorial Bolívar, 1946. 250pp. Memoirs. Period Covered: 1914–1945.

With nostalgia author, lawyer, judge, schoolteacher, and civic-minded Veracruzano recalls city. Hotels, plazas, parks, songs, naval school, airline service, and Ateneo names of individuals comprise memoirs. He defended poet Salvador Díaz Mirón for alleged physical attack on high school student.

508. Domínguez Aragonés, Edmundo (1938–). *Encuentros: los de primera plana*. México: Gernika, 1991. 166pp. Memoirs. Period Covered: 1951?–1990?

In acquaintance with celebrities, journalist scatters autobiographical data in forty-six word portraits, from José Agustín to Jacobo Zabludovsky.

509. Donner, Florinda. *Being-in-Dreaming*. San Francisco: Harper, 1991. 303pp.

Donner is selected as special initiate into arcane rites popularized in Carlos Castaneda's works. Goes back and forth from Arizona to Sonora often in confounding apprenticeship into other realities. No date possible because of irrelevance of chronological time.

510. Dorador, Silvestre (1871–1930). *…Mi prisión, la defensa social y la verdad del caso..* México: Departamento de Tallares Gráficos de la Secretaría de Fomento, 1916. 253pp. Memoirs. Period Covered: 1911–1915.

Founder of press, Propagandista de las Sociedades Mutualistas de Artesanos y Obreros, and founder of colony for laborers, he became Maderista in Revolution. Accused of collusion with revolutionaries, he was imprisoned in 1913. Details tenure as municipal president of Durango and prison experience. Later became senator.

511. Dorenbaum, Jaime (1900?–1973). *De Polonia a Cajeme: memorias de Jaime Dorenbaum*. México: Centro de Documentación e Investigación de la Comunidad Ashkenaszi de México, 1998. 190pp.

Posthumously published manuscript translated from Yiddish to Spanish. Arrived in Mexico as young man in 1923. Began working as peddler in Mexico City. Sold shoes, had store in Cajeme, Sonora (Cuidad Obregón), and returned to Mexico City. Successful immigrant and relationship with family, Jewish community, and other Mexicans. Contemporary history intervenes too much as Dorenbaum sustains interest with anecdote and enthusiasm.

512. Dornbierer, Manou (1936–). *Los indignos: novela autobiográfica*. México: Editorial Grijalbo, 1995. 312pp. Autobiographical Novel. Period Covered: 1959–1971?

Woman involved in cultural life and under alter ego of Valeria gives life in *roman a clef* of 1960s. Verifiable environment and events of critical decade end c.1968, year of Tlateloco.

513. Doubleday, Abner; Joseph E. Chance. *My Life in the Old Army…*. Ft. Worth: Texas Christian University Press, 1998. 403pp.

Five of ten chapters memoirs of West Point grad related to Mexican-American War. In 1845, Doubleday sent to Corpus Christi, Texas, as part of Zachary Taylor's army of occupation. In 1846, called to Rio Grande in Mexican-American War. Other chapters relate to battles of Monterrey and Buena Vista. Yet most unique chapter on Saltillo, site of military occupation. His chapter, "Roguery and Rascality in Mexico," bespeaks of theme and content.

514. Drees, Charles William; Ada M.C. Drees. *Thirteen Years in Mexico (from Letters of Charles W. Drees).* New York: Abingdon, 1915. 276pp.

Mexican Protestants have yet to share religious experience through autobiography. Best commentaries from American Protestant missionaries in Mexico such as title above. Methodist missionary there from 1874 to 1886 made Protestant activities explicit: work with Indians, establishment of orphanage and theological seminary, administrative efforts, overt anti–Protestantism of natives, and overseeing of mission efforts in Vera Cruz, Orizaba, Guanajuato, Querétaro, and other sites. One of best Protestant autobiographies of Mexico.

515. Dromundo, Baltasar (1906–1987). *Mi barrio San Miguel.* México: Antigua Librería Robredo, 1951. 136pp. Memoirs. Period Covered: 1910?–1914.

Writer evokes childhood neighborhood in Mexico City: architecture, family, local personalities, noises, food, Madero, etc. Nostalgia obliterates unhappiness or unpleasantness.

516. Dromundo, Baltasar (1906–1987). *Mi calle de San Ildefonso.* México: Editorial Guaranía, 1956. 263pp. Memoirs. Period Covered: 1923–1928.

Writer, politician, lawyer, and orator in Vasconcelos campaign entered Escuela Nacional Preparatoria in 1923. Pays tribute to school and generation that achieved university autonomy. Nostalgically evokes neighborhood, faculty, courses, classmates, books, and popular culture of students. Sharply drawn portraits of Frida Kahlo and Carmen Jaime, members of *cachuchas.*

517. Dromundo, Baltasar (1906–1987). *Rescate del tiempo.* México: Imprenta Madero, 1980. 180pp. Memoirs. Period Covered: 1911–1979.

Writer represents self in mosaic of 161 chapters each centering on person, event, or experience. Portrays famous Mexicans in anecdote.

518. Dumas, Alexandre. *Diario de Marie Giovanni: viaje de una parisiense.* México: Banco de México, 1981. 527pp.

Takes place in 1854 when French adventuress lands in Acapulco and proceeds to Mexico City. Notes route, climate, Indians, *costumbrismo,* surroundings of capital. Meeting Santa Anna and José Yves Limantour suggests status of traveler.

519. Duncklee, John. *Coyotes I Have Known.* Tucson: University of Arizona Press, 1996. 150pp.

Recovers years as cattleman along Sonora Arizona border in 1950s. Crisscrosses line with equal savvy in order to buy or to sell cattle or to complete one of jobs called for by occupation. Spontaneity, good humor, love for job, storytelling, integrity, rapid thinking, and some wanderlust fit him into category of turn-of-century cowboy with all of positive attributes. Doesn't idealize self in colorful memoir.

520. Dunn, H.H. *Crimson Jester, Zapata of Mexico.* New York: National Travel Club, 1934. 304pp.

Contrary to today's image of Zapata as hero and revolutionary martyr, Dunn's book humanizes and even debunks warlord. Journalist Dunn with Yaqui Juan accompanied Zapata from 1910 to 1918 on exploits and records them as observer and participant.

521. Duval, B. R. *A Narrative of Life and Travels in Mexico and British Honduras.* Boston: Brown, 1881. 70pp.

As title suggests, memoirs are only partly devoted to Mexico. Because of financial reverses in 1864 and possible spiritual needs of Southerners living in Mexico, author and family removed to this country. Methodist impulse enormous: "I had hoped to preach, in Spanish, to tens of thousands of the Mexicans, and to see thousands of them converted…" (p.30). During family's stay in Córdova, he observed climate, agriculture, and French troops.

522. Duvall, Marius. *A Navy Surgeon in California, 1846–1847: The Journal of Marius Duvall.* San Francisco: Howell, 1957. 114pp.

Medical doctor tells little of his practice in his diary from April 1846 to March 1847. He did attend family of Gen. Mariano Vallejo. Duvall often describes what he hasn't seen. He notes internal conflicts in Anglo California. A racist, he defends Anglo against Indian and Californians.

523. Echeagaray Y Ricardos, Miguel María de (1814–1891). *Memorias.* México: Editorial Citlaltépetl, 1973. 102pp. Memoirs. Period Covered: 1847.

In *Apuntaciones para la defensa del general Echeagaray escritas por él mismo* (1861) author vindicates self as officer who fought Americans at Molina del Rey and Chapúltepec in Mexican-American War. Considered traitor by Juárez government.

524. Echeverría, Alicia (1910?–?). *De burguesa a guerrillera….* México: Mortiz, 1986. 154pp. Autobiography Proper. Period Covered: 1915–1958?

Covers life with introspection and honesty. Daughter, wife, mother, grandmother, and confidante experienced traditional roles of women; but also was student, teacher, writer, businesswoman, foreigner, and guerrilla fighter. Develops life from comfortable childhood in Michoacán to poverty and ignorant, sadistic nuns in U.S. parochial schools, to middle-class survival in Vera Cruz, to marriage and Mexico City and finally to guerrilla movement in Guatemala. Frankness in negative revelations of family life. Highlights female relationships.

525. Echeverría A. Marquina, Javier (1895?–?). *¡Viva Carranza! Mis recuerdos de la Revolución.* México, 1963. 263pp. Memoirs. Period Covered: 1913–1961.

Carrancista military man with obligatory lauds for Carranza. Personal elements of more interest. Begins chapter in philosophical mood putting national events into universal context.

526. Ediger, Donald. *The Well of Sacrifice.* Garden City, NY: Doubleday, 1971. 288pp.

With modern equipment and enthusiastic bunch of colleagues, Ediger testifies to value of technology and need for variety of talents, e.g., archaeology, diving, engineering, and chemistry to rescue more artifacts and unfold Maya history.

527. Edwards, R. M.; Stewart Lillard. *"Down the Tennessee:" The Mexican War Reminiscences of an East Tennessee Volunteer.* Charlotte, NC: Lillard, 1997. 146pp.

Some of volunteers arrived after Mexican-American War. Author, a hospital steward and member of Tennessee Volunteer Infantry, served in Mexico from December 1847 to August 1848. He was scheduled to attack Orizaba to capture Gen. Santa Anna. Later he spoke of destruction of Mango de Clava, Santa Anna's hacienda. Difficulty of nine-month enlistment summed up in one sentence: "I myself on my arrival at Vera Cruz weighed 185 pounds, now would not weigh over 130 pounds" (p.58).

528. Edwards, William Seymour. *On the Mexican Highlands.* Cincinnati: Jennings and Graham, 1906. 283pp.

Author wrote above title between two other travel books, one on the Yukon and one on Scandinavia. He crosses Mexico, views bullfight, and shuttles through Michoacán, where he visits mines and Morelia. Toluca and Cuernavaca complete informative sojourn. Leaves some of self and almost no criticism of Porfiriato.

529. Eisenberg, Abel (1918–?). *Entre violas y violinas: crónica de un músico mexicano.* México: EDAMEX, 1990. 158pp. Memoirs. Period Covered: 1930–1988.

Violist and symphony director, Mexican-born author practiced profession also in Cuba and Dominican Republic. Mentions Jascha Heifetz, Carlos Chávez, and Julián Carrillo; but shows adoration for Silvestre Revueltas.

530. Elizondo, Juan Manuel (1910–?). *Memorias improvisadas: mi universidad.* Monterrey: Universidad Autónoma Nuevo León,

2000. 251pp. Memoirs. Period Covered: 1918?–1936?

Focus on politics in Monterrey by activist in Federación de Estudiantes Revolucionarios (FER) with ties to Partido Comunista Mexicano (PCM). He had role in creation of University of Nuevo León, founding of union for miners and Socialist Party for Workers. Details on politics at regional level from individual who interacted with major figures of period: Cárdenas, Calles, Vasconcelos, and Lombardo Toledano.

531. Elizondo, Salvador (1932–). *Elsinore un cuaderno*. México: Ediciones del Equilibrista, 1988. 51pp. Memoirs. Period Covered: 1947?

As teenager, writer spent several years in military school near Lake Elsinore in California. Typical pranks of cadets who abuse rules of institution. Recreates mood of immediate post-war Los Angeles.

532. Elizondo, Salvador (1932–). *Salvador Elizondo*. México: Empresas Editoriales, 1966. 61pp. Autobiography Proper. Period Covered: 1936?–1966?

Creativity is foremost: poetry, function of its creator, painting, film and its criticism, reading preferences, and writing of *Farabeuf*. Preference for emotional life: solitude, secret inner world he created, and perception of insanity. Hatred of school, travels in Europe and U.S., love for ex-wife, need for alcohol, marriage, birth of daughters, and scholarship from Centro Mexicano de Escritores comprise concrete part of life. Author confesses that 1966 autobiography somewhat premature. New one, *Autobiografía precoz* (2000), manifests maturity of sixty-seven-year-old writer over his thirty-three-year-old self.

533. Elliott, Richard Smith; Mark L. Gardner; Marc Simmons. *The Mexican War Correspondence of Richard Smith Elliott*. Norman: University of Oklahoma Press, 1997. 292pp.

Letters, published in *St. Louis Reveille*, were written by Elliott between June 7, 1846, and July 13, 1847. One of Missouri volunteers, he marched from Ft. Leavenworth, Kansas, to New Mexico and was a member of army of occupation. As dispatches to newspaper,

these brief letters intrigue reader with their clarity and their variety of topics: medicine, entry through Raton, planting of flag on palace of Armijo, food, Mexican foe, music, drills, recreation, campaign in Chihuahua, etc. One of better autobiographies of Mexican-American War.

534. Elorduy, Aquiles (1875–1964). *Puntadas de mi vida*. México: Impreso en los Tallares Gráficos de la Nación, 1963. 28pp. Anecdote. Period Covered: 1890–1960?

Writer, lawyer, and politician unfolds self in autobiographical anecdotes to be master of *salida* or repartee. In sporadic fashion talks about schooling, political life, and other less formal incidents.

535. Elorriaga Berdegué, Jorge Javier (1960–). *Ecos de Cerrohueco: el presunto juicio de un zapatista*. México: Ediciones Roca, 1996. 190pp. Memoirs. Period Covered: 1995.

Accused of leadership of EZLN (Ejército Zapatista de Liberación Nacional) in Chiapas, journalist and wife imprisoned by frightened government. Writers and illustrators for leftist periodicals in Mexico City, both denied affiliation with rebels. Arrest and imprisonment subject of document.

536. Elton, James Frederick. *With the French in Mexico*. London: Chapman and Hall, 1867. 206pp.

Few diaries, at least in English, reveal day-to-day trials of French. Elton travels from Vera Cruz to Mexico City and then to North. Notes surroundings, occasionally customs, and plight of French. Highly readable account of 1867.

537. Emory, William H. *Notes of a Military Reconnaissance from Fort Leavenworth, in Missouri, to San Diego....* Washington, DC: Wendell and Van Benthuysen, 1848. 614pp.

One-sixth of volume relates to scientific trip narrated in first person. Reconnaissance lasts from August 2, 1846, to December of 1847. Climate, vegetation, heights, latitude, and longitude occupy author as much as journey. Sojourn begins in New Mexico with reference to Santa Fe, Bernalillo, and Socorro as well as actions of Manuel Armijo. To West through Arizona and finally into San Diego and Los Angeles. Notes Indian tribes. More geography than autobiography.

538. Emrich, Harry. *Wanted: Missionary to Mexico: No Experience Necessary!* Longwood, FL: Longwood, 1992. 144pp.

"Two weeks after that wonderful day of Salvation, Mariedna and I were on our way south" (p.17). One of opening sentences guides reader to experiences of Methodist evangelist. From 1971, Emrich and wife evangelized in Tamaulipas, Nuevo León, Jalisco, Chihuahua, and Coahuila. Also visited prison and exorcised demons.

539. Enríquez Perea, Alberto (1880–1959 Dates of Reyes) *Itinerarios filosóficos: correspondencia José Gaos/ Alfonso Reyes, 1939–1959.* México: El Colegio de México, 1999. 271pp. Letters. Period Covered: 1939–1959.

Named president of recently created La Casa de España en México (later El Colegio de México), Reyes offered academic position to exiled philosopher, José Gaos. Twenty-year correspondence reveals life of professor of philosophy: research, publications, teaching, colleagues, students, and professional examinations. Letters divided evenly between two mutually supportive scholars.

540. Erives, Oscar. (1941–). *El otro Oscar: peripecias de un teatrista chihuahuense.* Chihuahua, CHH: Ediciones del Azar, 2001. 142pp. Memoirs. Period Covered: 1957–1994?

Given impossibility of priesthood, author opts for teaching and working in theatre at all levels. Director, actor, and student in Mexico City, he was active in regional theater in Chihuahua and also toured with group in Europe. Regional does not always imply amateur, for author worked with dramas of internationally known playwrights.

541. Escalante Marín, Pastor (1918–?). *Líos de un cura progresista.* Selección y prólogo, Alberto Cervera Espejo. Mérida, 1981. 221pp. Memoirs. Period Covered: 1934.

Born in Yucatan, he studied for priesthood in Spain during Civil War. Returning to Mexico, he exercised curate in Tixkobob, city east of Mérida. Active in Vatican Council,

admired Helder Câmara, Brazil's progressive priest. Author combated both Masons and Presbyterians in Mexico.

542. Escandón y Barrón, José Manuel, Marquis de Villavieja (1857–?). *Life Has Been Good: Memoirs of the Marqués de Villavieja.* London: Chatto & Windus, 1938. 336pp. Memoirs. Period Covered: 1861?–1938.

Member of Mexican nobility gives accurate title to memoirs. Born in Mexico and spending youth under Porfiriato, he spent years abroad in England, Spain, and France. Noted for love of horses and shooting, he introduced polo into Spain. Life is doing what one wants and mingling with nobility.

543. Escobedo, José G. (Dates?). *La batalla de Zacatecas (treinta y dos años después).* México, 1946. 123pp. Memoirs. Period Covered: 1914.

Journalist recalls incident when Victoriano Huerta usurped presidency, and Constitutionalist forces with Pancho Villa, Felipe Angeles, and Pánfilo Natera tried to dislodge him. With clarity and precision, author records taking of Zacatecas by Constitutionalist forces.

544. Escudero Luján, Carolina (1905–?). *Carolina Escudero Luján: una mujer en la historia de México....* Morelia: Instituto Michoacano de Cultura, 1992. 283pp. Oral Autobiography. Period Covered: 1905–1984.

Chihuahuense benefited from liberal education in Mexico City and El Paso, Texas. Worked as secretary and then married Francisco José Múgica, governor of Baja. Widowed, she ran for elective office and later worked for CREFAL (Centro Regional de Alfabetización Funcional en las Zonas Rurales de América Latina). Early feminist for political activities. Guadalupe García Torres synthesizes life of subject but no methodology.

545. Espejel y Alvarez, Manuel (1910 Birth of María Teresa de Landa). *Confidencias de "Miss México" narradas a un periodista.* México: Imprenta La Providencia, 1929. 96pp. Oral Autobiography. Period Covered: 1910–1928.

Pseudonymous author interviews imprisoned Miss México, María Teresa de

Landa. She married Gen. Moisés Vidal; he accused her of adultery in newspaper article; she shot him. Many soap opera elements: beautiful woman, adoring parents, convent education, idyllic life, and tragedy. Reminiscent of Moreno's *La tragedia de mi vida*.

546. Espejo, Beatriz (1938–). *Confiar en el milagro: entrevista con Beatriz Espejo*. Colima, COL, 1998. 108pp. Interview. Period Covered: 1945–1996?

Professor, editor, essayist, and short story writer, prompted by questions, talks of following: formation, publications, editorship, generation, literary genres, and writing. Refers often to favorite author, Inés Arredondo, and likewise to competitors in disfavor.

547. Espejo, Beatriz (1938–). *De cuerpo entero: Beatriz Espejo*. México: Ediciones Corunda, 1991. 58pp. Autobiographical Essay. Period Covered: 1944?–1991.

Short story writer speaks of gentle childhood: parents and grandparents, church, servants, education, reading, and travel.

548. Espinosa Yglesias, Manuel (1909–?). *Bancomer: logro y destrucción de un ideal*. México: Planeta, 2000. 230pp. Memoirs. Period Covered: 1909–1999.

With industrialist William Jenkins of Puebla, Espinosa Yglesias, heir to film theaters, moved into banking. Developed Mexico's successful Bancomer. In 1982, Bancomer taken over by state with low compensation for owner. Reprivatized bank under President Salinas Gotari did not enrich original owner.

549. Espinoza, Sánchez (1923?–?). *Recuerdos*. México: Instituto Municipal de Arte y Cultura, 1998. 189pp. Memoirs. Period Covered: 1939–1943?

Interested in Baja and its cities Tijuana and Mexicali as much as own autobiography. Describes generation in ITI (Instituto Técnica Industrial de Tijuana), secondary school similar to military academy. Teachers, courses, recreation, and pranks populate partial history of Tijuana.

550. Espinoza Valle, Víctor Alejandro (1907 Birth of Castañeda). *Don Crispin: una crónica fronteriza....* Tijuana: El Colegio de la Frontera Norte, 1990. 166pp. Oral Autobiography. Period Covered: 1907–1987.

Born in Estanzuela, Zacatecas, don Crispín worked on railways thirty-nine years on San Diego-Yuma route. Notes evolution of work and impressions of border cities of Nogales, Ciudad Juárez, Mexicali, and Tijuana. Union man, he advocated statehood for Baja. Final two chapters on border culture and Crispín's experiences as folk healer. Dictated to his grandson.

551. Esquivel, Laura (1950–). *Intimas suculencias: tratado filosófico de cocina*. Madrid: Ollero & Ramos, 1998. 158pp. Trans: *Between Two Fires: Intimate Writings on Life, Love, Food and Flavor*. Translated by Stephen A. Lytle. New York: Crown, 2001. Memoirs. Period Covered: 1953?–1997?

Composes memoir harmonious with novel, *Como agua para chocolate*. Fourteen independent chapters on recipes, preparation, and memory of food, family, and philosophy. Refers to new man as one who can integrate his past, his learning, lost savors, forgotten music, faces of grandparents, and gesture of dead. Philosophy both structures and permeates memoirs.

552. Esquivel Obregón, Toribio (1864–1945). *Adorada Laurita: Epistolario familiar de Toribio Esquivel Obregón, 1883–1946*. México: Instituto Nacional de Antropología e Historia, 1996. 272pp. Letters. Period Covered: 1883–1946.

First half, courtship and marriage, from 1883 to 1907. Fiancé and husband treats themes of absence and health and well being of chosen. Lawyer, vice president of Partido Antireeleccionista (1909–1910), secretary of treasury for five months under Huerta, and author in exile in New York from 1913 to 1924. Second half of greater interest: Washington, D.C., El Paso, Texas, the Revolution, Cuba, and New York. In U.S., unhappy about Revolution and in disharmony with environment.

553. Esquivel Obregón, Toribio (1861–1945). *Mi labor en servicio de México*. México: Ediciones Botas, 1934. 173pp. Memoirs. Period Covered: 1908–1914?

Represents life in critical moments of twentieth century history: anti-reelection campaign against Díaz, *Decena Trágica*, and government of Victoriano de la Huerta. Lawyer questions motives of anti-reelection-ists and readiness of populace for political change. Held cabinet position in administration of Victoriano de la Huerta, whose inconsistencies and brutalities led to author's resignation and exile. Certain of moral stance, he composes verbal portraits.

554. Estela (1968–?). "La neta, ora si yo no tengo cariño." En *¿Qué transa con las bandas?* de Jorge García-Robles. México: Editorial Posada, 1985. Pp.63–97. Oral Autobiography. Period Covered: 1968–1984.

García-Robles neglects methodology in collection of confessions of juvenile gang members. Forced from home at age of six, Estela lived as gang member and as prostitute. Enjoyment as pariah and boredom with honest work link her to picaresque.

555. Estrada, Alvaro (1895?–1985 Dates of Sabina) *Vida de María Sabina: la sabia de los hongos*. México: Siglo Veintiuno Editores, 1977. 164pp. Trans: *María Sabina: Her Life and Chants*. English edition by Alvaro Estrada. Santa Barbara, CA: Ross-Erikson, ca.1981. Oral Autobiography. Period Covered: 1900?–1976.

Mazatec Indian María traces major contours of life: parents, marriages, and children. Evokes much of cultural context of village. Healer with mushrooms and visions, María refers constantly to spirit world, either benevolent or evil for man.

556. Estrada, Francisco Javier (1801–1885). *Recuerdos de mi vida*. Universidad Autónoma de San Luis Potosí, 1954. 319pp. Autobiography Proper. Period Covered: 1801–1870.

Semi-orphan grew up without family. Educated sporadically, he worked in pharmacy, became owner of new printing press in San Luis Potosí, studied medicine, and fought on side of Iturbidistas. Involved in politics of San Luis Potosí. Autobiography, reflecting own life rather than outside experiences, original for nineteenth century Mexico. Clear style.

557. Estrada, Isabel Avila de (1922–?). "Interview with Isabel Avila de Estrada." Waco, TX: Institute for Oral History, Baylor, 1981. 95pp. Memoirs. Period Covered: 1922–1981.

Wife of Baptist minister Leobardo Estrada Díaz recalls past as it relates to church. Born in Torreón, Coahuila, she details youth, surreptitious exposure to Protestantism, and conversion in spite of father's opposition. At seminary in El Paso, Texas, married Leobardo Estrada and shared work of pastorates there, Dallas, Los Angeles, and New York. Student, missionary, wife, and mother, she represents traditional values of women. Interview by L. Katherine Cook.

558. Estrada, Julio (Dates?). *Cien días de safari*. México, 1948. 443pp. Memoirs. Period Covered: 1947.

Combines hunter, traveler, and anthropologist in three-month and 6,000-mile safari in East Africa. In exciting adventures meets natives and details landscape. Justifiably cites Stanley and Livingston and Theodore Roosevelt as inspiration.

559. Estrada, Leobardo (1915–?). "Interview with Leobardo Estrada." Waco, TX: Institute for Oral History, Baylor, 1981. 175pp. Memoirs. Period Covered: 1915–1981.

Thomas L. Charlton conducted five-hour interview with Estrada, Mexican-American Baptist minister. Born in Culiacán, Sinaloa, he and family moved to Laredo and to Corpus Christi. Held pastorates in Alpine (Texas), El Paso, Dallas, Los Angeles, and New York. President of Mexican Baptist Convention of Texas, 1949–1951 and 1957–1958, he touches on Baptist church and Hispanic community. Recalls Revolution and 1930 Depression in Corpus Christi.

560. Estrada, Xavier (1940–). *Desde otro punto de vista*. México: Editorial Diana, 1990. 213pp. Memoirs. Period Covered: 1940–1989?

Dwarf Estrada born into upper middle-class family with no previous history of this physical condition. Society's negative reactions to him and struggle to endure comprise life story. Final ninety-two pages a history of nanism (dwarfishness).

561. Evans, Albert S. *Our Sister Republic: A Gala Trip through Tropical Mexico in 1869–70....* Toledo, OH: Columbian Book, 1870. 518pp.

Author accompanied Wm. H. Seward of Alaska-purchase fame to Mexico from 1869 to 1870. Because Seward treated Mexico so well in decade of 1860s, his entourage well received. Party lingered in western and central Mexico: Colima, Guadalajara, Guanajuato, Querétaro, Mexico City, Puebla, and Orizaba. More travel than autobiography, *Our Sister Republic* compendium of Mexican culture including architecture, people, and customs. Ignacio Altamirano and Benito Juárez part of scene. Noted thieving Mexicans and also disreputable type of American attracted to this country.

562. Evans, George W.B.; Glenn S. Dumke. *Mexican Gold Trail: The Journal of a Forty-Niner.* San Marino, CA: Huntington Library, 1945. 340pp.

Much of diary takes place in Chihuahua. Gold-seeker Evans chose overland route to California. Of value is description of landscape, water, Indians, and general survival tactics. Little patience with non-Europeans and mixed bloods.

563. Evans, Rosalie Caden; Daisey Pettus. *The Rosalie Evans Letters from Mexico.* Indianapolis: Bobbs-Merrill, 1926. 472pp.

Foreigners in Puebla felt effects of Revolution. Young Rosalie Caden married Henry Evans, member of English family prosperous under Díaz. As owner of hacienda in Puebla valley at San Pedro Coxtocan, Evans improved property. With his death in 1917, widow was determined to save inheritance from redistribution. Fought at all levels of government parceling of hacienda from 1918 to 1923. Eventually lost struggle vividly recounted in this book.

564. Fabela, Isidro (1882–1964). *Isidro Fabela: epistolario a su discípulo Mario Colín.* Atlacomulco, MÉX: 1962. 85pp. Letters. Period Covered: 1942–1960.

Writer, politician, and diplomat corresponded sporadically with Mario Colín. Letters reveal much of author: work on International Court of Justice, understanding of political system, and constant encouragement of Colín, travels, and family.

565. Fabela, Isidro (1882–1964). *Mis memorias de la Revolución.* México: Editorial Jus, 1977. 316pp. Memoirs. Period Covered: 1902–1914.

Secretary of foreign affairs remembers younger years as Maderista, fervent Carrancista, and deputy to Congreso de la Unión. Narration follows chronological but fragmented path. Soldier, man of letters, journalist, and professor disappoints. Enlivens reportage with anecdotes but impersonal dominates. Brief collection of letters gives more of intimate Fabela.

566. Falconer, Thomas. *Letters and Notes on the Texan Santa Fe Expedition, 1841–1842.* Chicago: Rio Grande, 1963 (1930). 159pp.

Britisher Falconer joined expedition whose purpose was to win for Texas some of Santa Fe trade and perhaps claim dominion over this territory. Texans captured by Mexicans and marched to Mexico City. Entries from June 18, 1841, to March 9, 1842, relate to departure, capture, march to Mexico City, and sailing from Vera Cruz.

567. Farías, Luis M. (1920–1999). *Así lo recuerdo: testimonios políticos.* México: Fondo de Cultura Económica, 1992. 349pp. Memoirs. Period Covered: 1920–1991.

Regiomontano, lawyer, senator, majority leader in senate, member of PRI since 1951, and radio/TV commentator follows traditional format of memoir, i.e., shares only key moments of life. Unlike other memoirists, he tries to show how political system functions.

568. Farías y Alvarez del, Ixca (1874–1948). *Casos y cosas de mis tiempos.* Concejo Municipal de Guadalajara: Editorial Agata, 1992. 239pp. Memoirs. Period Covered: 1880–1936?

Inspector of colonial monuments, director of Museum of Guadalajara, and founder of open air painting school incorporates youth in focusing on Guadalajara of Porfiriato. Chapters on schools, personalities, Chapala, 1903 *Ateneo*, bullfighting, fiestas, arrival of railroad, and tobacco shop evoke *costumbrista* Guadalajara in direct dialog with reader. Prose of professional writer.

569. Feijoo Andrade, Rosa (Dates?). *SIDA: testimonio de una madre: dramático caso de la vida real.* México: EDAMEX, 2003. 227pp. Diary. Period Covered: 1968–1993.

Mexican woman married to Peruvian diplomat assigned to various posts. Crux of story is son who declares himself to be homosexual and eventually contracts AIDS. Mother, now divorced, struggled with problems: son's sexual orientation and eventual death from AIDS.

570. Félix, María (1914–). *Todas mis guerras.* México: Clio, 1993. 219pp. Memoirs. Period Covered: 1914–1992?

From Sonora and Jalisco, film idol to several generations missed nothing in life: fame, marriage, maternity, wealth, acquaintance and friendship with famous, travel, subject of portraits by Rivera and Dalí, and even a reading of Kafka. Illustrated volumes illuminate luxury of possessions, physical perfection, and film achievements.

571. Fell, Claude (1882–1959 Dates of Vasconcelos) (1889–1959 Dates of Reyes). *Escrits oublies: correspondance entre José Vasconcelos et Alfonso Reyes.* México: Institut Francais Français d'Amérique Latine, 1976. 198pp. Letters. Period Covered: 1916–1959.

Vasconcelos and Reyes exchange letters and notes. Thirty-seven from Vasconcelos and twelve from Reyes span active years of writers. Topics: publications, mutual acquaintances such as Pedro Henríquez Ureña and Antonio Caso, and cultural items. Postmarked Mexico and Spain, letters exude frankness of two close friends.

572. Ferlinghetti, Lawrence. *The Mexican Night: Travel Journal.* New York: New Directions, 1970. 58pp.

One of founders of Beat Generation, and reader of John Dos Passos, Ferlinghetti composes Mexico's most unusual travel journal. Although in prose, work more like poetry, his native genre. *Mexican Night* thus reflects poetic Ferlinghetti in breathless journeys into Mexico from 1961 to 1969. Standard tourist stops and themes defamiliarized in highly personal perspective.

573. Fernández Ledesma, Gabriel (1900–1982). *Viaje alrededor de mi cuarto (París, 1938).* Instituto Cultural de Aguascalientes, 1958. 101pp. Memoirs. Period Covered: 1938.

Aguascalientes artist and representative to Europe of LEAR (Liga de Escritores y Artistas Revolucionarios) in 1938–1939 leaves curious memoir. Details Parisian residence, Hotel St. Placide. Style, mood, and desire to capture charm of ordinary recall Azorín and Maillefert.

574. Fernández MacGregor, Genaro (1883–1959). *El río de mi sangre.* México: Fondo de Cultura Económica, 1969. 542pp. Memoirs. Period Covered: 1883–1956?

Scholar and writer's autobiography reflects early interest in books. Typifies Latin American male with intellectual scope of Renaissance type. Public man here: diplomat, lawyer, and rector of university. Yet he is in love and devoted to wife. Presents acceptable and even laudatory view of self. Since personality does not emerge from text, he sums up character in last chapter.

575. Fernández MacGregor, Genaro (1883–1959). *Notas de un viaje extemporáneo.* México: Editorial Stylo, 1952. 567pp. Memoirs. Period Covered: 1950?

El rio de mi sangre author travels to Europe in final years and leaves impressions of Spain, England, France, and Italy. Registers reactions to tourist sites. Diplomat, writer, teacher, and ex-rector of University of Mexico verifies what he has read.

576. Ferreira, Zeferino Diego (1892–1973); **Laura Cummins.** *Don Zeferino: villista, bracero y repatriado.* Tijuana: Universidad Autónoma de Baja California, 1981. 24pp. Oral Autobiography. Period Covered: 1892–1973.

Rapid account of don Zeferino: born into poverty in Guanajuato, miner in Michoacán, revolutionary under Villa, bracero in U.S., repatriated and resident of *ejido* in Baja. According to editor, don Zerferino emerges both as individual and generic Mexican in Revolution.

577. Ferrer Rodríguez, Eulalio. *Páginas del exilio.* México: Alfaguara, 1996. 460pp.

Naturalized Mexican suggests success of Spanish exiles. As writer and TV personality, he is accepted by literati and is member of several national academies of language. As advertising executive, one of few businessmen with memoirs. Arrival in Mexico, journalism, contact with other exiles, work in TV, and advertising comprise direct autobiography. Articles of meetings with celebrated Mexicans supplement self-portrait of Ferrer. Constant gratitude for Mexico. Earlier work, *Del diario de un publicista* (1933), has similar information with emphasis on author's success in advertising.

578. Ferry, Gabriel. *Vagabond Life in Mexico.* New York: Harper, 1856. 344pp.

Title owes much to picaresque novel. Author covers gambit of social levels in various locales and includes anecdotes such as Mexican monk, thieves' lawyer, miners of Rayas, etc. In spite of document's affinity with fiction, author spent seven years in Mexico and renders descriptions of natives. Mexico City prominent as is Vera Cruz. Wonderful index to mid-nineteenth century Mexican society!

579. Fierro Santiago, Felipe (1962–). *Tierra mojada...crónicas y vivencias.* México: Imprenta Candy, 1998. 75pp. Memoirs. Period Covered: 1970s.

Place contends with and even dominates author's personality in described area, villages in Guerrero near la Costa Grande. Thirty-one brief chapters at times *costumbristic* give essence of social protest: violence against *campesinos*, guerrillas, and the disappeared. Schoolteacher-author focuses on environment and oppression, not teaching.

580. Fierro Villalobos, Roberto (1897–1985). *Esta es mi vida.* México: Tallares Gráficos de la Nación, 1964. 385pp. Memoirs. Period Covered: 1910–1959.

Celebrated pilot recalls beginnings of aviation in Mexico. Lindberg's equivalent, he headed air academy in Monterrey and also

served as chief of air force. History of aviation more than development of life.

581. Figueroa, Gabriel (1908–1997). *Conversaciones con Gabriel Figueroa/Alberto Isaac.* Universidad de Guadalajara, 1993. 130pp. Interview. Period Covered: 1933–1992.

Illustrious cameraman converses on film career in Mexico and U.S. Some of most notable topics include *Rancho Grande, El indio,* Hollywood Ten (ten connected with film industry in 1947 invoked First Amendment in refusing to give evidence to Un-American Activities Committee), John Huston, Erich Von Stroheim, Bruno Traven, and Luis Buñuel.

582. Figueroa, Gabriel (1908–1997). *La mirada en el centro.* México: Editorial Porrúa, 1993. 253pp. Memoirs. Period Covered: 1933–1983.

Cameraman repeats some of *Conversaciones.* Discusses in chronological order screen triumphs and even disasters. Film credits include *María Candelaria, The Night of the Iguana,* and *Coronación.* Included photos testify to expertise with camera.

583. Finerty, Catherine Palmer. *In a Village Far from Home: My Life among the Cora Indians of the Sierra Madre.* Tucson: University of Arizona Press, 2000. 206pp.

Widow abandons comforts in U.S. to work among Cora/Huichol Indians in Nayarit in Jesús María. Untrained, she practices medicine in make-do environment. She observes: "The most arresting discovery I made was that Jesús María was Mexico upside down...the land belonged not to the *mestizos* but to the Indians, the whole big Cora zone" (p.19).

584. Fisher, Richard V. *Out of the Crater: Chronicles of a Volcanologist.* Princeton University Press, 1999. 179pp.

Writes on Mexico. One chapter, "El Chichón, Southern Mexico," has adventurous author in state of Chiapas. Climbs and describes volcano in 1983.

585. Flandrau, Charles Macomb. *Viva Mexico!* New York: Appleton, 1908. 293pp.

Harvard-educated Charles Flandrau

travels in Porfirian Mexico and recounts impressions. Unlike contemporary travelers, has persistent sense of humor and pays no homage to Diaz. Author describes his coffee plantation. Mixes with Mexicans and tempers negative remarks with comparisons to U.S. Berates ignorance of Gringos about Mexico. Each nationality thinks it sets standard for honesty. Supports solitude but derides thieves' appeal to honor. Classic reissued twenty-one times since 1908 and in Spanish in 1994.

586. Fleetwood, Hugh. *A Dangerous Place.* London: Hamilton, 1985. 198pp.

Another irascible Englishman thrusts himself on Mexico and writes travel autobiography concentrating on negative. Fleetwood, in Mexico in 1980, returned four years later and contrasted the two Mexico's. Mexico City, Oaxaca, Chiapas, Yucatan, Guanajuato, Vera Cruz, and Sonora comprise geographical settings. Yet he ponders presence of Indian and even theorizes over natives' bad taste in art. He wonders if Europe signifies civilization. He mingles with Latin American exiles who despise Mexico. British novelist unimpressed with Frida Kahlo.

587. Flores, Edmundo (1918–?). *Historias de Edmundo Flores: autobiografía, 1919–1950.* México: Martín Casillas Editores, 1983. 454pp. Autobiography Proper. Period Covered: 1919–1950.

First of three projected volumes that will bring Flores's life up to present. Initial volume (1983) arouses expectation that Mexican autobiography may shift to candor in views of self and family. Ph.D. in economics from University of Wisconsin and author of six books on Mexico, he recreates childhood, years at Chapingo's national school of agriculture, and graduate work at University of Wisconsin. Includes love life.

588. Flores, Edmundo (1918–?). *Historias de Edmundo Flores: autobiografía, 1950–1973, v.2.* México: Editorial Posada, l986. 558pp. Autobiography Proper. Period Covered: 1950–1973.

Second of economist's projected trilogy. Periodization of second volume corresponds

to six-year terms of presidents Flores served: Miguel Alemán, López Mateos, Díaz Ordaz, and Echeverría Alvarez. As in first volume, Flores more open and intimate than other autobiographers in relating personal life. Work in agriculture and in teaching.

589. Flores, Manuel María (1840–1885). *Rosas caídas*, ed. de Margarita Quijano. México: Imprenta Universitaria, 1953. 255pp. Memoirs? Period Covered: 1864–?

"Autobiographical pages" most accurate for writings. Have more intimacy of diary than external focus of memoirs. Exuberant emotion and subjectivity of romantic period of literature. Love life portrayed.

590. Flores López, Alfonso (1914–?). *La radio y yo.* Monterrey, México, 1987. 164pp. Memoirs. Period Covered: 1914–1987.

Radio announcer recalls career in first fifty-one pages. In Monterrey, San Luis Potosí, and Mexico City, he worked as announcer in early radio, a heretofore neglected area.

591. Flores Magón, Enrique (1877–1952). *Peleamos contra la injusticia….* México: Libro Méx, 1960, (1958) 2 v. Oral Autobiography. Period Covered: 1885–1952.

In *Peleamos* he fights against Porfirio Díaz to impose new regime. Liberal Party activist spent years in U.S. editing *Regeneración*, eluding authorities, or serving time in prison. Memoirs illuminate struggle against Porfiriato and collusion of U.S. in dictator's support. Same title republished as *Combatimos la tiranía*, 1958.

592. Flores Magón, Ricardo (1873–1922). *Correspondencia de Ricardo Flores Magón: (1904–1912).* Universidad Autónoma de Puebla, 1989. 462pp. Letters. Period Covered: 1904–1912.

Jacinto Barrera Bassols edits collection with introduction and indexes of contents, places, and surnames. Other two collections cover years 1904–1921 and 1919–1922, but present concentrates on earlier years from exile to U.S. and launching of military campaign in Baja. 1908–1911 hiatus corresponds to prison years. Postmarked Texas (Brownsville, Del Rio, El Paso and San Antonio), St. Louis, Los Angeles, and Canada (Toronto and Montreal), letters suggest Flores Magón's erratic hegira. Subversion of dictatorship dominates.

593. Flores Magón, Ricardo (1873–1922). *Epistolario revolucionario e intimo.* México: El Autor, 1925. 3 v. or 240pp. Letters. Period Covered: 1919–1922.

Letters of anarchist exude passion of true believer and deserve place in prison literature. From Leavenworth, Kansas, in 1920s, he believed anarchy would win as capitalism would fail. Letters specify no plan, but rather convictions, deteriorating health, belief in anarchy, hope of early release through lawyer, Harry Weinberger, constant refusal to recant from earlier position, and faith in comradeship. Correspondents, Gus Teltsch, Elena White, Nicolás Bernal, Irene Benton, Erma Barsky, Harry Weinberger, and Winnie E. Branstetter, a who's who of anarchists. Mexican background obscured because international anarchy obliterates nationality and family.

594. Flores Magón, Ricardo (1873–1922). *Epistolario y textos....* México: Ediciones Antorcha, ca.1978. 243pp. Letters. Period Covered: 1904–1921.

Many documents originated by author; others by those around him. Reveal little about anarchist cause but mainly persecution of him and followers at home and in U.S. Main correspondent María Brousse Talavera is Ricardo's love. Letters filled with emotion, admonishments to be discreet in cause of anarchism, and persecutions in U.S. Summarizes life and relation to anarchism in best and most autobiographical letter from Leavenworth to lawyer Weinberger.

595. Flores Rivera, Salvador (1921–1987). *Relatos de mi barrio.* Ageleste, 1994 (1972). 162pp. Memoirs. Period Covered: 1921–1979?

Composer of more than 600 songs and urban folklorist leaves document consistent with interests and talents but casual in chronological order: poverty, semi-orphaned childhood, first jobs, entrepreneurship, and success as composer. Theme of Mexico City barrios where author lived superior to all others.

596. Flores Salinas, Berta. *Cartas desde México: dos fuentes militares para el estudio de la Intervención francesa, 1862–1867.* México: Editorial Porrúa, 2001. 204pp.

Collection of sixty letters of Gen. Henri Agustín Brincourt and his family. He had prominent role in organizing state of Puebla and Tlaxcala after siege of Puebla in 1863. He notes his presence: commander of state of Puebla and problem of fortifying city; invaders' conflict with clergy; fighting in Oaxaca, Querétaro, Guanajuato, Aguascalientes, and Zacatecas; and himself in charge of an area larger than France. Personal touch is eagerness to complete tour of duty and return to France to be with family.

597. Flores Tapia, Oscar (1917–1998). *La casa de mi abuela.* México: Editorial Cultura, 1983. 120pp. Memoirs. Period Covered: 1921–1926.

Teacher and politician from Saltillo, Coahuila, evokes childhood with grandmother. Extended family revolves around strong personality of multifaceted female. Innocence of childhood in nostalgic view of provincial life.

598. Fonville, Nina. *Hold Fast These Earth-Warm Stones.* San Antonio: Naylor, 1949. 231pp.

In mid–1940s mother and ten-year-old son spend several months in Mexico City with doctor's family. Train trip down with stop in Monterrey and trips later to Cuernavaca and Taxco complete itinerary. Fonville details traditional customs and also brings Mexican history indirectly to reader's attention.

599. Foppa, Alaíde (1934 Birth of Cuevas). *Confesiones de José Luis Cuevas.* México: Fondo de Cultura Económica, 1975. 216pp. Oral Autobiography. Period Covered: 1973–1974.

Spurred by illusion of impending death, artist talks freely to Foppa about family, loves, Latin American trips, art, films, etc. Frank and scandalous Cuevas constantly debunks and entertains.

600. Forbes. *A Trip to Mexico: or Recollections of a Ten-Months Ramble in 1849–50.* London: Smith Elder. 1851. 256pp.

Barrister begins in Azores and ends in San Blas. Author lacks superiority complex of most British travelers and praises natives as miners more reliable than Englishmen. Vera Cruz, Mexico City, Guanajuato, and Tepic comprise itinerary. He speaks of natives, roads, and buildings. Four chapters devoted to Tepic. More travel than autobiography.

601. Foster, Harry L. *A Gringo in Mananaland.* New York: Dodd Mead, 1924. 357pp.

Harry and Eustace romp through Sonora, Sinaloa, Mexico City, and Vera Cruz. They find humor in all situations and also in Mexican character: lack of concern about bandits, adjusting truth to please listener, and ability to live wholly in present. Flee Mexico because of fear of vengeful Carranza.

602. Foster, John Watson. *Diplomatic Memoirs.* Boston: Houghton Mifflin, 1909. 2 v.

Represented U.S. in Mexico under presidency of Lerdo de Tejada, 1872–1876. Foster mixed autobiography with descriptions of Mexico: Benito Juárez, Santa Anna, Porfirio Díaz, and visits to states of Michoacán, Guerrero, and Oaxaca. Educated author shows nineteenth-century interest in travel. Mexican years only one portion of two-volume memoir.

603. Fox Quesada, Vicente (1942–). *A los Pinos: recuento autobiográfico y político.* México: Océano, 1999. 224pp. Memoirs. Period Covered: 1942–1999.

Only essentials of life: reared in Guanajuato, educated at Jesuit college, post-grad work at Harvard, salesman and chief executive of Coca Cola in Mexico, rejection of offer to head Coca Cola for Latin America, successful candidate for senator on PAN ticket, governor of Guanajuato in 1995, and finally president. May be different from PRI predecessors but memoirs follow pattern of autobiography and presidency, i.e., minimal personal life and much political life.

604. Fraenkel, Michael. *Journal: The Mexican Years, 1940–1944.* La Jolla, CA: Laurence McGilvery, 1986 (1944). 391pp.

German-Jewish Fraenkel resided in Mexico. In spite of title, this country not his major focus. In addition to philosophical

topics, he meditates on Shakespeare (Hamlet), Goethe, D.H. Lawrence and Henry Miller. About ten percent of journal devoted to Mexico and usually in morbid comment: travel, stunning moments, desolate landscape in spite of beauty, and character of inhabitants.

605. Franck, Harry Alverson. *Trailing Cortez through Mexico.* New York: Frederick A. Stokes, 1935. 373pp.

Author paid tribute to Bernal Díaz del Castillo and W.H. Prescott. Harry and Rachael Franck contemptuous of Sanborn-visiting tourists. Want challenge of walking Cortez's route from Vera Cruz to Mexico City. Hardships with eventual success. "…for after all, nothing is much more absurd than plodding along on foot amid the dust of automobile transportation. So we laid down the rule that we would ride wherever there was riding just as the Conquistadores would have done; and did" (p.viii).

606. Franco Nájera, Evila (1888–1989). *Evila Franco Nájera: A pesar del olvido.* México: Instituto Nacional de Estudios Históricos de la Revolución Mexicana, 1995. 84pp. Memoirs. Period Covered: 1888–1940.

Rural schoolteacher from Teloloapan, Guerrero, arranged testimony into three time frames: 1888–1910, birth to celebration of Mexican independence; 1911–1920, Revolution; and 1921–1940, conflicts between national authorities and local interests. Always supported Revolution and people and hated priests opposed to her goals. Fluid testimony evokes personality as well as Guerrero during critical years.

607. Franco Sodja, Carlos (1917–1957 Dates of Infante). *Lo que me dijo Pedro Infante.* México: Editores Asociados, 1977. 120pp. Oral Autobiography. Period Covered: 1917–1957.

Created posthumous autobiography based on research and on remembered conversations with Infante. "Memoir" belongs to as-told-to-another category. Singer/actor anecdotally mentions family, film, and love affairs.

608. Franco Torrijos, Enrique (1930–). *Odisea en Bonampak: narración inédita de* *una azarosa expedición.* México, 1950. 154pp. Memoirs. Period Covered: 1950?

Author and ten members of Grupo Alpino Inmexssal (Club Excursionista de Empleados del Seguro Social) visit Bonampak in Chiapas, home of Lacandones. Constant use of *I* and *We* to narrate travel incidents and anthropology lends personal tone to expedition.

609. Freg Castro, Luis (1890–1934). *Vida dramática y muerte trágica de Luis Freg....* Por Armando de María de Campos. México: Compañía de Ediciones Populares, 1959. 132pp. Memoirs. Period Covered: 1906?–1934.

Bullfighter in both Spain and Mexico, fifty-seven-times gored Freg Castro earned nickname don Valor. In conversations with Armando María y Campos, he concentrates on bullring. Ignores youth and development focusing on rise as celebrity. Methodology and intervention in arrangement of memoirs unmentioned.

610. Frémont, John Charles; Samuel M. Smucker. *The Life of Col. John Charles Fremont, and His Narrative of Explorations and Adventures.... The Memoir of Samuel M. Smucker.* New York: Miller Orton & Mulligan, 1856. 493pp.

Mapmaker and explorer of West reached Mexican California in 1843 when, accompanied by guide Kit Carson, he reconnoitered land between Mississippi valley and Pacific Ocean. Last part of book relates to California, where Frémont carefully chronicled landscape and vegetation and noted Indians, Spaniards, and army recruits.

611. French, Samuel Gibbs. *Two Wars: An Autobiography of General Samuel G. French...Mexican War....* Nashville: Confederate Veteran, 1901. 404pp.

Three and one half chapters of above on Mexican-American War. Matamoros, Palo Alto, Resaca, and Monterrey scenes of major battles. Bullfights, Gen. Taylor's brilliance, taking of Monterrey, and Mexico's surrender. Final episodes relate to removal of a ball from author's leg in Saltillo and departure for U.S.

612. Frías, Heriberto (1870–1925). *Miserias de México.* México: Ediciones Botas, 1916.

132pp. Autobiographical Novel. Period Covered: 1894–1906.

One of three autobiographical novels, *Miserias* chronologically falls between *Tomóchic* and *El triunfo de Sancho Panza.* Frías represents realities of Mexico through alter ego, Miguel Mercado. Influence of naturalism patent in realistic details of Miguel's alcoholism and use of drugs. Novel/autobiography condemns journalism. Though rooted in Mexico City, action shifts to Mazatlán, where author returns after failure as dramatist. Final chapters, composed of pseudo short stories, more memoir than autobiography.

613. Frías, Heriberto (1870–1925). *Tomóchic.* México: Editorial Porrúa, 1968 (1893). 153pp. Trans: *Tomochic: a Novel.* English edition by Barbara Jamison and Antonio Saborit. New York: Oxford University Press, 2002. Autobiographical Novel. Period Covered: 1891–1892.

Autobiography disguised as novel, *Tomóchic* author's military experiences in Díaz's 1892 effort to punish Indians of Guerrero, Chihuahua, for rebelling against authority. Frías imprisoned because of denunciation. Author intensified criticism of Díaz regime in various revised editions to 1911.

614. Frías, Heriberto (1870–1925). *El triunfo de Sancho Panza.*México: Imprenta de L. Herrer, 1911. 232pp. Autobiographical Novel. Period Covered: 1906–1909.

Autobiographical novel tracing years in Mazatlán as journalist. Society of Sinaloa's port city exposes corruption through young and idealistic Miguel Mercado. Title refers to city's victory over Mercado, a twentieth century don Quixote.

615. Frías, José D. (1891–1936). *Crónicas de un corresponsal mexicano en la Primera Guerra Mundial.* México: Departamento de Distrito Federal, 1983. 214pp. Memoirs. Period Covered: 1918–1922.

Anthologizes fifty articles of Paris years published in *El Universal,* oldest daily newspaper in Federal District. Collectively form memoir of poet/journalist who enjoyed France's cultural and everyday life. Permeated with Frías's presence, subjective essays reminiscent of Janet Flanner's "Letters from Paris" in the *New Yorker*.

616. Frías Conor, Billy (Dates?). *Un yucateco en Zacatecas....* México: Ediciónes Botas, 1940. 289pp. Memoirs. Period Covered: 1939?

Lawyer educated in U.S. likes Zacatecas. Pastiche of recollections, dialogs, individual letters, quotations, and book reviews, memoirs emphasize locale more than personality. Final part paean to Rotarians.

617. Frías y Soto, Luciano (Dates?). *Costumbres queretanas de antaño.* Querétaro, QUE: Ediciones Cimatario, 1947. 61pp. Memoirs. Period Covered: 1845–1895.

Nostalgically recalls Querétaro: preparations for trip to Mexico, evenings, theater, birthdays, school, and Holy Week. Book more on childhood city than author's personality.

618. Fuentes, Carlos (1928–). *Carlos Fuentes: territorios del tiempo: antología de entrevistas.* México: Fondo de Cultura Económica, 1999. 310pp. Interview. Period Covered: 1928–1998.

Seventy year old honored in anthology of sixteen interviews, which reveal much of life: childhood, family, Mexican heritage, religion, readings, especially *Quijote*, and much on own published works. Non-autobiographical elements relate to Mexican history, international relations, and world literature. Only three essays in Carlos Fuentes's *En esto creo* (2002) directly autobiographical: Buñuel's filming of *Nazarín* with author's first wife, Rita Macedo as actress; maternal and paternal family tree; and most poignantly, his children including death of young Carlos Fuentes Lemus.

619. Fuentes, Carlos (1928–). *Diana o la cazadora solitaria.* Mexico City: Aguilar, Altea, Taurus, 1994. 235pp. Trans: *Diana the Goddess Who Hunts Alone.* English edition by Alfred Mac Adam. New York: Farrar, Straus and Giroux, 1995. Autobiographical Novel. Period Covered: 1968–1980s.

Novelist confesses affair with American actress Jean Seberg. Three-month tryst,

because of filming in Mexico, allows Fuentes to sermonize on world problems, to portray tragic Seberg, and to divulge intimate details of relationship. Compares Hispanic Catholic self to Swedish Lutheran Seberg from Iowa.

620. Fuentes, Carlos (1928–). *Perspectivas mexicanas desde París: un diálogo con Carlos Fuentes.* México: Corporación Editorial, 1973. 159pp. Interview. Period Covered: 1934?–1973.

Fragments of life emerge through questions. Parents, privileged childhood, marriage, children, writings, especially *La región más transparente*, and admiration for Juan Rulfo. Dialog on Mexican culture, politics, and economics.

621. Fuentes Mares, José (1918–1986). *Intravagario.* México: Editorial Grijalbo, 1986. 187pp. Memoirs. Period Covered: 1918–1986.

From Chihuahua City was rector of University of Chihuahua, founder of newspaper *Novedades de Chihuahua,* and author of books on Mexican history. First part focuses on university days in Mexico City in 1930s. Praise for Antonio Caso. Second part on books.

622. Furber, Percy Norman. *I Took Chances, from Windjammers to Jets.* Leicester, UK: Backus, 1954. 301pp.

British-born Furber entrepreneurial in Mexico. Started in 1892 in quicksilver in San Luis Potosí; in 1894, searched for oil in Tampico; in 1903, invested in silver mines in Durango; in 1906, explored for coal in Puebla. Furber knew important Mexicans including Porfirio Díaz, and José and Julio Limantour. Anecdotes about snakes and bandits.

623. Gaitán Lugo, Rito (1929–). *Anécdotas de mi pueblo.* México: Editorial Libros de México, 1978. 147pp. Memoirs. Period Covered: 1939–1978?

Man of several trades and professions nostalgically evokes Charcas, Guanajuato, mining village north of San Luis Potosí. Rural ambience, types of people, and anecdotes pervade more than author's personality.

624. Galarza, Ernesto (1905–1984). *Barrio Boy.* University of Notre Dame Press, 1971. 275pp. Autobiography Proper. Period Covered: 1905–1918?

Mexican-American sociologist and educator spent part of childhood in Nayarit before immigrating to Arizona and California. *Barrio Boy*, though *costumbrista*, belongs to autobiography with author's concentration on own development. Observer and recorder of Mexican ambience in which he was reared on both sides of border: family, duties, and gender roles.

625. Galeana, Benita (1905?–1995). *Benita.* México: Imprenta MELS. 1940. 238pp. Trans: *Benita.* English edition by Amy Diane Prince. Pittsburgh: Latin American Literary Review Press, 1994. Memoirs. Period Covered: 1905?–1940?

Opposed to every president from Calles to Cárdenas, she tells of poor youth, migration to Mexico City, and activities on behalf of Communist Party. Early years prologue to later party commitment. Several accomplishments: spirit to escape oppressive rural background, ability to live economically without skills, oratory that arouses workers, and literacy.

626. Galeana, Benita (1907–1995). *Entrevista a una mujer comunista.* México: Universidad Autónoma Chapingo, 1996. 44pp. Interview. Period Covered: 1915?–1994.

Speaks succinctly on variety of topics: childhood, Mexico City, presidents and their reactions to communism, orientation to communism, 1968 travels, Noriega and Panama, jail, and celebrity friends. More extensive autobiography in *Benita*.

627. Galicia Espinosa, Rutilo (1899–?). *El almacén de mis recuerdos.* México: Instituto Nacional de Estudios Históricos de la Revolución Mexicana, 1997. 60pp. Memoirs. Period Covered: 1899–1949?

Born in Amecameca, Mexican author recalls Revolution and Zapatistas, work as carpenter, Ford Motor Company from 1926 to 1949, traveling salesman, and employee of publishing company. Resourceful, honest, and hardworking, he relates life directly. Testimony received Salvador Azuela Prize in 1996.

628. Galindo, Miguel (1883–1942). *A través de la sierra (diario de un soldado).* Colima, COL: Imprenta de El Dragón, 1924. 312pp. Memoirs. Period Covered: 1915.

Believing that soldiering was superior to medicine, doctor was Zapatista in Morelia and Oaxaca. Outstanding in field of memoirs of Revolution, writings have more involvement of author. Cultured Galindo aware of country's problems and pessimistic about Revolution. With an eye for landscape and historical detail, he is more of stylist than other memoirists. For him racial problem will diminish with ongoing mixture between upper and lower classes.

629. Gallegos C. José Ignacio (1900?–?). *La Casa de la monja….* Durango, DUR: Talleres del Estado, 1968. 368pp. Memoirs. Period Covered: 1905–1967?

View of Durango with past and customs equally important as life story. Locates family, schooling, boyhood friends, and courtship in regionalist setting. Focus on youth and pleasurable external environment. Preoccupying problem was eventually successful courtship.

630. Gallo, Delfino (Dates?). *Las huellas de mi caminar. (Perfil de una época).* Universidad de Guadalajara, 1986. 165pp. Memoirs. Period Covered: 1924–1976.

Guadalajara surgeon reminisces. Mixes medical topics with autobiography: medical school, conferences, operations, and realization of building of Guadalajara sanitarium.

631. Gallo Sarlat, Joaquín (Dates?). *Un año más y un año menos.* México: Editorial Libros de México, 1973. 116pp. Memoirs. Period Covered: 1970.

After twenty-seven years of university teaching, author retires and makes pilgrimage throughout native Mexico and Spain: Sevilla and Santiago de Compostela in Spain and Guadalajara and Oaxaca in Mexico.

632. Gallo Sarlat, Joaquín (1882–1965 Dates of Gallo Monterrubio). *El ingeniero Joaquín Gallo Monterrubio: astrónomo, universitario y hombre cabal.* México: Editorial Libros de México, 1982. 175pp. Hybrid. Period Covered: 1882–1965.

Created in tribute to 100th anniversary of birth of astronomer, book labeled quasi-autobiography. Educated in Mexico and U.S., he worked at National Observatory of Astronomy. Gallo Sarlat structures text with biography of prominent father. Gallo Monterrubio wrote of travels, publications, eclipses, philosophy, and astronomy.

633. Galván, Jorge (1935–). *De Memoria: autobiografía en tres llamadas y siete cuadros....* México: Casa Juan Pablos Centro Cultural, 2001. 399pp. Memoirs. Period Covered: 1947?–2001.

Several playwrights and directors have written autobiographies. Galván most thorough in giving examples of theater at regional level. Brought up with connections to theater and worked in profession in Querétaro, Campeche, Mérida, and Aguascalientes. Influential in *el teatro popular,* bringing theater to people. Many documents impede reading but much of Mexico's latter twentieth century theater here.

634. Gamboa, Federico (1864–1939). *Impresiones y recuerdos.* México: E. Gómez de la Puente, 1922 (1893). 274pp. Memoirs. Period Covered: 1880–1893?

In twenty-seven chapters young Gamboa divulges little of self in exterior events. Writes of travels (New York, Guatemala, London, Paris, and Buenos Aires). Gives impressions such as Spanish language of Argentina. Most personal items are two love affairs reacted through prism of Romanticism, i.e., attraction to fallen women. Interesting but nonrevealing memoir.

635. Gamboa, Federico (1864–1939). *Mi diario.* Imprenta de La Gaceta de Guadalajara, 1907–20. 3 v. Journal. Period Covered: 1901–1911.

Three volumes from 1901 to 1911. Outstanding novelist of realist period, Gamboa both dramatist and journalist. In diplomatic positions from 1888 to 1913: Guatemala, Argentina, Brazil, U.S., Spain, Belgium, and Holland. Three diaries or "journals" for lack of intimacy connect more to diplomatic world than to literary world. *Santa* and other novels mentioned cursorily. Diaries testify to loyalty that Porfirio Díaz inspired in associ-

ates. Ignacio Mariscal, secretary of foreign relations and Gamboa's protector, mentioned frequently. Perspective of Díaz supporter of more value than emergence of personality.

636. Gamboa, Joaquín (1911–1949). *Memorias de un locutor.* México: Ediciones Botas, 1949. 235pp. Memoirs. Period Covered: 1943–1949.

Served as war correspondent for magazine *Hoy.* Representing BBC branch in Mexico City, he worked as announcer in London. Career and impressions of British comprise memoirs.

637. Gangemi, Kenneth. *The Volcanoes from Puebla.* London: Boyars, 1979. 181pp.

Twenty-four year old travels alone in Mexico on motorcycle. Main love is undemanding vehicle that gives freedom and contact with Mexicans. Book structured like encyclopedia with 175 topics alphabetically arranged. Each entry relates to experiences with hotel, food, landscape, cities, towns, or tourist sites. In collective reading emerges personality of Mexico and author.

638. Gaona, Rafael (1923–?). *De cuerpo entero: Rafael Gaona.* México: Ediciones Corunda, 1991. 58pp. Memoirs. Period Covered: 1928–1945.

Novelist focuses on youth: parents, grandmother, books, schooling, poetry, Alfonso Reyes, and employment with fruit company. Departure for Mexico City in 1945 ends memoirs.

639. Gaos, José. *Confesiones profesionales.* México: Tezontle, 1958. 180pp.

Gives philosophical background in Spain; then includes Mexican years from 1938 to 1958. Notes discovery of Leopoldo Zea. Also wrote prologue to psychological autobiography, *Un hombre perdido en el universo* by Miguel Angel Cevallos (1954).

640. Gaos, José; Alfonso Rangel Guerra. *Epistolario y papeles privados.* México: UNAM, 1999. 557pp.

Spanish-exile philosopher Gaos, settling in Mexico and appointed to UNAM, sustained correspondence relating to his profession with Mexican intellectuals: Alfonso

Reyes; Antonio Caso; Daniel Cosío Villegas; Arnaldo Orfila Reynal, Argentine-born director of Fondo de Cultura; Leopoldo Zea; Samuel Ramos; Salvador Azuela; and Fernando Salmerón. To each of these he wrote three to fifteen letters.

641. Gaos de Camacho, Angeles
(Dates?). *Una tarde con mi padre: recuerdo de José Gaos.* Monterrey: Universidad Autónoma de Nuevo León, 1999. 93pp. Memoirs. Period Covered: 1900–1969.

Daughter of José Gaos, Republican exile, philosophy professor, and writer, records brief memoir of father that incorporates most of his life. Valencia, Paris, and finally Mexico are venues for nomadic Gaos family. Through impressions of her father and recovery of memory through conversations with other family members, Gaos de Camacho necessarily traces her autobiography. Includes painful separation of parents in Mexico. Interesting lives of father and daughter, but technique of reviving father through imaginary monologue in second person of greater originality.

642. García, Elvira (1907 Birth of Gabilondo Soler). *Es Cri-Cri.* México: Editorial Posada, ca.1985. 164pp. Interview. Period Covered: 1907–1985.

Begun as radio program, *Retrato hablado* documents full-life biography of Cri-Cri. From Orizaba, Vera Cruz, Gabilondo started life as boxer and bullfighter. In 1930, he joined radio station XETR as *Guasón del Teclado.* Four years later at XEW became known as "Cri-Cri," composer of children's songs. *Es Cri-Cri* focuses on life of entertainer and educator of children.

643. García, Inocente (1791–1878). *Hechos históricos de California: as Told to Thomas Savage, 1878....* Santa Barbara, CA: Flair Studio of Printing, 1974? 194pp. Memoirs. Period Covered: 1807–1878.

One of Bancroft's "as told to" autobiographies. Seventy-eight year old led adventurous life as merchant, soldier, Indian fighter, farmer, and partisan of Frémont. Narration never lags; he, or editor, knows what to select. Garcia's story is fifty-eight pages of 194-page book.

644. García, Manuel Edmundo.
(1900?–?). *Charlas de cacería.* Monterrey: El Autor, 1972. 262pp. Memoirs. Period Covered: 1907?–1970.

Fanatic hunter and fisherman in both Nuevo León and Coahuila covers lifetime in these sports. Almost every animal from this area present here including jaguar. Chapters devoted to each type of game with notes on terrain, habits, and firearms and skills needed for capture and slaughter.

645. García, Mario T. (1918 Birth of Corona). *Memories of Chicano History: The Life and Narrative of Bert Corona.* Berkeley: University of California, 1994. 369pp. Oral Autobiography. Period Covered: 1910–1990.

Born in El Paso, Corona has ties with Mexico since Protestant mother and grandmother both emigrated from here. Union organizer and political activist, Corona worked for Mexican-American Youth Conference, Community Service Organization, and Mexican-American Political Association (MAPA). Agreed to narrate life to Mario T. García, who taped fifty-five hours of interview and described role in recording and transcribing Corona's life. Parallels between two men facilitated realization of project.

646. García, Octavio (1899–?). *Otros días: Memories of "other days" from Mexico in Revolution to a Life of Medicine in Texas.* Westford, MA: Grey Home Press, 1984. 303pp. Memoirs. Period Covered: 1905?–1984.

Born in Mier, Tamaulipas, he studied in Saltillo, Coahuila, participated in Revolution and emigrated to U.S. Near Sebastian, Texas, worked on father's ranch; later attended St. Mary's College in San Antonio and received medical degree from St. Louis University. Practiced medicine in McAllen, Texas.

647. García Alonso, Aida (1890 Birth of Manuela Azcanio Alias) *Manuela, la mexicana.* Habana: Casa de las Américas, 1968. 444pp. Oral Autobiography. Period Covered: 1890–1945?

Tabasco-born Manuela Azcanio Alias at young age immigrated to Cuba, where she lived thirty-one years in poor neighborhood called Las Yaguas. Exemplifies talent of poor for survival in fascinating life (servant, cook, suffragette, street vendor, and nurse). García Alonso notes neither techniques nor intervention in final manuscript, which received Casa de Las Américas Award in 1968.

648. García Carrera, Juan (1898–1985 Dates of Sabina). *La otra vida de María Sabina.* México, 1986. 188pp. Memoirs. Period Covered: 1898–1985.

From Huautla de Jiménez, Oaxaca, María Sabina experienced brief celebrity as priestess and healer through magic mushrooms. García Carrera, María's godson/protegé, denounces abusers of healer: her family, president's sister, anthropologists, filmmakers, and even Estrada. All used María, who died unrewarded and in regret of sharing secret mushrooms with foreigners. Confessions interspersed with memoirs of García Carrera.

649. García Cumplido, Guadalupe Gracia (1881–1948). *Autobiografía, narraciones, documentos de....* México: Rámirez Editores, 1982. 481pp. Memoirs. Period Covered: 1890?–1947.

Success story of penniless lad from Durango who graduated from National School of Medicine in Mexico City and served in medical corps as Carrancista in Revolution until 1916. During career involved in military medicine.

650. García de Ortiz, Tere (Dates?). *¡Dios ya lo sabía! El don de un Niño especial.* México: Buena Prensa, 2000. 274pp. Memoirs. Period Covered: 1989–1992.

Author and husband move from Mexico City to Ciudad Juárez. She affiliates with Movimiento de Renovación en el Espíritu and intensified Catholic faith. Wise move assists acceptance and even happiness at giving birth to child with Down's syndrome.

651. García Diego y Moreno, Francisco (1785–1846). *The Writings of...Obispo de Ambas Californias,* translated and edited by Francis J. Weber. Los Angeles: Weber, 1976. 192pp. Letters. Period Covered: 1820–1846.

Appointed first bishop of upper and lower California in 1841, he spent much of life on behalf of church in California. Mainly letters relating to California, collection includes José Figueroa, Pío Pico, and José María Híjar. Church affairs dominate correspondence, but author's personality emerges.

652. García G. Rodolfo (Dates?). *Entre dos estaciones.* Toluca, México: Graficarte, 1986. 115pp. Memoirs. Period Covered: 1925?–1955?

Nostalgic view of Toluca and railroading by son of division foreman. Idyllic life of small capital in post-Porfirian years: theater with silent films, church, animals, fiestas, family, school, and train routes. He describes education and beginnings as journalist/writer, years as director of library, and final selection of career in teaching.

653. García Icazbalceta, Joaquín (1825–1894). *Cartas de Joaquín García Icazbalceta a José Fernández Ramírez, José María de Agreda, Manuel Orozco y Berra, Nicolás León, Agustín Fischer, Aquiles Gerset, Francisco del Paso y Troncoso.* Comp. y anotadas por Felipe Texidor. México: Editorial Porrúa, 1937. 433pp. Letters. Period Covered: 1850–1893.

Letters of one of foremost historian/biographers and collector of colonial documents. Icazbalceta's intellectual interests evident here in correspondence with other scholars, who are all humanists, historians, or booklovers. More life of mind even though occasionally he notes management of haciendas or familial problems. Letter of April 10, 1893, to Nicolás León, his major correspondent, betrays suffering human being more than man of letters.

654. García Icazbalceta, Joaquín (1825–1894). *Mes y medio en Chiclana, o, por un aficionado a pasearse.* México: J. García Pimentel y Braniff, 1987. 43pp. Memoirs. Period Covered: 1835.

Researcher, historian, and prolific author started writing precociously. At age of ten he left Mexico with parents for Cadiz. Here family visited Chiclana de la Frontera. Brief facsimile description of landscape and buildings plus activities.

655. García Naranjo, Nemesio (1883–1962). *En los nidos de antaño.* Monterrey: Tallares de El Porvenir, 1959. 375pp. Memoirs. Period Covered: 1883–1959?

Collection inspired by fiftieth anniversary as journalist. Intimate for focus on four generations of family, memoirs suggest love for home, country, and past. Subjects idealized in NGN's attempted recall or in deference to taboo of expressing negative sentiments about family. Letters, portraits, tributes, and reminiscences reveal more about family in Mexico than about García Naranjo family.

656. García Naranjo, Nemesio (1883–1962). *Memorias.* Monterrey: Tallares de El Porvenir, 1956–1963. 9 vols. Memoirs. Period Covered: 1883–1946?

Founder of *La tribuna* and *La Revista Mexicana* and contributor to many other newspapers and magazines of Mexico, he also directed writing talents to history, political science, essay, theater, and nine volumes of memoirs. V.1. 1883–1896? *Panoramas de la infancia.* In introduction justifies presence in Huerta regime. Gives autobiographical information such as birth, childhood, and excellent description of Lampazos, Nuevo León, and Encinal, Texas. V.2. 1897–1902. *El colegio civil de Nuevo León.* As title implies, writes of childhood in *colegio* and describes teachers and their faults. V.3. 1903–1906. *La vieja escuela de jurisprudencia.* Notes in detail years in law school in Mexico City with portraits of law professors and colleagues before fall of dictator. V.4. 1906–1909. *Dos bohemios en París.* Impressions of travels in New York, Paris, and London. Return to Mexico and continuation of law school. Job in National Museum and more sketches of contemporaries. Often in touch with literati. V.5. 1909–1910. *El crepúsculo porfirista.* Notes last moments of Porfiriato indicating conservative position and admiration for dictator. V.6. 1911–1913. *Exaltación y caída de Madero.* Married and also elected senator, NGN describes meeting with Victoriano Huerta. V.7. 1913–1914. *Mis andanzas con el general Huerta.* Treats of rise and fall of Huerta with positive analysis of president's character. Minister of education, NGN goes into exile. V.8. 1914–1923. *Nueve años de destierro.* Exile first to Buenos Aires, then to New York, and finally to San Antonio, Texas, where he founds and edits *La revista mexicana.* V.9. 1924–1946? *Mi segundo destierro.* After

brief stay in Mexico, NGN, once again exiled by Calles, lives as journalist in New York. Later works for American oil firm in Venezuela. More analysis of Revolution.

657. García Narro, Anita (1908–1986). *Anita la corredora.* Chihuahua, CHH: Editorial Camino, 1992. 128pp. Memoirs. Period Covered: 1908–1986.

Although victim of infantile paralysis, she realized ambition to help others by becoming teacher of Indians within vicariate of Tarahumara in Chihuahua (Sisoguichi and Bawinokachi). Involvement with Tarahumara also included medical services. In spite of primitive conditions and health problems, she summarizes a happy life. Father Brambilia has tribute to her.

658. García Olivera, Vicente (1916–?). *Anecdotario de un anestesiólogo.* México: Editorial Diana, 1996. 228pp. Memoirs. Period Covered: 1916–1991?

Medical doctor pioneered anesthesiology for over fifty years. Excellent student who struggled for education, he indicates evolution of field of expertise in achievements. Prologuist notes value of autobiography for students of medicine. Fascinating even for non-specialists.

659. García Orosa, Luis Alberto (Dates?). *Periodismo en paños menores.* México: EDAMEX, 1990. 166pp. Memoirs. Period Covered: 1962–1990.

As reporter or editor for *La Nación, El Universal Gráfico, Ovaciónes, Pórtico de América, Jueves de Excelsior* and *Visión,* he gives insider's view of Mexican journalism.

660. García Ponce, Juan (1932–). *Juan García Ponce.* México: Empresa Editoriales, 1966. 62pp. Autobiographical Essay. Period Covered: 1932–1966?

Typical of Empresa Editoriales series, writer notes salient moments in formation. Short story writer, dramatist, novelist, and essayist, he concentrates on intellectual development: desire to write and early successes, reading preferences, and work on *Revista de la Universidad.* He has considered problems of autobiography and understands travail of recreation of life. Need for larger project of full-scale life.

661. García Ponce, Juan (1932–). *Personas, lugares y anexas.* México: Mortiz, 1996. 165pp. Memoirs. Period Covered: 1932–1996.

Approaches life thematically rather than chronologically: childhood in Yucatan, removal to Mexico City, Vera Cruz, Christmas, sports, family, and friends, such as Marta Traba and Jorge Ibargüengoitia. Sensitive portrayal and reordering of life in peripatetic autobiography.

662. García Ramos, Juan (1915–?). *Paisajes en la senda de mi vida: memorias.* Universidad de Colima, 1994. 204pp. Memoirs. Period Covered: 1921?–1986?

Querétaro-born medical doctor probably best known as researcher and professor. In 1944, Dr. Arturo Rosenblueth, largest influence in career, invited him to join department of physiology of National Institute of Cardiology. Likewise, mentor in 1961 prompted him to collaborate in founding of CINESTAV, Centro de Investigaciones y Estudios Avanzados. García Ramos mixes autobiography, anecdote, and essays in thematic rather than linear approach to life.

663. García Riera, Emilio (1929–). *El cine es mejor que la vida.* México: Cal y Arena, 1990. 175pp. Memoirs. Period Covered: 1945?–1987?

Spanish-born movie critic has lived in Mexico since 1939 and mixes autobiography with film criticism. Three parts of memoirs, "Vida," "Cine," and "La política," surrender autobiographical data of international film critic: family, school (frustration with school of economics), return to Spain, stay in Dominican Republic, and career.

664. García Roel, Adriana (1916–). *Apuntes ribereños.* Monterrey: Sistemas y Servicios Técnicos, 1955. 299pp. Memoirs. Period Covered: 1950?

Monterrey journalist praises more relaxed atmosphere of Tampico, Tamaulipas, where she visited. More than just traveler, she immerses self in life of port city. Results in hybrid account mixing description of port with contact with natives and foreigners.

Anecdotes and forays into literature both vary and proportion reading. More balanced memoir than most of its twentieth century counterparts.

665. García Ruiz, Ramón (1908–?). *Mis ochenta años: memorias.* Guadalajara: UNED, 1993. 273pp. Memoirs. Period Covered: 1908–1988.

Although memoirs read like annotated resume, subject has most varied career of any educator in this bibliography: expert in rural education in 1926; inspector and instructor of Secretaria de Educación Pública in 1929; director of inspection for states of Mexico, Morelos, and Jalisco; coordinator general of secondary and normal education, 1961–1964; and position with educational body of UNESCO. Also in complementary positions: co-founder of Confederación Mexicana de Maestros; creator of cultural contacts between Mexico and Panama; and founder of Mexican Academy of Education. Wrote books on pedagogy.

666. Gardner, Erle Stanley. *The Land of Shorter Shadows.* New York: Morrow, 1948. 228pp.

More intimate view of Baja from U.S. writer. Author of more than a hundred mysteries, Earle Stanley Gardner loved Baja and wrote six books on exploration there. Written between 1948 and 1965, six travel journals have following in common: love of Baja and desert, need for congenial companions, admiration for natives, and impulse to be physically challenged by primitive Baja. Traveled state either in traditional vehicle or specially built terrain buggy and helicopter. In 1969 work, met President Miguel Alemán. Six travel memoirs include following: *The Land of Shorter Shadows* (1948). *Neighborhood Frontiers* (1954). *Hovering over Baja* (1961). *Off the Beaten Track in Baja* (1967). *Mexico's Magic Square* (1968), and *Host with a Big Hat* (1969).

667. Garfias, Valentín R. (1883–?). *Garf from Mexico.* México: Editorial Jus, 1950. 261pp. Memoirs. Period Covered: 1883–1947?

La Paz and Mexico City early locations for young Garf, who eventually immigrates to San Francisco to learn English. With a bachelor's and two advanced degrees from

Stanford, he becomes successful petroleum engineer. Tells of wife, family, prosperity, and Mexico. Memorable experience was 1906 San Francisco earthquake. Early autobiography of Mexican-American.

668. Garibaldi, Giuseppe. *A Toast to Rebellion.* Indianpolis: Bobbs-Merrill, 1935. 327pp.

Grandson of unifier of Italy, Giuseppe (José) Garibaldi includes Mexico in memoir. Arrived in Mexico in 1910 and fought on side of Madero at Casas Grandes and Juárez, Chihuahua. Freebooter mentions Abraham González, Pascual Orozco, Pancho Villa, Mormons, and *Cristeros.*

669. Garibay, Ricardo (1923–1999). *Beber un cáliz.* México: Mortiz, 1965. 182pp. Memoirs. Period Covered: 1962–1963.

Short story writer, poet, essayist, and journalist draws on talents as poet in *Beber un cáliz.* In brief account of father's death, he evokes own emotional responses in poetic imagery. As focus of memoir, father catalyzes reactions of family.

670. Garibay, Ricardo (1923–1999). *Cómo se gana la vida.* México: Mortiz, 1992. 282pp. Memoirs. Period Covered: 1930–1988.

Exuberant memoir in which freewheeling Garibay bares self: writing, books, films, prostitutes, boxers, parents, journalism, and fellowship from Centro Mexicano de Escritores. Much humor and idiomatic Mexican Spanish.

671. Garibay, Ricardo (1923–1999); **Socorro Arce; Rocío Aceves.** *La conquista de la palabra: entrevista con Ricardo Garibay.* Universidad de Colima, 1999. 117pp. Interviews. Period Covered: 1965–1996.

Author of forty-five books from various genres talks about agony of creation and the reason he writes: "…si no pudiera escribir más, la vida no tendría ningún sentido" (p.23). Mentions his maestros, including Alfonso Reyes and Carlos Pellicer. Discusses thirteen of his books from *Beber un cáliz* (1965) to *Treinta y cinco mujeres* (1996). Occasionally lashes out at other writers such as Juan Rulfo and deplores Mexican system of literary prizes.

672. Garibay, Ricardo (1923–1999). *Fiera infancia y otros años.* 3a ed, México: Océano, 1987 (1982) 134pp. Autobiography Proper. Period Covered: 1927–1941.

Autobiography Proper results from intensity of childhood experiences. Further volumes of equal intensity on other stages in Garibay's life necessary to maintain his life story. Remarkable document for kaleidoscopic impressions of childhood, fragmentation, sporadic dialog, and minimal portraiture. Love, family, religion, and schooling in San Pedro de los Pinos and other parts of Mexico City. Style and technique superior to content.

673. Garibay, Ricardo (1923–1999). *¡Lo que ve el que vive!* México: Excelsior, 1976. 318pp. Memoirs. Period Covered: 1966–1975.

Journalist, film writer, essayist, and short story writer becomes travel writer divulging self and environment in Cuba, U.S., France, Russia, China, Hong Kong, Ecuador, Argentina, Brazil, and Venezuela. Most intriguing is Cuba and Fidel Castro. Rapid and dialogued style unequal to prose and sensitivity of *Beber un caliz.*

674. Garizurieta, César (1904–1962). *Recuerdos de un niño de pantalón largo….* México: Editorial Ruta, 1952. 210pp. Memoirs. Period Covered: 1904–1919?

Labeled "autobiographical pages," *Recuerdos* covers too short a period for complete autobiography. Son of Vera Cruz schoolmaster orphaned Garizurieta attended school sporadically. Pícaro for variety of jobs, cunning, and humor, author evokes customs of Vera Cruz. Centering on self-development removes book from mere *costumbrismo.*

675. Garizurieta, César (1904–1961). *Un trompo baila en el cielo.* México: Ediciones Botas, l942. 102pp. Memoirs. Period Covered: 1909?–1915?

Cuasi-novel/cuasi-autobiography, *Un trompo* poetically evokes childhood in Vera Cruz. Much of world evolves around child's dreams and storytelling of illiterate albeit older companion. Autobiography of imagination complements more material world delineated in *Recuerdos de un niño de pantalón largo.*

676. Garmabella, José Ramón (1910–1978 Dates of Quiroz Cuarón). *Dr. Alfonso Quiroz Cuarón: sus mejores casos de criminología.* México: Editorial Diana, 1980. 197pp. Memoirs. Period Covered: 1910–1948?

First professional detective of Mexico and author of various books on criminology, Quiroz Cuarón dictates memoirs. Spending brief time on childhood, birth in Chihuahua, and father's murder, he fascinates with most interesting cases: assassination of Trotsky and search for identity of Bruno Traven, Mexico's mysterious resident author.

677. Garmabella, José Ramón (1897–1986 Dates of Leduc). *Por siempre Leduc.* México: Editorial Diana, 1995. 304pp. Memoirs. Period Covered: 1897–1986?

Taping 1500 hours with Renato Leduc, Garmabella rescued some of journalist and poet's anecdotes. Organized under categories of Revolution, presidents, the Left, Paris, journalism, intellectuals, women, friendship, bulls, and bohemia, anecdotes profile their creator: itinerant, iconoclastic, succinct, and acerbic.

678. Garmabella, José Ramón (1897–1986 Dates of Leduc). *Renato por Leduc: apuntes de una vida singular.* México: Océano, 1982. 364pp. Oral Autobiography. Period Covered: 1897–1980?

Journalist and popular poet Renato Leduc in 1,500 hours of tape recording exposes life through anecdotes. Is Garmabella mere recorder or also organizer of life of self-styled bohemian? Arranged by theme, stories fall under eleven categories with journalism and poetry as most important. Uninhibited confessor/storyteller Leduc talks about Revolution, politics, women, and bulls. Succinct and frank.

679. Garmabella, José Ramón (1908 Birth of Eduardo Téllez Vargas). *¡Reportero de policia! el güero Téllez.* México: Océano, 1982. 265pp. Oral autobiography. Period Covered: 1908–1974.

Garmabella, collecting journalistic adventures of famous Eduardo Téllez Vargas, notes almost nothing of methodology. Crimes and other cases of sensationalist reporter make absorbing reading: Angel

falling in earthquake of 1957, assassination of Trotsky, collapse of Cárdenas dam, and some of most lurid murders.

680. Garrido, Felipe (1942–). *La musa y el garabato.* México: Universidad de Guadalajara. Fondo de Cultura Económica, 1992. 279pp. Memoirs. Period Covered: 1946?–?

Short story writer, essayist, journalist, and translator creates hybrid autobiography with unusual memoirs. In 175 portraits, disperses poignancy of childhood, observations, and discovery. Collective evocations with neither chronology nor development.

681. Garrido, Luis (1898–1973). *El tiempo de mi vida: memorias.* México: Editorial Porrúa, 1974. 440pp. Memoirs. Period Covered: 1898–1973.

Professor, university rector, civil servant, and author of law books connects with variegated aspects of life. Eleven-page index suggests number of personalities he knew. Intimate self never appears.

682. Garro, Elena (1920–). *Memorias de España 1937.* México: Siglo Veintiuno Editores, 1992. 159pp. Memoirs. Period Covered: 1937.

Seventeen-year-old girl with youthful husband Octavio Paz traveled to Spain with other intellectuals belonging to LEAR (Liga de Escritores y Artistas Revolucionarios) for the second Congreso Internacional de Escritores para la Defensa de la Cultura. In kaleidoscopic form, Garro narrates adventures noting Paris and various locales in Spain. Interacts with other members of LEAR, José Mancisidor, Juan de la Cabada, Fernando Gamboa, José Chávez Morado, Silvestre Revueltas, Carlos Pellicer, María Luis Vera, and Susana Gamboa. Daughter of Spanish father, Garro visited family in Spain. Patricia Rosas Lopátegui's *Yo sólo soy memoria: biografía visual de Elena Garro* (2000) mixes both biography and autobiography. Photos captioned by Garro highly autobiographical.

683. Garza, Catarino (1859–1902?). "Memorias de Catarino E. Garza." En *En busca de Catarino Garza* by Celso Garza Guajardo. Monterrey: Universidad Autónoma de

Nuevo León, 1989. 145pp. Memoirs. Period Covered: 1877–1888.

Tamaulipan journalist and anti–Díaz revolutionary lived both in Mexico and U.S. Working for newspapers in Laredo, Eagle Pass, Corpus Christi, and San Antonio, Garza in 1891, two years following date of memoirs, led revolutionary/ bandit force into Mexico. One of first autobiographies of Mexican in U.S. Polemical Garza notes injustice on both sides of border.

684. Garza, Julián (1935–); **Guillermo E. Hernández.** *Diez Mil millas de música norteña: memorias de Julián Garza.* Universidad Autónoma de Sinaloa, 2003. 196pp. Oral Autobiography. Period Covered: 1940–2002?

Hernández, provocateur of this life, allows subject to narrate in his own words. Educated in the streets, Garza expresses himself colloquially as he focuses on two trades generally overlooked in Mexican autobiography: truck driver and *corridista* (composer and singer of ballads). Inspiration, creation, recordings, and popularity in song writing.

685. Garza, Ramiro (1930–). *Solar poniente.* 2ed. Monterrey: Impresos y Tesis, 1982 (1953). 87pp. Memoirs. Period Covered: 1936–1946?

Attempts to recreate from imagination Villa de García, Monterrey, hometown of parents and grandparents. Evokes idealized village with family and local personalities through poetical descriptions.

686. Garza H. Luis Lauro (1927 Birth of Juan de la Rosa Tellez). *Cristal quebrado: testimonio de un vidriero regiomontano.* México: Siglo Veintiuno Editores, 1988. 252pp. Oral Autobiography. Period Covered: 1941–1979.

Laborer speaks of craft and relations with management. Subject Juan De la Rosa Tellez, glassworker, labor organizer, baseball player, and prisoner tells story to Luis Garza. Latter explains techniques in oral memoir.

687. Garza Ríos, Celso (1912–?). *La huella de mis pasos por las calles y barrios de mi pueblo.* Sabinas Hidalgo, COA: Ediciones Minas Viejas, 1989. 54pp. Memoirs. Period Covered: 1912–1976.

Dictated by unschooled author to fam-

ily, memoirs form part of popular history: "This is the history of a man in his time and his circumstances of his will to live" (p.l). Proletarian author disenchanted with Revolution and its effects on his class.

688. Garzón Chávez, Leobardo (1927?–). *Ayutla: una cita con el recuerdo.* México: Rovelo Ediciones de México, 1991. 125pp. Memoirs. Period Covered: 1927–1941.

Son of schoolmaster recalls childhood in Ayutla, Guerrero, in 1930s. Autobiography with anthropology, sociology, and folklore as he focuses on customs and incidents of native region.

689. Gascón Mercado, Julián (1925–). *Un manojo de recuerdos: 11 relatos y un cuento.* México: Costa-Amic, 1978 (1957). 149pp. Memoirs. Period Covered: 1932–?

Subtitle of 1957 edition, *11 relatos y un cuento*, best describes medical doctor's autobiography. In Nayarit, he resurrects incidents and personalities. Belongs to nineteenth century romanticism with *estampas* or *cuadros de costumbre*.

690. Gascón Mercado, Julián (1925–). *Minutero de antaño.* México: Costa-Amic, ca.1978. 129pp. Memoirs. Period Covered: 1930?–1935?

Born in Nayarit, surgeon and governor of home state from 1964 to 1970, he continues autobiography in eight stories set near Tepic. Humorous incidents from youth cohere into *costumbrista* narrative: animals, death, and religious pilgrimage to Talpa.

691. Gascón Mercado, Alejandro (1932–). *Por las veredas del tiempo.* Tepic: Universidad Autónoma de Nayarit, 2000. 690pp. Memoirs. Period Covered: 1947–2000.

Nayarit-born author spent life as leftist politician and journalist. At age fifteen helped organize Partido Popular and served on central committee for twenty years. Also involved self in Partido del Pueblo Mexicano (PPM), Partido Socialista Unificado de Mexico (PSUM), and Partido de la Revolución Socialista (PRS). Memoirs relate to liberal politics on local and state levels. Idol is Vicente Lombardo Toledano.

692. Gavira, Gabriel (1867–1956). *General de brigada Gabriel Gavira, su actuación político-militar revolucionario.* México: Tallares Tipográficos de A. del Bosque, 1933. 234pp. Memoirs. Period Covered: 1867–1932.

One of founders of Círculo Liberal Mutualista of Orizaba, provisional governor of San Luis Potosí and Durango, head of expeditionary forces of Northwest during Villa years, and Chief of Staff of War Department. Further autobiographical data in *Polvos de aquellos lodos-unas cuantas verdades.*

693. Gaxiola, Francisco Javier (1898–1978). *Memorias.* México: Editorial Porrúa, 1975. 236pp. Memoirs. Period Covered: 1898–1948.

Lawyer who rose to be secretary of economics (Consejo Nacional de Economía) in cabinet of Avila Camacho intersperses personal life with public life. Perspective on political life.

694. Gerzso, Gunther (1915–?); **José Antonio Aldrete-Haas.** *Conversaciones con José Antonio Aldrete-Haas.* México: Ediciones de Samarcanda, 1996. 45pp. Interview. Period Covered: ?

Unusual interview that totally avoids all factual data concerning painter: date of birth, family, education, and career. Document explores processes of creation and abstraction.

695. Gibson, George Rutledge. *Over the Chihuahua and Santa Fe Trails, 1847–1848....* Albuquerque: University of New Mexico Press, 1981. 111pp.

Mexican-American War rescued Gibson from law practice. Mustered in Missouri, he became part of Col. Stephen Kearny's Army of West and set out for New Mexico. March and peaceful conquest of New Mexico under Kearny and then segued into march to Chihuahua City under Alexander Doniphan in early 1847. Lt. Gibson's details both marches and journalistic background, evident in vivid account of landscape, battles, animals, food, and Mexicans.

696. Gil, Miguel (Dates?). *La tumba del Pácifico...en su viaje a las Islas Marías.* Méx-ico: Ediciones de La Prensa, 1931–1932. 2 v. Memoirs. Period Covered: 1930.

Reporter traveled to Islas Marías and first volume describes journey by land, air, and water. On Pacific islands off Nayarit coast, he visits penal colony. Meets Francisco J. Múgica, head of prison, and illustrious inmate, Concepción Acevedo y de la Llata. Gil focuses on daily life of notorious Madre Conchita.

697. Gilb, Dagoberto; César Augusto Martínez. *Gritos: Essays.* New York: Grove, 2003. 247pp.

Author writes highly autobiographical essays often relating to Mexico and border: El Paso, cockfighting, work, and much about mother from Mexico City. Frankness pervasive. Uncomplicated but vigorous prose.

698. Gilders, Michelle A. *Reflections of a Whale-Watcher.* Bloomington: Indiana University Press, 1995. 269pp.

Unique travel memoir of Baja California. From 1989 to 1992, Gilders perused coastline in the *Don José* and *Searcher.* Her dual purpose of observing nature and sounding alarm for protection of marine life equals exclusion of natives and all of Baja non-relevant to environment. Bahia Magdalena, Laguna San Ignacio, Isla San José, and Cabo San Lucas figure prominently. Final chapter title, "The Human Problem," signals author's stance.

699. Gilliam, Albert M. *Travels in Mexico, during the Years 1843 and 44....* Aberdeen: Clark and Son, 1847. 312pp.

We meet Santa Anna again in 1846. Gilliam is nineteenth century gentleman traveler personified. Journey from 1843 to 1844 takes him from Vera Cruz to Mexico City and then northward as far as Guaymas and Tampico. Well read; knows Mexican history; scrutinizes landscape, people, and customs. From small incident makes harsh judgment on Mexicans. Delightful read with discussion of Santa Anna.

700. Gillow, Eulogio G. (1841–1922). *Reminiscencias del Ilmo. y Rmo. Sr. Dr. D. Eulogio Gillow y Zavalza, Arzobispo de Antequera (Oaxaca).* Los Angeles, CA: Imprenta y

Linotipia de El Heraldo de México, 1920. 296pp. Oral Autobiography. Period Covered: 1841–1919.

Son of English immigrant father and aristocratic Mexican mother, Gillow had continental education. Personal wealth, hacienda at Chautla, and family connections suggest prelate favored under Porfiriato. Appointed bishop of Oaxaca in 1887 and archbishop in 1891. Exiled to Los Angeles.

701. Gillpatrick, Owen Wallace. *The Man Who Likes Mexico….* New York: Century, 1911. 374pp.

Does all of tourist things but also mingles with Mexicans. Itinerary of Durango, Querétaro, Jalisco, Aguascalientes, and Mexico City allows for multiple exposures to culture. Usual Gringo praise for achievements of Porfirio Díaz: schools and compulsory education, safety for foreigners, railway systems, and thirty years of peace. Exciting pages on lost mines in Durango.

702. Giménez, Manuel María. …*Memorias del…ayudante de campo del general Santa Anna, 1798–1878.* México: Vda. de C. Bouret, 1911. 285pp.

Memoir of Spaniard who lived through many of Mexico's political and military episodes of nineteenth century from 1818 to 1878: battle against Iturbide, independence of Mexico, aid to Santa Anna, war against France, war against Mexico, support of Maximilian, the Reforma, and cooperation with Gen. Porfirio Díaz.

703. Glantz, Margo (1930–). *Las genealogías.* México: Martín Casillas Editores, 1981. 246pp. Trans: *Family Tree: An Illustrated Novel.* English edition by Susan Bassnett. London: Serpent's Tail, 1991. Memoirs. Period Covered: 1850?–1981.

Hybrid genre, for although Glantz focuses on parents and Russian Jewish background and adjustment to Mexico, she reveals self in interaction with family and environment. Recaptured time in parents' fragmented conversations and monologues. Author's life takes form through schooling, family's ambulatory life style, Jewishness, and visit to New York. Informality of style and non-chronological approach falsely imply

chaotic effort. Organic and carefully structured memoirs.

704. Glantz, Susana (1934 Birth of Manuel Escalante). *Manuel, una biografía política.* México: Editorial Nueva Imagen, 1979. 226pp. Oral Autobiography. Period Covered: 1934–1976.

Through Manuel's narration to Glantz, reader perceives personality and context in which it functions: environment (sugar *ejido* in Jilquilpan near Los Mochis, Sinaloa) and subject as labor leader. Glantz attempts to orient reader to relatively new genre within autobiography.

705. Godines, Prudencio (Dates?). *Que poca mad…era: la de José Santos Valdés.* 2 ed. México, 1961. 165pp. Memoirs. Period Covered: 1959–1967.

Communist for twenty-seven years expressed disenchantment with party. Fascinating chapter on aborted communist attack against federal soldiers in Madera, Chihuahua, paralleling assault on Moncada Barracks in Cuba. Wounded Godines escapes, hides, and denounces communism. Pejorative title relates to José Santos Valdés's supposedly spurious account.

706. Godoy, Mercedes (1900?–?). *When I Was a Girl in Mexico*: Boston: Lothrop Lee and Shepherd, ca.1919. 139pp. Memoirs. Period Covered: 1906–1910.

Daughter of Mexican diplomat posted to Havana and Washington, D.C., portrays happy childhood in Mexico, U.S., and Cuba in lightly *costumbrista* work.

707. Gómez, Marte Rodolfo (1896–1973). *Anecdotario de San Jacinto.* México: Editorial Porrúa, 1958. 148pp. Memoirs. Period Covered: 1909–1914.

From Cuidad Reynosa, Tamaulipas, he studied from 1909 to 1914 at San Jacinto, National School of Agriculture. Gómez reacts to classmates, teachers, studies, and Revolution in brief account of school from end of Porifirato through Huerta. Incidents or personalities in anecdote.

708. Gómez, Marte Rudolfo (1896–1973). Entrevista en James W. Wilke y Edna Monzón Wilkie's *Frente a la Revolución mexicana: 17 Protagonistas de la etapa constructiva, v.3.* México: Universidad Autónoma Metropolitana, 2002 (1969). Pp.133–203. Interview. Period Covered: 1896–1947?

Probably no other Mexican politician so involved in country's agricultural life. Covers minimal personal life: birth in Tamaulipas, demanding father, education, marriage, and children. Career more dominant: director of school of agriculture, head of agrarian reform in Tamaulipas, consultant for Portes Gil, secretary of agriculture under Avila Camacho, and author of books on this subject. Also governor of Tamaulipas and ambassador to France. Gómez noted career and opinions in context with presidents and revolutionary leaders.

709. Gómez, Marte Roldolfo (1896–1973). *Vida política contemporánea: cartas de Marte R. Gómez.* México: Fondo de Cultura Económica, 1978. 2 v. Letters. Period Covered: 1923–1973.

Professional agronomist, head of railways, and also ambassador to France, Austria, and United Nations. Above labels deceptively limit cultural life as indicated by letters. Name indexes to two volumes like a who's who of national culture. In correspondence, style goes beyond formulaic of office holder, and collectively letters delineate rich personality.

710. Gómez Arias, Alejandro (1906–1990). *Memoria personal de un país con Víctor Díaz Arciniega.* México: Editorial Grijalbo, 1990. 293pp. Oral Autobiography. Period Covered: 1906–1988.

Lawyer, professor, orator, admirer of José Vasconcelos, and one of founders of Popular Party (PPS) produces satisfying memoirs: constant presence of personality, superb description of university years with focus on Antonio Caso, desire to interpret rather than merely describe, and succinctness in expression. Credit to editor Víctor Díaz Arciniega, who notes methodology in introduction.

711. Gómez González, Filiberto (Dates?). *Rarámuri, mi diario tarahumara.* México: Tallares Tip. de Excelsior, 1948. 309pp. Memoirs. Period Covered: 1937.

Author-teacher traveled to several Tarahumara villages and recorded experiences. More than reporter, he interacted with Indians as sympathetic observer and defender of their customs and culture.

712. Gómez Haro, Claudia (1918–2001 Dates of Juan José Arreola) *Arreola y su mundo.* México: Alfaguara, 2001. 275pp. Memoirs. Period Covered: ?

Arreola uses Gómez Haro as foil to speak subjectively on many topics: Borges, films of 1930s, images of Christ, sports, wine, Virgin of Guadalupe, Neruda, etc. In writing on multiple and disparate topics, Arreola reveals much of self.

713. Gómez Junco, Horacio (1930–). *Desde adentro.* Monterrey: Fondo Estatal Para la Cultura y los Artes de Nuevo Leon, 1997. 358pp. Memoirs. Period Covered: 1943–1996.

Tells of affiliation with el Instituto Tecnológico y de Estudios Superiores de Monterrey (Tech). Both student and administrator at institution founded in 1943, author confides political problems of university and his exodus after twenty-year tenure.

714. Gómez Maganda, Alejandro (1910–1985). *Una arena en la playa: continuación de mi voz al viento.* México: Editora Cultural Objetiva, 1963. 285pp. Memoirs. Period Covered: 1929–1936?

Political life dominates book especially after writer becomes partisan of Lázaro Cárdenas. Memoirs end at moment of Spanish Civil War.

715. Gómez Maganda, Alejandro (1910–1985). *¡España sangra!* Barcelona: Commissariat de Propaganda de la Generalit de Catalunya, 1938. 99pp. Memoirs. Period Covered: 1936.

On behalf of government, he flies to Bolivia as delegate to Asamblea Internacional Americana. Visits New York, Cherbourg, Paris, and Lisbon. As consul to Spain and Portugal, he favors Republican forces. Emotional prose relates more to place than self.

716. Gómez Maganda, Alejandro (1910–1985). *Mi voz al viento: apuntes de mi vida y algo más.* México: Editorial Cultura Objetiva,

1962. 266pp. Memoirs. Period Covered: 1900–1929.

First of three volumes, *Mi Voz* evokes family environment of early Guerrero years. Poverty due to premature death of father sets tone of struggle. Student leader and later diplomat, he ends first narrative cycle in Argentina and U.S.

717. Gómez Maganda, Alejandro (1910–1985). *Torbellino un hombre de 30 años.* México: Ediciones Quetzal, 1941. 255pp. Genre: Memoirs. Period Covered: 1910–1940.

Second of five-volume autobiographical suite of politician and diplomat. Desperate childhood in Guerrero, military school in San Jacinto, president of National Student Convention in Morelia, senator from Guerrero, partisan of Cárdenas, and Consul General in Spain during Civil War. External more important than self.

718. Gómez Maganda, Alejandro (1910–1985). *El vino del perdón.* México: Ediciones Joma, 1971. 301pp. Memoirs. Period Covered: 1936–1968.

Consul in Spain during Spanish Civil War and intimate friend of Presidents Cárdenas, Avila Camacho, and Alemán, author unrestrained in exhibiting emotions. Strong likes and dislikes. More valuable as account of politics than as revelation of Mexican being in third volume of memoirs.

719. Gómez Morín, Manuel (1897–1972). Entrevista en James W. Wilkie y Edna Monzón de Wilkie's *México visto en el siglo XX.* México: Instituto Mexicano de Investigaciones Económicas, 1969. Pp.41–231. Interview. Period Covered: 1897–1964.

Wilkies provide only autobiography extant of influential politician: one of seven sages, Vasconcelista, founder of PAN, UNAM rector, head of department of statistics, etc. Early years in Chihuahua city of Batopilas, Vasconcelos, Calles, Cárdenas, Avila Camacho, and PAN among other topics.

720. Gómez Ocón, Tegro (1909–?). *Mi viejo Mazatlán: memorias del Tegro.* Mazatlán: Sociedad Histórica Mazatleca, 1997. 175pp. Memoirs. Period Covered: 1899–1996.

Member of upper class in Mazatlán,

Guerrero, he notes Ocón side of family and ties to Porfirio Díaz. Incorporates life of author with life of Mazatlán. Provincial existence enhanced by trip to U.S. and Europe and meetings with Mexican and American celebrities.

721. Gómez Palacio, Martín (1893–1970). *Viaje maduro.* México, 1919. 257pp. Memoirs. Period Covered: 1938.

Poet, novelist, and short story writer in diary form records trip to Turkey, Greece, Holy Land, Italy, France, and England.

722. Gómez Z. Luis (1905–?). *Sucesos y remembranzas.* México: Secapsa, 1979. 2 v. Memoirs. Period Covered: 1898–1978?

Railroading at age of twelve in 1917, he writes more a history of railroads than own life. Involved in railroad labor unions.

723. Gomezperalta, Mauro (Dates?). *Cuatro años y un embajador, 1967–1971.* México, 1973. 233pp. Memoirs. Period Covered: 1967–1971.

Ambassador in two different assignments: Dominican Republic and Poland. In former, he tends to be autobiographical in problems within Trujillo's country; in second, evolves tract on life in communist country.

724. Góngora, Pablo De (1860–1939). *Memorias de un ministro.* México: Tallares Tipográficos de L. Catano, 1936. 287pp. Memoirs. Period Covered: 1890–1910?

Journalist and founder of newspaper *Novedades*, also undersecretary of Gobernación and secretary to governor of Puebla. Wise and vigorous personality shows patronage side of politics. Pseudonym for Jesús M. Rábago.

725. Gonzáles, Ramón (1922–). *Between Two Cultures: The Life of an American-Mexican as Told to John J. Poggie, Jr.* Tucson: University of Arizona Press, 1973. 94pp. Oral Autobiography. Period Covered: 1922–1963.

Pseudonymous Ramón Gonzáles born in Guanajuato but spent most of life in California. Family problems, deportation, work in Mexico as well as in U.S., and poverty. Neither Mexican nor American, indefinite in self-identity.

726. González, Agustín (1859–1926). *Memorias de mi vida.* Toluca: Cuadernos del Estado de México, 1957. 238pp. Memoirs. Period Covered: 1842–1870.

In tradition of *cuadros de costumbres* and stylistically one of better autobiographies of nineteenth century. Born in Tlalnepantla, Mexico, he writes of French invasion from 1864 to 1866. Focuses on early schooling. Outside of Victoriano Salado Alvarez, no other Mexican concentrates as much on education. Clear and careful writing primer on education especially Lancastrian system. Incorporates family relationships.

727. González, Hugo Pedro (1909–?). *Un mucho de mi vida y un poco de la política.* Tamaulipas: Instituto Tamaulipeco de Cultura, 1993. 256pp. Memoirs. Period Covered: 1909–1991.

From Nuevo Laredo, author in politics from presidencies of Emilio Portes Gil to Gustavo Díaz Ordaz: governor of state from 1945 to 1947, judge, and ambassador to Bolivia and Indonesia. Much more of youth of author, family, education, colleagues, and marriage. Politics at state and city levels.

728. González, Jesús Héctor (1903–1987 Dates of Felipe González) *Don Felipe González: mis 70 años como ganadero de Coaxamalucan (1917–1987).* Tlaxcala, TLA: Tallares Gráficos del Edo. de Tlaxcala, 1988. 82pp. Oral Autobiography. Period Covered: 1903–1987.

From Coaxamalucan, Tlaxcala, author fascinated by cattle breeding and bullfighting. Claims bullfighting in state began on grandfather's ranch. Author's son made notes of cattleman's story.

729. González, Luis (1925–). "Luis González: Minuta de un viaje redondo." En *Egohistorias: El Amor a Clío,* coordinated by Jean Meyers. México: Centre D'Etudes Mexicaines et Centroaméricaines, 1993. Pp.59–81. Memoirs. Period Covered: 1925–1993.

Historian and author of *Pueblo en vilo: Microhistoria de San José de Gracia* (1968) relates childhood in provincial and Catholic Jalisco and high school and university in Guadalajara. Entering Colegio de México in 1946, he studied with Daniel Cosío Villegas.

González spent sabbatical in hometown San José de Gracia and wrote classic *Pueblo en vilo,* a universal history within regional history.

730. González, Manuel W. (1889–?). *Con Carranza: episodios de la revolución constitucionalista, 1913–14.* Monterrey: Cantú Leal, 1933–1934. 2 v. Memoirs. Period Covered: 1913–1914.

Belonged to Army of Northeast and as Carranza partisan describes incidents of Revolution in North. Has eye for anecdote and style that approaches novel. Too many names and tributes burden personal account.

731. González, Manuel W. (1889–?). *Contra Villa, relatos de la campaña, 1914–1915.* México: Ediciones Botas, 1935. 379pp. Memoirs. Period Covered: 1914–1915.

Too detailed memoirs of Carrancista. Informative value for Revolution rather than interpretation or single life.

732. González Calzada, Manuel (1915–1981). *Café París Express: Tragicomedia en dieciséis años.* México: Federación Editorial Mexicana, 1973. 127pp. Memoirs. Period Covered: 1938–1953.

Anecdotes and portrayals originate in Café París Express, gathering place of intellectuals. Writer/journalist audited or exchanged repartee with Andrés Henestrosa, Daniel Castañeda, Gerónimo Baquiero Fóster, Estela Ruiz, León de la Selva, León Felipe, César Garizurieta, Pedro Rendón, and Epigmenio Guzmán.

733. González Cedillo, Guillermo (Dates?). "Cuatro pueblos en la Lucha zapatista." En *Con Zapata y Villa: tres relatores testimoniales.* México: Instituto Nacional de Estudios Históricos de la Revolución, 1991. 48pp. Memoirs. Period Covered: 1900–1919?

Focuses on four villages on Lake Texcoco: San Sebastían Tecolixtitlan, Santa María Aztahuacán, Santa Marta Acatitla, and Santiago Acahualtepec. Two women from here worked in home of Porfirio Díaz; and even as Zapatistas, accompanied him into exile in Paris in 1911. Much of narration refers directly to Emiliano Zapata.

734. González Chávez, Rafaela (1912–). *Testimonio zapopano. Rafael González Chávez platica con Ana María de la O Castellanos.* Zapopan, JAL: El Colegio de Jalisco, 1994. 102pp. Memoirs. Period Covered: 1912–1993.

Provincial life and autobiography in personal narrative of Zapopan, site near Guadalajara that harbors sanctuary of Our Lady of Zapopan. Life incorporates much of history of town: houses, businesses, famous citizens, medicine, religion, clothes, feast days, and bars. Interviewer's presence and interference unnoted in text.

735. González-Crussi, Francisco (1936–). *The Dead and Other Mortal Reflections.* New York: Harcourt Brace, 1993. 179pp. Memoirs. Period Covered: 1945–1991.

Immigrated to U.S. in 1973. As pathologist accustomed to autopsy and as child in Mexico recalling death of young classmate, he incorporates much of self and native country.

736. González-Crussi, Francisco (1936–). *Partir es morir un poco.* México: UNAM, 1996. 185pp. Memoirs. Period Covered: 1936–1994.

Son of pharmacy owner became prominent medical doctor. Experiences in Mexico, France, U.S., and Canada recounted in style more characteristic of professional writer than doctor. Marital problems and divorce.

737. González-Crussi, Francisco (1936–). *There Is a World Elsewhere: Autobiographical Pages.* New York: Riverhead Books, 1998. 209pp. Memoirs. Period Covered: 1936–1965?

Eleven self-contained autobiographical essays complement author's two previous works. Mexico City and U.S. serve as venue for bilingual bicultural Mexican author who honed medical degrees in U.S. Family pharmacy, Jewish neighbors, education, medical stories, and death predominate. Eponymous last essay summarizes book and interprets immigrant experiences.

738. González de Alba, Luis (1944–). *Los dias y los años.* México: Ediciones Era, 1971. 207pp. Memoirs. Period Covered: 1968.

Nineteen sixties university student in novelized format spells out events that climaxed in Tlateloco in 1968. Notes both involvement and imprisonment: locale, political parties, and national leaders such as Javier Barrios Sierra, UNAM rector and sympathizer with students.

739. González Flores, Manuel (1907–1972). *Una pareja de tantos.* México: Editorial Yolotepec, 1950. 285pp. Memoirs. Period Covered: 1930s.

Lawyer, writer, and translator recounts adventures as laborer in Chicago in 1930s. Comments ambivalently on U.S. environment and on types of Mexicans there. Visits Langston Hughes in New York City.

740. González Garza, Roque (1885–1962). "Los lastres de una revolución ingenuamente política." En *Los revolucionarios* by Daniel Cazes. México: Editorial Grijalbo, 1973. Pp.75–126. Oral Autobiography. Period Covered: 1886–1911.

From Saltillo and orphaned, worker challenged injustice of employers. Madero confidant, he knew many personalities and witnessed events leading up to Revolution. Narration ends with election of De la Barra.

741. González González, José (Dates?). *Lo que dije del negro y de otros.* México: Solares Editores, 1984. 191pp. Memoirs. Period Covered: 1952?–1982?

For twenty-eight years on Mexico City's police force and addresses related issues: condemnation of Arturo Durazo Moreno, chief of police accused of corruption; praise for Gen. Renato Vega Amador, who tried to reform police; system of stealing involving police and creation of *halcones*, special force of young male recruits.

742. González Lobo, Salvador (Dates?). *Memorias de un rector.* Saltillo: Universidad Autónoma de Coahuila, 1980. 400pp. Memoirs. Period Covered: 1930?–1980.

Appointed president of newly created University of Coahuila, author combines history of higher education in Coahuila with own life. Nothing outside of university impinges on narration. Hybrid document reminiscent of memoirs of politicians.

743. González Martínez, Enrique
(1871–1952). *La apacible locura.* México: Ediciones Cuadernos Americanos, 1951. 156pp.
Memoirs. Period Covered: 1909–1949?

El hombre del bujo connects with familial
aspects of life while this book concerns creative activities, literary contemporaries and
diplomatic career. He labels work, "…[una]
consignación reminiscente de una vida al
mandato de vocación…" (p.25). He transfers
to reader's custody reminiscences of life as
poet. Two worlds, creative and diplomatic,
balanced and intertwined with Spanish king
and other luminaries: Mario Vigil, López-
Portillo y Rojas, López Velarde, Leopoldo
Lugones, Luis Urbina, Manuel Jose Othón,
José Juan Tablalda, and Efrén Rebolledo.
Gives chronological history of writings, notes
critics, and tries to define *poetry*.

744. González Martínez, Enrique (1871–
1952). *El hombre del buho: el misterio de una
vocación.* Guadalajara: Departamento de Bellas Artes del Gobierno del Estado, 1973
(1944). 181pp. Autobiography Proper. Period
Covered: 1871–1911?

Traces life in Guadalajara and Mocorito
from birth to 1911. Family life in detailing
characteristics of parents. Noting efforts to
become medical doctor, he develops creative
life from first bad verse to finding of own
voice in third book, *Silenter.*

745. González Parrodi, Carlos (1923–
1998). *Memorias y olvidos de un diplomático.*
México: Fondo de Cultura Económica, 1993.
532pp. Memoirs. Period Covered: 1923–1992.

Spent life in diplomatic corps: England,
Portugal, Argentina, France, Panama, Poland,
and Finland. Memoirs outstanding for diplomat. Notes work and problems of career in
foreign service; reacts to foibles of colleagues
and incorporates their personalities; analyzes
national character of countries; and finally,
depicts self honestly.

746. González Peña, Carlos (1885–1955).
El patio bajo la luna. México: Editorial Stylo,
1945. 242pp. Memoirs. Period Covered:
1890–1902?

Nostalgic, poetic evocation of childhood. Collection series of essays on Lagos de
Moreno, Jalisco, author's birthplace. Fairs,

houses, walks, church bells, music, etc.,
transformed through prism of time by novelist, journalist, and literary critic.

747. González Peña, Carlos (1885–1955).
Por tierras de Italia, Portugal y España. México: Editorial Constancia, 1952. 294pp. Memoirs. Period Covered: 1951.

Novelist and literary critic narrates trip.
Work sufficiently subjective to be labeled
autobiography rather than guidebook. Scenes
in *El patio bajo la luna* (preceding title) more
evocative and subjective. Two years before
Por tierras de Italia, he published *París y Lon-
drés: cuadros de viaje* (1950), barely autobiography. Inventories cultural opportunities of
both cities: small museums, artists' quarters,
and even city planning. Betrays Mexican
preference for France but always loyal to own
culture.

748. González Peña, Carlos (1885–1955).
*La vida tumultuosa: seis semanas en los Esta-
dos Unidos.* México: Ediciones Botas, 1918.
330pp. Memoirs. Period Covered: 1918.

Author circles U.S. from Texas and
Louisiana to Washington, New York, Pennsylvania, Mid-West, West, and Southwest;
exits through San Antonio, Texas. Place
dominates narrative intentioned to explain
U.S. to Mexico. Enough of journalist remains
in travel paragraphs to classify work as travel
memoir.

749. González Ramírez, Eulalio
(Piporro) (1921–?). *¡Autobiogr… ajúa! y
anecdo…taconario.* México: Editorial Diana,
1999. 474pp. Memoirs. Period Covered:
1921–1997.

Book jacket suggests multiple roles:
bracero, reporter, radio announcer, actor,
comedian, composer, singer, scriptwriter,
poet, and peasant. Loosely held together
autobiography replete with snapshots. Born
in Los Herrera, Nuevo León, Piporro notes
films as his forte. Lists sixty-seven films from
1950 to 1990.

750. González Ramírez, Manuel (1904–
1979). *Recuerdos de un preparatoriano de
siempre.* México: UNAM, 1982. 143pp. Memoirs. Period Covered: 1920–1968?

Lawyer, man of letters, and professor, he

belonged to *Los Cachuchas*, gang of class-mates with brilliant careers: Alejandro Gómez Arias, Miguel N. Lira, José Gómez Robleda, Alfonso Villa, Agustín Lira, Jesús Ríos y Valles, Carmen Jaime, and Frida Kahlo. Creates intellectual ambience by citing professors and ideas that nurtured generation. Captures spirit of prep school of l920s.

751. González Rodríguez, Raúl (1952–). *Así gané: mi espíritu de lucha— y voluntad de triunfo.* Monterrey, 1986. 141pp. Memoirs. Period Covered: 1952–1986.

From rural family of China, Nuevo León, he attended University of Nuevo León. In 1969, discovered talent as runner and directed career to winning of gold medal in 1984 at Los Angeles Olympics. Development as runner in various international competitions.

752. González Rubio, Enrique; María Sabina. *La magia de los curanderos mazatecos: después de María Sabina.* México: Publicaciones Curz O., 2001. 157pp. Memoirs. Period Covered: ?

Author alternates chapters between descriptions of shamans and their art and chapters on his interviews and transcendental experiences in shamanism: use of magic mushrooms; visit with spirits of a dead shaman; dreams; witnessing a *nahual* becoming a cat; consumption of mushrooms and walk in moonlight; stories of hobgoblins; Day of Dead, etc.

753. González Salazar, Pablo (1859–1922). *El general don Luis Caballero se rebela: diario.* Ciudad Victoria: Universidad Autónoma de Tamaulipas, 1976. 75pp. Diary. Period Covered: 1918–1920.

Describes impartially one incident of Revolution in Tamaulipas. Assassination of Gen. Emiliano P. Nafarrete precipitated rebellion against President Carranza. One of initiators of rebellion was Gen. Luis Caballero in succinct and unemotional diary.

754. González-Ulloa, Mario (1913–?). *Barro de cirujano.* México: E.D.I.A.P.S.A., 1954. 134pp. Memoirs. Period Covered: 1936?–1953?

Plastic surgeon diffuses memoirs

through fourteen story-type experiences (*relatos*). Each involves an incident with patient whose life changes through surgery.

755. González Urueña, Jesús (1868–1957). *Memorias.* México, 1947. 413pp. Memoirs. Period Covered: 1868–1943?

From Morelia, Michoacán, he received degree in medicine in 1893 and specialized in dermatology in Paris. Practiced medicine for over fifty years with cognate duties: professor of medicine, medical inspector of primary schools, and research and writing including *La lepra en México* (1941). Memoirs incorporate other schooling, family, various postings in provinces, and travel. Expansive in recounting life in detail and in profiles of personalities.

756. Goodspeed, Bernice I. *Criada.* Mexico: American Book and Printing, 1950. 381pp.

Rather than chapter of book or paragraph under larger theme of living in Mexico, maid is focus of *Criada*. Definitive study, at least in autobiographical form, of statistically elusive but always-present maid. Author in Mexico in 1930 when began saga of hired help. After apprenticeship with domestics, Goodspeed achieves success in Dominguita, loyal employee and subject of book's dedication.

757. Gordon, Alvin J.; Ralph Gary. *Never Lose Your Discouragements....* Sonoma, CA: Arcus, 1989. 239pp.

In 1950s, author opened restaurant and inn in historic Los Alamos. Gordon and spouse trained local help; found imaginative ways to do hotel laundry; prepared dishes; searched Hermosillo, Guyamas, and Navojoa for food and ingredients; battled city hall and warded off competitors who threatened assassination. An earlier but less autobiographical publication, *Our Treasure House* (1955) tells of the founding of the restaurant and initial successes with cooking and attracting customers. Many regional recipes.

758. Gordon, Alvin J.; Darley Fuller Gordon; Kenneth Macgowan. *Our Son Pablo.* New York: McGraw-Hill, 1946. 235pp.

Darley's "adapt" Tarascan youth and

bring him to Berkeley to study at University of California. He learns; they also learn. Pablo returns to Michoacán and is disillusioned in struggle to alleviate condition of Indian. Realizes difficulty of naïve goal after experience.

759. Gorostiza, José (1901–1973). *Epistolario (1918–1940)*. Edición y notas de Guillermo Sheridan. México: Consejo Nacional, 1995. 451pp. Letters. Period Covered: 1918–1940.

Third collection of letters of poet. One hundred and fifteen written to Gorostiza while he composed total of sixty-nine mainly to Carlos Pellicer, Jaime Torres Bodet, Genaro Estrada, and Carlos Chávez, members or supporters of los Contemporáneos. Government officials or other writers less frequent correspondents. 1918 to 1940 covers Gorostiza's most important creative period, chairmanship of Belles Artes, and service in diplomatic corps. Sheridan superbly edited with many explanatory footnotes.

760. Gorostiza, José (1901–1973). *José Gorostiza, cartas de primeros rumbos: correspondencia con Genaro Estrada*. México: UNAM, 1991. 38pp. Letters. Period Covered: 1925–1931.

Poet and diplomat corresponds in eleven letters with Genaro Estrada, undersecretary of foreign relations. Letters collectively suggest human being eager to please cultural mentor yet unhesitant to enumerate problems of family and foreign environment.

761. Gorostiza, José (1901–1973). *José Gorostiza y Carlos Pellicer* (1899–1977) *Correspondencia, 1918–1928*. Edición de Guillermo Sheridan. México: Ediciones del Equilibrista, 1993. 229pp. Letters. Period Covered: 1918–1928.

Sheridan edited exchange of forty-two letters and postcards of Gorostiza and Pellicer. Natives of Villahermosa, Tabasco, and in government service, poets mix ordinary with comments on publications and affection for one another. Sheridan analyzes contrastive personalities in introduction.

762. Gracia, María (1896–1977 Dates of Wilebalda Rodríguez Jiménez). *La noble tarea de educar: recuerdos y vivencias de una maestra jalisciense*. México: Instituto Nacional de Antropología e Historia, 2000. 220pp. Memoirs. Period Covered: 1896–1977.

Born in Mexticacán, Jalisco, Rodríguez Jiménez spent life at some level of Mexican education: attended grade school in village; at age thirteen began ten-year stint as teacher's aid in sister's school; graduated from normal school in Guadalajara; she taught in Guadalajara; finally, worked with teachers' union. Testimony one of most indepth and best in Mexican education.

763. Grajeda, María Magdalena (Dates?). *¿Vale la pena ser monja?* México: Editorial Posada, 1989. 182pp. Memoirs. Period Covered: 1962–1975.

From middle-class family, she enters order of Sisters of Charity in Chihuahua City. Sixteen-year convent tenure exposes environment of hypocrisy and rivalry rather than Christian charity. Spanish-born nuns like conquistadors.

764. Grant, Ulysses S. *Memoirs and Selected Letters….* New York: Library of America, 1990 (1885). 2 v.

Eight chapters of Grant's work relate to Mexican-American War. At Rio Grande at start of War, he participated in battles at Cerro Gordo and Mexico City. Writing in an engaging fashion, Grant notes conflicts between Scott and Taylor and is generous in assessment of Mexicans. After war he attended bullfight and scaled Popocatapetl.

765. Greene, Graham. *The Lawless Roads: A Mexican Journey*. London: Longmans Green, 1939. 306pp.

In 1938, Catholic convert Greene visited Mexico, mainly Tabasco, state of extreme anticlericalism. Fondness for Catholicism and perceived abuse of Roman Catholic Church by government give essence of *The Lawless Road*. Yet from Greene's bad experience came *The Power and the Glory* (1940).

766. Gregg, Josiah. *Diary & Letters of Josiah Gregg*. Norman: University of Oklahoma Press, 1941–1944. 2 v.

Best part of two-volume relates to Mexican-American War, in which he accompanied

Gen. John E. Wool to Chihuahua. Gregg is harsh judge of leaders and campaigns. Other pages devoted to Gregg as physician in Saltillo, visit to Mexico City, and leader of scientific expedition.

767. Griego, Alfonso (1906–). *Good-bye My Land of Enchantment: A True Story of… Territory of New Mexico.* N.p.: The Author, ca.1981. 132pp. Memoirs. Period Covered: 1825–1979?

New Mexican Hispano traces roots to early nineteenth century in idyll of village life and family. Living off land, Griego family incarnates type of Hispanic existence that lasted into twentieth century. *Good-bye* is *costumbrista* and qualifies as Mexican for its pre–Guadalupe Hidalgo portrayal.

768. Griffin John S.; George Walcott Ames. *A Doctor Comes to California….* San Francisco: California Historical Society, 1943. 97pp.

Not many memoirs extant of doctors in Mexican-American War. Griffin part of Army of West that marched from Ft. Leavenworth to New Mexico and California in 1846 under Stephen Kearny. Describes march, terrain, and, of course, his practice of medicine.

769. Grigsby, Robert Faires. *R.F. Grigsby's Sierra Madre Journal,* Sebastopol, CA: Pleasant Hill, 1976. 88pp.

Focuses on Chihuahua and its mines. Author visits various mines and becomes quite technical in presentation of smelting. In passing gives positive account of state's capital.

770. Grosso de Espinoza, Anita (1910–?). *Reflections by Mama Espinoza….* Ensenada, BC: Arte y Publicidad Gráfica, 1994. 92pp. Memoirs. Period Covered: 1896–1993.

Narrator lived on both sides of California/Baja border but spent life in El Rosario, Baja. Speaks of marriage, children, food, flood of 1992, and contacts with U.S. Latter includes Flying Samaritans, Californians alleviating poverty in El Rosario. Interesting part of Mama Espinoza's story is Catholic family's conversion to born-again-Protestants: "When he [her son] returned to El Rosario, he shared his new faith with his father, who also

accepted Jesus Christ as personal Lord and Savior" (p.80).

771. Guerra González, Luis (1916–?). *Andanzas rurales de un maletín.* Hermosillo, SON: Grafiteck, 1999. 57 pp. Memoirs. Period Covered: 1916–1998.

Eighty-two-year-old doctor's memoirs of fifty-eight years in medicine as radiologist. Educated at UNAM, he did *servicio social* (residency) in Sonora, where he practiced medicine in Ures, Sahuaripa, and Hermosillo.

772. Guerra Leal, Mario (1928–1992). *La grilla.* México: Editorial Diana, 1978. 389pp. Memoirs. Period Covered: 1947–1977?

Journalist, lawyer, and politician intimate with politics for over thirty years: president of Federación del Partidos del Pueblo Mexicano, secretary to Gen. Henríquez Guzmán, president of Partido Nacional Anticomunista, and presidential candidate for Partido Demócratico Cristiano. Gives more of political system than most memoirists.

773. Guerra Leal, Mario (1928–1992). *Más allá de la grilla.* México: Editorial Diana, 1984. 153pp. Memoirs. Period Covered: 1950–1979.

Lawyer and critic of political system exposes imprisonment in el Reclusorio Preventivo Norte. Images of favorites among presidents rarely harmonize with official histories. Action mainly in 1970s but reflects upon earlier decades.

774. Guerrero, Euquerio (1907–?). *Imágenes de mi vida.* México: Editorial Porrúa, 1986. 297pp. Memoirs. Period Covered: 1907–1986.

Lawyer, professor, writer, rector of University of Guanajuato, supreme court justice, and senator was born in Guanajuato. Representing government of President Luis Echeverría, he traveled to Europe, South America, and to Muslim world. In 1979, he began working for Instituto Nacional de la Senectud (National Institute for Aged). Memoirs as much of place as of person.

775. Guerrero, Guadalupe (Dates?). *Notas de la montaña.* Chihuahua, CHH:

Instituto Chihuahuense de la Cultura, 1998 (1993). 91pp. Diary. Period Covered: 1990.

Sent from Mexico City as representative of family planning agency (DIF), she finds self among poor and indigenous of Chihuahua. Introductory note captures essence of book: "Estas *Notas*.... intimistas y un tanto herméticas, son mis impresiones sentidas ante la pobreza y el abandono de la familia campesina" (p.11). Sensitive recorder of self and rural personalities, who populate entries.

776. Guerrero, Salvador (1919–). *Memorias: A West Texas Life.* Ed. by Arnoldo de León. Lubbock: Texas Tech University Press, 1991. 126pp. Memoirs. Period Covered: 1915–1989.

Born in Coahuila in 1917, he spent first seven years of life in Mexico. Revolution forced family to move to Villa Acuña and finally to San Angelo, Texas. Success story of immigrant who survived in Anglo culture: segregated schools, Protestantism, high school graduation, WWII and army, and civic leadership in Odessa, Texas. Member of G.I. Forum, radio host, and county commissioner.

777. Guerrero Tarquín, Alfredo (1909–1983). *Memorias de un agrarista....* México: Instituto Nacional de Antropología e Historia, 1987. 2 v. Memoirs. Period Covered: 1913–1938.

First of three-volume autobiography, compiled with aid of three anthropologists, reveals life of self-taught man of people, who witnessed later years of revolutionary process in Guanajuato. Presidente municipal of San Luis de la Paz and secretary general and treasurer of two rural organizations. In land redistribution (*ejido*), local hostility such as *Cristeros* inhibited ideals of movement. Second volume continues struggle for land reform.

778. Guerrero Tarquín, Alfredo (1909–1983). *Reminiscencias de un viaje a través de la Sierra Gorda por Xichú y Atarjea.* México: Instituto Nacional de Antropología e Historia, 1988. 355pp. Memoirs. Period Covered: 1938.

After events of *Memorias,* he is commissioned to inspect agrarian communities in area in title. "He narrates the situation that he finds. The new agrarian policies are seen as reflected in places he visits. But narration goes beyond this in that it constitutes an introduction to the region that makes the reader feel he has been there." (p.7)

779. Guijosa, Marcela (1951–). *Altar de muertos: memorias de un mestizaje.* México: Documentación y Estudios de Mujeres, 1994. 116pp. Autobiography Proper. Period Covered: 1951?–1976?

Autobiography for intense scrutiny of pre-teenage and adolescent years. Daughter of Spanish father and Mexican mother, she traces both racial and cultural heritage in sharp depiction of family members and middle-class milieu. Metaphorical title suggests recall of dead family members.

780. Guillén, Fedro (1920–1994). *La semilla en el viento.* México: Ediciones Gaita y Menhir, 1959. 61pp. Memoirs. Period Covered: 1913–1958?

Short story writer, journalist, and poet conjures much of poet for feelings more than actions dominate. Eight chapters, mainly in Chiapas during parents' exile in Huerta years, comprise volume. Dying father axis of narration.

781. Guillén Martínez, Nicasio (Dates?). *Historia de mi vida.* México: Editorial El Pueblo, 1969. 234pp. Memoirs. Period Covered: 1943–1961.

Author falsely accused of theft and sentenced to jail. Here he learns vicious ways and becomes successful thief in capital and Guadalajara. Narration on degeneracy, loves, thefts, henchmen, and final sentencing for period of thirty years. Book found under title, *¡Maldito delator!* by Carlos Cuevas Paralizábal.

782. Guiteras, Holmes, Calixta (1900 Birth of Manuel Arias Sohóm). *Los peligros del alma: visión del mundo de un tzotzil.* Habana: Instituto Cubano del Libro, 1972. 309pp. Trans: *Perils of the Soul.* New York: Free Press of Glencoe, 1961. Oral Autobiography. Period Covered: 1900–1956?

At request of anthropologist Robert

Redfield, she interviewed Manuel Arias Sohóm, Tzotzil from Chiapas. In interview with questions present, Manuel reveals much about his own and family's lives and focuses on spiritual world. More than presentation of Manuel's worldview, book serves as manual for oral autobiography. Author understands entire process of genre and need to convey procedure to reader.

783. Guízar Oceguera, José (Dates?). *Episodios de la Guerra Cristera y….* México: Costa-Amic, 1976. 172pp. Memoirs. Period Covered: 1923–1976.

Militant *Cristero* initiates reader into history of movement. Much of action in Cotija, Michoacán, where author helps found Liga Defensora de la Libertad Religiosa. Evaluates results of movement from perspective of fifty years.

784. Guridi y Alcocer, José Miguel (1763–1828). *Apuntes de la vida de….* México: Moderna Librería religiosa de J.L. Vallejo, 1906. 192pp. Memoirs. Period Covered: 1763–1801?

Enlightenment produced Guridi y Alcocer. Born in Tlaxcala, he received three bachelor's degrees from University of Mexico. Priest and doctor of theology, he held high-church offices as well as membership in Cortes of Cadiz. One of few memoirs prior to Independence. With ideas of Rousseau and picaresque, he gives something of self and society that produced him.

785. Gurrión, Evaristo C. (1879–1913). *Memorias…acerca de la vida política de su hermano Adolfo del mismo apellido.* México: Ayuntamiento Popular de Juchitán Oaxaca, 1983. 43pp. Memoirs. Period Covered: 1879–1914.

Author involves self and family in rendering life and details of martyred brother, Adolfo C. Gurrión. School teacher from poor family, he opposed dictatorship and corresponded for anarchist newspaper, *Regeneración*. In 1913, Federals took him from prison and shot him. Remainder enumerates honors paid to Adolfo in Juchitán.

786. Gutiérrez, Celedonio (1908–?). *A Narrative of Human Response to Natural Dis-* *aster: The Eruption of Paricutín….* College Station: Texas A&M University Press, 1972. 78pp. Memoirs. Period Covered: 1939–1944.

Survivor and observer of Paricutín eruption in Michoacán speaks autobiographically: background of village of Zicosto, eruption (vapors and lava), evacuations, religious reactions, livestock, and abandonment and destruction of San Juan Parangaricutiro.

787. Gutiérrez Camacho, Esperanza (Dates?). *Cartas para mi hijo.* México?, 1981. 79pp. Letters. Period Covered: 1958–1981.

Type of autobiography more typical for women than men. Women write about adored subject, husband, father, son, or lover, and, in passing, scatter fragments of their lives. Earliest letters start with son's infancy and latest when he is twenty-three years old and started in career. With advice according to age of son, letters combine to form moral autobiography of writer.

788. Gutiérrez de Mendoza, Juana Belén (1875–1942). "Autobiografía: apuntes." En *Juana Belén Gutiérrez de Mendoza, 1875–1942: Extraordinaria precursora de la Revolución mexicana de Angeles Mendieta Alatorre.* México: Impresores de Morelos, 1983. 36pp. Memoirs. Period Covered: 1901–1913.

Her autobiography only one portion of book, which has accompanying documents plus brief biography of subject. Fascinating self-taught woman from San Juan del Río, Durango, who sold goats in 1901 to buy printing press and denounce dictatorship. Friend of Flores Magóns and member of Liberal Party Ponciano Arriaga, Juana Belén deported. Harassment from authorities did not stop newspaper *Vesper*.

789. Gutiérrez Elías, Humberto (1911–?). *Memorias de mis tiempos: la medicina en Chihuahua.* Chihuahua, CHH: El Autor, 1997. 2 v. Hybrid. Period Covered: 1911–1993?

Photographs, newspaper clippings, articles, and history of medicine. Doctor's life data scattered throughout two volumes. Description of education especially in medical school and much on Chihuahua medicine. Narrator appears in anecdote.

790. Gutiérrez Gutiérrez, José G.
(Dates?). *Recuerdos de la gesta cristera.*
Guadalajara: Trinidad Elizondo G., 1972.
137pp. Memoirs. Period Covered: 1926–1927.

Author's actions as *Cristero* arose from government's implementation of anti-church articles of 1917 Constitution. Spy-thriller document as M.D. attempts to avoid and to combat Calles-inspired persecution. Two elements stand out: sincerity of *Cristeros* and organization of women into feminist brigades.

791. Gutiérrez Herrera, Luis (1913–?).
Un son de recuerdos. Naucalpan, MÉX: Ediciones El Aduanero, 1996. 79pp. Journal. Period Covered: 1913–1989.

From Tepeji del Río, Hidalgo, he composes journal rather than diary. Chronologically recorded events relate more to activities in city than personal life of author. Laboring man and musician with four years of formal education, he writes of school, family, church, government, and neighborhood.

792. Gutiérrez Verduzco, Mariano
(Dates?). *El sendero de un viajero.* Guadalajara: Instituto Jalisciense de Antropología e Historia, 1983. 130pp. Journal. Period Covered: 1950?–1980?

Guadalajara author early in life found profession: traveling salesman. For thirty years, he covered northern and northwestern Mexico on train. Journal serves as *derrotero* where he mentions routes, trains, city sizes, businesses, hotels, and personalities. Supplementary material included in chapter "A manera de anécdotas."

793. Guzmán, Eulalia (1890–1985). *Lo que vi y oí.* México: Tip.SAG, s.d.R.L., 1941. 123pp. Memoirs. Period Covered: 1936–1939.

Commissioned by Alfonso Caso and José Vasconcelos, teacher and archeologist Guzmán made several expeditionary trips to Europe on behalf of Mexican culture. Upon returning home in 1940, she registered impressions of European reactions to Mussolini and Hitler. Highly anecdotal, snapshots of Fascist Europe suggest indignation of free world towards aggression that precipitated WWII. Collected articles cohere into memoir.

794. Guzmán, Humberto (1948–). *De cuerpo entero: Humberto Guzmán.* México: Ediciones Corunda, 1990. 63pp. Memoirs. Period Covered: 1954–1989.

Novelist and short story writer reveals own theme in inner title of autobiography, "Confesiones de una sombra (…o de una generación)." In pessimistic book his other self, i.e., writing self, is dark shadow. In locating writing *I*, self distorted in hallucination. Reveals little of family but much on unfair imprisonment and treatment in Acapulco jail. Prison chapters interwoven with 1968 Tlateloco as observed by nine-year-old writer. Menacing and victimizing experiences core of autobiography.

795. Guzmán, José María (Dates?). *Breve y sencilla narración del viage que hizo a visitar los santos lugares de Jerusalén.* México: Imprenta de Abdiano, 1837. 54pp. Memoirs. Period Covered: 1834–1835.

Roman Catholic priest, in pilgrimage to Holy Land via Europe, stops at sites relating to Christ. Visits other countries of Levant, where he finds Christians living under control of Turks. Valuable for Mexican and Roman Catholic perspectives.

796. Guzmán, Martín Luís (1887–1976).
El águila y la serpiente. México: Editorial Anahuac, 1949. 469pp. Trans: *The Eagle and the Serpent.* Translated from Spanish by Harriet de Onís. Garden City, NY: Dolphin Books, 1965, (1928). Memoirs. Period Covered: 1913–1915.

Written in 1929, *El águila y la serpiente* is one of best and most controversial creations. Polemics stem from hybrid nature, both novel and autobiography. In first person narration, he focuses on youthful self involved in Revolution in North. Presence and reaction to events and personalities, especially Villa, favor autobiography or history. Talent as stylist, as recreator of scenes, and as inventor of novelistic but picaresque plot line indebt memoirs to novel.

797. Guzmán, Martín Luís (1887–1976).
Apuntes sobre una personalidad. México, ca.1955. 49pp. Autobiographical Essay. Period Covered: 1895?–1954?

Succinctly author gives early context for

present formation. He loved beauty and reading. One of gods was to be a liberal like Guillermo Prieto. Guzmán tries to assess his own pro–Villa stance.

798. Guzmán, Martín Luís (1887–1976). *Medias palabras: correspondencia 1913–1959.* Edición, prólogo (epistolar), notas y apéndice documental de Fernando Curiel. México: UNAM, 1991. 205pp. Letters. Period Covered: 1913–1959.

Arranged chronologically and geographically, letters postmarked Mexico, Mexico-Paris, Manhattan-Madrid, Madrid-Paris, Madrid-Buenos Aires, and Madrid-Rio de Janeiro. Guzmán wrote sixty-two letters; Reyes, forty-three. Correspondence reveals more of Guzmán, struggling writer in exile to "mentor" Reyes, compassionate and full of advice. Reyes penned best and most autobiographical letters in 1930 detailing antipathy for politics. Curiel superbly edited collection.

799. Guzmán, Martín Luís (1878–1915 Dates of Villa). *Memorias de Pancho Villa.* 9 ed. México: Compañía General de Ediciones, 1966, (1936). 950pp. Trans: *Memoirs of Pancho Villa.* Translated by Virginia H. Taylor. Austin: University of Texas Press, 1970; ca.1965. Oral Autobiography. Period Covered: 1895–1915.

Labeled *memoirs*, book in technique and in use of primary sources is oral autobiography. According to Guzmán, every word here verified either by testimony of eyewitness or by document. In conversations with Villa, Guzmán tried to transcribe them in general's words. Result is exciting document of Mexican autobiography. With picaresque structure, book created through Villa's narration: episodes from childhood, struggle for justice, battles in Revolution, and justification of actions. *Memorias* populated with luminaries of period.

800. Guzmán-C., S. *A Vagabond in Mexico.* Seattle: Nomads, 1993. 144pp.

American went to Mexico and worked illegally, searching for new life. Survived with manual labor in Sonora, Baja, Sinaloa, and Nayarit. Alone and knowing Spanish, was close to variety of bosses. Mexico from perspective of illegal alien.

801. Hagan, Robert. *The Diary of Robert Hagan, Assistant Surgeon, …in the War with Mexico, 1847–1848.* Rye, NY, 1946. 56 leaves.

Typescript of experiences of medical doctor who accompanied troops through following sites: Vera Cruz, Jalapa, Perote, Puebla, Mexico City, and return to Vera Cruz and to New Orleans. As a doctor, he inventories illness and especially notes fever and diarrhea and graphically describes an amputation. Beyond his profession, he details battles and notes Gen. Scott's unpopularity because of early armistice. Also gives reader tour of Mexico City.

802. Hail, John B. *To Mexico with Love: San Miguel with Side Dishes.* New York: Exposition, 1966. 219pp.

Floridian spouses return to San Miguel de Allende for winter. Humorous experiences as paean to Gringo-created mecca in Guanajuato: magnificent self-supported library, house and garden tours, religious self-expression of Protestants, and confusion with language suggest Gringo accommodation to hospitable environment.

803. Hale, Howard. *Long Walk to Mulegé: A True Story of Adventure and Survival in Baja California.* Santee, CA: Pinkerton, 1980. 151pp.

Hale is no professional writer, But among many popular books on Baja, *Long Walk* stands out. Young author and companion journey on foot from Ensenada to Mulegé, distance of 1,000 miles. Search for remnants of Catholic missions motivated trip. Written sixty years after trek, memoirs fresh, vigorous, humorous, and informative: landscape, wild animals, natives, climate, burros, and undiscovered Baja.

804. Hall, Arthur C. *Those Wonderful Years in Mexico.* Tucson: Sundance, 1997. 250pp.

Mining engineer exercised profession with ASARCO (American Smelting and Refining Company) from 1934 to 1951. For seventeen years he and family lived in Charcas, Guanajuato; Angangueo, Michoacán; and Hermosillo, Sonora. Simplifies mining engineering. Harmonious relationship sustained with Mexicans and other Americans.

805. Halsell, Grace. *The Illegals.* New York: Stein and Day, 1978. 216pp.

Halsell does undercover work here. Autobiography and sociology mix as reporter makes contact with Mexicans who wish to enter illegally. Interviews undocumented, dialogs with them, visits homes, and places self in their predicament. Many ideas covered.

806. Hamilton, Charles W. *Early Day Oil Tales of Mexico.* Houston: Gulf, 1966. 246pp.

Adventures recorded here include chapters on finding oil, exploration hazards, fish and pests, bandits, guerrillas and rebels, etc. Topics held together chronologically by presence of Hamilton, who tells good story in setting similar to Wild West.

807. Hanut, Erkyk. *The Road to Guadalupe: A Modern Pilgrimage to the Goddess of the Americas.* New York: Tarcher/Putnam, 2001. 190pp.

Cynical view of experience in above title. Autobiography and history blend in alternating chapters. History of miraculous appearance of Mary in Mexico in century of Conquest. Additional chapters when Hanut meets other Mexicans and seeks contemporary views of miracle at Tepeyac. Purity of religious experience diluted when author seeks wisdom of *curanderos* and *brujos*.

808. Harding, Bertita Leonarz (1902–?). *Mosaic in the Fountain.* New York: Lippincott, 1949. 320pp. Autobiography Proper. Period Covered: 1906?–1914?

Of German and Hungarian ancestry, she arrived in Mexico as child. Father had employment as engineer; mother, Magyar countess, commissioned by Austrian Hapsburgs to recover jewels left by ill-fated Maximilian. Most of memoir focuses on Harding and family in Mexico City and in Monterrey. Eloquent chapters on German school in Mexico City and French convent school in Monterrey.

809. Hardy, Robert William Hale. *Travels in the Interior of Mexico....* Glorieta, NM: Rio Grande, 1977 (1829). 558pp.

British author, with desire to travel and to educate reader about Mexico in 1820s,

traverses much of country but spends time mainly in northwest: Mexico City, Michoacán, Jalisco, Sinaloa, Sonora, Upper and Lower California, Chihuahua, Guanajuato, and Vera Cruz. Lt. Hardy visited shortly after independence and met major political figures. More fascinating are anecdotes about Indians and his experiences with herbs to cure ailments. Again, Frances Calderón de la Barca is not only outstanding foreign observer of nineteenth century Mexico.

810. Harkort, Eduard. *In Mexican Prisons: The Journal of Eduard Harkot, 1832–1834.* College Station: Texas A&M University Press, 1986. 194pp.

Santa Anna both praised and abused here. German leaves record of adventures in Mexico and Texas: director of mines, lieutenant colonel of engineers and artillery in Santa Anna's army, and prisoner in Perote near Jalapa, Vera Cruz, and in Puebla. Multitalented Harkort was scientist, painter, soldier, and active and recording participant of surroundings.

811. Harlan, Jacob Wright. *California '46 to '88.* San Francisco: Bancroft, 1888. 242pp.

As title suggests, small part of autobiography relates to Mexico. Gives ancestry and then difficult childhood. A book on California induced author and some of family to journey there in 1845. Many difficulties and information on Donnor Party. They arrived in San Francisco in 1846. He joined Frémont's battalion in Monterey. Dedication of book: "To Gen. John C. Frémont, my chief in days of yore." In 1847, he was mustered out. Garrulous old-timer with many anecdotes. Much information from point of view of foot soldier.

812. Haro Oliva, Antonio (1910–?). *Del brazo y por la vida: Nadia y Antonio.* México: Editorial Diana, 1994. 270pp. Memoirs. Period Covered: 1910–1994.

Military attaché in France (1938–1941), Olympic-class fencer, and theater backer has intriguing life. One of most interesting chapters locates him in France during 1940 German invasion. Involved in Mexican dramatic theater along with French-born wife Nadia, Haro Oliva valuable for culture.

813. Harper, Henry Howard. *A Journey in Southeastern Mexico....* New York: De Vinne, 1910. 100pp.

Eastern-bred farmer reconnoiters Mexico for investment in agriculture. He and companions contract boatman to carry them from Tampico to Tuxpam, Vera Cruz. Humorous encounters with natives, insects, animals, and smallpox plague journey. In Tuxpam, Harper warns of doing business in Mexico: "Our modern methods and ideas assimilate with those of Mexico very slowly, if at all"(pp.64–65). Logic of local practices should be blueprint for investor who would make radical changes. He bought ranch but primitive conditions frightened away family in eventually successful endeavor.

814. Harper Burgueño, Carlos Oscar (1934–). *Más allá de los muros.* México: Instituto Politécnico Nacional, 1985. 101pp. Memoirs. Period Covered: 1934–1984.

Geologist, champion javelin thrower, and former football star seriously injured in car accident in 1967. Invalid gives major contours of life.

815. Harris, Dilue Rose. *Life in Early Texas: The Reminiscences of Mrs. Dilue Harris.* Texas State Historical Assoc.; Quarterly, n.p., 1970–1976? (1900). 88pp.

Arrived in Matagorda, Texas, from New Orleans and diary covers years 1833 to 1838. Much on Mexican Texas. Description of family, neighbors, school, and farming while showing racial sensitivity to Indians, Blacks, Mexicans, and Whites. Notes tensions building up to Alamo and battles of Alamo and San Jacinto. Author's family out of fear left home in March of 1836 and did not return until a month after. Mentions Santa Anna, Sam Houston, and Deaf Smith.

816. Haven, Gilbert. *Our Next-door Neighbor: A Winter in Mexico.* New York: Harper, 1875. 467pp.

American interest in exporting Methodism. Worthy subtitle of foray into nineteenth century Mexico might be "The Prospects for Protestantism in a Romanist Country." Methodist minister Haven visits major cities, seeks out Protestants, and measures progress. Although anti–Catholic stance intrudes constantly, he writes and notes as much as any other traveler of that century.

817. Henestrosa, Andrés (1906–?). *Cartas sin sobre: confidencias y poemas al olvido.* México: Editorial Porrúa, 1996. 190pp. Letters. Period Covered: 1925–1929.

Fourth and penultimate autobiography consists of twenty letters. Many repeated in earlier collection. Most interesting and original here, "Confidencias" pertains to years in Spain. Lyrical quality. Author's personality further illuminated in Martha Chapa's *De domingo a domingo, conversaciones con Andrés Henestrosa* (2001). Compatible interviewer and interviewee dialogued from 1985 and to 1990. Talks about self, Indian background, love for indigenous languages, and intimate knowledge of celebrated Mexicans such as Antonieta Rivas Mercado, Olga Costa, José Vasconcelos, and Olga and Rufino Tamayo.

818. Henestrosa, Andrés (1906–?). *Divagario.* México: El Dia en Libros, 1989. 246pp. Memoirs. Period Covered: 1910?–1989.

In weekly articles from 1985 to 1989, teacher and journalist renders fragmented autobiography. One-third of entries refer to self: books, birthplace, writings, family, travel, and obituaries on intimates. Adventures with books give more of author. *Divagario* augments other autobiographies.

819. Henestrosa, Andrés (1906–?). *Entonces vivía yo en Ixhuatán y me llamaba Andrés Morales: carta a Cibeles.* México: Editorial Praxis, 1994. 33pp. Memoirs. Period Covered: 1900?–1920?

With usual poetic style and clarity, he recaptures story of parents' courtship through eyes of mother. Complements *Tres cartas.*

820. Henestrosa, Andrés (1906–?). *Prosa presurosa.* Villahermosa: Gobierno del Estado de Tabasco, 1991. 193pp. Essays. Period Covered: 1980–1981.

Of four autobiographical works, *Prosa* parallels most closely *Divagario* (1989). Themes of books, writing, family, travel, and obituaries appear among anthology of articles taken from column, "Sombras y reflejos" of *Excelsior.* Ninety brief essays tribute him as stylist unusual in journalism. Title contradicts precision of writings and profundity of thoughts.

821. Henestrosa, Andrés (1906?–?) *3 cartas autobiográficas.* México: Secretaría de Educación Pública, 1967. 67pp. Letters. Period Covered: 1906–1915.

Writer, magazine editor, and professor of literature in three letters evokes much of childhood in Oaxaca. Brief and exquisitely written letter, "Retrato de mi madre," shows pride in Indian heritage. In 1979, he published *El remoto y cercano ayer* (Porrúa) comprised of three essays mentioned here plus new one, "Una confidencia a media voz." In letter to Estela Shapiro, he talks about pitiful condition of man, beauty of words, and about experiences in New Orleans in 1936 together with intimate friendship with landlady. Author in essay, *Sobre el mi* (1966), recalls incident of childhood when he annoyed pretentious aunt, who in turn verbally lacerated him. Aunt's abuse of possessive *mi* stimulates autobiographical recall.

822. Henríquez Ureña, Pedro (1889–1959 Dates of Reyes). *Epistolario íntimo, 1906–1946: Pedro Henríquez Ureña and Alfonso Reyes.* Santo Domingo: UNPHU, 1981. 3 v. Letters. Period Covered: 1906–1946.

Prologue summarizes: "Collection contains correspondence of an entire life that crossed between Pedro Henríquez Ureña and Alfonso Reyes, two glories of Spanish American letters and thought of our century" (p.5). Reyes reveals more of self than in autobiographies. Postmarked Cuba, Spain, France, Argentina, and Brazil, letters disclosed intellectual life but also details of family, surroundings, and opinions on political events.

823. Henriquez Ureña, Pedro; Enrique Zuleta Alvarez. *Memorias; diario: notas de viaje.* México: Fondo de Cultura Económica, 2000. 223pp.

Dominican writer landed in Mexico in 1906 and indulged in rich intellectual life. Taught, collaborated on journal, helped found Ateneo de la Juventud, and interacted with major young intellectuals. Much recorded in fourth chapter of memoirs and in diary from 1909 to 1911, both collected in above title.

824. Henry, W.S. *Campaign Sketches of the War with Mexico.* New York: Harper, 1981 (1847). 331pp.

Memoirs in frank adoration of Gen. Taylor. Thus northern Mexico, specifically Monterrey and Saltillo, is scenario for action in Mexican-American War. Yet Henry knows how to write and does much with landscape, climate, and anecdote.

825. Heredia Bucio, Rubén (1907–?). *Mi vida en el recuerdo.* Morelia: Michoacana de San Nicolás de Hidalgo, 1987. 336pp. Memoirs. Period Covered: 1907–1954.

Farmer, schoolteacher, and principal from Morelia details three stages of life: infancy, adolescence/youth, and maturity. Although Revolution, love and courtship, and business ventures occupy life, learning prevails. Has much of Morelia's history.

826. Hermosillo, Heriberto (1960–); **Elsa Ponce de Hermosillo.** *Por tu gracia: relato de una vida revolucionada por la misericordia de Dios.* Miami: Editorial Vida, 2003. 143pp. Memoirs. Period Covered: 1960–2002?

Unusual testimony of contradictory career of co-founder of band Torre Fuerte and an active evangelist preacher with Hispanic congregations. He has preached in Argentina and now has congregation in McAllen, Texas. Product of dysfunctional family but filled with forgiveness.

827. Hernández, Octavio Andrés (1917–1992). *Entre la vista y la nada: los primeros 97 dias de mi negra negrura.* México: Editorial Porrúa, 1987. 335pp. Memoirs. Period Covered: 1922?–1982?

Congenital eye problem impedes normal education for jurist. Even as autodidact, he acquired sufficient learning to become lawyer. He relives ninety-seven days of blindness with philosophical dialog and thoughts on suicide.

828. Hernández, Tony (Dates?). *A mi manera...: la vida de un homosexual.* México: Costa-Amic, 1988. 87pp. Memoirs. Period Covered: 1950?–1987?

Hides autobiographical data to maintain anonymity. From provincial town, he suffered because of effeminate mannerisms. Moving to Mexico City, found employment and engaged in active homosexual life. Cross-sectioning sexual adventures, the writer describes temporary relationships and venue, macho types that attract him, and society's abuse of gays.

829. Hernández, Víctor (1890–?). *Andanzas de un ferrocarrilero.* Guadalajara, México: Tallares Linotipográficos Radio, 1951. 381pp. Memoirs. Period Covered: 1905–1949.

Sixteen year old started working for railway in northern Mexico. Section foreman, fireman, engineer, inspector, and negotiator for union did spectrum of railroading. History of heavy industry informs memoirs. Apprenticeship and success interest more than union years. Replete with documents.

830. Hernández Colunga, Felipe (Dates?). *Mexicaltzingo mi barrio.* Guadalajara: Colegio Internacional, 1983. 108pp. Memoirs. Period Covered: 1912–?

Inventories Mexicaltzingo, neighborhood or district in Guadalajara: streets, buildings, climate, games, other entertainments, Revolution, and celebrations. Own life enters with family, especially train-engineer father, education, and influence of Revolution.

831. Hernández E., Agustín (1921–?). *Remembranzas de mi vida: testimonio de un lerdense.* Ciudad Lerdo, DUR: Hernández E., 1992. 65pp. Memoirs. Period Covered: 1921–1991.

From Ciudad Lerdo in Durango, uneducated author survived various employments throughout northern Mexico: store clerk, railway man on Tijuana-Mexicali line, drugstore assistant, and salesman. Memoirs combine work, family, *costumbrismo,* and anecdote.

832. Hernández Gómez, Manuel (1950–). *Medio siglo: vivencias y testimonios.* México: Impre-Jal, 2000. 219pp. Memoirs. Period Covered: 1955?–1999?

Journalist for *El Informador* notes highlights of life: youth, *preparatoria,* college,

reprobate years, and conversion to Protestantism. Written four books relating to history, ethics, and religion.

833. Hernández Hernández, Claudio (1928?–). "El trabajo escolar de un maestro rural." En *Los maestros y la cultura nacional 1920–1950, v.3.* México: Museo Nacional de Culturas Populares, ca.1987. Pp.51–90. Memoirs. Period Covered: 1928–1950.

"El trabajo escolar" concerns family, education, and teaching experiences. From state of Tlaxcala, he was certified as rural teacher. Various positions in Tlaxcala and Puebla, including one where *Cristeros* threatened teachers, lend perspective on education.

834. Hernández Leal, Jesús (1898–?). "Entrevista con Jesús Hernández Leal." Waco, TX: Institute for Oral History, Baylor, 1979. 27pp. Memoirs. Period Covered: 1898–1979.

Another interview of Mexican Baptists by Leobardo Estrada. From Uruapan, Michoacán, Hernández Leal tells of childhood, call to ministry, education, and marriage. Held several pastorates and briefly served as president of Lacy Seminary in Mexico. From Catholic family, wife Dionisia Ramírez notes difficulties in converting to Protestantism.

835. Herr, Robert Woodmansee (1906–?). *An American Family in the Mexican Revolution.* Wilmington, DL: SR Books, 1999. 263pp. Hybrid. Period Covered: 1910–1932.

Four voices combine in family autobiography. Sons Robert and Richard reminisce while parents present selves in written documents of years in Guanajuato. Elder Herr, U.S. mining engineer, worked at El Cubo as superintendent who interacted with government officials, rebels, and mine employees. All four recall turbulent years including Huerta, Villa, Obregón, and *Cristeros.*

836. Herrera, Juan Felipe. *Mayan Drifter: Chicano Poet in the Lowlands of America.* Philadelphia: Temple University Press, 1997. 272pp.

Poet connects with Mexico through Mexican-born parents and through journey to Chiapas. His goal: "I want to reinvent the

Mexican southlands as much as I want to reinvent the position that I hold as a brown man from 'El Norte'" (p.6). Autobiography and travel closely unite in prose document.

837. Herrera de la Fuente, Luis (1916–?). *La música no viaja sola*. México: Fondo de Cultura Económica, 1998. 173pp. Memoirs. Period Covered: 1881–1995?

Composer, orchestra director, founder of Chamber Orchestra of Radio University and concert pianist composes one of best autobiographies of Mexican musician. Reaches back into family before his birth; details and interprets career going beyond mere chronicle; conveys vaster experience.

838. Herrera Sánchez, Raymundo (Dates?). *Mis amigos periodistas*. Editores de Escritores y Autores de Morelia, 1989. 52pp. Memoirs. Period Covered: 1939–1974?

Teacher in Colegio de San Nicolás de Hidalgo, radio announcer, and journalist focuses on journalistic activities in Morelia.

839. Herrera-Sobek, María (Dates?). "An Oral History Interview with a Composite Bracero." In *The Bracero Experience: Elitelore Versus Folklore*. Los Angeles: University of California, 1979. Pp.39–74. Memoirs. Period Covered: 1947–1950?

Author visited Huecorio, Michoacán, grandfather's village in 1969. His presence and bracero background inspired and facilitated project of interviewing braceros. In monologue, representative bracero tells of experiences in U.S. and then returns to Mexico. Three other autobiographies also exploit fictionalization of generic subject: Vaca del Corral, Máximo Peón, and Robert Ai Camp.

840. Hickman, Katie. *A Trip to the Light Fantastic: Travels with a Mexican Circus*. London: Flamingo, 1994, (1993). 301pp.

She illuminates more of *Circo Bell*. Traveling with circus, she introduces main characters in exotic world: owner, clown, trapeze artist, dancers, contortionists, elephant keeper, and circus hands.

841. Hidalgo y Esnaurrízar, José Manuel (1826–1896). *Un hombre del mundo escribe sus impresiones y cartas*. México: Editorial Porrúa, 1960. 424pp. Memoirs. Period Covered: 1861–1896.

Written as letters, collection actually suits characteristics of memoir. José Hidalgo, whose Spanish father prospered under Iturbide, was secretary of Mexican Legation in France. He and other aristocratic exiles connived to stem republicanism by imposing European monarch. Moved in best circles and wrote gossipy letters about royalty and fellow émigrés. Record of cultured Mexican in Europe.

842. Higuera Gil, Roberto (Dates?). *Hacienda El Forlón: fundación, mis recuerdos, la decadencia y su fin*. Ciudad Victoria: Gobierno del Estado de Tamaulipas, 1998. 158pp. Memoirs? Period Covered: 1900–1998?

History of Tamaulipan family hacienda that sporadically melds into memoirs as author connects his life to ancestors and to properties. Autobiography in memories of father and grandparents, their anecdotes, childhood stays at El Forlón, and games and recreation. Major value is founding, growth, and administration of hacienda and its deterioration with Revolution.

843. Higuera Gil, Roberto (Dates?). *Su casona, La Vega, La Labor y Huanimba: memoria de la familia Gil-Reyes*. Ciudad Victoria: Instituto Tamaulipeco para la Cultura, 2001. 98pp. Memoirs. Period Covered: 1880–1979.

Autobiography of prosperous Tamaulipan family. Author gives genealogy of four grandparents and chronologically proceeds to present when he and spouse build retirement home near Ciudad Victoria. Houses, gardens, labor, seasons, flora and fauna, and even ecology comprise narration. Author related to former President Emilio Portes Gil.

844. Hill, D.H.; Nathaniel Cheairs Hughes; Timothy Johnson. *A Fighter from Way Back: The Mexican War Diary....* Kent, OH: Kent State University Press, 2002. 231pp.

"Scrupulous to the point of obsession Hill consistently made his daily entries, recording not only clashes with higher authority but also routine activities of daily life — the places he went, the sights he saw, and the people he met"(p.xiii) summarizes preface of one of better diaries of Mexican-American War. Somehow author more involved with environment. Lt. Hill witnessed much of this war: Monterrey, Saltillo, Vera Cruz, Cerro Gordo, Puebla, and Mexico City.

845. Hilton, John W. *Sonora Sketch Book.* New York: Macmillan, 1947. 333pp.

Under influence of 1920s and 1930s, he images a Mexico back to nature. Each chapter is self-contained unit on some facet of northern state: natives, photography, reptiles, customs, domesticated animals, bird hunting, etc. Sonoran personalities appeal to Hilton.

846. Hinojosa, Francisco (1954–). *Mexican Chicago.* México: Conaculta, 1995. 164pp. Memoirs. Period Covered: 1996–1997.

Writer visits Chicago and interacts with Mexican-Americans and their culture. With companion, glimpses museums; enjoys regional cuisine; hears blues and mariachis; interviews political and cultural leaders; discovers local hero, martyred Rudy Lozano; visits Pilsen; and participates in Diálogo México-Chicago. Involved narrator blends travel, essay, anecdote, and autobiography.

847. Hitchcock, Ethan Allen; W. A. Croffut. *Fifty Years in Camp and Field, Diary....* New York: Putnam, 1909. 514pp.

Approximately a hundred pages by author relates to Mexican-American War. Officer at Rio Grande, Vera Cruz, Cerro Gordo, and Mexico City. As Scott's Inspector General, he had job of overseeing readiness of entire command. Close to Scott, Hitchcock worked with treaty proceedings. Diary, filled with original quotes, also has many explanatory paragraphs by Croffut.

848. Hogan, Michael. *Mexican Mornings: Essays South of the Border.* San Diego: Intercambio, 2001. 199pp.

Wrote essays as high school English teacher in Guadalajara. Involve incursions into self in constant revelation in backdrop of Mexico: teaching, battling insects, imposing Gringo customs, fathoming machismo, Judas burning, and looking at street people. Personal outlook attuned to Mexico.

849. Holder, Maryse. *Give Sorrow Words: Maryse Holder's Letters from Mexico.* New York: Grove, 1979. 302pp.

"These pages are the account of a woman on her way to death, a death not only imposed but sought after" (p.9) writes Kate Millet as she introduces this title, most self-analytical autobiography written by foreigner in Mexico. Holder self dissects as she wanders from one pleasure spot to another—Acapulco, Oaxaca, Merida and Mexico City—in sexual forays with both females and males, often predatory beach boys. In successful quest for death, psychoanalyzes Mexicans as lovers and women as feminists. Drugs, liquor, and unlimited sex recall sixties more than 1970s, decade of author's sojourn. Holder writes brilliantly with sporadic insights into Gringo presence in Mexico.

850. Holderman, Jennifer. *Jennifer Holderman: estudio de un caso.* Manuel Esparza, editor. México: Instituto Nacional de Antropología e Historia, Centro Regional de Oaxaca, ca.1975 and 1979. 169pp.

Mexican anthropologist Esparza, finding Jennifer a hippie living in Oaxacan commune, interviewed her for ten months. Reverse situation of Oscar Lewis. Of Austrian Jewish descent via New York, she expresses disenchantment with contemporary society: anger at university, boredom with education, sexual freedom, drug use especially in Mexico, and desire for social change.

851. Holding, Nannie Emory. *A Decade of Mission Life in Mexican Mission Homes.* Nashville: Publishing House Methodist Episcopal Church, 1895, 275pp.

Author's fervor for Methodism in above title. Her institution made forays into Laredo, Texas, and states of Nuevo León, Chihuahua, Coahuila, and Durango. Striking is number of American women involved in endeavor. Beyond proselytizing, mission work involved education, nursing, and care of orphans.

852. Hopkins Durazo, Armando (1920–). *Mis incursiones en la política sonorense, 1958–1997.* Hermosillo, SON: Impresos Chávez, 1998. 135pp. Memoirs. Period Covered: 1958–1997.

Engineer involved self in local politics in Magdalena, Sonora, and maximized career as federal deputy. In between served on local PRI committee; state congress; director of ISSSTESON (Social Security and Social Services for Workers of Sonora); secretary of development for state, and member of executive board of PRI. Career suggests politics at local and state levels. Unique for goal to do good rather than well. Chapter on fear of centralism.

853. Hornaday, William Temple. *Camp-Fires on Desert and Lava.* New York: Scribner, 1909 (1908). 362pp.

Geography, wildlife, and vegetation occupy and internationalize naturalist. Traditional Mexico not found in focus on Pinacate region of Arizona and Sonora. Adventures of men willingly submitting to unknowns and sufferings of trek into desert. Product of Teddy Roosevelt era and big game hunting, Hornaby is anachronistic. Shows sensitivity to protection of wildlife.

854. Horney, Renate. *Lazarus, What's Next? A Memoir.* Laguna Beach, CA: Laurel, 1999. 261pp.

Daughter of psychiatrist Karen Horney, Renate lived in Mexico from 1939 to 1973. Mexico City, Cuernavaca, and Ajijic backdrop for marriages, family, mother, filming Tarascans and Mayan with husband, and stint as travel agent.

855. Horton, Inez. *Copper's Children: The Rise and Fall of a Mexican Copper Mining Camp.* New York: Exposition, 1968. 202pp.

Another perspective on small-town Sonora. Spunky Horton married and lived in Nacozari from early 1900s to 1930s. Adjustment to foreign environment and even love for it. Husband worked in copper mines; she gave piano lessons and taught school. Sporadically refuged in U.S., she lived through Revolution with good humor. Sometimes evades life and writes chapters on Mexico and its politics. Vignettes of Nacozari's American colony and its social structure.

856. Horton, Lewis. *Escape from Mexico.* Berkeley, CA: Creative Arts Book, 2001. 123pp.

Mexicali's darker side exposed here. Sol-

dier on leave crosses over from army exercises in Mojave Desert to Mexicali as a lark. Confusion over marijuana and he is thrust into jail and battles normal U.S. and Mexican bureaucracies to gain freedom. With connivance of family, escapes to Los Angeles. Horrific prison conditions converted to humor through constant references to Hollywood movies of prison or comparisons of his condition with B. Traven's hero in *March of the Montería.*

857. Howard, Josefina; Lila Lomelí. *Rosa Mexicano: A Culinary Autobiography with 60 Recipes.* New York: Viking, 292pp.

Spanish-born Josefina Howard's work merits mention. Food and life intermingle in recipe book/memoir, wherein discovery of Mexican foods, preparation, and translation to New York structure adventure.

858. Huerta, Aldolfo de la (1881–1955). *Memorias de don Adolfo de la Huerta según su propio dictado.* México: Ediciones Guzmán, 1975, 337pp. Memoirs. Period Covered: 1908–1950?

Third-person memoirs dictated to de la Huerta's secretary, Roberto E. Guzmán. Cover mainly years 1908–1923: revolt against dictatorship, efforts to pacify Yaquis, union with Carranza against Victoriano Huerta, governor of Sonora, and collaboration with Obregón against President Carranza and De la Huerta-Lamont Treaty. Little introspection or interpretation or portraits of contemporaries. Memoirist's image diluted by intervention of secretary: recreated dialogs lend fictional air of novel. Self rarely emerges.

859. Huerta, Elena (1908–?). *El círculo se cierra.* Saltillo: Universidad Autónoma de Coahuila, 1990. 198pp. Memoirs. Period Covered: 1908–1985.

Telephone operator, union organizer, artist, Marxist, painter, world traveler, and mother led exciting life. Born in Saltillo at end of Porfiriato, she traveled to U.S., Scandinavian countries, China, Cuba, and Soviet Union. Initiative of determined woman equals success.

860. Huerta, Victoriano (1854–1915). *Memorias del general Victoriano Huerta.* San

Antonio: Impreso por la Librería de Quiroga, 19–? 96pp. Memoirs. Period Covered: 1910–1915?

With style more that of professional writer than a military man, Huerta in apocryphal memoirs describes turbulent 1910–1915 years. Revelations of love for alcohol and fondness for killing also lend suspicion to document. Negative self-exposure unusual in Mexican autobiography.

861. Hughes, Langston. *The Big Sea: An Autobiography.* New York: Knopf, 1940. 335pp.

Afro-American sallies into Mexico. College-age Hughes taken to Mexico by divorced father, successful entrepreneur in adopted country. Mexico City, Cuernavaca, and Toluca, loci of Hughes's journey, offer glimpses of stratified and racist society. Anecdotes about German colony in Toluca, where Hughes taught English, enliven narrative about frazzled father-son relationship.

862. Hummel, F.C. *Memories of Forestry and Travel: Uganda, Mexico....* New York: Radcliffe Press, 2001. 249pp.

Author in small way illuminates neglected field. British-educated Hummel and family lived in Mexico from 1961 to 1966, and he gives "...a brief account of my family life, work, including efforts to place forestry into the broader context of its contribution to rural development, nature conservation and international co-operation..." (p.xi). Employee of Food and Agricultural Organization (FAO) of United Nations relates professional life and adjustments to another culture.

863. Humphrey, Zephine. *'Allo Good-by.* New York: Dutton, 1940. 284pp.

Mature couple travels by car from Laredo to Mexico City. Taxco, Cuernavaca, and Puebla complete itinerary of admirers of Indians, beneficiaries of uncomplicated civilization. When queried if she liked Mexico, Humphrey responded, "No...but I have never been in a country which interested me so keenly" (p.241). Curious title relates to Taxco children greeting Humphreys with prologue as request for money.

864. Hunter, Ben. *The Baja Feeling.* Ontario, CA: Brasch and Brasch, 1978. 334pp.

Married couple from Los Angeles with intensifying relationship with Baja. Make short jaunts to peninsula and by last chapter, build house in Ensenada. Title answers question: "What miracle transported me from the miasma [Hollywood] to this paradise" (p.11)?

865. Hunter, Helen. *Betrayal in the Parsonage.* Mukilteo, WA: Wine Press, 1999. 245pp.

Not every autobiography of Protestants in Mexico is hopeful. Hunter wanted to be Wycliffe translator but married Mexican evangelist. Two served congregations in Federal District, La Paz, but also Texas and California. Story differs from other Protestant testimonies because preacher husband was philanderer and wife beater.

866. Hupu (1926–?). *Autobiografía de un cabrón.* N.p., 1998. 309pp. Memoirs. Period Covered: 1926–1994?

Anonymous author burdens autobiography with essays denouncing evils of Mexican society. Follows loose chronological order but dedicates most chapters to topics: women, world leaders, wretched world, publicity, etc. Born into hacendado family in Bajío, he earned living in various capacities: General Motors of Mexico, hotel management, tourism in Guadalajara, coordination of events such as Olympics, and publicity agent. Memoirs closely resemble those of Mexican politicians for lack of focus on self and use of life story to attack enemies.

867. Ibacache, María Luisa (1889–1959 Dates of Reyes). "Gabriela Mistral y Alfonso Reyes vistos a través de su epistolario: una amistad más que literaria." Ph.D. Dissertation, George Washington University, 1986. 698 leaves. Letters. Period Covered: 1924–1959.

Final 216 pages comprise affectionate correspondence of Reyes with Spanish America's first Nobel prize-winning author. From Mexico City, Rio de Janeiro, and Buenos Aires, Reyes fulfills part of epistolary exchange. Mistral reveals more of self than her correspondent; constant and supportive Reyes encourages her writing, recalls mutual acquaintances, and shares moments of his family.

868. Ibargüengoitia, Jorge (1928–1983). *Autopsias rápidas: selección de Guillermo Sheridan.* México: Vuelta, 1988. 290pp. Memoirs. Period Covered: 1969–1976.

Posthumous collection of selected articles written between 1969 and 1976 for *Excelsior.* Functions as life writing, for in editorial essays he reveals much of self: family, career, film criticism, relationships with literature, and, more directly, how he writes. "Confesiones de un 'Boy Scout'" most autobiographical. Pervasive humor and sarcasm.

869. Ibargüengoitia, Jorge (1928–1983). *La casa de usted y otros viajes.* México: Mortiz, 1991. 338pp. Memoirs. Period Covered: 1969–1976.

Author writes of self sporadically but with caustic humor in third and final collection of journals edited by Guillermo Sheridan. As in Salvador Novo, travel writing a form of autobiography by not distancing self from foreign experience with guidebook prose. Focuses on Mexico City, Acapulco, and Revolution through family's hacienda.

870. Ibargüengoitia, Jorge (1928–1983). *Misterios de la vida diaria.* México: Mortiz, 1997. 277pp. Memoirs. Period Covered: 1969–1976.

Another posthumous collection of *Excelsior* editorials that reflects opinion and life of creator. Pieces organized by category: what is expected, how to educate children, homage to commerce, national showcase, and events and commentaries. Agile pen of sardonic humorist.

871. Icaza, Alfonso de (1897?–?). *Así era aquello...sesenta años de vida metropolitana.* México: Ediciones Botas, 1957. 318pp. Memoirs. Period Covered: 1890–1952.

Rather than concentrating on self, remembers aristocratic childhood during Porfiriato: music, architecture, personalities, theater, medicine, political life, transportation, etc. Registers cultural life of Mexico.

872. Icaza, Claudia de (1911–1953 Dates of Jorge Negrete). *Cartas de amor y conflicto.* México: EDAMEX y Claudia de Icaza, 1993. 205pp. Letters. Period Covered: 1941–1952.

Artist of *música ranchera* and star in forty films, Jorge Negrete married Gloria Marín and together they made four films including *¡Ay, Jalisco, no te rajes¡* Present collection includes forty-seven letters to her mixed with appropriate biography. Postmarked New York, Havana, Lima, Buenos Aires, Montreal, Paris, Madrid, London, San Antonio, Reno, and Los Angeles, they incarnate his love for Marín and reaction in her absence. Except for occasional mention of place, films, and illness, few other items interrupt love expressed. Replete with photographs, biography/autobiography imitates screen life. Film as popular culture.

873. Iduarte, Andrés (1907–1984). *Don Pedro de Alba y su tiempo.* México: Editorial Cultura, 1963. 135pp. Memoirs. Period Covered: 1928–1960.

Ostensibly life of famous educator and writer, Pedro de Alba book compatible with genres of biography and autobiography. In affectionate recall of his *maestro* in preparatory school and university, Iduarte evokes memories of own student life and companions. In more optimistic tone, *Don Pedro* begins where *El mundo sonriente* ends.

874. Iduarte, Andrés (1907–1984). *Familia y patria.* México: Secretaría de Comunicaciones y Transportes, 1975. 209pp. Memoirs. Period Covered: 1910–1974.

Prolific autobiographer vacillates between memoir and essay in present collection. Accurate title summarizes family members and author's preoccupation with his Mexican identity. Democratic attitude manifests in constant depreciation of illustrious family tree, mainly on Foucher side. Even with two classic essays, "Yo soy indio" and "Sí, soy indio," *Familia y patria* inferior in both style and cohesion to *Un niño de la Revolución mexicana.*

875. Iduarte, Andrés (1907–1984). *Lunes de "El Nacional."* México: Secretaría de Educación Pública, 1975 (1970). 191pp. Memoirs. Period Covered: 1923–1970?

Journalist and Columbia University professor collects essays that reveal much autobi-

ography: life in New York, politics, and His-
panamericanism.

876. Iduarte, Andrés (1907–1984). *México
en la nostalgia.* México: Editorial Cultura,
1965. 112pp. Memoirs. Period Covered: 1910–
1964?

Author of *Un Niño en la Revolución
mexicana* offers intimate glimpses of childhood with parents and cousin. Early school
also has role. Autobiographical moments
published independently between 1935 and
1941 while author abroad representing government. Mixture of autobiography and
essay on meaning of Mexico hybridizes collection.

877. Iduarte, Andrés (1907–1984). *El
mundo sonriente.* México: Fondo de Cultura
Económica, 1968. 111pp. Memoirs. Period
Covered: 1923–1928.

Iduarte continues autobiography, *Un
niño en la Revolución mexicana.* In exception
to almost all of contemporaries, unafraid of
spelling out emotions as in adolescent love.
In several episodes he tells of Garrido Canabal, leftist from author's native state of
Tabasco. Law school and noteworthy students of his generation present. Frankness in
portrayal and talent as writer combine in one
of best autobiographies.

878. Iduarte, Andrés (1907–1984). *Un
niño en la Revolución mexicana.* México:
Obregón, 1954. 133pp. Trans: *Niño, Child of
the Mexican Revolution.* Translated and
adapted by James F. Shearer. New York:
Praeger, 1971. Autobiography Proper. Period
Covered: 1907?–1930?

One of best autobiographies. Brief chapters from childhood to early manhood with
believable change in character when subject
loses innocence. Adoration of Porfirio Díaz
gradually turns to acceptance and eventual
shame. Through child's eyes, Revolution a
negative force. Author with hindsight recaptures past, imposing adult ideas and judg-
ments on childhood. Major theme, growing
up in Mexico, developed through word pictures of family and author and education
in Villahermosa, Vera Cruz, Campeche,
and Mexico City. Father best drawn character.

879. Iduarte, Andrés (1907–1984). *Semblanzas.* México: Editorial Galache, 1984.
329pp. Memoirs. Period Covered: 1928–1973.

Much that Iduarte writes is autobiography. Collects forty-two biographical sketches
published in periodicals between 1961 and
1971. Humanist scholar and teacher of Spanish American literature at Columbia University, he knew many intellectual
contemporaries from the Americas. In
sketching them, he presents self and disperses
autobiographical data throughout text.

880. Iglesias, José María (1823–1891).
Autobiografía…. México: Antigua Imprenta
de E. Murguía, 1893. 78pp. Memoirs. Period
Covered: 1823–1885.

Covers genealogy and childhood in one
page and then begins career: councilman,
journalist, member of Junta de Crédito, secretary of Department of Interior, supreme
court judge, liberal in War of Reform, official
in ambulant government of Juárez, congressman, minister of gobernación, and vice president. Reveals accomplishment rather than
personality. Occasional excellent summary of
public personage such as Juárez or Lerdo de
Tejada. Bitter and resigned at end.

881. Imamura, Federico. *Casi un siglo de
recuerdos….* Monterrey: Ediciones, 1994.
225pp.

Only Japanese-Mexican to write autobiography. Success story of ambitious immigrant. Arriving in Mexico at age of twenty,
fell into bondage under another Japanese
immigrant. Imamura worked as farmer,
bread maker, restaurant owner, and finally as
pastry chef. Attack on Pearl Harbor mandated involuntary removal to Mexico City.
After war became owner of chain of pastry
shops in Monterrey. Educated in both Japanese and Spanish, he tells unique story with
frequent returns to Japan.

882. Ingersoll, Ralph. *In and under Mexico.* New York: Century, 1924. 235pp.

Mine expert exposes system as practiced
in 1920s. Foreigners automatically received
more benefits than natives; one strong entrepreneur could parcel laborers and receive
quota for each day they work. More intriguing, Ingersoll comments on local labor force:

"That was my introduction to the fact that all Mexicans are children and have to be treated accordingly" (p.45). Like Horton, Ingersoll understood co-patriots: "Pasts were easy to talk of and hard to prove. At once their early lives became intensely rosy; there was not the slightest doubt that they were all used to much better things, much more exclusive friends, and in general an entirely different (and higher) rung of the social ladder. They all wanted more than anything else to be back in that rarefied air they had left, and were obviously putting up with the others at Monte and making the best of a bad deal" (pp.138–139).

883. Isunza Aguirre, Agustín (1917?–?). *Ateneo de mis mocedades.* México: Ediciones Asociación Regional de Ateneístas del DF, 1959. 140pp. Memoirs. Period Covered: 1932–1937.

Nostalgic view of adolescent years in Ateneo Fuente School in Saltillo. Sympathetic portrayal of curriculum, professors, school chums, and author. History of Ateneo Fuente.

884. Iturbide, Agustín de (1783–1824). *The Memoirs....* Washington, DC: Documentary Publications, 1824. 157pp. Memoirs. Period Covered: 1821–1823.

Because of Antonio López de Santa Anna, disgruntled Emperor Iturbide went into exile in Italy in 1822. Composed memoirs or manifesto addressed to Mexicans. Locates self within political turmoil of period and bemoans ill preparedness of Mexicans for self-government. One of earliest memoirs of politician who set pattern for this type of document: elevating oneself and beliefs while deploring one's adversaries and their beliefs.

885. Iturbide, Eduardo (1878–1952). *Mi paso por la vida.* México: Editorial Cultura, 1941. 275pp. Memoirs. Period Covered: 1878–1940?

Lateral descendant of Emperor Iturbide recalls Porfiriato and circle that frequented Jockey Club. Briefly governor of Distrito Federal of México, he arranged Treaty of Teoloyucan for evacuation of Federal troops from Capital. Exiled to U.S., had contacts with major officials in Washington. Interesting memoirs, especially eventful escape to U.S. Final chapters comprised of polemics on 1930's Mexico.

886. Jackson, Everett Gee. *Burros and Paintbrushes: A Mexican Adventure.* College Station: Texas A&M University Press, 1985. 151pp.

Texan and artist spends four years in Mexico beginning in 1923. Guadalajara, Guanajuato, Mexico City, and Tehuántepec stopping places for acquaintance with Mexicans, assorted Gringos, and burros, and for painting landscapes and other subjects. Distills beauty of Mexico from point of view of artist: "To walk through those streets [Guanajuato] on a bright, sunny day was like hearing Chopin's music with your eyes" (p.50). Language and cultural clash pervasive. Delight for concern for *lo mexicano*.

887. Jackson, Everett Gee. *It's a Long Road to Comondú: Mexican Adventures since 1928.* College Station: Texas A&M University Press, 1987. 160pp.

This text continues the above but with frequent trips to Baja. Comondú, at southern end of Upper Baja, suggests that one can never know this state. Other excursions and revisits to Chapala and Palenque. Expresses more sensitivity to beauty of environment or Maya art than other Gringo travelers.

888. Jackson, Joseph Henry. *Mexican Interlude.* New York: Macmillan, 1936. 232pp.

Ideal travel writer. Process of journey more important than destination. Scenery and chance encounters occupy him as much as a cathedral. Neither gushing nor sneering, picks up much of Mexico in anecdote about courtesy or family. Diego Rivera, Frida Kahlo, and John Steinbeck mentioned.

889. Jacobs, Bárbara (1947–). *Vida con mi amigo.* Madrid: Santanilla, 1994. 105pp. Memoirs. Period Covered: 1960?–1993?

Mexican author dialogs with imaginary friend evoking titles and authors of books she has read. Although other aspects of culture occasionally impinge, books dominate and reveal Jacob's literate nature.

890. Jacobs, Donald Trent. *Primal Awareness*. Rochester, VT: Inner Traditions, 1998. 273pp.

Survivor of near-death experience in 1983 makes pilgrimage to Tarahumara lands in Copper Canyon of Chihuahua. In proximity to Indians as well as to nature, he discovers new vision or awareness of another reality. New consciousness, summed up in acronyms CAT-FAWN, suggests harmony with nature. Autobiography as he learns from shamans.

891. Jacques, Mary J. *Texan Ranch Life with Three Months through Mexico in a "Prairie Schooner."* London: Cox, 1894. 363pp.

Englishwoman Mary J. Jaques along with servant left England in 1889 to work as governess in Texas. Nineteen-month tenure allowed her to see Mexico. Entered at Piedras Negras and continued south to Monterrey, Saltillo, Bajío, and Mexico City. Jaques, with nineteenth century penchant to instruct, includes history, landscape, customs, and anecdotes in her book.

892. James, Neill. *Dust on My Heart: Petticoat Vagabond in Mexico*. New York: Scribner, 1946. 310pp.

Combines qualities of travel writer, anthropologist, and adventurer. Also studies Otomies of Orizabita, an Indian tribe central Mexico. Brief stay in Mexico City. James disabuses subtitle of book, *Petticoat Vagabond in Mexico*, with adventures. Jaunt through Sierras; foray in mountaineering detailed in chapter, "Inside Popocatepetl Volcano;" and mandatory reconnaissance of recently sprouted Paricutín.

893. Jamieson, Milton. *Journal and Notes of a Campaign in Mexico...*. Cincinnati: Ben Franklin Printing House, 1849. 105pp.

Ohio volunteers go to Mexico with twelve-month hitch. Sail down Mississippi, arrive in Vera Cruz, and then follow path of war to Jalapa, Cerro Gordo, Perote, Puebla, and Mexico City. Land and its customs attract author as much as battles: insects, hospitals, norther, executions, fandango, pulque, and Mexico City.

894. Jamieson, Tulitas; Evelyn Payne. *Tulitas of Torreón: Reminiscences of Life in Mexico*. El Paso: Texas Western Press, 1969. 146pp.

Jamieson shuttles between San Antonio, Texas, and Torreón in story of family comfortable on both sides of border. Daughter of Fred Wulff, prosperous engineer educated in Germany, Tulitas at home in three languages: German, Spanish, and English. Anecdotes about Torreón interest most, e.g., schools, local mores, servants, medicine, other foreigners and their support of Díaz, Revolution, and Pancho Villa.

895. Janssens, Victor Eugene Agustin (Dates?). *The Life and Adventures in California of Don Agustin Janssens, 1834–1856;* Ed. by William H. Ellison and Francis Price. Translated by Francis Price, San Marino, CA: Huntington Library, 1953. 165pp. Memoirs. Period Covered: 1822–1856.

Belgian immigrated to Mexico at eight years of age and at seventeen migrated to California with Híjar and Padres colony. Rancher and businessman, he lived under three governments, Mexico, California, and U.S. Interests for details on Indians, government, church, and agriculture in informal style. Document prompted by Hubert H. Bancroft.

896. Jara, Pepe (1928–). *El andariego*. México: Aguilar, León y Cal Editores, 1998. 373pp. Memoirs. Period Covered: 1928–1997.

Son of career military grew up in Nuevas Casas Grandes, Chihuahua. Music dominated life of popular singer and player of boleros. Exercised talents in Ciudad Juárez, Mexico City, Torreón, San Antonio (Texas), and Central America. Chapters on playing music in upper class bordellos. Member of trio, Los Pepes and Los Duendes, Jara married and with family. Friends of Chavela Vargas and Alvaro Carrillo. Good for popular culture.

897. Jaramillo, Rubén M. (1900?–1962). *Autobiografía*. México: Editorial Nuestro Tiempo, 1973. 167pp. Memoirs. Period Covered: 1914–1962.

Evangelical did not believe in writing in first person. Rural labor organizer and martyr from Morelos, he worked for both Cárdenas and Avila Camacho. Assassinated along with family in 1962, he reputedly left interrupted autobiography.

898. Jaurrieta, José María (Dates?). *Con Villa (1916–1920), memorias de campaña.* Xoco, México: Consejo Nacional para la Cultura y las Artes, 1997. 281pp. Memoirs. Period Covered: 1916–1920.

"A book that tells the truth cannot be bad" (p.23) begins memoirs of years close to Villa. Little known about Chihuahuense, who claims to have attended military academy in Chapultepec. Title pinpoints recalling Villa in anecdote. Superior military memoirs for writing and sustaining interest.

899. Jenks, Randolph; Beverly J. Powell. *Desert Quest: The Hunt for True Gold.* Grand Rapids, MI: Zondervan, 1991. 174pp.

Religion attracted Jenks to Sonora as indicated in memoirs. Author labels contact with state as "an experiment in practical Christianity" (p.9). Ostensibly searching for alternative route from family's gold mine in Sierra Madres of Sonora. Book allows Jenks to meet Indians of Sonora and include them in adventures. Accepts everyone and memoirs filled with anecdote, folklore, and nature.

900. Jiménez, Luz (1890?–1965). *De Porfirio Díaz a Zapata: memoria nahuatl de Milpa Alta.* Recopilación y traducción: Fernando Horcasitas. México: UNAM, 1974 (1968). 154pp. Trans: *Life and Death in Milpa Alta; A Nahuatl Chronicle of Díaz and Zapata.* Translated and ed. by Fernando Horcasitas. Oral Autobiography. Period Covered: 1905–1919.

Nahuatl-speaking woman first gives cultural life of Milpa Alta: education, food, Lord of Chalma, and family. In second part, she incorporates Revolution and village through invasions of Zapatistas and Carrancistas. Village profiled in more detail than narrator's personality.

901. Jiménez Moreno, Wigberto (1909–1985). "Entrevista a Wigberto Jiménez Moreno por Alicia Olivera." En *Caminos de antropología, entrevistas a cinco antropólogos/compiladores,* Jorge Durand y Luz Vázquez. México: Instituto Nacional Indigenista, 1990. Pp.63–129. Interview. Period Covered: 1909–1973.

Historian, ethnologist, and linguist makes preparation for these subject fields and notes some of Mexico's other luminaries in them. Paying debt to Alfonso Caso, he particularizes achievements of his generation.

902. Jiménez Rueda, Julio (1896–1960). *El México que yo sentí, 1896–1960: testimonios de un espectador de buena fe.* México: Consejo Nacional para la Cultura y las Artes, 2001. 257pp. Memoirs. Period Covered: 1909–1959.

Novelist, dramatist, professor, director of Escuela de Verano, and diplomat to Argentina and Uruguay approaches life chronologically and develops each career theme as separate chapter. Family and personal life, premature death of two children, for example, rarely impinge on professional life.

903. Jodorowsky, Alejandro. *La danza de la realidad: psicomagia y psicochamanismo.* Madrid: Ediciones Siruela, 2001. 437pp.

Interest in shamanism present in memoirs of Chilean Jew, resident in Mexico. He neglects both theater and film, his normal subjects, to explore shamanism.

904. Johnson, Fred E. *Hardrock: About Mining.* Tombstone, AZ: Tombstone Printers, 1991. 95pp.

Although first chapter locates young mining engineer in Philippines and Brazil, remainder of book takes place in Mexico. Involves him and spouse and their years 1960 to 1971 in Río Verde in San Luis Potosí. Maintains interest: history, relations with natives, mining for fluorspar, servants, illnesses, transportation, etc. "While we prospected for ore I was general manager (gerente), surveyor, mine superintendent, bookkeeper, geologist and cook" (p.39).

905. Johnson, Larry P. *Mexico by Touch: True Life Experiences of a Blind American Deejay.* N.p., 2003. 242pp.

Title captures uniqueness of Johnson's experience: blind disk jockey in Mexico. He lived in capital from 1957 to 1974, married a national, had children, received masters from Mexico City College (Universidad de las Américas), and worked as deejay for station XEL Radio Capital. More than other memoirist, he captures emotions of being foreign student in Mexico City. Includes interviews with Stevie Wonder and Paul Anka.

906. Johnston, Abraham Robinson; Marcellus Edwards Ball; Philip Gooch Ferguson; Ralph P. Bieber (eds). *Marching with the Army of the West, 1846–1848.* Glendale, CA: Clark, 1936. 368pp.

Abraham Robinson Johnston: March of army from Ft. Leavenworth, Kansas, to New Mexico. Armijo fled before them making an easy entry from Ratón to Santa Fe. General declared himself governor. Marcellus Ball Edwards: His companion piece to above tells of his march from Missouri to New Mexico (Ratón, Las Vegas, Santa Fe, Albuquerque, Socorro) and to Chihuahua City under Col. Alexander Doniphan. His adventure-filled memoirs read like novel: Kearney's speech to New Mexicans, description of Santa Fe, feats of horsemanship, landscape, flora, fauna, and Mexican customs. Philip Gooch Ferguson: Ferguson goes from Missouri to Las Vegas, Santa Fe, Albuqueruqe, El Paso, and Chihuahua City. He is more into arts than other two authors: books, leisure time, and Thespians. On his sojourn he meets Kit Carson and Governor Armijo. Some Mexican customs and details of fandango.

907. Jones, Mother. *Autobiography of Mother Jones.* New York: Arno, 1969 (1925). 242pp.

Author testifies in court about Mexico. Central point is arrest and imprisonment of Manuel Sarabia in Douglas, Arizona. Criticizes U.S. for helping President Díaz murder agitator.

908. Jones, Mother; Edward M. Steel. *The Correspondence of Mother Jones.* University of Pittsburgh Press, 1985. 360pp.

Has themes similar to above entry for years, 1911–1921: visit to imprisoned Flores Magón, doubt about Mexican anarchists, efforts to free Mexican agitators imprisoned in U.S., and denouncement of fanaticism.

909. Jones Garay, Lupita (1967–). *Palabras de reina.* México: Planeta, 1993. 183pp. Memoirs. Period Covered: 1986–1991.

Achieved international success in beauty contests: Miss Baja California, La Señorita México in 1990, and finally first Mexican to be Miss Universo (1991). Memoirs and photos collaborate to form insider's perspective on competitive world of beauty contests. Advises aspirants of select sorority; denounces Comité Señorita México for its indifferent and even hostile treatment of beauty winners; and emphasizes supportive family. Much for popular culture.

910. Jordan, Ora Scally. *Looking Back: A Collection of Memories from the Diaries....* Riverside, CA: The Author, 1984. 226pp.

Matzatlán more eloquently mentioned in autobiography than any other Sinaloa city. Topolobampo has unique history in above title. Young married woman member of Owens Southwestern Utopia Colony, a community based on cooperation rather than socialism or capitalism. Non-judgmental diary filled with activities of women's lives including work and recreation. Lacking interest in Mexico or its cultures, Americans lived in insulated community. Interruptions by encroaching Revolution or presence of ships in harbor.

911. Juana Inés de la Cruz, Sister (1651– 1695). *The Answer=La respuesta.* New York: Feminist Press at the City of New York, 1994 (1700). 96pp. Letters. Period Covered: 1654–1691.

Oldest feminist document of Americas in which Sor Juana tells her story and with baroque language and logic defends women's right to think for selves. Supreme irony/sarcasm in nun's pose of humility. Letter provoked by reprimand from Archbishop Aguiar y Seijas for her attack on Antonio Vieira, intellectual showpiece of Jesuit Order, for his disquisition on Christ's greatest gift to humanity.

912. Juárez, Benito (1806–1872). *Apuntes para mis hijos: datos autobiográficos del benemérito de las Américas....* México: Editorial Cronos, 1955. 174pp. Memoirs. Period Covered: 1806–1864.

Most personal of pages concern his youth, early education, and study for legal profession. Rest deals with political life. Later entries factual accounts with little assessment.

913. Juárez, Benito (1806–1872). *Correspondencia Juárez-Santacilia 1858–1867.* México: Secretaría de Marina, 1972. 425pp. Letters. Period Covered: 1858–1867.

Mainly letters of official nature between Juárez and son-in-law and secretary, Pedro Santacilia. Written during decade of Intervention, they show affairs of state but occasionally compassionate family man emerges. Should be used in conjunction with *Apuntes para mis hijos.* Juárez's wife has collection of nineteen letters published in *Margarita Maza de Juárez* (1972). Written between July 8, 1862, and June 15, 1866, they complement letters he wrote to her when he fled north during French Intervention. Her letters filled with love and concern for Juárez and some details of daily life.

914. Junco, Alfonso (1896–1975). *Los ojos viajeros.* México: Editorial Jus, 1951. 223pp. Memoirs. Period Covered: 1938–1950.

Historian, poet, journalist, director of Catholic-oriented journal *Abside* also belonged to la Academia de la Lengua. Devout Catholic traveled to Spain in 1950 for special holy year for Virgin of Guadalupe. Attending masses and visiting shrines, he recalls medieval pilgrim. Other aspects of Spanish culture attract him. Admiration for dictator Francisco Franco. First part refers to pilgrimages to other parts of Europe and to Central America.

915. Junco, Alfonso (1896–1975). *Un poeta de casa.* México: Finisterre, 1968. 44pp. Memoirs. Period Covered: 1897–1948.

Initiated into Mexican Academy of Language in 1950, he presented self through above speech. Poet at home refers to Junco's father, Celedonio Junco de la Vega, merchant/banker and also versifier. Several pages express son's delight in father's talent and influence.

916. Junco, Alfonso (1896–1975). *Tiempo de alas.* México: Editorial Jus, 1973. 277pp. Memoirs. Period Covered: 1947–1971.

Monterrey-born poet traveled to Peru, Ecuador, Venezuela, Argentina, Spain, and other parts of Europe as well as points within own country. As published author and member of Academia Mexicana de la Lengua, he had access to many literati. Two themes stand out: devout Catholicism and fervor for *hispanidad,* or positive characteristics of all Spanish-speaking people.

917. Kahan, Ari. *Wulf Kahan, My Father.* Mexico: Imprebal, 1996. 283pp.

Ari Kahan collects multiple voices of family and friends of personality in title. Lithuanian and Jewish, Wulf arrived in Mexico in 1926. His father Szewel Kahan started used car parts business that Wulf expanded into truck and car dealership and became active in AMDA (Asociación Mexicana de Distribuidores de Automotores). Shows family and business success of immigrant, who occasionally speaks for self through remembered conversations.

918. Kahlo, Frida (1907–1954). *El diario de Frida Kahlo: un íntimo autorretrato.* Madrid: Debate, 1995. 296pp. Trans: *Diary of Frida Kahlo: An Intimate Self-Portrait.* New York: Abrams, 1995. Diary. Period Covered: 1940?–1954.

Colored facsimile of diary with writing, drawings, and paintings. Sarah Lowe glossed and translated Spanish text and wrote interpretive essay in English version. Meaning inaccessible because poetic and at times incoherent entries originate from subconscious and not from verifiable reality. Understanding of artist useless without present book. Carlos Fuentes's introductory essay in English locates Kahlo within Mexican milieu.

919. Kahlo, Frida (1907–1954). *Escrituras.* México: UNAM, 1999. 316pp. Letters. Period Covered: 1922–1946.

Largest collection so far of documents created by Kahlo. Alejandro Gómez Arias, Leo Eloesser, Bertram and Ella Wolfe, Nikolas Muray, and Diego Rivera are her favorite correspondents. She presents self better here than in all of secondary works based on her life. In love with Gómez Arias, desperate for money, mother-lover to Diego, confidante of Ella Wolfe, and confused and angered by Breton coterie, Kahlo exhibits many moods. Excellent editing.

920. Kahlo, Frida (1907–1954). *The Letters of Frida Kahlo: cartas apasionadas/selected and edited by Martha Zamora.* San Francisco: Chronicle Books, 1995. 159pp. Letters. Period Covered: 1924–1948.

Legend becomes more human in letters to Alejandro Gómez Arias, Isabel Campos, Leo Eloesser, Ella Wolf, Diego Rivera, Carlos Chávez, Lucienne Bloch, Nikolas Muray, Emmy Lou Packard, and Miguel Alemán. Suffering, concern for Diego, painting, friendship and feelings towards others dominate as well as humor. Essential reading for details about Rivera. Pleas to President Alemán to save Diego's Del Prado mural.

921. Kalmar, Stephen S. *Goodby Vienna!* San Francisco, CA: Strawberry Hill, 1987. 251pp.

Austrian-born author refugeed in Mexico from 1940 to 1948, where he interacted with other Jews and also German exiles. Details business ventures: honey, cigarette lighters, rosaries, export of curios, export of cut steel, dead flies for fishing, etc.

922. Kamstra, Jerry. *Weed: Adventures of a Dope Smuggler.* New York: Harper & Row, 1974. 267pp.

Autobiography, Mexican culture, and foremost, an exposé of cultivation, processing, and marketing of marijuana, combine in *Weed*. Kamstra, with contract from *Life* magazine to film plant in Mexico, had motive for marijuana run and research opportunity for book. Adventure, landscape, gamut of Mexicans in Sierras and Guerrero, and author's detours from weed to peculiarities of Mexicans. Over 200 natural hallucinogens bless or curse Mexico.

923. Keiffer, Elisabeth. *Year in the Sun.* Indianpolis: Bobbs-Merrill, 1956. 175pp.

Writer, painter-husband, and infant son abandon tense New York City to spend year in Cuautla, Morelos. Knowing no Spanish, they learn as they live by renting house and hiring servants. Memoir focuses on antics of natives, procession of unreliable illiterates who steal but call it borrowing. Inexpensive but primitive and unsatisfactory life style results.

924. Kelley, Francis Clement. *The Bishop Jots It Down: An Autobiographical Strain on Memories.* New York: Harper, 1939. 333pp.

Two chapters relate to Mexico: school for exiled seminarians in Castroville, Texas, persecution of church by government, and heroic actions of Mexican hierarchy. Criticizes Woodrow Wilson and William Jennings Bryan for indifference to persecution. Kelley author of *Blood-drenched Altars: Mexican Study and Comments* (1935).

925. Kelley, Jane Holden (Dates?). *Yaqui Women: Contemporay Life Histories.* Lincoln: University of Nebraska Press, 1978. 265pp. Trans: *Mujeres yaquis: cuatro biografías contemporáneas.* Spanish edition by Carlos Valdés. México: Fondo de Cultura Económica, 1982. Oral Autobiography. Period Covered: 1880–1920.

Kelley, collaborating with Rosalio Moisés on *Tall Candle*, composed oral autobiographies of four Yaqui women: Dominga Tava, Chepa Moreno, Dominga Ramírez, and Antonia Valenzuela. Technically biographies because of third person narration, these in reality differ little from *I* narratives. Kelley balances Yaqui culture/history with individual personality. First 113 pages discuss anthropological format and technique.

926. Kendall, George Wilkins; Lawrence Delbert Cress. *Dispatches from the Mexican War.* Norman: University of Oklahoma Press, 1999. 448pp.

Author was correspondent for New Orleans *Picayune* and wrote more than 200 dispatches from Mexico. He also pioneered getting news rapidly from Mexico to New Orleans. War itinerary was this: Matamoros, Reynosa, Camargo, Monterrey, Tampico, Veracruz, Cerro Gordo, Jalapa, Puebla, and Mexico City. More than military man, Kendall had flexibility of movement, incentive for news, and journalist's need to be constantly interesting. Anecdotes, climate, landscape, anti–Mexican sentiments, patriotism, and gossip characterize dispatches. At times vividness interrupted by Kendall's writing on events he hasn't witnessed.

927. Kenly, John Reese. *Memoirs of a Maryland Volunteer. War with Mexico, in the years 1846–7–8.* Philadelphia: Lippincott, 1873. 521pp.

Kenly proceeded to Matamoros, Camargo, Monterrey, Monte Morelos, Victoria, and Tampico. In chain of conquests, he writes of climate, landscape, transportation, and battles. Enlistment expired, he returned to Maryland and recruited volunteers to enter through Vera Cruz. Remained in army of occupation until June of 1848. Officer Kenly knew and admired Gen. Taylor and visited with Santa Anna at his hacienda. Much on Mexico and author composes in more leisurely fashion than most memoirists of this war.

928. Kennedy, Diana. *My Mexico: A Culinary Odyssey with More than 500 Recipes.* New York: Clarkson Potter, 1998. 550pp.

Mixes food and autobiography. British-born Diana Kennedy has lived in Mexico since 1957 and authored six cookbooks. Leads food tour of Mexican states, revealing kitchen secrets and own life.

929. Kennedy, Diana. *Recipes from the Regional Cooks of Mexico.* New York: Harper, 1978. 288pp.

Earlier same author wrote above title. Kennedy confesses that *Cusines of Mexico* did not include regional areas. "This is therefore...a collection of completely new recipes gathered during five years of wandering and learning—updating my palatte so to speak" (p.1). Gives recipes from regions far from capital. Ingredients, advice, and autobiography.

930. King, Carole Call (1900–1993 Dates of Anson B. Call). *A Good, Long Life: The Autobiography of Anson B. Call, Jr., 1900–1993.* N.p.: The Author, 1994. 270pp. Oral Autobiography. Period Covered: 1900–1923.

First twenty-three years spent in Mexico has value for this bibliography. Born in Colonia Dublán, Chihuahua, Call gives detailed accounts of Mormon Mexico: daily life, first exodus (1912), return to Dublán, second exodus (1914), bishop father, Villa in Dublán, Pershing in Dublán, high school at Juárez Academy, and missionary work in Mexico.

931. King, Rosa E. *Tempest over Mexico: A Personal Chronicle.* Boston: Little, Brown, 1935. 319pp.

Spunky woman had business in Cuernavaca. English, widow and mother of two, Mrs. King moved there in 1910. From her tearoom and gift shop, she became owner of Bella Vista Hotel. Success assured until Revolution in 1910 as her beloved Cuernavaca in state of Morelos was focal point of marauding Zapatistas from neighboring Anenecuilco.

932. Kingdon, Maud Kenyon. *From Out the Dark Shadows.* San Diego: Frye & Smith, 1925. 233pp.

American Kingdon accompanied husband to Sonora, where he was superintendent of Cananea mine. He rejected miners' strike demands in 1914 and jeopardized his and spouse's lives. Revolution, larger context for episode, told from regional point of view through inclusion of Maytorena, Calles, Carranza, and Villa. Climax of memoirs when author meets Villa.

933. Kino, Eusebio Francisco; Ernest J. Burrus. *Kino Reports to Headquarters: Correspondence from New Spain to Rome.* Rome: Institutum Historicum Societatis Jesu, 1954. 135pp.

Jesuit Eusebio Francisco Kino arrived in New Spain in 1681, and in 1683 made expedition to Californias and helped settle region. Letters run from 1683 to 1704 and suggest versatility of author: priest, missionary, geographer, farmer, ethnologist, economist, and historian. Letters still very readable today.

934. Kirkham, Ralph W. *The Mexican War Journal and Letters....* College Station: Texas A&M University Press, 1991. 141pp.

Graduate of West Point, he takes note of his surroundings, visits churches, attends Episcopal services, and writes profusely to his wife. His prolonged stay in Puebla, May 19 to August 6, 1847, gives him time to know city. Following this, he moves to Mexico City, participates in battles, and leaves there in 1848. One of few officers who noted Mexico City's cultural institutions.

935. Kirkham, Stanton Davis. *Mexican Trails: A Record of Travel in Mexico, 1904–7....* New York: Putnam, 1909. 293pp.

Known sites described by self-styled lotus-eater. Ignoring poverty and social injustice, pursues mood and beauty in Mexico ready to explode under enforced calm of Porfiriato. Notes efficacy of *rurales* who shoot criminals on sight but focuses on buildings and Indians. Marked contrast with Turner's *Barbarous Mexico.*

936. Kitchel, Jeanine Lee. *Where the Sky Is Born: Living in the Land of the Maya.* Haiku, HI: Enchanted Island, 2004. 217pp.

One of most recent books on living in Mexico and without condescension towards natives. Author and spouse leave California in 1985 and build house in Puerto Morelos, Quintana Roo. Focuses on problems of acquiring land and building to withstand hurricanes but always with affection for Mexico. Kitchel notes accumulation of books relating to Yucatan.

937. Knab, Timothy J. *Mad Jesus: The Final Testament of a Huichol Messiah from Northwest Mexico.* Albuquerque: University of New Mexico Press, 2004. 279pp. Oral Autobiography. Period Covered: 1970–2000?

Dual autobiography. Story of Mad Jesus, a Huichole Shaman, whose conveyed life often parallels the Christian Jesus. Peyote-consuming Indian leader combines pre–Columbian and Christian elements in story. A teacher and leader with a following, he died violently at hands of police thirty years after anthropologist author met him. Knab's own story involves meeting Jesus, studying Huichole cosmology, interviewing messiah, and thirty years later, searching for him. Knab's methodology in own words: "...I have constructed a narrative using many different sources: tapes, interviews, field notes, and documents, as well as techniques from fiction, biography, history and travel writing" (p.4). Contrastive document to that of Guiteras Holmes (q.v.).

938. Knab, Timothy J. *A War of Witches: Journey into the Underworld of the Contemporary Aztecs.* San Francisco: Harper, 1995, 224pp.

Anthropologist journeys into Aztec cosmology from 1974 to 1977 in state of Puebla. Using Nahuatl rather than Spanish when researching Aztec world, he asserts: "Here, on the fringes of the old empire, the ancient religion of the Aztecs was still alive. It had not been eradicated by the Conquest" (p.14). For five years he interviewed shamans, witches, and curanderos and in his dreams even visited Tlalocan, Aztec underworld.

939. Kochi, Paul (1889–?). *Imin no aiwa= An Immigrant's Sorrowful Tale.* Los Angeles, 1978. 53pp. Memoirs. Period Covered: 1912–1918.

Okinawa-born knew he could not enter U.S. legally. In 1917, he landed in Salina Cruz, Mexico, made way to U.S. border, and crossed through Calexico in 1918. Tale of disaster of traipsing one year through Mexico and surviving boat accident unique. Pauses to note kindness of Mexicans who befriended him.

940. Kollonitz, Paula Grafin; Joseph Earle Ollivant. *The Court of Mexico.* London: Saunders Otley, 1868. 303pp.

Kollonitz, part of entourage of Empress Carlota, perfected travel writing, i.e., she combined travel with autobiography. After lady-in-waiting's account of voyage to Mexico, landing at Vera Cruz, and journeying to Mexico City, reader knows acerbic and intelligent woman who spent five months in Mexico in 1864. Comments on conditions and character wound Mexican sensibilities even today.

941. Komes Peres, Maruch (Dates?). *Ta jlok 'ta chobtik ta k' u' Il. Maruch Komes Peres=Bordando milpas: un testimonio de María Gómez Pérez*; recopilado, redactado y traducido por Diana Rus y Xalink Guzmán. San Cristóbal de las Casas, CHP: Taller Tzotzil, INAREMAC, 1990. 34pp. Oral Autobiography. Period Covered: ?–1990.

From Los Altos de Chiapas, Chamula weaver María in native Tzotzil describes process from raising sheep to preparing wool. History of Tzotziles and family relations emerges in bilingual account.

942. Koons, Carolyn A. *Tony, Our Journey Together.* San Francisco: Harper, 1984. 214pp.

Koons adopts nine-year-old boy from Mexicali prison. She describes two struggles: her efforts to bring Tony to U.S. and her program for facilitating his assimilation.

943. Kraig, Bruce; Dudley Nieto.
Cuisines of Hidden Mexico: A Culinary Journey to Guerrero and Michoacán. New York: Wiley, ca.1996. 278pp.

Two states provide culinary challenge for authors at work on a documentary, *Hidden Mexico.* Travel, history, anthropology, food, recipes, and autobiography in all six chapters. Acapulco, Taxco, Pátzcuaro, and Uruápan main sites on journey that starts in Mexican Chicago.

944. Krauze, Ethel (1954–). *De cuerpo entero: Ethel Krauze.* México: Ediciones Corunda, 1990. 57pp. Memoirs. Period Covered: 1910?–1990.

In style not unlike Margo Glanz in *Genealogías,* Krauze traces immediate Jewish ancestry from czarist Russia to Mexico. In Yiddish-Spanish environment, young writer introduces family. Main love for María, Indian-Mexican Catholic maid. Krauze's resentment of heritage evident in attitude towards Jewish school she attended involuntarily.

945. Krauze, Ethel (1954–?); Socorro Arce; Rocío Aceves. *Lo lúdico, lo visceral, en su imaginería: entrevista con Ethel Krauze.* Universidad de Colima, 2000. 111pp. Interview. Period Covered: 1963–1996.

Novelist, short story writer, poet, and autobiographer focuses on her writings, her inspiration, and her methodology in creation. Some space on creation of women characters and on Jewish women writers of Mexico. Education, childhood, family, feminism, and Jewish background other themes.

946. Krauze, Helen (1928–). *Viajera que vas….* México: Editorial Diana, 1998. 276pp. Memoirs. Period Covered: 1935–1997.

Polish-born journalist Helen Kleimbort de Krauze immigrated to Mexico at young age. Little here of early years; for book consists of travel essays on Mexico, U.S., Canada, South America, Europe, USSR, and East (Israel, Japan, Honk Kong, Thailand, and India). Description and interviews.

947. Krusensterna, Ken. *Terror in Mexico: The Kidnapping of Ken Krusensterna.* Phoenix: Stand International, 2000. 222pp.

Victim relates violence towards American CEO of international transportation corporation who was held hostage and mistreated in Reynosa. Efforts of closely-knit family facilitated freedom as well as discovery that Mexican partner collusive in 1990's kidnapping.

948. Krutch, Joseph Wood. *The Forgotten Peninsula: A Naturalist in Baja California.* New York: Sloane, 1961. 277pp.

Krutch attempts to essence Baja after ten visits. Road transportation, mansions, name lore, plants and unique boojum (tree named for make-believe creature in Lewis Carroll), early Jesuits, whales, and villages. Mixes biographies of Baja personalities with history and other materials and includes autobiography. Best writing and most unique information in chapter "Plants, queer, queerer and queerest." Nature is Krutch's forte and inspires his writing.

949. Labarthe R., María de la Cruz (1929 Birth of Ysidro García) *Notas sobre el proceso de industrialización de León: autobiografía de un obrero del calzado.* León, GUA: Colegio del Bajío, 1985. 53 leaves. Oral Autobiography. Period Covered: 1929–1980.

"La intención original…fue la de publicar UN proceso industrial al tiempo que manifiesta la percepción personal de un obrero…" (p.3): Labarthe gives context and life. García, in own testimony as shoemaker, talks of apprenticeship, work in factory, leader of union, participation in cooperative, and efforts to be independent shoemaker and seller.

950. Lagos de Minvielle, Socorro (1950?–). *Memorias de Socorrito.* México: Offset Setenta, 1980. 53pp. Memoirs. Period Covered: 1950–1980?

From mid to late twentieth century, document difficult to date. From wealthy influential family, Socorro enjoyed privileges of education and travel. Married, had children, and used her degree in economics. Frustration as career woman. Realistic appraisal of bureaucracy, family relationships, and friendships.

951. Laidley, Theodore; James M. McCaffrey. *Surrounded by Dangers of All Kinds: The Mexican War Letters of Lieutenant Theodore Laidley.* Denton: University of North Texas Press, 1997. 185pp.

Twenty-three letters dating from August 23, 1845, to May 13, 1848, comprise collection and are postmarked Brazos San Iago, Tampico, Vera Cruz, Pass of Sierra Gordo (Cerro Gordo), Jalapa, Perote, Puebla, and Mexico City. Longest stays were Puebla, seven months; and Mexico City, five months. West Point graduate Laidley writes letters to his father and expresses emotions, illnesses, conflicts of officers, and customs of Mexicans. Churches attracted him. Well edited with explanatory texts before and after.

952. Lamarque, Libertad. *Libertad Lamarque.* Buenos Aires: Vergara, 1986. 351pp.

Ninety-three-year-old Lamarque died in 2001. Tango singer and actress lived in Mexico from 1946 to 1982, when she retired to her native Argentina. In Mexico, a second home for her, she made forty-one films.

953. Lamas Guzmán, Félix (Dates?). *Memorias de Estanzuela: risas, rezos y cánicas.* Colotlán: Universidad de Guadalajara, 2002. 179pp. Memoirs. Period Covered: 1960s?

One of most detailed accounts of family life and growing up in a village in Jalisco, Estanzuela. Context superior to development of personality as author inventories ruralness: trucks and roads, grocery store, fireworks, baker, farm animals, children, game, harvest, school, Xmas, and shepherding. Sociological value.

954. Lamb, Dana Storrs; Ginger Lamb. *Quest for the Lost City.* New York: Harper, 1951. 340pp.

Quest for the Lost City is quest for self achieved through survival skills. Young couple by foot, mule, and Model T Ford end up in Chiapas. With little knowledge of terrain and few tools, they pass excruciating time in jungle. Climax of insect-ridden trip is lost city, which they named Lasch-tu-Nich, Place of Carved Stones (probably Chiapas).

955. Landeta, Matilde (1913–1999); **Julianne Burton-Carvajal; Mauricio**

Montiel Figueiras; Gustavo García. *Matilde Landeta, hija de la revolución.* México: Conaculta, 2002. 169pp. Interviews. Period Covered: 1913–1997.

One of few Mexican women directors tells story: birth into aristocratic family, marriage, and divorce, but mainly her career in production of films. As director, she has three commercial movies to her credit, *Lola Casanova* (1948), *La Negra Angustias* (1949), and *Trotacalles* (1951).

956. Lane, Walter P. *The Adventures and Recollections of General Walter P. Lane, a San Jacinto Veteran....* Austin, TX: Jenkins, 1970? 180pp.

Lane fought in War for Texas Independence. Yet larger portion of book on Mexican-American War. One sentence suggests tone, "Twenty Mexicans were round me when I rose, but it so surprised them to see a dead boy rise..." (p.13). Apparently he led Rangers into Mexico and acted as an independent force during this war. He was at Camargo, Monterrey, and did reconnaissance in San Luis Potosi. Adventure of capturing soldier/ brigand Juan Flores. Lane also challenged orders of Gen. Zachary Taylor. Reads more like dime novel than autobiography.

957. Lara. J. Andres (1895–?). *Prisonero de callistas y cristeros.* México: Editorial Jus, 1954. 117pp. Memoirs. Period Covered: 1926–1929?

Adventures of Jesuit priest stationed at Mission Tarahumara during *Cristero* rebellion. Captured, harassed, and freed first by Callistas, Lara sent on mission to convince Bajío *Cristeros* of superior strength of government forces. Suffers almost same fate with *Cristeros* as with Callistas.

958. Lara, Jorge Zadik (1889–1959 Dates of Alfonso Reyes). *La polémica.* México: Universidad Autónoma Metropolitana, 1984. 169pp. Letters. Period Covered: 1922–1957.

Controversy on what literature should be and its esthetics, e.g., use of local color in Mexico. Reyes praises and encourages his contemporary, Mayanist and literary critic, Ermilo Abreu Gómez. Sustaining various ideas about literature, Reyes is personable correspondent in letters postmarked Spain, Mexico, France, Brazil, and Argentina.

959. Lara Zavala, Hernán (1946–).
Equipaje de mano. Toluca: Instituto Mexiaquense de Cultura, 1995. 47pp. Memoirs. Period Covered: 1994?

Expert on British literature attended conference on this topic at Cambridge. Accommodations, international colleagues, and papers presented comprise themes of book. Mentions Salman Rushdie, P.D. James, and Terry Eagleton among others.

960. Lara Zavala, Hernán (1946–). *Erotismo de hilo fino: entrevista con Hernán Lara Zavala.* Universidad de Colima, 1990. 111pp. Interview. Period Covered: 1946–1997.

Writer studied engineering but switched to humanities and British literature as graduate student. Has published short stories, essays, and novel. Interview encompasses following: schooling, travel, women and subtle sexuality as suggested by title, literary influence, generation of '68, and authors known personally and through publications.

961. Larbaud, Valery (1881–1957 Dates of Reyes). *Correspondance, 1923–1952: Valery Larbaud, Alfonso Reyes: avant-propos de Marcel Bataillon,* introd. et notes de Paulette Patout. Paris: Didier, 1972. 328pp. Letters. Period Covered: 1923–1952.

Twenty-six letters of Alfonso Reyes resulted from friendship with Valery Larbaud, French novelist and creator of South American millionaire traveling in Europe. Reyes's love of literary themes and delight in friendship emerge.

962. Larralde, Elsa (Dates?). *My House Is Yours.* Philadelphia: Lippincott, 1949. 250pp. Memoirs. Period Covered: 1940s.

Nuevo León born woman, recovering from divorce, retires to tranquility of Acapantzingo, village near Cuernavaca. Purchase of house and subsequent remodeling and staffing puts her in contact with array of eccentric villagers. Gossip about Maximilian's Indian mistress and illegitimate son.

963. Lasater, Annette Nixon; Watt M. Casey, Jr. *Two to Mexico.* San Angelo, TX: The Author, 1979. 180pp.

Adventurous American couple decides to ranch in Coahuila. Know little Spanish;

know little about Mexican culture. Ideal scene for humor. Three chapters stand out for understanding contrasting cultures: "Doing Business—Their Way," "Living under 'The System,'" and "Living with 'The System.'"

964. Lawrence, D.H. *The Letters of D.H. Lawrence.* Ed. by James T. Boulton. New York: Cambridge University Press, 1979– 2000. 8 v.

Letters (V.4, 1921–1924) (1987) has a block of correspondence from March 24 to November 20, 1923. Mainly from Lake Chapala but also Mexican City, Navojoa, Mazatlán, Tepic, and Guadalajara, they show excitement of Mexico, constant presence of Indian, and work on *The Plumed Serpent* (1925). Vol 5, 1924–1927 of same series contains Oaxaca period from October 1924 to March 1925. In these letters, he mentions settling in Oaxaca, Zelia Nuttall, Edward Weston, illnesses, violence of post-revolutionary years, essays submitted to *Vanity Fair* and later anthologized in *Mornings in Mexico* (1927), and work on novel *The Plumed Serpent.*

965. Lazcano Ochoa, Manuel (1912–). *Una vida en la vida sinaloense.* Culiacán: Tallares Gráficos de la Occidente, 1992. 255pp. Memoirs. Period Covered: 1912–1990.

Constant politician focuses on political life in Sinaloa and career: attorney general, secretary of state, state senator, leader of state legislature, president of PRI in Sinaloa, and national committeeman from states of Aguascalientes and Colima. Politics at state level emerges. Sociological value in racism towards Greeks and Chinese.

966. Lazo, Rina; Abel Santiago. *Rina Lazo, sabiduría de manos: conversaciones con Abel Santiago.* Oaxaca: Instituto Oaxaqueño de las Culturas, 1998. 193pp.

Guatemalan painter and etcher learned mural art from Diego Rivera and aided in Hotel del Prado murals. Friend and colleague of Frida Kahlo.

967. Leal, Felícitos (1918–1989 Dates of Godoy). *Emma Godoy en vivo.* México: Editorial Jus, 1990. 241pp. Oral Autobiography. Period Covered: 1956?–1988?

Mainly poet but also novelist, Godoy concerns self with values and existential thoughts rather than concrete reality. Leal, conscientious as autobiographer of another, explains use of Godoy's voice, which carries narration. Interrogator and recorder, Leal taped last decade of conversation. Materials cohere in associational form.

968. Leal, Luis (1907–?). *Don Luis Leal: una vida y dos culturas.* Tempe, AZ: Bilingual Press, 1998. 153pp. Interview. Period Covered: 1907–1998.

Víctor Fuentes interviews Luis Leal, Mexican-born university professor and literary critic. From Linares, Nuevo León, he completed high school, college, and advanced degrees in U.S. Interview crisscrosses Mexico and U.S. as he divulges life and opinions. Critic of both Mexican and Mexican-American literature, he comments on ties between two countries.

969. Lechuga Chapa, Celso (1894–1991). *Memorias de Celso Lechuga Chapa.* Juárez: Puentelibre, 1995. 101pp. Memoirs. Period Covered: 1894–1984.

Railroad man from Chihuahua late in life completed memoirs and arranged them into nine chronological segments from early years to retirement. Poor and independent, he loved railroad and wrote dispassionately on Revolution. Family problems also impinge on autobiography. Notes and bibliography.

970. Leduc, Renato (1897–1986). *Cuando éramos menos.* México: Cal y Arena, 1989. 169pp. Memoirs. Period Covered: 1897–1914.

Journalist, telegrapher, and Villista tells of youth. Antidote to nostalgic evocation of Porfiriato, Leduc recounts schooling, early work, Revolution, friendships, and love affairs. Readable autobiography.

971. Lee Mancilla, Manuel (1921–?); **Maricela González Félix**. *Viaje al corazón de la península….* Mexicali: Instituto de Cultura de Baja California, 2000. 66pp. Oral Autobiography. Period Covered: 1910–1995.

Son of Chinese immigrant and Mexican woman incorporates both China and Mexico in testimony. Life story and sociology mix as he narrates father's immigration from China

to Baja, dynamics of transplanted Chinese colony, struggle for survival in agriculture and business, and local prejudice against Chinese. Mexicali, Tecate, and Vizcaíno locales for life story.

972. Lemus Olvera, Rafael (1955–). *Cuando las puertas se abren.* México: Editorial Oasis, 1984. 63pp. Memoirs. Period Covered: 1983.

Journalism student brutally arrested by Dirección de Investigaciones para la Prevención de la Delincuencia (DIPD). Accused of plotting to kidnap but with no substantiating evidence, author in detention for six days in 1983.

973. Leñero, Vicente (1933–). *De cuerpo entero: Vicente Leñero.* México: Ediciones Corunda, 1992. 56pp. Memoirs. Period Covered: 1957–1991.

Scenes from the Life of a Writer subtitles autobiography of dramatist. With humor he evokes early experiences at writing, motive behind drama *Los albañiles,* and friendship with Manuel Puig. Debunks sainthood of Juan José Arreola, Juan Rulfo, and Gabriel García Márquez. Notes hierarchy among writers in relation to literary agent Carmen Barcells.

974. Leñero, Vicente (1933–). *Lotería: retratos de compinches.* México: Mortiz, 1995. 135pp. Memoirs. Period Covered: 1960?–1990?

In sixth autobiographical effort since 1967, dramatist diffuses life through sketches of intellectuals. Half of eighteen entries reveal moments in professional life. Seven Mexicans and two foreigners, writers, publishers, and film/theater directors act as foils to explicate personality: Elías Nandino, Joaquín Diéz-Canedo, Ignacio Retes, Julio Scherer García, María Elvira Bermúdez, José Estrada, José Agustín, Manuel Puig, and Carmen Barcells.

975. Leñero, Vicente (1933–). *Vicente Leñero.* Azcapotzalco, DF: Universidad Autónoma Metropolitana, 1985. 28pp. Interview. Period Covered: ?–1984.

As part of format of series, he answers questions relating to his art. Speaks about

Father Morelos, his Catholicism, most famous work *Los albañiles*, and career as journalist.

976. Leñero, Vicente (1933–). *Vicente Leñero*. México: Empresas Editoriales, 1967. 62pp. Autobiographical Essay. Period Covered: 1967.

Short story writer, novelist, and playwright, renders unique account. Traditionally depicted life: childhood, family, and intellectual influences subordinated to detailed struggle to write essay. Combats verbally with relentless alter ego that sneers at his creations.

977. Leñero, Vicente (1933–). *Vivir del teatro*. México: Mortiz, 1982. 255pp. Memoirs. Period Covered: 1969–1981.

Playwright notes experiences in theater. Behind-the-scenes view privileges reader to gestation and realization of major productions: *Pueblo rechazado*, *Los albañiles*, *El juicio*, *Los hijos de Sánchez*, etc.

978. Leñero, Vicente (1933–). *Vivir del teatro II*. México: Mortiz, 1990. 224pp. Memoirs. Period Covered: 1981–1988.

Continuation of first volume of life in theater. Second volume on following plays: *Los vagabundos*, *Martirio de Morelos*, *¡Pelearán diez rounds!*, *Señora*, *Jesucristo Gómez*, *Las noches blancas 2*, *¿Te acuerdas de Rulfo, Juan José Arreola?* Like companion, *Vivir II* exposes politics behind theatrical productions.

979. León Flores, Ricarda (1905–?); **Juan Silverio Jaime León**. *Testimonios de una mujer yaqui*. México: Conaculta, 1998. 81pp. Oral Autobiography. Period Covered: 1905–1940?

Yaqui relationship with government traced from Porfirio Díaz through Lázaro Cárdenas. Only Cárdenas opted for fair treatment of this tribe. Ricarda tells of enslavement under Díaz, escape from Yucatan and difficult return to Chihuahua, Revolution, marriage, children, poverty, and final gift of land.

980. León Ossorio (y Aguero), Adolfo (1895–1981). *Balance de la revolución, 1910–1981: memorias*. México, 1981. 213 pp. Memoirs. Period Covered: 1910–1981.

Revolutionary, newspaper editor, Carrancista, orator, and poet in tendentious memoirs leaps from Mexico to Colombia to Central America. One of last to eat with fleeing Carranza; toured part of Latin America as orator and poet; assassinated Ramón Segués; attacked Ruiz Cortines; and suffered exile to Revillagigedo Islands. Erratic life equals erratic memoirs.

981. León Ossorio (y Aguero), Adolfo (1895–1981). *Mis Confesiones*. México, 1946. 79pp. Memoirs. Period Covered: 1910–1945.

Recounts adventures as Maderista and anti–Obregonista and later political preferences. Distinguishes self in two ways from memoir writers of same period: traveled outside of Mexico to U.S., Cuba, and Central America; writes well. Memoirs free of documents, quotations, and lists of soldiers' names.

982. León Ossorio (y Aguero), Adolfo (1895–1981). *¡Secuestro! Historia de una gran infamia*. México: 1971. 109pp. Memoirs. Period Covered: 1959.

Maderista and revolutionary disagreed in published letter with former President Adolfo Ruiz Cortines. Both Ruiz Cortines and President Adolfo López Mateos connived to kidnap and imprison him on uninhabited Revillagigedo Islands off Mexico's Pacific coast. Victim laments misadventure.

983. León-Portilla, Miguel (1926–). "Miguel León-Portilla." En *Egohistorias: El Amor a* Clio, coordinated by Jean Meyer. México: Centre D'Etudes Mexicaines et Centroaméricaines, 1993. Pp.82–122. Memoirs. Period Covered: 1926–1992.

Devotes self to major projects. Two activities manifest fruits of research: discovery and exposition of pre–Columbian philosophy of Indians and insistence year 1992 not be dedicated solely to Spain's role in discovery but in theme, "Encuentro de Dos Mundos." Historian-philosopher and collaborator with Angel M. Garibay, León-Portilla author of *Visión de los vencidos* (1959) and *Los antiguos mexicanos a través de sus crónicas y cantares* (1961).

984. León Toral, José de (1901–1929). *El jurado de Toral y la Madre Conchita: lo que se* *dijo y lo que no se dijo en el sensacional juicio: versión taquigráfica textual.* México: s.n., (1928?). 2 v. Memoirs. Period Covered: 1928.

Member of Liga Nacional Defensora de la Libertad Religiosa in 1928 assassinated re-elected President Alvaro Obregón at San Angel restaurant. Court trial proceedings in which the accused through interrogation notes relationship with Madre Conchita and asserts independence of action. Executed in 1929.

985. León Uranga, Luis L. (1890–1981). *Crónica del poder: en los recuerdos de un político en el México revolucionario.* México: Fondo de Cultura Económica, 1987. 479pp. Memoirs. Period Covered: 1888–1979.

Agronomist, head of Department of Agriculture for state of Sonora, senator, secretary of agriculture, interim governor of Chihuahua, and founding member of Partido Nacional Revolucionario expelled from Mexico along with Gen. Calles in 1936. Resumed career upon return in 1940. Absence of chapters on childhood and family. Insertion of relevant documents.

986. León Uranga, Luis (1890–1981). Entrevista en James W. Wilkie y Edna Monzón Wilkie's. *Frente a la Revolución mexicana 17 protagonistas de la etapa constructiva, v.3.* México: Universidad Autónoma Metropolitana, 2002. Pp.205–315. Interview. Period Covered: 1890–1952.

Some autobiography but more of León's opinions on politicians and politics. Birth in Chihuahua, brief genealogy, education, and entrance into agricultural school of one of founders of PRI. Active in land redistribution, subject speaks mainly of Calles and Cárdenas years and constantly defends former. In final pages, he summarizes marriage and exile to United States.

987. Lepe, José I. (1902–?). *Reflexivo hurgar en mis recuerdos.* México, 1974. 96pp. Memoirs. Period Covered: 1902–1973.

Military man and expert on horses has written articles and compiled reference books on topic. Memoirs/scrapbook relates to equitation in Mexico.

988. LePlongeon Alice D. *Here and There in Yucatan: Miscellanies.* New York: Bouton, 1886. 146pp.

Wife of archaeologist Augustus Le Plongoen, who discovered chac-mool. She justified trip and key word in title is *miscellanies*. Every academic field of interest covered in unselected sweep of peninsula: turtle catchers, Cozumel, evil eye, pygmies, idolatry, bondage, eclipses, and evocation of spirits. Writes for unsophisticated public.

989. Lerdo de Tejada, Sebastian (1823–1889). *Memorias de Sebastián Lerdo de Tejada.* México: Editorial Citlatepetl, 1959. 259pp. Memoirs. Period Covered: 1823–1877?

Apocryphal memoirs attributed to Adolfo Carrillo, journalist and contemporary of former confidant of Juárez. Author with more "don de la palabra" than most politicians or diplomats. Witty, aphoristic, and scandalous in comments about contemporaries and Mexican character. Divided between Lerdo's years at home and exile in U.S., delightful memoirs example of variety within Mexican autobiography.

990. Lerma, Olga Yolanda (1898?–?). *Vida de un reportero.* México, 1953. 62pp. Memoirs. Period Covered: 1908–1950.

Life of ambitious, lower class woman who wishes to become reporter. Beginning career in Chihuahua, she flees to U.S. to escape Villa's wrath. In Los Angeles, efforts to own newspaper disastrous. Returns to Mexico City and spends rest of life as reporter.

991. Leví Calderón, Sara (1942–). *Dos mujeres.* México: Editorial Diana, 1990. 237pp. Trans: *The Two Women.* Translated by Gina Kaufer. San Francisco: Aunt Lute Books, 1991. Autobiographical Novel. Period Covered: 1950–1990?

From wealthy Jewish family, sociologist and writer reflects on own life in *Dos mujeres.* Married and with two almost-grown sons, she prefers lesbian relationship. Love for female artist and entire family's rejection of her life style dominate novel.

992. Lewis, Oscar (1900–1962 Dates of Guadalupe). *A Death in the Sanchez Family.* New York: Random House, 1969. 119pp.

Trans: *Una muerte en la familia Sánchez.*
México: Mortiz, 1969. Oral Autobiography.
Period Covered: 1962.

Lewis continued contact with Sánchez
family after publication of *The Children of
Sanchez* in 1961. *A Death* centers upon
Guadalupe and lonely demise in Mexico City
slum. Niece and two nephews each react in
separate monologues under "The Death,"
"The Wake," and "The Burial." Brutality of
detail and sincerity of survivors make a dis-
concerting collective autobiography of family.

993. Lewis, Oscar (1915? Birth of Jesús
Sánchez). *Los hijos de Sánchez: autobiografía
de una familia mexicana.* México: Fondo de
Cultura Económica, 1965. 531pp. Trans: *The
Children of Sanchez; Autobiography of a Mexican Family.* New York: Random House,
ca.1961. Oral Autobiography. Period Covered:
1900–1958?

"...My purpose is to give the reader an
inside view of family life and of what it
means to grow up in a one-room home in a
slum tenement in the heart of a great Latin
American city which is undergoing a process
of rapid social and economic change." Questions prompted responses and tape-recorded
autobiographies of four children. Each confesses in three separate parts. Multiplicity of
views in brutal environment.

994. Lewis, Oscar (1889 Birth of Martínez). *Pedro Martínez: un campesino mexicano y su familia.* Ortiz, 1964. 459pp. Trans:
*Pedro Martínez: A Mexican Peasant and His
Family.* New York: Random House, ca.1964.
Oral Autobiography. Period Covered: 1887–
1963.

Final tape-recorded autobiography of
rural family that lived through Revolution.
Village environment, Revolution and its
effects, religion, and personal problems made
concrete through sequential narrations of
Pedro, Esperanza, and Felipe. In contrast to
Sánchez, counterparts living in urban slum,
the Martínez family is rural Indian with various levels of fluency in Nahuatl. Central is
Pedro, father, Zapatista, Protestant convert,
and sometime leader in village. Violence,
brutality, and realism of environmental
detail. Both Martínez and Sánchez families
introduced earlier in *Five Families.*

995. Lewis, Tracy Hammond. *Along the
Rio Grande.* New York: Lewis Publishing,
1916. 215pp.

Journalists also participated in this
melee. "To gather material for this book the
author wandered in July and August, 1916,
along the Rio Grande as a warless war correspondent" (p.ix). Dispatches written each day
sent to *New York Morning Telegraph.* Lewis
intrigues as he images the border and relation
to American troops stationed there. Reflects
acceptable sentiment of time: inferiority of
Mexican and his culture. He quotes ranger
story, "We met two Mexicans on the road, but
we didn't have time to bury them" (p.176).

996. Licea, Vicente (Dates?). *El sitio de
Querétaro: apuntes relativos a aquel episodio.*
México: Tip. Berrueco Hnos., 1887. 50pp.
Memoirs. Period Covered: 1867.

Medical doctor in memoir to Porfirio
Díaz defends self of charge that he delivered
Gen. Miguel Miramón to Republicans who
successfully besieged Querétaro. Licea claims
he was forced to doctor Miramón and then,
unable to help imperialist general escape, was
accused of betraying him. Highly readable
apology.

997. Liceaga, Eduardo (1839–1929). *Mis
recuerdos de otros tiempos: obra póstuma.*
México, 1949. 276pp. Memoirs. Period Covered: 1851?–1903?

Important in medicine both before and
during Porfiriato: professor, president of
Academia Nacional de Medicina and Mexican
Red Cross, and founder of Consejo Superior
de Salubridad. Career and congresses with
little of personal self.

998. Liggett, William Verner. *My Sev-
enty-Five Years along the Mexican Border.*
New York: Exposition, 1964. 139pp.

Lived in Cananea, Sonora, from 1910 and
into Revolution. Ran dray line between Naco,
Arizona, and Cananea and witnessed early
riots in 1906. Much on Col. Kosterlitzky,
chief of *rurales*; some on mine owner
William Green; and many incidents related
to author's business.

999. Limantour, José Yves (1854–1935).
Apuntes sobre mi vida pública. México: Edito-

rial Porrúa, 1965. 359pp. Memoirs. Period Covered: 1892–1911.

Author confesses "...even less may one consider these writings as social science or as autobiography. They are simply narrations of happenings of general interest..." (p.xv). Covering ca.1892 to 1911, recounts incidents of career as noted in chapter titles: "Los científicos, su origen," "Política de Hacienda..." etc. Chapters unrelieved by any revelation of personality. Contemporary public figures also absent.

1000. Linck, Wenceslaus; Ernest J. Burrus. *Wenceslaus Linck's Diary of His 1766 Expedition to Northern Baja California.* Los Angeles: Dawson's Book Shop, 1966. 115pp.

One of earlier memoirs of Baja emphasizes German Jesuit's Catholicism and its truths, landscape with frequent mention of water, treacherous or docile Indians, and other anecdotes.

1001. Lincoln, John. *One Man's Mexico: A Record of Travels and Encounters.* London: Sydney Bodley Head, 1967. 238pp.

Graham Greene praised above title, "*One Man's Mexico* seems to me the best book on Mexico written this century." No stereotypical routes crowded with tourists, but more tailored itinerary with Sonora's Seri Indians and their poverty, Mixtecas and mushrooms, and Chetumal Maya and Rio Bec ruins. Gloom mixed with snippets of history and flashes of interpretation, e.g., Mexicans are guilty of building cart before they even have a horse. Lincoln achieves epiphany in final chapter in visit to Cobá. Stay from 1958 to 1964 far outlasted that of Graham Greene and Evelyn Waugh.

1002. Lindbergh, Anne Morrow. *Bring Me a Unicorn: Diaries and Letters of Anne Morrow Lindbergh, 1922–1928.* New York: Harcourt Brace Jovanovich, 1972. 259pp.

First diary of Anne Morrow Lindbergh, who as daughter of Ambassador Dwight Morrow, observed Mexico from December 19, 1927, to December 28, 1927, and from March to April, 1928. Landscape, Xmas, meeting Col. Lindbergh, bullfight, and reception at embassy. Second stay includes Vera Cruz and Cuernavaca. Thoughtful, sensitive

comments by recent Smith graduate. December portion of diary published as separate, *Christmas in Mexico, 1927* (1971).

1003. Linke, Lilo. *Magic Yucatan: A Journey Remembered.* New York: Hutchinson, 1950. 160pp.

In English language, Yucatan is subject of treasure and adventure. Not for German Linke, who tries to grasp essence of Mexico's most rebellious state by looking at education, village, Indian and white relations, water, etc. Realistic portrayal of Maya and their efforts at literacy emerges. Linke integrates self with villagers and finds reality uncommon for storied state.

1004. Lira, Miguel Nicolás (1905–1961). *Epistolario: cartas escogidas 1921–1961.* Tlaxcala, TLA: Gobierno del Estado de Tlaxcala, 1991. 360pp. Letters. Period Covered: 1921–1961.

Editors Jeanine Gaucher-Morales and Aledo O. Morales collected 282 letters written to or by Lira. Correspondents in world of letters and often drama: María Luisa Ocampo, Salvador Novo, Alfonso Reyes, Rosario Castellanos, and Jaime Torres Bodet among others. Novelist, playwright, poet, and editor, Lira's themes relevant to these. Literary review *Huytlale* and loyalty to Tlaxcala appear frequently.

1005. Lira, Miguel Nicolás (1905–1961). *Itinerario hasta el Tacaná: notas de viaje.* México: Ediciones de Andrea, 1958. 63pp. Memoirs. Period Covered: ?

Time has no importance in prose poem in which Lira moves from native Tlaxcala to Chiapas and to volcano Tacaná that sentinels Mexican-Guatemala border. Subjectively registers impressions in trip more mental than physical.

1006. List Arzubide, Germán (1898–1998). Entrevista en James W. Wilkie y Edna Monzón Wilkie's *Frente a la Revolución Mexicana: 17 protagonistas de la etapa constructiva,* v.2. México: Universidad Autónoma Metropolitana, 2001. Pp.247–301. Interview. Period Covered: 1898–1945?

Man of letters, journalist, and communist notes relationship with *el estridentismo,* one of manifestations of poetry under *vanguardismo* after WWI. Also observes book that catapulted Zapata from bandit to hero of Revolution. Affiliated with communism, he muses on Left in Mexico, Cárdenas, and Vasconcelos.

1007. Little, Harry Lee. *Rima, The Monkey's Child.* Edmonton: University of Alberta Press, 1983. 123pp.

Vegetarian and conscientious objector looked for ideal place for family, wife, and two children. Southern Mexico, home of Lacandon Indians in Chiapas, proved suitable. Outsiders acquire spider monkey. Human traits seen in monkey and also something of jungle and inhabitants.

1008. Lizárraga García, Benjamín (1928–). *Una mujer, un maletín, una historia*—. México?: s.n., RM Editores, 2001. 263pp. Memoirs? Period Covered: 1952–2001.

An M.D. from Pitiquito and Caborca, Sonora mixes autobiography with history of medicine in his region. Chapter titles suggest varied perspective: "Community Service," "Pitiquito Yesterday," "Personalities," "My Return as a Doctor," "Anecdotes," "ISSSTE (Instituto de Seguridad y Servicios Sociales para los Trabajadores del Estado)," "IMMS (Instituto Mexican del Seguro Social)," etc. Informative for medicine at provincial level. Forty pages on religious pilgrimage on horseback.

1009. Loera Y Chávez, Agustín (1894–1961). *Estampas provincianas.* México: Editorial Cultura, 1953. 57pp. Memoirs. Period Covered: 1900?

Diplomat and publisher evokes native Aguascalientes in six chapters relating mainly to families and locale. Filters Aguascalientes through young self recalling Spaniard Azorín and own countryman Maillefert.

1010. Lombardo de Miramón, Concepción (1835–1921). *Memorias de….* México: Editorial Porrúa, 1980. 678pp. Memoirs. Period Covered: 1835–1917.

Married to Miguel Miramón, military man, president, conservative, and supporter of Maximilian. Through life with him she sees and records nineteenth century society. As aristocrat, she moved in circles of power. Detailed memoirs fast moving and of *costumbristic* value.

1011. Lombardo Toledano, Vicente (1894–1968). Entrevista en James W. Wilkie y Edna Monzón de Wilkie's *México visto en el siglo XX.* México: Instituto Mexicano de Investigaciones Económicas, 1969. Pp.233–409. Interview. Period Covered: 1894–1964.

Best autobiography extant of one of most prominent Marxists and one of Seven Wise Men. Autobiographical data but in relation to political and economic life: initiation into Marxism, labor movement, governor of Puebla, and familiarity with presidents Portes Gil through Avila Camacho. Oral portraits of Garrido Canabal, Saturnino Cedillo, José Vasconcelos, Manuel Gómez Marín, Alfaro Siqueiros, and Diego Rivera.

1012. Lomelí Cota, Alejandro (1916–). *Bajo la hierba duerme una flor: biografía.* México: Editorial Río Colorado, 1989. 159pp. Memoirs. Period Covered: 1890?–1970?

In portraying mother, journalist gives fragments of own life. Narration centers on self-sufficient and folkloric doña Berna who spent life in Sinaloa. Brief self-contained chapters encompass benevolent universe.

1013. Lomelí Garduño, Antonio (1908?–?). *Prometeo mestizo: estampas de la vida de un mexicano.* México: Costa-Amic, ca.1975. 107pp. Memoirs. Period Covered: 1913–1975?

Lawyer, professor, and federal senator for Guanajuato recounts childhood, education, military experiences, political life, Indian-Spanish heritage, and convictions. Most self-revelatory chapter is "El mestizaje."

1014. Long, James Irvin; John Townsend Long. *Pioneering in Mexico.* Los Angeles: Long, 1942. 120pp.

Concerns American author's career as mining engineer in Parral, Chihuahua, in latter half of nineteenth century. Long also influential in bringing railway to this city, and he and brothers engaged in other commercial enterprises. Praise for Porfirio Díaz as well as Luis and Enrique Terrazas.

1015. Longinos Martínez, José; Lesley Byrd Simpson. *Journal: Notes and Observations of the Naturalist of the Botanical Expedition.…* San Francisco: Howell-Books, 1961. 114pp.

Charles III's Enlightenment sent José Longinos Martínez on scientific expedition to Californias in 1787. Madrid surgeon recorded observations in journal. Journeyed from Mexico City to San Blas, Cape San Lucas to Mission San Miguel (Baja), and San Diego to Monterey. Some autobiography among notes on climate, vegetation, landscape, and natives.

1016. Longoria, Arturo. *Adios to the Brushlands.* College Station: Texas A&M University Press, 1997. 118pp.

Mexican-American has ties to Mexico: maternal grandparents fled Revolution, family-owned ranch in Tamaulipas, and, foremost, concern for environment that transcends border between two countries. From south Texas, Longoria loves nature and specifically brushlands, which allow literal interpretation of book's title. Relationship to regional ecology overwhelms Mexican-American sociological issues.

1017. Longoria, Arturo. *Keepers of the Wilderness.* College Station: Texas A&M University Press, 2000. 115pp.

"This book reflects my ideas and philosophies about nature…" (p.3). In journey south of border to brushlands, Longoria meditates on nature and man's abuse of it. Twelve days of journey structure book into essays on man and nature and the unequal relationship that leads to diminishment of latter. Final chapter, "The Months that Followed," proclaim type of victory when author convinces developer father to place his brushlands property into nature conservancy.

1018. López, Arcadia H. (1909–?). *Barrio Teacher.* Houston: Arte Público, 1992. 81pp. Memoirs. Period Covered: 1909–1991.

Born in Sabinas, Hidalgo, in 1909, she fled to San Antonio, Texas, with family in 1913. Aside from occasional returns to birthplace, taught school for forty-six years in San Antonio. Female version of Horatio Alger but in education. She struggled to finish high school, earned advanced degrees, and became pioneer in bilingual education. Story reflects invisibility of border in continuation of Mexican culture into southwest U.S.

1019. Lopez, Enrique Hank. *Conversations with Katherine Anne Porter: Refugee from Indian Creek.* Boston: Little, Brown, 1981. 326pp.

Diego Rivera knew Katherine Anne Porter, who lived briefly in Mexico and moved in his circle and that of other literati: Manuel Gamio, Jorge Enciso, Moisés Sáenz, Miguel Covarrubias, José Alfaro Siqueiros, and Felipe Carrillo Puerto. In addition to teaching, she cultivated writing and found inspiration for *Flowering Judas* (1930). Enrique Hank Lopez calls this her autobiography. Two chapters on Mexican years, 1920–1923. Thirty pages of *Letters of Katherine Anne Porter* (1990) relate to Mexico. Written between May 30, 1930, to August 28, 1931, letters show a garrulous Porter indulging literary friends with her life in Mexico: housing, Indians, artists, Guggenheim Fellowship, and literature.

1020. López Aranda, Susana (1925 Birth of López Tarso). *El cine de Ignacio López Tarso.* México: Universidad de Guadalajara, 1997. 148pp. Filmography. Period Covered: 1925–1996.

Illustrated work of film and stage actor includes introduction and biographical note. Autobiographical core is Ignacio López Tarso's comments on forty-nine of films from *La desconocida* in 1954 to *Santo Luzbel* in 1996. Each with credits, summary, and his autobiographical notes. Interacted with film celebrities from Mexico, U.S., and Spain.

1021. López Aviña, Antonio (1915–?). *Remembranzas de un Obispo.* México: Editorial Diana, 2001. 433pp. Memoirs. Period Covered: 1926–1993.

Ordained in 1939, parish priest in Gómez Palacio, bishop of Zacatecas, 1955–1961, and archbishop of Durango in 1961. Attended Vatican II and also noted visit of Pope Paul II to Durango. Most interesting chapter on *Cristeros* and church's compromise with state, period that coincided with entry into priesthood.

1022. López de Nava Baltierra, Rodolfo (1893–1965). *Mis hechos de campaña: testimonios....* México: Instituto Nacional de Estudios Históricos de la Revolución Mexicana, 1995. 171pp. Memoirs. Period Covered: 1911–1952.

Career military figure, who started as telegrapher, fought in Revolution under Genevieve de la O and Emiliano Zapata. Assigned to Guadalajara, participated in campaign against *Cristeros*. Edited by son, memoirs manifest constant presence of observer/participant.

1023. López Díaz, Pedro (1928–?). *Huellas de un destino: memorias.* Guadalajara? México: Variant Editorial, 2000. 486pp. Memoirs. Period Covered: 1928–1955.

First volume of memoirs that should be continued to present day. Writes well describing experiences as sailor, railway hand, and preparation for medical degree. Without wealth, he earned way through *preparatoria* and medical school. One of best-detailed views of medical school from classes to *servicio social* and professional exam.

1024. López Fuentes, Isaac (1899–?). *Facetas de mi vida de 83 años: autobiografía de....* México, 1983. 106pp. Memoirs. Period Covered: 1899–1977.

From Espinal, Oaxaca, he was telegraph operator for thirty-five years in home state and in Mexico City. Rose to rank of superintendent involved in labor movement and wrote book on development of telegraph service in Mexico. Refreshing innocence and gusto.

1025. López Gardea, Víctor (1900–). *Mis memorias de cacería.* Chihuahua? Impresora Fronteriza, 1974. 140pp. Memoirs. Period Covered: 1910– ?

Chihuahuense's fascination with life is hunting. Describes success with every type of animal native to northern Mexico and even jaguars in Nayarit. Anecdotes from direct experience and from stories heard.

1026. López Matoso, Antonio (1761–1825). *Viaje de Perico Ligero al país de los moros....* New Orleans: Tulane, 1972. 114pp. Journal. Period Covered: 1816–1820.

López Matoso, suspected of conspiracy against Spanish government in Mexico, exiled to Ceuta in 1816. Describes journey from Mexico City to Vera Cruz and Havana as well as return trip. Journal becomes autobiography. Editor Tatum captures López Matoso's self-portrayal: "...one of the most salient characteristics is the alternate jocose-tragic tone. In one paragraph López Matoso laments his hardships and sufferings and expresses truly painful emotions; in the next he attempts a pun or a joke and often ridicules himself and laughs at his own situation" (p.xi).

1027. López Pérez, Antonio (1924?–?). *Ja'k'u x'elan ta jpoj jbatik ta ilbajinel yu'un jkaxlanetik=Cómo defenderse del ladino.* San Cristóbal de Las Casas: INAREMAC, 1985. 58pp. Memoirs. Period Covered: 1933–1966.

Bilingual Spanish-Tzotzil testimony of Indian constantly persecuted by *Ladinos*. From Zinacantán, Chiapas, he became literate, attended school in Mexico City, taught in village, headed cooperative of five stores, and served as appointed secretary of village. Document emphasizes Indian struggle for justice.

1028. López Portillo, José (1920–). *Mis tiempos: biografía y testimonio político.* México: Fernández, 1988. 2 v. Memoirs. Period Covered: 1920–1986.

President from 1976 to 1982, he rose to office from other prominent positions. As politician, concentrates mainly on public personality. Private life obscured. Portion of first and all of second volume comprised of documents and explanations. Essay devoted to single theme, pertinent notes abstracted from diary, and, finally, retrospective view of events. Although last tome undigested, López Portillo involves more of personality than most other politicians in memoirs.

1029. López-Portillo y Rojas, José (1850–1923). *Egipto y Palestina: apuntes de viaje.* México: Díaz de León y White, 1874. 2 v. Memoirs. Period Covered: 1871–1874.

Writer of regionalist fiction of realist-naturalist period graduated from law school and traveled for three years. Two volumes on Egypt and Palestine serve as travel autobiography: recounting personal experiences, analyzing culture, and including dialog, notes, moods, and feelings.

1030. López Ramos, Ernesto (1919–?). *Crónica de la vida de un geólogo*. México: López Ramos, 1987. 290pp. Memoirs. Period Covered: 1925–1985.

Worked for Petroleos Mexicanos in 1944 in Chiapas, Tabasco, Vera Cruz, and Tamaulipas. Founded Sección de Geología de la Zona Norte in 1950 and headed other regional offices. Describes education, career activities, and travel to Europe, Central America, and Africa. Geologist autobiography rare in Mexico.

1031. López Romero, Félix J. (Dates?). *Los dias de ayer*. México: Costa-Amic, 1988. 214pp. Memoirs. Period Covered: 1865–1949.

History and autobiography in depiction of Chilpancingo, Guerrero, during early part of twentieth century. Journalist and poet recalls Chilpancingo of youth: family, landscape, neighborhoods, streets, childhood games, feast days, school and friends, walks, alameda, markets, bars, and incidents of historical interest. No social problems in past.

1032. López Salinas, Samuel (1900–?). *La batalla de Zacatecas: recuerdos imborrables que dejan impacto para toda la vida*. México: Ediciones Botas, 1964. 49pp. Memoirs. Period Covered: 1910–1914.

Revolution in Zacatecas told in concise prose by twelve-year-old boy. Victoriano Huerta occupied Zacatecas only to be defeated by Pancho Villa and Army of North in battle that destroyed Huerta's army.

1033. López-Stafford, Gloria (1937–). *A Place in El Paso: A Mexican American Childhood*. Albuquerque: University of New Mexico Press, 1996. 212pp. Memoirs. Period Covered: 1940–1949.

With widowed father, she reaches adolescence in El Paso and Juárez. Four parts of autobiography correspond to different locations where she lived on Anglo side of border. Mexican-American girl of pre–Chicano days loves El Paso but reacts to poverty and Anglo dominance. Highly *costumbrista*.

1034. López Velarde, Ramón (1888–1921). *Correspondencia con Eduardo J.Correa y otros escritos juveniles [1905–1913]*. Edición de Guillermo Sheridan. México: Fondo de Cultura Económica, 1991. 287pp. Letters. Period Covered: 1905–1913.

Guillermo Sheridan in 1988 discovered unpublished works (165 pages of letters and ninety-four pages of poetry and essays) of Zacatecan poet. López Velarde penned forty-five letters to Correa, Catholic poet, editor and founder of journals and newspapers in Aguascalientes. Velarde wrote letters after leaving seminary and starting law school. Editor notes contents in introduction: "The letters… insinuate who he is, what he thinks and what he feels and what he does…" (p.19).

1035. López Yescas, Ernesto (1912–1992). *Una vida entre libros II: testimonios….* Hermosillo: Centro INAH Sonora, 1995. 2 v. Oral Autobiography. Period Covered: 1912–1992.

Chapters chronologically structure life of Sonoran bibliographer, book collector, teacher, and priest: childhood, teaching, seminary, parish priest, and love of books. Narrates various stages of life with verve. First volume establishes importance as bibliographer and collector of books on Sonora. Well-edited oral autobiography.

1036. Lorang, Mary Corde, Sister. *Footloose Scientist in Mayan America*. New York: Scribner, 1966. 308pp.

Maryknoll Sister is nonspecialist who travels in Guatemala and Mexico. Visits, studies, and stimulates reader to do on-site inspection of Chichén Itzá, Uxmal, and Dzibilchaltun. One of few Maya "scholars" who sees unity of archaeological ruins of the Americas.

1037. Lores, Rosa María (1934–?). *De hadas, aromas y brazos de oro: (Campeche de mis recuerdos)*. Campeche, CAM: Publicaciones de la Universidad Autónoma de Campeche, 1998. 83pp. Memoirs. Period Covered: 1936–1986?

Author covers life in thematic chapters related to chronology. Traditional subjects in Campeche childhood: home, grandmother, servants, first communion, and birthdays.

One chapter on love for Greek culture. Married and with own children, she mocks magazine quizzes that suggest she should not be housewife. Unidealized contemporary account.

1038. Loret de Mola, Carlos (1921–1986). *Confesiones de un gobernador.* México: Editorial Grijalbo, 1978. 306pp. Memoirs. Period Covered: 1970–1976.

Journalist, congressman, and governor of Yucatán during presidency of Luis Echeverría Alvarez, author is honest. Confessional writings suggest workings of political system. Loyal to Yucatán, he complains of frustrations with national government.

1039. Loustaunau, Adolfo C. (1910–?). *Los dos mundo de Fitín: relato auto-biográfico.* Hermosillo, SON: 1986. 287pp. Memoirs. Period Covered: 1910–1968.

Without emotion he chronologically narrates life in two worlds: childhood and adolescence in Chihuahua and Sonora and maturity in Tucson, Arizona. Orphaned, author survives and prospers. Focuses on childhood but maintains reserve of memoirist. Emotional or personal elements absent from factual account.

1040. Love, Thomas Neely; Grady H. Howell. *A Southern Lacrimosa: The Mexican War Journal.* N.p.: Chickasaw Bayou, 1995. 313pp.

Doctor Love had a total of eighteen months of medical experience with a volunteer regiment from Mississippi. Part of army of occupation in northern Mexico, he exercised his profession from December 1846 to May 1847 in Matamoros and Monterrey. Problems of medical treatment, not battles were his major concern: selecting hospital sites, assigning medical personnel, and finding medical supplies. Two greatest afflictions were smallpox and diarrhea. Difficulties of transporting the ill.

1041. Loyola, Bernabé (Dates?). *El Sitio de Querétaro en 1867: memorias íntimas.* Querétaro, QUE: Ediciones Culturales del Gobierno del Estado, 1967. 78pp. Memoirs. Period Covered: 1867.

Liberal opposed to French Intervention, he witnessed siege of Maximilian and generals at Querétaro. Author's constant presence and interest in details make absorbing read. Loyola friend of Juárez's generals, Mariano Escobedo and Felipe B. Berriozabal. Centenary publication of memoirs previously serialized in newspaper.

1042. Lozano Rocha, Erasmo (1912–?). *Crónica de un viaje al Río San Miguel.* Hermosillo, SON: Instituto Sonorense de Cultura, 2000. 65pp. Memoirs. Period Covered: 1995.

Resident of Cananea, Sonora, has chance to see more of this state with a tour of Americans also interested in nature. Arizpe, Sinoquipe, Curcurpe, and Magdalena are sites along route. Author talks about travel, camping, nature, and Mexicans.

1043. Lozano Rocha, Erasmo (1912–). *Remembranzas-opiniones y críticas.* Cananea, SON: Lozano Rocha, Imparcolor, 1991. 468pp. Memoirs. Period Covered: 1877–1989?

Mix of autobiography, biographies of Mexicans, anecdotes, political life, and news clippings relevant to career. Lawyer born in Nuevo León but spent life in Texas, Mexico City, and Cananea, Sonora. Unique for Protestantism and relationship through blood or marriage to nucleus of Baptists in Nuevo León, e.g., Westrup and Rocha. Baptist education in Texas.

1044. Lucas, María Elena (1941–). *Forged under the Sun: The Life of María Elena Lucas: Forjado bajo el sol.* Ed. and with an introduction by Fran Leeper Buss. Ann Arbor: University of Michigan Press, ca.1993. 314pp. Oral Autobiography. Period Covered: 1941–1990.

Editor confesses role in realization of memoirs from taped interviews and writings of Lucas. Mexican-Anglo at home on either side of border, Lucas from family of migrant farm workers. Deprived childhood, futile early marriage, and desire to write comprise life of narrator who became labor organizer and settled in Brownsville, Texas. Epitomizes U.S. Mexicans of south Texas as poorest social and economic substratum.

1045. Lugo, José del Carmen (1813–?).
Life of a Rancher. Vida de un ranchero dictada por don José del Carmen Lugo.... Escrito por D. Tomás Savage para la Bancroft Library, años de 1877. *Southern California Quarterly,* XXXIII, (September 1950) pp.185–236. Memoirs. Period Covered: 1818–?

Lugo's description of skirmishes confusing with no time or historical locales. *Costumbrista* elements of interest and value: religion, women's work, agriculture, food, dress, and dances. Lugo is type of Quixote.

1046. Lugo de Santoyo, Alicia (1905–?).
Mexicali de mi juventud: relatos intrascendentes, 1922–1932. México: EDAMEX, 1988. 90pp. Memoirs. Period Covered: 1922–1932.

Spends youth in border cities Mexicali, Tijuana, and Ensenada. Secretary to Gen. Abelardo Rodríguez (future president) then governor of Baja and later secretary to Gov. Carlos Trejo Lerdo de Tejada. Trip to Europe in 1930s and marriage highlight tranquil life.

1047. Lumholtz, Carl. *New Trails in Mexico: An Account of One Year's Exploration in North-Western Sonora....* New York: Scribner, 1912. 411pp.

Title self describes. About half of book on trip to Sonora: Yaquis, Papagos, folklore, Sonoita, animals, landscape, archaeology, etc. Difficult to select single topic for multifaceted author who personalizes each experience from 1910–1911.

1048. Lumholtz, Carl. *Unknown Mexico: A Record of Five Years' Exploration among the Tribes of the Western Sierra Madre....* Glorieta, NM: Rio Grande, 1973 (1902). 2 v.

Earlier Carl Lumholtz and Frederick Starr researched various tribes of Mexico. Norwegian Lumholtz's work on Tarahumaras, Coras, Huicholes, Tarascans, and Aztecs. Lumholtz neither praised Porfirio Díaz nor condemned Indians. Anthropologist, historian, folklorist, archaeologist, and ethnologist, he studies Indian and understands them. Experiments with magic mushrooms of Huicholes and reactions.

1049. Luna Arroyo, Antonio (1905–1982 Dates of O'Gorman). *Juan O'Gorman: autobiografía, juicios críticos y Documentación....*

México: Cuadernos Populares de Pintura Mexicana Moderna, 1973. 528pp. Oral Autobiography. Period Covered: 1905–1970?

Architect and muralist taped memoirs at behest of Luna Arroyo. One hundred and twenty-six page document, comprised of clusters of information under thematic labels, suggests constant presence of Luna Arroyo, which doesn't distract from document's value for information. Discusses family and life in art and architecture.

1050. Luna Hernández, Antonio (Dates?). "Mi huella educativa en el tiempo." En *Los maestros y la cultura nacional,* 1920–1952, v.3. México: Museo Nacional de Culturas Populares, 1987. Pp.107–153. Memoirs. Period Covered: 1928–1963?

Author worked in teaching assignments in Vera Cruz and Chiapas frequently among Indians. Narrates career focusing often on extra-curricular requirements of position.

1051. Luna Morales, Ricardo (Dates?).
Mi vida revolucionaria.... Tlaxcala, TLA: Luna Morales, 1943. 127pp. Memoirs. Period Covered: 1910–1937.

Revolutionary activity dates from meeting with Aquiles Serdán. Author meets many other personalities in Revolution such as Madero, Obregón, Natera, etc. Rises in rank, heads various military sections of Mexico, and combats rebels.

1052. Luquín, Eduardo (1896–1971).
Autobiografía. México: Ecuador 0000, 1967. 454pp. Autobiography Proper. Period Covered: 1896–1959.

Espigas de infancia y adolescencia. 1896–1915. Birth in Sayula, Jalisco, childhood home, primary school, friends, adolescence, education, uncles, and beginning of military career in first of three autobiographies.

Corona de espinas. 1915?–1928? Fought in Revolution under Venustiano Carranza and in 1925 entered diplomatic corps. Noted poverty while in Paris and Madrid; after returning to Mexico was assigned to London. Maximizes travel and autobiography for presence saturates every moment in Europe. Knew several of Los Contemporáneos.

El regreso. 1918–1960. Longest of three books images diplomat at height of career in

Ecuador, Brazil, Spain, Hague, Chile, England, and Cuba. Knew significant writers and diplomats and describes them. Two other autobiographers equal or surpass him as sketch artists, Martín Luis Guzmán and Victorian Salado Alvarez. Luquín merits more attention as autobiographer.

1053. Luquín, Eduardo (1896–1971). *Diagrama*. México: Imprenta Mundial, 1930. 92pp. Memoirs. Period Covered: 1929?

Travel and meditation join. Recalls England as topic in grade school, crosses Atlantic, visits Stratford on Avon, yet remembers France and Belgium. Oxford similar to Bruges. Dialog with imaginary female correspondent establishes mood uncommon in Mexican travel literature.

1054. Luquín, Eduardo (1896–1971). *Tumulto: memorias de un oficial del Ejército Constitucionalista*. México: Imprenta Mundial, 1937. 119pp. Memoirs. Period Covered: 1909–?

Here novelist and short story writer prefers latter genre. In eight self-encapsulated chapters, modeled after short story in structure and dramatic tension, he recounts Carrancista days in battle.

1055. Lyon, G.F. *Journal of a Residence and Tour in the Republic of Mexico in the Year 1826....* London: Murray, 1828. 2 v.

One of first Britishers to explore Mexico and with an interest in mines. He left England in 1820 and started record of meanderings in journal of West coast, then to San Luis Potosí, Zacatecas, Guadalajara, and Mexico City. More than geography attracts restless traveler. All ethnic groups and unusual customs enliven *Journal of a Residence*.

1056. Macedo López, Juan (1910–?). *Viaje alrededor de la nostalgia*. Universidad de Colima, 1986. 2 v. Memoirs. Period Covered: 1923–1940?

Teacher, director of Colimas's normal school and public education for state, was also journalist. Like many regionalists, mixes autobiography with history, *costumbrismo*, and anecdotes. Focuses on city, poets, family, friends, and teachers in autobiographical but

independent essays that evoke yesteryear's Colima.

1057. Mackintosh, Graham. *Into a Desert Place: A 3000 Mile Walk around the Coast of Baja California*. Idyllwild, CA: Mackintosh, 1990. 312pp.

Always alone, he fends for self in emergencies. Rattlesnakes abound, virgin scenery inspires, gregarious or disgruntled natives and foreigners hinder or expedite journey of loner. Nature dominates as does author who survives self-imposed challenge.

1058. Mackintosh, Graham. *Journey with a Baja Burro*. San Diego: Sunbelt Publications, 2001. 358pp.

Completes six-month journey on foot from Tecate to Loreto, 1,000-mile trek. Entertains with history of Baja; regales with stories of filibuster William Walker; admires missions; dialogues with Mexicans; details essentials for living outdoors; and personalizes Misión, his Baja burro, pack animal, and companion.

1059. Madero, Francisco Indalecio (1873–1913). *Epistolario ed. por Agustín Yáñez y Catalina Sierra*. México: Ediciones de la Secretaría de Hacienda, 1963. 3 v. Letters. Period Covered: 1873–1910.

Selected letters with context and problems that occupied him at moment. Overall but especially in correspondence with family, emerge facets of martyr's personality. Accompanying memoirs illuminate salient points in career. Name index profiles Madero's relationship with various individuals. Gilberto López Alanís edited *Madero y los sinaloenses: 1909–1910* (1996). Forty-four of apostle's letters written to nine Sinaloenses comprise volume. Indicates Maderismo in Sinaloa rather than personal life. Heriberto Frías, Fidencio Schmidt, Benjamín Hill, and Manuel Bonilla frequent recipients.

1060. Madero, Gustavo A. (1875–1913). *Gustavo A. Madero: epistolario*. Selección y prólogo de Ignacio Solares. México: Editorial Diana, 1991. 239pp. Letters. Period Covered: 1901–1913.

Younger brother of President Francisco I. Madero, Gustavo, was senator, director of finances of brother's campaign, founder of Progressive Constitutional Party and secretary of treasury of provisional government in 1911. Letters to wife, Carolina Villarreal de Madero, suggest happy marriage and success as businessman. Postmarked Mexico and U.S., eighty-six letters delineate caring father and husband. Editor Solares corrects impression that Gustavo Madero exploited Revolution for own purposes. In 1991, Elena Garza Madero de Suárez, granddaughter of Gustavo, published *Gustavo y Francisco Madero: dos raíces, una idea: historia oral y epistolaria*. From Mexico or U.S., letters relate to major correspondents, Gustavo Madero and Carolina Villarreal de Madero.

1061. Madero, Pablo Emilio (1908–?). *500 (i.e. quinientas) horas de hielo*. Monterrey: Printagráfica, 1985. 365pp. Memoirs. Period Covered: 1982.

PAN ran Madero for presidency in 1982. Incorporates year of campaigning and dissatisfaction with PRI. Active in PAN in Nuevo León, Madero national senator from 1979 to 1982. Nephew of Francisco I. Madero tells of family's exile to U.S. in 1913. Peach trees need 500 hours of frost to produce explains metaphorical title.

1062. Madero Olivares, Enrique (1900–?). *Memorias*. México: Editorial Jus, 1983. 61pp. Memoirs. Period Covered: 1900–1970.

Mining engineer, industrialist, and president of Mexican Red Cross notes major contours of life. Cousin of martyred president and member of aristocracy of Monterrey with privileges of travel and education.

1063. Madrid Hurtado, Miguel de la (1934–). **Alejandra Lajous**. *Cambio de rumbo: testimonio de una presidencia, 1982–1988*. México: Fondo de Cultura Económica, 2004. 871pp. Memoirs. Period Covered: 1982–1988.

Former president in seventy-two chapters, or a month-by-month reportage of his six-year regime, defends self. More than predecessors, de la Madrid employs first person plural and singular in narration. Expresses opinions and also assesses personalities such as President Reagan or John Gavin.

One of longer political memoirs to date but with more refreshing subjectivity.

1064. Magdaleno, Mauricio (1906–1986). *Las palabras perdidas*. México: Fondo de Cultura Económica, 1956. 225pp. Memoirs. Period Covered: 1928–1930.

With perspective of twenty-seven years, writer recalls Vasconcelos's campaign after assassination of Obregón in 1928. Twenty-three-year-old Magdaleno worked in support of candidate. Memoirs salient for two reasons: capture spirit of Vasconselistas eager for reform; as professional writer, he communicates better than most memoirists.

1065. Magdaleno, Mauricio (1906–1986). *Tierra y viento*. México: Editorial Stylo, 1948. 244pp. Memoirs. Period Covered: 1936–1945.

Collection of articles fragmented. Visiting Querétaro, Vera Cruz, Oaxaca, San Luis Potosí, and other places, Magdaleno presents self in first person narrative and in subjective interpretation of locale.

1066. Magoffin, Susan Shelby. *Down the Santa Fe Trail and into Mexico: The Diary of Susan Shelby Magoffin, 1846–1847*. New Haven: Yale University Press, 1962. 294pp.

Document of educated and plucky eighteen year old married to Santa Fe trader who traveled from El Paso to Chihuahua City to Saltillo. "Quite apart from its worth as a trail journal, a Mexican War account and an insight into the political as well as economic role of the American borderlands merchant, Mrs. Magoffin's journal has a final merit as social history" (pp.xxx).

1067. Magruder, Henry R. *Sketches of the Last Year of the Mexican Empire*. Wiesbaden: Printed for private circulation, 1868. 135pp.

Perhaps granddaddy of all texts with exception of Cortez and Bernal Díaz del Castillo is Henry R. Magruder. Almost as interesting as Fanny Calderón de la Barca in his above title. Compresses geography and customs. Details trip from Vera Cruz to Mexico City with modes of travel, inns, and Indians. In capital delights with composite view of city and its peculiarities. Abundant rats, funeral of one of poorer classes, and other themes suggest that he never bores.

1068. Maillefert, Alfredo (1889–1941).
Ancla en el tiempo, gentes y paisajes. Morelia:
Michoacana, 1940. 192pp. Memoirs. Period
Covered: 1895?–1920?

Evokes Porfirian Michoacán of youth in
eighty-three word portraits of personalities.
Happy world untouched by realities of dictatorship: Morelia's doctors, street vendors,
poets, priests, and other assorted types
emerge in perfection of nostalgia. Qualifies as
autobiography for Maillefert's close relationship with individuals and environment.
Spaniard Azorín and fellow countryman J.
Rubén Romero justly mentioned here.

1069. Maillefert, Alfredo (1889–1941).
*Laudanza de Michoacán: Morelia, Pátzcuaro,
Uruapan*. México: UNAM, 1937. 148pp.
Memoirs. Period Covered: 1900s.

Memoirs too unpoetic term to describe
impressions that comprise book. Author
remembers three colonial cities of native
Michoacán. Mood and atmosphere superior
to tourist information. Intent was to intuit
rather than to visit cities.

1070. Maillefert, Alfredo (1889–1941). *Los
libros que leí*. México: Imprenta Universitaria, 1942. 255pp. Memoirs. Period Covered:
1910–1938?

He reacts to books and records feelings
and surroundings that engender them. Maillefert shares two dozen favorite European and
Mexican authors. Subjective reactions through
tastes in reading equal autobiography.

1071. Malanco, Luis (1828–1888). *Viaje a
Oriente*. México: Imprenta Agrícola-Comer-
cial, 1883. 2 v. Memoirs. Period Covered:
1875–1876.

Lawyer/diplomat, posted to Mexican
legation in Italy, traveled to Orient: Naples,
Alexander, Cairo, Port Said, Jaffa, Ramle,
Jerusalem, San Sabas, and Jericho. Travel
informed with romanticism characteristic of
period: love for exotic, interest in nature,
and show of emotion. Ignacio Altamirano's
introduction enhances volume.

1072. Maldonado, Enrique J. (1906–?).
Jirones de mi vida. México: Morales Hnos.,
1963. 2 v. Autobiography Proper. Period Covered: 1906–1963?

Born into poverty in Huatabampo,
Sonora, author plagued by hard work and
disaster in early years. Held many jobs from
low employments to purchaser for department of agriculture, registrar for school,
journalist, politician in Partido de la Revolución Mexicana, and several government positions. In second volume prosperous Malanco
goes to Europe and records travel. Self dis-
placed by locale.

1073. Maldonado, Gerardo (1938?–).
Anecdotario. Monterrey: Ediciones, 1989.
160pp. Memoirs. Period Covered: 1943?–1989?

Thirty anecdotes cohere for Monterrey
psychologist. Well-connected friendship with
Ofelia Guilmain, Juan Rulfo, and José Gál-
vez, and well-traveled with trips to Cuba,
China, Russia, and Poland, Maldonado distills experience from peak moments.

1074. Maldonado C., Arturo (1895?–?).
Memorias de un maestro. Chihuahua, CHH:
Imprenta Ruiz Sandoval, 1953. 127pp. Mem-
oirs. Period Covered: 1900–1953.

Completed teacher's training during
Revolution and taught from 1915 to 1953.
Names, places, and anecdotes of rural teacher.

1075. Maldonado Sánchez, Braulio
(1903–?). *Braulio*. México: Tallares Gráficos
del Gobierno de Baja California, 1986. 116pp.
Memoirs. Period Covered: 1903–1960?

Born in San José del Cabo and mainly
politician, he was federal deputy (senator)
and governor of Baja from 1953 to 1959.
Lawyer, soldier, co-founder of Leftist Socialist Party, and bracero in U.S., he enjoyed varied career. Little on family and personality.

1076. Maltos, Juan Pablo (1924?–). *Un
norteño tiene la palabra*. Ciudad Victoria:
Instituto Tamaulipeco de Cultura, 1991.
97pp. Memoirs. Period Covered: 1940?–.

Thirty-six episodes of *coahuileño* farm
laborer who worked as bracero in U.S. Setting
here and northern Mexico. Colloquial style
suggests that stories should be oral rather
than written.

1077. Mancisidor, Anselmo (1895?–?).
Viví la Revolución. México, 1959. 597pp.
Memoirs. Period Covered: 1913–1916.

Young man joins Constitutionalists on side of Venustiano Carranza in Revolution. First quarter of book relates to military experiences; remainder collection of documents.

1078. Mancisidor, José (1894–1956). *Ciento veinte dias* in *Obras Completas....* Xalapa: Gobierno del Estado de Vera Cruz, 1979 (1937). Memoirs. Period Covered: 1936?

Journalist, teacher, and revolutionary believed in communistic principles. Travel/observation in USSR not all praise. Interviews and history mingle with travel data.

1079. Manero de Gertz, Mercedes (1910–?). *El mundo en que he vivido*. México: Lasser, 1991. 219pp. Memoirs. Period Covered: 1910–1988.

Born to wealth and privilege, she recalls childhood in Toluca, Mexico City, and New York City because of Revolution. Interacted with all presidents from Abelardo Rodríguez to Miguel de la Madrid. Analyzes each *sexenio* with its social life. Because of German father-in-law, she dwells on anti–German sentiment provoked in Mexico by WWII. Life is absorbing for reader.

1080. Mangas Alfaro, Roberto (Dates?). *México en el Aconcagua. Los capítulos La Cumbre y Buenos Aires por Roberto García Juárez*. México: Ediciones Eugene, 1948. 236pp. Memoirs. Period Covered: 1947?

Patriot and believer in *Guadalupanismo*, author mountaineer. With colleagues in 1947, he set out to conquer Argentina's Aconcagua, highest peak in hemisphere and records ascent. Notes other achiever, Argentine Juan Jorge Link.

1081. Mangieri, Nick. *Passport to Danger: Diary of an Adventurer*. Williamsburg, VA: Valor, 2002. 295pp.

Five chapters set in Mexico: jaguar hunt in Chiapas and mastering of Mt. Orizaba in Vera Cruz. Hires native guides for both exploits.

1082. Mantecón Pérez, Adán (1895–?). *Recuerdos de un villista: mi campaña en la Revolución*. México, 1967. 125pp. Memoirs. Period Covered: 1910–1960.

Collage of poems, photographs, and impressions of Revolution recalled half century later. Writes with passion lauding Maderista-Villistas of Revolution. Fragmented memoirs center on battles such as Torreón and Zacatecas. Few personal incidents noted.

1083. Manzanero, Armando (1935–). *Con la música por dentro*. México: Planeta, 1994. 209pp. Memoirs. Period Covered: 1937?–1992.

Non-chronological account of Yucatecan singer and composer of popular songs during 1960s. Mixes childhood, adolescence, and family in Yucatan with career.

1084. Manzanero, Armando (1935–?). *Relatos de mi infancia*. México: Sansores & Aljure, 1997. 229pp. Memoirs. Period Covered: 1935–1945?

Yucatecan composer, singer, and piano player renders a non-chronological account with emphasis on childhood. More than successes of tours and song hits, he recalls growing up with parents and other family members.

1085. Manzanilla, Yanuario (1838–?). *Recuerdos de la campaña de los republicanos contra el imperio, en el estado de Yucatán*. Mérida: Imprenta Mercantil Guzmán, 1888. 229pp. Memoirs. Period Covered: 1862–1867.

Participated in French Intervention and feels that war, as fought in Yucatán, will be remembered in memoirs. Introduction most personal part.

1086. Manzanilla Domínguez, Anastasio (Dates?). *Aguas fuertes (gentes y cosas de Yucatán)*. México, 1919. 70pp. Memoirs. Period Covered: 1918–1919.

Socialist author profiles some of leading personalities of Yucatan: Carlos Castro Morales, Felipe Carrillo Puerto, Rafael Mediz Bolio, Hircano Ayuso, Florencio Avila Castillo, and Felipe Valencia López.

1087. Manzanilla Schaffer, Víctor (1924–?). *Confesiones políticas: síntesis de mis memorias*. México: Editorial Grijalbo, 1998. 449pp. Memoirs. Period Covered: 1924–1995.

Yucatecan professor and politician:

deputy or senator, 1967–1979; governor 1988–1991; member of central executive committee of PRI, 1971–1974; and ambassador to China, 1980–1982. Public life far overwhelms private life.

1088. Maples Arce, Manuel (1900–1981). *A la orilla de este río.* Madrid: Editorial Plenitud, 1964. 285pp. Memoirs. Period Covered: 1900–1913.

Unsatisfying autobiography of childhood in Papantla, Vera Cruz, because too dependent on external world. Family and early years Arcadian. Evocation of river in life and some perspective on Revolution from child's point of view. Second volume, *Soberana juventud*, reveals more of author.

1089. Maples Arce, Manuel (1898–1981). *Mi vida por el mundo.* México: Universidad Veracruzana, 1983. 379pp. Memoirs. Period Covered: 1935–1972?

Work continues *Soberana juventud.* Relies on memoir for life in diplomatic corps: Belgium, Poland, Italy, Portugal, England, Panama, Chile, Colombia, Japan, and Pakistan. External life but not creative life of poet. Mentions family and friends. *Vida por el mundo* proves thesis that adult years lack intensity of youth.

1090. Maples Arce, Manuel (1900–1981). *Soberana juventud.* Madrid: Editorial Plenitud, 1967. 292pp. Autobiography Proper. Period Covered: 1915?–1934?

Activities contributing to literary formation: education, reading, journalism, and acquaintance with intellectual figures. On final fringes of Modernism, poet eager for next stage of evolvement. Hints at insights into inspiration but exhibits little interior life. Sketches of Federico Gamboa, Emilio Rabasa, José Juan Tablada, and Rafael López. Diverse geographical foci: Mexico City, Jalapa, New York, and Paris. Active political career: secretario general in government of Vera Cruz (1925), state senator representing Acayucan and Minatitlán (1928), technical counselor of Narciso Bassols, secretary of education, and senator from Tuxpan (1932–1934), and various diplomatic posts. Chronologically developed.

1091. Marcos, Fernando (1915–?). *Mi amante, el fútbol.* México: Editorial Grijalbo, 1980. 200pp. Memoirs. Period Covered: 1920?–1970?

Sports announcer played soccer professionally both in minor and major leagues, and competed for World Cup in Italy in 1934. Referee, coach, and announcer, he knows soccer equally well with broadcasting.

1092. Marett, Robert Hugh Kirk. *An Eye-Witness of Mexico.* London: Oxford University Press, 1939. 267pp.

Englishman varies perspective on country, and more than most Americans, he has integrated self into culture. Married into aristocratic Mexican family, he speaks firsthand about land reform and loss of hacienda. Employee of British oil company speaks autobiographically on perils of Cárdenas's expropriation of 1938. No American sentimentality about Indian.

1093. Margadant S., Guillermo Floris; Lois Parkinson Zamora. *Guillermo Margadant y su mundo.* México: Editorial Porrúa, 2002. 320pp.

Possibly only Hollander to reside in Mexico and to recount his experiences in interviews. Law professor left his native country in 1947 and by way of Haiti arrived in Mexico in 1950. Temporary stay became permanent. Struggle for survival, ties with Jewish community, fascination with law, appointment to UNAM's law school and fifty years of teaching and research into Roman law and Mexico. Well-crafted book with conversations, testimonies, lectures, prologues, and letters.

1094. María de San José, Madre (1656–1719); Kathleen Ann Myers; Amanda Powell. *A Wild Country out in the Garden: The Spiritual Journals of a Colonial Mexican Nun.* Bloomington: Indiana University Press, 1999. 386pp. Diary. Period Covered: 1656–1717.

With Sor Juana's letter, *Wild Country* one of oldest autobiographical documents from Mexico written by a woman. Magnificent job of co-editing in two additional chapters on María's world and tradition of spiritual writing. Selected translation incorporates nun's pre-convent days, vocation, family, other nuns, religious authorities, and mystical experiences. Above title derived from Myers's 1986 Ph.D. dissertation from Brown University, "Becoming a Nun in Seventeenth Century Mexico." Sister María Joseph, born Juana Palacio Berruecos in Tepeacan near Puebla, describes early life and frustrations with family because of determination to enter convent. According to Myers, later volumes focus more on religious life.

1095. Marín, Guadalupe (1897–1981). *La única*. México: Editorial Jalisco, 1938. 251pp. Autobiographical Novel. Period Covered: 1920s.

Lupe Marín, married to Diego Rivera in 1922, exhibits her life in a *roman a clef*: her child by Diego, her second marriage and divorce, her excursion to Paris sponsored by Diego, her stay in New York with Diego and Frida, and finally, her return to Mexico. As first wife of the artist, she has a fascinating story.

1096. Marín, Mariano B. (1897–?). *Recuerdos de la revolución constitucionalista: segunda edición; La rebelión delahuertista en Tamaulipas*: tercera edición. Ciudad Victoria: Universidad Autónoma de Tamaulipas, 1977. 109pp. Memoirs. Period Covered: 1914–1934.

Soldier in Constitutionalist army under Gen. César López de Lara recounts adventures in Tamaulipas. Second half of book is role in Delahuertista rebellion. Exiled to U.S. for aborted movement against President Obregón.

1097. Marín, Rubén (1910–). *Los otros días: apuntes de un médico de pueblo*. 8ed. México: Editorial Jus, 1994 (1961). 565pp. Memoirs. Period Covered: 1931–1941?

Exercised profession for forty years, ten of them among miners in Sierra de Puebla. Columnist for *El Heraldo de México,* Marín is writer. Two professions, writer-doctor, combine in naturalistic document reminiscent of Zola's *Germinal*. He knows patients, poverty, and places them in context. Textured result more akin to novel than autobiography.

1098. Marín Rodríguez, Gregorio (1933?–). *Tiempo de hablar: otra cara del periodismo*. México?, ca.1988. 236pp. Memoirs. Period Covered: 1950–1964.

From San Luis Potosí, he worked at various jobs before becoming reporter. Involved in state politics in opposition to regional caudillo, Gonzalo N. Santos. Marín Rodríguez focuses on local personalities.

1099. Marnham, Patrick. *So Far from God: A Journey to Central America*. New York: Viking, 1958? 253pp.

One half of Patrick Marnham's book relates to Mexico. Highly literate author alludes to other British writers and Mexico. Scrutinizing Mexico City, Cuernavaca, and Oaxaca, he reveals menacing and surrealist incidents. Incisive on Indian and racial problems.

1100. Márquez Campos, Alfredo (1923–). *El soplo del viento: memorias*. México: Sansores & Aljure, 1998 (1994). 291pp. Memoirs. Period Covered: 1926–1994.

Michoacano M.D., writer, journalist, and editor of magazines, representative of OAS in Mexico and family man. Evokes government's persecution of *Cristeros* and specifically his family. Encouraged in writing by Mariano Azuela, he later founded and published twenty-one-year *La semana medical de México*.

1101. Marroquín Pámanes, Enrique (1903–?). *Anécdotas del güero Marroquín*. México: Dirección General de Culturas Populares de la SEP, 1988. 400pp. Memoirs. Period Covered: 1895–1988.

Chronological reconstruction of life around independent incidents that involve event or personality. Farmer, *hacendado*, pioneer aviator, and mainly a personality, Marroquín spent most of life in La Laguna in Coahuila-Durango. Knew Pancho Villa, Juan Andreu Almazán, Elías Calles, Cantínflas, Saturnino Cedillo, Avila Camacho, Miguel Alemán, Jesús Urueta, and Portes Gil. Center of narrative is Lázaro Cárdenas, whom he aided with land redistribution in 1930s. Good source for popular culture.

1102. Martín Montoro, Margarita. *Margarita Martín Montoro: una mujer — una aca-*

demia. Universidad de Guadalajara, 2001. 166pp. Memoirs. Period Covered: 1935?–2000.

Of high school age, author emigrated from Spain to Guadalajara, Mexico, in 1944. Narration focuses on academic life, from student to graduate to career. As M.D., surgeon, and midwife, she developed and taught courses for nurses at University of Guadalajara. Interests in gender studies and pedagogy. Professional life dominates over role as wife and mother. Much information on training of nurses.

1103. Martínez, Adrian (1932–). *Adrian: An Autobiography.* Austin, TX: Morgan, 1986. 140pp. Memoirs. Period Covered: 1932–1981?

Devoutly Catholic Mexican-American from south Texas (Laredo, San Ygnacio, and Zapata) narrates innocent life: family from Nuevo León and Coahuila, altar boy, musician, impact of WWII, 4-H Club, personalities in San Ygnacio, and pilgrimage to shrine of Virgin of Guadalupe.

1104. Martínez, Antonio; Joaquín de Arredondo; Virginia H. Taylor. *The Letters of Antonio Martínez, Last Spanish Governor of Texas.* Austin: Texas State Library, 1957. 354pp.

Thirty-two letters from San Antonio, Texas, validate desperation of one of Spain's frontier colonies: defense against Indians and Americans, bandits, constant lack of food and money, need for horses and mules, uninhabitable houses, deserters posted to San Antonio, and a bureaucracy that impeded Martínez's efforts. Loyal, astute, frank governor in hopeless situation.

1105. Martínez, Jesús Alberto (Dates?). *El rey del cabrito, biografía de Jesús Alberto Martínez.* Monterrey: Ediciones Castillo, ca. 2000. 191pp. Memoirs. Period Covered: 1930?–1999?

Born in Zuazua, Nuevo León, to modest family. By own efforts he opened *cabrito* restaurant in Monterrey and became successful restaurant owner. Parents, siblings, marriage, and own family. Briefly tried to be singing star on radio.

1106. Martínez, Jorge (1919–?). *El Orozco de Jorge Martínez.* Universidad de Guadala-

jara, 1997. 80pp. Memoirs. Period Covered: 1936–1939.

Painter worked as apprentice of José Clemente Orozco in execution of murals in Hospicio Cabañas. Portraying master, Martínez writes autobiographically: cultural environment, Orozco as man and master, techniques, apprentices, themes, composition, and anecdotes.

1107. Martínez, Luis María (1881–1956). *A propósito de un viaje.* 2ed. México: Administración de La Cruz, 1941 (1935). 171pp. Memoirs. Period Covered: 1935.

Archbishop of Morelia travels to U.S., Spain, France, Italy, and Egypt. Religious orientation to all tourist sites makes travel memoir. Own advice summarizes philosophy and technique of travel: "The most exquisite of our lives is inside of ourselves; the outside is only stimulus or nourishment, and at times an extension of our intimate lives" (p.8).

1108. Martínez, Miguel F. (1850–1919). *Memorias de mi vida.* México: Fondo Editorial Nuevo León, 1998. 460pp. Memoirs. Period Covered: 1850–1919.

One of co-publishers, la Escuela Normal "Miguel F. Martínez," suggests stature of subject in Nuevo León education. Director of normal school of Monterrey in 1881 and director of primary instruction in both Nuevo León and Mexico in 1901 assisted Enrique Rébsamen in drafting school laws for Federal District. Not intended for publication, unchronological memoirs some of best for turn-of-century education.

1109. Martínez, Zarela (1942?–). *Food from My Heart: Cuisines of Mexico Remembered and Reimagined.* New York: Macmillan, 1992. 354pp. Memoirs. Period Covered: 1931?–1992.

Culture, customs, food preparation, and zest for Mexico in life of celebrated chef make *Food from My Heart* engrossing. From conservative Sonoran ranch family and student in Guadalajara, she knew country intimately through foods. Now owner of restaurant in New York, author describes her life and shares cultural anecdotes and recipes. Autobiography and reference book on cuisine.

1110. Martínez Assad, Carlos R.
(1946–). *En el verano, la tierra.* México:
Planeta, 1994. 152pp. Memoirs. Period Covered: 1913–1993?

Mexican-Lebanese writer recalls Lebanese past of his country and his family. Narration on two levels: arrival of grandfather in Mexico from Lebanon and author's reverse trip. In grandfather's native country, author lives in present and in past.

1111. Martínez Caro, Ramón (Dates?).
Verdadera idea de la primera compaña de Tejas.... México: Imprenta de Santiago Pérez, 1837. 69pp. Memoirs. Period Covered: 1835–1837.

In 1836 Texas campaign, author fought in Battle of San Jacinto, which ensured Texan independence. Source cites present document as "requisitorio contra Santa Anna" (formal demand for punishment of an accused person). Mentions Cos, Urrea, and Filisola.

1112. Martínez Corbalá, Gonzalo
(1928–). *La historia que viví.* México: La Jornada Ediciones, 2003. 254pp. Memoirs. Period Covered: 1964?–1981?

Active PRI politician and ambassador to Cuba and Chile gives something of his life but much more of its context. Three parts to document: in Mexico more on Lázaro Cárdenas than on self; ambassador to Chile and sympathy for Allende regime; and Cuba and Castro.

1113. Martínez de Oliveros, Gloria
(1927–). *¡Tú me escogiste a mí, para esta misión sublime!* Guadalajara: Amate, 1996. 189pp. Memoirs. Period Covered: 1957–1972.

In 1957, gave birth to daughter who at five months was stricken with purulent meningitis, illness that affected all stages of development. Memoirs mirror struggle of Catholic mother to rehabilitate and to educate daughter.

1114. Martínez López, Adolfo (Dates?).
Vivir...Recordando escuela normal de Jalisco. Guadalajara: Unidad Editorial, 1988. 130pp. Memoirs. Period Covered: 1939–1987.

Normal School of Jalisco's birthday in 1987 coincided with president's "year of *normalismo.*" Pays homage to alma mater by remembering 1939–1945 generation, faculty, students, staff, educational plant, and certification as teacher. Affectionate recall of educational system.

1115. Martínez López, Joel (1928–).
Orígenes del presbiterianismo en México. Tamaulipas: Matamoros, 1972. Pp.2–13. Memoirs. Period Covered: 1928–1972.

First pages tell life from baptism to ordination and first parish in San Benito, Texas. Songs, Sunday school, Bible contests, knowledge of God through His word, call to ministry, seminary in Mexico City, and internship in Linares, Nuevo León, encapsulate Protestant in Mexico.

1116. Martínez Martínez, Jorge
(1917–). *Memorias y reflexiones de un obispo.* México: Editorial Villicaña, 1986. 526pp. Diary. Period Covered: 1984–1985?

First volume of diary of bishop required reading for understanding problems of contemporary priest and church dignitary. Martínez Martínez has dual concern of present-day church and his self-examination and efforts at change. Tone and content similar to second volume.

1117. Martínez Martínez, Jorge (1917–).
Memorias y tonterías de un obispo. 2a parte. México: Grupo Editorial Ecumene, 1990. 429pp. Diary. Period Covered: 1985–1986.

Twenty-month diary betrays profundity unsuggested by title. Scatters snippets of autobiography but predominating sentiment religious. Shares readings, thoughts on parishioners, duties, mystical role of church in revolutionary Mexico, daily activities, etc. Exemplary for mixing spiritual and mundane.

1118. Martínez Ortega, Judith (1908–?).
La isla y tres cuentos. México: Imprenta Universitaria, 1959. 134pp. Memoirs. Period Covered: 1931.

Writer spent 1931 as secretary to Gen. Francisco J. Mújica on penal colony Islas Marías. Impressions of enervating environment inside and outside of prison in realistic memoirs: punishment, rape, homosexuality, and prostitution. Chapters read independently or collectively.

1119. Martínez Portilla, Isabel María.
Dejando atrás Nentón: relato de vida de una mujer indígena desplazada. Málaga: Universidad de Málaga, 1994. 190pp.

Guatemalan Magdalena and her family, because of chaos in their country, lived for eight years on border with Mexico. In decade of 70s, Mexico offered refuge to Guatemalans. Magdalena, now located in Tabasco, lost both husband and son in same year. Survived with two unusual jobs. Devout Catholic was employed as catechist for confirmands. She and other friends organized and became seamstresses. One-third of book devoted to Mexico.

1120. Martínez Vásquez, Víctor Raúl
(Dates?). *Va de nuez: crónicas.* Universidad Autónoma Benito Juárez de Oaxaca, 1991. 135pp. Memoirs. Period Covered: 1986–1988.

Oaxacan *cronista* attempts to define "Mis crónicas iniciales representaron una especie de catarsis; respuestas sentimentales a situaciones de alegría, tristeza, frustración y rabia…" (p.11). Locates *crónica* within autobiography and pays tribute to Ricardo Pozas (q.v. *Juan Pérez Jolote*), who taught him methods of social science research. Filtered through Martínez Vásquez, Oaxaca becomes tangible: art, patriotic celebrations, weddings, Revolution through anecdotes, politics, and biographies.

1121. Mason, Gregory; Herbert Joseph Spinden. *Silver Cities of Yucatan.* New York: Putnam, 1927. 340pp.

Author with four colleagues including Herbert J. Spinden, noted Mayanist, in 1920s sailed coast of Quintana Roo Territory from Belize to Puerto Morelos. Expedition had two purposes: search for birds and for Maya ruins. Nucleus of enthusiasts found five Maya ruins: Acomal, Chakalal, Paalmul, and Xhert. Camaraderie of adventurers, interaction with Mayas, and roughing it in wilderness also comprise travel autobiography.

1122. Massolo, Alejandra (1946 Birth of la señora Aurora). *Memoria del Pedregal, memorias de mujer: testimonio de una colona.* México: Mujeres para el Diálogo, 1988. 32pp. Oral Autobiography. Period Covered: 1965–1982?

Thirty-eight-year-old Aurora of Pedregal de Santo Domingo de Los Reyes in Coyoacán in Mexico City. Belonging to poorest class, squatters, Aurora is articulate survivor. In slum area has four children, fights city government that destroys home, works to build school, and is politicized. Enhancing materials in introduction, description of Pedregal, and reflections of women's roles and bibliography. Massola mentions nothing on methodology.

1123. Mathewson, Donna. *Down Mexico Way.* New York: Comet Press Books, 1956. 213pp.

Early 1950s set time for humorous travel memoir of elderly lady. She crosses into Mexico in bus at Juárez and her adventures begin: Chihuahua, Mexico City, and Bajío comprise itinerary. She enjoys and describes Mexican customs and is not judgmental about host country.

1124. Mathias, Fred S. *The Amazing Bob Davis: His Last Vagabond Journey.* New York: Longmans Green, 1944. 326pp.

Fred S. Mathias is Bob Davis's Boswell. In 1920s, two men motor to Mexico starting in Coahuila with American rancher. Continue journey to Monterrey, Tamazunchale, Mexico City, Cuernavaca, and Taxco and home through Laredo. Davis, celebrity journalist, meets Ambassador Daniels in capital. Book, delight of information on Mexico, has uniqueness of presenting two autobiographies, author's and also Bob Davis's through first-person anecdote.

1125. Maury, Dabney Herndon. *Recollections of a Virginian in the Mexican, Indian, and Civil Wars.* New York: Scribner, 1894. 279pp.

West Point graduate of 1846 entered Mexican-American War. Monterrey, Victoria, Tampico, Vera Cruz, and Jalapa his major war scenes. Tells of landing at Tampico and massing of troops there. Incident with surgeon who wanted to amputate Maury's arm. Injury allowed for early discharge. One part of autobiography on Mexico.

1126. Mayo, C.M. *Miraculous Air: Journey of a Thousand Miles through Baja California,* *the Other Mexico.* Salt Lake City: University of Utah Press, 2002. 389pp.

Mayo moves in space, time, and culture through the peninsula. She meets natives and foreigners; recalls other books on the area. Chapters on whale watching, environmentalism, drugs, border, and martyred Luis Donaldo Colosio distinguish memoir from others on Baja.

1127. McCann, Irving Goff. *With the National Guard on the Border: Our National Military Problem.* St. Louis: Mosby, 1917. 271pp.

With Pershing in Mexico to chase Villa, author stationed in San Antonio, Texas, with National Guard unit. Colorful account of moving local militia, training in San Antonio, adjusting to climate, and preparedness along border.

1128. McClellan, George Brinton. *The Mexican War Diary....* Princeton: Princeton University Press, 1917. 97pp.

"McClellan could write" (p.3). This sentence, appearing in introduction, is verified. West Point graduate of 1846, he was positioned for upcoming war and served at Rio Grande, Victoria, Tampico, Lobos, Vera Cruz, and Cerro Gordo. He notes land, people, life of soldiers, disgrace of volunteers, and siege of Vera Cruz. Nothing of McClellan's brilliant war strategy for Scott in Mexico City.

1129. McClellan, Ginny. *Situation Normal, Mañana Mejor.* New York: Carlton, 1977. 95pp.

American couple with children spent 1947–1948 in Mazatlán, where husband had employment with fishing industry. Humorous adventures relating to shelter, servants, fiestas, thieves, social system, and improvised Gringo Xmas accumulate into enjoyable reading.

1130. McCormick, Patricia. *Lady Bullfighter: The Autobiography of the North American Matador.* New York: Holt, 1954. 209pp.

The McCormicks, as tourists in Mexico, took daughter to obligatory bullfight. Stereotypical event triggered passion for bullfighting in Patricia. Autobiography is woman coming of age in 1950s and eager to participate in masculine sport. Apprenticeship and acceptance into exclusive coterie of *toreros* and successes in rings of Mexico.

1131. McDonald, Marquis; Glenn N. Oster. *Baja: Land of Lost Missions.* San Antonio: Naylor, 1968. 161pp.

In early 1950s, Marquis McDonald and Glen N. Oster visit fifteen of Baja's thirty-seven missions from north to south and describe trip. Much detail on locating missions, combating elements, and interacting with natives.

1132. McElroy, Clarence L. *Seventeen Days in the Mexican Jungle.* Greenfield, IN: Mitchell, 1933. 172pp.

In 1932, author commissioned to fly plane to Honduras. Crashed in Oaxaca killing co-pilot, but McElroy survived seventeen days. Details experience and credits Gerardo Enríquez, Indian who saved him. Survival amazed even natives. Much of human spirit and also history of early flying in Latin America.

1133. McGary, Elizabeth Visere. *An American Girl in Mexico.* New York: Dodd Mead, 1904. 150pp.

Upper-class family of Monterrey depicted here. Monolingual Texan in Monterrey for year with family that allows observations of customs and courtship. Novel and picturesque setting attract her; poverty and racial attitudes of Mexicans repel her.

1134. McKay, Hugh Dixon. *Stranded in Mexican Revolution, 1923–1924.* Wilton, CN: Printed by Helkin, 1969. 108pp.

Hugh McKay, sales representative for Vicks VapoRub in Yucatan, witnessed Revolution when Adolfo De la Huerta declared against Alvaro Obregón in 1923. Experienced much of brief affair and admired Felipe Carrillo Puerto. Humorous incidents of promoting foreign product before days of radio and TV.

1135. McKellar, Margaret Maud; Dolores L. Latorre. *Life on a Mexican Ranche.* Bethelhem, PA: Lehigh University Press, 1994. 238pp.

Scottish-born family buys 400,000-acre ranch El Nacimiento in Coahuila and moves there in 1891. Abandons ranch abruptly in 1894 with murder of Mr. McKellar. Interactions with other foreigners, natives, and Blacks reveal part of cultural complexity of Mexican society. Incidents of ranch life enliven book.

1136. McKinlay, Arch. *Visits with Mexico's Indians.* Glendale, CA: Wycliffe Bible Translators, 1945. 127pp.

One of Cameron Townsend's first followers to publish memoirs, Arch McKinlay evangelized in states of Vera Cruz, Puebla, and Jalisco. Title page annotates author as missionary to Mexico and teacher at Camp Wycliffe. Arch McKinlay is in Cuautla: "...to search out Indians...to teach them the way of salvation through Christ...and give them the Word of God...in their own language" (p.7). Autobiographical anecdotes that relate to author's project.

1137. McSherry, Richard; David Holmes. *El puchero; or, A Mixed Dish from Mexico....* Philadelphia: Lippincott, Grambo, 1850. 247pp.

Medical doctor in Mexican-American War in 1847. In Vera Cruz, Perote, Puebla, and capital, McSherry writes memoirs different from others. He is more attentive to wounded and medicine. Also, he is more expansive on Mexicans and their culture. Delightful!

1138. Meade, George Gordon; George Meade. *The Life and Letters of George Gordon Meade, Major-General United States Army.* New York: Scribner, 1913. 2 vols.

Few officers in Mexican-American War left long documents. Meade as an officer wrote almost 200 pages of letters on conflict and specifically in northern Mexico from 1845 to 1847: Matamoros, Reynosa, Camargo, Ceralvo, Marín, Monterrey, Montemorelos, Victoria, and Tampico. More background on war than in other memoirists. Meade's rank put him in contact with Zachary Taylor, almost his idol.

1139. Medina Rivera, Lucy (1906?–?). *Un espíritu en vuelo.* Toluca: Universidad Autónoma del Estado de México, 2000. 114pp. Memoirs. Period Covered: 1906–1998.

Born in Mexico, grew up in U.S., and returned to Mexico as adult. Aviation interested her at young age. She divorced, married military officer, had two children, and enjoyed married life.

1140. Mediz Bolio, Antonio (1884–1957). *A la sombra de mi ceiba: relatos fáciles.* México: Ediciones Botas, 1956. 286pp. Memoirs. Period Covered: 1900?–1940?

Politician, diplomat, poet, dramatist, and expert on Mayans (*La tierra del faisán y del venado*), Mediz Bolio has fragmented memoir. Each independent *relato* focuses on personal experience of author: childhood in Yucatan, diplomatic corps, Revolution, and Yucatecan culture. Thematically joined *relatos*.

1141. Mejía, Francisco (1822–1901) *Memorias de don Francisco Mejía, secretario de hacienda de los presidentes Juárez y Lerdo.* México: Ediciones del Boletín Bibliográfico e la Secretaría de Hacienda y Crédito Público, 1958. 183pp. Memoirs. Period Covered: 1822–1887.

Active and varied life: studied pharmacy, worked in customs, fought Americans in invasion of 1847, served as inspector of customs, helped Juárez in War of Reform, fought French, and, finally, became secretary of treasury under Juárez. Focus on public life.

1142. Mejido, Manuel (1932–). *El camino de un reportero.* México: Editorial Grijalbo, 1984. 332pp. Memoirs. Period Covered: 1954–1972.

Creative and enterprising reporter roamed world in search of stories. Each of twenty-one chapters involves international event usually outside Hispanic world. Memoir for focus on external for limited number of years.

1143. Méliès, Erot (1960–1992). *Memorias sensuales de Erot Méliès.* Toluca: Ediciones del H. Ayuntamiento de Toluca, 1995. 63pp. Memoirs. Period Covered: 1900?–1967?

Unique document. Few authors concentrate on childhood; fewer broach erotic themes and sensual memories: parents and sex, breast-feeding, discovery of differences in sexes, church confirmation, an X-rated film, and homosexual uncle.

1144. Melo, Juan Vicente (1932–1996). *Juan Vicente Melo*. México: Empresas Editoriales, 1966. 61pp. Autobiographical Essay. Period Covered: 1940?–1966.

Short story writer, magazine editor, and surgeon concentrates on family, intellectual development, and writing. Structured approach to life of writer; essay with elements of traditional autobiography: genealogy, education, career patterns, and literary influences.

1145. Mena Brito, Bernardino (1887–1979). *Paludismo (Novela de la tierra caliente de México)* México: Ediciones Botas, 1940. 314pp. Memoirs. Period Covered: 1913.

Journalist and soldier's memoir shares characteristics of fiction. Maderista, he enters Revolution in Campeche. Crux of memoir on death march through jungle of southern Mexico and Guatemala and his illness. Critic compares *Paludismo* to José Eustacio Rivera's *La vorágine* (1924). Disconnection between first part "La selva," second part "La costa," and "Epílogo."

1146. Mena Brito, Bernardino (1887–1979). *Los vivos mandan*. México, 1921. 88pp. Memoirs. Period Covered: 1920–1921?

Concerns appointment by Carranza as counsel in New York. Yucatecan's first paragraph explains necessity of publication. Detractors doubted patriotism and attitude in handing over Consulate General of New York to successor. Enemies originated in Agua Prieta where Obregón, Calles, and De la Huerta refused to recognize Mena Brito's superior, Carranza.

1147. Menchaca, Antonio (1800–1879). *Memoirs*. San Antonio: Yuanaguana Society, 1937. 31pp. Memoirs. Period Covered: 1811–1836.

Eyewitness to several of San Antonio events: independence from Spain and Battle of Alamo. Menchaca vivifies narration with colorful but violent anecdotes. More history than memoir.

1148. Méndez M., Miguel (1930–). *Entre letras y ladrillos: autobiografía novelada*. Tempe, AZ: Bilingual Press, 1996. 120pp. Trans: *From Labor to Letters: A Novel Autobi-ography* English edition by David William Foster. Tempe, AZ: Bilingual Press, 1997. Memoirs. Period Covered: 1930–1995?

Follows contours of life along Arizona-Tucson border. Born in Bisbee, Arizona, he moved to Sonora during Depression. Life vacillates between manual labor and academia. Only academic catapulted to university-level teaching without formal education. Free association style demands much of reader.

1149. Mendoza, Adalberto R. (1885–1957). *Autobiografía de Adalberto R. Mendoza*. México: Instituto Nacional de Estudios Históricos de la Revolución Mexicana, 1998. 72pp. Memoirs. Period Covered: 1914–1924.

Three interweaving threads run through text of railway employee: family, Revolution and job. Beginning in San Luis Potosí and Tamaulipas, chief dispatcher in Cárdenas, inspector of transportation, conductor, head of trains (la División México-Querétaro), and finally, superintendent.

1150. Mendoza, Lydia (1916–). *Lydia Mendoza: A Family Autobiography*. Compiled and introduced by Chris Strachwitz and James Nicolopulos. Houston: Arte Público, 1993. 409pp. Oral Autobiography. Period Covered: 1928–1984?

"Lydia Mendoza was the first woman performer of vernacular music to emerge as a star from the fledgling business of commercial recording of Mexican-American country music" (p.ix). Lydia dominates but other members of family under focus for careers in music. From San Antonio, Texas, family toured Southwest, California, and Mexico to perform. From interviews with family, autobiography incorporates popular lore of Mexico in songs and variety acts. Family endured and thrived in occasionally hostile Anglo environment.

1151. Mendoza, María Luisa (1930–). *Confrontaciones: María Luisa Mendoza*. Azcapotzalco, DF: Universidad Autónoma Metropolitana, 1985. 36pp. Interview. Period Covered: 1930–1985.

Reveals autobiographical data such as writing since age fifteen. She decries Mexican misuse of Spanish, love for culture of Spain, trip to Soviet Union, and Tlateloco in country's history. Guanajuato-born journalist also novelist and founder of two magazines.

1152. Mendoza, María Luisa (1930–). *De cuerpo entero: María Luisa Mendoza*. México: Ediciones Corunda, 1991. 55pp. Memoirs. Period Covered: 1927–1991.

From Guanajuato, novelist, journalist, lecturer, politician, and interior decorator reveals intellectual habits, reading, writing and creating. Abstract life weighs more than concrete one: fragments of thoughts about other authors and momentary revelations of self generally displace both Mexico and immediate surroundings. Intellectual and emotional self emerges.

1153. Mendoza, María Luisa (1930–). *Dos palabras dos: (crónica de un informe, por) María Luisa Mendoza (y) Edmundo Domínguez Aragonés* (Dates?). México, 1972. 139pp. Memoirs. Period Covered: 1972.

Unique New Journalism approach, *Dos palabras dos* documents two reporters trailing President Luis Echeverría Alvarez. Contribution of each journalist never clearly delineated. Dually produced document relates as much to journalism as to Echeverría's personality or programs.

1154. Mendoza, María Luisa (1930–). *Raaa, Reee, Riii, Rooo Rusia (URSS)*. México: Fondo de Cultura Económica, 1974. 63pp. Memoirs. Period Covered: 1973.

Journalist selected to visit Russia and write articles for *El Universal*. First pages autobiographical in emotion about trip. Rest of document on visits to standard tourist sites such as Lenin's Tomb. Allusions to Russian literature enrich memoirs.

1155. Mendoza Barragán, Ezequiel (1893–?). *Testimonio cristero: memorias del...*; presentación de Jean Meyer. México: Editorial Jus, 1990. 421pp. Oral Autobiography. Period Covered: 1922–1929.

Jean Meyer meets don Ezequiel in 1973 and compiles book based on writings and conversations of *Cristero* from Coalcomán, Michoacán. Testimony of Catholic peasant who became *Cristero* in 1922 and fought troops of President Plutarco Elías Calles. Insider's view from perspective of victims of persecution. Difficult to detect interference or presence of recorder.

1156. Mendoza Guerrero, Telésfor (1914?–?). *Los maestros y la cultura nacional: primera época: relato de las experiencias vividas*. México, 1986. 87pp. Memoirs. Period Covered: 1920–1980.

Has variety of experiences with education: elementary teacher in rural, semi-rural, and urban settings; high school teacher; normal school professor; state superintendent of education of Sonora; and coordinator for basic education (literacy and training) for Mexico.

1157. Mendoza-López, Margarita (1910?–1985). *El teatro de ayer de mis recuerdos*. México: Editorial Porrúa, 1985. 159pp. Memoirs. Period Covered: 1890–1967?

Remembers theater through lives of parents, Luiz Mendoza López, promoter and creator of musicals, and Bertha Mendoza López, costumer and theater operator. Family toured Mexico and U.S. Theater history superior to development of author's personality.

1158. Mendoza Vargas, Eutiquio (1892–?). *Gotitas de placer y chubascos de amargura: memorias de la Revolución mexicana en las Huastecas*. México, 1960. 150pp. Memoirs. Period Covered: 1910–1957.

Active moments of Revolution predominate. Cursorily covers early life and then leaps into Revolution as Maderista. As writer, he is primitive painter. Much aware of own presence, he is center of action. Goes beyond dull chronology with eye for minutiae. No stylist, he lures by directness of prose and enthusiasm for subject.

1159. Menéndez González, Antonio (1926–1973). *El diario de un conscripto*. México, 1946. 319pp. Diary. Period Covered: 1944–1946.

Many military officers record memoirs but few recruits or draftees register experiences. Yucatecan and drafted, author with day-to-day entries inventories military life from ranks. Leaving Yucatan and going directly to Mexico City, he joins medical corps. Anecdotal, personal, and absorbing, diary complements life stories of military available in this bibliography.

1160. Merriam, Charles B. *Machete: "It Happened in Mexico."* Dallas: Southwest, 1932. 231pp.

Charles Merriam, pseudo doctor, writes of medical adventures in Oaxaca, Isthmus of Tehuántepec. Young man visits brother on sugar plantation and discovers that though not medical doctor, he can heal natives. Curing one sick man brings more clientele. Memory enables recall of medical folklore in U.S. Ingenuity of "doctor," local culture, and individuals fascinating. Title refers to level of culture as well as inevitable weapon of defense.

1161. Merritt-Hawkes, Onera Amelia. *High Up in Mexico.* London: Nicholson & Watson, 1936. 277pp.

Her "In the Beginning" sets tone, mood, and critical attitude. "The first time I went to Mexico I thought it was hell, HELL, HELL; the second time I knew it was pretty near paradise, and, during the following months there were all kinds of ups and downs between the two" (p.1). Merrit-Hawkes, with eye for sordid detail or defining negative insight, conjures up naturalism. Chihuahua, Mexico City, Cuernavaca, Cholula, Taxco, Oaxaca, Morelia, and Páztcuaro cast in negative light.

1162. Mesa Andraca, Manuel (1893–1984). *Relatos autobiográficos con las compañías petroleras: mi vinculación con la reforma agraria.* México: Editoriales Nuestro Tiempo, 1981. 168pp. Memoirs. Period Covered: 1918–1922?

Active in both oil and agriculture, author recounts beginnings of career. Narrative useful for perspective on both bastions of economy. Little of family, personal life, or personality here. After 1922, involved in agriculture and in national and international politics.

1163. Michel de Rodríguez, Isaura (1913–). *Cuentos e historias verdaderos.* México: Tradición, 1984. 187pp. Memoirs. Period Covered: 1913–1984?

Sporadically locates life in Ejutla (Jalisco), Colima, and San Francisco, California. Devout Catholic pens chapters with moralistic tone in context where correct behavior easily determined. Convent-educated and with several family members in clergy, she laments persecution of church.

1164. Mier Noriega y Guerra, Fray Servando Teresa de (1763–1822) *Memorias.* México: Editorial Porrúa, 1946. 2 vols. Trans: *The Memoirs of Fray Servando Teresa de Mier.* English edition by Helen Lane. New York: Oxford University Press, 1998. Memoirs. Period Covered: 1794–1805.

Of three autobiographies of Mier, *Apología, el Manifiesto apologético* and *Memorias,* last-mentioned one most complete. Figure of Enlightenment and Independence details background of exile to Spain, e.g., public skepticism of apparition of Virgin Mary. Describes imprisonment in San Juan de Ullúa and in Spain plus visits to France, Rome, and Portugal. Focuses more on surroundings than on self. Travel writer's penchant for good story, e.g., French rabbi's wanting Mier to marry his daughter. Deserves attention as period document and for contacts with eminent figures. *Manifesto apologetic* takes life to 1816. *Cartas del doctoral fray servando Teresa de Mier al cronista de India, D. Juan Bautista Muñoz sobre la tradición de Ntra. Sra, de Guadalupe de México escritas desde Burgos año de 1797* (1875) give more autobiographical data.

1165. Miguel (1968–). "Ya tengo mi lugarcito en el infierno." En *¿Qué transa con las bandas?* de Jorge García-Robles. México: Editorial Posada, 1985. Pp.177–204. Oral Autobiography. Period Covered: 1976–1985.

Adolescent from broken family takes drugs and learns to steal. In life of crime, fatalistic narrator foresees own death.

1166. Miles, Beryl. *Spirit of Mexico.* London: Murray, 1961. 208pp.

Author's interest in famous orator, Jesús Urueta, led her to his daughter Margarita. Miles's stay in Mexico proves fruitful: Oaxaca, Chiapas, Tula, Cholula, Ixtapalapa, Nogales and Monte Alban figure within spontaneous itinerary. Best chapter on medieval/Renaissance theater in Guanajuato.

Closure with Miles's and her hostess Margarita's visit to Jesus Urueta's birthplace in Chihuahua.

1167. Millán Peraza, Miguel Angel (1911–1982). *¡A Tijuana! (nosotras las gringas)*. Tijuana: Tallares Gráficos de California, 1992. 89pp. Memoirs. Period Covered: 1950s.

Journalist and poet and editor of periodical *Letras de Baja California* reinvents self in fictitious creation, Maximinio Lozada. Tijuana, city of 60,000 in 1950, evoked in realistic and pungent memoirs.

1168. Miller, Loye Holmes. *Lifelong Boyhood: Recollections of a Naturalist Afield*. Berkeley: University of California Press, 1950. 226pp.

"What if I was two or three weeks late for classes? I had had a wonderful summer and had exposed certain brain cells to a great variety of interesting pictures which time and subsequent experiences have continued to develop" (p.103): Loye Holmes Miller ends chapter on Baja in above work. He went as bird collector in summer of 1896, and comments on much natural life but also natives and *costumbrismo*. Perfect meld of autobiography and nature.

1169. Miller, Max. *Land Where Time Stands Still*. New York: Dodd Mead, 1943. 236pp.

With two naturalists, he ventured into Baja before WWII. Mission San Borjas, El Mármol, Comondú, Magdalena Island, and La Paz complete itinerary. Scatters landscape, history, sociology, and self. Salutary attitude cautions visitors to Mexico. "We of the truck were the intruders. We had not been invited; we had not been expected…" (p.6).

1170. Miller, Robert; Fred E. Basten. *Gringo: A Young American's Flight from Hell….* Beverly Hills, CA: Noble House, 1979. 241pp.

Negative view of Mazatlán. In 1975, vacationing Robert Miller was arrested for possession of one marijuana cigarette. Thus started sojourn in Campo Militar and Cárcel Público Municipal. During months of imprisonment, he tried cooperating with bureaucratic system for freedom. Nightmare of torture, neglect, and unscrupulous lawyers ended with escape to U.S.

1171. Miramón, Miguel (1832–1876). "Cartas del general Miguel Miramón a su esposa." En *Memorias de Concepción Lombardo de Miramón*. México: Editorial Porrúa, 1980. 193pp. Letters. Period Covered: 1858–1867.

Conservative general and president fought Juárez and Liberals. Partisan of Maximilian, he was shot at Querétaro in 1876. Collection suggests devoted husband and father. Postmarked Mexico, U.S., and Europe, letters indicate gentler side of general in politics. Excited by pope at mass in Rome.

1172. Miranda, Gregorio (1944–?). *Un profe…misión cumplida*. Tepic, NAY, 2000? 170pp. Memoirs/Diary. Period Covered: 1955–1994.

Nayarit-born schoolteacher talks about thirty years of work at all educational levels from primary through normal. Taught school and prepared self for advanced levels of teaching both in Nayarit and Guanajuato. Daily routine of teacher emphasized.

1173. Moats, Alice-Leone (1908–1989). *A Violent Innocence*. New York: Duell, Sloan and Pearce, 1951. 312pp. Memoirs. Period Covered: 1908?–1921.

Mexican-born daughter of privilege recalls childhood in Mexico City from Porfiriato to fall of Carranza in 1921. Though native, she views Mexico from perspective of outsider. Hotel Geneve brat, she is educated at home by semi-prepared tutors. Revolution impinges on idyllic setting and at times forces family to asylum in U.S. Globe-trotting Moats has two other memoirs. *Blind Date with Mars* (1943) humorously recounts her efforts to get a visa to go to Russia in 1940 and her wars in that country with U.S. ambassador and Russian censors. Later *No Passport for Paris* (1945) unfolds in Spain and France in 1943. Journalist in espionage in Nazi-occupied France.

1174. Modotti, Tina; Edward Weston; Antonio Saborit. *Mujer sin país: las cartas a Edward Weston y otros papeles personales*. México: Cal y Arena, 2001, 1992. 287pp.

Tina Modotti speaks for self in above title. Photographer and militant communist penned letters from 1921 to 1938 to lover and mentor Weston but also to others. Early 1920s to 1930 with beleaguered Tina hounded into exile to Berlin. Mexican decade with love, professional growth, and ties to intellectual and artistic worlds of capital. Well-edited and indexed edition.

1175. Moheno, Querido (1874–1933). *Mi actuación política después de la Decena Trágica*. México: Ediciones Botas, 1939. 201pp. Memoirs. Period Covered: 1913–1914.

Prolific journalist, politician, and head of Foreign Relations under President Huerta from 1913 to 1914. Anti-Maderista, Moheno defends Huerta against charges of collusion in death of Madero. Memoirs mix with pertinent documents.

1176. Moisés, Rosalio (1896–1969). *A Yaqui Life: The Personal Chronicle of a Yaqui Indian*. Lincoln: University of Nebraska Press, 1977 (ca.1971). 251pp. Memoirs. Period Covered: 1896–1952.

Trilingual Yaqui writes story with aid of anthropologist. Born in Colorado, Moisés spent most of life in Sonora-Arizona area. He migrated to Mexico, where he found hardships greater than in U.S. Returned to Lubbock, Texas. Account of Yaqui culture and poverty on both sides of border.

1177. Mojarro, Tomás (1932–). *¡Mis veladores!: al poder popular*. México: Editorial Grijalbo, 241pp. Interview. Period Covered: 1932–1998?

Focuses on proletarian beginnings, apprenticeship, and success as mechanic, education, family, and anecdotes of Juan Rulfo, first writings, and Emmanuel Carballo. Interview mainly expresses political ideas.

1178. Mojarro, Tomás (1932–). *Tomás Mojarro*. México: Empresas Editoriales, 1966. 61pp. Memoirs. Period Covered: 1934?–1966.

Moments from childhood to publication of first novel, *Malafortuna* (1964). Includes education, dreams of U.S., experience in seminary, training as mechanic, introduction to literature, removal to Mexico City and acquaintance with Emmanuel Carballo.

Picaresque life moves geographically from Jalapa to Guadalajara to Mexico City. Thirty-four year old records self in most formative moments.

1179. Mojica José (1895–1974). *Yo pecador: autobiografía*. México: Editorial Jus, 1956. 662pp. Trans: *I, a Sinner…Autobiography*. Translated by Franchon Royer. Chicago: Franciscan Herald, 1963. Memoirs. Period Covered: 1895–1942.

Incorporates significant moments of life until entry into Franciscan order in 1942, decision precipitated by mother's death. Of illegimate birth and with difficult childhood, Mojica becomes both film and opera star.

1180. Molina Font, Julio (1897–?). *Halachó, 1915*. México: Editora Internacional de México, 1955. 112pp. Memoirs. Period Covered: 1914–1915.

Title taken from Halachó, Yucatán, scene of seventeen-year-old author's introduction to carnage and Revolution. Narrative focuses on capture and impending death. Facility with words and ability to create tension indicate potential novelist.

1181. Monaghan, Jay. *Schoolboy, Cowboy, Mexican Spy*. Berkeley: University of California Press, 1977. 218pp.

Twenty-four-year-old Swarthmore student spends summer on Mexican border at El Paso in 1911. He witnessed beginnings of Revolution with Madero's *insurrectos* against *Federales*. Arrested as spy and released, he runs into some of early notables of Revolution such as Madero, Villa, and Pascual Orozco. Another adventure takes him into Mormon Chihuahua. Much humor.

1182. Moncada, Carlos (1931?–). *30 años en esto: autobiografía periodística*. Hermosillo: Gobierno del Estado de Sonora, 1984. 209pp. Memoirs. Period Covered: 1953–1983.

Journalist and author of six books on Mexico covers years in Sonora and Mexico City. Distinct from other journalists in life writing, he attempts to provide primer of journalism: vocation, important newspapers of D.F., portraits of colleagues, women journalists, author and foreign journalists, techniques, politics, and ethics.

1183. Monroy Rivera, Oscar (1933–).
Esas voces lejanas: Autobiografía III. México:
Alta Pimería Pro Arte y Cultura, 1987. 245pp.
Memoirs. Period Covered: 1963–1977.

In vein similar to *Sueños sin retorno,* he
continues memoirs. Loyal Sonorense and
critic of Mexican culture, he wrote *El señor
presidente enanonia.* Combative author mixes
letters, poetry, and narrative.

1184. Monroy Rivera, Oscar (1933–).
Sueños sin retorno: autobiográfico II. México:
Alta Pimería Pro Arte y Cultura, 1986. 122pp.
Memoirs. Period Covered: 1948–1963.

Poet, essayist, and fanatic Vasconcelista
focuses on years from age fifteen to age
thirty. Student in Hermosillo, Guadalajara,
and later Mexico City, he became criminolo-
gist. Scatters poetry and patriotism throughout text.

1185. Monsiváis, Carlos (1938–). *Carlos
Monsiváis.* México: Empresas Editoriales,
1966. 62pp. Memoirs. Period Covered:
1940?–1966.

Essayist and critic of contemporary
Mexico selects significant events from life:
Protestantism, reading preferences, leftist
leanings, schooling, films, New York City,
etc. Manner of writing: inserting English
phrases, compounding adjectives, humor,
and invective reveal more of personality than
content of short chapters.

1186. Montalbán, Ricardo (1920–?).
Reflection: A Life in Two Worlds. Ricardo
Montalbán with Bob Thomas. Garden City,
NY: Doubleday, 1980. 164pp. Memoirs.
Period Covered: 1920–1980.

Son of Spaniards, actor spent first eighteen years in Mexico, mainly in Torreón. As
teenager moved to California and became
interested in theater and film. Also mentions
marriage and family. Title refers to spiritual
life.

**1187. Monteforte Toledo, Mario;
Mathias Goeritz.** *Conversaciones con
Mathias Goeritz.* Coyoacán: Sigla Veintiuno,
1993. 140pp.

Mario Monteforte Toledo's interview of
exiled German-Jewish artist in *Conversaciones con Mathias Goeritz* (1993). Dialog

covers diverse topics: major beliefs, politics,
profession, art movements, modernity, etc.

1188. Montemayor, Carlos (1947–).
Encuentros en Oaxaca. México: Editorial
Aldus, 1995. 140pp. Memoirs. Period Cov-
ered: 1994?

Poet, writer, journalist, and anthologist
also brought literature to Mixes, Zapotecs,
Chinantecas, and Mayas. Specifies stimulating Indians in creating literature. Working
from indigenous tongues into Spanish, he
discovers facets of psychology and speech of
native peoples. Sensitivity to language and
discussion of encounter make *Encuentros*
mandatory reading for understanding Indians.

1189. Montenegro, Roberto (1886–1968).
Planos en el tiempo. México: Imprenta Arana,
1962. 88pp. Memoirs. Period Covered:
1905–1918.

Of same generation as Diego Rivera,
author is writer. Describes arrival in Mexico
City, success as art student, and scholarship
to Europe. Artwork, opinions of other artists,
and impressions of Paris and Spain integrated
with personality. More autobiography than
travel.

1190. Monterroso, Augusto. *La letra e:
fragmentos de un diario.* México: Ediciones
Era, 1987. 204pp.

Similar to Iduarte as professor and
writer is Augusto Monterroso. Guatemalan
has resided in Mexico since 1952. Active in
literature, he has publications comprised of
criticism but also creative works. Above consists of subjective essays composed between
1983 and 1985. Shows grasp of literary topics
while revealing much autobiography in
ostensibly simple style.

1191. Montes, Amparo (1920?–?). *Mi
vida. En versión de Zita Finol.* México:
EDAMEX, 1988. 126pp. Oral Autobiography.
Period Covered: 1940–1987.

Radio singer collaborates with Zita Finol
to record memoirs. Born into modest family
from Chiapas, Montes reached celebrity as
vocalist on radio in 1940s and 1950s. Happy
moments of life and interaction with other
celebrities.

1192. Montes de Oca, Marco Antonio
(1932–). *Marco Antonio Montes de Oca.*
México: Empresas Editoriales, 1967. 60pp.
Memoirs. Period Covered: 1932–1967.

Autobiographical pages give vision of
poet's world. Words and images more important than routine aspects that comprise every
life. Poetry is imagined side of reality. Barely
mentioning family, concentrates on formation in poetry and preference for verse of
Octavio Paz.

**1193. Montes de Oca y Obregón, Igna-
cio** (1840–1921). *Epistolario de Ipandro
Acaico.* Introducción, transcripción y notas
de Joaquín Antonio Peñalosa. San Luis
Potosí, SLP: Estilo, 1952. 139pp. Letters.
Period Covered: 1861–1875.

One section, "Cartas de Montes de
Oca," comprises sixteen letters written to
father. Postmarked Rome, Florence, Alexander, Jerusalem, Tula, and Ciudad Victoria,
formal letters expose young priest intellectu-
ally alert and eventually bishop of Tamaulipas. Guanajuantan-born Montes de Oca,
humanist and chaplain for Maximilian, went
into exile during Revolution.

1194. Montes Zamora, Benjamín
(1942–). *Autonovela en refranes.* Guadalajara: Suárez-Muñoz Ediciones, 1989. 254pp.
Memoirs. Period Covered: 1942–1989?

Catholic priest attempts to recapture
past by narrating in proverbs. From Comala,
Colima, describes humble beginnings, family,
orphanhood, women, call to priesthood, and
studies in Zapotiltic. Average of six proverbs
per page.

1195. Montes Zamora, Benjamín
(1942–). *Auto-novela en refranes.* 2a parte.
Guadalajara: Suárez-Muñoz Ediciones, 1993.
271pp. Memoirs. Period Covered: 1974–
1992.

Same technique of placing proverbs with
autobiography as in earlier work. Includes
seminary work in Tula, Hidalgo, and eight
pastoral assignments: Tonaya, Jalisco; El
Ranchito, Michoacán; El Beaterio en Colima,
Colima; Villa Victoria, Michoacán; Villa de
Alvarez, Colima; Ahuijulo, Jalisco; Coalata,
Colima, and Tecomán, Colima. Homilies and
proverbs with autobiography.

1196. Montesinos, José María (1848–?).
*Memorias del sargento José María Monte-
sinos.* Gobierno del Estado de Chiapas, 1984
(1935). 279pp. Memoirs. Period Covered:
1866.

For verve, passion, and narrative talent,
one of better memoirs of nineteenth century.
Sergeant, with many other Yucatecans,
opposed reelection of Juárez as president of
Mexico and Pantaleón Domínguez as governor of Yucatan. Montesinos first fought on
side of Eutimio Yáñez and later Julián Gra-
jales and Sebastián Escobar. In introduction
Fernando Castañón compares Montesinos
with Bernal Díaz del: "...he not only carried
a rifle but also notebook in which to record
his immediate impressions" (p.l6).

1197. Montiel, Gustavo (1914–). *Cintalapa de mis recuerdos y su valle.* México: Gustavo Montiel, ca.1968. 168pp. Memoirs.
Period Covered: 1936.

Prolific travel author through memory
and diary recalls year in Cintalapa, Chiapas,
as civil engineer. Self, environment, friends,
events, works, word lore, and poetry fuse
into collage of autobiography. Perspective on
small city and region in 1936.

**1198. Montiel, Sara; Pedro Manuel Vil-
lora.** *Memorias: vivir es un placer.* Barcelona:
Plaza y Janés, 2000. 412pp.

Spanish actress promoted and developed
screen career in Mexico of 1950s. Met Gabriel
Figueroa among other celebrities and starred
in *Furia roja.* Found one of her loves, Spanish
poet León Felipe.

1199. Montoya, María Tereza (1898–
1970). *El teatro en mi vida.* México: Ediciones
Botas, 1956. 365pp. Chronicle. Period Covered: 1900–1956?

Life in theater done without help of editor. Chronological approach with little personality development or history of theater.
Attentive to theme, she stays so close to subject that she ignores family. Perspective of life
in theater unsatisfying because she broaches
no difficult questions. Formula rarely varies:
city, name of drama, roles, and applause.
Nothing of art of actor nor status of drama
in Mexico. No inclusion of famous
friends.

1200. Mora, Gabriela de la (1926–). *Para ser maestro: memoria de práctica profesional, servicio social y examen recepcional.* México: Editorial Oasis, 1968. 229pp. Memoirs. Period Covered: 1926–1965?

Thirty-eight year old enters teaching and outlines career from normal school to practical experience to completion of professional exams. Teaching in rural areas of Pihuamo and La Barca, Jalisco, he interlaces memoirs with lesson plans and pedagogy.

1201. Moraga, Cherrie (1952–). *Loving in the War Years: lo que nunca pasó por sus labios.* Boston: South End, 1983. 152pp.

Essays and poems comprise sporadic autobiography of Chicana-lesbian who mingles life story with essays on Chicanismo. California-born Moraga's bitter confession and analyses incorporate women from both sides of border. In same style and anger as *Loving in The War Years*, *The Lost Generation* relates more to Mexico. Moraga finds past in pre–Columbian myths. Search for self, "Chicana, lesbian, half-breed, poet," and discussion of whither Chicano Movement dominate as themes. Antipathy to patriarchal Chicano system and its heterosexism.

1202. Morales, Dionicio (1918–). *Dionicio Morales: A Life in Two Cultures.* Houston: Piñata Books, 1997. 199pp. Memoirs. Period Covered: 1918–1997.

Mexican-American from California and constant activist on behalf of people lives in both cultures. Son of Mexicans and multiple ties to this country make him eligible for present bibliography. Notes prejudice, struggle for education, braceros, work with ex-convicts and elderly, and founding of Mexican American Opportunities Foundation in Los Angeles.

1203. Morales, Melesio (1838–1908). *Mi libro verde.* México: Conaculta, 1999. 230pp. Memoirs. Period Covered: 1866–1876.

Only nineteenth century musician to write autobiography. Climax of career was second opera *Ildegonda*, success of which enabled him to study in Italy through sponsorship of wealthy Mexicans. Returned to native land and helped found el Conservatorio Nacional de Música y Declamación. Documents and reviews of concerts. Expresses culture of music of nineteenth century Mexico.

1204. Torres Vda. de Morales, Esther (1897–?). "¿Aparte las mujeres?" En *Vivencias de la Revolución* de Jorge Basurto. México: Instituto Nacional de Estudios Históricos de la Revolución Mexicana, 1993. Pp.51–77. Interview. Period Covered: 1897–1917.

Basurto questions tobacco factory worker and seamstress on conditions of working class women during Revolution and their efforts to unionize. Labor activist Torres recalls participation. "La conciencia tranquila," supporting story of her sister Ignacia Torres Vda. de Alvarez, adds precision to vivid account.

1205. Morely, Sylvanus Griswold. *In Search of Maya Glyphs: From The Archaeological Journals of Sylvanus G. Morley.* Santa Fe: Museum of New Mexico Press, 1970. 170pp.

Sylvanus Morely made several exploratory trips to Maya area between 1916 and 1932: Uaxactun, Tuluum, Xullton (*sic*), Piedras Negras, and Calakmul. Describes trips, ideas, and ruins.

1206. Moreno, Joaquín (1809–?). *Diario de un escribiente de legación....* México: Secretaría de Relaciones Exteriores, 1925. 286pp. Diary. Period Covered: 1833–1836.

Diary because much of personal self present here in observations: cultural life, illness, and reactions to people and to sights in Paris and Rome. Insightful twenty-four year old, at times prescient about conduct of mentor, Lorenzo de Zavala, who in 1835 played part in Texas separatism.

1207. Moreno, María del Pilar (1907–). *La tragedia de mi vida.* México: Compañia Editorial Phoenix, 1922. 70pp. Memoirs. Period Covered: 1907–1922.

Lived pampered life indulged by father, politician and head of periodical *El Heraldo de Mexico*. Politician Teed Lora gunned down adored father. In retribution, fifteen-year-old Maria del Pilar shot Teed Lora. Both patriarchal system and Latin interpretation of vengeance encompassed in soap opera, *La tragedia*.

1208. Moreno Villa, José. *Vida en claro; autobiografía.* México: El Colegio de México, 1944. 278pp.

Spanish painter, poet, and writer refuged in Mexico in 1939 and in twenty pages of *Vida en claro* delves into experience: poet's sensitivity to details, living accommodations, work as intellectual in lectures and writing and teaching in Casa de España (Colegio de México), and interaction with capital's literati. Most important was Genaro Estrada. Assimilation to Mexico, marriage, and family.

1209. Morones, Felipe (1886–?). *Capítulos sueltos: o, apuntes sobre la persecución religiosa en Aguascalientes.* Aguascalientes, AGU, 1955. 230pp. Memoirs. Period Covered: 1926–1927.

Final eighty-three pages with independent incidents connected to *Cristero* movement explain title. First part on Catholic priest from Encarnación, Jalisco, who suffered persecution in Aguascalientes and Zacatecas. He and followers in hegira from village to village to escape pursuers.

1210. Morris, Ida Dorman. *A Tour in Mexico.* New York: Abbey, 1902. 322pp.

Typical book of period. Author and husband, following zigzag course to Mexico City through major northern and central cities, arrive at destination. Attitude towards Mexico typifies Gringo before 1910. Diaz, godsend to Mexico, governs over Mexicans who need him. "There are two classes of people to whom life is one long afternoon. The very rich and the very poor. The one because they need do nothing, and the other because they have nothing to do" (p.80).

1211. Morris, Mary. *Nothing to Declare: Memoirs of a Woman Traveling Alone.* Boston: Houghton Mifflin, 1988. 250pp.

Morris seeks to find self in San Miguel de Allende and Mexico City with occasional sallies into Guatemala and Honduras. Yet Mexico always emerges in inventory of local items such as crippled drummer or blind man. Tourist Mexico left to other writers. Integrates self into lives of natives in San Miguel. Through best friend, an unmarried mother, she exposes problems of men and women. Lover Alejandro allows her to ana-

lyze own contradictory emotions about love. In spite of preference for self-revelation, Morris more sharply images Mexico here than do other authors dedicated to that purpose.

1212. Morrow, Elizabeth. *The Mexican Years: Leaves from the Diary of Elizabeth Cutter Morrow.* New York: Spiral, 1953. 72pp.

Shuttling between U.S. and Mexico from 1927 to 1930, wife of Dwight Morrow records experiences. Foremost wife and mother and secondarily hostess with duties of husband's office imposed upon her.

1213. Morton, Lyman. *Yucatán Cookbook: Recipes & Tales.* Santa Fe, NM: Red Crane Books, 1996. 233pp.

Six autobiographical chapters on travel, Merida, food, its preparation, Day of the Dead and other fiestas, and Yucatecan personalities punctuate cookbook with recipes arranged under traditional topics such as meats, vegetables, etc. Author started coming to Mexico after WWII.

1214. Morton Morales, Alejandro (1884–1964). *Memorias de un revolucionario.* Nuevo Leon: Editora González, 1997. 46pp. Memoirs. Period Covered: 1910–1920.

From Sabinas Hidalgo, he joined Revolution in 1910 and became colonel under Antonio I. Villarreal. Fought against Huertistas and Villistas in North. Writes better than most soldiers in movement. Places self in center of action and creates readable document.

1215. Moser, Edwa. Mrs. *The Mexican Touch.* New York: Duell, Sloan and Pearce, 1940. 279pp.

Cuernavaca attracts determined foreign females. She and three children spend year in Mexico with unusual goal, "...we sought to discover an explanation of the Mexicans' technique of living..." (p.5). Search starts in Mexico City but moves to Cuernavaca, where family rents *The Quinta Delicia.* Portrayal, not of grandiose Borda gardens or Cortes's Palace with Rivera mural, but everyday scenes with noises, pets, markets, servants, neighbors, schools, and foreigners.

1216. Múgica Velázquez, Francisco José (1884–1954). *Diario de Campaña del General....* Villahermosa: Universidad Juárez Autónoma de Tabasco, 1984. 86pp. Diary. Period Covered: 1913–1916.

Michoacanan joined Maderistas and rose to captain as aid to Carranza and to chief of operations under Lucio Blanco in North. Objectivity and lack of emotion coincide more with journal than intimate diary. Includes names of other officers, location, weather, towns, battles, terrain, strategy, and buildings. *Estos mis apuntes* (1997) has more writing of colorful revolutionary. Sporadic diary, 1911–1913, 1923–1924, 1925, 1925–1928, 1934 and 1951, includes above text. Intense years showcase Múgica's talents as diarist: personal involvement, action, details, people, and variety. Well-edited edition by Anna Ribera Carbó.

1217. Múgica Velázquez, Francisco José (1884–1954); **Javier Moctezuma Barragán**. *Francisco J.Múgica, un romántico rebelde.* México: Fondo de Cultura Económica, 2001. 695pp. Hybrid. Period Covered: 1906–1949.

Collections of documents generated both by Múgica and correspondents. Revolutionary, politician, military officer, and director of Islas María's prison, subject reveals self mainly in thematic sections on Revolution, military, and letters to family and friends. Correspondents such as Carranza, Pino Suárez, Obregón, Calles, and Abelardo Rodríguez suggest Múgica's distinguished position. Naturally, thirty-page "Íntimo" with letters to family and eulogy to Amado Nervo best represent author.

1218. Mújica Montoya, Emilio (1926–). *Corriendo las bases: vivencias y opiniones.* México: Ediciones El Caballito, ca.1990. 154pp. Memoirs. Period Covered: 1926–1989?

Economist confesses that memoir born from ten-day dictation in order to "...give proof of certain experiences that might be of general interest and to give opinions about topics of certain importance" (p.7). Reflects on current economic problems. Lauds three economists: José Attolini, Jesús Silva Herzog, and Ricardo J. Zevada.

1219. Muñiz, Marco Antonio (1933–). *¡Soy un escándalo — dicen! Marco Antonio Muñiz*; por Guillermo Saad. México: Grupos Editorial Siete, ca.1992. 288pp. Oral Autobiography. Period Covered: 1946–1990.

Little discussion of methodology for oral memoir of member of singing group *Los Tres Ases* founded in 1952. Left award winning group in 1960 and became soloist. On career beginning in 1946, he talks about women and family and his interlude as an entertainer in a Mexico City bordello.

1220. Muñiz-Huberman, Angelina (1936–). *Castillos en la tierra (seudomemorias).* México: Ediciones del Equilibrista, 1995. 226pp. Memoirs. Period Covered: 1942.

Attempts to recapture childhood. Given difficulty of recalling what she was at age six, she resorts to two ploys: labels efforts *seudomemorias* admitting partial fabrication; and evokes generic childhood, one without actions but of responses to situation. Geographical location in various parts of Mexico, adult friends, peers, schooling, and illness sum up world of Algerian. Unadorned prose and simple vocabulary reinforce narrative's goals.

1221. Muñiz-Huberman, Angelina (1936–). *De cuerpo entero: Angelina Muñiz-Huberman.* México: Ediciones Corunda, 1991. 47pp. Autobiographical Essay. Period Covered: 1940?–1990?

Explores unique background: Jewish-Spanish parents exiled because of Civil War, three years in Cuba, and entering grade school in Mexico. Other world is creation and writing: ability to be anywhere and adapt self, writings as child, travel and perceptions about language, constant reading, college and literature, literary critic, first publications, and hints at sources of creation.

1222. Muñoz, Esau P. (1884–1967). *Historias de fe y amor, al principio del evangelio en el norte de México....* México: Casa Unida de Publicaciones, 1987. 229pp. Memoirs. Period Covered: 1828–1906.

Ended life as Methodist minister serving in Villaldama and Monterrey, Nuevo León, Torreón, Coahuila, and in U.S. Both Jewish and Catholic, Muñoz's family in nineteenth century converted to Protestantism. Traces Protestant origins and evolution of family in

Catholic milieu of northern Mexico. As Presbyterian/Methodist, they suffered rejection and persecution even from relatives.

1223. Muñoz, Ignacio (1892–1965). *Verdad y mito de la revolución mexicana (relatada por un protagonista), v.2.* México: Ediciones Populares, 1960. Memoirs. Period Covered: 1913–1914?

Journalist and soldier that fought on side of Villa has hybrid memoir in two volumes. First is history; second with author as participant/observer is "autobiography." Opinionated Muñoz writes with more expertise than other memoirists and maintains interest with anecdotes.

1224. Muñoz Cota, José (1907–1993). *El espectro de las horas muertas.* Universidad Autónoma Benito Juárez de Oaxaca, 1993. 190pp. Memoirs. Period Covered: 1913?–1992.

Orator and scholar focuses on intellectual development. Attended school in Mexico City and selected by Gonzalo Báez Camargo to attend Instituto Metodista Mexicano in Puebla. *Preparatoria* in capital exposed him to Samuel Ramos, Antonio Caso, and Horacio Zúñiga. Notes informal education at Café Alfonso attended by *los cachuchas*. Final chapter on oratory. Curious autobiography, rejecting concept of recovering one's life, suggests education of a generation. Although prolific journalist and ambassador to three Latin American countries, he mentions none of this.

1225. Muñoz Cota, José (1907–1993). Entrevista en James W. Wilke y Edna Monzón Wilkie's *Frente a la Revolución Mexicana: 17 protagonistas de la etapa constructiva, v.1.* México: Universidad Autónoma Metropolitana, 1995. Pp.224–276. Interview. Period Covered: 1926–1952.

"Los puestos que tuve, o que desempeñé durante el régimen cardenista, fueron muy modestos, muy sencillos" (p.227). Humility and proximity to power open interview. Active in politics since 1920s, he talks about 1930 with Cárdenas in Michoacán and analyzes Abelardo Rodríguez, Cárdenas, and Emilio Portes Gil. Private secretary to former, Muñoz Cota attended Congreso de Estudiantes Socialistas en Tabasco under Garrido Canabal. Other items: teaching in Oaxaca, Zapatista sentiments, and role of his generation, 1922–1924, in revolutionary process.

1226. Muñoz Muñoz, Joaquín (Dates?). *Juan Gabriel y yo.* México: Praxis, 1985. 251pp. Memoirs. Period Covered: 1978–1984.

Intimate friend of musician Juan Gabriel. Loosely tied narrative follows two lovers through nightlife in various cities of Mexico, U.S., Venezuela, Colombia, Ecuador, Argentina, Chile, and Spain. Glimpses of gay life.

1227. Murbarger, Nell. *30,000 Miles in Mexico: Adventures of Two Women and a Pickup-Camper in Twenty-Eight Mexican States.* Palm Desert, CA: Desert Magazine, 1961. 310pp.

Subtitle captures contents: 1961 publication concerns fifty-one-year-old daughter and seventy-four-year-old mother who venture through Mexico without incident. Beauty of environment and odd pair's innate trust of honesty in people make travel memoir antidote to frequent anti–Mexican comments of foreigners. Camper held survival items and also assortment of inexpensive toys showered on children in opportune moments. Joy of Mexico's presence equaled only by joy of two women in one another's company.

1228. Murguía, Alejandro. *The Medicine of Memory: A Mexican Clan in California.* Austin: University of Texas Press, 2002. 228pp. Memoirs. Period Covered: 1955?–1995?

Unusual autobiography might be characteristic of new type of Mexican-American self-history. Author feels united with entire Spanish-speaking world and not just narrow Chicanismo. Reading of Gabriel García Márquez's *100 Years of Solitude* awakened him to wider world. Father's Mexican roots traced and author revisited ancestral home in Guadalajara. Main thread is growing up in California and leaving segments of state's history. Life with widowed father, frustration with education, introduction to Chicano movement, gradual politicization and universalization, and work on behalf of Nicaragua in Los Angeles.

1229. Nabhan, Gary Paul. *The Desert Smells like Rain: A Naturalist in Papago Indian Country.* San Francisco: North Point, 1982. 148pp.

Author lives with Papagos of Arizona and Sonora. In first person, he manifests two loves: one for desert and other for Papago's wisdom for suvival. Folklore, children, food, climate, and terrain deserve separate chapters. Nature, sociology, and autobiography blend here.

1230. Nacaveva, A. (Dates?). *Diario de un narcotraficante.* México: Costa-Amic, 1967. 371pp. Memoirs. Period Covered: 1950s.

Two years in life of drug dealer. Captured, he repents and recounts adventures in various aspects of trade.

1231. Nacif Elías, Jorge (1907–1994). *Crónicas de un inmigrante libanés en México....* México: J. Nacif Mina en colaboración con el Instituto Cultural Mexicano Libanés, 1995. 127pp. Memoirs. Period Covered: 1921–1994.

Young Lebanese immigrant arrives in search of parents. Mexico City and Mérida sites of hardworking salesman. Marries Mexican Lebanese and supports family with modest income. Tribute to success in alien culture.

1232. Nájera, Indiana (1906–?). *Carne viva.* México: Imprenta Cima, 1943. 224pp. Autobiography Proper. Period Covered: 1912–1943?

Poet, novelist, short story and script writer left autobiographical documents. In *Páginas íntimas* (following title), writing one of concerns; in present work, unhappy life dominates. Tempestuous relation with grandparent, children, and herself as product of failed marriage, Nájera directs thoughts to relationships with men. Analyzes love and its emotions.

1233. Nájera, Indiana (1906–?). *Páginas íntimas.* México: Costa-Amic, 1970. 260pp. Autobiography Proper. Period Covered: 1912?–1969?

Journalist also published poetry, short stories, and novels. Unorthodox Nájera supported self and children by writing and by selling books. Sporadic education. Often broached sociological themes in publications. Not a docile female!

1234. Nava Moreno, Joaquín (?–1917– Death of Castro). *Heliodoro Castro, general zapatista guerrerense: relato testimonial.* Ajuchitlán, GRO: Ediciones El Balcón, 1995. 199pp. Oral Autobiography. Period Covered: 1912–1917.

Zapatista belonging to Jesus H. Salgado's command, Castro engaged in combat in Guerrero. Too focused on tactics and supply to neglect of human element.

1235. Navarrete, Heriberto (Dates?). *Los cristeros eran así....* México: Editorial Jus, 1968. 105pp. Memoirs. Period Covered: 1926–1929.

Series of loosely tied anecdotes comprise memoir that complements earlier *Por Dios y por la patria.* Each chapter revolves around nonfictional heroic incident in daily life of *Cristeros* of Jalisco.

1236. Navarrete, Heriberto (Dates?). *En las Islas Marías.* México: Editorial Jus, 1965. 95pp. Memoirs. Period Covered: 1926–1927.

Persecuted Catholics and members of La Liga Nacional Defensora de la Libertad Religiosa acted upon advice to take up arms. Denounced and captured by police, thirteen lay persons and priests sent to las Islas Marías.

1237. Navarrete, Heriberto (Dates?). *Jesuita rebelde.* Guadalajara, Impre-Jal, 1983. 117pp. Memoirs. Period Covered: 1927–1972.

In 1932, young president of A.C.J.M. (Asociación Católica de la Juventud Mexicana) became Jesuit. From novitiate in Ysleta, Texas, to studies in Guadalajara and West Baden, Indiana, he speaks of education and joys of his order. Assigned superintendent of Carlos Pereyra High School in Torreón, Coahuila.

1238. Navarrete, Heriberto (Dates?) *Por Dios y por la patria, memorias de mi participación en la defensa de la libertad de concien-*

cia y culto.... México: Editorial Jus, 1961. 276pp. Memoirs. Period Covered: 1926–1929.

Jesuit recalls *Cristero* rebellion in Jalisco provoked by government persecution of clergy. Refers to activities of Asociación Católica de la Juventud Mexicana in 1921. Second part on his participation in armed rebellion. Anti-*Cristero* Saturnino Cedillo combated movement in Guanajuato, Jalisco, and San Luis Potosí.

1239. Navarrete, Raúl (1942–1981). *Raúl Navarrete.* México: Empresas Editoriales, 1968. 60pp. Autobiographical Essay. Period Covered: 1944?–1967.

Novelist's fragmented and impressionistic view of childhood lends dream-like quality to essay. Relating poverty of childhood, he sketches extended family. Describes writing experiences, but little noted of early intellectual influences.

1240. Navarro Corona, Rafael (1910?–?). *Recuerdos de un futbolista.* Monterrey: Impresora Monterrey, 1965. 345pp. Memoirs. Period Covered: 1914?–1945?

Covers large portion of life but focuses only on football. One of few autobiographies written by athlete.

1241. Navarro Martínez, Miguel (1901–?). *Relatos y anécdotas de un cantor, 1901–1954.* México: Instituto Nacional de Estudios Históricos de la Revolución Mexicana, 1990. 166pp. Memoirs. Period Covered: 1906–1954.

Peasant, songwriter and musician, Zapatista, farmer, wool gatherer, freighter, gardener, labor union leader, and organizer of religious pilgrimages. From Calimaya, Mexico, he mixes experiences with *corridos* of own creation.

1242. Navarro Torrent, Andrés. *Diario: diario patético de un emigrante.* Las Palmas: Ediciones del Cabildo Insular de Gran Canaria, 1991. 148pp.

In 1888, he emigrated from native Las Palmas in Canary Islands. Medical doctor, he had illusion that he could improve fortunes in Mexico. Aptly titled autobiography details disappointment and spends little time on environment or landscape of Mexico from 1888 to 1889.

1243. Nelligan, Maurice (1956–1977 Dates of Lupita). *Lupita: confesiones de una joven mexicana.* México: Editorial Diana, 1979. 247pp. Oral Autobiography. Period Covered: 1956–1977?

Seeing Mexicans as victims of stereotyping in psychology, Nelligan attempted to present unique life of subject somewhat representative of human experience. Lupita, campesina from Vera Cruz, passes through stages of childhood, school, adolescence, courtship, marriage, and childbirth. Daughter of indulgent *hacendado*, Lupita tried to adjust to various women in temporary marital relationship with father. Became economically self-supporting. Nelligan psychologically interprets each chapter.

1244. Neri Vela, Rodolfo (1952–); Carlos Elizondo. *El planeta azul: misión 61-B.* México: EDAMEX, 1986. 184pp. Trans: *The Blue Planet: A Trip to Space.* New York: Vantage, 1989. Memoirs. Period Covered: 1952–1986.

Crew member of *Atlantis* achieved celebrity in 1985 with voyage of U.S. space shuttle. Details preparation, flight, and nature of experience in space. Astronaut graduated from UNAM in 1975 and received advanced degrees in England. Notes childhood and dedication to science, topic rare in Mexican autobiography.

1245. Neruda, Pablo. *Confieso que he vivido: memorias.* Barcelona: Editorial Seix Barral, 1974. 511pp.

Neruda mentions some of same personalities in "México florido y espinoso," one chapter of memoirs. Appointed consul to Mexico, he is foremost a poet and images in short chapter verify calling. In 1976, he published *Mexico florido y espinudo* with an autobiographical essay on his presence in Mexico and encounter with country's greatest activity in the arts, muralism. Majority of pages incorporate Mexico chronologically as theme of poems on Conquest, Independence, Juárez, and Zapata. "México" (1940) is most autobiographical poem.

1246. Nervo, Amado (1870–1919). *Desde nuestras sendas soledades: Amado Nervo y Unamuno, epistolario.* Salamanca: Pontífica de Salamanca: 2000. 129pp. Letters. Period Covered: 1903–1914.

Mexican poet and Spanish philosopher exchange letters. Nervo touches various themes: children's books, poetry of Unamuno, *Vida de don Quijote y Sancho*, his arrival in Spain as first secretary of Mexican Legation, Basque character of philosopher, understanding *El sentimiento trágico de la vida*, love for France, and firing of Unamuno as president of Salamanca.

1247. Nervo, Amado (1870–1919). *Un epistolario inédito: XLIII carta a don Luis Quintanilla.* México: Imprenta Universitaria, 1951. 104pp. Letters. Period Covered: 1900–1915.

Letters written by poet and held by widow of Quintanilla. Nervo typical artist living modestly in Paris and intimate with important literary figures such as Rubén Darío and Díaz Rodríguez. Occasionally mentions works, especially "Hermana agua." Notes and recommends readings. Letters with moods and insights tell little of Nervo's life.

1248. Nervo, Amado (1870–1919). *Mañana del poeta: páginas inéditas, publicadas y glosadas por Alfonso Méndez Plancarte.* México: Ediciones Botas, 1930. 323pp. Memoirs. Period Covered: 1886.

Concentrates on frustrated love for Lola. More of romantic pose and overflowing emotions than life of poet. Persona reveals personality more than realistic image.

1249. Neuman, Alma. *Always Straight Ahead: A Memoir.* Baton Rouge: Louisiana State University Press, 1993. 165pp.

Author has sympathetic view of Germans in Mexico. Once married to James Agee, she went to Mexico with photographer Helen Levitt in 1940s. Married Bodo Uhse, German exile, and concentrates somewhat on German refugee colony in the captital. Scenes shift between Mexico City and Cuernavaca. Friend of Lupe Marín and Pablo Neruda, she worked in gallery that represented Rivera and Orozco.

1250. Neville, Harvey. *Mexican War Diary of 1st Lieutenant Harvey Neville....* N.p., 1950–1959? 44pp.

Served from June 27, 1846, to July 17, 1847. Five months in U.S. In October, crossed into Mexico from Presidio and remained in northern part: Monclova, Parras, Buena Vista, Monterrey, Camargo, and exited through Matamoros to New Orleans. Major battle Buena Vista. Much landscape and some customs.

1251. Nicolaita, Viejo (1895?–?). *Recuerdos Nicolaitas por un Nicolita viejo.* Morelia: Michoacana de San Nicolás de Hidalgo, 1978. 96pp. Memoirs. Period Covered: 1906–1912.

Anonymous author remembers Michoacán *colegio* years in biographical sketches of eight professors. Interactions with them create memoirs of regional high school education during Porfiriato.

1252. Nieto de Leyva, Dalia (Dates?). *Por qué me hice periodista.* s.n., Gráficas Económicas de Tijuana, 1994. 119pp. Memoirs. Period Covered: 1947–1992.

From Tijuana, she celebrated forty-fifth anniversary as newspaper reporter in 1992. Highlights exciting journalistic moments of career and profiles political character of city. Mentor was Renato Leduc.

1253. Nieto de Vázquez, Gloria (Dates?). *Los caminos altos: el relato de una madre.* Deerfield, FL: Editorial Vida, 1995. 137pp. Memoirs. Period Covered: 1985–1988.

Mother of child afflicted with lipidosis, lipid storage disease, tells of struggle with illness. Parents and child shuttle between U.S. and Mexico until daughter's death. Assembly of God mother infuses much of belief in narration.

1254. Nissán, Rosa (1939–). *Hisho que te nazca.* México: Plaza y Janés, 1996. 294pp. Autobiographical Novel. Period Covered: 1959–1995.

Sephardi continues story begun in *Novia que te vea.* Journalist and photographer narrates life after leaving husband and children and restrictive Jewish environment. One long monologue.

1255. Nissán, Rosa (1939–). *Novia que te vea.* México: Planeta, 1992. 181pp. Trans: *Like a Bride: and Like a Mother.* English edition by Dick Gerdes. Albuquerque: University of New Mexico Press, 2002. Autobiographical Novel. Period Covered: 1945?–1959?

Journalist and photographer develops life of Jewish girl in Mexico. Resents isolation caused by Jewishness in Latin Catholic culture. Middle-class family, victim of low ambitions for females, e.g., acquires secretarial skills.

1256. Nissán, Rosa (1939–). *Las tierras prometidas: crónica de un viaje a Israel.* Barcelona: Plaza y Janés, 1997. 145pp. Memoirs. Period Covered: 1996.

Spent twenty-nine days in Israel. Mexican Jew searches for family, roots, self, and meaning of Jewishness. Interacts with natives and visits kibbutz.

1257. Noriega Hope, Carlos (1896–1934). *El mundo de las sombras: el cine por fuera y por dentro.* México: Ediciones Botas, 1920. 183pp. Memoirs. Period Covered: 1919–1920.

Journalist and short story writer satirizes adventures in anecdotes in early years of Hollywood filmmaking.

1258. North, Arthur Walbridge. *Camp and Camino in Lower Californa....* New York: Baker & Taylor, 1910. 346pp.

Camp and Camino "reflects the many-faceted author, Arthur Walbridge North: traveler, outdoorsman, ecologist, hunter, social observer, patriot, romantic, athlete, and lawyer, as well as amateur naturalist, ethnologist and historian" (p.8). Quote foreshadows contents in one of first travel books. North writes for popular audience and captures interest immediately: "Down the camino we plunged, following hard in the wake of our thirst-crazed burros" (p.165).

1259. Norton, L.A. *Life and Adventures of Col. L.A. Norton.* Oakland, CA: Pacific, 1887. 492pp.

Literate volunteer from Illinois pens memoirs and one-third of them on Mexican-American War. Norton in oft-mentioned battlegrounds, Tampico, Cerro Gordo Perote, and Mexico City. Has storyteller's eye for good anecdotes and scatters them freely through narration. Customs, beautiful women, execution of Irish soldier for killing of Mexican, visit to Cholula and pyramids, cockfight, tiger hunt, etc. Autobiography one of most exciting of war.

1260. Novo, Salvador (1904–1974). *Continente vacío (viaje a Sudamérica).* Madrid: Espasa Calpe, 1935. 252pp. Memoirs. Period Covered: 1934.

Confesses and practices that travel writings are conversations with self. Subjectivity regarding place, people, and ideas exposes more of Novo than topic he treats. Perceptive comments on Rio de Janeiro, Buenos Aires, and Montevideo render more of author's personality. Abundant use of *yo* in confession and interaction with environment make Novo's writings autobiographical.

1261. Novo, Salvador (1904–1974). *Espejo: poemas antiguos.* México: Taller de la Mundial, 1933. 48pp. Poetry. Period Covered: 1906–1918?

Unique in autobiography, collection of poetry incorporates childhood of author. Each poem, following chronological sequence, establishes moment or period of life. Topics: provincial environment, school, first communion, friendship, and love, among twenty subjects. Addresses anguish of creation in most famous selection, "La poesía."

1262. Novo, Salvador (1904–1974). *La estatua de sal.* México: Consejo Nacional para la Cultura y las Artes. 1998. 141pp. Memoirs. Period Covered: 1904–1945.

Exposes homosexual life in which he names lovers as well as gays prominent in intellectual life. Humor, frankness, and pathos combine in description of intramundane Mexico City. Honesty extends to unidealized picture of parents' marriage and family life. Sensitive and necessary introduction by Carlos Monsiváis.

1263. Novo, Salvador (1904–1974). "Este y otro viajes." En *Toda la prosa.* México: Empresas Editoriales, 1964. (1938). Pp.331–416. Memoirs. Period Covered: 1938.

Twenty-three dispatches to periodicals

in 1938 reveal humor, personality, and regional Mexico. Sporadic character of articles, different times and themes, do not achieve unity of Novo's best autobiography, *Continente vacío. Este y otros viajes* sparkles with verve and subjectivity.

1264. Novo, Salvador (1904–1974). *Jalisco-Michoacán*. In *Toda la prosa*. México: Empresas Editoriales, 1964 (1933). Pp.417–456. Memoirs. Period Covered: 1933.

Novo accompanied Bassols on four-day trip to rural schools mainly in Michoacán. Subjective and autobiographical dispatches of trip commenting on geography, local personalities, schools, and villages. Pervasive acrid comments in magnificent prose.

1265. Novo, Salvador (1904–1974). *Return Ticket*. México: Editorial Cultura, 1928. 139pp. Memoirs. Period Covered: 1927.

Young Novo embarks on trip to Hawaii. Memoirs more than travel diary for revelation of personality. In train trip through native Torreón, reminisces about childhood and moments of Revolution. Reaction to minutiae rather than major sites personalizes journey. Too brief to be monograph, "Memoir," necessitates inclusion. Retraces youth from Torreón to capital and recognizes mother as culprit. Relives school days and broaches taboo topic: homoerotic Mexico. According to editor, manuscript still considered unpublishable in Mexico. Salvador Novo, "Memoir," in *Now the Volcano; An Anthology of Latin American Gay Literature*, pp.11–47.

1266. Núñez Guzmán, J. Trinidad (1898?–?). *Mi infancia en la Revolución: apuntes de un muchacho pueblerino*. México: Libro Mex, 1960. 117pp. Memoirs. Period Covered: 1910-.

Attempting to recapture emotions as child, recalls outbreak of Revolution and gradual impingement on life of family in Zacatecas and Guadalajara. In clear style, memoir follows tradition of *costumbrismo*. With echoes of *Al filo de agua, Mi infancia* appropriately prologued by Agustín Yáñez.

1267. Núñez y Domínguez, Roberto (1893–1970). *Como vi la República Española*

(película impresionista). México: Imprenta Mundial, 1933. 85pp. Memoirs. Period Covered: 1931–1932.

Visits Spanish Republic and attempts to sense mood of country in elections, burning of convents, strikes, and leaders: Fernando de los Ríos, Julio Alvarez del Vayo, Cardinal Pedro Segura y Sáenz, and President Niceto Alcalá Zamora. Includes adulatory tribute to poet, "Con Luis G. Urbina en España."

1268. Núñez y Domínguez, Roberto (1893–1970). *Sol y luna de España*. Madrid, 1957. 156pp. Memoirs. Period Covered: 1952?

Veracruzano went to Spain in 1931 and returned in 1952 as chief correspondent for *Excelsior* in Madrid. Thirty-two *crónicas* on cities, authors, religious sites, students, books, and fairs evidence Núñez y Domínguez as Hispanophile. Spain predominates over author's personality.

1269. Obeso Rivera, Sergio (1931–). *Sergio, arzobispo de Xalapa: su vida, su pensamiento, su actuación pastoral: entrevistas*. Xalapa, VER: Ediciones San José, 1992? 172pp. Interviews. Period Covered: 1931–1991.

Ordained in 1954, he held status positions within Catholic Church: president of Jalapa seminary, bishop of Papantla (1971–1974), assistant to archbishop of Jalapa (1974–1979), and archbishop of Jalapa (1979). No radical Catholic, archbishop avoids controversial answers to problems of national church as well as universal church. Advocates study of church's spiritual role rather than sociological role in Mexico.

1270. Obregón, Alvaro (1880–1928). *Ocho mil kilómetros en campaña*. México: Fondo de Cultura Económica, 1970. 618pp. Memoirs. Period Covered: 1911–1916.

Divided into three chronological sections: campaigns against Orozco, Huerta, and Zapata, Convention of Aguascalientes, and Villa. Describes men, battles, and causes, leaving little information about self. Unreflective military man in clear style.

1271. O'Bryon, Eleanor Dart. *Coming Home to Devil Mountain*. Tucson: Harbinger House, 1989. 97pp.

Religious mountain climber tells story.

She and fiancé tried to conquer mountain in Baja in 1967. Separated from companion, O'Bryon spent three weeks without food.

1272. Ocampo, Melchor (1814–1861). *Mis quince dias de ministro remitido.…* México: Estab. Tip. de A. Boix, 1856. Pp.3–35. Memoirs. Period Covered: 1855.

Governor of Michoacán and key figure in *Reforma*, he displays liberal bent in defining spectrum of positions in politics and in opposition to conservative Ignacio Comonfort.

1273. Ocampo, Melchor (1814–1861). "Viaje de un mexicano a Europa." En *Obras completas de don Melchor Ocampo, v.1.* Morelia: Comité Editorial del Gobierno de Michoacán, 1985–1986, (1840). Pp.271–311. Letters. Period Covered: 1840.

Eleven letters postmarked France and Italy to Ignacio Alas, insurgent and public figure. Without tourist information but observations on food, hospitals, and visit to Doctor José Maria Luis Mora. Vents anticlericalism in Rome. Raul Arreola Cortés edited and prologued work.

1274. Ocaranza Carmona, Fernando (1876–1965). *La novela de un médico.* México: Tallares Gráficos de la Nación, 1940. 318pp. Memoirs. Period Covered: 1878?–1914.

Covers thirty-six years of life as doctor and rector of University of Mexico but does not develop personality. Receiving medical degree, he notes little of self in achievement of goal. Indicates individual training and something of life of *médico* in military. Nothing on status of medicine during Porfiriato or reflections on dictator's policy on Yaquis. Maintains interesting narrative chronologically arranged in locales of Toluca, Mexico City, and Bácum (Sonora in war against Yaquis), Jalapa, and Guaymas.

1275. Ocaranza Carmona, Fernando (1876–1965). *La tragedia de un rector.* México: Tallares Linotipográficos Numancia, 1943. 532pp. Memoirs. Period Covered: 1914–1938?

Public life: M.D., research as physiologist, secretary of faculty of medicine, participation in various medical societies, and

ascent to president of University of Mexico. Conflicts with colleagues because of successes. Rectorship beset with intrigue. No comments on science and state of medicine. Inclusion of verbatim texts inhibits flow of narrative.

1276. Och, Joseph; Theodore E. Treutlein. *Missionary in Sonora.* San Francisco: California Historical Society, 1965. 196pp.

Earlier victim of expulsion was Jesuit Joseph Och. In above title, he renders three parts of memoirs: first in Germany, then in Spain, finally in Mexico and Sonora until expulsion of Jesuits in 1767, and return to Spain. Father Och missionized in Sonora for eleven years.

1277. O'Hea, Patrick A. *Reminiscences of the Mexican Revolution.* Mexico: Distributors: Centro Anglo-Mexicano del Libro, 1966. 212pp.

Another Brit in Mexico who writes well, O'Hea spent years 1909 to 1920 there. Overseer of hacienda in Laguna region, headed La Jabonera, company in Torreón, Coahuila, and vice counsel for Britain in Gómez Palacio, Durango. O'Hea did not fight in Revolution but saw much of it from vantage of northern Mexico. Knew many revolutionaries but mainly Pancho Villa. Analysis of Villa suggests both acumen and style: "If therefore I am asked for a definition of the man — Pancho Villa — my reply can only be — 'which one'? For the man underwent the mutations of his own process of success or failure" (p.160).

1278. Ojeda, Jorge Arturo (1943–). *Cartas alemanas.* México: Secretaría de Educación Pública, 1972. 210pp. Memoirs. Period Covered: 1970?

Novelist, short story writer, and essayist combines travel and autobiography from trip to Europe: Germany (Munich and Murnau), Spain, Italy, and Czechoslovakia. Relates to travel and involvement with other students. Young man sensitive to meaning of 1968 for his generation.

1279. Ojeda, Jorge Arturo (1943–). *Vuelo lejano.* México: Conaculta, 2002. 246pp. Letters. Period Covered: 1962–1994.

Letters, without dates, place of origin, or name of recipient, arranged in reverse chronological order. Mainly from Europe (France, Germany, England, Belgium, Holland, and Russia), China, India, and U.S., documents concentrate on Germany, where he lived as student of culture and language. Subjective letters relate to solitude, homosexuality, and comments on literature. Journalist and writer talks about two favorite subjects: Octavio Paz and Juan José Arreola.

1280. Ojeda Bonilla, Víctor (1861–?). *Recuerdos e impresiones.* Mérida: Famboa Guzmán, 1921. 152pp. Memoirs. Period Covered: 1861–1906.

From Espita, Yucatán, he mixes history, *costumbrismo*, and autobiography. Teacher in both Motul and Espita became lawyer and traveling justice of peace. Describes trip to Mexico City and Europe. Conscious of Indian wars in Yucatan.

1281. Ojeda de Gironella, Alicia (1906?–?). *Recetas y recuerdos de Alicia Ojeda De Gironella relatado a Jorge DeÁngeli.* México: Casa Autrey, 1998. 188pp. Memoirs. Period Covered: 1920–1993?

Society matron in early nineties looks back on life as hostess and cook in Mexico City and Cuernavaca. Although mainly privileging reader with recipes, she periodically interrupts culinary ventures with page of memoirs: learning to cook; family; reunions and individual members; teaching a Gringa to cook; introducing children to kitchen; food in Barcelona; and special guests such as León Felipe and Ofelia Medina.

1282. Oliva Poot, Paul (1954–). *Más allá de la escuela.* Bacalar, ROO: Cafcude, 1995. 81pp. Memoirs. Period Covered: 1969–1974.

Native of Chetumal, Quintana Roo, graduated from normal school at age nineteen and was assigned to rural school in Yokdzonot in Temozón, Yucatán. Relates teaching and interactions with community. Anecdotes comprise last third of memoirs.

1283. Olivera Figueroa, Rafael (Dates?). *Memorias de la lucha libre.* México: Costa-Amic, 1999. 223pp. Memoirs. Period Covered: 1933–1995.

Referee and sports reporter explores wrestling as spectator sport in Mexico: "He tratado de recoplar batallas sangrientas, hechos insólitos, desplantes geniales, anécdotas increíbles, ideas constructivas, críticas veraces y entrevistas fabulosas…"(p.9). Accordingly history, film, referees, and wrestlers in jovial account.

1284. O'Neill, Carlota. *Una mexicana en la Guerra de España.* México: La Prensa, 1964. 223pp.

Nationalized Mexican wrote *Trapped in Spain* (1973), translation of above title. Incarceration in women's prison in Melilla (Spanish port on Moroccan coast) from 1936 to 1937 provides theme. Shows capriciousness of Franquistas. *Los muertos también hablan* (1971) continues O'Neill's tragic saga: widow of supposed "red" under constant surveillance and narrow escape from Spain to Venezuela with two daughters.

1285. O'Reilly, Edward S. *Roving and Fighting: Adventures under Four Flags.* New York: Century, 1918. 354pp.

Nineteen ten embryonic Revolution attracted attention of Major Edward S. O'Reilly, who found self in Chihuahua as correspondent for Associated Press. Maderista, he fought on side of Villa and even in charge of regiment of foreigners. Journalistic background served in composing memoirs with much immediacy. Portraits of Villa in final pages.

1286. Orozco, Esther (Dates?). *Si la mujer está—: Chihuahua, abriendo caminos en la lucha por la democracia.* Chihuahua, CHH: Doble-Hélice Editores, 1999. 166pp. Memoirs. Period Covered: 1979–1998.

Distinguished scientist in molecular biology was candidate of PRD (Partido de la Revolución Democrática) for governor of Chihuahua. New party attempted to break deadlock of PRI and PAN. Details of campaign and speeches.

1287. Orozco, José Clemente (1883–1949). *El artista en Nueva York….* México: Siglo Veintiuno Editores, 1971. 187pp. Trans: *The Artist in New York: Letters to Jean Charlot and Unpublished Writings, 1925–1929.* Translated by Ruth L.C. Sims. Austin: University of Texas Press, 1974. Letters. Period Covered: 1925–1929.

Letters reveal more personality than formal *Autobiografía*. Expresses attachment and trust in Jean Charlot, main correspondent. Orozco communicated mixed feelings about New York City, hatred of Diego Rivera, distrust of Frances Toor, ambivalence toward Anita Brenner, and love for Alma Reed. Frustration with art world intensified by Rivera's acceptance in New York and public's preference for folkloric Mexico. Comments on art exhibitions and praises French artists. Success in art exhibit.

1288. Orozco, José Clemente (1883– 1949). *Autobiografía*. México: Ediciones Era, 1970. 126pp. Memoirs. Period Covered: 1883–1936.

Clarity of style and frankness of opinion. Fifteen chapters on art and less on travels in U.S. and Europe. Twentieth century art and muralist movement but little of Orozco as human being. Tells nothing of family. Early interest in drawing and painting suggests artist in formation. No self-revelation through minor points. Joy with New York snow tells more about man than reaction to art. Further glimpses of self in enthusiasm for Harlem Blacks and other ethnic groups.

1289. Orozco, José Clemente (1883– 1949). *Cartas a Margarita, 1921/1949*. México: Ediciones Era, 1987. 362pp. Letters. Period Covered: 1921–1949.

Third autobiographical tome repeats information in *El artista en Nueva York (cartas a Jean Charlot y tres textos inéditos)*. Written to wife, Margarita Valladares, with focus on frustrated artist living in New York and wary of exploitation. Topics: painting, contact with friends, promotion of works, and questions concerning family in Mexico. Themes lack poignancy of collection with Jean Charlot.

1290. Orozco, José Clemente; Alma M. Reed. *José Clemente Orozco*. New York: Delphic Studios, 1932. 272pp.

Alma Reed also reveals self in her association with master. Friendless artist arrived in New York and through Anita Brenner met

Alma Reed. She became his patroness and guardian and even opened gallery in which to exhibit his work. Reed followed him everywhere and felt his defeats as keenly as he did. New York years as well as murals in Pomona, N.Y., and Hanover, N.H., occupy many pages. Cabañas painting in Guadalajara and commission to execute mural in Bellas Artes end book. Reed's idolization of Orozco justified in his immediate success and later fame.

1291. Orozco, José Clemente (1883– 1949). *Textos de Orozco*. México: UNAM, 1983. 183pp. Interviews/Letters. Period Covered: 1924–1946.

Miscellanea that supplement other autobiographies. Much autobiographical data scattered throughout text. Fifteen letters to Justino Fernández, postmarked Mexico and New York, 1940–1949. Militant expression of Orozco's art view is shown in 1944 interview with Antonio Rodríguez.

1292. Orozco, Margarita Valladares de (Dates?). "Memorias/testimonios." En *Cartas a Margarita*. México: Ediciones Era, 1987. 70pp. Letters. Period Covered: 1915–1969.

Two autobiographies in *Cartas a Margarita*. First seventy pages, Orozco's widow gives context for major portions of husband's letters. Notes family background, meeting with Orozco, and mainly his presence or absence during years in U.S.

1293. Orozco y Jiménez, Francisco de (1864–1936). *Memoir of the Most Reverend....* N.p., 1918. 54pp. Memoirs. Period Covered: 1916–1917?

Archbishop of Guadalajara arrested five times by police. Informs reader of activities after accused of betraying government. Records services to church. Document bereft of interesting fine points or personal items.

1294. Ortiz de Montellano, Bernardo (1899–1949). *Epistolario*. México: UNAM, 1999. 348pp. Letters. Period Covered: 1924–1949.

Two-hundred-fifteen letters of poet, critic, editor, and translator of poems of T.S. Eliot. Dates cover author's productive literary period as one of *Contemporáneos* and editor of journal with same name. Edited *Letras de*

México and founder and collaborator of
Cuadernos Americanos in 1941. Most frequent
correspondents José Gorostiza, Juan Marinello, Alfonso Reyes, and Jaime Torres
Bodet.

1295. Ortiz Rubio, Pascual (1877–1928).
*Memorias, 1895–1928 y Memorias de un peni-
tente.* México: Academia Nacional de Historia
y Geografía, 1963. 208pp. Memoirs. Period
Covered: 1895–1928.

External life presented chronologically
rather than psychological focus. During Revolution, Ortiz Rubio was ambassador to Germany (1924) and Brazil (1926). Major topics
end before presidential period of 1929. Separate book bound with this, *Memorias de un
penitente* (1916), more autobiographical. Four
months in prison as enemy of President Victoriano de la Huerta. Memoirs realize potential when confined politician writes of daily
prison routine. Forced to deeper self-analysis,
he shares hopes, disappointments, relationships, and reading preferences. Intimacy
makes memoirs more valuable than ones
based on external action.

1296. Osbaldeston Mitford, W.B.J.
Dawn Breaks in Mexico. London: Cassell,
1945. 228pp.

In 1925, when Britain once again recognized Mexico, Osbaldeston Mitford was Honorary Attaché under Sir Esmond Ovey. *Dawn
Breaks in Mexico* affords view of period.
Much on Mexico; some autobiography; relations with British colony in capital; acquaintance with Obregón and Calles as well as
Valente Quintana, head of Mexico City secret
police; and friend of Ambassador Dwight
Morrow and family.

1297. O'Shaughnessy, Edith. *Diplomatic
Days.* New York: Harper, 1917. 337pp.

Shows enjoyment of being wife of American diplomat. She liked entertaining those of
her own class, enjoyed new countries, read
serious books on Mexico, sprinkled letters
home with French phrases and deplored loss
of Porfirio Díaz and arrival of new order.
From comments on menus and outings,
efforts at parenting four-year-old son, bridge
parties, gossip about president's wife ignorant of style, and political philosophical

thoughts, she never bores. Tensions between
Mexico and U.S.

1298. O'Shaughnessy, Edith. *A Diplomat's Wife in Mexico: Letters from the American Embassy at Mexico City....* New York:
Harper, 1916. 355pp.

O'Shaughnessy, as wife of American ambassador in Mexico and with access to pow-
erful, had strong admiration for President
Huerta, who showed more authority than
insipid Madero. Book serves as lens to spy on
diplomatic corps in Mexico, its functions and
social life. Mrs. O'Shaughnessy always fascinates. Racism characteristic of period.

1299. Osuna, Andrés (1872–1946). *Por la
escuela y por la patria (autobiografía).* México: Casa Unida de Publicaciones, 1943.
324pp. Memoirs. Period Covered: 1876?–1941?

Professor of Escuela Normal Nocturna
of Monterrey, director general of education in
Federal District and states of Coahuila and
Nuevo León, and provisional governor of
Tamaulipas. Self in struggle for education
and career as teacher or administrator.
Intrigues against schoolmasters and directors
dominate more than educational needs. Lived
in U.S. for several years as translator of
Protestant literature but never discusses conversion to Protestantism. Personal life rarely
noticed.

1300. Oswandel, J. Jacob. *Notes on the
Mexican War, 1846–47–8.* Philadelphia, 1885.
642pp.

One of longest and best autobiographies
from Mexican-American War with entries
beginning December 11, 1846, and ending
July 24, 1848. Span allows comments from
enlistment down to gradual withdrawal from
Mexico and return to U.S. Letters and notes
comprise volume that details more than other
memoirs: trek from Vera Cruz, San Juan de
Ulloa, Cerro Gordo, Perote, Puebla, and
Mexico City; history of Mexico; prisoner
exchange; dissatisfaction with government
contractors; frequent presence of Santa Anna,
Scott, and Taylor; gambling; bullfight; etc.
Offensive use of word *greaser.*

1301. Otaola, Simón; José de la Colina.
La librería de Arana: historia y fantasía.

Madrid: Ediciones del Imán, 1999. 370pp.

Otaola in first person narrates vicissitudes of bookstore of José Ramón Arana, another émigré. From book peddler to bookstore owner, Arana is centerpiece of intellectual nucleus of Spaniards refuged in Mexico ca.1944. Through Otaola's conversational style or master-of-ceremonies mode are presented various male personalities of vivacious exile group: *tertulias*, El Ateneo Español de México, formation of publishing group (El Aquelarre), and cell of fanatic Madrileños. Shows intellectual vitality of anti–Franquistas abroad.

1302. Otaola, Simón. *Los tordos en el pirul.* México: Ediciones de La Colección Aquelarre, 1953. 350pp.

Rightful for Otaola in *Los tordos en el pirul* (1953) to pay homage to Azorín, master of small things. Otaola's Mexican village, San Felipe, Guanajuato, gives motive to parade of fellow townsmen as they relate to him. Poetical account of persons, streets, moods, and time of day. Among many Mexican autobiographies that follow this pattern, *Los tordos* is one of best.

1303. Othón, Manuel José (1858–1906). *Epistolario: glosas, esquemas, índices y notas de Jesús Zavala.* México: UNAM, 1946. 122pp. Letters. Period Covered: 1894–1906.

Forty-three letters written to poet friend Juan B. Delgado. Shows working writer discussing problems of verse, vocabulary, and publications.

1304. Oviedo Mota, Alberto (1882–1953). *El trágico fin del general Gertrudis G. Sánchez/dos capítulos de las memorias del coronel médico cirujano.* Michoacán: Editorial Revolucionario, 1939. 60pp. Memoirs. Period Covered: 1915.

Battles and death of Gen. Gertrudis Sánchez, chief of Constitutionalist Revolution in Michoacán. Physician author accompanies Sánchez in battles against Huerta. Oviedo Mota exhibits more literary skills than contemporary memoirists: clarity of style, chapters of alternating description and action, and passion for cause and for Sánchez.

1305. Owen, Gilberto (1905–1952). *Cartas a Clementina Otero.* México: Instituto Nacional de Bellas Artes, 1982. 87pp. Letters. Period Covered: 1928.

Poet and member of *los Contemporáneos* wrote letters to actress Clementina Otero. Postmarked Mexico and U.S., letters expressed love for Otero. Ones from U.S. more commonplace with comments about alien culture.

1306. Pacheco, Cristina (1941–). *Confrontaciones.* Azcapotzalco, DF: Universidad Autónoma Metropolitana, 1987. 53pp. Interview. Period Covered: 1959?–1986?

Journalist since 1960 wrote under pseudonym of Juan Angel Real in *Sucesos*, did series entitled *Mar de historias* in *La Jornada*, and since 1980 has done TV series, *Aquí nos toca vivir*. Pacheco talks about poverty of family, mother's influence as storyteller, marriage to poet José Emilio Pacheco, work with women's magazines, etc.

1307. Pacheco Cruz, Santiago (Dates?). *Recuerdos de la propaganda Constitucionalista en Yucatan.* Mérida: Tallares Gráficos y Editorial Zamna, 1953. 493pp. Memoirs. Period Covered: 1914–1915.

Rural schoolteacher joined forces of Gen. Salvador Alvarado, head of army of Southeast and governor of Yucatan, 1915–1917. Author served as major translator to propagate Alvarado's program in Yucatan. Memoirs diluted because third and fourth parts are with idols, Salvador Alvarado and Felipe Carrillo Puerto.

1308. Pacheco Loya, César Francisco (Dates?). *Encuentro con un medio desconocido.* Chihuahua, CHH: Instituto Chihuahuense de la Cultura, 2002. 131pp. Memoirs. Period Covered: 1972.

Does *servicio social* (one year of medical service in village) in order to be licensed. From civilized Chihuahua (city), he is assigned village of Guachochi in Sierra Madre Occidental. Interference by military as he makes journey preludes year of deprivation and brutality: Tarahumara Indians, little medicine, bad nutrition, lice, cold climate, and always improvisational medicine. One of best for topic *servicio social*.

1309. Padrón González, Joel (1938–).
Desde la cárcel: una palabra para todos. México: Plaza y Valdés, 2003. 485pp. Diary.
Period Covered: 1965–1993.

Liberation theology not yet important subject in Mexican autobiography. Catholic priest here combines two related aspects of life: need for this movement in Chiapas and imprisonment because of his involvement. Prison diary from 1991 to 1992. San Cristóbal de las Casas and Simojovel, two places most frequently mentioned, have large Indian populations.

1310. Palacios, Adela (1908–?). *Normalista: tres relatos.* México: Unidad de Escritores, 1957 (1947). 136pp. Memoirs. Period Covered: 1927–1935?

Evokes normal school years and teaching. Receiving normal certificate in 1928, she captures spirit of school, its curriculum, and professors in Chapter "Normalista" and in Chapter "Maestra" concern for children.

1311. Palacios, Adela (1908–?). *Los palacios de Adela: apuntes autobiográficos.* México: Federación Editorial Mexicana, 1986. 123pp. Memoirs. Period Covered: 1908–1984?

Novelist, poet, and widow of Samuel Ramos. Frank and iconoclastic, deplores parents and conventions that stifle women. Different in content and style from other female autobiographers of generation, she mixes history, poetry, and life writing with delightful results.

1312. Palacios, Alfredo (1938?–) *¡Este soy yo!* México: Editorial Diana, 1994. 146pp. Memoirs. Period Covered: 1938?–1993.

From poor Vera Cruz family, he held low-paying jobs until discovery of talent as hairdresser. First pages note rise to success; final pages, relationship with celebrities.

1313. Palacios Mendoza, Enrique Juan (1881–1953). "Cien leguas de tierra caliente." En *Cien viajeros en Vera Cruz: crónicas y relatos, v.11, 1875–1967.* Editado por Martha Poblett Miranda. Xalapa Enríquez: Gobierno del Estado de Vera Cruz, 1992. Pp.63–168. Memoirs. Period Covered: 1911?

Archaeologist, historian, and inspector of prehistoric monuments makes excursion into jungles on banks of Tecolutla (Vera Cruz river). Interacts with other excursionists, describes landscape, pictures Indians, and encompasses culture of untamed region.

1314. Palafox García, Fidel (1895?–?). *Memorias de un revolucionario.* Puebla, PUE: Editorial Cajica, 1996. 291pp. Memoirs. Period Covered: 1910–1929.

From Tlaxcala, fifteen year old decides to become Maderista and even meets President Madero. Assumes anti–Zapatista stance because Revolutionary hero against Madero. Toward end of narration, becomes *Cristero.* Too much emphasis on history of Revolution dilutes anecdotes.

1315. Palavincini, Felix Fulgencio (1881–1952). *Mi vida revolucionaria.* México: Ediciones Botas, 1937. 558pp. Memoirs. Period Covered: 1901–1929.

Ardent Maderista, senator, journalist, diplomat, minister of public education, and author of several books. More historian than autobiographer. Lists of names and insertion of documents appropriate for chronological moment but interrupt readings.

1316. Palencia, Isabel de. *Smoldering Freedom: The Story of the Spanish Republicans in Exile.* New York: Longmans Green, 1945. 264pp.

Isabel Palencia and family arrived in Mexico via France and U.S. in 1939. Vivid description of Mexico and acceptance of refugees and survival. Exile, mother, and author reflects passion and partisanship.

1317. Palma, Erasmo (1928–). *Donde cantan los pájaros chuyacos.* Ediciones del Gobierno del Estado de Chihuahua, 1992. 110pp. Oral Autobiography. Period Covered: 1928–1986.

Incidents of life told to Margarita Aguilar, who arranged text and tried to maintain style of Indian. Narration, home, family, landscape, folklore, and drinking, mainly in 1930s in voice of young author. Dominant theme is *tesguino,* alcohol consumed by Tarahumarans. Indian telling own story rare in Mexican autobiography.

1318. Palmer, Ann; Jessica Herman.
Busted in Mexico. Albuquerque: Sun Books, 1978. 48pp.

Records imprisonment in Mexican jail. Caught for possession of drugs, she spent almost a year in prison. Speaks of condition of jail as well as disregard for rights.

1319. Palomar y Vizcarra, Miguel
(1880–1968). Entrevista en James W. Wilkie y Edna Monzón de Wilkie's *Mexico Visto en el siglo XX.* México: Instituto Mexicano de Investigaciones Económicas, 1969. Pp.411–490. Interview. Period Covered: 1880?–1958.

Only autobiography extant on militant Catholic. Subject gives conservative anti–Juárez and pro–*Cristero* perspective. One of founders of Partido Católico in 1911, researcher on A.C.J.M. (Asociación Católica de la Juventud Mexicana), and vice president of la Liga Nacional Defensora de la Libertad Religiosa. Perceives José León Toral, assassin of President Alvaro Obregón, as hero.

1320. Palomares, José Francisco
(1801–?). *Memoirs of José Francisco Palomares….* Los Angeles: Glen Dawson, 1955. 69pp. Memoirs. Period Covered: 1808–1846.

Californiano, Indian fighter, and soldier recalled adventures. Fighting invading Americans in California most credible part of memoirs. Other incidents less verifiable. Episodes of mutual brutality between Indian and White, pornographic story of snake, and use of *cabestros* (trained cattle to control herds) from subject's eagerness to entertain rather than to corroborate history. Lapsed time, Palomares's old age, and tendency to exaggerate lend air of lore to memoirs. Good read.

1321. Pani, Alberto J. (1878–1955).
Apuntes autobiográficos: exclusivamente para mis hijos. México: Editorial Stylo, 1945. 712pp. Memoirs. Period Covered: 1878–194?

Against dictatorship of Porfirio Díaz and serving presidents from 1911 to 1933, Pani wrote two volumes of memoirs. More history of Revolution than history of self. Government posts from 1911 to 1932 dominate. Major portion of interest to historians. *Lo autobiográfico* and *lo mexicano* in following sections: childhood, collector of art, and civil

engineer and construction of Hotel Reforma in 1930s. No references to mood or boredom or development as personality; prefers exterior self.

1322. Pani, Alberto J. (1878–1955). *Mi contribución al nuevo Régimen (1910–1933).* México: Editorial Cultura, 1936. 395pp. Memoirs. Period Covered: 1910–1933.

Active in public life, undersecretary of public instruction, director of public works for Federal District, secretary of industry and commerce, minister in Paris, secretary of foreign relations, secretary of treasury, and ambassador to Spain. Wants to rectify allusions of Vasconcelos in *Ulises criollo.* Gives only public life.

1323. Pani, Arturo (1870–1962). *Ayer.* México, 1954. 387pp. Memoirs. Period Covered: 1885–1932.

Engineer, employee of Secretaría de Comunicaciones y Obras Públicas, and member of diplomatic corps, Pani details childhood, home in Aguascalientes, early education, and service as diplomat mainly in Paris. Focuses more on other families than own.

1324. Pani, Arturo (1879–1962). *Una vida.* México, 1955. 209pp. Memoirs. Period Covered: 1844–1911.

Through concentrating on family, he deflects narration from self. Exposes proximate genealogy and then network of relationships in immediate family. Biography/ memoir gallery of portraits of upper class family of Porfiriato. Some funny; others pathetic.

1325. Pani, Mario (1911–1993). "Entrevista con el arquitecto Mario Pani." En *Testimonios vivos: 20 arquitectos/entrevistas realizadas por Lilia Gómez y Miguel Angel Quevedo.* México: Secretaría de Educación Pública, 1981. Pp.93–110. Interview. Period Covered: 1925–1979.

Paris-trained architect reveals accomplishments in interview. Author of buildings throughout republic: la Ciudad Universitaria, Hoteles Reforma and Prado, Tlatelolco, and Ciudad Satélite. Anecdote about Diego Rivera and Hotel Prado murals.

1326. Pani, Mario (1911–1993); **Graciela de Garay Arellano**. *Historia Oral de la ciudad de México: testimonios de sus arquitectos, 1940–1990*. México: Conaculta, 2000. 124pp. Interview. Period Covered: 1940–1990.

Of four architects who render lives in autobiography, Pani best explains field as profession: training, patronage, competition, challenges in realization of structure, and organization of profession. French-trained Pani designed famous buildings and sites: Hotels Reforma and Plaza, la Ciudad Universitaria, and master plan for earthquake-destroyed Managua.

1327. Pappatheodorou, Theodoro. *Memorias de un inmigrante griego llamado Theodoro Pappatheodorou*. Juquilpan, MIC: Centro de Estudios de la Revolución Mexicana Lázaro Cárdenas, 1987. 440pp.

At age of twenty-two left Greece for Mexico, where he engaged in business, cultivated silkworms, and farmed. Lived in Michoacán and Sinaloa. Comments on relationships with other Greeks. No rags to riches but immigrant who assimilated into native culture. Guadalupe García Torres places subject in sociological context but mentions little of methodology.

1328. Pardinas, Miguel Agustín (1915–1965). *Un testigo de Cristo: autobiografía, 1915–1966*. México: Buena Prensa, 1967. 198pp. Memoirs. Period Covered: 1939–1965.

Jesuit priest, Pardinas was missionary among Tarahumaras, Chinese, and Filipinos. Mainly in China and efforts at converting natives and expulsion by communists. Reveals individual assured of mission and unsympathetic to non–Catholic cultures. Narrative chronological and external.

1329. Parker, Morris B. *Morris B. Parker's Mules, Mines, and Me in Mexico, 1895–1932*. Tucson: University of Arizona Press, 1979. 230pp.

Mining engineer spent most of career in Sonora and Chihuahua and in areas contiguous with Arizona, New Mexico, and Texas. Mining techniques, labor problems, Yaqui Indians, and Revolution conflate in novelesque narrative. In touch with significant *politicos* and business figures of region, he names and sketches them.

1330. Parmenter, Ross. *Lawrence in Oaxaca: A Quest for the Novelist in Mexico*. Salt Lake City: Smith/Peregrine Smith Books, 1984. 384pp.

Search for author can be biographical and autobiographical as in this title. Since British author spent winter here, 1924–1925, Parmenter attempts to retrace steps based on Oaxaca writings. Lawrence rightfully dominates, but some of Parmenter emerges in verification and interpretation of novelist's writing experiences.

1331. Parmenter, Ross. *Stages in a Journey*. New York: Profile, 1983. 269pp.

Parmenter travels for colonial architecture of Agustinians, Dominicans, and Franciscans in Michoacán, Guerrero, and Puebla. He seeks to find self. "I had set out, half heartedly, to learn about Mexico, but I had ended by learning from Mexico" (p.268). Stages in title refer to self-illumination rather than geographical space. Closing lines convey relationship with Mexico. "...I had sought my answers...and the answers had come to me effortlessly in the times I had abandoned the search and come to look upon the world with Mexican eyes" (p.268).

1332. Parmenter, Ross. *Week in Yanhuitlán*. Albuquerque: University of New Mexico Press, 1964. 375pp.

Former music critic for *New York Times* records impressions verbally and visually. Unknown town near city of Oaxaca shelters gem of Dominican monastery both unrepaired and under researched. Parmenter rectifies latter. Self and monastery emerge as author delights in discoveries of physical nature of church and psychological nature of seeing. Monastery and self dominate. Yet Parmenter includes history of Dominicans. Indivualized host and hostess who guard colonial structure and "adopt" curious Gringo with whom they share treasure.

1333. Parodi, Enriqueta de (1899–1976). *Alcancía: Prosas para mis hijos*. Hermosillo, SON, 1945. 144pp. Memoirs. Period Covered: 1920?–1936?

Sonoran writer now completes generational cycle of life. In 1937, she wrote *Madre: Prosas* describing role as child; in *Alcancia*, role as mother. Thirty sketches of mother-child relationship tribute to motherhood and self-fulfillment.

1334. Parodi, Enriqueta de (1899–1976). *Madre: Prosas.* México: Tipografía Julia Marta, 1937. 131pp. Memoirs. Period Covered: 1910?–1937?

In twenty-nine chapters, Sonoran journalist traces life from childhood to maternity. Mother dominates each impression and even more so following her death. Describing motherhood in Mexican context, document paean to universal maternity.

1335. Paso, Franco del (Dates?). *Spiritualia: memorias de un seminarista.* Cuernavaca: El Autor, 1995. 186pp. Memoirs. Period Covered: 1990s?

Chronological time meaningless in these confessions of a seminarian. Most topics abstract: apprenticeship for sainthood, classics, confessions, Christians and stoics, pretending love, concerns, etc. Leaving seminary, death of one of seminarians, and author's final abandonment of priestly enterprise more concrete.

1336. Patán, Federico (1937–). *De cuerpo entero: Federico Patán.* México: Ediciones Corunda, 1991. 58pp. Memoirs. Period Covered: 1939–1990.

Novelist, short-story writer, essayist, poet, and translator, Patán, son of Spanish exiles in Mexico, mixes intellectual development (education, love for reading, and efforts at creation) with biography concerning family. Economic struggles forced family to live in Chihuahua, Mexico City, and Vera Cruz.

1337. Pattie, James O. *The Personal Narrative of James O. Pattie.* Missoula, MT: Mountain, 1988 (1833). 200pp.

Takes author in 1828 from Baja to Mexico City and to Vera Cruz for return to U.S. Narrative anti–Mexican. Travel difficulties, e.g., while in Baja, author imprisoned.

1338. Paya Valera, Emeterio (1932–). *Los niños españoles de Morelia: (el exilio*

infantil en México). México: EDAMEX, 1985. 256pp. Memoirs. Period Covered: 1936–1985.

In 1937, author was one of 456 Spanish children refuged in Mexico. From then until today, lived in Morelia and in return trip to Spain discovered his Mexican identity. Memoirs encompass provisions for young exiles and their adjustment to Morelia.

1339. Payno, Manuel (1810–1894). "Un viaje a Vera Cruz en el invierno de 1843." En *Cien viajeros en Veracruz: crónicas y relatos, v.10.* Editada por Martha Poblett Miranda. Jalapa Enríquez: Gobierno del Estado de Vera Cruz, 1992. Pp.27–73. Memoirs. Period Covered: 1843.

Diplomat and novelist visited Vera Cruz noting regional personality, climate, clothing, history, customs, and lack of beautiful women. Delightful work authored by one of major nineteenth century novelists. Payno occasionally reveals own mood.

1340. Paz, Ireneo (1836–1924). *Algunas campañas: memorias escritas por Ireneo Paz.* México: El Autor, 1884–1885. 3 v. Memoirs. Period Covered: 1884–1885.

Young Paz, grandfather of Octavio Paz, describes experiences during French Intervention. Favored liberals in struggle against conservatives in nineteenth century. Adventures in Guadalajara, Colima, Mazatlán, and San Luis Potosí read like novel. Journalist Paz writes well and presents self at best. Salvador Ortiz Vidal condensed three volumes into one.

1341. Paz, Octavio (1914–1998). *Itinerario.* México: Fondo de Cultura Económica, 1993. 274pp. Memoirs. Period Covered: 1918?–1993.

Nobel Prize winning essayist and poet intermittently presents self and generation through autobiographical essays that comprise hybrid memoir. Narration conforms to chronology of author's life: early education, bouts with history, impact of 1930s on generation, scholarship to Spain, Paris and Satre in 1945, inspiration for *The Labyrinth of Solitude* (1956), India, 1968 and leaving public service, and involvement with journals *Plural* and *Vuelta*. Most formal autobiography so far and one of best analyses of communism's influence on Mexican intellectuals, writings may be labeled inferior Paz. Metaphorical language absent here.

In *Vislumbres de la India* (1995), inventories arrival and departure from this country in chapters "Los antípodas de ida y vuelta" and "Despedida."

In Braulio Peralta's *El poeta en su tierra: diálogos con Octavio Paz*, poet talks about self, family, and relationships with other writers: Pablo Neruda, Julio Cortázar, and Arthur Lundkvist.

Paz considers book of poems, *Ladera este* (1969), autobiographical.

1342. Paz, Octavio (1914–1998). *Memorias y palabras: cartas a Pere Gimferrer 1966– 1997.* Barcelona: Seix Barral, 1999. 425pp. Letters. Period Covered: 1966–1997.

Thirty-one years of letters with Paz as friend and mentor to precocious Catalan poet, Gimferrer, born in 1945. Older poet coaxes, chides, and constantly encourages prodigy. Paz talks about own intellectual life and publications such as *Plural* (1971) and *Vuelta* (1976). Of more interest than relationship is Mexican's preoccupation with art of poetry. Fifth autobiography of Paz supplements most closely *One Word to the Other.*

1343. Paz, Octavio (1914–1998). *One Word to the Other.* Mansfield, TX: Latitudes, ca.1992. 43pp. Translation of *De una palabra a otra.* Memoirs. Period Covered: 1925?– 1990?

Essay concerning personal evolvement with poetry. English, French, Spanish, Chinese, Japanese, and pre–Columbian poetry all influenced him. Particularly cites José Juan Tablada for introducing him to haiku. Paz searches for metaphysical definition of term *poet.*

1344. Paz, Octavio (1914–1998). *Xavier Villaurrutia en persona y en obra.* México: Fondo de Cultura Económica, 1978. 85pp. Trans: *Hieroglyphs of Desire: A Critical Study of Villarrutia.* Translated by Eliot Weinberger & Esther Allen. Port Townsend, WA: Copper Canyon, 1993. Memoirs. Period Covered: 1931–1948.

In writing intellectual biography of Xavier Villaurrutia, Paz gives much of own life. Ideas all appear to be derived from primary sources, i.e., Villaurrutia's poems and dramas or what Paz himself remembers of *los Contemporáneos.* Hence indirect memoir comprised of Paz's reminiscences and interpretation of Villaurrutia's creation and occasionally Mexican and Hispanic culture. Essayist rather than poet present.

1345. Paz Garro, Helena (1948–). *Memorias.* México: Oceáno, 2003. 463pp. Memoirs. Period Covered: 1948–1998.

Resurrects life mainly as it relates to celebrity parents, Elena Garro and Octavio Paz. Mexico, Berkeley, New York, Paris, and travels in Orient and Europe contexts for unhappy childhood in conflicted marriage. Helena chooses sides. She prefers mother's family and despises all of *los* Paz including father. Paris years, longest in book, suggest vibrant cultural life of ambassador. Writing runs in family.

1346. Pazuengo, Matías (Dates?). *Historia de la Revolución en Durango.* Cuernavaca, 1915. 115pp. Memoirs. Period Covered: 1910–1914.

Pro-revolutionary soldier, he describes the war and effects on Durango. Observer/participant sparks interest in anecdotal moments such as disposal of bodies or assimilation of captured enemy troops. At times historian, one who describes events that he did not observe, takes over.

1347. Peck, John J. *The Sign of the Eagle: A View of Mexico, 1830–.* San Diego: Union-Tribune, 1970. 168pp.

Mexico City appears in letters, dated from August 1846 to February 1848, composed by Lt. Peck who fought in Mexican-American War on both fronts, Monterrey and Mexico City. Loves war and notes few of agonies. Has sophistication to speak highly of Mexicans. Book well annotated with lithographs by German, Carl Nebel.

1348. Pedrero, Felipe Alfonso (1918–?). *Diario de Felipe Alfonso Pedrero, estudiante, attaché civil de la Legación de México en Berlin, Alemania.* Mérida, 1934. 43pp. Diary. Period Covered: 1934.

Sixteen year old from wealthy family hopes to find career in Germany. Climate and failing health necessitate return to Mexico. Comments on luxury accommodations of ship, occasionally notes Hitler's Germany, and records his deteriorating condition as well as love for family.

1349. Peissel, Michel. *The Lost World of Quintana Roo.* New York: Dutton, 1963. 306pp.

Britisher treads from Yocac, Quintana Roo, to San Pedro in Belize in three months. Aspiring archaeologist ferrets out Maya ruins. Two enemies confront him: tenacity and primitiveness of jungle and presence of *chicleros* or bandits.

1350. Pelé; Robert L. Rish. *My Life and the Beautiful Game: The Autobiography of Pelé.* Garden City, NY: Doubleday, 1977. 371pp.

One chapter relates to World Cup in Mexico in 1970 and Brazil's victory over Uruguay. President Díaz Ordaz presented trophy to Brazilians.

1351. Pellicer, Carlos (1897–1977). *Cartas desde Italia.* México: Fondo de Cultura Económica, 1985. 120pp. Letters. Period Covered: 1927–1928.

Editor Clara Bargellini defines good travel literature: "...es claro que para Pellicer el año en Italia fue algo más. Fue una búsqueda de sí mismo a través de los lugares y personajes históricos que encontró" (p.7). Postmarked Milan, Padua, Venice, Florence, Assisi, and Rome, letters are written to Arturo Pani, Mexican consul in Paris, friend Guillermo Dávila, and Juan Pellicer, younger brother.

1352. Pellicer, Carlos (1897–1977). *Correo familiar, 1918–1920.* México: Factoria Ediciones, 1998. 245pp. Letters. Period Covered: 1918–1920.

In three-year period, young poet sends ninety-three letters to family, mainly mother Deifilia Cámara de Pellicer, father Carlos Pellicer Marchena, and brother Juan José Pellicer. From New York, Bogota, and Caracas, letters manifest devoted son close to family and especially to mother. Sent to Bogota to represent Mexican Federation of Students, he records intellectual life, Catholicism, and achievements as student.

1353. Pellicer, Carlos (1895–1977). *Correspondencia, 1925–1959.* México: Del Equilibrista, 1997. 85pp. Letters. Period Covered: 1925–1959.

Serge I. Zaitzeff edits collection. Thirty-eight letters postmarked Mexico, France, Italy, Spain, and Brazil exchanged between Reyes and Pellicer. Friendship and active literary life manifest.

1354. Peña, José Enrique de la (1807–1841). *With Santa Anna in Texas: Personal Narrative of the Revolution.* Translated and edited by Carmen Perry. College Station: Texas A&M University Press, 1975. 202pp. Memoirs. Period Covered: 1836.

According to translator Perry [de la Peña's] "...diary has survived in spite of Santa Anna (q.v.), Filisola (q.v.) and others who were determined that it be destroyed..." (p.xi). Lt. Colonel participated in Texas campaign and scathingly appraised Mexican officers. *With Santa Anna*, with style, perception of detail, and honesty of emotions, is one of best of nineteenth century. Published in English since owner of manuscript was Texan. Introduction synthesizes: "It is not the report of an officer who had to justify his military orders...but that of an able and introspective soldier" (p.xiii).

1355. Peña, Margarita (1937–). *Desde Bloomington.* Universidad Autónoma de Ciudad Juárez, 1992. 46pp. Memoirs. Period Covered: 1985–1989.

Writer and professor spent sabbatical year at University of Indiana. Incorporates academic environment, but Mexican-Americans interest her most. In El Paso, Texas, links Mexican and American cultures and seeks vestiges of own family.

1356. Peña, Margarita (1937–). *En nombre de Eleguá: crónicas.* México: Instituto Nacional de Bellas Artes, 1995. 85pp. Memoirs. Period Covered: 1988–1989.

Records sabbatical year at University of Indiana. Twenty-five essays read independently or as whole, subjectively incorporate year: trees, messages, and signals, El Paso, voodoo (Title refers to an African god), Joaquin Corolla, Chicago, etc. Textured and moody rendition of surroundings.

1357. Peña de Villarreal, Consuelo

(1896–?). *La Revolución en el Norte*. Editorial Periodística e Impresora de Puebla, 1968. 468pp. Memoirs. Period Covered: 1903–1916?

Pro-revolutionary witness creates hybrid document. It is as though she had read history and takes on role of historian rather than memoirist. Interrupts chronology to record anecdotes, lament a death, or sketch portrait.

1358. Peña González, Abelardo de la

(1927–). *Chapala olvidada*. Chapala, JAL: El Autor, 1998. 167pp. Memoirs. Period Covered: 1927–1997.

Mexican-American returns to native Chapala and recalls youth. As retiree wanting to resettle here, records struggle and success in cleaning up environment.

1359. Peñafiel, Francisco A. (1904?–?).

Un dia después de siempre. México: Claves Latinoamericanas, 1987. 119pp. Memoirs. Period Covered: 1904?–1981.

Born into poverty in state of Hidalgo, he and family moved to Mexico City in 1920s. Portions of youth spent in Cuba and France. Communist, journalist, and promoter of Mexican films traveled to China, Russia, Poland, and Japan. Captures mood of Mexico in 1930s and 1940s. Valuable chapter, "La undécima muse," on relationship with poet, Concha Urquiza.

1360. Peniche Vallado, Leopoldo

(1908–?). "Memorias inoportunas." En *Teatro y vida: ensayos-artículos*. Mérida: Liceo Peninsulares de Estudios Literarios, 1957. Pp.165–206. Memoirs. Period Covered: 1915?

Yucatan playwright recalls youth in six chapters of memoirs: Argumedo and Revolution, carnivals in Mérida, Progreso, *la preparatoria*, Oswaldo Baqueiro Anduze, and Pastor Bautista.

1361. Peniche Vallado, Leopoldo

(1908–?). *Sombras de palabras: memorias y antimemorias*. Mérida: Maldonado Editores, 1987. 224pp. Memoirs. Period Covered: 1908–1975?

University student, playwright, and politician with memories of Yucatan. No other autobiographer registers more intensely preparatory and university years of 1920s and 1930s. In minutiae, recalls dispute between President Miguel Alemán and González Beytia, governor of Yucatan. Final pages on writing career.

1362. Peón, Máximo (Dates?). *Cómo viven los mexicanos en los Estados Unidos*. México: Costa-Amic, 1966. 270pp. Memoirs. Period Covered: 1943.

Pseudonymous author recalls halcyon days of WWII when Mexican laborers, needed by country under stress, suffered little discrimination. Employment as railroad worker in West and Northwest. Focuses more on immigrant than Mexican-American.

1363. Peralta, Elda (1930–?). *Luis Spota: Las sustancias de la tierra: una biografía íntima*. México: Editorial Grijalbo, 1990. 359pp. Memoirs. Period Covered: 1910?–1985.

Biography of writer Luis Spota, but companion Elda Peralta also tells of herself. Pages focus on love and quarrels. U.S. educated, professional tennis player, stage and film actress, and playwright, Peralta precise about own life: bourgeoisie mother with pretensions of aristocracy, father as an ambulant government employee, three successful sisters, and Luis Spota, axis of her existence. Independent and talented Peralta has no need of Spota for fame.

1364. Peralta, Olivia (1917–?). *Mi vida con José Revueltas*. México: Plaza y Valdés Editores, 1997. 132pp. Memoirs. Period Covered: 1937–1947.

Married to José Revueltas from 1937 to 1947, author narrated decade in 1991. Brings out facets of Revueltas's life: communist, writer, and fanatic for betterment of mankind. Wife, mother, and supportive of Revueltas tells of marriage that ended in divorce. Preparation as schoolteacher led to fifty-year career in teaching.

1365. Perea, Hector (1887–1976 Dates of Guzmán). *Martín Luis Guzmán: Iconografía*. México: Fondo de Cultura Económica, 1987. 167pp. Memoirs/Photographs. Period Covered: 1887–1976.

Selections of best of autobiographical writings. From *Apuntes sobre una personali-*

dad, *A orillas del Hudson*, *El águila y la serpiente*, *La sombra del caudillo* and *Crónicas de mi destierro*, interviews and letters, recasted pieces along with multiple photographs fuse into enhancing but fragmented image of Guzmán. Photographs also exhibit contemporary personalities of period.

1366. Pereau, Charla; James F. Scheer. *Charla's Children*. Minneapolis: Jeremy Books, 1981. 218pp.

Spouses open and operate orphanage in Colonia V. Guerrero in Baja. Unique memoirs for two reasons: first account of Americans working with Mexican orphans; only memoir of Lutheran missionary efforts in Mexico.

1367. Perera, Victor; Roberto D. Bruce S. *The Last Lords of Palenque: The Lacandon Mayas of the Mexican Rain Forest*. Boston: Little, Brown, 1982. 311pp.

Two anthropologists spent 1977 and 1978 in Chiapas. Short chapters on place names, human subjects, activities or concepts comprise long study. Perera profiles Gertrude Duby Blom, widow of anthropologist and champion of rights of Lacandones. Trove of Lacandon culture and folklore through tutor, Old Chan K'in.

1368. Pérez, Luis (1904–?). *El Coyote, the Rebel*. New York: Holt, 1947. 233pp. Autobiography Proper. Period Covered: 1909–1929.

Eleven year old joins federal army in northern Mexico. Picaresque life of Chicano/Mexican with Mexico and Southwest as scenarios. Converts to Protestantism, attends public schools and college, learns English, suffers from fraud, and becomes citizen. Good humor.

1369. Pérez, Ramón (Tianguis) (Dates?). *Diario de un mojado*. Houston: Arte Público, 2003. Unpaged. Trans: *Diary of an Undocumented Immigrant* English edition by Dick J. Reavis. Houston: Arte Público, 1991. Genre: Memoirs. Period Covered: 1980s.

One of most complete autobiographical documents of immigrant in U.S. Leaves Oaxaca with hopes to earn money to be carpenter. Leads picaresque existence because of instability in Gringo environment. From Texas to California to Oregon and back to Mexico, holds multiple jobs, sees underbelly of life, suffers from *migra*, and experiences exploitation again when he returns home.

1370. Pérez, Ramón (Tianguis); Dick J. Reavis. *Diary of a Guerrilla*. Houston: Arte Público, 1999. 144pp. Memoirs. Period Covered: 1970s.

Same narrator appears in *Diary of an Undocumented Immigrant*. Scenario changes to Mexico and specifically to Oaxaca. Zapotec Indian, "...was a courier and agitator in [Florencio] Madrano's ranks." Emphasizes conflict over land and ethnicity.

1371. Pérez Estremera, Manuel; Arturo Ripstein (1943–). *Correspondencia inacabada con Arturo Ripstein*. Huesca, España: Festival de Cine de Huesca, 1995. 206pp. Interview. Period Covered: 1965–1994.

Autobiography here in confession and conversation with three different interviews. Ripstein, director of fifteen films and one documentary, *El Lecumberri*, talks about Luis Buñuel, Gabriel García Márquez, and Juan Rulfo. Probably all of his films mentioned throughout interview.

1372. Pérez Olivares, Porfirio (1910–?). *Memorias: un dirigente agrario de Soledad de Doblado*. Xalapa, VER: Veracruzana, 1992. 190pp. Memoirs. Period Covered: 1910–1978?

Unusual peasant from Soledad de Doblado, Vera Cruz. Literate he headed police department and three times president (mayor) of his town. As politician, active in peasant labor movement.

1373. Pérez Romero, Ricardo (1960–); **Lorenzo Armendáriz.** *La lumea de noi= Nuestra gente: memorias de los ludar de México*. México: Conaculta, Fonca, 2001. 103pp. Memoirs. Period Covered: 1895–2000.

In only Gypsy autobiography in Mexico, two men describe their lives and those of their families in brief essays accompanied by photographs. Emigrating from Rumania, family made living first with circus animals and then with itinerant film theatre. They traversed Mexico and by various devices attracted locals to improvised cinema to view restored and drastically reduced popular

films. Author began work with family in
1974. In 1989, family abandoned cinema for
variety act.

1374. Pérez Solís, Ivan (Dates?). *Intimidades de un médico: 46 casos de la vida real.*
México: Costa-Amic, 1967. 255pp. Memoirs.
Period Covered: 1950?–1967?

Each chapter self-contained incident
from life of narrator. Tells of experiences in
medical practice in Tijuana.

1375. Pérez Tamayo, Ruy (1924–?). *La
segunda vuelta: notas autobiográficas y comentarios sobre la ciencia en México.* México: El
Colegio Nacional, 1983. 209pp. Memoirs.
Period Covered: 1933–1972.

Rare scientist (pathologist) to record
memoirs. Leaves document on career as surgeon who studied in Mexico and U.S. Encompasses intellectual development in interaction with teachers and mentors and in
humanities. Tamaulipan native with thoughtful approach to science and medicine. Returns to research after hiatus of twenty-five
years.

1376. Pérez Tejada, José (1900?–?). *Los
revolucionarios: crónica de un general constitucionalista.* Los Mochis, SIN: Universidad de
Occidente, 1985. 352pp. Memoirs. Period
Covered: 1914–1946?

Constitutionalist fought against Zapata
in Revolution, 1910–1920. From 1918 to 1955,
served as chief investigator for public security in Mexico City, fought against Saturnino Osornio in Querétaro, and posted to
Hermosillo, Sonora. Subject often plays
role of historian as much as observer/participant. Personal perspective of indicated
period.

1377. Perry, Nancy Whitlow. *Missionaries
Are Human Too: Glimpses of Life in Mexico.*
s.l., 1978. 144pp.

Another aspect of Baptist life in above
title. In 1970s, she and husband had call to
Mexico. In Yucatan, Mexico City, Guadalajara, and Oaxaca, prominence given to missionary's family: food, shelter, travel, minister's kids, friends, and frustrations. In
anecdotal style incorporates several miracles.

**1378. Perry, Vincent D. and Eleanor
Swent.** *A Half Century as Mining and Exploration Geologist with the Anaconda Company.*
Berkeley, CA: Regional Oral History Office,
1991. 128pp.

Geologist author, employee of Anaconda, transferred from Butte, Montana, to
Cananea, Sonora, and remained there from
1928 to 1937. Almost thirty pages of oral history relate to technicalities of mining. But
Perry also comments on living conditions
and foreign community in Cananea. Grateful
for good job during Depression.

1379. Pesado, Isabel (?–1913). *Apuntes de
viaje de México a Europa en los años de
1870–1871 y 1872 por....* París: Garnier Hnos.,
1910. 625pp. Memoirs. Period Covered:
1870–1899.

Trip to continent and eastern belt of
U.S. by wealthy Veracruzana with pseudonym, Duquesa de Mier. Tour lasted two
years, and family returned to Paris in 1885
and remained until 1899. Description of
churches and other monuments. Poet of
romantic period reflects culture of upper
class Mexican in Europe during Porfiriato.

1380. Pettersson, Aline (1938–?). *De
cuerpo entero: Aline Pettersson.* México: Ediciones Corunda, 1990. 64pp. Memoirs. Period
Covered: 1938–1989.

In search of self, explores larger terrain
than do most writers in series. Reading, writing, and solitude axis of memoir, but novelist
displays developing self in mundane aspects:
adolescence, travel, illness, marriage, and
divorce.

1381. Philipon, M. M. (1862–1937 Dates
of Cabrera de Armida). *Una vida, un mensaje: Concepción Cabrera de Armida.* México:
Concar A.C., ca.1976. 285pp. Trans: *Conchita:
A Mother's Spiritual Diary.* New York: Alba
House, 1978. Diary/Autobiography. Period
Covered: 1894–1937?

Wife, mother, and grandmother with
duties incumbent upon each role, Conchita
with vigorous spiritual life. Arranged into
themes of mysticism, second part reflects
inner life. Thematic cohesiveness violates
chronology and progressive spiritual development. Intervention of two Catholic reli-

gious in editing diary adulterates pristine form intended by Cabrera de Armida.

1382. Pico, Pío (1801–1894). *Don Pio Pico's Historical Narrative.* Translated by Arthur P. Botello. Glendale, CA: Clark, 1973. 171pp. Memoirs. Period Covered: 1801–1845.

At age seventy-six, Californiano reminisces and dictates memoirs. Last Mexican governor of California and administrator of Mission San Luis Rey, Pico concentrates on Mexican period though lived under U.S. rule for twenty-nine years. Disjointed and garrulous document recounts political and personal incidents.

1383. Pike, Eunice V. *Not Alone.* Chicago: Moody, 1956. 127pp.

From 1936 to 1939, author and friend Florrie live with Mazatec Indians in Chalco, Oaxaca, in order to translate New Testament into language of this tribe according to Wycliffe Bible Translators. They must build glossary, write a primer, and face issue of tone in Mazatec language. By 1946, book of Mark translated and women spent more time teaching Gospel.

1384. Pike, Eunice V. *An Uttermost Part.* Chicago: Moody, 1971. 192pp.

Continues story of *Words Wanted.* Pike and companion selected towns of Chalco and Río Sánchez for proselytizing. Earlier visit to Mazatec region promoted translation of three books of Bible into native language. From 1950 to 1964, American missionaries, products of Wycliffe movement, preached, taught, and continued translating Bible into Mazatec. Anecdotes of mission work, acceptance, and opposition.

1385. Pike, Eunice V. *Words Wanted.* Chicago: Moody, 1958. 159pp.

Author states reason. "My purpose for studying both the language and the customs of the Mazatec Indians was to translate the New Testament for them" (p.7). From 1940 to 1949, author and colleague lived among non–Spanish-speaking tribe in Oaxaca. Two women had threefold job: learn to speak Mazatec language, complete grammar and dictionary of language, and translate and teach Gospel. Show devotion and excitement

of discovery in recording what was once only an oral language.

1386. Pillsworth, Elizabeth G. *Interiors: An Exploration of Life and Death in Southern Mexico.* Amherst, MA, 1994. 118pp.

Pillsworth lived in Tocuaro, Michoacán. In relating community values in courtship, death, fights, and fiestas, she reveals much of state and something of her life. Justifies her experiences: "Simply by living with them, sharing in their chores and gossip, arguments and celebrations, I was able to learn more than I ever had in hours and hours of library research or meticulously planned interviews" (p.115).

1387. Pimentel Aguilar, Ramón (1897–1986 Dates of Leduc). *Así hablaba Renato Leduc: un diálogo vivo con el legendario poeta y periodista.* México: EDAMEX, 1990. 124pp. Oral Autobiography. Period Covered: 1910?–1980.

Frankness and colorful language, frequent use of *cabrón* and *chingado*, characterize autobiography. Provides context for Leduc's forays into past: childhood in last years of Porfiriato, telegrapher, participant in Revolution in Chihuahua, bureaucrat in Paris who knew André Breton and other surrealists, and outspoken journalist in Mexico City.

1388. Pineda Campuzano, Zoraida (1910?–?). *Memorias de una estudiante de filosofía.* México: Editorial Fernández, 1963. 480pp. Memoirs. Period Covered: 1915?–1941?

Author identifies career in education of children but pens garrulous and humorous memoir of adolescent and college years. Attempts to recall conversation in order to novelize memoir. Struggle for master's degree in philosophy most valuable account of document.

1389. Pineda Ramírez, Ildefonso (1919–?). *Un sacerdote nacido tres veces: la asombrosa verdad humana de los mensajeros de la verdad divina.* México: Editorial Jus, 1987 (1988). 2 v. Autobiography Proper. Period Covered: 1919–1975.

Jesuit recaptures total life from birth to maturity through theme of Roman Catholicism. From Chilapa, Guerrero, grows up in

Catholic environment similar to Yáñez's *Al filo de agua*. Destined for priesthood, studies in Mexico, U.S., and Rome. Teacher and priest shuttles between all three countries but focuses on Montezuma Seminary in New Mexico. Stages in religious development reflected in title.

1390. Pinkson, Tom Soloway. *The Flowers of Wiricuta: A Journey to Shamanic Power with the Huichol Indians of Mexico.* Rochester, VT: Destiny Books, 1997 (1995). 287pp.

Author searches for other reality in pilgrimage to Indians in Central Mexico in 1990. They use peyote "...to get a more accurate reading of the nature of reality" (p.147). Title of self-help book signifies making one's own flowers blossom.

1391. Piñón, Fernando (1944–?). *Child of the Half Millennium: What It Means to Be Mexican American.* México: Plaza y Valdes, 2001. 234pp. Memoirs. Period Covered: 1950–2000.

Mexican-American born in Mexico but grew up in Laredo, Texas. Close ties to Mexico through family and through forays into Mexico as journalist and search for links here with Mexican-Americans. Snippets of autobiography, but goal is "...what it is and how it feels to be Mexican-American in the United States" (p.23). Two points: Mexico to blame for *charro* complex or "the acceptance of futility and frustration" (p.127). Anglo-American to blame for perceiving non–Anglo cultures as threatening.

1392. Pismis, Paris (1901–1999). *Reminiscences in the Life of Paris Pismis: A Woman Astronomer.* México: UNAM, 1998. 103pp. Memoirs. Period Covered: 1912–1989.

Born in Turkey and against all conventions, Pismis became astronomer. In 1942, settled permanently in Mexico, where exercised career for over sixty years. Professor at UNAM internationally famous in field. Life parallels study of astronomy in adopted country since 1942. Answers no obligatory questions such as foreigners adjusting to Mexico or women succeeding in male-dominated field.

1393. Pitner, Ernst; Gordon Estherington-Smith. *Maximilian's Lieutenant: A Personal History of the Mexican Campaign,* Albuquerque: University of New Mexico Press, 1993. 201pp.

Another foreigner's view of period. Austrian volunteer Pitner spent three years in Mexico, 1864–1867, stationed in various parts of Republic from Campeche to Matamoros. Complains about military duty and comments on Mexico in letters and diaries.

1394. Pitol, Sergio (1933–). *Sergio Pitol.* Prólogo de Emmanuel Carballo. México: Empresas Editoriales, 1967, ca.1966. 60pp. Memoirs. Period Covered: 1933–1966.

Short story writer lived in Rome, Peking, and Warsaw and outlines life: Italian descent, love of reading, formal and informal education, frustration with Mexican left, friendship with Carlos Monsiváis, and early efforts at writing. More recent, 303-page *El arte de la fuga* (1996) comprised of essays from decade of 1990s. Present here in autobiographical data and in reading tastes and writing. *El arte* indirect autobiography.

1395. Poinsett, Joel. *Notes on Mexico Made in the Autumn of 1822.* New York: Praeger, 1969, (1825). 359pp.

Joel Poinsett completed a secret mission to Mexico to determine politics of Iturbidistas. Document of educated and intelligent observer acquainted with writings of Humboldt. Not only politics but also history, terrain, vegetation, modes of travel, and personalities attract him. He met Santa Anna. Vera Cruz, Mexico City, Guanajuato, and exit through Tampico comprise itinerary.

1396. Pollard, Hugh B.C. *A Busy Time in Mexico: An Unconventional Record of Mexican Incident.* London: Constable, 1913. 243pp.

Journalist and freebooter Pollard travels for adventure such as delivering money to dangerous places like Chiapas. Biased traveler redeems self in last chapters when he witnesses Revolution from beginnings to Diaz's flight to Vera Cruz. Encapsulates unforgettable scenes. At times equals contemporary, John Reed in *Insurgent Mexico*. Both writers had much in common: journalists from Anglo-speaking world and voluntarily in

Mexico for adventure, write about Revolution for foreigners.

1397. Ponce, José Bernardo (1934 Birth of Cuevas). *José Luis Cuevas, ¿genio o farsante? Charlas con el polémico pintor.* México: Signos, 1983. 125pp. Interview. Period Covered: 1939–1981.

Cuevas mixes interview and oral autobiography as he expounds/polemicizes with old and new themes: attachment to Yucatan, grandmother's birthplace; attack on President José Lopéz-Portillo; Marta Traba; politics; psychiatry; journalism; New York and art; cinema; Salvador Dali; and Premio Nacional de Arte. Ponce, arranging twenty interviews into twenty-six chapters, contextualizes topics and provokes comments.

1398. Ponce de León, Soledad (1903–?). "*Recordar es vivir.*" En *Los maestros y la cultura nacional, 1920–1952*, v.1, *El Norte*. México: Museo Nacional de Culturas Populares, 1987. Pp.17–37. Memoirs. Period Covered: 1931–1936.

Sinaloense spent over thirty years working with children in rural schools. Reluctance of many areas to accept teachers and education. Inventiveness in stimulating children and in preparing materials. Self-taught, she lacked credentials for university degree.

1399. Poniatowska, Elena (1933–). *Elena Poniatowska.* Azcapotzalco, DF: Universidad Autónoma Metropolitana, 1984. 50pp. Interview. Period Covered: 1954–1984.

Journalist responds to questions typical of format of series. Tlateloco and 1968, Luis Buñuel, Octavio Paz, assassinated Buendía, status of women in society, urge to write, politics, and attitudes toward poverty.

1400. Poniatowska, Elena (1933–). *La "Flor de Lis."* México: Ediciones Era, 1990. 261pp. Autobiographical Novel. Period Covered: 1937–1949?

Events of *Fleur de Lis* closely pattern author's life: French Polish ancestry, removal to Mexico because of WWII, education in Mexico and in U.S., two siblings, attachment to favorite servant, etc. Even non–Mexican education of very bright child verifiable. Catalytic and exotic intrusion of Father Teufel

upsets ostensible decorum of upper class family.

1401. Poniatowska, Elena (1900 Birth of Jesusa Polancares). *Hasta no verte, Jesús Mío.* México: Ediciones Era, 1969. 315pp. Trans: *Here's to You, Jesusa!* Translated by Deanna Heikkinen. New York: Farrar, Straus and Giroux, 2001. Oral Autobiography. Period Covered: 1905?–1965?

Labeled by some critics as novel, *Hasta* also qualifies as autobiography. Recorder and organizer of Jesusa's life story, Poniatowska visited her subject three times a week. Resultant document superb. Author hears and filters language with all nuances to written form. From Tehuántepec and motherless at age of five, Jesusa spends most of life in Mexico City. *Soldadera*, spiritualist, laundress, and totally independent female.

1402. Poniatowska, Elena (1920 Birth of Soriano). *Juan Soriano, niño de mil años.* México: Plaza y Janés, 1998. 294pp. Oral Autobiography. Period Covered: 1920–1997.

Guadalajaran-born painter Soriano reveals life to Poniatowska: family, Guadalajara, Mexico City, homosexual loves, and acquaintance with celebrities Diego Rivera, Kahlo, Paz, Pellicer, Nandino, Lupe Marín, etc. Memoirs more internal and personal than normal for genre in Mexico. Chapters by Poniatowska, subject's confessions, dialogs with interviewer, and comments by others about him comprise self-illustrated document.

1403. Poniatowska, Elena; Mariana Yampolsky. *Mariana Yampolsky y la buganvillia.* México: Plaza y Janés, 2001. 119pp.

Photographer and also engraver, Mariana Yampolsky in Mexico in 1945 at age of twenty. (Auto)biography and photos comprise text with comments by Yampolsky and Poniatowska. Former speaks of arrival, discovery of aptitude for photography, friendships, and accomplishments.

1404. Poniatowska, Elena (1933–). *Me lo dijo Elena Poniatowska: su vida, obra y pasiones contadas por ella misma.* México: Ediciones del Milenio, 1997. 95pp. Interview. Period Covered: 1937?–1996.

No other woman writer has done as much with autobiography as Elena Poniatowska. Interviewer Esteban Ascencio notes goal: "…to introduce to the reader to the life, the ideas and the works of Mexico's most important contemporary journalist." She divulges childhood, reading interests, and acquaintance/friendship with Paz, Fuentes, Rulfo, Buñuel, Carlos Salinas de Gotari, and Díaz Ordaz. Focuses on creation of best work, *Night of Tlateloco* (1971).

1405. Poole, Annie Sampson. *Mexicans at Home in the Interior.* London: Chapman & Hall, 1884. 183pp.

Englishwoman of genteel tastes shares impressions. Unlike most nineteenth century foreign writers, Poole had advantage of spending time in one place, Guanajuato, where husband employed. Much *costumbrismo* here; however, memoir also replete with brigands and murderers. Poole has negative opinion of Mexicans from servants to ugly babies to general untidiness in dress. Text suggests French Intervention. In spite of slanderous context, book always interests.

1406. Portales, Urbano J. (1906–). *Andares de un "falluquero", autobiografía.* Monterrey, 1960. 2 v. Memoirs. Period Covered: 1906–1961.

Born and reared in poverty, Mexican Horatio Alger gained modest living as traveling salesman. In 1935, he opened Empacador Zapor, Monterrey cannery that brought him wealth. Neither family nor personal life but business success is focus. Second volume on travels in Europe less interesting.

1407. Portes Gil, Emilio (1890–1978). Entrevista en James W. Wilkie y Edna Monzón de Wilkie's *México visto en el siglo XX.* México: Instituto Mexicano de Investigaciones Económicas, 1969. Pp.491–600. Interviews. Period Covered: 1891–1940?

Covers life and career in interview: fragments of childhood, Sandino, formation of PNR (Partido Nacional Revolucionario) *Sinarquismo*, socialism, Cárdenas-Calles conflict, Vicente Lombardo Toledano, etc.

1408. Portes Gil, Emilio (1890–1978). *Quince años de política mexicana.* México:

Ediciones Bota, 1941. 575pp. Memoirs. Period Covered: 1928–1936.

Memoirs and documentary for author incorporates texts from political life. Provisional president from 1928 to 1930 after assassination of Alvaro Obregón. Defends political career. Reveals larger moments but shows little of workings of government or major facets of political personality.

1409. Portes Gil, Emilio (1890–1978). *Raigambres de la revolución en Tamaulipas: autobiografía en acción.* México: Lito Offset Fersa, 1972. 407pp. Memoirs. Period Covered: 1895–1932.

Born in Ciudad Victoria, Tamaulipas, he focuses on native state: schooling, labor problems, candidacy as national senator, organization of Partido Socialista Fronterizo, agrarian reform, and governor. President from 1928–1930 writes memoirs typical of politicians: defense of own career and inclusion of undigested materials. Focus on successful political career rather than youth.

1410. Portilla, Jorge (1943–). *De cuerpo entero.* México: Ediciones Corunda, 1992. 64pp. Memoirs. Period Covered: 1943–1992?

Writer, translator, alcoholic, and prisoner in Lecumberri confides intellectual formation in love for reading and hatred of schools. Analysis of solitude originates in large unhappy family with superbly drawn parents. Has sense of sin and unworthiness coupled with religious visions.

1411. Portilla, Juan de la (Dates?). *Episodio histórico del gobierno dictatorial del señor don Ignacio Comonfort en la República Mexicana, años de 1856 y 1857.* México: Imprenta de I. Cumplido, 1861. 204pp. Memoirs. Period Covered: 1856–1857.

Passionately defends self and superior, Juan Bautista Traconis. Portilla, secretary to Gov. Traconis of Puebla, incurred wrath of President Ignacio Comonfort over *bienes eclesiásticos* (church funds) in Puebla. Earlier friendship with Comonfort makes plea moving.

1412. Pozas A., Ricardo (1912–1994). "Entrevista a Ricardo Pozas por Luis Vázquez." En *Caminos de la antropología: entre-*

vistas a cinco antropólogos/compiladores, Jorge Durand y Luis Vázquez. México: Instituto Nacional Indigenista, 1990. Pp.131–137. Interview. Period Covered: 1914–1989.

Author of classic, *Juan Pérez Jolote* (1948), provides clues to interest in anthropology and notes influence of Sol Tax and quarrel with Aguirre Beltrán. Focuses on Pozas's reactions to innovations in anthropology.

1413. Pozas A. Ricardo (1900? Birth of Pérez Jolote). *Juan Pérez Jolote: biografía de un tzotzil*. México: Fondo De Cultura Económica, 1952. 119pp. Trans: *Juan the Chamula: An Ethonological Recreation of the Life of a Mexican Indian*. Berkeley: University of California Press, 1962. Oral Autobiography. Period Covered: 1900–1916?

Narration of Chamula Indian who escapes home to avoid father's beatings and gradually finds self in Spanish-speaking world and culture. In return to village, reintegrates into original culture. Portrayal more of customs than personality of typical representative.

1414. Prado Vertiz de Lezama, María (1904?–?). *Los años azules*. Cuernavaca: Quesada Brandi, 1968. 98pp. Memoirs. Period Covered: 1905?–1916?

Mature woman remembers happy childhood during Porfiriato. Disconnected humorous incidents from innocent childhood in wealthy environment comprise chapters. Death of brother is only sorrow.

1415. Pratt, Erma E. *Waiting for God: A Journal of Missionary Work among the Totonac Indians*. Dallas, OR: The Author, 1998. 110pp.

More personalized look at one of followers of Townsend. Quote best sums up this life: "It shows the impact of evangelism and caring by some of Wycliffe Bible translators" (p.7). Organization inspired her when she attended conference in Mexico City. Details tenure in La Unión, village in East Central Mexico. Missionizing, nursing, and teaching inform memoir. Goal of Wycliffe to translate Bible into Totonac.

1416. Preaty, Amy. *Mexico and I*. Philadelphia: Dorrance, 1951. 258pp.

Follows traditional tourist itinerary: Guadalajara, Mexico City, Taxco, Cuernavaca, El Bajío, Puebla, and Oaxaca. Each place personalized by own impressions and insertion of illuminating anecdotes. Book typical of 1950s. Some excellent b/w photos.

1417. Prescott, William Hickling (1825–1894 Dates of Ignacio Icazbalceta). *Correspondencia entre los historiadores William H. Prescott y Joaquín García Icazbalceta, 1847–1856* prólogo de Ignacio Bernal y García Pimentel. México: Instituto Mexicano Norteamericano de Relaciones Culturales, 1984. 77pp. Letters. Period Covered: 1847–1856.

Both giants as historians in respective countries, two intellectuals exchange ideas, articles, and books. Longer work, *Correspondencia mexicana (1838–1856)* (2001) includes many other correspondents: Fanny and Angel Calderón de la Barca, John Lloyd Stephens, Lucas Alamán, and Charles Dickens among others.

1418. Prida Santacilla, Pablo (1886–1973). *Y se levanta el telón: mi vida dentro del teatro*. México: Ediciones Botas, 1960. 346 pp. Memoirs. Period Covered: 1914–1955.

Actor concentrates on theater in Mexico but also in Cuba and U.S. Performed in *zarzuelas* or *el género chico* español (musical comedies) in Mexico City and in provinces in 1920s. Includes newspaper clippings.

1419. Pride, Nigel. *A Butterfly Sings to Pacaya: Travels in Mexico, Guatemala, and Belize*. London: Constable, 1978. 367pp.

"…I developed a special interest in the Maya and a determined resolve one day to return to make a more thorough study of their achievements" (p.12). In 1974, he, along with spouse and four-year-old son, makes visual images of façade decorations in Southeast Mexico. Much autobiography.

1420. Prieto, Carlos (1937–). *Alrededor del mundo con el violonchelo: notas y comentarios de giras musicales*. México: Alianza Editorial Mexicana, 1988. 328pp. Memoirs. Period Covered: 1985.

Cellist made concert tour in 1985 beginning in Mexico, then to U.S., Colombia,

USSR, France, China, and India. In each location notes program, public, and incidents related to concert. Tends to interrupt memoir with pages of history or economics especially in exotic lands.

1421. Prieto, Guillermo (1818–1897). *Cartas públicas y privadas*. En *Obras completas de Guillermo Prieto*. México: Consejo Nacional para la Cultura y las Artes, 1997. 451pp. Letters. Period Covered: 1847–1897.

Three hundred sixty-one letters of liberal writer and politician (friend of Juárez and opponent of Porfirio Díaz) to other famous liberals of period: Manuel Doblado, Melchor Ocampo, José María Vigil, Ignacio Ramírez, etc. Political life dominates with something of personal. Letters grouped by recipient rather than by year.

1422. Prieto, Guillermo (1818–1897). *Crónicas de viajes*. En *Obras completas*. México: Consejo Nacional para la Cultura y los Artes, 1994 (1887). 398pp. Memoirs. Period Covered: 1877–1878.

Visited Louisiana, Ohio, Washington, D.C., New Jersey, and New York. Constantly present in writings, he observes North Americans without judging them. Zest of discoverer who narrates achievements. Unlike Lorenzo de Zavala and Justo Sierra O'Reilly (*Impresiones*), Prieto shows little or no influence of Alexis de Tocqueville (1835).

1423. Prieto, Guillermo (1818–1897). "Una excursión a Xalapa en 1875." En *Cien viajeros en Veracruz: crónicas y relatos v.10, 1839–1875*. Editado por Martha Poblett Mirando, Jalapa Enríquez: Gobierno del Estado de Veracruz, 1992. Pp.125–233. Memoirs. Period Covered: 1875–1876.

Articles published serially in *La Revista Universal* comprise unit in travel book. Chatters away leaving portraits of Xalapa's environment and personalities. Giving opinion, he dialogs and completely immerses self in material.

1424. Prieto, Guillermo (1818–1897). *Memorias de mis tiempos, 1828–1840, 1840–1853*. México: Editorial Patria, 1948 (1853). 2 v. Memoirs. Period Covered: 1828–1853.

Nineteenth century journalist and founder of periodicals, poet, minister of interior, senator, minister of foreign relations, and friend of Juárez has written two volumes of memoirs. Noted are relationship with many intellectuals of period and something of own character. Index to cultural life of period in descriptions.

1425. Prieto, Guillermo (1818–1897). *Mi guerra del 47*. México: UNAM, 1997 (1875). 178pp. Memoirs. Period Covered: 1847.

First serialized in 1875, *Mi guerra* one of best eyewitness documents on War with U.S. told by famous author. Marks entrance of Americans into Mexico City in 1847. Humor, fine points, and rapid characterization pervasive. Never abandons post of observer/participant to become historian.

1426. Prieto Laurens, Jorge (1895–1990). *Anécdotas de Jorge Prieto Laurens*. México: Costa-Amic, 1977. 197pp. Memoirs. Period Covered: 1909–1939.

Recounts thirty years as revolutionary (Zapatista) and politician often against established government. Introduces prominent revolutionaries in anecdote. Exiled to U.S. in 1920s; worked as radio announcer in Los Angeles until return to Mexico in 1933. Knew Saturnino Cedillo and favored Juan Andreu Almazán for presidency in 1940.

1427. Prieto Laurens, Jorge (1899–?). *Cincuenta años de política: memorias políticas*. México: Editora Mexicana, 1968. 422pp. Memoirs. Period Covered: 1895–1964?

Active politician, e.g., senator, head of senate, mayor of Federal District, governor of San Luis Potosí, etc. Supported three unpopular figures for Mexican presidency: Adolfo de la Huerta, José Vasconcelos, and Ezquiel Padilla. In exile was journalist in Houston, Texas. Detailed memoirs more history than autobiography.

1428. Prieto Quimper, Salvador (1887–1951). *El Parral de mis recuerdos: datos para la biografía de una noble ciudad de provincia*. México: Editorial Jus, 1948. 304pp. Memoirs. Period Covered: 1913–1945.

"Es una evocación de la niñez de los años felices que cerraron el siglo xix y dieron principio al siglo xx. Es un homenaje…a sus padres y a las familias que formaron el entorno social de los Prieto Quimper…" (p.10). As quote suggests, benign recall of Parral through eyes of middle-class child. Rarely uses personal *I* but readers aware that all scenes filtered through him in inventory of Parral: landscape, business, medicine, entertainments, society, churches, schools and students, and illustrious Parralenses. Best known as journalist.

1429. Pruneda, Salvador (1895–1985). *Huellas.* México: Editorial México Nuevo, 1936. 159pp. Memoirs. Period Covered: 1910–1934?

Title describes style and form of memoirs. Varying numbers of staccato paragraphs of sparse dialog and minimal description comprise each chapter. Carrancista against Villa and artist in post-revolutionary years complains about degeneration of Revolution.

1430. Puga, María Luisa (1944–). *De cuerpo entero: María Luisa Puga.* México: Ediciones Corunda, 1990. 56pp. Memoirs. Period Covered: 1944–1989?

Novelist and short story writer, as indicated by subtitle of autobiography, *Literary Space*, focuses on craft and creation of writing. Nomadic Puga goes beyond travel in description of major European capitals by subjectively reacting to environment. Travel and autobiography fused. Puga journeys to interior self to find writer.

1431. Purcell, William. *Frontier Mexico, 1875–1894: Letters.* San Antonio: Naylor, 1963. 295pp.

Author proved Coahuila offered opportunities beyond ranching. Irish-born Purcell arrived in Mexico in 1862. In 1866, moved from Matamoros to Saltillo and in three decades became involved in major industries of area: mining, cotton, cattle, and banking. In this book, he suggests commercial interests and shows a vision of the future. Letters also evidence courtesy and solicitude for others.

1432. Puxley, W. Lavallin. *The Magic Land of the Maya.* London: Allen and Unwin, 1928. 244pp.

Concentrates more on eternal in Maya area. Landscape, vegetation, Indian lore, insects, and even fish occupy slowly paced journey. In avoiding day's events, Brit's musings still have currency.

1433. Quevedo, Miguel Angel de (1862–1946). *Relato de mi vida.* México, 1943. 92pp. Memoirs. Period Covered: 1862–1943.

Engineer during Porfiriato helped clean port of Vera Cruz of sandbars, established fish hatcheries, founded and headed school of forestry, and beautified train stations. Born in Guadalajara, orphaned Quevedo educated in France. Concentrates on career in Mexico.

1434. Quezada, Abel (1920–1991). *Confrontaciones.* Azcapotzalco, DF: Universidad Autónoma Metropolitana, 1987. 7pp. Interview. Period Covered: 1956–1987?

Caricaturist responds to questions regarding career and problems of contemporary Mexico. Pays tribute to Germán Butze, world's best caricaturist for Quezada. Noting own successes and their sources, Charro Matías and Gastón Billetes, author speaks of liberal politics and authors who influenced him.

1435. Quinn, Anthony (1915–2001). *One Man Tango: Anthony Quinn with Daniel Paisner.* New York: Harper Collins, 1995. 388pp. Trans: *Tango de un hombre.* México: Edivisión, 1995. Memoirs. Period Covered: 1913?–1994.

Differs from *Original Sin,* Quinn's earlier autobiography for recent materials and strategy of narration. *One Man Tango* has little of self-excoriating alter ego of first work. Instead Quinn alternates chapters of past, birth in Mexico, migration to U.S., and successful film and stage career with present life, marriage, and moments in Italian villa. Sporadic awareness of Mexico, e.g., roots, family, and role in film *Viva Zapata.* Constantly interacts with other film and stage celebrities.

1436. Quinn, Anthony (1915–2001). *The Original Sin, A Self Portrait.* New York: Bantam, 1974. 373pp. Trans: *El pecado original: autobiografía.* Santiago de Chile: Pomaire, 1973. Autobiography Proper. Period Covered: 1916–1972?

Began life in Chihuahua and fled with family to El Paso, Texas, because of Revolution. Settled in Los Angeles. Rise from poverty due to acting. Straight narration of engrossing life would suffice without relentless psychologizing of imaginary boy/imp who bedevils Quinn with taunting questions and deprecatory comments. Fifty-six year old focuses on childhood and adolescence.

1437. Quintana, José Miguel (1908–?). *Mis recuerdos de la casa del Correo Viejo 13.* México: Vargas Rea, 1958. 78pp. Memoirs. Period Covered: 1910–1925.

Poetic evocation of family and home in Mexico City. From perspective of child, author nostalgically recalls patriarchal grandfather, aunts and uncles, house, and furniture. World almost perfect except for death of grandfather.

1438. Quintana, Valente (1889–1968). *Memorias de Valente Quintana.* México: Ediciones Populares, 1961 (1925). 243pp. Oral Autobiography. Period Covered: 1920s.

Famed for investigating assassinations of Alvaro Obregón (1928) and José Antonio Mella (1929), policeman focuses on less celebrated crimes. In account to Ignacio Muñoz, colloquial author outsmarts adversaries and solves crimes. Style reminiscent of el Güero Téllez.

1439. Quintero Rodríguez, Luis Roberto (1940–?). *Los doce sueños de un cardiólogo.* Tabasco: El Autor, 1992, 303pp. Memoirs. Period Covered: 1970–1988?

Cardiologist compresses twelve experiences with heart patients in various worldwide clinics. Memoir appropriate vehicle for cardiovascular surgeon.

1440. Quirós, Carlos Alberto (1888–1975 Dates of Rodolfo Gaona). *Mis 20 años de torero....* México: Biblioteca Popular de El Universal, 1925. 391pp. Oral Autobiography. Period Covered: 1897–1925.

Writer prompts Gaona to narrate life in form of memoir. Leonés bullfighter studied with Saturnino Frutos (Ojitos), began career in 1905 in Mexico, and to Spain in 1908, where he retired in 1925. Gaona registers sensitivity to public. Meets and chats with Porfirio Díaz in 1910 in final chapter.

1441. Quiroz(z), Alberto (1907–). *Los intelectuales.* México: Costa-Amic, 1978. 252pp. Memoirs. Period Covered: 1905–1977.

Prolific author dispenses self in 188 portraits or anecdotes. Knows many intellectuals, interacts with them, and introduces them in gentle portraits. Author's personality incremental in brief chapters.

1442. Ramírez, Carlos (1909?–?); **Jorge Uzeta.** *He pasado muchas tristezas: acercamiento a una historia de vida en el occidente de México.* Universidad de Guanajuato, 2001. 48pp. Oral Autobiography. Period Covered: 1909–1995?

Peasant narrator spent life, aside from brief sojourn in U.S., in Jalisco, Michoacán, and Guanajuato. Told in own peculiar language, life shows variety: work on hacienda, devout Catholicism, *Cristero* rebellion, tenant farmer, bracero in California in 1940, stone mason, and livestock owner. Interviewer Uzeta gives some methodology.

1443. Ramírez, Juan (1908–?). *Remembranzas de un hombre del Bajío.* México: Litografía Helio, 1995. 66pp. Memoirs. Period Covered: 1914–1995.

From Bajío de Bonillas in Guanajuato and self-taught in music. Played trumpet and trombone with mariachis in Mexico City. Schooling, Revolution, marriage, and bracero in U.S. among lesser incidents.

1444. Ramírez Arellano, Petra (1860–1935). *Diario de mamá Petrita, 1881–1934.* Instituto de Cultura de Durango, 200. 491pp. Diary. Period Covered: 1881–1934.

Life spanned Porfiriato and post-revolutionary years. Middle-class widow with many children lived in Zacatecas, Aguascalientes, Irapuato, and Mexico. Diary testament to strength of family and survival skills. Church pervasive in life of matriarch. Revolution and *Cristero* rebellion peripheral themes.

1445. Ramírez de Aguilar, Fernando (Jacobo Dalevuelta) (1887–1953). *Cariño a Oaxaca, escrito para viandantes.* México: Ediciones Bota, 1938. 172pp. Memoirs. Period Covered: 1938?

Retablo (decorative structure behind altar) describes book composed of nineteen lyrical scenes of Oaxaca. Subjectivity, travel, and autobiography combine in descriptions of climate, landscape, churches, cities, and humans. Echoes two other writers in technique and style: Azorín and Alfredo Maillefert.

1446. Ramírez de Aguilar, Fernando (Jacobo Dalevuelta) (1887–1953). *Desde el tren amarillo: crónica de guerra.* México: Botes e Hijo, 1924. 138pp. Memoirs. Period Covered: 1910–1924.

Minor classic of Revolution, *Desde el tren amarillo* (presidential train) refers to journalist's wanderings and testimonies of upheaval. More than simple reportage, he witnesses battles, landscape, and moods. *Soldaderas*, Yaquis, campfires, and weather as notable as strategy and carnage. "La fría mañana de Huamantla," "Pénjamo, la histórica," y "La acción de Palo Verde," suggest perspective.

1447. Ramírez Heredia, Rafael (1942–). *De cuerpo entero: Rafael Ramírez Heredia.* México: Ediciones Corunda, 1990. 64pp. Memoirs. Period Covered: 1942?–1989?

In third person, he reveals personality interested in creativity, drinking, bullfighting, and womanizing. Notes schools and father. Experiences concerns of writing and self-encounter through anguish.

1448. Ramírez Heredia, Rafael (1942–). *Por los caminos del sur, vámonos para Guerrero.* México: Alianza Editorial Mexicana, 1990. 235pp. Memoirs. Period Covered: 1980s?

One of best examples of travel/autobiography. Visiting Taxco, Olinalá, Atoyac, Chilpancingo, Acapulco, and El Río Balsas, he combines geography and tourism. Filters all impressions through constant subjectivity; writes in style both accelerated and breathless.

1449. Ramírez Ramírez, Guillermo (Dates?). "Mis experiencias en el estado de Oaxaca." En *Los maestros y la cultura nacional, 1920–1952, v.5. Sureste.* México: Museo Nacional de Culturas Populares, 1989. Pp.187–214. Memoirs. Period Covered: 1928–1945.

Detailed account of teaching positions in Oaxaca: Chacalapa, region de La Chinantla, Tiltepec, Tepanzacoalco, El Carrizal, Tepantlali, and Cuajimoloyas. Environment and peculiar problems of each location evident. Emphasizes enormity of task: hygiene and health, teaching of Spanish to Indians, literacy for adults, and work with children. One of better testimonies in series for completeness.

1450. Ramos, Jorge (1958–). *Atravesando fronteras: la autobiografía de un periodista en busca de su lugar en el mundo.* New York: Rayo, 2002. 320pp. Memoirs. Period Covered: 1958?–2001.

Journalist and anchorman talks about career in U.S. and in Mexico. Worked for radio and TV in Mexico and then at age of twenty-four tried Los Angeles. Worked for Cuban TV in Miami. Writes of family, race prejudice, and own identity, i.e., Mexican, Hispano, or Latino. Many other topics, but view of two worlds, Mexico and U.S., best.

1451. Ramos, Jorge (1958–). *Lo que vi: experiencias de un periodista alrededor del mundo.* México: Editorial Grijalbo, 1999. 344pp. Memoirs. Period Covered: 1978–1999.

Trained in U.S. and Mexico, journalist travels world, focuses on current events, gives opinions, and reveals bits of self. Latin America, U.S., Asia, Africa, and Europe scenario for eventual and fragmented autobiography.

1452. Ramos, Rafael A. (1895?–1979). *Del arcón de mis recuerdos.* México: Federación Editorial Mexicana, 1980. 119pp. Memoirs? Period Covered: 1900–1970?

Eighty-year-old doctor reflects upon life but with interruptions in chronology and theme. Yucatecan attended medical school in Chicago and practiced medicine for fifty years in U.S. Vague about details, gives anecdotes from youth, talks philosophically about pain, questions memory, and writes independent chapters on Mayan folklore. Evocative memoir at times reminiscent of Castellanos's *Balún Canán.*

1453. Ramos Romo, Jesús (1902–?). *Relatos de don Jesús Ramos Romo: narración e* *historia personal.* Ed. by Guillermo Ramos Arizpe. Jiquilpan, MIC: Archivo de Historia Oral, 1986. Pp.25–207. Oral Autobiography. Period Covered: 1902–1984.

Editor spotted Ramos Romo as natural storyteller and so enlisted him for larger enterprise. Seven chapters relate to early years in San Agustín de las Cuevas, Jalisco, work as muleteer, stonemason in Guadalajara and Jiquilpan, bracero in California, return to Jiquilpan, and union activities. Vernacular narration. Final fifty pages oral history and autobiography.

1454. Ramos Sánchez, Alfonso (1925–?). *Memorias de un ganadero.* Chihuahua, CHH: Doble Hélice, 1999. 243pp. Memoirs. Period Covered: 1925–1995.

Hacienda appears frequently as theme in Mexican autobiography, but little attention to cattle raising. Chihuahuense spent entire life working with cattle. Son and father of ranchers. For five terms president of Cattlemen's Union of Chihuahua.

1455. Ramsey, Leonidas; James Anthony Kelly. *Time Out for Adventure: Let's Go to Mexico.* Garden City, NY: Doubleday, Doran, 1934. 315pp.

Title justifies word *adventure* in last chapter when he and companion foolishly opt for trip from Tehuantepec to Oaxaca over mountains. Rest of book much tamer with two American men in Mexico to look for contrary concepts of time. Unextraordinary itinerary carries them also to Monterrey, Guanajuato, Celaya, Acámbaro, Pátzcuero, Mexico City, Mérida, and Campeche. Chapter on Mexico City exemplifies book: praise for beauty of capital, survey of hotels, some history, entertainments including cockfights and sports, and favorite alcoholic drinks.

1456. Rangel, Salomón H. (1918–). *Forjando mi destino (Apuntes de mi vida).* México: Epessa, 1989. 635pp. Memoirs. Period Covered: 1918–1976.

Farmer, journalist, and politician follows form of memoir in first 122 pages of book. Remainder comprised of undigested miscellany: news clippings, speeches, and letters. Rises from poverty to become successful farmer; fights established PRI (Partido Rev-olucionario Institucional) and major representative in San Luis Potosí, Gonzalo N. Santos. Rangel active in *Sinarquismo,* counter-revolutionary movement of 1937.

1457. Rangel Frías, Raúl (1913–1993). *Los hijos del desierto: conversaciones con don Raúl Rangel Frías.* Guadalupe, NLE: Presidencia Municipal de Guadalupe, 1993. 133pp. Interview. Period Covered: 1913–1986?

Interviewer Celso Garza Guajado sums up subject: "La vida de…está ligada al origen y desarrollo de la Universidad Autónoma de Nuevo León, la Ciudad Universitaria, la Biblioteca Público, la Escuela de Verano, la Capilla Alfonsina y la creación de la Facultad de Filosfía y Letras" (p.vii). Topics structure interview.

1458. Rangel Guerra, Alfonso (1928–). *Ensayo de una vida: conversaciones con Alfonso Rangel Guerra.* Monterrey: Universidad Autónoma de Nuevo León, 1996. 104pp. Interview. Period Covered: 1887–1996.

Nuevoleonese, lawyer, professor, university president, diplomat to Spain, and writer in humanities. Five conversations with Celso Garza Guajardo in 1996 create book. In dialog, Rangel Guerra touches upon family, childhood, education (reading, schools, films, radios, and libraries), Spain, and work on *Armas y letras,* journal of creative literature.

1459. Rangel Guerra, Jorge (Dates?). *Opera en Monterrey, 1953–1989.* Monterrey: Secretaría de Educación y Cultura, 1990. 125pp. Memoirs. Period Covered: 1960–1989.

Unusual memoirs by two different authors. Díaz Du-Pond covers opera from 1953 to 1980; Rangel Guerra, 1960 to 1989. Year-by-year account involving selves with operas and their stars. Vaguely autobiographical.

1460. Rankin, Melinda. *Twenty Years among the Mexicans, A Narrative of Missionary Labor.* Cincinnati: Central Book Concern, 1875. 233pp.

Foremost Presbyterian missionary in Mexico was Melinda Rankin, whose Victorian autobiography manifests certainty of her task near border: Brownsville, Texas; Matamoros, Tamaulipas; and Monterrey, Nuevo

León. Avowed Protestant, she battled anti–Mexican attitudes, Baptists, and Roman Catholics: "The spirit of popery was fully alive, and in violent activity to counteract my influence" (p.71).

1461. Rascón Banda, Hugo (1948–). *De cuerpo entero: Hugo Rascón Banda.* México: Ediciones Corunda, 1990. 54pp. Memoirs. Period Covered: 1948–1990.

Born in Uruachich, Chihuahua, dramatist in imaginary interview/inquisition profiles life: parents and grandparents, experiences in theater, writing for film, and creating novels. Concentrates on drama and problems of beginning playwright.

1462. Ratz, Konrad. *Correspondencia inédita entre Maximiliano y Carlota.* México: Fondo de Cultura Económica, 2003. 367pp.

Over 225 letters and telegrams almost equally divided between the monarchs. Letters begin in 1859, but majority between 1864 and 1867. Except for her final European pilgrimage, most of Carlota's letters postmarked Mexico City; in contrast, Maximilian letters from many parts of Mexico including El Bajío, Hidalgo, Veracruz, and Morelos (Cuernavaca): "…revelan su ansiedad y entusiasmo por reconstruir un país que se encontraba fragmentado…" (p.14). Great mutual affection.

1463. Reachi, Santiago (1898–?). *La revolución, Cantínflas y JoLoPo (JOsé LOpez POrtillo).* México: Editores Asociados Mexicanos, 1982. 232pp. Memoirs. Period Covered: 1904?–1982.

Narrates exciting life. Guerrerense fled from father and then Revolution. In U.S., represented tire company internationally. Helped launch Cantínflas's film career. Supreme capitalist, he moved to Tijuana and attempted to promote community.

1464. Rébora, Hipólito (1890?–?). *Memorias de un chiapaneco.* México: Editorial Katún, 1982. 247pp. Memoirs. Period Covered: 1896–1946.

Simultaneous memoirs of author-politician and hometown, Tapachula, Chiapas. Focuses on Revolution and aftermath. Good for regional-level politics.

1465. Reed, John. *Insurgent Mexico.* New York: Appleton, 1914. 325pp.

Writer allies self with Villistas and Constitutionalistas in one of best narratives of Mexican Revolution. Six parts: Desert War; Francisco Villa; Jiménez and Points West; A People in Arms; Carranza — An Impression; and Mexican Nights. Character sketches, tad inferior to those of Martín Luis Guzmán, make him competitor in perceiving cataclysm.

1466. Reich, Sheldon. *Francisco Zúñiga, Sculptor: Conversations and Interpretations.* Tucson: University of Arizona Press, 1980. 153pp.

Although from Costa Rica, sculptor Zúñiga had Mexican-born father and moved to father's country in 1935. Answers questions relating to life and to sculptures and propounds esthetics of this art. Reich and Zúñiga sustained thirty-five hours of conversation to realize fifty-six-page interview.

1467. Reid, Elizabeth Hyde. *Mayne Reid; A Memoir of His Life.* London: War and Downey, 1890. 277pp.

Author of novels and boys' books penned experiences in Mexican-American War in 1847: San Juan de Ulloa, Lobos Islet off of Vera Cruz, Antón Lizardo, Vera Cruz, Cerro Gordo, Jalapa, Perote, Puebla, and Mexico City. In storming of Chapultepec, Reid wounded and died in Mexico. Writes dramatically.

1468. Reid, Samuel C. *The Scouting Expeditions of McCulloch's Texas Rangers….* Philadelphia: Zieber, 1970 (1848). 251pp.

Of many autobiographies in English on Mexican-American War, Reid's is one of few by a Ranger. Although Reynosa, Matamoros, Camargo, and China receive attention, Monterrey is centerpiece of Rangers' campaign. McCulloch, named chief of Taylor Scouts, did yeoman service in noting Santa Anna's army and perhaps saving Taylor. Reads like an adventure novel.

1469. Revere, Joseph Warren. *Keel and Saddle: A Retrospect of Forty Years of Military and Naval Service.* Boston: Osgood, 1872. 360pp.

Virginian and graduate of West Point, Revere is type of freebooter whose adventures take him to Mexican California and Mexico. Mazatlán, San Blas, Manzanilla, Mapimi, San Juan de los Lagos, Mexico City, Guanajuato, Morelia, Perote, and Vera Cruz suggest range of travel. Curiously he joined Mexican army and resigned from it with retirement of friend and patron, Mariano Ariste. Stories and remembered conversations approach novel.

1470. Revueltas, José (1914–1976). *Cartas a María Teresa.* México: Ediciones Era, 1985. 116pp. Letters. Period Covered: 1947–1972.

One of main twentieth century writers and avowed communist in posthumous letters reveals self. Passionate, frank, loving, unhappy, and at times critical of family. Written mainly to second wife, María Teresa Retes, collection suggests nomadic existence: cities in Mexico, Berlin, Prague, Budapest, Trieste, Havana, and San Jose, California.

1471. Revueltas, José (1914–1976). *Conversaciones con José Revueltas/Gustavo Sainz....* México: Veracruzana, Centro de Investigaciones Lingüístico-Literarias, 1977. 153pp. Interviews. Period Covered: 1950–1976?

Through thirteen interviews, controversial writer and Marxist airs views on philosophy, love, novels, critics, prison, and Faulkner.

1472. Revueltas, José (1914–1976). *Las evocaciones requeridas (Memorias, diarios, correspondencia).* México: Ediciones Era, 1987. 2 v. Hybrid. Period Covered: 1928–1975.

Two volumes concentrate on author and convey personality in sinewy and passionate prose. Various media and disjunctions of time and tone fragment image in multiple topics: Islas Marías, site of author's imprisonment in 1934; trip to USRR in 1935 as delegate of Mexican Communist Party; letters to first wife Olivia Peralta; letters to second wife Teresa Retes; Lecumberri; twenty-page autobiography; and miscellaneous letters to family.

1473. Revueltas, María (Dates?). "Una familia chocarrosa" En *"El naranjo" en flor: homenaje a los Revueltas* by José Angel Leyva.

Durango, DUR: Secretaría de Educación, Cultura y Deporte, 1994. Pp.47–71. Memoirs. Period Covered: 1910?–1993.

Self-confessed *hermana doméstica* of Revueltas family contributes memories and interpretation of parents and illustrious siblings. Durango and Mexico City venues for recall of brilliant family in historical fact and anecdote that emphasize favorites, personalities, and conflicts.

1474. Revueltas, Rosaura (1920–1996). *Los Revueltas (Biografía de una familia).* México: Editorial Grijalbo, 1980. 327pp. Memoirs. Period Covered: 1922?–1965?

Concentrates on self only in final section. In chronological order lists main events of life: marriage, family, dancing, film, theater, travels, Bertold Brecht, Fidel Castro, etc. Interesting narrative; self-portrait rapid, sporadic, and unreflective. Reveals self in memoirs of other famous members of family: Silvestre, Fermín, José (most celebrated family member and close to Rosaura), and Consuelo. Drawn from diaries and letters, portraits semi-autobiographical. Immediately preceding entry ("*El naranjo" en flor*), essential companion to present title, has both biography and autobiography.

1475. Revueltas, Silvestre (1899–1940). *Cartas intimas y escrites.* México: Fondo de Cultura Económica, 1982. 100pp. Letters. Period Covered: 1916–1937.

Three types of materials: introduction by novelist brother José that complements other two sections and yet in tone and content reveals as much about novelist as about musician; eighteen letters without responses; and brief essays by Silvestre. Readings locate Revueltas in world of music. Violinist, composer, and director of national symphony of Mexico. In *José Revueltas en el banquillo de los acusados y otros ensayos* (1987), Eugenia Revueltas wrote of self and of father in one chapter, "Silvestre."

1476. Revueltas, Silvestre (1899–1940). *Epistolario.* Recopilación y notas de Juan Alvarez Coral. México: UNAM, 1974. 109pp. Letters. Period Covered: 1937.

Musicians also writers. As Secretario General de la Liga de Escritores y Artistas

Revolucionarios (LEAR), Revueltas went to Europe in 1937 to aid Spanish Republic. With mastery and originality of style, boldly expresses thoughts and emotions to wife, Angela Acevedo. Postmarked New York, Paris, and Spain, letters some of best of twentieth century Mexico.

1477. Revueltas, Silvestre (1899–1940). *Silvestre Revueltas por él mismo: apuntes autobiográficos...de un gran músico/recopilación de Rosaura Revueltas.* México: Ediciones Era, 1989. 262pp. Autobiography/Diary/Letters. Period Covered: 1899–1946.

More definitive than two preceding titles, collection repeats some of same material. Autobiographical essay accompanied by letters to musician's family, Jule Klarecy, Nicolas Slonimsky, and Angel Acevedo; diary of trip to Spain in 1937; diary of stay in sanitarium in 1939; and Rosaura Revueltas's interview with Manuel Falcón, head of sanitarium. Excellent photos illustrate member of brilliant family.

1478. Reyes, Alfonso (1889–1959). *Albores, segundo libro de recuerdos.* México: El Cerro de la Silla, 1960. 160pp. Memoirs. Period Covered: 1885–1900?

Fragments of life of multi-faceted author. Monterrey scenario for evocation of childhood: family, dwellings, servants, games, climate, etc. Sharpness of impressions and style.

1479. Reyes, Alfonso (1889–1959). *Una amistad porteña: correspondencia entre Alfonso Reyes y Roberto F. Giusti.* México: El Colegio Nacional, 2000. 105pp. Letters. Period Covered: 1920–1959.

Another contribution to growing corpus of Reyes's correspondence. Polymath Reyes, ambassador to Argentina in 1927, exchanges letters with Robert Giusti, Argentine literary critic responsible for journal *Nosotros.* Love of literature attracted two writers, who talk of Amado Nervo, Pedro Henríquez Ureña, and Valery Larbaud, gift books to one another, and translations.

1480. Reyes, Alfonso (1889–1959). *Berkeleyana.* México: Gráfica Panamericana, 1953. 40pp. Memoirs. Period Covered: 1941.

In 1941, University of California at Berkeley conferred honorary doctorate on Reyes. Commitments in Mexico gave author limited days traveling for event. Delightful account of rapid car trip and encounter with tailors and academicians. High degree of writing and self-irony.

1481. Reyes, Alfonso (1889–1959). *Cartas a la Habana: epistolario de Alfonso Reyes con Max Henríquez Ureña, José Antonio Ramos y Jorge Mañach.* México: UNAM, 1989. 160pp. Letters. Period Covered: 1930–1954.

Exchange of letters with each of following: Henríquez Ureña, Ramos, and Mañach. Collection concentrates on Reyes imaged as generous scholar towards Cuban colleagues. Explains abstention from political life after death of father, Bernardo Reyes.

1482. Reyes, Alfonso (1889–1959); **Victoria Ocampo**. *Cartas echadas: correspondencia, 1927–1959.* México: Universidad Autónoma Metropolitana, 1983. 78pp. Letters. Period Covered: 1927–1959.

Letters between two intellectual luminaries of twentieth century. Ocampo's *Sur* receives attention within topic of creativity. Personal touches about each pervasive, but less apparent for Reyes.

1483. Reyes, Alfonso (1889–1959); **Genaro Estrada** (1887–1937). *Con leal franqueza: correspondencia entre Alfonso Reyes y Genaro Estrada*: compilación y notas de Serge I. Zaitzeff. México: El Colegio Nacional, 1992. 485pp. Letters. Period Covered: 1916–1927.

Letters (226) postmarked Madrid, Mexico, and Paris exchanged between two diplomats and writers. Reyes posted to Spain, France, and Argentina; Estrada, creator of doctrine to recognize new governments automatically, undersecretary of foreign relations. Intimates confess personal lives: daily work, literature, and gossip of mutual acquaintances. Zaitzeff edited letters with introduction, footnotes, and index.

1484. Reyes, Alfonso (1889–1959); **Ignacio H. Valdés**. *Correspondencia, Alfonso Reyes — Ignacio H. Valdés, 1904–1942.* Monterrey: Universidad Autónoma de Nuevo León, 2000. 292pp. Letters. Period Covered: 1904–1942.

Present has some of earliest letters. Barely fifteen when pens first letter to Monterrey friend. Eternally encouraging and book-loving Reyes emerges. Includes samples of poetry and struggle with creation. Edited edition by Aureliano Tapia Méndez.

1485. Reyes, Alfonso (1889–1959). *Diario.* Universidad de Guanajuato, 1969. 330pp. Diary. Period Covered: 1911–1930.

Leaves imprimatur, but diary lacks charm and intimacy of *Parentalia* and *Albores.* Anecdotal entries on years in Monterrey, New York, Madrid, and Rome and on writing and lecturing. End rather than process of intellectual life.

1486. Reyes, Alfonso (1889–1959). *Epistolario Alfonso Reyes, José M.A. Chacón/Zenaida Gutiérrez-Vega.* Madrid: Fundación Universitaria Española, 1976. 285pp. Letters. Period Covered: 1914–1959.

Few collections reveal so much of intellectual life. In forty-five-year relationship, Reyes refers to publications and to luminaries attracted to diplomatic posts in Spain, Argentina, and Brazil. Trajectory of developing and sustained friendship with Cuban critic and essayist José M. Chacón just as significant.

1487. Reyes, Alfonso (1889–1959). *Fronteras conquistadas: correspondencia Alfonso Reyes-Silvio Zavala, 1937–1958.* (1909 Birth of Zavala). Compilación, introducción y notas de Alberto Enríquez Perea. México: El Colegio de México, 1998. 344pp. Letters. Period Covered: 1937–1958.

Letters (207) between Reyes and historian Silvio Zavala, founder and director and president of Centro de Estudios Históricos of Colegio de México. Letters divided into two parts: 1937 to 1950 with Reyes in Buenos Aires but back to take charge of Casa de España, and 1951 to 1958 with Zavala back in Europe for research and diplomatic duties. Reflects more of personality of Zavala, researcher and bibliophile, than humanist Reyes of Colegio de México.

1488. Reyes, Alfonso (1889–1959). *Grito de auxilio: correspondencia entre Alfonso Reyes y Juana de Ibarbourou.* México: El Colegio

Nacional, 2001. 115pp. Letters. Period Covered: 1928–1959.

A total of forty-five letters, thirty-seven from Ibarbourou to Reyes and eight from Mexican to Uruguayan poet. Unusual Reyes' collection for infrequency of his correspondence and for his correspondent's direct emotional need of him, i.e., Ibarbourou's terror and superstition. Other themes: literature and Reyes's sponsorship of her for Nobel Prize.

1489. Reyes, Alfonso (1889–1959). *Historia documental de mis libros [1955–1959].* En *Obras completas de Alfonso Reyes, v.24.* México: Fondo de Cultura Económica, 1990. Pp.149–351. Memoirs. Period Covered: 1903–1957.

Surveys life through writings. Arranging materials chronologically, he is precise about writing context of geographical surroundings, friendships, and contacts. Fifteen chapters either carry title of year, e.g., "El año de 1923," name of book, e.g.,"*Visión de Anáhuac*" or geographical locale, e.g., "Paris y Roma (1924–1925)." Profiles intellectual self through history of writings.

1490. Reyes, Alfonso (1889–1959); **Gustavo Baz** (1894–1987). *Inteligencia española en México: correspondencia, Alfonso Reyes-Gustavo Baz (1939–1958).* Madrid: Fundación Histórica Tavera, 2001. 179pp. Letters. Period Covered: 1939–1958.

Reyes, president of La Casa de España en México (El Colegio de México) and Baz, president of UNAM, exchange correspondence relating to placement of Spanish exiles in these two institutions and also in other parts of Mexico. Pro forma correspondence in which authors plea for employment for illustrious academics: Antonio Madinaveitia, José y Francisco Giral, Agustín Millares Carlo, José Medina Echavarría, Manuel Márquez, Manuel de Rivas Cherif, Isaac Costero, José Gaos, María Zambrano, and José Moreno Villa.

1491. Reyes, Alfonso (1889–1959). *Memorias de cocina y bodega.* México: Tezontle, 1953. 177pp. Memoirs. Period Covered: 1900–1953.

Travels, gastronomic experiences, anecdotes, and frequent mention of books from many cultures of western world comprise delightful document.

1492. Reyes, Alfonso (1889–1959). *Páginas sobre una poesía: correspondencia, Alfonso Reyes y Luis Cernuda (1932–1959)*. Sevilla: Renacimiento, 2003. 206pp. Letters. Period Covered: 1932–1959.

Cernuda in Mexico in 1954 needed financial aid. Reyes, on behalf of the Colegio de México, offered exiled Spaniard scholarship to write on subject of contemporary Spanish poetry from Bécquer to 1954. Fifty-two letters, mainly between Reyes and Cernuda, indicate progress of exile's research with constantly warm replies from Reyes.

1493. Reyes, Alfonso (1889–1959). *Parentalia, primer capítulo de mis recuerdos*. México: Los Presentes, 1954. 74pp. Memoirs. Period Covered: 1889–1910?

Sets pattern for sequel *Albores*. Fragmented and desultory approach to childhood. Writes of family in amused tone and reveals personality in anecdotal sketches.

1494. Reyes, Alfonso (1889–1959); **Daniel Cosío Villegas** (1898–1976). *Testimonios de una amistad: correspondencia Alfonso Reyes-Daniel Cosío Villegas, 1922–1958*. México: El Colegio de México, 1999. 252pp. Letters. Period Covered: 1922–1958.

Exchanges (134) between two intellectuals, who had in common the Colegio de México and its presidency. During the thirty-six-year period, Reyes was in the diplomatic service in Spain, France, Argentina, and Brazil. For the same period, Cosío Villegas founded the department of economics at UNAM and also the publishing house, Fondo de Cultura Económica. He edited the multivolume *Historia Moderna de México*. The two men incorporate the following themes in their letters: literature, diplomacy, La Casa de España and El Colegio de México. Surely not as revelatory as the Alfonso Reyes-Pedro Henríquez Ureña correspondence; also, should be used as adjunct to Cosío Villegas's *Memorias*.

1495. Reyes, Alfonso (1871–1952). *El tiempo de los patriarcas: epistolario, 1909–1952*. México: Fondo de Cultura Económica, 2002. 454pp. Letters. Period Covered: 1905–1952.

To date, best collection of Reyes's correspondence is with Pedro Heníquez Ureña. Present title competes for profundity of friendship and elegance of prose. Two poets/diplomats exchange letters postmarked Mexico City, Paris, Madrid, Santiago, and Buenos Aires. Themes include exchange of books, esthetics, journals, reactions to book reviews, readings, and less abstract idea of friendship and even locations. "Que siga lloviendo en su milpa literaria" (p.240) suggests metaphoric value of prose. Letters published first serially in journal *Abside*, a Catholic- inspired publication.

1496. Reyes, Alfonso (1889–1959); **Jesús Silva Herzog** (1892–1985). *Vidas de cultura y pasión mexicanas: correspondencia Alfonso Reyes/Jesús Silva Herzog, 1939–1959*. México: El Colegio de Mexico, 2001. 123pp. Letters. Period Covered: 1939–1959.

Forty-nine letters comprise exchange of two public servants, who discuss various themes: collaboration between department of economics at UNAM and Colegio de México and founding of *Cuadernos Americanos*. Most passionate letter is Reyes's indignation and defense of father accused of betraying his country in one issue of said journal. Much courtesy and elegant language.

1497. Reyes, Bernardo (1849–1913). *Defensa que por sí mismo produce el C. general de división Bernardo Reyes, acusado del delito de rebelión, México, octubre de 1912*. México: Tip. G. y A. Serralde, 1912. 35pp. Memoirs. Period Covered: 1909–1912.

Career military officer, both provisional and elected governor of Nuevo León and secretary of war, eloquently defends self. In prose, worthy of father of Alfonso Reyes, old general generates memories of political and military life. Executed prior to *Decena Trágica*. "Bernardo Reyes visto por sus hijos" in *El gobernador Bernardo Reyes y sus homólogos de la frontera norte* (1991), pp.305–342. Includes three affectionate essays, "Charlas de la siesta," "Oración del 9 de febrero" de Alfonso Reyes, and "La jornada del domingo" de Rodolfo Reyes. Autobiographical writing illuminates two sons and father.

1498. Reyes, Judith (1920?–1988). *La otra cara de la patria: autobiografía*. México: El Autor, 1974. 270pp. Memoirs. Period Covered: 1923–1970?

Singer la Tamaulipeca, journalist, and balladeer writes social protest memoirs. From proletarian background in Tampico, moves to two major arenas of life, Chihuahua and Mexico City, where she battles social injustice through ballads and other activities. In Chihuahua in 1964, opposes *latifundistas* and failure of PRI to redistribute land. Continues struggle in Mexico City and incorporates Tlateloco of 1968.

1499. Reyes, Rodolfo (1878–1954). *De mi vida, memorias políticas, 1899–1914*. Madrid: Biblioteca Nueva, 1929. 2 v. Memoirs. Period Covered: 1899–1914.

Lawyer and minister of justice in Huerta regime recounts climactic moments of career. In first volume perceives father Bernardo Reyes as martyr to Revolution. Beyond profiling own life, Rodolfo Reyes favors personal interpretation of *Decena Trágica*. Notes defects of Madero and Huerta.

1500. Reyes Aguilar, Saúl (1903–?). *Mi madre y yo; sucesos históricos en la Mixteca*. México: Ediciones Botas, 1972. 560pp. Memoirs. Period Covered: 1903–1924.

Life in Oaxaca but mainly in relation to Revolution. First on side of Federals, family later supports Carranza. Story of sufferings of one family and author's super adoration of mother.

1501. Reyes Aurrecoechea, Alfonso (1916–1991). *Conversaciones con Alfonso Reyes Aurrecoechea/Celso Garza Guajardo*. Monterrey: Universidad Autónoma de Nuevo León, 1991. 132pp. Interview. Period Covered: 1916–1990.

Nuevo León historian interviews Reyes Aurrecoechea, whose main career as journalist manifest in publications: *El Porvenir*, *Tribuna*, *Armas y Letras*, *El Tiempo*, *Resurgimiento*, and *Roel*. Son of Methodist minister educated at El Colegio Laurens in Monterrey. Functions as history of Nuevo León journalism and as biography of many personalities that Reyes knows.

1502. Reyes de la Maza, Luis (1932–). *Memorias de un pentonto*. México: Editorial Posada, 1984. 296pp. Memoirs. Period Covered: 1800?–1979?

From San Luis Potosí, best known as critic and historian of theater. Head of Supervisión Literaria de Televisión and director of radio and television for government. Genealogical research exposes examples of foolishness in family and chance for humor. Insider's view of theater.

1503. Reyes López, Venustiano (1916–?). *Venus Rey, vida y secretos*. México: EDAMEX, 2001. 120pp. Memoirs. Period Covered: 1925–1986?

Orphaned Veracruzano became professional musician with studies in own country and in U.S. Director of symphonic orchestra of Bellas Artes had own band. Active in musicians' union and in politics.

1504. Reyes Navarro, Angel (1924–). *Yo recuerdo*. Colima, COL: Editorial Gobierno del Estado, 1995. 311pp. Memoirs. Period Covered: 1924–1994.

President of University of Colima from 1965 to 1968 composes memoir of undigested minutes of regime. Talks about family and occasionally self but focus is on external.

1505. Richardson, William H. *Journal of William H. Richardson, a Private Soldier in Col. Doniphan's Command*. Baltimore: Robinson, 1847. 84pp.

Richardson left Maryland in 1846 and from Ft. Leavenworth arrived in New Mexico and joined Doniphan's march to Chihuahua. Participated in battle of Sacramento in Chihuahua. After Mexican-American War returned through Monterrey, Camargo, and Rio Grande. Notes Indians, food, landscape, boredom, and a bullfight that violated Sabbath.

1506. Riestra, Ernesto (1901–?). *Mi batuta habla*. México: Editorial Diana, 1974. 303pp. Memoirs. Period Covered: 1913–1972.

Musician directed one of most famous conjuntos in Mexico City from 1933 to 1950. Describes trip to New York in 1919 and learning to play several instruments. Toured with band in U.S. before return to Mexico.

1507. Ríos, Alberto (1952?–). *Capirotada: A Nogales Memoir*. Albuquerque: University of New Mexico Press, 1999. 145pp. Memoirs. Period Covered: 1952–1995?

Ríos mestizo by birth and location. English mother and Mexican father reared him in Nogales, Arizona, twin city of Nogales, Sonora. Five-part recall evokes separate moments of growing up on bicultural border. Dually used *capirotada*, also title of one chapter, reflects culture and structure of book.

1508. Ripley, Eliza. *From Flag to Flag: A Woman's Adventures and Experiences in the South during the War, in Mexico, and in Cuba*. New York: Appleton, 1889. 296pp.

Confluence of two events, Civil War in U.S. and French Intervention in Mexico. Three chapters relate to husband's work, procuring supplies for Confederacy from Mexico. Ripleys cross over Piedras Negras and Matamoros. Rugged conditions on both sides of border.

1509. Rittlinger, Herbert. *Jungle Quest: A Search for the Last of the Mayas*. London: Odhams, 1961. 258pp.

German author and party riverboat through Lacandon country for pictures and adventures. Undaunted by deprivation, suffering, and death. Meet remnants of Maya-related Lacandones and achieve rapport with disappearing tribe.

1510. Riva Palacio, Vicente (1832–1896). *Epistolario amoroso con Josefina Bros, 1853–1855*. Mexico: Consejo Nacional para la Cultura y las Artes, 2000. 270pp. Letters. Period Covered: 1853–1855.

Future romantic novelist, historian, and ambassador begins penning love letters to sweetheart and wife, Josefina Bros Villaseñor. Letters, static in content, express love, absence, worry about health, and forgiveness for supposed wrongs of twenty-one-year-old author. Repetition and sentimentality in single representative quote suggests entire collection. "Josefinita de mi corazón, esposa de mi alma, mi vida, mi aliento, mi todo" (p.54).

1511. Rivas, José (1915–). "Entrevista con José Rivas." Waco, TX: Baylor, Institute for Oral History, 23pp. Memoirs. Period Covered: 1915–1978.

One of six autobiographies of Mexican-American Baptists by Leobardo Estrada for Institute of Oral History at Baylor University. Succinctly Rivas notes early life, marriage and family, call to ministry, and education as Protestant. Life develops in Saltillo, Monterrey, Ciudad Victoria, El Paso, Houston, and Brownwood (Texas).

1512. Rivas Hernández, Eulalio (Dates?). *Grillos y gandallas: lecciones de político "a la mexicana."* México: Costa-Amic, 1984. 374pp. Memoirs. Period Covered: 1956–1984.

Divulges inside view of politics. Concentrates on political life during college career, but most of document concerns life after graduation.

1513. Rivas Mercado, Antonieta (1898–1931). *Obras completas de María Antonieta Rivas Mercado*. Compiled by Luis Mario Schneider. México: Editorial Oasis: 1987. 466pp. Diary. Period Covered: 1927–1930.

Most autobiographical of *Obras* is "87 cartas de amor." Literate and sensitive woman — patroness of arts, translator, and writer — pens letters to artist lover, Manuel Rodríguez Lozano. Totally devoted and dependent upon him. Mexican culture brought in marginally especially during sojourn in New York City, where she interacted with Mexico's intellectual expatriates. Last twenty-seven pages of *Obras* intense diary penned in Paris prior to suicide in Notre Dame. Evokes literate woman concerned about contemporary affairs, determined to follow schedule of intellectual development, and honest about sexual emotions. Compared to diary, earlier letters suggest relatively calm woman.

1514. Rivera, Diego (1886–1957). *Correspondence*. México: El Colegio de México, 1999. 330pp. Letters. Period Covered: 1910–1957.

One hundred seventy-three letters comprise unedited collection. Reflect indirect autobiography by presenting self through letters or through narration to another. Correspondence does not show radical and iconoclastic artist, image he cultivated. Most personal letters to Angelina Beloff and to Alfonso Reyes suggest care about relations. Remainder of letters, routine or perfunctory, on painting: restoration, rejection of certain exhibits, purpose of art, and Soviet art.

1515. Rivera, Diego (1886–1957). *My Art, My Life: An Autobiography with Gladys March.* New York: Citadel, 1960. 318pp. Memoirs. Period Covered: 1886–1954.

First person narration and self-hyperbole suggest authorship of Rivera. Incidents from youth, introduction to painting, years in Europe, meeting with Kahlo, and tempestuous moments in U.S. comprise document. Presents self as *enfant terrible*, e.g., four year old enters church in Guanajuato and denounces Virgin. Predicts WWI and later warns friends about Hitler. Images generated by ego rather than actual circumstances.

1516. Rivera Marín, Guadalupe; (1924–) Marie-Pierre Cole. *Las fiestas de Frida y Diego: recuerdos y recetas.* New York: Clarkson Potter, 1994. 223pp. Trans: *Frida's Fiestas: Recipes and Reminiscences of Life with Frida Kahlo.* New York: Clarkson Potter, 1994. Memoirs. Period Covered: 1942–1943?

Culinary memoir of life with father Diego Rivera and stepmother Frida Kahlo. Hostess rather than agonized painter dominates pages of dinner parties and other entertainments with prominent guests in Blue House in Coyoacán. Tucked in anecdotes within chapters structured through twelve national fiestas with recipes and food photographs, Lupe's life finds purpose only in contact with famous parents.

1517. Rivera Silva, Manuel (1913–). *Perspectiva de una vida: biografía de una generación.* México: Editorial Porrúa, 1974. 254pp. Autobiography Proper. Period Covered: 1900–1970?

Lawyer and scholar on criminal law composes unique autobiography. Influenced by Miguel Angel Cevallos, author perceives life as generic process passing through stages: infancy, primary schooling, adolescence, prep school, law school, profession, marriage, teaching, and maturity. Factual material impedes attempts to establish *ser* at various

moments of life, e.g., chapter on matrimony mentions neither fiancée nor courtship but process in search for love. Subtitle *Biography of a Generation* sets generic tone for work.

1518. Robertson, John Blout. *Reminiscences of a Campaign in Mexico.* Nashville: York, 1849. 288pp.

Some of memoirists, in addition to chauvinism, knew how to write. Such is Robertson with Tennessee infantry slogging through Mexico: Reynosa, Carmargo, Cerralvo, Monterrey, Montemorelos, Victoria, Tampico, and Vera Cruz. Climax is Monterrey, where Tennessee infantry supported Gen. Taylor. Author uses *we* more than *I*. Simultaneously historian, sociologist, and autobiographer.

1519. Robertson, Thomas A.; Dorothy Mae Utt. *Tepic Journal: Memories of Mexico: Excerpts from a Larger Manuscript Written in 1979–80.* Canoga Park, CA: Wilkin, 1984. 107pp.

Three members of Robertson family contributed to manuscript. Nayarit and Baja venues from 1923–1941. Railroad building in Tepic; enjoyment of nature in Baja.

1520. Robertson, William Parish. *A Visit to Mexico, by the West India Islands, Yucatan and United States....* London: Simpkin Marshall, 1853. 2 v.

British author in Mexico from 1848 to 1849 and only in last chapter reveals purpose of his visit: Mexico's capabilities of paying its foreign debts. Hence travel and autobiography at times subordinate to politics and a specific focus on mining with chapters on Real del Monte (Hidalgo) and Fresnillo (Zacatecas). Yet he interacts with Mexicans and describes individuals. Campeche, Vera Cruz, Puebla, and Mexico City major stopping places.

1521. Robinson, Ione. *A Wall to Paint On.* New York: Dutton, 1946. 451pp.

Robinson worked on Diego Rivera's murals in Mexico City from 1929–1932. With humor and keenness, she encompasses Mexican years and talks about the artist and his circle. Robinson, in close contact with Mexican Communist Party through courtship and marriage to Joe Freeman, in charge of Russian news agency, *Tass*.

1522. Robinson, Jacob S.; Carl Cannon. *A Journal of the Santa Fe Expedition under Colonel Doniphan.* Princeton University Press, 1932 (1848).

Document runs from June 22, 1846, to June 16, 1847. Composed by highly literate soldier, who in comments is as much of an anthropologist as soldier. Landscape, climate, but mainly Indians and their customs interest him most. Trajectory starts in Kansas and continues to Las Vegas, Santa Fe, El Paso, and Chihuahua. With victory there, troops withdraw through Camargo, Reynosa, and arrive in New Orleans. One of classic autobiographies of Mexican-American War.

1523. Robles de Flores, Norma (Dates?). *Con tan sólo seis años.* Ciudad Mante, TAM, 2000. 285pp. Memoirs. Period Covered: 1996.

From Nuevo León, author autobiographizes her trials with a six-year-old daughter diagnosed with leukemia. Struggle takes place in Monterrey as well as in Texas with parents expending all of their resources and hopes. Book ends with death of child.

1524. Robles Garnica, Héctor Guillermo (Dates?). *Guadalajara, la guerrilla olvidada: presos en la isla de la libertad.* México: Ediciones La Otra Cuba, 1996. 141pp. Memoirs. Period Covered: 1968–1975.

Tlatelolco in 1968 motivated authors to join AP (Fuerzas Armadas del Pueblo), a guerrilla force in Guadalajara. Through subsequent capture and exchange of prisoners, he ended up in Castro's Cuba. Rest of story relates to Cuban and other bureaucracies that impeded his freedom until 1974.

1525. Robles Zarate, Alfredo (1903–?). *50 años después...o la Revolución en casa.* México: Impresora y Editora Mayo, 1964. 286pp. Memoirs. Period Covered: 1910–1914.

Quotations and other undigested materials create prototypical memoir of Revolution. Action begins with apprehension of seven-year-old boy's father in Zacatecas. Pro-Revolutionary, Robles Zarate and family flee village and situation normalizes when father is safe. Turmoil of Revolution in one family.

1526. Robson, Bobby; Bob Harris. *So Near and Yet so Far: Bobby Robson's World Cup Diary 1982–86.* London: Willow, 1986. 219pp.

Englishman played and coached soccer. Diary of year's preparation and performance at 1986 World Cup Finals in Mexico. Includes Monterrey and Mexico City. Practice, frustration with playing field, description of individual players, press, and hotels comprise diary entries.

1527. Rodman, Selden. *Mexico Journal: The Conquerors Conquered.* New York: Devin-Adair, 1958. 298pp.

Rodman interweaves travel information, history, current events, and celebrities with emphasis on latter. He knows everyone in Mexico, including artists, writers, politicians, architects, anthropologists, etc. They willingly extend him interviews so book is a who's who of Mexico in mid–1950s.

1528. Rodríguez, Abelardo L. (1889–1967). *Autobiografía.* México: Distribuido por Novaro Editores, 1962. 466pp. Memoirs. Period Covered: 1889–1951.

Successful military man, politician, and businessman, Rodríguez lived in U.S. for seven years. Career inventory: brigadier general, chief of operations in various areas of Mexico, governor of Baja, undersecretary of war, secretary of industry and commerce, and president when Pascual Ortiz Rubio resigned. Chronologically arranged chapters hide personal Rodríguez. Occasional glimpse of self when challenges superior officer or delineates character of northern peon. In "Lo más íntimo de mi vida," describes three marriages, first two, disasters; third, happy. Many chapters listing of accomplishments or impressions with intervention of self. Clear style and puritanical view of life distance author from reader.

1529. Rodriguez, Jose Maria (1829–1913). *Rodriguez Memoirs of Early Texas.* San Antonio: Passing Show, 1913. 76pp. Memoirs. Period Covered: 1835–1910?

One of prominent families in San Antonio in autobiography touches upon much of Texas history: War of Independence, Battle of San Jacinto, statehood, and Viduarri Revolution. Includes personal touches such as kinship, social relationships, San Antonio landmarks, and genealogy of prominent Mexican families.

1530. Rodríguez, José Policarpio (1829–1914). *A Tejano Son of Texas: An Autobiography.* Texas Tejano.com, 2002. 88pp. Memoirs. Period Covered: 1829–1914?

Rodríguez was born in Zaragoza, Coahuila, when this state was joined with Texas. Life exemplifies frontiersman: battles with Indians, U.S. Army and development of roads, Texas Tejano Ranger, surveyor, guide and scout, rancher, County Commissioner, and Justice of Peace. In 1877, Roman Catholic Rodríguez converted to Methodism and became preacher. Vivid narration with many anecdotes. Action mainly in Coahuila and Texas with San Antonio mentioned frequently.

1531. Rodríguez, Luis I. (1905–1973). *Ballet de sangre: la caída de Francia.* México: Ediciones Nigromante, 1942. 252pp. Memoirs. Period Covered: 1940.

Educator, politician, and ambassador to France under Cárdenas, 1939–1940, pens emotional memoir of German campaign in spring of 1940. In dramatic prose, presents self as active participant.

1532. Rodríguez, Marcos (Dates?). *Yo fui empleado de gobierno....* México: Costa-Amic, 1977. 123pp. Memoirs. Period Covered: 1935.

Claims anecdotes true but names of participants changed in confessions of government employee. University professor agreed to accept employment in bureaucracy at request of former schoolmate well positioned in government. Humorous account of rivalry, *personalismo*, and inefficiency among *corbatas* exposes more of political system than any dozen political memoirs.

1533. Rodríguez, Richard (1944–). *Days of Obligation: An Argument with My Mexican Father.* New York: Viking, 1992. 230pp.

More than memoir, these chapters meditate on Mexico and U.S. along with the diverse cultures each country spawned. Through family, mainly father, Mexican-

American childhood, Mexican past of California, locals of Tijuana, Michoacán, and Mexico City, Rodriguez ponders who he is and how Mexicans and we are defined by culture.

1534. Rodríguez, Sara (1940?–). *Ricardo Rodríguez: la curva de la muerte.* México: Editorial Diana, 1995. 224pp. Memoirs. Period Covered: 1957–1962.

Married to race car driver Ricardo Rodríguez (1942–1962), Sara develops life in relation to more famous husband. Winner at age fifteen of international competition in California and also of LeMans in France suggest early triumphs. Married couple spent time at automobile racing in France and Italy. Cid of race car driving killed during practice session in Mexico in 1962. Sara's problems with husband's family enliven reading.

1535. Rodriguez Familiar, Ramón (1898–1986). *Diario de un viaje.* México, 1945? 105pp. Memoirs. Period Covered: 1945.

Career military officer and two other Mexican generals comprised mission to visit European war fronts at invitation of U.S. government. Germany, France, and Czechoslovakia scenario where author meets Patton, Eisenhower, Bradley, destruction, death camps, and military operations.

1536. Roffe, Reina (1918–1985 Dates of Juan Rulfo). *Autobiografía armada.* Argentina: Ediciones Corregidor, 1973. 100pp. Autobiographical Essay. Period Covered: 1818–1972?

Fragments of autobiography of Juan Rulfo collected from various publications. Reveals portions of childhood in Jalisco and talks about personal formula for writing. Freely speaks of creation of *Pedro Páramo* and *El llano en llamas.* Alludes to projected novel, *La cordillera.*

1537. Roffiel, Rosa María (1945–). *Amora.* México: Planeta, 1989. 162pp. Autobiographical Novel. Period Covered: 1988?

Author of *Ay Nicaragua, Nicaragüita* discloses lesbian life in humorous novel that explores one perspective or interpretation of Sapphic Mexico. *Amora* profiles degrees of lesbianism between/among various characters. Male remains intrusive outsider and secondary choice as lover. Confessing autobiographical nature of novel, writer claims that almost all persona belong to real world.

1538. Roffiel, Rosa María (1945–). *¡Ay Nicaragua, Nicaragüita!* México: Claves Latinamericanas, 1980. 122pp. Memoirs. Period Covered: 1979–1980.

Revolting against bourgeois upbringing, journalist self encounters in Nicaragua. In seventy-three chapters loosely tied, she describes moments, personalities, and places in Revolution. Total image creates disarrayed world in belated need for change. Staccato-like sentences accelerate both reading and accumulation of impressions.

1539. Rojas, Arnold. *Last of the Vaqueros.* Fresno, CA: Academy Library Guild, 1960. 165pp.

Mexican-American born in Pasadena, California, had roots in both Sonora and Sinaloa, where family originated. Through knowledge of horses and riders discloses life and links art of vaquero with Mexico. Most autobiographical chapters: "Mostly about Horses," "Mostly about Riders," and "Lore and Legends" image young Rojas learning craft interacting with other vaqueros.

1540. Rojo de Santos, Anita (Dates?). *Madre e hijo luchan contra la leucemia.* San Mario, CA: Publicaciones Media Graphics, 1992. 89pp. Memoirs. Period Covered: 1984–1985.

Sinaloa mother discovers young son with leukemia. Inventories emotional journey from detection to eventual recovery.

1541. Romano Moreno, Armando (1920–). *Anecdotario estudiantil.* Universidad Autónoma de Puebla, 1985. 2 v. Memoirs. Period Covered: 1934–1943.

Of 1939–1943 law school generation of University of Puebla, author collected and recorded stories of college years. Two volumes with history of Puebla, classes, professors, classmates, humor, and nostalgia. Chronicles generation as much as single individual. Prep school years at times included.

1542. Romero, José (Pepe) (1911–?). *Mexican Jumping Bean.* New York: Putnam, 1953. 282pp. Memoirs. Period Covered: 1911–1952.

Lived in U.S. as child and acquired native English. Returning to Mexico City, became journalist with column "Un momento" in *The Mexican Herald*. In fun memoirs interacts with Mexican and foreign celebrities as he crisscrosses capital in search of scandal and other types of news. Title summarizes author's personality and mobility in multiple topics of culture.

1543. Romero, José Rubén (1890–1952). *Apuntes de un lugareño.* Barcelona: Imprenta Núñez y C., 1932. 360pp. Trans: *Notes of a Villager: A Mexican Poet's Youth and Revolution.* Kaneohe, HI: Plover, 1988. Memoirs. Period Covered: 1900–1913.

Early life and mainly Revolution. Self-referencing narrator conforms more to pícaro than standard observer/participant of memoir. Adventures, attitudes, humor, and static development as human being based on picaresque. Evocation of rural Michoacán and inhabitants more valuable than Romero's sympathies as Maderista. Humor, style, and occasional breathless metaphor make delightful reading.

1544. Romero, José Rubén (1890–1952). *Desbandada.* México: Editorial Porrúa, 1960 (1934). 150pp. Memoirs. Period Covered: 1913–1915.

Like *Apuntes de un lugareño*, *Desbandada* concerns bucolic life of pre–Revolutionary Tacámbaro in Michoacán. Yet final chapters destroy early tranquility in violent scenes. Chronological order and factuality suggest memoirs. Simple style betrays classical substratum.

1545. Romero, José Rubén (1890–1952). *Rostros.* México: Imprenta Aldina, Robredo y Rosell, 1942. 177pp. Memoirs. Period Covered: 1908–1942.

Reminisces on life as writer and focuses on major works. Notes autobiographical in trajectory of publications. Titillates with choice of erudite and almost obscure words that fit precisely in rustic context.

1546. Romero de Flor; Figueroa, Gabriel (1907–1997). *Gabriel Figueroa: hacedor de imágenes: conversaciones.* Santafé de Bogotá: Empresa Editorial P.E.N., 1996. 199pp. Interview. Period Covered: 1907–1997?

Mexico's foremost cameraman chats about favorite themes: childhood, Hollywood, best film directors, Luis Buñuel, Bruno Traven, María Félix, Dolores del Río, and unprecedented accomplishment of Mexican films of 1940s.

1547. Romero de Terreros, Juan (1818–?). *Apuntaciones de viaje en 1849.* México: Real Academia de la Historia, 1919. 36pp. Memoirs. Period Covered: 1849.

Romero de Terreros or el Duque de Regla travels from Mexico to Madrid: Mexico City to Vera Cruz, Havana, New York, London, and Madrid. Details, such as quarantine in Spain, interest more than memoir.

1548. Romero Flores, Jesús (1885–1987). *Maestro y amigos (Recuerdos y semblanzas de algunos escritores).* México: Costa-Amic, 1971. 461pp. Memoirs. Period Covered: ?–1904.

Gives fragments of life as he moves with literati. Focusing on single individual, each chapter becomes forum for ideas and moment in intellectual development. In creating collective biography, he records own autobiography.

1549. Romo de Alba, Manuel (1890?–?). *El gobernador de las estrellas: autorretrato, Guadalajara, México, febrero de 1962.* México: Gráfica Panamericana, 1986. 350pp. Memoirs. Period Covered: 1896–1930?

Jaliscense mentions birth, ambition to attend agricultural school, Revolution, and efforts at journalism. The second part, after Constitution of 1917, places him on right and on side of *Cristeros* against Calles's government. Anti-Semitic Romo de Alba uniquely theorizes Calles's anticlericalism.

1550. Ronstadt, Frederico, José María (1868–1954). *Borderman: Memoirs of Frederico José María Ronstadt.* Albuquerque: University of New Mexico Press, 1993. 154pp. Memoirs. Period Covered: 1864–1889?

Born in 1868 in Las Delicias, Sonora, to Frederick August Ronstadt, German immigrant, and Margarita Redondo, daughter of *hacendado.* Focusing on childhood first in Sonora and Baja and after 1882 in Tucson and El Paso, writing memorializes successful Mexican-American who grew up on both sides of border. Education, frontier violence, business, family, friends, and music comprise document. Incorporates regional history of Mexico and U.S.

1551. Rosado, José María (1847–?). "A Refugee of the War of Castes Makes Belize His Home;" In *The Memoirs of J.M. Rosado.* Belize City: Belize Institute for Social Research and Action, 1970. 19pp. Memoirs. Period Covered: 1854–1894.

Santa Cruz Maya during War of Castes capture eight-year-old Rosado. Life among captors, Talking Cross miracle that united Mayas, and later years in Belize comprise memoirs written in 1915.

1552. Rosado, Nidia Esther (1918–). *Huellas en el umbral: autobiografía.* Mérida: El Autor, 1996. 132pp. Memoirs. Period Covered: 1918–1937.

Third-person narration tells of physical and intellectual growth of Yucatan girl, who finishes normal school and becomes schoolteacher. Context of girlhood in Yucatan includes family and also political movements. Better written than most self-inspired endeavors of this nature.

1553. Rosado, Nidia Esther (1918–?). *Registrando cajones: mis memorias en recortes.* Mérida: El Autor, 1998. 274pp. Hybrid. Period Covered: 1981–1982.

Hybrid describes assortment of letters written and received by author and articles published in periodicals. Collectively gives fragmented autobiography. She exercised dual role of creator and critic of literature in Mérida. *Registrando* suggests fomenting of literature at regional level. Journalism betrays gentle critic who would rather encourage than annihilate provincial talent.

1554. Rosales Alcaraz, José (1928–). *La huella de mis pasos.* Archivo Histórico del Municipio de Colima, 2000. 56pp. Memoirs. Period Covered: 1900–1987.

Honest and uncomplicated life retold with short chapters and direct syntax. He introduces us to four grandparents, parents, and then himself in setting in which he spent most of life, Coquitmatlán-Colima area of Nayarit. Appraisals, generally more favorable to women then men, note presence of womanizers in family. Preparation for teaching, rural schools, and retirement after thirty-seven years occupy much of memoirs. Only earthquakes and *Cristero* rebellion interrupt tranquil and successful existence.

1555. Rosas Landa, José (Dates?). *Apuntes y recuerdos. (Memorias de las revoluciones del plan de la Noria y de Tuxtepec).* Guadalajara, 1902. 87pp. Memoirs. Period Covered: 1872.

Student and colleague join forces of Porfirio Díaz in Plan de la Noria against President Sebastián Lerdo de Tejada. Humorous account of military ineptness of young recruits. Descriptive text alternates with remembered dialog.

1556. Rosas Solaegui, Guillermo (1897–?). *Un hombre en el tiempo.* México: Costa-Amic, 1971. 347pp. Memoirs. Period Covered: 1897–1971.

Native Oaxacan with strong loyalties to state, author remembers Revolution in which he participated momentarily. As career military, he was sent to various states disturbed by labor disputes. As violinist, he promoted music in Oaxaca. Narrates little of personal life and concentrates on external.

1557. Roy, Manabendra Nath. *M.N. Roy's Memoirs.* New York: Allied, 1964. 627pp.

In 1917, Indian radical left New York City for Mexico. He joined Mexican Socialist Party and in 1918 attended its first conference. Roy converted Socialist Party to Communist Party and headed delegation to Communist International in Moscow. In 1919, he left Mexico, where he claimed to have found a new outlook on life: "…there was a revolution in my mind…" (p.217). One-fourth of autobiography devoted to Mexico.

1558. Royer, F. *The Mexico We Found.* Milwaukee: Bruce, 1948. 210pp.

Memoir that incorporates drama in remote part of Mexico. In Chiapas, author occupied in making documentary on life of Bartolomé de las Casas. Fascination of problems of endeavor in Mexico marred by author's obtrusive Catholicism.

1559. Royer, Mae R. *In the Heart of Mexico.* Lititz, PA: Klopp Printing, 1984. 175pp.

In northern Mexico, another missionary at work. Mae Royer, missionary nurse for Evangelical Congregational Church, stationed in village near Tamazunchale, San Luis Potosí, for first assignment. Experiences include medicine, healing, and proselytizing. Anecdotes of illnesses, anti–Protestantism, and friendship among natives.

1560. Rubio, Abel G.; Thomas H. Kreneck. *Stolen Heritage: A Mexican-American's Rediscovery of His Family's Lost Land Grant.* Austin, TX.: Eakin, 1986. 224pp.

Autobiography and biography of author's ancestors, de la Garza and Becerra of Refugio, Texas. Adventures validate family's claims to lands illegally dispossessed in nineteenth century. Starts in 1821 and ends temporarily in 1978 with judgment in favor of O'Connor Ranch.

1561. Ruiz, Bernardo (1953–). *De cuerpo entero: Bernardo Ruiz.* México: Ediciones Corunda, 1990. 58pp. Memoirs. Period Covered: 1953–1989.

As creator of both fiction and poetry, he focuses on intellectual formation: reading, formal education, dedication to literature in college, literary friends, contributor/editor to journals, and writing. Love for words here marginalizes parents, siblings, travel, marriage, and children.

1562. Ruiz, Eduardo (1879–1942). *Un convoy militar: de Veracruz a Encarnación. Toma de Aguascalientes.* Guadalajara, 1915. 109pp. Memoirs. Period Covered: 1915.

Guaymas-born colonel fought on side of Obregon against Victoriano Huerta. Title sums up ride from Veracruz, Veracruz to Encarnación, Jalisco. Autobiography, conversation, politics, the military and, most certainly, the train structure exciting narrative. One of better memoirs of Revolution.

1563. Ruiz, Ramón Eduardo. *Memories of a Hyphenated Man.* Tucson: University of Arizona Press, 2003. 242pp.

Academic was son of Mexican immigrants and grew up near border in southern California. Title suggests his loyalty to both countries. He inventories slights because of his Mexican background and speaks to development of Chicano Studies. Notes ties with Mexico: family, study, sabbatical, book on Mexican-American War, and sufficient time there to note prejudice against Mexican-Americans. Insider's view of academia.

1564. Ruiz Camarena, Merced (1881–?). *Tuyo o de nadie: cartas a Mercedes Martínez Carrillo.* México: Instituto Nacional de Antropología e Historia, 1997. 103pp. Letters. Period Covered: 1907–1912.

"La vida íntima, particular, anónima…" (p.13) are words that describe humble traveling salesman in Guanajuato. Merced met Mercedes Martínez Carrillo in 1907, date of first letter of correspondence that lasted until 1912 and touched various themes: courtship, position of her parents, fiestas, fairs, advice, circus, and prayer to Saint Michael.

1565. Ruiz Massieu, Mario (1950–1999). *Confesiones a manera de testamento.* México: Océano, 2000. 128pp. Memoirs. Period Covered: 1999.

Confessions of brother of assassinated José Francisco Ruiz Massieu, who was married to sister of former President Carlos Salinas de Gotari. Author, long-time member of PRI and accused of drug trafficking, denounced PRI and went into exile in U.S. The introductory note, that the work is the political testament of someone who knows the Mexican government, unmasks it, and gives some unusual opinions difficult to refute.

1566. Ruiz Webber, Patricia (1954–). *Fragmentos para un reloj de arena.* México: EDAMEX, 1999. 100pp. Memoirs. Period Covered: 1954–1998.

Hourglass with sand particles on move serves as metaphor for life: separate incidents, monumental or insignificant, related without concern for chronology. Multi-talented as dancer, singer, actress, and painter, she tries to recover life after car accident that provoked both amnesia and epilepsy. Self-illustrated with her paintings.

1567. Ruiz y Flores, Leopoldo (1865–1941). *Recuerdos de recuerdos.* México: Buena Prensa, 1942. 181pp. Memoirs. Period Covered: 1865–1936.

Religious held positions in Catholic Church in Mexico: secretary of V Concilio Mexicano and bishop of León (1900), Monterrey (1911), and Michoacán. Cursory account of life potentially fascinating. Needs more on hierarchy's attitude towards Madero, fight against Calles, and some of interior life of prelate exiled three times.

1568. Rulfo, Juan (1917–1986). *Aire de las colinas: cartas a Clara.* México: Plaza y Janés, 2000. 341pp. Letters. Period Covered: 1944–1950.

Author of two books now has another albeit posthumous. Has eighty-one letters to Clara Aparicio, who became author's wife. Engagement, marriage, birth of two children and something of daily life present here. However, love is dominant theme. Prose not equal to *El llano en llamas* (1953) or *Pedro Páramo* (1955).

1569. Russek, Jorge (1932–1998). *Una vida de película: autobiografía.* México: EDAMEX, 1997. 184pp. Memoirs. Period Covered: 1932–1996.

Sixteen year old attended Harvard Military Academy in California. Thus set pattern: life and work on both sides of border. Born in Guaymas, Sonora, acted in both Mexican and American films. American film successes more notable than Mexican: *Hour of the Gun* (1967), *Guns for San Sebastian* (1968), *The Wild Bunch* (1965), and *Pat Garrett and Billy the Kid* (1973).

1570. Russell, Phillips; Leon Underwood. *Red Tiger: Adventures in Yucatan and Mexico.* New York: Brentano's, 1929. 335pp.

Red Tiger is thoughtful journey through Yucatan. Exudes period's delight in *lo mexicano.* When recrosses border to U.S., he laments: "Everywhere is evidence of the desire of men to separate themselves from contact with the earth" (p.335). Russell enjoys environment of ruins, fishing, hunting, and interacting with Mexicans.

1571. Ruxton, George Frederick Augustus; Horace Kephart. *Adventures in Mexico.* New York: Outing, 1915. 292pp.

Ruxton sets British standard for criticizing Mexicans. Trip's foray into exotic landscape. Never meets dull Mexican on trek from Vera Cruz to Mexico City, Durango, and Chihuahua. Information, such as hungry donkeys eat one another's tails, scattered in text.

1572. Ruy Sánchez, Alberto (1951–). *De cuerpo entero.* México: Ediciones Corunda, 1992. 64pp. Memoirs. Period Covered: 1951–1991.

Writer begins autobiography in Sahara, desert reminiscent of Baja. Physical and psychological travel dominates in which mood and place in Africa take preference to more traditional autobiographical data.

1573. Ryan, William Redmond. *Personal Adventures in Upper and Lower California, in 1848–9.* New York: Arno, 1973 (1850). 347pp.

Dates place narration immediately following independence of California. Yet Ryan is really describing Mexican California: landscape, Indians, fandango, women, clothes, hatred of Americans, honor, and justice. He was in both upper and lower California. Apparently author was volunteer in Mexican-American War and notes advantages of this condition.

1574. Sabella, Salvatore. *El otro mundo de Salvatore Sabella.* Monterrey, 1990. 157pp.

Twenty-three year old emigrates from Naples in 1954. Marries in Monterrey, has family, and survives by selling watches and jewels. Success story of immigrant.

1575. Sacks, Oliver W. *Oaxaca Journal.* Washington, DC: National Geographic, 2002. 159pp.

Not everyone goes to Oaxaca for mushrooms. Pteridology never with jauntier exposé. Author makes science exciting as he takes reader on botanical fern expedition to Oaxaca. Travels with compatible and noncompetitive group to Mexico's Zapotec capital and notes environment overlooked in other travel books. Known for its churches, Oaxaca here suffers comeuppance. Fern enthusiasts tolerate tour through colonial gem only to exit and study vegetation. Sacks tells much of pteridology, something of Oaxaca, and more of self in ten-day trip.

1576. Sainz, Gustavo (1940–). *Gustavo Sainz.* México: Empresas Editoriales, 1966. 62pp. Autobiographical Essay. Period Covered: 1945?–1965?

Popular culture, varied reading, and book collecting in self-inventory at age of twenty-six. Rebelliousness and iconoclasm paralleled in first work, *Gazapo.* Focus on childhood with less than idyllic home life. Few topics taboo for Sainz.

1577. Salado Alvarez, Victoriano (1867–1931). *Correspondencia de don Victoriano Salado Alvarez, 1894–1931.* Estudio y compilación de Juan López. Guadalajara, 1992. 1168pp. Letters. Period Covered: 1889–1931.

VSA was senator, secretary general of state of Chihuahua under Enrique Creel, secretary in Mexican embassy in Washington, and minister to Guatemala and Brazil. One hundred fifteen letters to variety of individuals including Luis González Obregón, Alfonso Junco, and Ignacio Lozano; plus letters from Enrique Creel (one hundred twenty-nine), Celedonio Junco de la Vega, and J. Ballescá. Many correspondents appear only once; some are governmental institutions. No prolonged exchange with any one individual equals little revelation of personality.

1578. Salado Alvarez, Victoriano (1867–1931). *Memorias de Victoriano Salado Alvarez....* México: E.D.I.P.S.A., 1946. 2 v. Memoirs. Period Covered: 1867–1910.

Lawyer, journalist, educator, politician, and diplomat one of best memoirists. Positions that he occupied—first secretary of Washington embassy, secretary of foreign affairs, and member of Academy of Language and Literature—put him in contact with influential of Porfiriato. As portraitist he creates cameos of leading personalities of epoch. Essential for understanding intellectual formation of upper class during dictatorship of Díaz.

1579. Salazar, Diana Martha (1938–). *Aquel Saltillo de ayer....* DIF. Saltillo, 1992. 206pp. Memoirs. Period Covered: 1950s.

Through fictitious creation named Susanita, Salazar remembers Saltillo, her home at twelve years of age. Four- hundred-fifteenth anniversary of northern city amiably recorded in tribute. Grandfather's house, newspapers, church and feast days, food, dances, and other details comprise life of Saltillo plus its recorder.

1580. Saldaña, José P. (1891–?). *El cronista centenario: 1891- 1991: don José Pedro Saldaña Treviño.* Monterrey: Producciones Al Voleo-El Troquel, 1991. 192pp. Memoirs. Period Covered: 1891–1991.

Chronicler of Monterrey wrote sixteen books on history. Recovers a hundred years concentrating on various themes: early life, family, bookkeeper, politician, Revolution, and editor of *El Sol de Monterrey*.

1581. Salinas de Gotari, Carlos (1948–). *México: un paso difícil a la modernidad.* México: Plaza y Janés, 2000. 1,393pp. Memoirs. Period Covered: 1989–2000.

Defense of regime with few touches on personal life. Sets record in length for political autobiography and shows benefits of technology in long bibliography and in twelve-page name index. First person singular mixes with overriding topics of 1988–1994 presidency: NAFTA, social challenge, Chiapas, *magnicidio* (Donaldo Colosio), presidential elections of 1994, Zedillo and tradition of persecution of exiting President Raul Salinas, and challenges for twenty-first century.

1582. Salinas Price, Hugo (1932–). *Mis años con Elektra.* México: Editorial Diana, 2000. 184pp. Memoirs. Period Covered: 1952–1997.

Descendant of Baptist family and one of heirs of Salinas Rocha fortune talks about main impulse in life: business. He quit school to start career. When father, Hugo Salinas Rocha, euchred out of Salinas Rocha stores, author started successful Elektra. Details growth of appliance store.

1583. Salinas Rocha, Irma (1921–). *Mi padre.* Monterrey: Oficio Ediciones, 1992.

414pp. Memoirs. Period Covered: 1863–1949.

Focusing on father, Benjamin Salinas Westrup, *Tal cual* author tells her story more sedately in noting history of family. Descendants of Tomás Westrup, one of introducers of Protestantism into Mexico, family of Salinas Rocha became one of leading capitalists of Monterrey. Baptist, Mason, and Rosicrucian father founded Salinas Y Rocha department store. Much history of Monterrey.

1584. Salinas Rocha, Irma (1921?–). *Tal cual: vida, amores, cadenas.* México: Tinta Libre, 1977. 370pp. Memoirs/Letters. Period Covered: 1932?–1970?

One can pick up Mexican autobiography with comfortable assumption that writers will reveal nothing of personal lives. Wonderful jolt to pattern here. Daughter of wealth in Monterrey, Protestant, and U.S. educated, Salinas Rocha is maverick. In memoirs and letters confesses love for three men: husband, Baptist minister, and lawyer. Articulate, frank, and outrageous, Irma combines Celestina and Molly Bloom.

1585. Salm-Salm, Agnes Elisabeth. *Ten Years of My Life.* New York: Worthington, 1877. 385pp.

Outsider close to throne tells story. Felix and Agnes Salm-Salm achieved fame in Mexico, where they gravitated to Maximilian's retinue. Salm-Salm tried to save condemned Emperor from avenging Juárez. Agnes's pleas in person futile; efforts to spirit fallen monarch out of Querétaro also aborted.

1586. Salvatierra, Juan María de. *Selected Letters about Lower California.* Los Angeles: Dawson's Book Shop, 1971. 279pp.

Italian-born Jesuit Salvatierra helped establish Loreto, earliest mission town in Baja. Four letters, composed in last two months of 1697, appear in this title. Reveal both author and circumstances: geography, religiosity of period, Indians, and joys at proselytizing.

1587. Samaniego, Leopoldo de (Dates?). *Buenos, malos y regulares: estampas sanmiguelenses.* México: Norte Revista Hispano-

Americano, ca.1969. 86pp. Memoirs. Period Covered: 1926?–1930.

　　Recounts anecdotes of grandparents that have origin in Porfiriato or before. Nostalgic recall of happy humorous childhood in picturesque family. Playful title sets tone.

1588. Sanborn Helen J. *A Winter in Central America and Mexico.* Boston: Lee and Shepard, 1886. 321pp.

　　One fourth of book relates to Mexico. Sanborn typical nineteenth century traveler in curiosity about new lands and in eagerness to record impressions. Short journey from Vera Cruz to Mexico City and then environs of capital. Clarity, sense of humor, description more than autobiography, and tendency for rapid judgment characterize writing. Occasionally Mexicans fare badly from Yankee perspective.

1589. Sánchez, Mary (1918–?). *Vivir por un ideal: mis memorias.* México: EPESSA, 1996. 308pp. Memoirs. Period Covered: 1929–1991?

　　Book surprises. Format and tradition suggest marriage, children, family, and happy life. Sánchez's life is different; related to family of Saturnino Cedillo of San Luis Potosí, she has insider's view of cacique's death in 1938. Husband, Zeferino Sánchez Hidalgo, was *Sinarquista,* journalist, and perpetual candidate of PAN (Partido Acción Nacional) in Tijuana. Author was *Sinarquista* and active in PAN politics.

1590. Sánchez Andraka, Juan (1950?–). *Zitlala, por el mágico mundo indígena guerrerense.* México: Fondo de Apoyo Editorial del Gobierno del Estado del Guerrero, 1983. 144pp. Memoirs. Period Covered: 1980?

　　Confesses interest in world of Indians. Makes known experiences with Indians of Zitlala near city of Chilapa in Sierra Madres. Interacts with natives, responds to them, and produces more than travel literature.

1591. Sánchez García, Jesús (1932–). *¡Mi chingada gana! y otros textos para combatir el insomnio.* México: Olivares Impresos, 2002? 167pp. Memoirs. Period Covered: 1932?–2003.

　　From Jerez, Zacatecas, Sánchez García lived in Mexico City in 40s and 50s and later returned to his native state. Worked in government for many years: customs, military, director of state police of Zacatecas, and finally municipal president of Jerez. Anecdotal author reveals much of each job. Also enthusiastic horseman.

1592. Sánchez Hernández, Nestor (1920–). *Memorias de un combatiente.* Oaxaca: Carteles del Sur, 1976. 386pp. Memoirs. Period Covered: 1920–1965?

　　Mexico's support of Spanish Republic generated few memoirs of participants in 1936–1939 Civil War. Journalist joined Mexican army in 1934; in 1938 left for Spain stopping first in Cuba, U.S., and France. Fought in Battle of Ebro and remained in northern Spain until return in 1939. Arranges chapters in non-chronological order.

1593. Sánchez-Navarro, Carlos (1816–1876). *La guerra de Tejas: memorias de un soldado.* México: Editorial Jus, 1960. 103pp. Memoirs. Period Covered: 1835.

　　Author apparently included journal of José Juan Sánchez-Navarro in disastrous campaign in Texas. Member of *hacendado* family of Coahuila, he was inspector of garrisons when problem of Texas arose. Many personal touches, dialog, and author's interpretation of dream of Vicente Filisola lighten memoir.

1594. Sánchez S., Teodoro (1925–). *Alma del teatro Guiñol Petul.* Tuxtla Gutiérrez, CHP: Instituto Chiapaneco de Cultura, 1993. 102pp. Memoirs. Period Covered: 1939–1981.

　　From *ejido* in Ixtapa, Chiapas, and working for telephone company as well as serving in army, author focuses on twenty-five years in Centro Coordinador Indigenista Tzeltal-Tzotzil, part of Instituto Nacional Indigenista in San Cristóbal de Las Casas. Interested in puppet theater as vehicle for educating Indians and discovered talent in communicating directly with them. Rosario Castellano briefly involved in project.

1595. Sánchez Salazar, Leandro A. (Dates?). *Así asasinaron a Trotski.* México: Populibros La Prensa, 1955 (1950). 256pp.

Trans: *Murder in Mexico: The Assassination of Leon Trotsky*. Translated by Phyllis Hawley. London: Secker and Warburg, 1950. Memoirs. Period Covered: 1940.

Head of police secret service had opportunity to investigate assassination of Trotsky in August of 1940. Memoir structured like detective novel. Sánchez Salazar tells of death of Trotsky as well as capture and conviction of assassin.

1596. Sánchez Vázquez, Adolfo. *Recuerdos y reflexiones del exilio*. Barcelona: Cop d'Idees: 1997. 190pp.

Exiled to Mexico from Spain in 1939. Indicates gratefulness to President Cárdenas for treatment of Spanish exiles including himself. The writer gives intellectual life and involvement in Mexico: received Ph.D. in philosophy and taught at Universidad Michoacana; researched for Instituto de Investigaciones Estéticas; and became Marxist publishing *Las ideas estéticas de Marx* in 1965.

1597. Sanderson, Ivan Terence. *Living Treasure*. New York: Viking, 1941. 290pp.

One third devoted to Yucatan. A quote evokes author's mood and sense of humor, "…we take our work very seriously, but…we do not take ourselves at all seriously" (p.14). As naturalists, Sanderson and spouse look at life in tropical forest and jungle and find buzzards, flies, rabbits, skunks, frogs, etc. They interact with natives and find clean villages as well as dirty villages. They respect Mayas' ability to classify and know numerous animals and their environment. Lay person's approach to natural history.

1598. Sandford, Jeremy. *In Search of the Magic Mushroom: A Journey through Mexico*. New York: Potter, 1973? 176pp.

Sandford achieves hallucinatory view in quest. Not standard tourist itinerary through country but more of demimonde: i.e., houses of ill repute, obscene nightclub acts, rockets, and hippy-like Gringos, either receiving or paying alimony. Yet the mushroom, its history and potential to alter reality, parallels land journey of irascible English writer.

1599. Sandoval Avila, Alejandro (1957–). *De cuerpo entero*. México: Ediciones

Corunda, 1992. 56pp. Memoirs. Period Covered: 1963?–1992.

Poet and novelist, Sandoval concentrates on childhood/ adolescent years in Aguascalientes. From accumulation of images comes fragments of childhood: Las Nubes, secret place for drinking and perversions, illness and recuperation to become tennis star, fair of Aguascalientes, and two grandmothers.

1600. Santa Anna, Antonio López de (1794–1876). *Historia militar y política (1810–1874): Guerra con Tejas y los Estados Unidos*. México: Editorial Porrúa, 1974 (1905?). 276pp. Memoirs. Period Covered: 1810–1874.

Describes and defends political and military exploits: presidency, exile, Texas, French Intervention, etc. *Guerra con Tejas* comprised mainly of letters. Little of personal life revealed.

1601. Santamaría, Francisco Javier (1889–1963). *Memorias, acotaciones y pasatiempos*. México: Consejo Editorial del Gobierno del Estado de Tabasco, 1981. 5 v. Memoirs. Period Covered: 1895?–1962.

Historian, lexicographer, bibliographer, member of Academia de la Lengua, and governor of home state of Tabasco in hybrid form presents fragments of life. Poetry, anecdotes, and diary entries combine to personalize active scholar. Stories relating to childhood in Macuspana, Tabasco, prove most engrossing.

1602. Santamaría, Francisco Javier (1886–1963). *La trajedia de Cuernavaca en 1927 y mi escapatoria célebre*. México, 1939. 175pp. Memoirs. Period Covered: 1927.

Lawyer, professor, and member of Academy of Language barely escaped firing squad in Huitzilac, Morelos, when accused of partisanship for Gen. Francisco R. Serrano, alleged rebel against Obregón in 1927.

1603. Santleben, August. *A Texas Pioneer: Early Staging and Overland Freighting Days on the Frontiers of Texas and Mexico*. New York: Neale, 1910. 321pp.

German immigrant living in Castroville, Texas, August Santleben and partner established stage line between U.S. and Mexico in 1867. Carried goods and money between San Antonio and Chihuahua City until 1876. Filled with geography and anecdotes about robbers and Indians.

1604. Santos, Gonzalo N. (1895–1978). *Memorias.* México: Editorial Grijalbo, 1984. 975pp. Memoirs. Period Covered: 1897–1968.

Self-made political success, Santos with no recognizable formal education was senator from home state San Luis Potosí. Served as governor of SLP, executive committee of PNR (National Revolutionary Party), and minister to Belgium. Ex-revolutionary on side of Carranza, Santos near presidents from Obregón to Ruiz Cortinas. One of longest memoirs in Mexican autobiography.

1605. Santos, John Phillip. *Places Left Unfinished at the Time of Creation.* New York: Viking, 1999. 284pp.

Title focuses loosely on author, San Antonio-born Mexican-American obsessed with solving puzzle of grandfather's suicide in 1939. Horizontal experiences incorporate Texas, New York, Mexico, and England. Vertical time takes family back to pre-colonial Mexico and up to contemporary period. Garcías and Santos meet in author and two families, tinged in magic realism, generate characters as bizarre and beloved as those of García Márquez. Classic Mexican-American autobiography unites both countries.

1606. Santos Ramos, Hermelindo (1901–?). *Así construimos una nueva sociedad.* México: Instituto Nacional de Antropología e Historia, 1998. 325pp. Autobiographical Novel. Period Covered: 1901–1938.

Suggests history through lives of nonfamous. He entered Revolution in 1910 as mascot and remained until 1919 as Constitutionalist in Celaya, León, Aguascalientes, Saltillo, Gómez Palacio, Torreón, Tehuantepec, and Acapulco. Rest of memoirs categorizable under civilian life, women, illness, and religion. Had candy stand; worked in soap factory and on railroad. Two common-law wives, one church-sanctioned wife, and several children comprised married life. Healed by curandero, illnesses lead to Protestant fanaticism.

1607. Santos Rowe, Manuel (1914–?). *Recuerdo a San Luis.* Gobierno del Estado de San Luis Potosí, 1991. 118pp. Memoirs. Period Covered: 1914?–1990.

Recovers memories that give more history of San Luis Potosí than of his life. Nostalgia centers him until 1938 in idealized provincial city filtered through his presence: families, women, churches, city centers, sounds, gardens, and notable persons.

1608. Santos Santos, Pedro Antonio (1854–1922). *Memorias.* San Luis Potosí, SLP: Consejo Estatal para la Cultura y las Artes, 1990. 159pp. Memoirs. Period Covered: 1888–1913.

From anti–Porfirian family and member of San Luis Potosí's *hacendado* class, he inherited father's political beliefs. As favorite son, he dominates memoirs of Santos Santos killed in combating Victoriano Huerta in 1913. Life of anti-dictator Mexican and Revolution.

1609. Sarmiento, J. Esteban (Dates?). *Un sacerdote en la URSS y otros viajes.* Hermosillo, SON: Idea Activa, 1986. 273pp. Memoirs. Period Covered: 1962–1963.

Sarmiento acted as Archbishop D. Juan Navarrete's secretary and theological consultant on trip to Europe, Colombia, and USSR. Published in *El Imparcial*, collected articles underline loyalty to Catholicism.

1610. Sato Parra, José Ramón (1923–). *Relatos e ilustraciones de viajes a través del mundo.* México: Lar Corporative Gráfico, 1999. 365pp. Memoirs. Period Covered: 1961?–1999?

From the state of Sinaloa, Sato Parra was active in medical profession for fifty years. His many professional organizations gave him and his family the opportunity for international travel: U.S., Canada, South America, Europe, Middle East, Far East, and India. Japanese-Mexican Sato Parra speaks only of itineraries.

1611. Savala, Refugio (1904–1980?). *The Autobiography of a Yaqui Poet;* edited with background and interpretation by Kathleen Sands. Tucson: University of Arizona Press, 1980. 228pp. Memoirs. Period Covered: 1904–1967.

Personalizes Yaqui experiences. Editor Sands insists: "The narrative which follows is essentially what Refugio wrote for Mrs. Painter [woman who inspired Savala]. Some deletions and changes have been made to make it read smoothly, and structure of separate parts has been reformed into logical chapters" (p.viii). Victims of Porfiriato's policy towards Yaqui, family emigrated from Sonora to Arizona. Family life, work on railways, agriculture, religion, military life, Yaqui culture, and writing comprise memoirs.

1612. Schaller, Susan. *A Man without Words.* New York: Summit Books, 1991. 203pp.

Author works with deaf Mexican national. Analyzes experiences with Ildefonso, an illegal alien in California. By use of American Sign Language she reached prelingual adult. Much speculation on topic of language as requirement for thought.

1613. Schell, Rolfe F.; Lois Schell. *Yank in Yucatán: Guide to Eastern Mexico.* Fort Myers Beach, FL: Island, 1973. 309pp.

Campeche, Yucatan, Quintana Roo, Cozumel, and Isla de las Mujeres sites of author's travels. Describes terrain, interacts with natives, enjoys local culture, visits Maya ruins, scuba dives, explores legends such as one of little people, and engages in big game hunting. Through anecdote and description Schell's personality emerges.

1614. Scherer García, Julio (1896–1974 Dates of Siqueiros). *La piel y la entraña (Siqueiros).* México: Era, 1965 (1996). 137pp. Oral Autobiography. Period Covered: 1900?–1964?

Visiting jailed Siqueiros (1959–1964) in Lecumberri, journalist Scherer García confesses, "The book is made up of memories, emotions, tragedies, fantasy all mixed together" (p.12). In no chronological order, fifty anecdotes create militant and opinionated muralist. Mexico, France, and U.S. locales for stories of painting, friendships, enemies, and family. Much pungent humor. Scherer García gives no methodology.

1615. Schmidtlein, Adolfo. *Un médico alemán en el México de Maximiliano: cartas de Adolfo Schmidtlein a sus padres, 1865–1874.* México: C. Amor S., 1978. 384pp.

Author received medical degree in 1864 and answered Maximilian's call for doctors in Mexico. Letters run from 1865 to 1874. He remained after debacle of Puebla, city where he exercised his profession as well as in Mexico City. With love for Mexico, he married Gertrudis García Teruel. Letters show affection for family, relationship with prosperous German colony, comments on inadequacy of French rule, social life through Teruel family, *costumbrismo*, and spouse and children. One of best autobiographies of Germans in Mexico.

1616. Schueler, Donald G. *The Temple of the Jaguar: Travels in Yucatan.* San Francisco: Sierra Club Books, 1993. 253pp.

Sierra Club imprimatur identifies title as search and assessment of Yucatan's environment, i.e., conservation of both land and species. And title is metaphor: "...the not quite acknowledged search for an animal that was to me mysterious and magical as a unicorn, the incarnation of everything in the world that was still beautiful and wild" (p.253). He seeks primitive Yucatan through major cities, and, in subjectivity, describes self.

1617. Schwatka, Frederick. *In the Land of Cave and Cliff Dwellers.* Glorieta, NM: Rio Grande Press, 1977 (1893). 391pp.

Travel in nineteenth century style far more important than portrayal of author's personality. Sonora and Chihuahua with Mayo, Tarahumara, and Yaqui demand his attention. Hermosillo, Guaymas and Mormon colonies noted along with Chihuahuense villages and towns all with *chic* suffix such as Carichic and Cuishuiriachic. Introduction captures value of expedition: "But his account of an eventful, dangerous and fascinating hike in Mexican wilderness is bright and breezy and interesting to read" (p.11).

1618. Scott, Ruby. *Jungle Harvest: God's Word Triumphs in Tila Hearts.* Wheaton, IL: Conservative Baptist Home Mission Society, 1988. 127pp.

Author and companion, Wycliffe Bible

Translators, settled with two goals in a Tila Chol Indian village in Chiapas: translate the New Testament into the local language and, naturally, convert the natives to Protestantism. Interesting account of painful accumulation of words, and anecdotes about increasingly accepting Indians aided by missionaries who also answer secular needs.

1619. Scott, Winfield. *Memoirs of Lieut.-General Scott, LL.D.* New York: Sheldon, 1864. 2 v.

Americans had other concerns in war. Commander of U.S. Army in Mexican War (1847), Scott captured Vera Cruz, was victorious at Cerro Gordo and Chapultepec, and occupied Mexico City. Here he gives landscape but notes enemies beyond Mexican foes: Gen. Zachary Taylor and President Polk.

1620. Scribner, B. F. *Camp Life of a Volunteer: A Campaign in Mexico, or A Glimpse at Life in Camp.* Austin, TX: Jenkins, 1975 (1847). 75pp.

Gives foot soldier's view. His area is Texas and northern Mexico: Matamoros, Saltillo, Palo Alto, Camargo, and Buena Vista. A willing soldier, Scribner describes funerals, trying to learn Spanish, weather, transportation, diversions, regimental rivalries, customs of Mexicans, etc

1621. Sedelmayr, Jacobo; Daniel S. Matson; Bernard Fontana. *Before Rebellion: Letters & Reports of Jacobo Sedelmayr, S.J.* Tucson: Arizona Historical Society, 1996. 61pp.

1745 to 1751 covers experiences of German priest. Assignment is to make *entradas* in Pimería Alta or southwest Arizona and northwest Sonora. Accordingly he reports: geography, religious needs, baptism, catechism, confirmation, confession, and personal concerns for salvation. Personality evident in desire to obey orders and to show courage.

1622. Segura, Vicente (1883–1957). *Memorias de Vicente Segura, niño millonario, matador de toros, general de la Revolución.* México: Compañía Editora y Distribuidora de Publicaciones, 1960. 135pp. Memoirs. Period Covered: 1883–1909.

Bullfighter relates life to Armando de María y Campos. Childhood covered briefly and remainder of book devoted to bullfighting either in narration or press clippings.

1623. Segura Gómez, Jorge (1928 Birth of Gallardo Villarreal). *Pura gente de tren: don Manuel Gallardo Villarreal: testimonios.* Monterrey: Universidad Autónoma de Nuevo León, 1998. 99pp. Oral Autobiography. Period Covered: 1928–1996?

Railroading occupies small place in autobiography. Coaxed from devotee of railroad, present combines autobiography, *costumbrismo*, and folklore. From Monterrey, Gallardo Villarreal worked in northeast Mexico in variety of railway jobs: junction guard, crew foreman, signalman, brakeman, conductor, and union delegate.

1624. Segura Gómez, Jorge (1915 Birth of García Canales). *Remembranzas lampacenses: testimonios de don Vidal García Canales.* Monterrey: Universidad Autónoma de Nuevo León, 1998. 183pp. Oral Autobiography. Period Covered: 1928–1998.

Author briefly introduces subject and labels him chronicler, minstrel, storyteller, balladeer, poet, and lover of life. Family man, García Canales worked in both Matamoros, Tamaulipas, and Lampazos, Nuevo León. Credits Masons with much of development. Self-educated and proud of library. Thematic rather than chronological approach to autobiography and *costumbrismo*.

1625. Serdán, Félix (1917–?); **Renato Ravelo Lecuona**. *Félix Serdán: memorias de un guerrillero.* México: Causa Cuidadana APN, 2002. 217pp. Oral Autobiography. Period Covered: 1917–1995.

Peasant leader who followed tradition of Zapata and Rubén Jaramillo, Serdán's comrade assassinated along with family in 1962. From Galeana, Morelos, Serdán in struggle for labor rights since age eighteen. Guerrilla, *ejidatario*, bracero, and lately, fighter for Indians in Chiapas, Serdán also influential in forming union of *ejidos* and communities. Ravelo Lecuona confesses technique of collection of interviews and conversations recorded by diverse people who knew author.

1626. Serrano, Irma; Elisa Robledo
(1934? Birth of Serrano). *A calzón amarrado.*
México: Avelar Hnos. Impresos, 1978. 296pp.
Oral Autobiography. Period Covered:
1940?–1978?

Irma Salinas Rocha has competitor for
frankness and savory detail in life writing.
Film and stage actress and singer, Serrano
spends little time on childhood and focuses
mainly on loves and career. In monologue
with interviewer Elisa Robledo, Serrano in
tattletale anecdotes involves several names in
amorous affairs. Both love and career follow
similar formula: opportunity, risk, and success. In same vibrant and chatty style and
constant desire to outrage, Irma supplements
first work with *Sin pelos en la lengua* (c.
1978). Exposes escapades only suggested in
earlier autobiography. Picaresque heroine
moves from adventure to adventure and successfully advances self and career. Frankness
about sex life and antipathy to own family
unusual within Mexican autobiography.

1627. Serrano Martínez, Celedonio
(1913–). *El cazador y sus perros.* México: Fernández Editores, 1979 (1959). 131pp. Memoirs. Period Covered: 1926?

Poet, teacher, essayist, and student of
Mexican ballad contributes uniquely to autobiography in present work. Recalls rural
scene where he hunted with two dogs,
Confite and Salvador. In short poetic chapters, he communicates with two animals in
countryside jaunts. Evocation more than plot
justifies book.

1628. Sharp, Robert L. *Bob Sharp's Cattle
Country: Rawhide Ranching on Both Sides of
the Border.* Tucson: University of Arizona
Press, 1985. 286pp.

California-born Sharp wanted to be cowboy. Without experience he and pal went into
cow business near Cananea, Sonora in 1920s.
He liked adopted country for landscapes and
people. Inferior cattle, border between markets, land hostile to Gringo, and unsteady
politics. With humor he survived until 1929
when employed by Baca Float in Arizona.

**1629. Sheldon, Charles; Neil B. Car-
mony; David E. Brown.** *The Wilderness of
the Southwest: Charles Sheldon's Quest for*

*Desert Bighorn Sheep and Adventures with the
Havasupai and Seri Indians.* Salt Lake City:
University of Utah Press, 1993. 219pp.

Four chapters of memoirs relate to Mexico, Arizona-Sonora Border and state of Sonora. Harvard educated Sheldon hunted and
researched mountain sheep in this area from
1913 to 1922. Description of nature and sheep.

**1630. Shepherd, Gary; Gordon Shep-
herd.** *Mormon Passage: A Missionary Chronicle.* Urbana: University of Illinois Press, 1998.
454pp.

No other autobiography expresses in
such detail struggles to convert Mexicans to
Protestantism. In 1960s, two Utah brothers
missionized Mexico: preparation including
language training, distributing tracts, proselytizing through sequeled lessons, conflict
with Catholics and competing evangelistic
Protestants, and adjustment to environment.

1631. Shepherd, Grant. *The Silver
Magnet.* Ayuntamiento de Chihuahua, 1994.
302pp. Trans: *Batopilas: magnate de plata.*
Translated by Concepción Montilla de Camú.
Chihuahua, CHH: Centro Librero La Prensa,
1978. 387pp.

Author's father moved family from
Washington, D.C. to Batopilas, Chihuahua,
in 1880. Father, mine superintendent, provided opportunity for large family to grow
up in Mexican frontier. *Silver Magnet* is
exciting autobiography: laborers, food,
regional personality, and trips to U.S. Chihuahua and the West in the U.S. much in
common from survival to heroic manhood.
Author lauds Porfirio Díaz as peacemaker of
Mexico. Supports Chihuahua governor,
Enrique Creel, and despises Pancho Villa.

1632. Sheppard, Carrie Lee. *A Missionary's Experience in Mexico.* Guthrie, OK:
Faith, 1973. 60pp.

Focuses on Baja. Member of Church of
God, she spent years 1963 to 1972 in Santa
Catarina, Pátzcuaro, Rosarito, and Ojos
Negros. Passion of true believer.

1633. Sheridan, Clare. *My American
Diary.* New York: Boni and Liveright, 1922.
359pp.

Niece of Lady Randolph Churchill,

Sheridan well-connected British traveler on three-month visit to Mexico between trips to U.S. Because she wrote *Mayfair to Moscow*, she had context for judging Mexico's Revolution. Feted by American and British colonies, she was also lionized by Mexicans. Alberto Pani, Obregón, de la Huerta, Bonilla, and José Vascancelos find entry in her diary. Sheridan goes beyond luxury and tourist Mexico in visit to oil camps of Tampico.

1634. Sherman, William T. *Memoirs of General William T. Sherman, by Himself.* Bloomington: Indiana University Press, 1957 (1875). 409pp.

"Early Recollections of California, 1846–1848" is one chapter of above title. This has to be one of tamest documents of Mexican-American War. Assigned from Pittsburg to California, Sherman does no fighting and nothing of importance strategically. He mentions Sutter and discovery of gold and Mormons who were discharged in 1847.

1635. Shields, Karena. *The Changing Wind.* New York: Crowell, 1959. 215pp.

Underage narrator and setting reminiscent of Rosario Castellano's *The Nine Guardians.* Shields, her parents, and sister move from U.S. to Chiapas, where father has job with American company during Porfiriato. *Changing Wind* concerns conflictive meetings between White and Indian worlds in Revolution. Magic world that Indian supposedly inhabits dominates plot, theme, and mood.

1636. Sierra, Justo (1848–1912). *Correspondencia con José Yves Limantour* (1885–1935). México: UNAM, 1996. 236pp. Letters. Period Covered: 1892–1906.

Justo Sierra, Secretary of Public Instruction and Bellas Artes, and José Yves Limantour, Secretary of Treasury, both high officials in Díaz regime, exchanged 187 letters. Two notables write pro forma letters relating to office. Personality rarely emerges.

1637. Sierra, Justo (1848–1912). *Epistolario con Porfirio Díaz, Obras Completas XV.* Recopilación de Catalina Sierra de Peimbert y Cristina Barros. México: UNAM, 1993. 289pp. Letters. Period Covered: 1885–1911.

During Porfiriato, he held positions that put him in contact with dictator: senator, supreme court justice, and secretary of education and Bellas Artes. Themes deriving from offices reflected in letters which collectively read as memoir. Relates to arts: suggests that certain musician be sent to Europe to study or announces arrival of copies of Mexican sculpture for 1904 Louisiana Purchase Exposition.

1638. Sierra, Justo (1848–1912). *Epistolario y papeles privados.* Edición establecida por Catalina Sierra de Peimbert. México: UNAM, 1949. 585pp. Letters. Period Covered: 1867–1912.

Minister of education, lawyer, diplomat, and writer. Like father, he left autobiographical document. From posthumously collected letters emerges sensitive renaissance-type humanist in touch with major literary and political personalities of Mexico. Reading of collection suggests Sierra the writer.

1639. Sierra Flores, José (1928?–). *De médico, poeta y... tampiqueño: relatos de un cirujano.* Tampico: 1997? 215pp. Memoirs. Period Covered: 1948–1996.

Autobiography and place compete for attention in regional volume. Discharges medical career in first half: medical school in San Luis Potosí, internship in Aquismón, SLP, return to Tampico to practice medicine, medical adventures, and rector of la Universidad del Noreste. Family plays small role. Nostalgia for bygone Tampico comprises rest.

1640. Sierra O'Reilly, Justo (1814–1861) *Diario de nuestro viaje a los Estados Unidos (La pretendida anexión de Yucatán).* México: Antigua Librería Robredo, 1938. 125pp. Diary. Period Covered: 1847–1848.

In 1847, arrived in Washington on three-pronged mission: U.S. would withdraw from Island of Carmen, Yucatan would be defended from reprisals from Mexico, and U.S. would aid Yucatan in Caste Wars. Consisting mainly of frustrations in Washington, diary reveals contacts with city and these personal touches lend autobiographical value. In second volume, more expansive in recalling life in Washington: weather, personalities, customs, and own moods in style uncommon for Mexican diplomats.

1641. Sierra O'Reilly, Justo (1814–1861). *Impresiones de nuestro viaje a los Estados Unidos de América y al Canadá.* Campeche: Por Pedro Méndez, 1850–1851. 4 v. Echazarreta, 1851. Memoirs. Period Covered: 1847.

Like de Toqueville, Justo Sierra traveled and commented on Mexico's enemy: geography, government, cities, prisons, schools, statesmen, and other more ordinary human beings. At moment of Mexican-American War, belonged to generation that admired U.S. with ideas of Enlightenment. Composes document that improves fellow Mexicans. Memoirs reflect current genres of novel, history, travel, and political discourse. More on outer world than on self.

1642. Silva, Federico (1923–?). *México por Tacuba: pasajes autobiográficas.* México: Conaculta, 2000. 187pp. Memoirs. Period Covered: 1934?–1999?

Sculptor and muralist painter disavows chronological organization to material in favor of own artistic development. Notes small moments of childhood such as trip to Vera Cruz or ride on streetcar. Married to daughter of Vicente Lombardo Toledano, Silva interacted with artists: David Alfaro Siqueiros, Mathías Goertz, Pablo O'Higgins, and Diego Rivera.

1643. Silva Herzog, Jesús (1892–1985). Entrevista en James W. Wilkie y Edna Monzón de Wilkie's *México visto en el siglo XX.* México: Instituto Mexicano de Investigaciones Económicas, 1969. Pp.601–708. Interview. Period Covered: 1892–1952?

Economist and politician speaks of childhood and career: Revolution, formation of Partido Nacional Revolucionario, Lázaro Cárdenas, Manuel Avila Camacho, and Miguel Aleman.

1644. Silva Herzog, Jesús (1892–1985). *Mis ultimas andanzas,* México: Siglo Veintiuno Editores, 1973. 350pp. Memoirs. Period Covered: 1947–1972.

Prolific and versatile intellectual of twentieth century. Writer on agrarianism and petroleum synthesizes twenty-five years of cultural life. Emissary represented country in many foreign missions and knew everyone of intellectual importance. Interests multiple: economics, poetry, history, and contemporary events. Organizes materials chronologically in text occasionally interrupted with verbatim inclusion of documents.

1645. Silva Herzog, Jesús (1892–1985). *Una vida en la vida de México.* México: Siglo Veintiuno Editores, 1972. 347pp. Memoirs. Period Covered: 1892–1964.

Una vida begins as autobiography, i.e., concentration on childhood, familial relations, and finding of self. Honesty about difficult early years and relationship with father unique in Mexican autobiography. Writings soon switch to more comfortable mode of memoir. In multiple careers: teacher, writer, economist, and diplomat. External life or public image dominates.

1646. Simental, José Claro (1914–). "Experiencias de maestros y alumnos en las escuelas rurales" En *Los maestros y la cultura nacional, 1920–1952, v.1, Norte.* México: Museo Nacional de Culturas Populares, 1987. Pp.221–248. Memoirs. Period Covered: 1930–1952?

At age sixteen, Simental began career as rural teacher in Durango. More than personal experiences he writes about duties of rural teachers: hygiene, medicine, carpentry, agriculture, land redistribution (*ejido*), and adult education. They battled illiteracy, *Cristeros,* priests, *hacendados,* and *marijuaneros,* all opposed to education.

1647. Siqueiros, David Alfaro (1896–1974). *Me llamaban el Coronelazo (memorias).* México: Biografías Gandea, 1977. 613pp. Memoirs. Period Covered: 1892?–1961?

Incorporating anecdotes of colorful grandfather, author spends little time on childhood. Launches into tumultuous career as painter, soldier, political activist, and citizen- at-large. Determined and opinionated in artistic and political spheres, he selects high points of long and tendentious career. Eventful life plus natural narrative ability creates readable memoirs.

1648. Siqueiros, David Alfaro (1896–1974). *Mi respuesta: la historia de una insidia.*

¿Quiénes son los traidores a la patria? México: Ediciones de Arte Público, 1960. 135pp. Memoirs. Period Covered: 1921–1960.

Polemical speeches but with sufficient autobiographical material to read selectively for two reasons: muralist movement in Mexico and artist's experiences in U.S.

1649. Siqueiros, David Alfaro (1896–1974). *Palabras de Siqueiros.* Selección, prólogo y notas de Raquel Tibol. México: Fondo de Cultura Económica, 1996. 537pp. Letters. Period Covered: 1936–1964.

Thirty-six letters to individuals and two open letters to Cuban artists and to artists of world comprise small part of text. Dogmatic in art and politics. Personal correspondence with women: María Asúnsola, Blanca Luz Brum, Angélica Arenal, and María Teresa León.

1650. Siqueiros, David Alfaro (1896–1974). *La trácala: mi réplica a un gobierno fiscal-juez.* México, 1962. 78pp. Memoirs. Period Covered: 1919–1962.

Polemical artist claims to be imprisoned by government for efforts on behalf of political prisoners and defense of constitutional rights. In four-hour self-defense, denounces government and includes much as artist.

1651. Siurob, José (1886–1966). *Memorias de la vida revolucionaria.* México, 1963. 61pp. Memoirs. Period Covered: 1909–1934.

Governor of Guanajuato, Querétaro, and territory of Quintana Roo and head of Department of Health under Cárdenas focuses on revolutionary experiences as general in Maderista forces. Aggressive anti-clericalism.

1652. Skeaping, John Rattenbury. *The Big Tree of Mexico.* Bloomington: Indiana University Press, 1953. 333pp.

Above title is source for understanding Oaxaca. One of givens is impossibility for outsider, Mexican or foreigner, to penetrate Indian culture. Britisher John Skeaping foils dictum. Knowing little Spanish and less of indigenous language, he settles in Oaxaca and integrates self into Indian family. Anecdotes reveal Indian character.

1653. Slocum, Marianna C.; Grace Watkins. *The Good Seed.* Orange, CA: Promise, 1988. 260pp.

Of Wycliffe autobiographies, this one is best. Encapsulates much of evangelical experience of outsiders in Mexico. Two women, nurse and teacher, establish selves among Tzeltales of Chiapas. Combined memoir includes following: translation of Bible into native language, efforts at winning converts, process of conversion and its sociological implications, hostility and violence against them by Roman Catholics, ties to U.S., and profundity of beliefs of missionaries.

1654. Smart, Charles Allen. *At Home in Mexico.* Garden City, NY: Doubleday, 1957. 215pp. .

Fifty-year-old author, disgruntled with career and identity, travels from Ohio to Guanajuato. From 1949 to 1953, he and spouse live in San Miguel de Allende. Published author writes better than most Gringos on Mexico. Records many of usual themes of language, maids, repairmen, other Gringos, etc. Most interesting chapter on Siqueiros and Art School supported by G.I. monies. Writing and painting and understanding of Mexicans.

1655. Smith, E. Kirby; Emma Jerome Blackwood; R.M. Johnston, eds. *To Mexico with Scott: Letters of Captain E.Kirby Smith to His Wife.* Cambridge: Harvard University Press, 1917. 225pp.

Uneventful in his career until outbreak of Mexican-American War, Smith fought at Palo Alto, Resaca de la Palma, Matamoros, Camargo, Monterrey, Saltillo, Vera Cruz, Perote, Puebla, and Mexico City. Reader unhappy to learn that this lieutenant colonel was killed at Molina del Rey. He notes climate, vegetation, death, and "popish idolatry of Mexicans;" often describes locales.

1656. Smith, Francis Hopkinson. *A White Umbrella in Mexico.* Boston: Houghton Mifflin, 1899. 227pp. .

Artist Smith illustrated his travel autobiography. In manner of roving artists, he sat under white umbrella. Visiting Aguas Calientes, Zacatecas, Mexico City, Puebla, Toluca, and Morelia, painter/author differs from other travel writers. Moves slowly savoring each bit of architecture, landscape, or human being. Painter's training invited him to scrutinize each object. Avoids deprecating Indians.

1657. Smith, Franklin; Joseph E. Chance. *The Mexican War Journal of Captain Franklin Smith.* Jackson: University Press of Mississippi, 1991. 267pp.

Smith spent Mexican-American War mainly in north at Camargo from August 11, 1846, to February 6, 1847. Educated and a quartermaster, he recounts war from Rio Grande: geography; meeting officers including Gen. Taylor, Sam Houston, and Mirabeau Lamar; liquor; steamboats on Rio Grande for supplies and soldiers; and Mexican customs such as burials.

1658. Smith, H. Allen. *The Pig in the Barber Shop.* Boston: Little, Brown, 1958. 316pp.

Prolific writer had sufficient prestige to enjoy access to many of Mexico's famous of late 1950s: Pepe Romero, Diego Rivera, Santiago Reachi, Alma Reed, Cantinflas, Anita Brenner, and others. Visits country and celebrities but always with humor as suggested by title. Mexico City, Pátzcuaro, and Taxco stimulate Smith's humor at expense of self, wife, and Mexicans.

1659. Smith, J. Gregory. *Notes of Travel in Mexico and California.* St. Albans, VT: Printed at the Messenger and Advertiser Office, 1886? 123pp.

Well-heeled and moralistic traveler journeys by train from El Paso to Mexico City in pre–Porfirian Mexico. Superintendent of Mexican Central railways accompanied her; she had access to Escandón mansion in capital. Author angry about liquor and also sensitive to native thieves. Notes brutalizing effects of bullfight. Experiences of traveler both fascinated and repelled by Mexico.

1660. Smith, Jack Clifford. *God and Mr. Gomez.* New York: Watts, 1982 (1974). 216pp.

When Americans build homes in foreign countries, they must tolerate eccentricities of natives. Title accentuates predicament. Baja lover Jack Smith acquired house lots from Mr. Gomez and left him in charge of con-

structing ideal home on Pacific Coast, thirty miles south of Ensenada. Delays, bureaucracy, and Gomez's undimming optimism make humorous read.

1661. Smith, Lonnie C. *Anecdotes of a Missionary....* McAllen, TX: The Author, 1987. 204pp.

"These stories are based on the life and ministry of Lonnie C. Smith Sr. and his family, who have labored in Mexico since May 1956 in cooperation with the Baptist Bible Fellowship International" (p.1). Anecdotes (365) comprise document of missionary work in Tampico and Monterrey. Each anecdote preceded by Bible verse that foretells contents. Narratives encompass variety of themes: proselytizing, character of Mexican, adjusting to new environment, and rearing family.

1662. Smithers, Wilfred Dudley. *Pancho Villa's Last Hangout on Both Sides of the Rio Grande in the Big Bend Country.* Alpine, TX, 1964. 95pp.

Smithers, man of many trades, lived on border and frequently crossed into Mexico. One expedition resulted in sunstroke, an ailment that exposed him successfully to *curandera.* He tells of cures and notes use of rattlesnakes as alternative medicine.

1663. Smithwick, Noah; Nanna Smithwick Donaldson. *The Evolution of a State, or, Recollections of Old Texas Days.* Austin: University of Texas Press, 1983 (1900). 264pp.

One of few Texan autobiographies that incorporates years before independence, 1827–1861. Author humorous and garrulous with many anecdotes mainly from San Antonio, Austin, and Bastrop. Smithwick exercised many offices: medicine, blacksmith, Indian fighter, landowner, justice, and miller. Mentions Stephen Austin's colonists and their Catholicism, Afro-Americans escaping to Mexico, Indian wars, and antagonisms building up to Alamo. Fun to read.

1664. Sodi, Federico (1890–?). *El jurado resuelve: memorias.* México: Editorial Oasis, 1977. 268pp. Memoirs. Period Covered: 1927?–1960.

Criminal lawyer and novelist recounts

six of more sensational cases of career in police story form. Involved in cases for attraction to law and studies. View of legal system and suits that arouse publicity and scandal of peripheral interest.

1665. Sodi de Pallares, María Elena (1910?–). *Vida y escenas burguesas.* México, 1932. 94pp. Memoirs. Period Covered: 1915?

Writer and journalist remembers childhood and father, Demetrio Sodi, minister of justice under Porfirio Díaz. Recalls family, religion, fiestas, and vacations.

1666. Solana, Rafael (1915–1992). *Crónicas de Rafael Solana.* México: Publicaciones Mexicanas, 1991. 284pp. Memoirs. Period Covered: 1961–1991.

Claudio Rodríguez and Mireya Rodríguez collaborated in selection of articles by Rafael Solana from newspaper *El Día.* Journalist and dramatist, Solana worked in many aspects of both areas. Autobiographical articles reflect knowledge of literature, acquaintance with other illustrious Mexicans, and opinions on politics. Shows graciousness often lacking in Mexican journalism when treating competition.

1667. Solares, Ignacio (1945–). *De cuerpo entero: Ignacio Solares.* México: Ediciones Corunda, 1990. 55pp. Memoirs. Period Covered: 1949?–1990.

Writer (journalist, dramatist and novelist) renders unorthodox autobiography developing in each chapter an exotic theme: facing death with humor; spiritism (relating both to father and to Francisco Madero); existential search for the *I*; sexual fantasies in church; experiences with alcoholism; bullfighting; and sources for *Casas de encantamiento.* Sum of chapters creates puzzling human.

1668. Solórzano de Cárdenas, Amalia (1917?–). *Era otra cosa la vida.* México: Nueva Imagen, 1994. 127pp. Memoirs. Period Covered: 1916?–1993.

In chronological sequence lays out life: youth in Tacámbaro, Michoacán, family, school, meeting with Cárdenas, courtship, marriage, birth of Cuauhtémoc, and life with president. No secrets or surprises about for-

mer first lady or famous husband. Illustrated with b/w photos.

1669. Soltero, F.H. *Los peregrinos in Mexico.* Indianapolis: Pilgrim Holiness Church, 1958. 71pp.

Persistence and labor of American Protestants obvious in above title. Soltero's thirty-seven years in northern Mexico comprised of visits to penitentiary, preparation of natives for ministry, working with Indians, publishing, attending district conferences, and house-to-house visits to seek converts.

1670. Sotelo Arévalo, Salvador (1904–1965). *Historia de mi vida: autobiografía y memorias de un maestro rural en México, 1904–1965.* México: Instituto Nacional de Estudios Históricos de la Revolución Mexicana, 1996. 159pp. Memoirs. Period Covered: 1904–1965.

Rural schoolteacher, spirited author lived in Michoacán during Revolution and aftermath. Pro-revolutionary in Cárdenas's land reform and fanatically anticlerical Catholic liberal, he is atypical schoolteacher. Revealing details about implementation of program of Revolution. Well footnoted.

1671. Soto Soria, Alfonso (1926–?). *Una vida, muchas vidas: memorias.* Cuenca, Ecuador: Centro Interamericano de Artesanías y Artes Populares, 1997. 255pp. Memoirs. Period Covered: 1926–1990?

Has led varied existence: designer/ drawer (artist), museum director, traveler, cultural anthropologist, and consultant for U.N. Abilities enabled him to work with National Museum of Anthropology and design displays for several Indian cultures. As anthropologist studied with Huicholes, Yaquis, Coras, and Otomies. As consultant to U.N., influenced cultural preservation in Americas, e.g., book published by Centro Internacional de Artesanías y Artes Populares of Cuenca, Ecuador.

1672. Soustelle, Jacques. *México, tierra India.* México: Secretaría de Educación Pública, 1971. 296pp.

Frenchman Jacques Soustelle visited Mexico on various anthropological missions in 1930s and published *Mexique, terre indi-*

enne in 1936. In 1971, work appeared in Spanish with Roldolfo Usigli's *México, tierra India*. Frenchmen and wife study Otomi of central Mexico and later Lacandones of Yucatan.

1673. Spasek, Edward. *It's Fun to Fly in Mexico!* San Francisco: Avion Aids, 1967. 163pp.

Ventured into Mexico in plane in 1950s and 1960s. Aerial view of sites in Baja, Sinaloa, Chihuahua, Yucatan, and Jalisco. Stunning perspectives include Copper Canyon, Chichen Itza, and Uxmal. Minimal Spanish no problem for pilot, who once "lost" airfield at Ciudad Obregón, Chihuahua.

1674. Spratling, William. *File on Spratling: An Autobiography.* Boston: Little, Brown, 1967. 235pp.

Taxco deserves more attention in autobiography. This book answers need. Impetus behind silver revival in Taxco, he talks of collecting Precolumbian artifacts, rescuing skills of Eskimo craftsmen, interacting with native and foreign celebrities, and Taxco.

1675. Squier, Emma-Lindsay. *Gringa: An American Woman in Mexico.* Boston: Houghton Mifflin, 1934. 263pp.

Squier distinguishes self from other travel writers. Rather than car or train, she first pursues Mexican cities by boat. Covers usual tourist routes. Yet Mexico as theme somehow more organic. Any diversion into Mexican history or culture triggered by an incident, e.g., evokes Villa and President Obregón because moment calls for it. Constant sense of humor and self-corrections reflected in deprecatory title "Gringa."

1676. Stacy-Judd, Robert Benjamin. *The Ancient Mayas, Adventures in the Jungles of Yucatan.* Los Angeles: Haskell-Travers, 1934. 277pp.

Fifty-year-old Robert Stacy-Judd sallied into Yucatan in 1930s. In contact with jungle, he dialogued with natives, mentioned other archaeologists (Franz Blom, Herbert J. Spinden, and Edward H. Thompson, et. al), and explored and described ruins of Chichén Itzá, Uxmal, and Izmal.

1677. Stacy-Judd, Robert Benjamin. *Kabah: Adventures in the Jungles of Yucatan.* Hollywood, CA: House-Warven, 1951. 360pp.

Complements above title. Architect Stacy-Judd introduced Mayan themes into California structures. Exploring Mayan ruins such as Kabah, Chichen Itza, and Uxmal, he gives small incidents and interacts with other experts such as Franz Blom.

1678. Starr, Frederick. *In Indian Mexico: A Narrative of Travel and Labor.* Chicago: Forbes, 1908. 425pp.

Book resulted from years of labor. World traveler explored Japan, Congo, Philippines, Korea, and Mexico. Chapters, running from 1895 to 1901, blend sociology and anthropology. Concentrating on tribes of southern Mexico, he followed triple agenda: measure 125 men and women in each settlement; take pictures (portraits, context, dress, etc.), and make plaster busts of five Indians of each tribe. Interesting observations and his convoluted efforts to gain cooperation of tribes. Letters from federal, state, and local chiefs of districts attempted to assuage Indians to facilitate task. Both Starr and Lumholtz write in autobiographical vein.

1679. Stavans, Ilán (1961–). *On Borrowed Time: A Memoir of Language.* New York: Viking, 2001. 263pp. Memoirs. Period Covered: 1961–2000.

Mexican-born author of Jewish descent reflects on his multicultural background including love of languages and words. The Jew in Mexico is another theme. Familial ties, especially with father, brother, and Yiddish-speaking grandmother, also significant in international writer who has chosen New York as his home. More recent *Ilan Stavans: Eight Conversations* (2004) by Neal Sokol enlarges on themes in memoirs: Jewish heritage, books, and *lexicomania*. New themes: *hispanidad*, role of intellectual, and biography as a genre.

1680. Steele, C. William. *Yochib, the River Cave: An Account of the Exploration of the Sumidero Yochib of Mexico....* St. Louis: Cave Books, 1985. 164pp.

Yucatan scenario for adventures in this title. Speleologist as author explores major river cave. Landscape, adventures, and team-work.

1681. Steinbeck, John; Edward Flanders Ricketts. *Sea of Cortez: A Leisurely Journal of Travel and Research....* New York: Viking, 1941. 598pp.

Steinbeck collaborated with Edward F. Ricketts here. Scientist and writer, ostensibly interested in marine biology, sails waters of Baja guided by one precept: "... and we were determined not to let a passion for unassailable truths draw in the horizons and crowd the sky down on us" (p.3). Efforts result in musings and mini-essays on life, death, value of science, and scientific method. Most of log readable; some pages inscrutable for philosophical content. And Baja as geographical locale less important than journey itself with scientific end of collecting and cataloging marine species.

1682. Stephenson, Fairfax. *Carmen with a Shrimp in Her Mouth.* N.p.: Gotuit Enterprises, 1977. 98pp.

Author sees culture through foreign eyes. American Stephenson accompanies Mexican husband to home in Cuidad del Carmen. New world for her: availability of servants, need to shop daily for groceries, plumbing, fund raising *a la mexicana*, and social customs.

1683. Steven, Hugh. *Doorway to the World: The Mexicano Years: The Memoirs of W. Cameron Townsend, 1934–1947.* Wheaton, IL: Harold Shaw, 1999. 236pp.

Townsend originated Summer Institute of Linguistics, non-profit organization to study Indian languages to translate Bible. Author Hugh Steven bases much of his information on documents generated by Townsend. Accusation of cultural imperialism forced Institute's closing in 1979.

1684. Stevenson, Sara Yorke. *Maximilian in Mexico: A Woman's Reminiscences of the French Intervention, 1862–1867.* New York: Century, 1899. 327pp.

Valuable for perspective. Knowledgeable woman discusses political situation and glimpses of personal life emerge: quarters,

social activities, and friendships. Personal view of disaster.

1685. Stilwell, Hart. *Fishing in Mexico.* New York: Knopf, 1948. 296pp.

Sportsmen of Mexico often mention hunting but rarely fishing. Therefore, above title necessary. Stilwell exercises enthusiasm for fishing in all parts of Mexico: west coast, east coast, and interior. Both anecdotal and informative, he surveys regions and species of fish. First person narrative.

1686. Stone, Martha. *At the Sign of Midnight: The Concheros Dance Cult of Mexico.* Tucson: University of Arizona Press, 1975. 262pp.

Dancing can take many forms from Europeanized Contreras to Indianist authors. For twenty-five years, Martha Stone followed and studied Concheros, pre–Columbian dance group that allows women to perform and uses *concha* as mandolin. In above title, task is clearly stated: "...she has participated in the *danzante* ceremonial life and their daily human problems. She has risen through the ranks, gaining new knowledge and perspectives at each stage" (p.ix).

1687. Storm, Marian. *Hoofways into Hot Country.* Mexico: Bland Brother, 1939. 521pp.

Author covers Michoacán in above title. Never casual traveler, she submerged self totally in environment. Present text takes her on horseback journey through this state. And what an indirect way to note landscape, vegetation, food, geography, inhabitants, lore, and much on pack animals, guides, and mule drivers. Book replete with place names and small adventures that happen to anyone who travels slowly and carefully. Probably no native of Michoacán has done so much in detailing local terrain as foreigner Marian Storm.

1688. Storm, Marian. *Prologue to Mexico: The Story of a Search for a Place.* New York: Knopf, 1931. 328pp.

Marian Storm travels alone in Mexico and Guatemala. Quest takes her throughout Mexico until she finds Eden: Uruapan. Critic noted that Storm is not interested in social problems or progress of Revolution. Her forte is capturing sense of place. Uruapan almost saccharine with its Indians, food, flowers, history, and place names. Preferred chapter for its grit is "Tampico Blazes." "I came to Tampico, and it seemed to sear me, the desperate, glaring, mechanized metropolis of oil" (p.6). "Not wholesome Mexican maize cakes, but Gringo doughnuts, sandwiches, and sodas for daily bread" (p.7).

1689. Stuart, David E. *The Guaymas Chronicles: La mandadera.* Albuquerque: University of New Mexico Press, 2003. 394pp.

Little life writing on Guaymas. Young Stuart lived here in 1960s and 1970s as vagrant from anthropological studies and as hustler earning money in any way possible. Adventures evidence glimpses of inside Guaymas: *cantinas*, prostitution, street people, and distressed Gringos victimized by local bureaucracy. Most vivid personality aside from author's is Lupita, plucky *gamina* or errand runner, whom Stuart befriended. Disclaimer important: "This volume is nonfiction, but I have novelized the story in significant ways" (p.xii).

1690. Su, Margo (1929–1993). *Alta frivolidad.* México: Cal y Arena, 1990. 199pp. Memoirs. Period Covered: 1949–1989.

Writer and fanatic of theater briefly describes Poza Rica, Vera Cruz home of large family. Adolescent goes to Mexico City and seeks job as chorus girl. From vaudeville to more serious *Equus*, does gamut of theater jobs and shares perspective for forty-year period. Marriage, family, and two sons distract little from theater in vivacious prose and with humor. Source for popular culture.

1691. Suárez, Luis (Dates?). *Cárdenas: Retrato inédito: testimonios de Amalia Solórzano de Cárdenas y nuevos documentos.* México: Editorial Grijalbo, 1987. 418pp. Hybrid. Period Covered: 1911–1970.

Hybrid letters and speeches of Lázaro Cárdenas, summary of events by compiler/author Suárez, and interviews and testimony of widow, Amalia Solórzano de Cárdenas. Extrapolated from text, interviews and comments make weak autobiography. Glimpses of widow of one of Mexico's most popular presidents. Adoring woman acquired profile only because of husband. Lázaro Cárdenas more humanized here than in either of his works, *Apuntes* and *Epistolario.*

1692. Suárez, Luis (1886–1957 Dates of Diego Rivera). *Confesiones de Diego Rivera.* México: Editorial Grijalbo, 1975 (1962). 192pp. Memoirs. Period Covered: 1886–1956.

In sporadic confessions, Rivera fails to integrate life. At promptings of Suárez, artist describes early years in Guanajuato, close relationship with father, years in Europe, muralist movement, expression in art, and trip to Russia for cancer treatment. Maintains pose as *enfant terrible*. Much of material noted in autobiography co-authored with Gladys March.

1693. Suárez, Luis. *Puente sin fin: testigo activo de la historia.* México: Editorial Grijalbo, 2000. 256pp.

Another naturalized Mexican, Spanish republican Suárez refuged here in 1939. In new country has career as national and international journalist in all news media including TV. Detailed history of exciting life.

1694. Suárez Aranzola, Eduardo (1894–1976). *Comentarios y recuerdos (1936–1946).* México: Editorial Porrúa, 1977. 450pp. Memoirs. Period Covered: 1926–1946.

Trained lawyer active in national and international affairs of Mexico: delegate to Hague Conference on International Law, delegate to General Claim Commission between his country and Great Britain and France, one of founders of International Monetary Fund, and secretary of treasury under Cárdenas and Avila Camacho. Focus on public life with important events in which he participated.

1695. Suárez Fernández, Luis (1917–1997 Dates of Peralta). *Alejo Peralta, un patrón sin patrones.* México: Editorial Grijalbo. 1992. 271pp. Oral Autobiography. Period Covered: 1917–1992?

Career of engineer, industrialist, and owner of more than fifty companies. Graduate of National Polytechnic Institute in 1935 took over presidency of school under Ruíz Cortines. Peralta owned two baseball teams.

Author Suárez Fernández taped Peralta and interviewed friends to write book that details business career but not human or personal side of subject.

1696. Susan. *Peace & the Puta & the Day of the Beautyful Jail.* Santa Fe, NM, 1970. 150pp.

Prostitution, not favorite topic of foreign writers in Mexico, appears in few autobiographies. Young American woman, part of hippy culture of period, accepts lovemaking with Mexicans as natural as drugs or as rejection of standards of morality.

1697. Sutton, George. *Mexican Birds: First Impressions. Based upon an Ornithological Expedition to Tamaulipas, Nuevo León, and Coahuila.* Norman: University of Oklahoma Press, 1951. 282pp.

Lovers of ecology rare in Mexican autobiography. American George Miksch Sutton, in three books on ornithology, manifests sensitivity to environment. The above title plus *At a Bend in a Mexican River* (1972), and *Portraits of Mexican Birds: Fifty Selected Paintings* (1975). Bird watching and autobiography rarely associated. "I have presented the materials autobiographically because bird students who visit Mexico for the first time will be apt to go through much that I went through in adjusting myself to the fact that many birds there are the same as, or very closely related to, those of the United States…(p.viii). As artist, draws or paints specimens; as scientist, creates appendix as guide to birds in Mexico. Each portrait accompanied by text that details birds. Experience of ornithology vehicle for memoir.

1698. Swan, Michael. *Temples of the Sun and Moon: A Mexican Journey.* London: Cape, 1954. 288pp.

British lone traveler, Swan makes way through Indian Mexico: Toltec, Aztec, Totonac, Olmec, Mixtecs, Zapotecs and Maya. He arrives, tells anecdote, and interacts with natives even in sordid surroundings, and notes beauty. Juxtaposition of Indian and European in text allusive with names from literature contributes to understanding Mexico. Swan not stereotypical, condemning Brit set loose in Mexico.

1699. Tablada, José Juan (1871–1945). *Cartas a Genaro Estrada,* México: UNAM, 2001. 152pp. Letters. Period Covered: 1921–1929.

Poet left diplomatic service to live in New York, where he owned a bookstore and wrote for magazines, both Mexican and American. Genaro Estrada was undersecretary of foreign affairs and apparently an intimate friend of poet's. Much on health but also much on cultural issues: lecture at Yale, interview with Mexican artists, promotion of career of Miguel Covarrubias, personal library, and collection of Japanese publications.

1700. Tablada, José Juan (1871–1945). "Cuarenta cartas inéditas de José Juan Tablada." En *José Juan Tablada en la intimidad by Nina Cabrera de Tablada.* México: Imprenta Universitaria, 1945. Pp.117–200. Letters. Period Covered: 1926–1928.

Poet's letters to following: Miguel Arce, Venustiano Carranza, Genaro Estrada, José María González de Mendoza, Guillermo Jiménez, Rafael López, Alfonso Reyes, Victoriano Salado Alvarez, Alejandro Traslosheros, and Artemio de Valle-Arizpe. Genaro García main correspondent. Tablada reveals personal side in letters from U.S. to friends.

1701. Tablada, José Juan (1871–1945). *En el país del sol.* New York: Appleton, 1919. 149pp. Memoirs. Period Covered: 1900.

Credited with introducing haiku to Spanish lyric poetry, he visited Japan in 1900. "Travel book" underestimates poetic qualities of writing. Landscape, temples, *costumbrismo*, theater, and individuals emerge along with author's personality in prose reminiscent of Modernismo.

1702. Tablada, José Juan (1871–1945). *La feria de la vida.* México: Ediciones Botas, 1937. 456pp. Memoirs. Period Covered: 1875–1937?

Poet and journalist develops little of life in chronological *La feria.* Figures at times profile selves in acute anecdote. Writer's eye for description noting architecture, painting, and other cultural aspects during and after Porfiriato. Condemns critics incapable of understanding work they evaluate. Little attention to Japan and experiments with haiku. Revolution unmentioned.

1703. Tablada, José Juan (1871–1945). *Obras IV: Diario (1900- 1944)*. Edición de Guillermo Sheridan. México: UNAM, 1992. 358pp. Diary. Period Covered: 1900–1944.

Sheridan located and edited unpublished manuscript. His comments, "En el Diario no estaba escribiendo, sino anotando una efervescencia que nada tenía que ver con la tiranía de la posteridad a que aspiraba" (p.11), or "...Tablada pertenece, pues, a esos que no desprecian lo insignificante..." (p.13). Writing years in Mexico, New York, and Venezuela generally unnoted in entries.

1704. Tablada, José Juan (1871–1945). *Las sombras largas*. México: Consejo Nacional para la Cultura y las Artes, 1993. 472pp. Memoirs. Period Covered: 1926–1928.

Articles first published by *El Universal*, one of Mexico City's oldest newspapers. Each self-contained essay cumulatively profiles his personality. Poet interacts with other writers or even objects to personalize each chapter. Mexican or foreign subjects mixed: Manuel Puga y Acal, Aureliano Urrutia, bullfighters, boxers, Algonquin Hotel, Xochimilco, and Alexander the Great suggest potpourri. Elevates qualities of journalism.

1705. Taibo, Paco Ignacio. *Ocurrencias: notas de viajes*. México City: Conaculta, 2000. 149pp.

Original travel writer is Spanish-born Taibo, who arrived in Mexico in 1958 at age thirty-four. Journalist, writer, TV personality, and movie critic proves self in itinerant writings. Style notable: brief essay on place; U.S., Mexico, Europe, or Orient; meeting with friend or noting of detail of famous city; immediate involvement with person or incident; ostensibly simple prose; and quick unexpected ending.

1706. Taibo, Paco Ignacio, II (1934 Birth of Cuauhtémoc Cárdenas). *Cárdenas de cerca: una entrevista biográfica*. México: Planeta, 1994. 157pp. Oral Autobiography. Period Covered: 1934–1993.

Cuauhtémoc Cárdenas Solórzano, son of idolized Lázaro Cárdenas, governor of Michoacán, engineer, and prime challenger of sixty-five-year-old PRI Party both in 1988 and 1994, hurries through life in short autobiography. Based on sixteen hours of recorded interviews in February, March, and April, book appeared timely for 1994 elections. Tells of early life, e.g., born in year father assumed office, family, and travels, but focus is politics.

1707. Taibo, Paco Ignacio, II (1949–). *De cuerpo entero: Paco Ignacio Taibo II*. México: Ediciones Corunda, 1992. 60pp. Memoirs. Period Covered: 1954–1992.

Spanish-born has lived in Mexico since ten years old. Founder of new detective story because of fourteen novels of this subgenre, he expresses self according to Ediciones Corunda format: education, reading, and literary creation. Autobiography anything but formulaic, for he immerses self into 1992 and self-delineates through political life, concerts, Mexican history, trip to Europe, and influence of the first Paco Ignacio Taibo. Dialogs with alter ego.

1708. Taibo II, Paco Ignacio (1949–). *68*. México: Planeta, 1991. 116pp. Memoirs. Period Covered: 1968.

By thirtieth anniversary of Tlatelolco (1998), only nine autobiographers incorporated cataclysmic event. Perspective of distance plus maturity of generation may prompt more reflection and interpretation. Nineteen years old at time of Tlatelolco, observer/participant writes of signature year as he attempts to answer questions relating to government's suppression of students.

1709. Talamas Camandari, Manuel (1917–?). *Mi vida en mosaico: historia de una vocación*. Juárez: Ediciones Procorsa, 1994. 332pp. Memoirs. Period Covered: 1917–1993.

Chronological account of youth who became priest and in 1957 bishop of Ciudad Juárez. Title refers to ninety-five brief chapters that comprise life from birth to celebration of fiftieth year in priesthood. Religious profession evident but little of human personality emerges. Bishop never expresses doubts about vocation or suggests involvement with changes in Catholic Church since 1950.

1710. Tallien, Teresa (Dates?). *Las Malvinas por dos mujeres: María Sáez de Vernet (1829), Teresa Tallien (1953)*. México: Editores Asociados Mexicanos, 1982. 126pp. Memoirs. Period Covered: 1953.

Journalist was second Latin American woman to write on Malvinas in twenty-eight-day trip in 1953. (First was María Sáez de Vernet in 1828). Evidences woman with mettle, unintimidated either by government bureaucracy or loneliness of locale, recording impression of disputed island.

1711. Tamayo, Rufino (1899–1991). *Rufino*. México: Grupo Editorial Siete, 1997. 67pp. Interview. Period Covered: ?

Questions and answers and explanatory paragraphs describe Isabel Arvide's interview with Tamayo in 1983. Many themes touched on lightly: passion, death, philosophy, leftist politician, business manager wife, government as art patron, watermelons, and eroticism. Little life writing on Tamayo compared to Rivera, Siqueiros, and Orozco.

1712. Tamayo, Rufino (1899–1991). *Textos de Rufino Tamayo*. Recopilación, prólogo y selección de viñeta de Raquel Tibol. México: UNAM, 1987. 146pp. Memoirs? Period Covered: 1926–1980?

One of foremost muralists scatters autobiographical data throughout text of diverse documents. Art predominates in theories and techniques and also in polemics with other great muralists. Opposed politically inspired art.

1713. Tapia, Rafael (1874?–1963). *Mi participación revolucionaria*. México: Editorial Citlaltépetl, 1967. 39pp. Memoirs. Period Covered: 1910.

Maderista general recounts preparatory moments to Revolution in 1910 in Orizaba, Vera Cruz: discovering anti–Porfirian sentiments and gathering and storing munitions.

1714. Tapia, Santiago (1820–1866). *Diario de prisionero (1864–1865)*. México: Instituto Poblano de Antropología e Historia, 1970. 57pp. Diary. Period Covered: 1864–1865.

Ardent liberal patriot and soldier opposed to collusion of countrymen with French invaders was civil and military governor of Michoacán and Jalisco. Imprisoned first in Belén de Los Mochis but later in fort of Loreto de Puebla. Notes patriotic fervor and prison life. Rarely dull.

1715. Taracena, Alfonso (1895–1995). *Autobiografía, cuentos*. México: Ediciones Botas, 1933 (1928). 187pp. Memoirs. Period Covered: 1905?–1910?

Comprises first eighty-three pages of journalist, historian, short story writer, and novelist of Revolution. Thirty-six year old mixes *costumbrismo* with autobiographical data to recall childhood in Cunduacán, Tabasco, education in San Juan Bautista (Villahermosa) and Mexico City, and unsuccessful love affair. Some luminaries in education appear. In 1928, Taracena published *Bajo el fuego de helios, novela con detalles de historia y de leyenda*. Appears identical to *Autobiografía, cuentos*.

1716. Taracena, Alfonso (1897–1995). *Mi vida en el vértigo de la revolución mexicana (anales sintéticos–1900–1930)*. México: Ediciones Botas, 1936. 715pp. Memoirs. Period Covered: 1900–1930.

Mixture of personal life and national history. Frequently performs role of historian in narrating unwitnessed events. Journalist, writer (novelist), and Vasconcelista, Taracena, from Cunduacán, Tabasco, reveals life but always with national events unfolding chronologically. Schooling, first love, and first novel share space with Revolution and political and literary personalities: Vasconcelos, Madero, Carranza, Villa, Zapata, Carlos Pellicer, Jaime Torres Bodet, etc.

1717. Taracena, Alfonso (1895–1995). *Viajando con Vasconcelos*. México: Ediciones Botas, 1938. 190pp. Diary. Period Covered: 1937.

Overlooked gem of autobiography. Title refers to fourteen-day journey with Vasconcelos and with editor Gabriel Botas to Laredo, Mobile, New York, and New Orleans. Vasconcelos's Xmas visit with son José pretexts diary entries recording Taracena/Vasconcelos dialog touching on U.S., women, and Mexican personalities. Former secretary of education and presidential candidate acerbically assesses contemporaries. In recalling bon mots of his hero, Taracena suggests own personality like Boswell in *Life of Johnson* (1791). *Viajando* probably inspired Alessio Robles's *Mis andanzas con nuestro ulises* (1938).

1718. Tarango Ponce, Eleázar (1921–). *En el inquieto río Urique.* México: Costa-Amic, 1965. 78pp. Journal. Period Covered: 1964.

He and companions try to conquer difficult terrain which surrounds Urique River and reach its source in Chihuahua. Adventures and some author intimacy with landscape.

1719. Tausend, Marilyn; Miguel Ravago. *Cocina de la familia: More than 200 Authentic Recipes from Mexican-American Home Kitchens.* New York: Simon & Schuster, 1997. 415pp.

Author pays debt to Mexico and specifically to Diana Kennedy, doyenne of Mexican food; then in brief autobiographical essays notes sojourns to cities in U.S. with large Mexican-American populations: impressions of each state with its Mexican culture and her meeting with families who prepare traditional foods. All Southwest states present plus Illinois, Washington, Michigan, Florida, New York, Oregon, and Idaho.

1720. Tavira, Juan Pablo de (1945–). *A un paso del infierno.* México: Editorial Diana, 1989. 161pp. Memoirs. Period Covered: 1976–1986.

Lawyer author devoted career to penology and since 1984 held positions in prison administration in Mexico City. In first fifty-three pages, "Mi vida en los presidios," concerned with prison reform and recounting experiences among prisoners. Remainder focuses on contacts with six prisoners.

1721. Taylor, Zachary. *Letters of Zachary Taylor, from the Battle-fields of the Mexican War.* New York: Kraus Reprint, 1970 (1908).

Covers 1846–1847 in northern Mexico. Introduction summarizes: battles, revelations of character, obedience to orders, family, politics, and conflicts with other generals. Nothing on terrain, climate, or character of Mexicans. Merits inclusion for status as general and president.

1722. Tello Díaz, Carlos (Dates?). *Apuntes de un brigadista: la cruzada de alfabetización en Nicaragua.* México: Consejo Nacional de Recursos para la Atención de la Juventud, 1985. 99pp. Memoirs. Period Covered: 1980.

One of first works of author of *El exilio: un relato de familia.* In 1980, participated in La Cruzada Nacional de Alfabetización en Nicaragua. Quote suggests both tone and intensity of effort: "...formaba parte de un programa de integración del pueblo en el proceso revolucionario, a través de la educación, la organización y la concientización política" (p.9). Camaradería among committed *brigadistas* and enthusiasm for theories of Paulo Freire. No autobiographies so far on Mexico's literacy campaign.

1723. Tennery, Thomas Douthit. *The Mexican War Diary....* Norman: University of Oklahoma Press, 1970. 117pp.

Runs from June 29, 1846, to July 1, 1847, and covers two fronts: northern Mexico with Matamoros, Camargo, and Tampico, and then Vera Cruz to Mexico City. He inventories climate, landscape, military details, illness and death, and officers such as Gen. Scott. Private Tennery gives us war and Mexico from perspective of foot soldier.

1724. Terrell, Alexander Watkins. *From Texas to Mexico and the Court of Maximilian in 1865.* Dallas: Book Club of Texas, 1933. 94pp.

Disgruntled general from Confederate army made pilgrimage to Mexico to determine possibilities for ex-Confederates. Climax is interview with Maximilian. Inquired about Emperor's accepting Confederates into French army in Mexico. Little known disenchantment with U.S.

1725. Terrones Benítez, Alberto (1887–1981). *Alberto Terrones Benítez: autobiografía de un constituyente.* Durango, DUR: n.p., 1985. 21pp. Memoirs. Period Covered: 1887–1973?

Of modest family in Durango, author became mining engineer and involved in pol-

itics. Signer of 1917 Constitution, he continued revolutionary radicalism into 1920s by
opposing Alvaro Obregón's return and
counter-revolution. Organized peasant union
in Durango.

1726. Theroux, Paul. *The Old Patagonian
Express: By Train through the Americas.*
Boston: Houghton Mifflin, 1979. 404pp.

Probably in mid–1970s, Paul Theroux
experienced travel that informs above title.
Three chapters, Nuevo Laredo to Mexico
City, from here to Vera Cruz, and finally to
Tapachula and Guatemala. No other famous
American writers more condemning of Mex-
ico than Theroux. Natives, foreigners, land-
scape, food, and travel unbearable.
Wonderful prose.

1727. Thomas, Estelle Webb. *Uncertain
Sanctuary: A Story of Mormon Pioneering in
Mexico.* Salt Lake City: Westwater, 1980.
146pp.

Recalls Mormon experience in Chihuahua. Family moved there in 1898 and
lived in four different colonies: Dublán, García, Pacheco, and Morelos. Details much of
life to exodus in 1912.

1728. Thompson, Edward Herbert. *People of the Serpent: Life and Adventure among
the Mayas.* Boston: Houghton Mifflin, 1932.
301pp.

Foreigners or outsiders also interested in
Maya. Prolific self-taught Mayanist and once
owner of Chichén Itzá ruins, Edward Herbert
Thompson was American consul in Yucatan.
Discovered several sites and managed to
dredge treasures from cenote. *People of the
Serpent* part archaeology and part autobiog-
raphy.

1729. Thompson, John Eric Sidney.
Maya Archaeologist. Norman: University of
Oklahoma Press, 1963? 284pp.

Mayanist spent twenty years in Yucatan.
Travel, autobiography, folklore, theorizing as
to purpose of structures, excavations, hybrid
religion, and interaction with natives in read-
able exploration of Maya culture. Knew major
Mayanists of era: Franz Blom, Alfonso Caso,
Thomas Gann, Sylvanus Morely, Ralph Roys,
Herbert Spinden, and Edward Thompson.

1730. Thord-Gray, Ivor. *Gringo Rebel:
Mexico 1913–1914.* Coral Gables, FL: University of Miami Press, 1960. 487pp.

Memoirs of Revolution by Swedish freebooter, who fought for both Villa and Carranza for two years of Revolution. Expert in
artillery, he knew both generals personally.
Involvement ends when he disembarks at
Vera Cruz to fight in WWI.

1731. Tibol, Raquel (1910–1954 Dates of
Kahlo). *Frida Kahlo: crónica,testimonios y
aproximaciones.* México: Ediciones de Cultura Popular, 1977. 159pp. Memoirs. Period
Covered: 1910–1954.

Brief collection (fifty-eight pages) of letters and fragments of diary of Frida Kahlo.
Friend of Kahlo and editor, Tibol enhances
primary sources with chapters on artist's life.
Kahlo focuses on Indian-Spanish-German
heritage, parents, sisters, and on crippling
accident. Family life unidealized.

1732. Tijerina, Reis López (1926–). *Mi
lucha por la tierra.* México: Fondo de Cultura
Económica, 1978. 575pp.

Garrulous but passionate memoirs of
Texas-born Pentecostal minister involved in
human rights. From cooperative settlement
in Arizona, he moved to New Mexico and
dramatized unlawful dispossession of Hispanic lands with his Alianza Federal de Mercedes. Carried plight to Mexico in call to
brotherhood with presidents of Mexico. Only
Mexican-American autobiography published
by major Mexican publishing house.

1733. Tijerina de la Garza, Méntor
(1921–). *Evocaciones del doctor Méntor Tijerina de la Garza.* Monterrey: Universidad
Autónoma de Nuevo León, 1997. 232pp.
Memoirs. Period Covered: 1921–1996.

Nuevoleonés M.D. talks about career:
public school education, medical school,
training in cardiovascular surgery, organization and building of teaching hospital, medical associations, doctors' union, and travels
relevant to medicine. Nothing on personal
life.

1734. Tirado, Thomas Charles (1933
Birth of Celsa). *Celsa's World: Conversations
with a Mexican Peasant Woman.* Tempe: Ari-

zona State University Press, 1991. 119pp. Oral Autobiography. Period Covered: 1937?–1990.

Peasant woman collaborates with U.S. history professor, who studied with Oscar Lewis. Celsa, with several husbands, cohabitants, and natural and adopted children, spent most of life in village of San Antonio in central Mexico. Peasant-view of world gathered and organized by Tirado: "...I tried a straight chronological approach; but found that she was much more interesting in giving me episodic accounts of her life.... I developed an indexing system that allowed me to *flag* each topic with its own unique identifying mark.... Once transcribed...it was...easy to pull together all the *flags* of a particular topic into its own chapter..." (pp.15–16).

1735. Tita (1924–). *Viva mi subdesarrollo: igual raya semenal para cada ser humano.* México: Editorial Tesis Resendiz, 1983. 205pp. Memoirs. Period covered: 1930?–1982.

Strange mixture of autobiography, philosophy, and editorials on Mexico's problems. Crippled bookbinder and scientist who doesn't believe in science, Tita speaks of happy childhood in Mixcoac, world travels, and rejection of own field of science. Semimystical apprehension of world.

1736. Todd Pérez, Luis Eugenio (1935–). *Crónica de una vida en campaña.* Monterrey: Ediciones Castillo, 1999. 286pp. Memoirs. Period Covered: 1998.

Medical doctor, educator, PRI senator (1982–1985), and ambassador to UNESCO, Monterrey author broke with PRI in 1997 to run for governorship of Nuevo León. New party, Partido de Trabajo (PT), defeated. Disappointed author speaks of disillusionment with PRI and unpreparedness of PT.

1737. Todd Pérez, Luis Eugenio (1935–). *Piso 8: un sexenio en la universidad .* Monterrey: Ediciones Castillo, ca.1982 and 1988. 199pp. Memoirs. Period Covered: 1973–1979.

Nuevoleonese M.D. and university professor since 1959 records presidency of la Universidad Autónoma de Nuevo León. Only ten university presidents have memoirs of tenure.

1738. Topete, Jesús (1925?–). *Aventuras de un bracero: relatos de seis meses en Estados Unidos.* México: Editorial AmeXica, 1949. 143pp. Memoirs. Period Covered: 1944.

Literate account of bracero who leaves Guadalajara to work in California. Experiences coincide with WWII when needed Mexican immigrants received humane treatment. Dishwasher, cook, and field hand, he had pleasant experiences. Condemnation of U.S., especially Mexican-Americans, pervades document. Gutierre Tibón's introduction sets tone of *Aventuras.*

1739. Topete, Jesús (1925?–). *Terror en el riel de "El Charro" a Vallejo: páginas de la lucha sindical.* México: Editorial Cosmonauta, 1961. 302pp. Memoirs. Period Covered: 1948–1959.

Polemical on government's fight with organized labor from Avila Camacho in 1940 to regimes of Miguel Alemán and Adolfo Ruiz Cortines. From Guadalajara, Topete lived through union's struggle against "el charrismo," or government's placing corrupt leaders on railroad men's union. Narrator envisions struggle from own perspective and devotes pages to unjust imprisonment.

1740. Toral de León, María (1865–1955). *Memorias de María Toral de De León, madre de José De León Toral.* México: Editorial Tradición, 1972. 143pp. Memoirs. Period Covered: 1888?–1929.

Mother of assassin of Obregón in key moments of life. Psychic powers: apparition of dead mother and prescience of son's assassination of Obregón. Few other facets illuminate tragedy of José. Narrates in third person.

1741. Toro, Alfonso (1567–1596 Dates of Luis de Carvajal). *La familia Carvajal, v.2.* México: Patria, 1944. pp.315–350. Trans: *The Enlightened: The Writings of Luis de Carvajal, El Mozo.* English edition by Seymour B. Liebman. Coral Gables, FL: University of Miami Press, 1967.

Appendix of second volume study (1944) has autobiography of Luis de Carvajal, relapsed Jew killed by Inquisition. Only Jewish memoirs of colonial Mexico. As young adult, Carvajal emigrated from Spain to Nuevo León. Something of Jewish life and sprinkled with religious and mystical terminology.

1742. Torre, Gerardo de la (1938–). *De cuerpo entero: Gerardo de la Torre*. México: Ediciones Corunda, 1990. 70pp. Memoirs. Period Covered: 1953–1990.

Short story writer and novelist outlines basics of life: petroleum worker, Marxist, baseball fan, and father. Recalls past and intercalates scenes from present in efforts to send his son to join estranged mother in Cuba.

1743. Torre, Nemesia de la (1955–). *¡Júzgueme!* N.p.: Impresos González, 1998. 165pp. Memoirs. Period Covered: 1935–1978.

In brief forty-three-year time period, narration touches upon four generations of Yucatecan family. Central character, Nemesia, with few opportunities, survives both in Yucatan and in California. Mother of three children and victim of alcoholic husband and lovers, she manages to find a better life in the U.S. Cunning and determination ameliorate some of her sufferings and intra-family intrigues. One of few autobiographies of a Mayan woman.

1744. Torre Blanco, José. *Unos de tantos: un médico republicano español refugiado en México*. México: Colección Málaga, 1976. 386pp.

Spanish immigrant doctor, interested in obstetrics, writes of career in adopted country. One-eighth of book dedicated to Mexico, where he exercised profession and became celebrated in field. Arriving in 1940, he was president of Centro Republicano Español and also belonged to Junta Español de Liberación. Antifranquista, he reveals Mexico's anti–Franco and pro–Republican stance.

1745. Torrentera, Guadalupe (1931–). *Un gran amor*. México: Editorial Diana, 1991. 143pp. Interview. Period Covered: 1931–1988?

Estela Avila interviews dancer who eventually married singer and actor Pedro Infante. Actor/husband takes over as main topic.

1746. Torres, Carmelo (1927–). *Audacia*. Hialeah, FL: Distribuido por Estudios Televisivos Internacionales, 1991. 266pp. Memoirs. Period Covered: 1927–1989.

Born to middle-class family in Jalisco, Torres traveling salesman and bullfighter. Memoirs/scrapbook consist of training, practice of profession outside of Mexico, and restless desire for travel. Illustrated by press clippings, posters, and photographs.

1747. Torres, Licha (Dates?). *Yo soy testigo*. Chihuahua, CHH: Editorial Camino, 1983? 73pp. Memoirs. Period Covered: 1972.

Twentieth century confessions of born-again Christian. From humble background, she rediscovered Christ and experienced visions and small miracles. Christ-centered woman notes only what relates to religion.

1748. Torres, Olga Beatriz (Dates?). *Memorias de mi viaje= Recollections of My Trip*. Translated by Juanita Luna Lawhn. Albuquerque: University of New Mexico Press, 1994 (1918). 142pp. Memoirs. Period Covered: 1914.

Serialized in 1918 in *El Paso del Norte*, *Memorias* now in book form. Translator Lawhn edited and wrote introductory context for understanding Torres's comments. Member of generation of El México de Afuera, Torres traveled from Vera Cruz to Texas City, Houston, and El Paso. Letters to Aunt Ciria note architecture, social class, race, language, and Mexican-Americans.

1749. Torres Bodet, Jaime (1902–1974). *Años contra el tiempo*. México: Editorial Porrúa, 1981. 246pp. Memoirs. Period Covered: 1943–1946?

First of four-volumes. Describes experiences as secretary of public education under President Avila Camacho: inexpensive editions of classics, reform of teacher training program, visits to rural schools, etc. Interesting for narrative flow and Torres Bodet's circle of luminaries, memoirs inferior to *Tiempo de arena*, which has more reflection and stylistic care in volume on childhood.

1750. Torres Bodet, Jaime (1902–1974). *El desierto internacional: memorias*. México: Editorial Porrúa, 1971. 442pp. Memoirs. Period Covered: 1948–1952.

Incorporates four years as head of UNESCO. Although position axial to memoirs, he includes many peripheral items:

travel, meetings with writers, comments on art, and honors. Personalizes external themes. With keenness and vivacity, decisively sketches each individual.

1751. Torres Bodet, Jaime (1902–1974). *Equinoccio.* México: Editorial Porrúa, 1974. 360pp. Memoirs. Period Covered: 1931–1943.

Fifth book completes gap between appearance of *Tiempo de arena* and *Años contra el tiempo.* Again centers on career in foreign relations: Madrid, Paris, Argentina, Belgium, and return to Mexico and WWII. Interesting because of acquaintance with important people, *Equinoccio* satisfies as memoirs.

1752. Torres Bodet, Jaime (1902–1974). *Tiempo de arena.* México: Fondo de Cultura Económica, 1955. 349pp. Autobiography Proper. Period Covered: 1904?–1929.

Although ends in 1929, first volume of several projected works. *Tiempo* shows formation of man of letters from earliest moments, compatibility with parents, early interest in reading and critiquing, associates with cognate interests, and formation of integrated human being. Tangential chapters that analyze art suggest development of poet.

1753. Torres Bodet, Jaime (1902–1974). *La tierra prometida.* México: Editorial Porrúa, 1972. 469pp. Memoirs. Period Covered: 1953–1964.

In fifth volume of memoirs sets forth years as secretary of education. Under President López Mateos, originated plans for inexpensive editions of classics and constructed classrooms. Attempted to make *normalistas* teach in provinces. Describes literary criticism, *Tres inventores de realidad*, and years in France in diplomatic corps. Sketches international personalities. Never negative, he either praises colleagues or is neutral. Well-written but inferior to *Tiempo de arena* in style and in self-imaging.

1754. Torres Bodet, Jaime (1902–1974). *La victoria sin alas: memorias.* México: Editorial Porrúa, 1970. 219pp. Memoirs. Period Covered: 1946–1948.

Memoirs during directorship of UNESCO precede *El desierto internacional.*

Recounts activities as secretary of state and Cold War during 1946–1948. Victory, flightless after WWII, prompted title. Incidents include Truman's visit to Mexico, Alemán's visit to U.S., UNESCO, Bogotazo, etc. Compassionate and pessimistic about humanity. Describes famous with rapid pen strokes. Volume satisfies less than *El desierto internacional* because of fewer intimacies and fewer interesting personalities.

1755. Torres Ladrón de Guevara, Xavier (Dates?). *Un ladrón en el Cabañas: anecdotario.* Guadalajara: Impreform Gráfica, 1997. 197pp. Memoirs. Period Covered: 1983–1985.

Art historian of colonial period to twentieth century, author accepted position as collaborator of cultural projects at Hospicio Cabañas. With humor and insight, relates twelve-year tenure in chapters on Jalisco art, exhibitions, administrators, Lupe Marín, José Clemente Orozco, etc.

1756. Torres Quiñones, Agustín (1925–). *Una vida, una época.* Culiacán, SIN: El Autor, 2003, 172pp. Genre: Oral Autobiography. Period Covered: 1925–2000?

Self-made man has worked since he was six years old. Only as adult was he able to complete law degree. Entire life in Sinaloa as active member and leader of FTB (Federación de Trabajadores del Estado de Sinaloa). As a politician he worked in PRM (Partido de la Revolución Mexicana) and under its new name PRI on executive board. Successful labor leader and politician at state level.

1757. Torres Rodríguez, Victoria (Dates?). "Escuela Artículo 123: de los campos de Petróleos Mexicanos, 1941–1945." En *Los maestros y la cultura nacional, 1920–1952, v.1. Norte.* México: Museo Nacional de Culturas Populares, 1987. Pp.143–171. Memoirs. Period Covered: 1941–1945.

Teacher after Revolution tries to fulfill duties in rural Vera Cruz oil fields. Bureaucratic misassignment and bad conditions mandate appointment to another school. Suggests commitment to certification and to variety of rural schools plus importance of political connections.

1758. Torres Vázquez, Nicolás (1910–). *Mis recuerdos del Mariachi Vargas de Tecalitlán (1920–1935): fragmentos de mi autobiografía.* California?: El Autor, ca.1991. 17pp. Memoirs. Period Covered: 1926–1935.

Excerpted and printed from unpublished autobiography. From poor family in Jalisco, he learned to play violin. Joining mariachi, traveled to Tuxpan, Tamanzila, Ciudad Guzmán, and Ensenada. In 1933, group journeyed to Mexico City and performed in Plaza Garibaldi, at Radio XEB, and in film, *Así es mi tierra.* Broke up in 1939. Bilingual edition.

1759. Torrescano, María del Carmen (1925–). *Mi vida.* México: EDAMEX, 1992. 344pp. Memoirs. Period Covered: 1925–1990?

Horatio Alger story *a la mexicana.* Illegitimate and in poverty, rose to success with beauty salons and psychotherapy. Untrained, married young and with family, she overcame obstacles.

1760. Torri (Maynes), Julio (1889–1970). "Epistolario." En *Diálogos de los libros*; compilador, Serge I. Zaitzeff. México: Fondo de Cultura Económica, 1980. 82pp. Letters. Period Covered: 1910–1959.

Writer, librarian, and professor for fifty-one years at UNAM sustained sporadic fifty-year correspondence with fellow *ateneísta* Alfonso Reyes. Both, mutual admirers and supporters, wrote autobiographical letters: moods, teaching, writing, friendships, bureaucratic obligations, and commonplace activities to earn living. Fifteen of letters from Reyes.

1761. Torri (Maynes), Julio (1889–1970). "Epistolario Julio Torri-Pedro Henríquez Ureña." En *El arte de Julio Torri* by Serge I. Zaitzeff. México: Editorial Oasis, 1983. Pp.117–150. Letters. Period Covered: 1911–1921.

Thirty letters, sixteen from Torri and fourteen from PHU, written between 1911–1921. Torri-PHU relationship allowed former to be honest about friendship and career. Writer, teacher, and intellectual, Torri reached low point in career during correspondence. Speaks of inability to earn living. Topic of friendship concerns Torri, who

regrets distancing of Antonio Castro Leal. Letters suggest nothing of Torri's successes mentioned in recent reference book: member of Ateneo de la Juventud, founder and head of Departamento de Bibliotecas, and excellent prose writer.

1762. Torri (Maynes), Julio (1889–1970). *Epistolarios.* México: UNAM, Coordinación de Humanidades, 1995. 511pp. Letters. Period Covered: 1910–1959.

Atenista influenced intellectual life both through writings and positions. Note category of correspondents: Alfonso Reyes, 1910–1959; Pedro Henríquez Ureña, 1911–1921; José Vasconcelos, 1917–1945; Rafael Cabrera, 1919–1925; and Xavier Icaza, 1916–1920. Twenty-one other literati in index. Reyes most voluminous. Most harmonious relationship with Pedro Henríquez Ureña. Frendship and intellectual activities pervasive. Edited by Serge I. Zaitzeff.

1763. Torriente, Loló de la (1886–1957 Dates of Diego Rivera). *Memoria y razón de Diego Rivera.* México: Editorial Renacimiento, 1959. 354pp. Oral Autobiography. Period Covered: 1886–1957.

Cuban Loló de la Torriente, interviewing Diego from 1944 to 1953, produced first oral autobiography of artist. She carefully attests to conception of work and process of realization. Confesses role not only as prompter but also editor. Diego's entire life here. Most complete of four Rivera autobiographies.

1764. Toscano, Salvador (1872–1947). *Correspondencia de Salvador Toscano, 1900–1911.* México: Instituto Mexicano de Cinematográfico, 1996. 72pp. Letters. Period Covered: 1900–1911.

Pioneer filmmaker and owner of movie theaters wrote sixty-one letters to mother. Dutiful son had theater in Mexico City and also wandered to other places to show films: Zamora, Teziutlán, Pachuca, Vera Cruz, Jalapa, Guadalajara, and Atilxco. Comments on problems and successes of films in each city.

1765. Toussaint, Manuel (1890–1955). *De casa a casa: correspondencia entre Manuel*

Toussaint y Alfonso Reyes. México: El Colegio Nacional, 1990. 110pp. Letters. Period Covered: 1917–1955.

Art historian wrote letters to Reyes between 1917 to 1922, and 1937 to 1955. Fifty-four letters, thirty-four from Toussaint and postmarked either Europe or Mexico, and twenty from Reyes, postmarked Buenos Aires or Mexico. Most interesting letters fall in 1917 to 1922 time frame. "In the letters that Toussaint sends regularly to Reyes we see an excellent correspondent who not only gives vivid impressions but also reveals himself" (p.12). Both self and professional life emerge.

1766. Toussaint, Manuel (1890–1955). *Viajes alucinados: rincones de España.* México: Editorial Cultura, 1924. 176pp. Memoirs. Period Covered: 1921.

Expert in colonial art and founder of Institute of Aesthetics Research journeyed to Spain and recorded impressions. In thirty-five chapters leaves portions of self but mostly focuses on tourist subjects. Given his love for beautiful, one of better travel writers.

1767. Townsend, Mary Ashley; Ralph Lee Woodward. *Here and There in Mexico: The Travel Writings of Mary Ashley Townsend.* Tuscaloosa: University of Alabama Press, 2001. 332pp.

In some ways this title ranks with *Life in Mexico* by Fanny Calderón de la Barca. Both upper class women enjoyed privileges in Mexico and chronicled adventures and details in much-cultivated form of nineteenth century travel writing. Educated Townsend journeyed several times to Mexico in last decades of nineteenth century. Familiar with Jalapa, Orizaba, Puebla, Cholula, and Mexico City, and observer of manners and customs. Social conscience reflected in comments on class, status of women, and condition of Indian.

1768. Tree, Isabella. *Sliced Iguana: Travels in Unknown Mexico.* London: Hamish Hamilton, 2001. 316pp.

Britsh woman observes and writes about Huicholes in just one of six locales that she visits and interprets. Chapter on Huicholes in Jalisco and Nayarit one of strongest. Discusses peyote.

1769. Trejo, Lydia (1906–1970). *Lo que vi en España: Episodios de la Guerra.* México: Editorial Polis, 1940. 140pp. Memoirs. Period Covered: 1936–1939.

Journalist went to Spain as secretary of Mexican consul. Leftist Trejo, disenchanted with Communist Party, classified Dolores Ibarruri (La Pasionaria) a fraud. With feelings for working classes and early feminist, author always in conflict with comrades of like sympathies. Personality emerges in visits to France and Civil War Spain.

1770. Trevi, Gloria (1970–). *Gloria.* México: Planeta, 2002. 267pp. Memoirs. Period Covered: 1986–2001.

Singer, film and TV star reveals life as entertainer. More than most starlets in autobiography, has to defend career and even freedom. She and manager, Sergio Andrade, accused of kidnapping, rape, and corruption of minors. Victimized Aline in *Mi despertar* and Karina Yapor in *Revalaciones* give their side of story. Trevi currently (2003) imprisoned in Brazil.

1771. Treviño, Alejandro (1867–?). *Cincuenta años en el ministerio.* El Paso, TX: Casa Bautista de Publicaciones, 1937. 258pp. Memoirs. Period Covered: 1883–1937.

Treviño and family became Baptists in 1869 in Apodaca, Nuevo León. Losing father, he moved to Monterrey in 1875 and for fifty years served church. Traces history of Baptist church in Nuevo León and Saltillo and mentions two influential foreigners: Santiago Hickey and Tomás Westrup. More than evangelization, movement included education, quarrels with Catholic priests, and international ties with Baptists in U.S., England, and Panama. Story of poor and closely-knit family. Descriptions of 1903 yellow fever and 1909 floods in Monterrey. One of best autobiographies of Protestant Mexicans.

1772. Treviño, Elizabeth Borton de. *My Heart Lies South: The Story of My Mexican Marriage.* New York: Crowell, 1953. 248pp.

American lived in Monterrey and wrote with delightful recall. Journalist Borton married young Regiomontaño from large patriarchal family. She adjusted to Monterrey and to Mexican ways. View of family, mourning

period for death, rearing of children, acceptance of macho interpretation of women, and
reasons for suffering contrast to Berkeley-
educated author's background.

1773. Treviño, Elizabeth Borton de.
Where the Heart Is. Garden City, NY: Doubleday, 1962. 286pp.

Treviño continues saga of *My Heart Lies
South* (1953). Scenario not Monterrey but
capital with same affection for Mexico of
American-born journalist married to Mexican. *Where the Heart Is* lacks impact and
intensity of discovery of first work. Adjustments to new environment continue but
always with justification of ways of adopted
country. Growing children, work, friendships, extended family, home, thieves,
tourists, and neighbors perceived by sympathetic and humorous narrator. Best forum for
Mexico in two chapters: "Mucha Mujer, Muy
Macho" and "God Willing."

1774. Treviño, Jacinto B. (1883–1971).
Entrevista en James W. Wilkie y Edna
Monzón Wilkie's *Frente a la Revolución mexicana: 17 protagonists de la etapa constructiva,*
v.3. México: Universidad Autónoma Metropolitana, 2002. Pp.313–368. Interview. Period
Covered: 1883–1958.

Politician and general in Revolution
talks some of personal life: birth in Coahuila,
hacienda converted to *ejido*, military school,
and strategist for battle that defeated Pancho
Villa. Maderista in Revolution, he also sided
with Carranza and later Obregón. Revealing
incident is refusal to condemn Lucio Blanco
for Obregón. Also talks about formation of
PARM (Partido Auténtico de la Revolución
Mexicana). Colorful anecdote about feud
with José Alessio Robles.

1775. Treviño, Jacinto B. (1883–1971).
Memorias. 2ed. México: Editorial Orión, 1961.
284pp. Memoirs. Period Covered: 1893–1960?

Career military officer, who at young age
rose to rank of general, fought on side of
Madero and Carranza and against Huerta.
Secretary of war and navy and chief of military operations in Chihuahua.

1776. Treviño, José Guadalupe (1881–
1953). *Monseñor Martínez, Semblanza de su*
vida interior. Madrid: Ediciones Studium,
1959. 290pp. Trans: *The Spiritual Life of
Archbishop Martínez.* Translated by Sister
Mary St. Danviel Tarrant. St Louis: Herder
Book, 1966. Memoirs. Period Covered: 1881–?

By its nature, biography of archbishop
and primate shares many aspects of autobiography. Contemporary mystic, Monseñor
Martínez properly follows tradition of Spanish mysticism in quoted paragraphs.

1777. Treviño, Luis Carlos (1916–?). *Luis
Carlos Treviño: la vida de un hombre enam-
orado de un micrófono: XEX probando.* Monterrey: Ediciones 1992. 115pp. Memoirs.
Period Covered: 1916–1992?

Radio announcer quickly covers childhood in Monterrey, interest in film, desire to
be announcer, career in Monterrey and in
Ciudad Juárez, marriage, and television.

1778. Treviño, Tomás D. (1935–).
Relatos de cacería en México. Monterrey:
Castillo, 1986. 135pp. Memoirs. Period Cov-
ered: 1955–1985.

For twenty-five years author has hunted
in San Luis Potosí, Tamaulipas, Coahuila,
and Nuevo León. Each chapter told as story
locating incident, place, companions, and
game.

1779. Treviño Carranza, Celia (1912–?).
Mi atormentada vida. México: Editorial Jus,
1958. 622pp. Autobiography Proper. Period
Covered: 1912–1956?

Middle generation of musical dynasty
recounts life from birth in Monterrey, Nuevo
León, to death of daughter. Successful violinist made international concert tours. Married
several times, was main economic support of
mother and daughter. Emotional retelling of
external life of independent and talented
woman.

1780. Trilling, Susana. *Seasons of My
Heart: A Culinary Journey through Oaxaca,
Mexico.* New York: Ballantine Books, 1999.
369pp.

Of excellent cookbooks on Mexico published in late twentieth century, above title
has a place. Well-illustrated material on beige
paper arranged into twelve sections relating
to various regions in Oaxaca. Autobiography

scattered in introduction to each region.

1781. Trueheart, James L.; Frederick C. Chabot. *The Perote Prisoners.* San Antonio: Naylor, 1934. 344pp.

Author, Texan from San Antonio, taken prisoner by Mexicans under Gen. Adrián Woll in 1842. Along with other prisoners marched through Mexico and incarcerated in Perote, Vera Cruz. Diary over years 1842 to 1844. In last year prisoners released and embark from Vera Cruz for New Orleans. Diarist comments on verifiable and withholds own emotions. Weather, marching, working, and chain gangs.

1782. Trujillo Muñoz, Gabriel (1958–). *Mexicali: crónicas de infancia.* Mexicali: Universidad Autónoma de Baja California, 1990. 93pp. Memoirs. Period Covered: 1964?–1990?

Mexicali divulges personality in "insignificant" moments to young narrator, son of migrants to border city. Neighborhoods, brewery, kite flying, films, school, border, birds, and impingement of international world serve as themes of brief but sculpted chronicles.

1783. T'Serstevens, A. *Mexico: A Three-Storyed Land.* Indianapolis: Bobbs-Merrill, 1962. 368pp.

T'Serstevens does more than guidebook. Writes well but opinionated. Joy of adventuring with cranky Frenchman in contradicting statements such as difficulty of finding good meal in Mexico or mestizos can be nuanced into three groups. Title relates to altitudes, stages of civilization, and peoples.

1784. Tully, Brock. *Coming Together: A 10,000 Mile Bicycle Journey.* West Vancouver, BC: Tully, 1989 (1972). 128pp.

Bicycling through Mexico unheard of. Yet Tully started tour in Vancouver, pedaled through U.S., and entered Mexico through Laredo. Alone and pedaling 100 miles per day, he covered much: north, central, west and east coasts, to extremes and Tehuantepec, and exited through Nogales, Sonora. Interviewed by Mexican TV, Tully, on sparse budget, cheered on by natives often hospitable.

1785. Tuñón, Julia (1904–1986 Dates of Fernández). *En su propio espejo: entrevista con Emilio "El Indio" Fernández.* Iztapalpa: Universidad Autónoma Metropolitana, 1988. 116pp. Oral Autobiography. Period Covered: 1904–1979.

Fernández began film career in U.S. during exile. In Mexico, directed and acted in several film classics: *Janitzio, María Candelaria, La perla,* and *La red.* While Tuñón in own words gives most of information, her subject, "El Indio" provides complementary data in italics. Book resulted from twenty hours of tapes.

1786. Turner, Henry Smith; Stephen Watts Kearny; Dwight Lancelot Clarke. *The Original Journals of Henry Smith Turner with Stephen Watts Kearny to New Mexico and California,* Norman: University of Oklahoma Press, 1966. 173pp.

Author most introspective and religious in autobiography of Mexican-American War. A West Point graduate, he was captain in First Dragoons in Mexican War. In California campaign he was brevetted major. In controversy between Kearny and Stockton, Turner on side of former. Letters run from June 30, 1846, to May 1, 1847.

1787. Turner, J. Neville. *Football: The Pain and the Pleasure, the World Cup Diaries of J. Neville Turner.* Upper Ferntree Gully, Victoria, Australia: Rex Thompson and Family, 1999. 202pp.

"I have been fortunate enough to attend four World Cups: Mexico (1986), Italy (1990), and U.S. (1994), and France (1998). In each case I traveled as an individual without advance tickets. Logistics of traveling from city to city and haggling for tickets occupied a great part of my diary entries-and in retrospect, added to the exhilaration" (p.5). Introductory sentence explains book. Englishman comments on sports and contacts with Mexicans and their culture. Even enrolled in a course on Golden Age literature.

1788. Turner, Timothy Gilman. *Bullets, Bottles, and Gardenias.* Dallas, TX: Southwest, 1935. 258pp.

Captures essence of reporter's forays into Mexico during first year of Revolution in El Paso/Juárez and other parts of North. Meets Madero, Orozco, Thord-Gray, Garibaldi, Carranza, Villa, Obregón, and Adolfo de la Huerta. "Romantic adventure… is the interplay of human elements more than the mechanical ones, the colors, the sounds, the smells, the hot rhythm of life itself" (p.vii). Style and content follow this definition.

1789. Turrent Rozas, Eduardo (1892–1974). *Añoranzas.* México, 1948. 122pp. Memoirs. Period Covered: 1898–1906?

As in *Veracruz de mis recuerdos*, Turrent Rozas extracts happy memories from past: Calería, Vera Cruz and childhood, Indian grandmother, pet dog, religious celebrations, primary school, and portraits of regional personalities. Author of novels and poems.

1790. Turrent Rozas, Eduardo (1892–1974). *Catemaco: retablos i recuerdos.* México: Editorial Veracruz, 1967. 178pp. Memoirs. Period Covered: 1898?–1906?

Collection of *relatos* forms continuous memoir of childhood in native Vera Cruz. Rural Mexico and autobiography combine in images of hunting, chickens, July celebrations, local authorities, washerwomen, and more. Nostalgia prevails over analysis.

1791. Turrent Rozas, Eduardo (1892–1974). *Veracruz de mis recuerdos.* México, 1953. 166pp. Memoirs. Period Covered: 1907–1910.

Self-taught writer nostalgically recalls Porfirian Vera Cruz, home of family and early employment. Like others of his generation, unaware of social problems of Porfiriato.

1792. Tyler, Daniel. *A Concise History of the Mormon Battalion in the Mexican War: 1846–1847.* Grantsville, UT: LDS Archive, 1881. 376pp.

Mustered in Nauvoo, Illinois, Mormon battalion marched through New Mexico, Arizona, and on to California, all Mexican territory. Not much on Mexico but much on trials of journey. Santa Fe, Tucson, San Diego, and Los Angeles major cities.

1793. Underhill, Ruth (1875? Birth of María Chona). *The Autobiography of a*

Papago Woman. Millwood, NY: Kraus Reprint, 1974 (1936). 64pp. Trans: *Biografía de una mujer pápago.* Traducción de Bárbara Dahlgren-Jordán. México: Sep Setentas, 1975. Oral Autobiography. Period Covered: 1881–1931?

Anthropological study in 1936 of culture of Papago Indians through Chona. Working through interpreter, Underhill did not balance culture and personality of Indians of Mexican Arizona border. Chon is individual, but document records Papago culture: food, hunting, warring, puberty rites, marriage, and singing. Underhill confesses insurmountable barriers in autobiographies of this nature: "Indian narrative style involves a repetition and a dwelling on unimportant details which confuse the White reader and make it difficult for him to follow the story" (p.3).

1794. Urbina, Luis Gonzaga (1864–1934). *Estampas de viaje: España en los días de la guerra.* Madrid: Biblioteca Ariel, 1920. 303pp. Memoirs. Period Covered: 1916.

In 1916, Urbina correspondent in Madrid for *El Heraldo de Cuba.* Chapters comprise separate scenes of Spain tied together by place and mood. Capturing Spain and war sentiment, he leaves autobiographical impressions in views of Cádiz, Barcelona, Madrid, and Toledo. Much more of author revealed in *Hombres y libros.*

1795. Urbina, Luis Gonzaga (1864–1934). *Hombres y libros.* México: El Libro Francés, 1923. 298pp. Memoirs. Period Covered: 1890?–1930?

Journalist, poet, and essayist leaves fragmented memoir in images and recollections of men of letters. In recording lives of best contemporaries, Urbina reveals personality. Collective reading of highly subjective word portraits manifests Urbina's intellectual personality.

1796. Urquiza, Concha (1910–1945). *Obras: poemas y prosas*; edición y prólogo de Gabriel Méndez Plancarte. 2ed. México: Editorial Jus, 1977 (1946). 481pp. Diary. Period Covered: 1937–1940.

Poet led troubled existence due to conflict between God's expectations and her inability to measure up to them. Within tradition of Spanish mysticism, her writings reflect a soul in love with Creator and yet unworthy of Him. Two sections of autobiographical writings: "Páginas epistolares" and "Páginas del diario." Former occasionally treats mundane matters; latter distills religious feelings in clearer prose style.

1797. Urquizo, Francisco Luis (1891–1969). *Ahora charlemos.* México, 1949. 225pp. Memoirs. Period Covered: 1913?–?

Carrancista, soldier, and prolific autobiographer sporadically reveals self in informal and loosely strung memoirs. To paraphrase introduction, these are *charlas de sobremesa* around imaginary table with guests who generally broach Urquizo's themes: old revolutionaries, military men, writers, *paisanos* (*Coahuilenses*), artists, colleagues, and old friends. Selections alternate between autobiographical and anecdotal.

1798. Urquizo, Francisco Luis (1891–1969). *De la vida militar mexicana.* México: Herrero Hermanos Sucesores, 1930. 234pp. Memoirs. Period Covered: 1920?

In contrast to other autobiographical works, *De la Vida militar mexicana* is encapsulated and narrated with chronological events each forming a short story. Twenty-three incidents, structured to create tension, lead to conclusion. Military experience (his adoration of Carranza) primary source for memoirs.

1799. Urquizo, Francisco Luis (1891–1969). *Madrid de los años veinte.* México: Costa-Amic, 1961. 178pp. Memoirs. Period Covered: 1920s.

Contrast to author's six military autobiographies for tranquil time in life of former general in Carranza's army. Describes Madrid and individualizes environment with personal experiences. Most delightful example of prolific memoirist.

1800. Urquizo, Francisco Luis (1891–1969). *Memorias de campaña de subteniente a general.* México: Fondo de Cultura Económica, 1971. 157pp. Autobiography/Novel. Period Covered: 1913–1920.

Autobiographical novel of wanderings of young Urquizo through northern Mexico on side of Maderistas or Carrancistas. Sufficient detail to give idea of violence and rapine of Revolution. Direct involvement in action and use of first person narration reinforce perspective. Confusion of genres caused by circularity of work and interjection of two semi-fictional characters, el tío Bernardo and soldadera Belén, who summarize action and lend comic relief.

1801. Urquizo, Francisco Luis (1891–1969). *México, Claxcalantongo, mayo de 1920.* 2ed. México: Editorial Cultural, 1943 (1932). 179pp. Memoirs. Period Covered: 1920.

More Revolution by idolater of Carranza. Novelist and memoirist has eye for trenchant detail. Major chapter concerns death of Carranza.

1802. Urquizo, Francisco Luis (1891–1969). *Páginas de la Revolución.* México, 1956. 274pp. Memoirs. Period Covered: 1910–1920.

Continues memoirs. Divided into three parts: triumph of Madero to Constitution of 1917, brief biography of Carranza, and constitutional government until death of Carranza. Idolizing latter, Urquizo personalizes more by own presence than do contemporaries. Value for details and for occasional subjective paragraphs.

1803. Urquizo, Francisco Luis (1891–1969). *"Recuerdo que...": Visiones de la Revolución.* México: Ediciones Botas, 1934, 2 v. Memoirs. Period Covered: 1910–1914.

Maderista officer from Coahuila, who became general in Carranza's forces, experienced Revolution in northern Mexico with references to Torreón, Chihuahua, Saltillo, Sonora, and border. Little of personal life or feelings. No overall plan for book, ideological approach to Revolution or tracing of anti–Federalist campaign in North. Chapters, linked by chronological style and author's presence, could be read separately. Value in detail and anecdote encapsulated in each chapter.

1804. Urquizo, Francisco Luis (1891–1969). *3 de Diana.* México: Publicaciones Mundiales, 1947. 417pp. Memoirs. Period Covered: 1939–1943?

Military figure in presidency of Avila

Camacho. Selected to represent Mexico in missions to U.S. and Central America. Reveals little of self, excluding childhood, family, and education, but some personality emerges in attitude and during incidents. Adamant about punishment of captain who tried to cause revolt in army. Unable or unwilling to see pernicious side of *caudillismo*. Evocation of pro-military attitude. Indicates Mexico's support of U.S. during 1940's war fervor. *3 de Diana* refers to one movement in reveille that signals success.

1805. Urrea, José (1797–1849). *Diario de las operaciones militares....* Victoria, DUR: Imprenta de Gobierno, 1838. 136pp. Diary. Period Covered: 1836–1937.

Member of expedition against Texas in 1836, Urrea fought at Alamo, Goliad, San Patricio, and San Antonio. Writes of Texas campaign and conflict with Vicente Filisola. Vilified by Filisola, he attempts to vindicate self. Present at every moment in first person singular. Succinct account with narrative value. Vicente Filisola also wrote about episode in *Memorias para la historia de la guerra de Tejas*. (1849).

1806. Urrea, Luis Alberto (1953?–). *Across the Wire: Life and Hard Times on the Mexican Border.* New York: Anchor Books, 1993. 190pp. Memoirs. Period Covered: 1978–1992.

Tijuana-born author and Baptist missionary writes of desperate living conditions on Mexican side of border near San Diego. Product of both sides of border, records anecdotes of encounters with Mexican personalities as well as their poverty and suffering. Final pages on author's family.

1807. Urrea, Luis Alberto (1953?–). *By the Lake of Sleeping Children: The Secret Life of the Mexican Border.* New York: Anchor Books, 1996. 187pp. Memoirs. Period Covered: 1990–1996?

Complementary addition to *Across the Wire* especially in relation to poverty. After autobiographical introduction, he tours garbage dump of Tijuana to meet some of its personalities of all ages. Urrea had Mexican father and American mother.

1808. Urrea, Luis Alberto (1953?–). *Nobody's Son: Notes from an American Life.* Tucson: University of Arizona Press, 1998. 188pp. Memoirs. Period Covered: 1953?–1975?

Third and most intimate autobiography of Tijuana-born and based Urrea. Childhood and parents, American-born mother, and Mexican father. Poverty, quarreling parents, parochial school education, and border predominate in excoriating detail and revelation. First border autobiography with infusion of magical realism.

1809. Urrea de Figueroa, Otilia (1890?–?). *My Youth in Alamos: La ciudad de los portales: With a Walking Tour of the Town.* Glendale, CA: Dolisa Publications, 1983. 74pp. Memoirs. Period Covered: 1895?–1918.

From upper class in Alamos, Sonora (mining center in northwest Mexico), she led idyllic life before Revolution. Combines personal experience with history and environment. Revolution forces family to Los Angeles, California.

1810. Urueta, Margarita (1913–?). *El juicio de mis tiempos.* México: Editorial Porrúa, 1998. 394pp. Memoirs. Period Covered: 1913–1992.

Daughter of orator Jesús Urueta, travel and residence in U.S. and Europe, marriage to diplomat, fiction writer, *vanguardista* playwright, and owner/operator of theater, Urueta has cosmopolitan existence. Little idealization of family life along with awareness of historical moment make unusual document.

1811. Urzáiz Jiménez, Carlos (1916?–). *Crónicas de un estudiante de medicina.* Mérida: Maldonado Editores, 1983. 171pp. Memoirs. Period Covered: 1938–1945.

Dissatisfied with memoirs composed as young man, doctor modifies them into less brutal document. Account of medical school, teachers, colleagues, and practice in Yucatan shares characteristics with novel.

1812. Usigli, Rudolfo (1905–1979). *Conversaciones y encuentros: Bernard Shaw, Lenormand, Jean Cocteau, Clifford Odets, Andre Breton, Elmer Rice, Paul Muni, B. Traven, T.S. Eliot.* México: Organización Editorial

Novaro, 1974. 164pp. Memoirs. Period Covered: 1944–1969.

Twentieth century dramatist presents self through contacts with other celebrities. Bernard Shaw recognizes Usigli's greatness before Mexico does in by far most impressive interview.

1813. Utah State Historical Society and California State University, Fullerton Oral History Program (1895 — Average Birth year of interviewed Mormons). 1976? Unpaged. Interview. Period Covered: 1895?–1971?

Black, Mary Ann Jones (Dates?). *Recolletions of Mexico and Early Blanding, Utah* (1976).

Bradford, Britta (1899–?). *Life in Colonia Diaz, Mexico and Blanding, Utah* (1973).

Burtenshaw, Bernice Mortensen (1897–?). *Mormon Exodus from Mexico to Blanding, Utah* (1974).

Harvey, Charles (1895–?). *Mormon Exodus out of Mexico.* (Southeastern Utah Oral History Program, 1972).

Nielson, Morgan L. (1895–?). *Reminiscences of Life in Old Mexico and Blanding, Utah* (1976).

Antipolygamy laws forced Mormons to immigrate to Mexico after 1885, but Revolution caused return to U.S. in 1912. Five Mexican-born Mormons relate experience of Mexico. Thematically united, brief interviews follow same format in recollections of seventy-five-year-old subjects. Juárez, Sanchón [La Ascensión], Corrales, Dublán, García, Pacheco, and Díaz serve as locales. Prompted by questions, respondents refer more to U.S. than to Mexico. From collective reading of five lives, Mormon culture in Mexico emerges: schooling, Juarez Academy, building of homes, family, and Revolution. Little interaction with Mexicans or use of Spanish language. Topics better expressed in Guy C. Wilson's *Memories.*

1814. Vaca de Corral, R. (Dates?). *¡Soy puro...mexicano! libro primero, las conciencias olvidadas.* México: Costa-Amic, 1976. 140pp. Collective Autobiography. Period Covered: 1976.

With generic pseudonym, author willing to attack political, social, and familial life of country. In brief chapters and with humor, he lists psyche of countrymen.

1815. Vail, Harley. *Mexico, Mayas, and Me.* Lyons, OR: Bethel, 1984. 133pp.

Assembly of God minister, spent twenty-five years in Mexico, 1947 to 1972. Much work in Merida in Bethel Bible Institute. Claims Mexico has 600 congregations of Assembly of God.

1816. Val G., E. Franz (1898?–1985 Dates of Sabina). *Conversaciones con María Sabina y otros curanderos: hongos sagrados.* México: Publicaciones Cruz O., 1986–1990. 170pp. Memoirs. Period Covered: 1972–1985.

From Fernando Benítez's book *Los hongos alucinantes,* author aware of magic mushrooms. Probes hallucinogenic world of Mazatec Indian through conversations with Sabina and experiences hallucinations by testing mushrooms.

1817. Valadés, José C. (1889–1976). *Memorias de un joven rebelde 1a parte: mis confesiones.* México: Universidad Autónoma de Sinaloa, 1985, (1966). 199pp. Autobiography Proper. Period Covered: 1880?–1913.

One of better autobiographers details youth in Mazatlán with sharp portraits of parents and four grandparents. From prosperous family, he sets forth childhood as do few Mexicans and mother's eventual exile to Los Angeles following father's death. Journalist, politician, diplomat, and activist on left also authored several books on Mexican history.

1818. Valadés, José C. (1889–1976). *Memorias de un joven rebelde 1a parte: mis confesiones.* México: Universidad Autónoma de Sinaloa, 1986. 193pp. Memoirs. Period Covered: 1913?–1927.

Grown up and once again in Mexico, he joins Ejército Constitucionalista, attends college, and involves self in leftist organizations. For brief chapters on Revolution and his political activities, memoirs lose intensity of first volume. He excels as autobiographer of youth and family life; as political memoirist, more ordinary.

1819. Valdés Galindo, María Esther (1917?–). "La escuela olvidada." En *Los*

*maestros en la cultura nacional, 1920–1952,
v.3.* México: Museo Nacional de Culturas
Populares, 1987. Pp.155–194. Memoirs. Period
Covered: 1935–1975.

Recently certified and desperate for job,
Valdés Galindo through ruse is assigned to
school for blind. With no preparation to
teach blind, she learns to make tangible what
is obvious for those with sight. In too-short
memoir, compresses forty years of experience
and sympathy.

1820. Valdovinos Garza, José (1899–
1977). *La generación nicolaita de 1913.*
Michoacana, 1959. 43pp. Memoirs. Period
Covered: 1900–1913?

Dedicated to inscribing customs of
native Michoacán, he recalls year of Constitutionalist Revolution (1913). Capturing
emotions of critical year, highlights changes
wrought in venerable academy. Names school
alumni of 1913 generation who later distinguished themselves: Cayetano Andrade,
Manuel Martínez Báez, Antonio Martínez
Báez, Eduardo Villaseñor, and Samuel
Ramos.

1821. Valdovinos Medina, Jovita
(1911–?). *Jovita la cristera: una historia
viviente.* Jalpa, ZAC: Medina, 1995. 155pp.
Memoirs. Period Covered: 1911–1987.

Spent much of life in Zacatecas, but also
lived on Mexican border and in Chicago.
Self-sufficient woman, who engaged in battles, ran bar, worked in laundry, and felt
more comfortable dressed as a man.
Although carries label *Cristera,* autobiography manifests none of convictions of rebels
against Calles from 1926 to 1929. Erodes
stereotypes of Mexican womanhood and
casts doubts on patriarchal system.

1822. Valenzuela, Jesús E. (1856–1911).
Mis recuerdos: manojo de rimas. México:
Conaculta, 2001 (1945). 220pp. Memoirs.
Period Covered: 1873–1898.

From Durango and Chihuahua, Valenzuela was writer and politician. Best known
for inspiring Modernist authors in two
sequeled periodicals, *La revista moderna* and
La revista moderna de México. In brief memoirs, evidences familiarity with writers and
politicians, Enrique C. Creel, Gabino

Barreda, Jesús Urueta, and Ignacio Altamirano among others.

1823. Valenzuela Rodarte, Alberto
(1904–?). *Un mexicano cualquiera; 16 años en
escuelas oficiales, 40 años jesuita.* México: Editorial Jus, 1964. 246pp. Memoirs. Period Covered: 1904–1963.

Negatively compares public school training (1908–1924) with later life in Jesuit Order
(1924–1964). Student both in *preparatorio*
and in medical school, he also taught. As
devout Catholic he makes reader more
knowledgeable of Jesuit life.

1824. Valle-Arizpe, Artemio de
(1888–1961). *Historia de una vocación.* México: Editorial F. Trillas, 1960. 59pp. Memoirs.
Period Covered: 1903–?

Lawyer, diplomat, but mainly writer of
colonial past bore title "Chronicler of Mexico
City." Used formula similar to Ricardo
Palma's *Tradiciones.* He recounts love for
humanities through favorite school subjects,
teachers, books, and encounters with colonial
period. Joy of thought and composition natural sequences to research.

1825. Vargas, Chavela (1919–?). *Y si
quieres saber de mi pasado.* Madrid: Aguilar,
2002. 296pp. Memoirs. Period Covered:
1919–2002.

Major purveyor of Mexican popular culture through song born in Costa Rica. Notes
love for Mexico, lesbianism, career as nightclub singer, recording star during 1940s and
1950s, and bouts with tequila: "Si, amigos
míos, he sido parrandera y borracha" (p.290).
Knows many other celebrities including
Diego Rivera and Frida Kahlo. Exceptional
frankness.

1826. Vargas, Pedro (1908–1989). *Pedro
Vargas: "Una vez nada más."* Con José
Ramón Garmabella. 2ed. México: Ediciones
de Comunicación, 1985 (1984). 399pp. Oral
Autobiography. Period Covered: 1911–1985?

Popular singer of songs by Agustín Lara,
Pedro Vargas chronologically begins career
from obscurity to international fame. Born in
San Miguel de Allende, fled to Mexico City,
and promoted in career by Mario Talavera
and José Mojica. Other chapters highlight

diversity and fame: radio, television, travel, and presidents. Superb for popular culture. Writer Garmabella does not discuss interventions.

1827. Vargas Dulché, Yolanda (1923–1999). *Cristal: recuerdos de una muchacha.* México: Costa-Amic, 1965. 225pp. Memoirs. Period Covered: 1923–1936.

Journalist, scriptwriter for soap operas and films, and cartoonist recreates childhood. For one year, family now separated from father lived in Los Angeles. Memoirs concentrate on author and reactions to problems.

1828. Vargas Saavedra, Luis (1889–1959 Dates of Alfonso Reyes). *Tan de usted: epistolario de Gabriela Mistral con Alfonso Reyes.* Santiago: Ediciones Universidad Católica de Chile, 1990. 240pp. Letters. Period Covered: 1923–1955.

Equally divided between two illustrious correspondents, over 100 letters in collection. Arranged by date and provenance: 1923 to 1939, Mexico and Europe; 1940 to 1945, Brazil, Mexico, Italy, and New York. Communications exude mutual respect and love; suggest friendship strong enough for frankness. Beautifully edited.

1829. Vargas Sánchez, Eduardo (1900–?). "La ciudad de México de 1900 a 1920." En *Mi pueblo durante la Revolución.* México: Instituto Nacional de Antropología, 1985. Pp.151–190. Oral Autobiography. Period Covered: 1900–1920.

Memoirs vivify Revolution. Born in 1900, author lived in Mexico City and evoked *Decena Trágica* and impact on civilian population. Villa and New Mexico enter narration plus two exotic items, Spanish novelist Vicente Blasco Ibáñez and Mexicans' interest in aviation.

1830. Varón Modiano, Alberto (1923–?). *Alberto Varón Modiano: Pláticas con Cristina Gutiérrez Zúñiga [y] Gloria González Tejeda.* Zapopan: Colegio de Jalisco, 1997. 162pp.

One of few oral autobiographies where editors note interferences with text. Guadalajaran Jew Varón Modiano recalls Sephardic background on both sides of family. Education, professional title, and business success

comprise much of document. Focus on Jewish life in this city and conflict/conciliation with Askhenazim.

1831. Vasconcelos, José (1882–1959). *Cartas políticas de José Vasconcelos.* Preambula y notas de Alfonso Taracena. México: Clásica Selecta. Editora Librera, 1959. 312pp. Letters. Period Covered: 1924–1936.

One of best represented in autobiography because of four volumes, he continues to reveal personality in letters to Alfonso Taracena, journalist, short story writer, and novelist. Showing passionate, opinionated, and choleric Vasconcelos, collection complements tomes of autobiography. Themes of letters: aborted political campaign of 1929, exile and survival in Latin America, hatred of U.S., pro–Spanish stance, publication of books (*La tormenta* and *Estética*), and hatred of old enemies. Has documents and replies from Taracena, loyal to volatile hero.

1832. Vasconcelos, José (1882–1959). *El desastre, tercera parte de Ulises Criollo, continuación de La Tormenta.* 3ed. México: Ediciones Botas, 1938. 819pp. Memoirs. Period Covered: 1923–1928.

Role in education most important subject and continuation of *Ulises criollo.* Secretary of public education attempts mass literacy program. Remainder touches on travels to U.S., Europe, and Israel. In final chapter, "La llama del destino," opinionated and polemical author selects self as major combatant against Mexico's enemies.

1833. Vasconcelos, José (1882–1959). *La flama: los de arriba en la Revolución; historia y tragedia.* México: Continental, 1959. 496pp. Memoirs. Period Covered: 1929–1938.

Successor to four-volume memoirs. Mature author opinionated and articulate in presidential elections and in exile. Echoes older themes such as hatred for Dwight Morrow. Ends in year of expropriation of oil under Cárdenas.

1834. Vasconcelos, José (1882–1959). *El proconsulado: cuarta parte de Ulises Criollo.* 2ed. México: Ediciones Botas, 1939. 777pp. Memoirs. Period Covered: 1928–1931.

Ends autobiographical suite in same vigorous prolix style. Candidature for 1929 presidency focuses document. Flaunts suspicion and hatred of Dwight Morrow, *el proconsulado*. Defeated author goes into exile.

1835. Vasconcelos, José (1882–1959). *La tormenta: segunda parte de "Ulises Criollo."* 4ed. México: Ediciones Botas, 1937 (1936). 592pp. Memoirs. Period Covered: 1882–1959.

Continues wanderings: U.S., Mexico, South America, and Europe. Focuses on love for Adriana (Antonieta Rivas Mercado) and her sporadic presence at his side. Passionate and opinionated author comments on Revolution and preferences among leaders, Madero and Eulalio Gutiérrez; casts Villa and Zapata as barbarians. Transplanted to Mexico and eroded by *pochismo* and *anglosajonismo*, peninsular Spanish culture preoccupies author.

1836. Vasconcelos, José (1882–1959). *Ulises Criollo: la vida del autor escrita por él mismo*. México: Ediciones Botas, 1936. 534pp. Trans: *A Mexican Ulysses, an Autobiography*. Translated by W. Rex Crawford. Bloomington: Indiana University Press, 1963. Autobiography Proper. Period Covered: 1881–1913.

One of best autobiographies in Spanish language. At center, he either participates in action or gives opinions. *Ulises criollo* a developed life expressed with clarity and precision. Exhibits much less reserve in writings than others. Notes negative feelings towards parents and siblings. Concentrates on childhood, reading interests, frequent moves within Mexico due to father's employment, law school, and early Revolution.

1837. Vázquez Barragán, Jesús (1939–). *Antes del olvido: memorias*. s.l., 2002? 87pp. Memoirs. Period Covered: 1939?–1996.

Born in Zapotlán el Grande, Jalisco, author spends little time on childhood and adolescence. Interested in voice, he moved to capital, where he studied and performed in opera as well as in musicals. Later he discovered talent for painting. Coincidentally from same Jalisco town as Juan José Arreola, mentioned several times in memoir.

1838. Vázquez Gómez, Francisco (1860–1933). *Memorias políticas (1909–1913)*. México: Imprenta Mundial, 1933. 599pp. Memoirs. Period Covered: 1909–1913.

Porfirio Díaz's doctor, Madero's minister of foreign relations, and León De la Barra's minister of education memorializes most chaotic years of career. Affiliated with political luminaries of early Revolution. Impersonal memoirs diluted with inclusion of documents and verbatim speeches.

1839. Vega Flores, Héctor (1918–). *Memorias de un desconocido*. Cuernavaca: El Autor, 1995. 155pp. Memoirs. Period Covered: 1918–1995.

Born to poverty in Zacualpan, Mexico, author managed to educate self sufficiently to teach school and to obtain law degree. Spent many years as lawyer in Yautepec, Morelos, lived in Cuernavaca, Mexico City, Jojutla, and Tetecala. Sudden anti–Catholicism and membership in Communist Party teasing topics.

1840. Vega González, Roberto (1919–). *Cadetes mexicanos en la guerra de España*. México: Compañía General de Ediciones, 1954. 221pp. Memoirs. Period Covered: 1934–1941.

Matriculated at military academy in 1934. Jeopardizing career, fled to Spain to fight for Republicans in Valencia, Teruel, Monreal, Pamplona, and Zaragoza. Writing in third person distances self from suffering.

1841. Vejar Lacave, Carlos (1908–?). *Bajo el signo de Esculapio: la medicina trágica y apasionante*. México: Costa-Amic, 1965. 274pp. Memoirs. Period Covered: 1930?–1964.

Doctor records experiences in medicine but with distinct philosophical approach. Author of several books with Mexican themes, Véjar Lacave product of broader humanistic culture than most of colleagues. Clear style.

1842. Velasco, Francisco de (1867–?). *Autobiografía*. Puebla, 1946. 135pp. Memoirs. Period Covered: 1872–1945.

Puebla aristocrat suffered from two events: French Intervention and subsequent punishment of family and 1910 Revolution. Active in city government, he edited newspaper and was head of Red Cross. Written in third person.

1843. Velasco Piña, Antonio (1935–?). *Cartas a Elisabeth.* México: Hoja Casa Editorial, 1990. 313pp. Letters. Period Covered: 1988–1990.

In two-year period lawyer wrote forty-eight letters to niece in U.S. Correspondence reveals mystical being in touch with Mexico through Indian cultures: "We are in transition from a stage of massification and standardization to one of recovery of what is sacred in Mexico" (p.179). Apostle scatters fragments of material life throughout letters.

1844. Velasco Ramírez, Raúl (1933–). *Mi rostro oculto: Raúl Velasco.* México: Editorial Diana, 1989. 264pp. Memoirs. Period Covered: 1939–1988.

Writer for film magazines, reporter for *Novedades* and *El Heraldo de México,* and TV. Personality for *Confrontación 68, Medianoche, Domingos espectaculares,* and *Siempre en domingo,* Velasco intersperses travel, early life, family, and career as TV personality. Involves self constantly with portrayed experiences. In recall of Mexico, foreign travel turns autobiographical.

1845. Velázquez, Carolina (1954–). *¿A dónde desea hablar?* México: Aguirre y Beltrán Editores, 1993. 111pp. Memoirs. Period Covered: 1979–1990?

Worked eleven years as long distance telephone operator in Mexico City. Humorous account manifests need for women to work outside home, difficulties of maintaining marriage, exploitation in work place, and function of labor unions.

1846. Velázquez Andrade, Manuel (1877–1952). *Remembranzas de Colima, 1895–1901.* México: Páginas del Siglo XX, 1945. 268pp. Memoirs. Period Covered: 1895–1901.

Educator writes of Colima's yesteryears. Events and personalities nostalgically recalled as author revisualizes them from fifty-year perspective.

1847. Velez, Joseph Francisco (1928–). *En la ruta de Pito Pérez: cuarenta años*

después. México: CEID, 1983. 102pp. Memoirs. Period Covered: 1983.

Rubén Romero's 1938 classic *La vida inútil de Pito Pérez* motivated Velez to seek traces of Romero, Pito, and their Michoacán context in 1983. Velez bused from Yuriria to Morelia with six intermediate stops. Notes sites familiar to Romero and Pérez and inconveniences and pleasures of road. Study climaxes in Pátzcuaro, where interviews centenarian José Reyes Tapia, relative of Pito Pérez.

1848. Veloz García, Rosa María (1902 Birth of Veloz García). *Relatos de mi padre: señor Juan Antonio Veloz F. Rosa María Veloz García.* Durango, DUR: Salas Offset, 1994. 76pp. Memoirs. Period Covered: 1911–1914.

Recalling stories of Revolution told by father, author recounts them in his name. In style and mood similar to Campobello's *Cartuchos,* she evokes rural Gómez Palacios, Durango, and plundering of revolutionary armies. Impassive nine-year-old girl views movement negatively.

1849. Vera y Zuria, Pedro (1874–1945). *Diario de mi destierro.* El Paso, TX: Editorial Revista Católica, 1927. 231pp. Diary. Period Covered: April 22, 1927-October 31, 1927.

Archbishop of Puebla exiled to U.S. under Calles. Diary or chronicles describes impressions of U.S. (mainly Catholic population and institutions) and records news of further religious persecution in Mexico. Totally excludes personal and whatever is irrelevant to Catholicism. Flat prose style stimulates little interest.

1850. Vérgez, José F. *Recuerdos de Méjico.* Barcelona: Imprenta de Henrich, 1902. 319pp.

Luckily for Mexico, Spaniard José F. Vérgez, editor of *Diario de la Marina* in Havana, invited to Mexico in 1873 to help inaugurate *Ferrocarril Mexicano.* Buoyant journalist, jubilant about Spain's contributions to this country, has nineteenth century penchant for description of exotic landscape and culture from Progreso to Vera Cruz to Mexico City. Subordinates personality to description in *Recuerdos de Méjico.*

1851. Veríssimo, Erico. *Mexico.* New York: Orion, 1960. 341pp.

José Vasconcelos attracted foreign writers such as Brazilian Erico Verissimo. Gives history through interview with Vasconcelos and compares him to Alfonso Reyes. Famous Brazilian observes, compares, and makes canny remarks throughout text. Covers some of same topics as other Mexican enthusiasts but style has pungency of experienced writer.

1852. Villa, Luz Corral, vda. de (1892–1981?). *Pancho Villa en la intimidad.* México, 1948. 273pp. Trans: *Pancho Villa, an Intimacy.* English edition by Richard H. Hancock. Chihuahua, CHH: Centro Librero, La Prensa, c. 1981. Memoirs. Period Covered: 1910–1923.

Villa's widow recalls girlhood and first meeting with Revolutionary hero. Recording exploits of husband, she either exonerates him from attributed wrongs or extenuates them. Like Villa's life, hers spent mainly in Chihuahua and northern Mexico and in exile in U.S. Own life conjured in remembrances of spouse.

1853. Villa Rojas, Alfonso (Dates?). "Entrevista a Alfonso Villa Rojas" por José Luis Domínguez. En *Caminos de la antropología: entrevistas a cinco antropólogos.* Compiladores Jorge Durand y Luis Vázquez. México: Instituto Nacional Indigenista, 1990. Pp.175–199. Interview. Period Covered: 1927–1980.

Native of Yucatan and specialist on Mayas mentions early formative contacts such as Sylvanus Morely, Sol Tax, and Bronislaw Malinowski. *Chankom, a Mayan Village* (1934) is most famous work.

1854. Villagrán, Vicente (1826–?). *Compendio histórico formado.* Pachucha: Gobierno del Estado de Hidalgo, 1992 (1874). 255pp. Memoirs. Period Covered: 1826–1874.

Few nineteenth century writings pertain to autobiography. Published in 1874, present work fills gap. From Huichapan, Hidalgo, Villagrán gives autobiographical data and military life. Memoirs filled with personal experiences and anecdotes redolent with Mexico: religion, myths, legends, family, politics, and social life. Written with verve.

1855. Villalobos, Jorge (Dates?). *Perseguidor perseguido: testimonios de un abogado*

investigador. México: Alta Pimería ProArte y Cultura, 1985. 183pp. Memoirs. Period Covered: 1974–1985?

Twenty-three stories of philosophical and honest lawyer working for police in Baja California and Sonora. Investigations cover range of fascinating cases: child who accidentally killed his brother, robbery in Acapulco of jewels of Tyrone Power and Linda Christian, Indian vendors slandered by disgruntled buyer, etc.

1856. Villalva, Antonio R. (1871–?). *Apuntes de un músico de la Revolución: septiembre a noviembre de 1914.* Gobierno del estado de Chihuahua, 1988. 54pp. Memoirs. Period Covered: 1914.

Military history and personal exploits dominate: "Dentro de…la Revolución, un lugar importante fue el que correspondió a las bandas militares… que… acompañaban siempre a la tropa tanto en la batalla como en el descanso…" (p.3). Musician and band director exercised talents in Brigada "Benito Juárez" of División del Norte. Transcribed by daughter Lourdes Villalva-Muguerza, diary focuses on music and daily activities of brigade.

1857. Villanueva, René (1933–?). *Cantares de la memoria: recuerdos de un folklorista.* México: Planeta, 1994. 402pp. Memoirs. Period Covered: 1963–1995.

Musician in 1966 founded Los Folkloristas to interpret and to spread folkloric music and new Latin American songs. In 1970, joined *Peña de los folkloristas*, vehicle for major artists of Latin American folk music. Music, tours (Latin America, U.S. and Europe), and other musicians dominate.

1858. Villanueva Cervantes Espinosa de los Monteros, Sebastiana. (1677–1737). *En religiosos incendios.* Ed. By Beatriz Espejo. México: UNAM, 1995. 247pp. Memoirs. Period Covered: 1686–1730.

Original title, *Vida de sor Sebastiana de las vírgenes, monja profesa en el convento de San José de Gracia de la ciudad de México, escrita por ella misma*, evokes medieval charm of document. Typical nun, considering self unworthy of Christ, seeks proper confessor. Centrality of religious life excludes almost all secular autobiography and climaxes in beatific vision.

1859. Villaseñor, Eduardo (1896–1978). *Memorias-testimonio.* México: Fondo de Cultura Económica, 1974. 446pp. Memoirs. Period Covered: 1916–1970.

Fragmented memoirs more like anthology of disparate chapters of life. Held various public positions: secretary of Nacional Council of Economics, undersecretary of Hacienda (treasury) y Crédito Público, and director of Banco de México.

1860. Villaseñor, Víctor (1903–1981). *Memorias de un hombre de izquierda.* México: Editorial Grijalbo, 1967–77. 2 v. Memoirs. Period Covered: 1902–1972?

Few can boast of life as active as Villaseñor: law school in U.S., track star, lawyer at claims commission, chief of archives at Department of Interior, charter member of Confederation of Mexican Workers, president of Amigos de la URSS, influential in two periodicals, *Futuro* and *Combate,* vice president of Partido Popular, head of Mexican railways, etc. Interprets moments of history he has lived. Two volumes reflect active life but little of personal life.

1861. Villaurrutia, Xavier (1903–1950). *Cartas de Villaurrutia a Novo,1935–1936.* México: Instituto Nacional de Bellas Artes, 1966. 78pp. Letters. Period Covered: 1935–1936.

One of best-known playwrights, member of los Contemporáneos, and co-founder of magazine *Ulises,* author studied drama at Yale. Letters to Salvador Novo reveal cultural life, love for theater, reactions to U.S., and affection for correspondent. In few pages, Villaurrutia self-defines more than most Mexicans in volumes of memoirs.

1862. Villegas de Magnón, Leonor (1876–1948?). *The Rebel.* Ed. and introduced by Clara Lomas. Houston: Arte Público, 1994. 297pp. Memoirs. Period Covered: 1876–1920.

Life spanned Revolution in which she served as nurse for Carrancistas. Wealthy, she was educated in Texas and lived in Mexico City at height of Porfiriato. Focuses on revo-

lutionary years; however, she showed survival skills following loss of family's fortune. Editor Clara Lomas introduces subject within context of feminism and Mexican autobiography. Female perspective on Revolution is rare.

1863. Villegas Oropeza, Miguel (1895–?). "Tapando agujeritos de la historia de la Revolución." En *Mi pueblo durante la Revolución.* México: Instituto Nacional de Antropología, 1985. Pp.233–276. Memoirs. Period Covered: 1913–1928.

In keeping with objectives of recording of memories of ordinary people, "Tapando" concentrates on Obregonista, who recalls Revolution from *Decena Trágica* to assassination of Obregón. Nomadic soldier fought in Mexico City; Saltillo, Coahuila; Torreón, Coahuila; Gómez Palacio, Durango; Laredo, Texas; Naco, Sonora; Empalme, Sonora; and Vera Cruz, Vera Cruz. Anecdotes, precision, and personal perspective.

1864. Villoro, Juan (1956–); **Elisa Ramos; Rocío Aceves.** *Certidumbre del extravío: entrevista con Juan Villoro.* Universidad de Colima, 2001. 94pp. Interview. Period Covered: 1962?–1995?

Above resulted from four-hour interview in 1998. Talks about family, education at the Colegio Alemán, blue collar work, and association with letters. Radio commentator, writer of literary supplements, creator of children's books, and author of novels, short stories, and hybrid mix of *crónica* and essay. Defines writers' work and his generation; also interprets twentieth century.

1865. Villoro, Juan (1956–). *Palmeras de la brisa rápida: un viaje a Yucatán.* México: Alianza Editorial Mexicana, 1989. 196pp. Memoirs. Period Covered: 1989.

Novelist and short story writer with Yucatecan grandmother has roots here. In personal and subjective style tells fragments of history, travel, Mayan archaeology, and word lore. Yet in each chapter, Villoro's presence turns account into memoir.

1866. Viveros, Marcel (Dates?). *Anatomía de una prisión: 1525 días en Lecumberri y Santa Martha.* México: Editorial Diana, 1972. 173pp. Memoirs. Period Covered: 1966.

Viveros is pseudonym of former prisoner. Focusing on injustices, violence, perversion, and privileges, author lacks sensitivity and insights characteristic of best prison narratives.

1867. Vivo, Buenaventura (?–1872). *Memorias de Buenaventura Vivo, ministro de México en España durante....* Madrid: Rivadeneyra, 1856. 486pp. Memoirs. Period Covered: 1853–1855.

Standard memoirs of diplomat in nineteenth century Spain. Little of personality emerges in objective account of three-year tenure.

1868. Viya, Miko (Dates?). *Diario de un director.* Puebla, PUE: Editorial Cajica, 1998. 370pp. Diary. Period Covered: 1951–1983.

"...quiero descubrirme ante el lector, como un trabajador y forjador de nuestra televisión" (p.8). Author was productive, for he lists ninety-one programs and series that he directed and contacts with 129 celebrities. Entries verify multileveled life: screenings, concerts, premiers of stage plays, sponsors, rehearsals, recordings, play writing, movie making, and continental travel.

1869. Viya, Miko (Dates?). *La televisión y yo: crónica de la televisión mexicana.* México: Costa-Amic, 1971. 181pp. Memoirs. Period Covered: 1950–1970.

Playwright worked for television in all aspects of production. Directed over seventy soap operas. Positive memoir mentions numerous TV personalities and other celebrities. Sophisticated craftsman, he periodically took trips to Europe to refresh creative energies.

1870. Vogt, Evon Zartman. *Fieldwork among the Maya: Reflections on the Harvard Chiapas Project.* Albuquerque: University of New Mexico Press, 1994. 451pp.

Vogt's autobiography could serve as manual for academics in fieldwork in Chiapas. Studying Tztoziles, Harvard professor introduced students to area, set up Harvard Research Ranch in Las Casas, carried Tzotzil speaker to university to facilitate teaching of language, and wrote book on Zinacantecos. Knew all of other anthropologists or archae-ologists working here. Integration of Mayan culture with U.S. university recognized by Mexican government's awarding Order of the Aztec Eagle in 1978.

1871. Volkow, Verónica (1955–). *Diario de Sudáfrica.* México: Sigla Vientiuno Editores, 1988. 179pp. Diary. Period Covered: 1986.

Africa not priority among Mexican autobiographers. Above title is exception. Poet and essayist spends three months in 1986 in South Africa. Autobiography through travels but mainly perceptions and insights into country. Close to people, she follows lives and writes negatively of apartheid. Notes built-in discrimination in language.

1872. Wagner, Henry Raup. *Bullion to Books: Fifty Years of Business and Pleasure.* Los Angeles: Zamorano Club, 1942. 370pp.

Seven chapters or almost one-fourth of book relate to Mexico. Wagner managed smelting for Guggenheims. Here until 1914, he witnessed much of Revolution including *Decena Trágica*. He has own interpretation of death of Madero and exonerates Henry Lane Wilson. Wagner also dealt with Villa, who wanted him to smelt confiscated ore. An avid book collector, engineer purchased from Genaro García.

1873. Wakefield, Celia. *Under the Tabachín Tree: A New Home in Mexico.* Berkeley, CA: Creative Arts Book, 1997. 121pp.

Retirement-age couple abandons Berkeley for Colima and gives us this city in 1975. Humorous run-ins with natives over repairs, language, rentals, and driving. Pleasant information on neglected site.

1874. Wald, Elijah. *Narcocorrido: A Journey into the Music of Drugs, Guns, and Guerrillas.* New York: Rayo, 2001. 333pp.

Self-explanatory title describes journey into Mexico in search for contemporary *corrido* (ballad). Travels widely: Sinaloa, Los Angeles, northern Mexico (Chihuahua and Torreón), Mexico City, and states of Michoacán and Guerrero. Seeks ballad writers, interviews them, attends performances, includes many of their *corridos* with translation and tries to gage popularity and evolution of music in particular geographical area. Profile of contemporary Mexico through popular traditional art form.

1875. Wallace, Dillon. *Beyond the Mexican Sierras.* Chicago: McClurg, 1910. 301pp.

Author and companions, fearing colonization schemes would ruin western Mexico, start in San Blas and journey to pristine area: Sinaloa, Durango, and Nayarit. Slowly paced trip allows for travel, enjoyment of scenery, description of customs, and autobiography. Praise for Porfirio Diaz and solvency suggests usual Gringo predisposition to laud dictator. Author noted abuse and enslavement of Yaqui.

1876. Wallace, Lew. *Lew Wallace: An Autobiography....* New York: Harper, 1906. 2 v.

Author of *Fair God,* novel of Conquest, and *Ben Hur* left law studies in Indiana to join Gen. Taylor at Matamoros. Camargo, Monterrey, Buena Vista, and interview with Taylor comprise Mexican-American War.

1877. Wallace, Mildred Young. *We Three: Papa's Ladies.* San Antonio: Naylor, 1957. 192pp.

Author and two teenage sisters move from New York to pre-revolutionary Cananea. Story switches from Sonora to New York, where women attend school. Description of mining city, something of its culture (*posadas*), trip to Guaymas, and arrival of Pancho Villa. Anecdotes on Chinese cook. Author taught grade school in Cananea during WWI.

1878. Ward, Gerald F. *Life in Mexico.* Seal Beach, CA: Jutras, 1973. 78pp.

Spent total of twenty-seven years in Sonora and Sinaloa. Mine manager, he was in charge of water system of Mazatlán. Excellent description of city, living conditions, interaction with natives, and nuclei of other foreigners, mainly Germans. Lived through second decade of Revolution. Good will in spirited American family.

1879. Warren, Nola. *The Foolishness of God.* Lake Mary, FL: Creation House, 2000. 151pp.

Narrates how she and husband, both graduates of International Bible College in San Antonio, Texas, came to proselytize in Durango, Mexico. Novel approach of dropping Bibles from plane to attract Catholics to convert. Catholic opposition to Protestant intruders. Much on daily routine of woman pastor, who leads life of circuit rider in 1960s.

1880. Waters, Frank. *Pumpkin Seed Point.* Chicago: Sage Books, 1969. 175pp.

Above is "...a personal narrative of my inner and outer experiences in this subterranean world of Indian America" (p.xi). Two loci: Arizona with Hopis and Chihuahua with Tarahumara. Traveling to mission Sisoguichi, he notes universality of Indian myths.

1881. Wauer, Roland H. *Naturalist's Mexico.* College Station: Texas A&M University Press, 1992. 304pp.

Covers much of country: Tamaulipas, Chihuahua, Baja, Jalisco, Colima, and Yucatan. Nature lover notes "...a biological paradise of enormous diversity" (p.xvii). Flora, fauna, and volcanoes all recorded with subjectivity.

1882. Webb, Georgia. *More than a Dozen: Fifty Years of Ministry in Mexico.* Springfield, MO: Tribune, 1998. 192pp.

Webb exemplifies factotum that American missionaries became: nurse, stepmother, cook, fundraiser, teacher, linguist, and peacemaker. Spent five decades in Tamaulipas, San Luis Potosí, Coahuila, Nuevo León, and Querétaro.

1883. Webb, James Josiah; Ralph Paul Bieber. *Adventures in the Santa Fé Trade, 1844–1847.* Lincoln: University of Nebraska Press, 1995 (1931).

Memoirs show trade between Santa Fe and Chihuahua near time of Mexican-American War. Webb and associate left Independence, Missouri, and arrived in New Mexico when army of Col. Kearny entered with merchants given duty free rights. Webb continued on to Chihuahua through El Paso. Taken prisoner by Mexican troops near Chihuahua City. Fear of capture of city by Americans forced him to San Juan de los Lagos, Jalisco, in 1846 for market. Returned to Santa Fe and Independence in 1847. Two chapters, "A Prisoner in Chihuahua" and "To the Fair of San Juan de los Lagos," cover trip.

1884. Webster, Frances Marvin Smith; Lucien Bonaparte Webster; Van R. Baker. *The Websters: Letters of an American Family in Peace and War, 1836–1853.* Kent, OH: Kent State University Press, 2000. 327pp.

Letters alternate between husband and wife in Indian Wars and in Mexican-American War. West Point graduate wrote letters from Texas and Mexico from May 17, 1846, to May 4, 1847. Matamoros, Monterrey, and Saltillo comprise war itinerary: "…he would be in Mexico for the next thirty-seven months fighting two battles and then enduring the boredom of occupation duty" (p.71). Letters mixture of war news and concern for family.

1885. Weckmann (Muñoz), Luis (1923–). *Diario político de un embajador mexicano, 1967–1988.* México: Fondo de Cultura Económica, 1997. 751pp. Diary. Period Covered: 1967–1988.

Diplomat and medievalist dispensed several assignments with government: 1967–1969, Israel; 1969–1973, Austria; 1973–1974, Germany; 1974, Iraq and Iran; 1974–1975, Cypress; 1975–1979, Iran; 1979–1980, UN; 1981–1986, Italy; and 1986–1988, Belgium. Diary packed with activities of energetic diplomat in multiple venues. Frustration and accomplishments in career superior to delineation of individual.

1886. Weeks, George F. *Seen in a Mexican Plaza: A Summer's Idyll of an Idle Summer.* New York: Revell, 1918. 120pp.

Spends tranquil summer in village of Cuatro Ciénagas. Seating self in plaza, he contemplates daily activities in confined space: birds, cripples, beggars, children, and open-air movie among others. Occasional moral-ladened anecdote interrupts description. Serenity shattered by thoughts on Crimean War and French Intervention and by violent death of companion.

1887. Weston, Edward. *Daybooks of Edward Weston.* Millerton, NY: Aperture, 1973. 2 v.

Struggles of artist clearly visible here. Photographer spent three years in Mexico, 1923–1926, and journal offers insights into life of man who must pay bills, keep up self-confidence, worry about separated family, party occasionally, and sell work. Constant companion, Tina Modotti, arranged exhibit of photos, and ensuing success attracted Weston to Mexico. Capital was main venue but excursions to Guanajuato, Puebla, Cholula, and Oaxaca. Both discernments and irritations with Mexicans and Mexico. Initial success gave him entrance to Mexicans and to foreigners helpful to career: Diego Rivera, Lupe Marín, Jean Charlot, Dr. Atl, Frances Toor, and Anita Brenner.

1888. Whitworth, William B. *Under an Aztec Sun: Adventures in Mexico.* New York: Vantage, 1965. 110pp.

Author not typical Gringo tourist who writes another book on Mexico. Although he mentions place, Durango, Mazatlán, capital, and Vera Cruz, sites and their culture not important. He meets Mexicans, mainly poor ones, and wins them over with generosity and empathy. Almost each of twenty-two chapters ends with victory for friendship.

1889. Wilhelmy, Adolfo (1884–?). *Teatro, periodismo y Revolución.* Editora de Mexicali, 1956. 219pp. Memoirs. Period Covered: 1913–1929.

From northern Mexico, Wilhelmy born in Sinaloa and spent much of life as journalist. Document indicates writer who knows how to structure story to build interest. He fought against Huerta on side of Abelardo Rodríguez, military commander of Baja. One chapter devoted to rebellion of José Gonzalo Escobar. More than soldier, Wilhelmy is journalist and go-between. Theater occupies small portion of memoir.

1890. Wilkins, James Hepburn. *A Glimpse of Old Mexico….* San Rafael, CA: The Author, 1901. 115pp.

Ten letters comprise this book. Something of self but more of Mexico in installments sent to newspaper: mining in San Dimas, Durango; government of Porfirio Díaz; lack of thrift as weakness in Mexican character; hunting and fishing, etc.

1891. Williams, Ben F.; Teresa Williams Irvin. *Let the Tail Go with the Hide: The Story of Ben F. Williams....* El Paso, TX: Mangan Books, 1984. 287pp.

Self-made subject living in Arizona and Sonora from 1902 to 1980, Williams man of many parts: cattleman, geologist, engineer, inventor, investor, and family man. Biggest venture in Mexico was purchase of 2,275,000 acre Palomas Ranch in Sonora. Much anecdote, dialog, and integrity.

1892. Williams, Morris; Frank Shaffer-Corona. *Lo llevo en la sangre: las memorias de Morris "moe" Williams, Jr.* Puebla, PUE: Familia Williams, 1988. 272pp.

Soccer well known in Mexico; basketball is scarce so above title addresses need. North Carolina-born and veteran of WWII attended Mexico City College in 1940s. Married Mexican, remained, and developed career: travel agent, athletic director, and coach at Universidad de las Américas in Puebla. Emphasizes acceptance of Blacks in adopted country.

1893. Wilson, Guy C. (1905–?). *Memories of a Venerable Father and Other Reminiscences.* Fullerton: Oral History Program of California State, 1988. 192pp. Interview. Period Covered: 1888–1986.

Talks of Mormons in Mexico, polygamy, and leadership. In more than five Mormon interviews, Wilson focuses on Mexican Mormon relations: attendance of natives at Mormon schools, success of Juarez Academy in Colonia Juárez, abandonment of colonies and difficulty of recuperation, use of two languages at stake meetings, and occasional intermarriage.

1894. Wilson, Henry Lane. *Diplomatic Episodes in Mexico, Belgium and Chile.* Garden City, NY: Double Page, 1927. 399pp.

Madero's nemesis recorded impressions. Half of Henry Lane Wilson's *Diplomatic Episodes* relates to Mexico. Appointed ambassador in 1910 by President Taft, Wilson suffered opprobrium of direct interference in death of Madero. Turbulent years in Mexico and denial of intervention in Madero's death figure here. In 1913, President Wilson asked for H. Wilson's resignation.

1895. Wise, H.A. *Los Gringos, or, An Inside View of Mexico and California....* New York: Baker and Scribner, 1850. 453pp.

Lieutenant in U.S. Navy, experienced Mexican-American War aboard ship that sailed from San Francisco to Mazola, Somalia. Participated in blockade of port. For unclear reasons, went on mission to Mexico City. Mixed with descriptions and anecdotes, autobiography emerges. Fanny Calderón de la Barca is not only good foreign writer in nineteenth century Mexico.

1896. Wislizenus, F.A. *Memoir of a Tour to Northern Mexico, Connected with Col. Doniphan's Expedition, in 1846 and 1847.* Glorieta, NM: Rio Grande, 1969 (1848). 141pp.

Title does not suggest scientific nature of author's trip. German-born author and M.D. practiced profession in U.S. Naturalist who wanted to study subject in Mexico. In spite of Mexican-American War, he journeyed from New Mexico to Chihuahua. Information on geography, flora, and fauna.

1897. Woldenberg, José (1952–). *Memoria de la izquierda.* México: Cal y Arena, 1998. 309pp. Memoirs. Period Covered: 1969–1991.

Political scientist in 1984 published *La desigualdad en México*, title that suggests his moral posture as he analyzes his country. He does more than write. In post '68 years: "...participé primero en la construcción y expansión de los sindicatos universitarios y...en los trabajos por remontar la atomización de la izquierda..." (p.12). He mentions el Movimiento de Acción Popular, El Partido Socialists Unificado de México, El Mexicano Socialista, and El Partido de la Revolución Democrática. Little autobiography on students and politics in Mexico.

1898. Wolfe, Bertram David. *A Life in Two Centuries: An Autobiography.* New York: Stein and Day, 1981. 728pp.

Bertram and Ella Wolfe arrived in Mexico in 1920. Communist and delegate to IV International, he also wrote for *El Machete*, one of main organs of Mexican Communist Party. Involved in labor dispute, he was expelled from country in 1925. He collaborated with Diego Rivera to write *Portrait of*

Mexico (1937) and *The Fabulous Life of Diego Rivera* (1963). Mexican years covered in three chapters in *A Life in Two Centuries* (1981).

1899. Woodcock, George. *To the City of the Dead.* London: Faber and Faber, 1957. 271pp.

Cristeros one of subjects for Brit, who crosses desert and journeys from central to southern Mexico. Sees two nations, conquered and conquerors in rural and urban Mexico. Touches themes often ignored by other foreign writers: *Quixotismo* of Mexicans, who love risk including lottery; *Sinarquismo*, or amalgam of Catholicism and Fascism that sprang from Cristero movement; films meant for middle class; abundance of bookstores; and Mexico's exile community refuged here but contemptuous of Mexicans.

1900. Worker, Dwight. *Escape.* San Francisco Book, 1977. 247pp.

Author foolishly enters Mexico in 1973 with hidden cocaine. Detected, arrested, and sentenced, he evokes Mexico's most notorious prison: beatings, torture, anti–Gringoism, homosexuality, fraudulent lawyers, and indifferent U.S. government. Cunning method of escape from Lecumberri.

1901. Wortman, Mary E. Vail; Orville Wortman. *Bouncing Down to Baja.* Los Angeles: Westernlore, 1954. 200pp. .

With El Jeep enter Baja in Tijuana and circle peninsula roughing it from Cabo San Lucas to Sinaloa (Mazatlán), Sonora (Hermosillo), and return to U.S. through Nogales. With no pretense of knowledge or culture, authors accept Mexicans as they are and with little Spanish communicate with them.

1902. Wright, Ronald. *Time among the Maya: Travels in Belize, Guatemala, and Mexico.* New York: Weidenfeld & Nicholson, 1989. 451pp.

In 1970 and 1985, author visited Mayas: Palenque, Bonampak, Nahá, Campeche, Cancún, Tulum, Cobá, and Mérida. Speaks of history and contemporary Mayas. *Time among the Maya* refers to perdurability of Indians.

1903. Xántus, János. *Travels in Southern California.* Detroit: Wayne State University Press, 1976. 212pp.

Hungarian author was first to describe Mexico to his countrymen. This naturalist, in America from 1851 to 1867, detailed flora and fauna and natives of Baja California. Nature predominates, but Xántus leaves some autobiographical data of encounters with wildlife, means of travel, need for prayers, mountain climbing, interaction with natives (Tejones), skill at healing, sending credentials to authorities, mining operations, etc.

1904. Yáñez, Agustín (1904–1980). *Flor de juegos antiguos.* México: Editorial Novaro México, 1942 (1965). 157pp. Memoirs. Period Covered: 1908?

Portrays Jalisco childhood through play activities for two seasons, Christmas Eve and summer (dog days), and games with water. One of most concentrated evocations of childhood in Mexican autobiography should be read along with *Por tierras de Nueva Galicia*. Both works prelude *El filo de agua*.

1905. Yáñez, Agustín (1904–1980). *Por tierras de Nueva Galicia.* Guadalajara: Editorial Hexágono, 1987. 181pp. Memoirs. Period Covered: 1909–1915?

Composed about 1930. For originality of prose, apprenticeship to *Al filo de agua* (1947), rhythm, and impressionism, writings fit in with best years of Mexican autobiography, 1928–1939. In images of landscape, seasons, music, churches, and personalities, evokes childhood in Catholic Jalisco. Scattered impressions essence author's native region.

1906. Yáñez Chico, Francisco (1908–?). *Historias escogidas del mariachi Franciso Yáñez Chico según los apuntes de Edgar Gabaldón Márquez.* Caracas: Castañón, 1981. 591pp. Oral Autobiography. Period Covered: 1908–1968.

From large and humble family from San Juan de la Vega, Guanajuato, author worked as ranch hand and as mariachi from 1938 to 1973. Much of career relates to Plaza Garibaldi in Mexico City. Mother doña Chucha Chico de Yáñez stands out. Amanuensis Gabaldón Márquez captures accent, vocabulary, and story-telling abilities of untutored subject's colloquial speech. Editor notes methodology and includes seventeen pages of notes, *Mexicanismos*, and *Guanajuatismos*.

1907. Yapor, Karina (Dates?). *Revelaciones: mis amargas experiencias con Gloria Trevi, Sergio Andrade y Mary Boquitas.* México: Editorial Grijalbo, 2001. 227pp. Memoirs. Period Covered: 1988–2000.

Accusations against Gloria Trevi and Sergio Andrade continue in *Revelaciones.* Twelve-year-old Yapor of Chihuahua idolized Gloria Trevi and accepted offer to become movie star. White slavery in Spain and in Mexico rather than fame was Yapor's destiny.

1908. Yetman, David. *The Guarijíos of the Sierra Madre: Hidden People of Northwestern Mexico.* Albuquerque: University of New Mexico Press, 2002. 270pp.

Much autobiography in above title. "The best way to get to know Cipriano was to hike with him through the monte. That way I could learn what he knew about the great Río Mayo tropical forest, about the Guarijíos and what it was like to be one" (pp.5–6). Thus he spends three years with this tribe of Sonora and Chihuahua. Some chapters are purely descriptive; others have much of experience of author who lives with tribe and records its culture especially their use of plants. Notes deculturizing effects of Protestantism.

1909. Yetman, David. *Sonora: An Intimate Geography.* Albuquerque: University of New Mexico Press, 1996. 248pp.

Introduction to Mexico's second largest state that borders Arizona and shares twin cities, Nogales/Nogales or Douglas/Agua Prieta. Covers Sonora and its multiple topics: Catholicism, Yaquis, Series, places, landscape, Mexican racism towards Indians, food, and history. List hints at dry factual study. Journalistic style invites easy apprehension of history, geography, and sociology through incident, dialog, and anecdote.

1910. Yetman, David. *Where the Desert Meets the Sea: A Trader in the Land of the Seri Indians.* Tucson: Pepper, 1988. 177pp.

Intrigued by Seris Indians of northern Sonora, author visited them in 1968 and returned many times in next five years: "This is a book about the Seris as I saw them" (p.8). Interests, both commercial (ironwood carvings and woven baskets) and anthropological, recorded here. Personality of both Indian tribe and author.

1911. Young, Biloine W. *Mexican Odyssey: Our Search for the People's Art.* St. Paul, MN: Pogo, 1996. 258pp.

In above title, two middle-aged housewives from St. Paul, Minnesota, adventure to Mexico to buy curios to sell at home. Success incremental with each return trip and with visits to folk artists whose creations stock shelves of "Old Mexico," their store. Apprenticeship as merchants and forays into Mexico make unique memoir. Details on folk artists and creations.

1912. Zabludovsky, Abraham (1924–). *Historia oral de la Ciudad de México: testimonios de sus arquitectos (1940–1990). Abraham Zabludovsky.* México: Lotería Nacional para la Asistencia Pública, Instituto Mora, 1991. 120pp. Interview. Period Covered: 1940–1990.

Son of Polish Jewish immigrants looks back on career as architect. Formation and philosophy about field balanced with projects: Mexican embassy in Brasilia, private residences, Complejo Residencial La Cantera, Central de Abasto, la Delegación Cuauhtémoc, El Infonavit, El Colegio de México, El Museo Tamayo, el edificio Cuadra, la biblioteca de la Ciudadela, y el Auditorio Nacional. Subject prompted by Graciela de Garay.

1913. Zabludowsky, Jacobo (1896–1974 Dates of Siqueiros). *Siqueiros me dijo....* México: Organización Editorial Novaro, 1974. 129pp. Interview. Period Covered: 1922?–1968.

In six interviews, Siqueiros talks of Mexican muralism, difference between acceptance of art in Mexico and in Europe, Russian art, and prison experience.

1914. Zaitzeff, Serge I. (1899–1977 Dates of Carlos Pellicer). *Correspondencia entre Carlos Pellicer y Germán Arcieniegas, 1920–*

1974. México: Conaculta, 2002. 222pp. Letters. Period Covered: 1920–1974.

Sixty-seven letters exchanged between poet Pellicer and diplomat, writer, and journalist, Arciniegas of Colombia. Young men knew each other in Colombia around 1918. Letters, in addition to friendship, discuss topics of faith in Latin American youth, unity of Latin America, literature, and student journal, *Universidad*.

1915. Zaitzeff, Serge I. (1889–1959 Dates of Alfonso Reyes)(1884–1961 Dates of Artemio Valle-Arizpe). *Cortesía norteña: correspondencia entre Alfonso Reyes y Artemio de Valle-Arizpe*. México: El Colegio Nacional, 1999. 131pp. Letters. Period Covered: 1918–1959.

Forty-one letters exchanged between polymath Reyes and diplomat and chronicler of city of Mexico, Valle-Arizpe. Mainly postmarked from within Mexico, letters also from Belgium, Spain, and Argentina. Two correspondents, contemporaries and *norteños*, broach following topics: books, periodical *Monterrey*, Spain and Civil War, and friendship.

1916. Zaitzeff, Serge I. (1896–1981 Dates of Castro Leal). *Recados entre Alfonso Reyes y Antonio Castro Leal*. México: El Colegio Nacional, 1987. 175pp. Letters. Period Covered: 1913–1959.

Diplomat and man of letters held prominent positions in both fields. Comprised of ninety-four letters, collection has fifty-five letters from Castro Leal, forty messages from Reyes, and one letter from Manuela Reyes. Pedro Henríquez Ureña introduced Castro Leal to English literature and to Reyes. Content of letters sporadically reveals literary life of Castro Leal: books, lectures, editing anthology of poetry, societies, teaching, research, and *los siete sabios*. Intimate and often expansive Reyes amicable if cryptic with Castro Leal.

1917. Zaitzeff, Serge I. (1892–1969 Dates of Icaza). *Xavier Icaza y sus contemporáneos epistolarios*. Xalapa: Universidad Veracruzana, 1995. 209pp. Letters. Period Covered: 1916–1952.

Poet, dramatist, novelist and short story writer, and author of multigenre *Panchito Chapopote*, sustained correspondence with six famous contemporaries: Alfonso Reyes, 1916–1952; Julio Torri, 1916–1920; Genaro Estrada, 1920–1948; Carlos Díaz Dufóo, Jr., 1919–1926; Francisco I. Icaza, 1919–1923; and Pablo Martínez del Río, 1916–1924. In letters, occasionally answered by correspondents, Icaza is active in Mexican literature and concerned about friendship Longest correspondence with Alfonso Reyes.

1918. Zaldívar F., José Antonio
(1910?–?). *Siete veranos entre paréntesis: semblanzas y anécdotas de Chapingo*. México: Editorial PAIM, 1954. 237pp. Memoirs. Period Covered: 1929–1935.

Loving tribute to Escuela Nacional de Agricultura de Chapingo, Mexico, and site of Diego Rivera's murals. Recalls nostalgically seven years spent at school with memories of classmates, professors, courses, pranks, and escapades into nearby Texcoco.

1919. Zapata, Luis (1951–). *De cuerpo entero: Luis Zapata*. México: Ediciones Corunda, 1990. 71pp. Memoirs. Period Covered: 1953?–1990.

Novelist and short story writer grew up in Chilpancingo, Guerrero. Movies influenced development. Like protagonist in Manuel Puig's *Betrayed by Rita Hayworth*, films consume youth and nurture creativity of Zapata. Autobiography, like well-crafted film script, climaxes when child Zapata comes upon decaying corpse.

1920. Zapata Vela, Carlos (1879–1968 Dates of Jara). *Conversaciones con Heriberto Jara*. México: Costa-Amic, 1992. 222pp. Oral Autobiography. Period Covered: 1914–1968.

Federal deputy, senator and governor of Vera Cruz, governor of Federal District, ambassador to Cuba, journalist, career military officer (general), and campaign manager for Avila Camacho, Jara presents self in fragmented autobiography. With questions, Zapata Vela chronologically develops life of Jara through five chapters: "Ingreso a la Revolución," "El magonismo," "Jara y Cárdenas."

1921. Zavala, Lorenzo de (1788–1836).
Viaje a los Estados Unidos del Norte de

América. México, 1846. 272pp. Trans: *Journey to the United States of North America*. English edition by Wallace Woolsey. Austin, TX: Shoal Creek, 1980. Memoirs. Period Covered: 1829–1932?

Politician of liberal stance is Mexican Alexis de Tocqueville. In memoirs, comments frequently on difference between U.S. and Mexico. Keen observer of geography, social classes, and political life, he focuses on U.S.

1922. Zeh, Frederick; William J. Orr; Robert Ryal Miller. *An Immigrant Soldier in the Mexican War*. College Station: Texas A&M University Press, 1995. 117pp.

German immigrant in need saves self by joining regiment headed for Mexico in 1846. He follows trajectory of war: Veracruz, Cerro Gordo, Jalapa, Puebla, and Mexico City with Churubusco, Molino del Rey, and Chapultepec. European background does not restrain him from making negative comments about Mexicans. According to editor, "Zeh's account mirrors the experiences of the lower ranks, underrepresented in the memoirs of literature of the Mexican War" (p.xvi).

1923. Zelayeta, Elena (1897–?). *Elena*. Englewood Cliffs, NJ: Prentice-Hall, 1960. 246pp. Autobiography Proper. Period Covered: 1897–1959?

Mature Zelayeta looks back at life and tries to reconstruct significant moments. Born in Spain and immigrating to Mexico as child, she and family settle in San Francisco. Successful restaurant owner until blindness was able to support self and two sons. Zelayeta's honesty about family often missing in Hispanic autobiography.

1924. Zelis S.J., Rafael de (1747–1798). *Viajes en su destierro*. Xalapa, VER: Veracruzana, 1988. 99pp. Memoirs. Period Covered: 1767–1777.

Joined Jesuit Order in Mexico in 1765 and two years later suffered expulsion. Comprised of nine trips, document one of few eighteenth century autobiographies extant. He details trip from Vera Cruz to Havana to Cádiz and to Italy. Ordained in Italy, Zelis does not focus on religion. Daily life and happenings on board ship and in transit comprise memoirs.

1925. Zepeda, Eraclio (1937–). *Eraclio Zepeda*. Azcapotzalco, DF: Universidad Autónoma Metropolitana, 1985. 52pp. Interview. Period Covered: 1960?–1984?

Journalist, teacher, radio announcer, actor, storyteller, and political activist fits well into format of series. Speaks of love and death but more experientially of oral and written verbal creation. Lay person's appreciation of classics, writing habits, Juan Rulfo, and art of conversation exemplified in self-portrayal.

1926. Zingg, Robert M. *Behind the Mexican Mountains*. Austin: University of Texas Press, 2001. 307pp.

In 1930, University of Chicago anthropologist Zingg spent nine months with Tarahumaras in Chihuahua. His field work serves as ethnography on tribe. He also leaves much autobiography in travelogue. Introduction states two reasons for reading biased author: Tarahumaras in 1930 and that period's colonial attitude about non–Western people.

1927. Zorrilla, José; Pablo Mora; Silva Salgado. *Memorias del tiempo mexicano*. México: Consejo Nacional para la Cultura y las Artes, 1998. 219pp.

Spanish poet and dramatist spent eleven years in Mexico, 1855–1866. Like Fanny Calderón de la Barca and other nineteenth century travelers, he is fascinated by *lo mexicano* and recreates towns near capital, haciendas, and nature, etc. Knew Maximilian and Carlota and appointed their personal poet. Presented his *Don Juan Tenorio* in palace.

1928. Zorrilla, Oscar (1934–1985); **María Andueza**. *Nuestros viejos días*. México: Coordinación de Difusión Cultural de Literatura. UNAM, 1989. 207pp. Genre: Letters. Period Covered: 1958–1961.

One hundred seven letters penned by twenty-four-year-old poet to Guadalupe Olivares suggest creator both immersed and inspired by love. One hundred twelve poems with similar theme and tone.

1929. Zúñiga, Olivia (1916–?). *Retrato de una niña triste*. Guadalajara: Ediciones Et caetera, 1951. 90pp. Autobiographical Novel. Period Covered: 1922?–1947.

Document fluctuates between consultation and convalescence at Mayo Clinic in Rochester, Minnesota, and home in Jalisco. Moments at clinic and childhood intertwine in sad confessions. Willful child and adolescent poorly adjusted to environment equals perceptive, sentient, and unhappy being. Medical treatment in U.S. avails little.

1930. Zúñiga, Silvia María (1910 Birth of Casilda Flores Morales). *Casilda la horchatera.* Oaxaca: Dirección General de Culturas Populares, 1989. 83pp. Oral Autobiography. Period Covered: 1890–1988?

Informal life of Oaxacan woman who sold fruit juices for forty years at Instituto de Ciencia y Artes del Estado. Born into poor family but still with strictures of Victorian era, she was beaten by mother for flirtations with son of wealth. Casilda blends autobiography with recall of disappeared Oaxaca. Evokes personalities and episodes of Instituto. Zúñiga includes questions but spends little on methodology.

1931. Zuno Hernández, José Guadalupe (1891–1980). *Reminiscencias de una vida.* Guadalajara, 1956. 185pp. Memoirs. Period Covered: 1897?–1923?

Author, painter, caricaturist, founder of periodicals, and politician, he skips over childhood and writes of anti–Porfirista activities and involvement in Revolution. Marks beginnings of career in journalism and art. Three later volumes are mixture of letters, lectures, tributes, decrees, description of paintings, and reminiscences of contemporaries. Distilled autobiography.

1932. Zwinger, Ann. *A Desert Country near the Sea: A Natural History of the Cape Region of Baja California.* New York: Harper & Row, 1983. 399pp.

Scientist as writer manifest in above title. Chapters indicate thoroughness in geographical coverage: Sierra, countryside, towns, Pacific, and Gulf of California. Autobiography and natural history inseparable. She explores and reacts to any item within purview. Mention of Joseph Wood Krutch and John Steinbeck suggests mentors in nature writing.

Appendix A:
Chronological Listing of Works

1691	Myers, Kathleen.	Becoming a Nun.
1700	Juana Inés de la Cruz.	Answer/La respuesta…
	Villanueva Cervantes, S.	En religiosos incendios.
1824	Bullock, W.	Six Months Residence and Travels in Mexico.
	Iturbide, Agustín de.	The Memoirs of Agustín de Iturbide.
1825	Poinsett, Joel.	Notes on México Made in the Autumn of 1822.
1828	Lyon, G.F.	Journal of Residence and Tour in the Republic…
1829	Hardy, Robert W.	Travels in the Interior of México, in 1825, 1826, 1827…
1837	Guzmán, José María.	Breve y sencilla narración del viage…
	Martínez Caro, Ramón.	Verdadera idea de la primera campaña de…
1838	Urrea, José.	Diario de las operaciones militares de la…
1840	Ocampo, Melchor.	Viaje de un mexicano a Europa.
1843	Calderón de la Barca, F.	Life in México.
1845	Carbajal, Francisco.	Vindicación de D. Francisco Carbajal.
1846	Gilliam, Albert M.	Travels in México City.
	Zavala, Lorenzo de.	Viaje a los Estados Unidos del Norte…
1847	Henry, W.S.	Campaign Sketches of the War with México.
	Richardson, William H.	Journal of William H. Richardson, A Private Soldier…
	Scribner, B.F.	Camp Life of a Volunteer.
1848	Emory, William H.	Notes of a Military Reconnaissance from Fort…
	Reid, Samuel C.	Scouting Expeditions of McCulloch's Texas Rangers…
	Robinson, Jacob S.	Journal of the Santa Fe Expedition under Colonel Doniphan.
	Wislizenus, Frederick A.	Memoir of a Tour to Northern México…
1849	Jamieson, Milton.	Journal and Notes of a Campaign in Mexico…
	Robertson, John Blout.	Reminiscences of a Campaign in México.
1850	McSherry, Richard.	El Puchero: or, a Mixed Dish from Mexico…
	Ryan, William Redmond.	Personal Adventures in Upper and Lower California…
	Wise, Henry Augustus.	Los gringos: or, an Inside View of México and California…
1851	Barrister, A.	Trip to México or Recollections of a Ten-Months…
	Carpenter, William W.	Travels and Adventures in México…
	Sierra O'Reilly, Justo.	Impresiones de nuestro viaje a los Estados Unidos…
1852	McManus, Jane Maria.	Eagle Pass: or Life on the Border.
1853	Prieto, Guillermo.	Memorias de mis tiempos, 1828–1840…
	Robertson, Wm. Parish.	Visit to Mexico by West India Islands, Yucatan…
1856	Ferry, Gabriel.	Vagabond Life in México.

1905	Santa Anna, Antonio.	Historia military y política.
	Blasio, José Luis.	Maximiliano íntimo, el emperador Maximiliano y su corte.
	Miksch, George Sutton.	Two Bird-Lovers in México.
1906	Audobon, John W.	Audobon's Western Journal: 1849–1850...
	Edwards, William S.	On the Mexican Highlands...
	Guridi y Alcocer, José M.	Apuntes de la vida de...
	Wallace, Lew.	Lew Wallace: An Autobiography.
1908	Flandrau, Charles.	Viva Mexico!
	Starr, Frederick.	In Indian México: A Narrative of Travel and Labor.
	Taylor, Zachary.	Letters of Zachary Taylor, from the Battle-fields...
1909	Carson, W.E.	Wonderland of the South.
	Channing, Arnold.	American Egypt: A Record of Travel in Yucatán.
	Foster, John Watson.	Diplomatic Memoirs.
	Hitchcock, Ethan Allen.	Fifty Years in Camp and Field...
	Hornaby, William T.	Camp-Fires on Desert and Lava.
1910	Dillon, Wallace.	Beyond the Mexican Sierras.
	Harper, Henry H.	Journey in Southeastern México...
	North, Arthur Wallbridge.	Camp and Camino in Lower California...
	Pesado, Isabel.	Apuntes de viaje de México a Europea en los años...
	Santleben, August.	Texas Pioneer: Early Staging and Overland Freighting.
1911	Anderson, Robert.	Artillery Officer in the Mexican War, 1846–184...
	Barton, Mary.	Impressions of México with Brush and Pen.
	Frías, Heriberto.	El triunfo de Sancho Panza.
	Giménez, Manuel María.	Memorias del coronel Manuel María Jiménez...
	Kirkham, Stanton Davis.	Mexican Trails: A Record of Travel...
1912	Blichfeldt, E.H.	Mexican Journey.
	Gillpatrick, Wallace.	Man Who Likes México...
	Lumholtz, Carl.	New Trails in México: An Account of One Year's...
	Reyes, Bernardo.	Defensa que por sí mismo produce el c. general...
1913	Meade, George G.	Life and Letters of George Gordon Meade...
	Pollard, Hugh B.C.	Busy Time in Mexico: An Unconventional Record...
	Rodriguez, Jose Maria.	Rodriguez Memoirs...
1915	Collins, Francis.	Journal of Francis Collins: An Artillery Officer...
	Huerta, Victoriano.	Memorias del general Victoriano Huerta.
	Pazuengo, Matías.	Historia de la Revolución en Durango.
	Ruiz, Eduardo.	Un convoy militar: de Veracruz a Encarnación.
1916	Aragón, Alfredo.	Escenas de la Rev mexicana, relatos de un testigo...
	Dorador, Silvestre.	Mi prisión, la defensa social y la verdad del caso...
	Frías, Heriberto.	Miserias de México.
	Lewis, Tracy Hammond.	Along the Rio Grande.
	Ortiz Rubio, Pascual.	Memorias de un penitente.
	O'Shaughnessy, Edith.	Diplomat's Wife in México.
1917	Brooke, George.	With the First City Troop on the Mexican Border.
	Cueva, Eusebio de la.	Por tierras de Quevedo y Cervantes.
	McCann, Irving Goff.	With the National Guard on the Border.
	McClellan, George B.	Mexican War Diary of George B. McClellan.
	O'Shaughnessy, Edith.	Diplomatic Days.
	Smith, E. Kirby.	To México with Scott: Letters of Captain E. Kirby Smith...
1918	González Peña, Carlos.	La vida tumultuosa: seis semanas en los Estados Unidos.
	O'Reilly, Edward S.	Roving and Fighting: Adventures under Four Flags.
	Orozco y Jiménez, F.	Memoir of the Most Reverend Francisco Orozco y Jiménez.
	Torres, Olga Beatriz.	Memorias de mi viaje.
1919	Díaz Barreiro, Francisco.	Un periodista mexicano en las frentes franceses.
	Godoy, Mercedes.	When I Was a Girl in Mexico.
	Gómez Palacios, Martín.	Viaje maduro.
	Manzanilla Domínguez, A.	Aguas fuertes (gentes y cosas de Yucatán).
	Romero de Terreros, Juan.	Apuntaciones de viaje en 1849.
	Tablada, José Juan.	En el país del sol.
1920	Davis, William Brownlee.	Experiences and Observations of an American Consular...
	Gillow, Eulogio G.	Reminiscencias del Ilmo. y Rmo. Sr. Dr. D. Eulogio...
	Noriega Hope, Carlos.	El mundo de las sombras; el cine...
	Urbina, Luis Gonzaga.	Estampas de viaje: España en los dias de la guerra.
1921	Beach, Rex.	Confessions of an Agitated Sportsman.
	Mena Brito, Bernardino.	Los vivos mandan.

	Núñez y Domínguez, R.	Como vi la República Española (película impresionista).
	Taracena, Alfonso.	Autobiografía, cuentos.
	Terrell, Alexander Watkins.	From Texas to México and the Court of Maximilian in 1865.
	Vázquez Gómez, Francisco.	Memorias políticas (1909–1913).
1934	Burns, Bob.	Battling the Elements.
	Esquivel Obregón, Toribio.	Mi labor en servicio de México.
	Pedrero, Felipe Alfonso.	Diario de Felipe Alfonso Pedrero…
	Squier, Emma-Lindsay.	Gringa: An American Woman in México.
	Romero, José Rubén.	Desbandada.
	Stacy-Judd, Robert.	Adventures in the Jungles of Yucatán.
	Trueheart, James L.	Perote Prisoners.
	Urquizo, Francisco.	"Recuerdo que…": Visiones de la Revolución.
1935	Bowman, Heath.	Mexican Odyssey.
	Brondo Whitt, Eulogio.	Nuevo León: novela de costumbres, 1896–1903.
	Cejudo, Roberto F.	Del "Diario de Campaña" del General de Brigada…
	Céliz, Francisco.	Diary of the Alarcón Expedition into Texas, 1718–1719.
	Franck, Harry A.	Trailing Cortez through México.
	Garibaldi, José.	Toast to Rebellion.
	González, Manuel W.	Contra Villa: relatos de la compaña, 1914–1915.
	King, Rosa.	Tempest over Mexico.
	Montesinos, José María.	Memorias del sargento José María Montesinos.
	Novo, Salvador.	Continente vacío (viaje a Sudamérica).
1936	Almada, Pedro J.	Con mi cobija al hombro.
	Barbour, Philip N.	Journals of the Late Brevet Major Philip Norbourne Barbour.
	Castillo y Piña, José.	Las oasis del camino.
	Edwards, Marcellus B.	Marching with the Army of the West.
	Ferguson, Philip Gooch.	Marching with the Army of the West.
	Góngora, Pablo de.	Memorias de un ministro.
	Guzmán, Martín Luis.	Memorias de Pancho Villa.
	Jackson, Henry Joseph.	Mexican Interlude.
	Johnston, Abraham R.	Marching with the Army of the West.
	Merritt-Hawkes, O.A.	High Up in México.
	Pani, Alberto J.	Mi contribución al nuevo régimen (1910–1913)…
	Pruneda, Salvador.	Huellas.
	Taracena, Alfonso.	Mi vida en el vértigo de la revolucion mexicana…
	Underhill, Ruth.	Autobiography of a Papago Woman.
	Vasconcelos, José.	La tormenta: segunda parte de "Ulises criollo"…
	Vasconcelos, José.	Ulises criollo: la vida del autor escrita por él mismo.
1937	Campobello, Nellie.	Las manos de mi mamá.
	Clark, Leonard.	Wanderer Till I Die.
	García Icazbalceta, J.	Cartas de Joaquín García Icazbalceta…
	Luquín, Eduardo.	Tumulto: memorias de un oficial del Ejército…
	Maillefert, Alfredo.	Laudanza de Michoacán: Morelia, Pátzcuaro, Uruapan.
	Mancisidor, José.	Ciento veinte dias.
	Menchaca, Antonio.	Memoirs.
	Palavincini, Felix.	Mi vida revolucionaria.
	Parodi, Enriqueta de.	Madre: prosas.
	Tablada, José Juan.	La feria de la vida.
	Treviño, Alejandro.	Cincuenta años en el ministerio.
1938	Alessio Robles, Vito.	Andanzas con nuestro…
	Beals, Carleton.	Glass Houses, Ten Years of Free Lancing.
	Carreño, Alberto María.	El cronista Luis González Obregón.
	Cooke, Philip St. George.	Cooke's Journal of the March of the Mormon Battalion…
	Cravioto Muñoz, Rafael.	Memorias de un adolescente.
	Escandón y Barrón, J. M.	Life Has Been Good: Memoirs…
	Gómez Maganda, A.	¡España sangra!
	Novo, Salvador.	Este y otros viajes.
	Ramírez de Aguilar.	Cariño a Oaxaca escrito a Oaxaca…
	Sierra O'Reilly, Justo.	Diario de nuestro viaje a los Estados Unidos.
	Taracena, Alfonso.	Viajando con Vasconcelos.
	Vasconcelos, José.	El desastre, tercera parte de Ulises criollo…
1939	Brondo Whitt, E.	Chihuahuenses y tapatíos (De Cuidad Guerrero…).
	Bush, Ira Jefferson.	Gringo Doctor.
	Greene, Graham.	Lawless Road.

	Kelley, Francis Clement.	Bishop Jots It Down: An Autobiographical…
	Marett, R.H.K.	Eye-Witness of Mexico.
	Moheno, Querido.	Mi actuación política después de la decena trágica.
	Oviedo Mota, Alberto.	El trágico fin del…
	Santamaría, Francisco.	La tragedia de Cuernavaca en 1927 y mi escapatoria célebre.
	Vasconcelos, José.	El proconsulado: cuarta parte de Ulises criollo…
1940	Beals, Carelton.	Great Circle: Further Adventures in Free-Lancing.
	Brondo Whitt, E.	La división del norte (1914) por un testigo presencial.
	Domínguez, Rafael.	Añoranzas del Instituto Juárez.
	Frías Conor, Billy.	Un yucateco en Zacatecas (impresiones de un visitante).
	Hughes, Langston.	Big Sea.
	Humphrey, Zephine.	'Allo Good-By.
	Maillefert, Alfredo.	Ancla en el tiempo, gentes y paisajes.
	Mena Brito, Bernardino.	Paludismo (novela de la tierra caliente…).
	Ocaranza Carmona, F.	La novela de un médico.
	Trejo, Blanca Lydia.	Lo que vi en España: episodios de la Guerra.
1941	Andreu Almazán, Juan.	Memorias; informe y documentos sobre la campaña…
	Castillo y Piña, José.	Mis recuerdos.
	Chávez, Ezequiel.	En respuesta.
	Cházaro Pous, Gabriel.	Pluviosilla, reminiscencias.
	Dame, Lawrence.	Yucatan.
	Galeana, Benita.	Benita (autobiografía).
	Gil Portes, Emilio.	Quince años de política mexicana.
	Gómez Maganda, A.	Torbellino un hombre de 30 años.
	Guzmán, Eulalia.	Lo que vi y oí.
	Iturbide, Eduardo.	Mi paso por la vida.
	Martínez, Luis M.	A propósito de un viaje.
	Sanderson, Ivan.	Living Treasure.
	Steinbeck, John.	Sea of Cortez: A Lesurely Journal of Travel…
1942	Cárdenas R., Antonio.	Alas sobre América.
	Diamant, Gertrude.	Days of Ofelia.
	Garizurieta, César.	Un trompo baila en el cielo.
	Long, James Irvin.	Pioneering in Mexico.
	Maillefert, Alfredo.	Los libros que leí.
	Rodríguez, Luis I.	Ballet de sangre: la caída de Francia.
	Romero, José Rubén.	Rostros.
	Ruiz y Flores, Leopoldo.	Recuerdos de recuerdos.
	Wagner, Henry Raup.	Bullion to Books: Fifty Years of Business and Pleasure.
	Yáñez, Agustín.	Flor de juegos antiguos.
1943	Almada, Pedro J.	99 días en jira con el presidente Cárdenas.
	Camacho, Ramiro.	Mi madre y yo: estampas históricas de provincia…
	Castillo, Guillermo J.	Chapingo: evocaciones de un profesor de zoología.
	Chávez, José Carlos.	Peleando en Tomochi.
	Griffin, John S.	A Doctor Comes to California…
	Ocaranza Carmona, F.	La tragedia de un rector.
	Luna Morales, Ricardo.	Mi vida revolucionaria: con aportaciones…
	Miller, Max.	Land where Time Stands Still.
	Moats, Alice-Leone.	Blind Date with Mars.
	Nájera, Indiana.	Carne viva.
	Osuña, Andrés.	Por la escuela y por la patria.
	Quevedo, Miguel.	Relato de mi vida.
1944	Claraval, Bernardo.	Cuando fui comunista.
	Denegri, Carlos.	Luces rojas en el canal: un reportaje.
	Fraenkel, Michael.	Journal: The Mexican Years, 1940–1944.
	González Martínez, E.	El hombre del buho: el misterio de una vocación.
	Gregg, Josiah.	Diary & Letters of Josiah Gregg…
	Moreno Villa, José.	Vida en claro: autobiografía.
1945	Maldonado, Víctor A.	Diario de un viaje a Latinoamérica.
	Mathias, Fred S.	Amazing Bob Davis: His Last Vagabond Journey.
	Audirac, Luis.	El fiel recuerdo.
	Charlot, Jean.	Charlot Murals in Georgia.
	Evans, George W.B.	Mexican Gold Trails: The Journal of a Forty-Niner.
	González Peña, Carlos.	El patio bajo la luna.
	McKinlay, Arch.	Visits with Mexico's Indians.

	Mitford, Osbaldeston.	Dawn Breaks in México.
	Moats, Alice-Leone.	No Passport for Paris.
	Orozco, José Clemente.	Autobiografía.
	Palencia, Isabel de.	Smouldering Freedom: The Story of the Spanish...
	Pani, Alberto J.	Apuntes autobiográficos: exclusivamente para mis hijos.
	Parodi, Enriqueta de.	Alcancía: prosas para mis hijos.
	Rodríguez Familiar, R.	Diario de un viaje.
	Tablada, José Juan.	Cuarenta cartas inéditas de José Juan Tablada.
	Toro, Alfonso.	La familia Carvajal...
	Valenzuela, Jesús E.	Mis recuerdos: manojo de rimas.
	Velázquez Andrade, M.	Remembranzas de Colima, 1895–1901.
1946	Chávez, Ezequiel.	¿De dónde venimos y a dónde vamos?
	Cox, Patricia.	Amanecer.
	Domínguez, Rafael.	Veracruz en el ensueño y el recuerdo...
	Escobedo, José G.	La batalla de Zacatecas (treinta y dos años después).
	Gordon, Alvin.	Our Son, Pablo.
	Hagan, Robert.	Diary of Robert Hagan, Assistant Surgeon...
	James, Neill.	Dust on My Heart: Petticoat Vagabond in Mexico.
	León Osorio, Adolfo.	Mis confesiones.
	Menéndez González, A.	Diario de un conscripto.
	Othón, Manuel José.	Epistolario: glosas. esquemas. índices...
	Robinson, Ione.	Wall to Paint On.
	Salado Alvarez, Victorian.	Memorias de Victoriano Salado Alvarez.
	Urquiza, Concha.	Obras: poemas y prosas.
	Velasco, Francisco de.	Autobiografía.
1947	Cuéllar, Alfredo B.	Impresiones y anécdotas de mi viaje al Brasil en 1922.
	Daniels, Josephus.	Shirt-Sleeve Diplomat.
	Dodge, David.	How Green Was My Father, A Sort of Travel Diary.
	Frías y Soto, Luciano.	Costumbres queretanas de antaño.
	González Urueña, Jesús.	Memorias.
	Hilton, John W.	Sonora Sketch Book.
	Palacios, Adela.	Normalista: tres relatos.
	Pérez, Luis.	El coyote, The Rebel.
	Urquiza, Concha.	Obras: poemas y prosas.
	Urquizo, Francisco.	3 de Diana.
1948	Bravo Izquierdo, Donato.	Lealtad militar (campaña en el estado de Chiapas...).
	Cantú, Juan Luis.	Memorias de un modesto e ignorado revolucionario...
	Estrada, Julio.	Cien dias de safari.
	Gómez González, Filiberto.	Rarámuri: mi diario tarahumaro.
	Magdaleno, Mauricio.	Tierra y viento.
	Mangas Alfaro, Roberto.	México en el Aconcagua.
	Prieto Quimper, Salvador.	El Parral de mis recuerdos...
	Royer, Franchon.	Mexico We Found.
	Stilwell, Hart.	Fishing in Mexico.
	Turrent Rozas, Eduardo.	Añoranzas.
	Villa, Luz Corral.	Pancho Villa en la intimidad.
1949	Alessio Robles, Miguel.	A medio camino.
	Alessio Robles, Miguel.	Mi generación y mi época.
	Audirac, Augusto.	Historia de un colegio.
	Bandelier, A.F.	Scientist on the Trail...
	Cárdenas Rodríguez, A.	Mis dos misiones: monografía aérea.
	Fonville, Nina.	Hold Fast These Earth-Warm Stones.
	Gamboa, Joaquín.	Memorias de un locutor.
	Gavira, Gabriel.	Polvos de aquellos lodos: unas cuantas verdades.
	Harding, Bertita Leonarz.	Mosaic in the Fountain.
	Larralde, Elsa.	My House Is Yours.
	Liceaga, Eduardo.	Mis recuerdos de otros tiempos: obra póstuma.
	Sierra, Justo.	Epistolario y papeles privados.
	Topete, Jesús.	Aventuras de un bracero: relatos de seis meses...
	Urquizo, Francisco Luis.	Ahora charlemos.
195?	Capistrán Garza, René.	Andanzas de un periodista y otros ensayos.
1950	Alessio Robles, Miguel.	Contemplando el pasado.
	Dr. Atl (Gerardo Murillo).	Gentes profanas en el...
	Brambila, David.	Hojas de un diario.

	Franco Torrijos, Enrique.	Odisea en Bonampak: narración inédita…
	Garfias, Valentín.	Garf from Mexico.
	González Flores, Manuel.	Una pareja de tantos.
	González Peña, Carlos.	Por tierras de Italia, Portugal y España.
	Goodspeed, Bernice I.	Criada.
	Lugo, José del Carmen.	Life of a Rancher. Vida de un ranchero…
	Miller, Loye Holmes.	Lifelong Boyhood: Recollections of a Naturalist Afield.
1950?	Neville, Harvey.	Mexican War Diary of 1st Lieutenant Harvey Neville…
1951	Bynner, Witter.	Journey with Genius: Recollections and Reflections…
	Dromundo, Baltasar.	Mi barrio de San Miguel.
	González Martínez, E.	La apacible locura.
	Hernández, Víctor.	Andanzas de un ferrocarrilero…
	Junco, Alfonso.	Los ojos viajeros.
	Lamb, Dana Storrs.	Quest for the Lost City.
	Moats, Alice-Leone.	Violent Innocence.
	Nervo, Amado.	Un epistolario inédito…
	Preaty, Amy.	México and I.
	Stacy-Judd, Robert.	Kabah: Adventures in the Jungles of Yucatán.
	Sutton, George Miksch.	Mexican Birds: First Impressions.
	Zuñiga, Olivia.	Retrato de una niña triste.
1952	Acevedo Escobedo, A.	Los días de Aguascalientes.
	Campbell, Henry Murray.	Mexican Cavalcade.
	Fernández MacGregor, G.	Notas de un viaje extemporáneo.
	Garizurieta, César.	Recuerdos de un niño de pantalón largo…
	González Peña, Carlos.	Por tierras de Italia, Portugal y España.
	Montes de Oca, Ignacio.	Epistolario de Ipandro Acaico.
	Pozas A. Ricardo.	Juan Pérez Jolote: biografía de un tzotzil.
	Rodríguez, Abelardo.	Autobiografía.
1953	Aguirre, Amado.	Mis memorias de campaña: apuntes para la historia.
	Bedford, Sybille.	Sudden View.
	Castillo, Porfirio del.	Puebla y Tlaxcala en los dias de la Revolución.
	Del Villar, Mary and Fred.	Where the Strange Roads Go Down.
	Flores, Manuel María.	Rosas caídas.
	Garza, Ramiro.	Solar poniente.
	Janessens, Víctor Eugene.	Life and Adventures in California…
	Lerma, Olga Yolanda.	Vida de un reportero.
	Loera y Chávez, Agustín.	Estampas provincianas.
	Maldonado C., Arturo.	Memorias de un maestro.
	Morrow, Elizabeth Cutter.	Leaves from the Diary of…
	Otaola, Simón.	La librería de Arana: historia y fantasia.
	Otaola, Simón.	Los tordos en el pirul.
	Pacheco Cruz, Santiago.	Recuerdos de la propaganda constitucionalists en Yucatán.
	Reyes, Alfonso.	Berkeleyana.
	Reyes, Alfonso.	Memorias de cocina y bodega.
	Romero, José.	Mexican Jumping Bean.
	Treviño, Elizabeth Borton.	My Heart Lies South: The Story of My Mexican Marriage.
	Tully, Brock.	Coming Together: A 10,000 Mile Bicycle Journey.
	Turrent Rozas, Eduardo.	Veracruz de mis recuerdos.
1954	Abreu Gómez, Ermilo.	La del alba sería.
	Agundis, Teódulo Manuel.	Sala de espera: páginas médicas.
	Cabrera de Tablada, Nina.	José Juan Tablada en la intimidad.
	Cevallos, Miguel Angel.	Un hombre perdido en el universo.
	Chadourne, Marc.	Anahuac: A Tale of a Mexican Journey.
	Correa, José Manuel.	Datos de la vida del cura de Nopala.
	Del Plaine, Carlos Werter.	Son of Orizaba: Memories of Childhood in Mexico.
	Estrada, Francisco.	Recuerdos de mi vida.
	Furber, Percy Norman.	I Took Chances from Windjammers to Jets.
	González-Ulloa, Mario.	Barro de cirujano.
	Iduarte, Andrés.	Un niño en la Revolución mexicana.
	Lara, J. Andrés.	Prisionero de callistas y cristeros.
	Pani, Arturo.	Ayer.
	Reyes, Alfonso.	Parentalia, primer capítulo de mis recuerdos.
	Swan, Michael.	Temples of the Sun and Moon: A Mexican Journey.
	Vega González, Roberto.	Cadetes mexicanos en la guerra de España.

	Isunza Aguirre, Agustín.	Ateneo de mis mocedades.
	Lerdo de Tejada, S.	Memorias de Sebastián Lerdo de Tejada.
	Luquín, Eduardo.	La cruz de mis vientos: memorias.
	Mancisidor, Anselmo.	Viví la revolución.
	Martínez Ortega, Judith.	La isla y tres cuentos.
	Serrano Martínez, C.	El cazador y sus perros.
	Shields, Karena.	Changing Wind.
	T'Serstevens, A.	México: Three-Storeyed Land.
	Torriente, Lolo de la.	Memoria y razón de Diego Rivera.
	Valdovinos Garza, José.	La generación nicolaita de 1913.
	Vasconcelos, José.	Cartas políticas de José Vasconcelos.
	Vasconcelos, José.	La flama: los de arriba en la Revolución.
1960	Alcantara Gómez, F.	Reminiscencias de un viaje.
	Alvarez del Castillo, Juan.	Memorias.
	Brown, James Stephens.	Giant of the Lord: Life of a Pioneer.
	Flores Magón, Enrique.	Peleamos contra la injusticia.
	García Naranjo, Nemesio.	Memorias.
	Hidalgo y Esnaurrízar, J.	Un hombre de mundo escribe sus impresiones y cartas.
	Mendoza Vargas, Eutiquio.	Gotitas de placer y chubascos de amargura…
	Muñoz, Ignacio.	Verdad y mito de la revolución mexicana…
	Núñez Guzmán, J. Trinidad.	Mi infancia en la Revolución…
	Portales, Urbano J.	Andares de un "falluquero," autobiografía.
	Prida Santacilia, Pablo.	Ya se levantó el telón: mi vida dentro del teatro.
	Reyes, Alfonso.	Albores, segundo libro de recuerdos.
	Rivera, Diego.	My Art, My Life: An Autobiography with Gladys March.
	Rojas, Arnold.	Last of the Vaqueros.
	Sánchez-Navarro, Carlos.	La guerra con Tejas: memorias de un soldado.
	Segura, Vicente.	Memorias de Vicente Segura, niño millonario.
	Siqueiros, David.	Mi respuesta: la historia de una insidia.
	Valle-Arizpe, Artemio de.	Historia de una vocación.
	Verissimo, Erico.	México.
	Zelayeta, Elena.	Elena.
1961	Beteta, Ramón.	Camino a Tlaxcalantongo.
	Brenton, Thaddeus Reamy.	Bahía: Ensenada and Its Bay: Freedom, Farce, Fiesta…
	Casasús de Sierra, M.	Las llaves perdidas.
	Guiteras Holmes, Calixta.	Perils of the Soul.
	Krutch, Joseph Wood.	Forgotten Peninsula: A Naturalist in Baja…
	Longinos Martínez, José.	Journal: Notes and Observations of the Naturalist…
	Marín, Rubén.	Los otros días: apuntes de un médico…
	Miles, Beryl.	Spirit of México.
	Murbarger, Nell.	30,000 Miles in México.
	Navarrete, Heriberto.	Por Dios y por la patria…
	Rittlinger, Herbert.	Jungle Quest: A Search for the Last of the Mayas.
	Thord-Gray, I.	Gringo Rebel (Mexico 1913–1914).
	Topete, Jesús.	Terror en el riel de "El Charro a Vallejo…"
	Treviño, Jacinto.	Memorias.
	Urquizo, Francisco L.	Madrid en los años veinte.
1962	Almada, Bartolomé, E.	Almada of Alamos: The Diary of don Bartolomé.
	Alvarez, Concha.	Así pasó mi vida.
	Alvarez, del Castillo, G.	Rincón de recuerdos.
	Aramburo Salas, F.	La Europa que yo vi: cartas…
	Bigler, Henry Wm.	Bigler's Chronicle of the West…
	Bravo, Ramón.	Bajo las aguas del Mar Rojo.
	Cárdenas D., Hipólito.	Mi padre y yo.
	Fabela, Isidro.	Isidro Fabela: epistolario a su discípulo Mario Colín.
	Ferlinghetti, Lawrence.	Mexican Night: Travel Journal.
	Gómez Maganda, A.	Mi voz al viento: apuntes de mi vida y algo más.
	Marín, Rubén.	Los otros días: apuntes de un médico de pueblo.
	Montenegro, Roberto.	Planos en el tiempo.
	Siqueiros, David Alfaro.	La trácala: mi réplica a un gobierno…
	Suárez, Luis.	Confesiones de Diego Rivera.
	Treviño, Elizabeth Borton.	Where the Heart Is.
1963	Arenas, Francisco.	La flota: cuadernos universitarios.
	Benítez, José R.	Cómo me lo contaron te lo cuento.

	Echeverría A., Marquina, J.	¡Viva Carranza! Mis recuerdos de la Revolución.
	Elorduy, Aquila.	Puntadas de mi vida.
	Gómez Maganda, A.	Una arena en la playa: continuación de mi voz al viento.
	Iduarte, Andrés.	Don Pedro de Alba y su tiempo.
	Madero, Francisco.	Epistolario.
	Maldonado, Enrique J.	Jirones de mi vida.
	Ortiz Rubio, Pascual.	Memorias de un penitente.
	Peissel, Michel.	Lost World of Quintana Roo.
	Pineda Campuzano, Z.	Memorias de un estudiante de filosofía…
	Purcell, William Louis.	Frontier Mexico, 1875–1894: Letters.
	Schell, Rolfe F.	Yank in Yucatan: Adventures and Guide…
	Siurob Ramírez, José.	Memorias de la vida…
	Thompson, J. Eric S.	Maya Archaeologist.
1964	Argudín, Raul S.	De la vida y aventuras de un médico de provincia.
	Brambila, David.	De la tierra herida.
	Bravo Izquierdo, Donato.	Un soldado del pueblo.
	Burns, Archibaldo.	En presencia de nadie.
	Bush Romero, Pablo.	Under the Waters of Mexico.
	Cordan, Wolfgang.	Cordan's Secret of the Forest: On the Tract of…
	Fierro Villalobos, R.	Esta es mi vida.
	Lewis, Oscar.	Pedro Martínez: un campesino mexicano y su familia.
	Liggett, William V.	My Seventy-Five Years along the Mexican Border.
	López Salinas, Samuel.	La batalla de Zacatecas: recuerdos imborrables…
	Maples Arce, Manuel.	A la orilla de este río.
	Robles Zarate, Alfredo.	50 años después … o la Revolución en casa.
	Roy, M.N.	Roy's Memoirs.
	Smithers, Wilfred Dudley.	Pancho Villa's Last Hangout on Both Sides…
	Valenzuela Rodarte, A.	Un mexicano cualquiera: 16 años en escuelas…
1965	Abreu Gómez, Ermilo.	Andanzas y extravíos: memorias.
	Garibay, Ricardo.	Beber un caliz.
	Iduarte, Andrés.	México en la nostalgia.
	Lewis, Oscar.	Los hijos de Sánchez: autobiografía…
	Limantour, José Yves.	Apuntes sobre mi vida pública.
	Navarrete, Heriberto.	El las islas Marías.
	Navarro Corona, Rafael.	Recuerdos de un futbolista.
	Och, Joseph.	Missionary in Sonora.
	Rodman, Selden.	Mexican Journal…
	Scherer García, Julio.	La piel y la entraña (Siqueiros).
	Tarango Ponce, Eleázar.	En el inquieto rio Urique.
	Vargas Dulché, Yolanda.	Cristal: recuerdos de una muchacha.
	Vejar Lacave, Carlos.	Bajo el signo de Esculapio…
	Whitworth, William B.	Under an Aztec Sun: Adventures in Mexico.
1966	Abert, J.W.	Western America in 1846–1847.
	Aguirre Benavides, Luis.	De Francisco Madero a Francisco Villa…
	Agustín, José.	José Agustín.
	Azcárate, Juan E.	Esencia de la Revolución.
	Bello Hidalgo, Luis.	Antropología de la Revolución de Porfirio Díaz a…
	Beteta, Ramón.	Jarano.
	Colorado Jr., Belisario.	Epistolario de viaje: un vivido relato…
	Elizondo, Salvador.	Salvador Elizondo.
	García Ponce, Juan.	Juan García Ponce.
	Hail, John B.	To México with Love: San Miguel with Side Dishes.
	Hamilton, Charles W.	Early Day Oil Tales of Mexico.
	Henestrosa, Andrés.	Sobre el mi.
	Linck, Wenceslaus.	Wenceslaus Linck's Diary of His 1766 Expedition…
	Lorang, Sister Mary Corde.	Footloose Scientist in Mayan America.
	Melo, Juan Vicente.	Juan Vicente Melo.
	Mojarro, Tomás.	Tomás Mojarro.
	Monsiváis, Carlos.	Carlos Monsiváis.
	O'Hea, Patrick A.	Reminiscences of the Mexican Revolution.
	Pattie, James O.	Personal Narrative of James O. Pattie of Kentucky.
	Peón, Máximo.	Cómo viven los mexicanos en los Estados Unidos.
	Pitol, Sergio.	Sergio Pitol.
	Sainz, Gustavo.	Gustavo Sainz.

	Author	Title
	Lomeli Garduño, Antonio.	Prometeo mestizo: estampas de la vida mexicana.
	Peña, José Enrique de la.	With Santa Anna in Texas: Personal Narrative…
	Rivas Mercado, Antonieta.	87 cartas de amor y otros papeles…
	Smith, Jack.	God and Mr. Gomez.
	Stone, Martha.	At the Sign of Midnight: The Conchero Dance Cult…
	Sutton, George Miksch.	Portraits of Mexican Birds: Fifty Selected Paintings.
	Wakefield, Celia.	Under the Tabachín Tree: A New Home in México.
1976	Alamillo Flores, Luis.	Memorias: luchadores ignorados…
	Arenas Betancourt, Rodrigo.	Crónicas de la errancia del amor y de la muerte…
	Berg, Richard.	Shwan: A Highland Zapotec Woman.
	Beteta, José Luis.	Viajes al México inexplorado.
	Black, Mary Ann Jones.	Recollections of Mexico and Early Blanding, Utah.
	Cruz, Roberto.	Roberto Cruz en la Revolución mexicana.
	Fell, Claude.	Escrit oublies: correspondance…
	García Diego y Moreno, F.	Writings of Francisco García Diego y Moreno…
	Garibay, Ricardo.	¡Lo que ve el que vive!
	González Salazar, Pablo.	El general don Luis Caballero se rebela…
	Grisby, R. F.	Sierra Madre Journal, 1864.
	Guízar Oceguera, José.	Episodios de la Guerra Cristera…
	Neruda, Pablo.	México florido y espinudo.
	Nielson, Morgan L.	Reminiscences of Life in Old Mexico and Blanding, Utah.
	Philipon, M.M.	Una vida, un mensaje: Concepción Cabrera de Armida.
	Reyes, Alfonso.	Epistolario, José M.A. Chacón…
	Sánchez Hernández, N.	Memorias de un combatiente.
	Torre Blanco, José.	Uno de tantos: un médico republicano español…
	Vaca del Corral.	Soy puro…mexicano: libro primero…
	Xántus, Janos.	Travels in Southern California.
1977	Agustín, José.	¿Quién soy yo?
	Beltrán, Enrique.	Medio siglo de recuerdos de un biólogo mexicano.
	Careaga, Gabriel.	Biografía de un joven de la clase media.
	Chávez, Carlos.	Mis amigos poetas: López Velarde, Pellicer, Novo.
	Cosío Villegas, Daniel.	Memorias.
	Fabela, Isidro.	Mis memorias de la Revolución.
	Franco Sodja, Carlos.	Lo que me dijo Pedro Infante.
	Marín, Mariano B.	Recuerdos de la revolución Constitucionalista…
	McLellan, Ginny.	Situation Normal, Mañana Mejor.
	Monaghan, Jay.	Schoolboy, Cowboy, Mexican Spy.
	Pelé.	My Life and the Beautiful Game: The Autobiography…
	Prieto Laurens, Jorge.	Anécdotas de Jorge Prieto Laurens.
	Revueltas, José.	Conversaciones con José Revueltas.
	Rodríguez, Marcos.	Yo fui empleado de gobierno.
	Salinas Rocha, Irma.	Tal cual: vida, amores, cadenas.
	Siquieros, David.	Me llamaban el coronelazo (memorias).
	Sodi, Federico.	El jurado resuelve: memorias.
	Stephenson, Fairfax.	Carmen with a Shrimp in Her Mouth.
	Suárez Aranzola, Eduardo.	Comentarios y recuerdos (1936–1946).
	Tibol, Raquel.	Frida Kahlo: crónica, testimonios y aproximaciones.
	Villaseñor, Victor Manuel.	Memorias de un hombre de izquierda.
	Worker, Dwight.	Escape.
1978	Bassi, Sofía.	Bassi…prohibido pronunciar su nombre…
	Bose, Johanne.	Farewell to Durango: A German Lady's Diary in Mexico…
	Campa S., Valentín.	Memorias de Valentín Campa: 50 años con…
	Campa S., Valentín.	Mi testimonio: experiencias de un comunista mexicano.
	Castro, Simón Hipólito.	De albañil al preso político.
	Chellet Díaz, Eugenio.	Instante recobrado: relatos.
	Cortés Leyva, Carlos R.	De El Salvador a Baja Californa Sur…
	Díaz Du-Pond, Carlos.	Cincuenta años de ópera en México…
	Flores Magón, Ricardo.	Epistolario y textos de Ricardo Flores Magón.
	Gaitán Lugo, Rito.	Anécdotas de mi pueblo.
	Gascón Mercado, Julián.	Minutero de antaño.
	Gómez, Marte R.	Vida política contemporánea: cartas de Marte R. Gómez.
	Guerra Leal, Mario.	La grilla.
	Halsell, Grace.	Illegals.
	Hunter, Ben.	Baja Feeling.

	Kelley, Jane Holden.	Yaqui Women: Contemporary Life Histories.
	Kennedy, Diana.	Recipes from the Regional Cooks of Mexico.
	Kochi, Paul.	Imin no aiwa=An Immigrant's Sorrowful Tale.
	Loret de Mola, Carlos.	Confesiones de un…
	Palmer, Ann.	Busted in Mexico.
	Paz, Octavio.	Xavier Villaurrutia en persona y en obra.
	Perry, Nancy Whitlow.	Missionaries Are Human Too.
	Pride, Nigel.	Butterfly Sings to Picaya: Travels in México…
	Quiroz(z), Alberto.	Los intelectuales.
	Rivas, José.	Entrevista con José Rivas.
	Schmidtlein, Adolfo.	Un médico alemán en el México de Maximiliano…
	Serrano, Irma.	A calzón amarrado.
	Serrano, Irma.	Recuerdos nicolaitas.
	Tijerina, Reies López.	Mi lucha por la tierra.
1979	Acosta, Helia d'.	Indiana y Concha: dos brillantes periodistas…
	Adalpe, Eliseo Castro.	Entrevista con Eliseo Castro Adalpe.
	Brimmer, Gaby.	Gaby Brimmer.
	Cruschetta, Angelina.	Agustín Lara y yo.
	Burciaga, José Antonio.	Drink cultura: Chicanismo.
	Burstein, John.	En sus propias palabras: cuatro vidas Tzotziles.
	Castro y Castro, Fernando.	Pensamiento, personas y circunstancias…
	Cedillo, Luciano.	¡Vaaamonos! Luchas, anécdotas y problemas…
	Davison, John.	Long Road North: The Story of a MexicanWorker's…
	DeVries, Lini.	Up from the Cellar.
	Domecq, Brianda.	Once días—y algo más.
	Gangemi, Kenneth.	Volcanoes from Puebla.
	Glantz, Susana.	Manuel, una biografía política.
	Gómez Z., Luis.	Sucesos y remembranzas.
	Henestrosa, Andrés.	El remoto y cercano ayer.
	Hernández Leal, Jesús.	Entrevista con Jesús Hernández Leal.
	Herrera-Sobek, María.	Oral History Interview with Composite Bracero.
	Holder, Maryse.	Give Sorrow Words: Maryse Holder's Letters from México.
	Lasater, Annette Nixon.	Two to Mexico.
	Lawrence, D.H.	Letters of D.H. Lawrence.
	Nelligan, Maurice.	Lupita: confesiones de una joven mexicana.
	Theroux, Paul.	Old Patagonian Express: By Train through…
1980	Abascal, Salvador.	Mis recuerdos, sinarquismo y colonia.
	Arenal, Angélica.	Páginas sueltas con Siqueiros.
	Azuela, Salvador.	La aventura vasconcelista, 1929.
	Cadwallader, Sharon.	Savoring México: A Travel Cookbook.
	Cardona Peña, Alfredo.	El monstruo en su laberinto.
	Castro, Carlo Antonio.	Che NDU, ejidatario chinateco.
	Castro, Carlo Antonio.	Lupe, la de Altontonga.
	Dromundo, Baltasar.	Rescate del tiempo.
	Garmabella, José Ramón.	Dr. Alfonso Quiroz Cuarón: sus mejores casos…
	González Lobo, Salvador.	Memorias de un rector.
	Hale, Howard.	Long Walk to Mulegé: A True Story of Adventure…
	Lagos de Minvielle, S.	Memorias de Socorrito.
	Lombardo de Miramón, C.	Memorias de Concepción Lombardo de Miramón.
	Marcos, Fernando.	Mi amante, el fútbol.
	Miramón, Miguel.	Cartas del general Miguel Miramón a su esposa.
	Montalbán, Ricardo.	Reflections: A Life in Two Worlds.
	Ramos, Rafael A.	Del arcón de mis recuerdos.
	Reich, Sheldon.	Francisco Zúñiga Sculptor: Conversations…
	Revueltas, Rosaura.	Los Revueltas (Biografía de una familia).
	Roffiel, Rosa María.	¡Ay Nicaragua, Nicaragüita!
	Savala, Refugio.	Autobiography of a Yaqui Poet.
	Thomas, Estelle Webb.	Uncertain Sanctuary: A Story of Mormon…
	Torri Maynes, Julio.	Epistolario.
	Zavala, Lorenzo de.	Viaje a los Estados…
1981	Cárdenas Hernández, G.	Adiós, Lecumberri.
	Castaños, Carlos Manuel.	Testimonios de un agrónomo.
	Cuevas, José Luis.	José Luis Cuevas Letters…
	Dumas, Alexandre.	Diario de Marie Giovanni: viaje de una parisiense.

Labarthe R. María de la.	Notas sobre el proceso de industrialización de León.
Madero, Pablo Emilio.	500 horas de hielo.
Marnham, Patrick.	So Far from God: A Journey to Central America.
Mendoza, María Luisa.	Confrontaciones.
Mendoza-López, Margarita.	El teatro de ayer de mis recuerdos.
Miguel.	Ya tengo mi lugarcito en el infierno.
Mother Jones.	Correspondence of Mother Jones.
Muñoz Muñoz, Joaquín.	Juan Gabriel y yo.
Anonymous.	La neta, estuviera...
López Pérez, Antonio.	Cómo defenderse del ladino.
Paya Valera, Emeterio.	Los niños españoles de Morelia.
Pellicer, Carlos.	Cartas desde Italia.
Pérez Tejada, José.	Los revolucionarios: crónica de un general...
Revueltas, José.	Cartas a María Teresa.
Romano Moreno, Armando.	Anecdotario estudiantil.
Sharp, Bob.	Bob Sharp's Cattle Country...
Steele, William C.	Yochib, The River Cave.
Tello Díaz, Carlos.	Apuntes de un brigadista: la cruzada de alfabetización...
Terrones Benítez, Alberto.	Alberto Terrones Benítez: autobiografía...
Vargas Sánchez, Eduardo.	La ciudad de México de 1900 a 1920.
Villalobos, Jorge.	Perseguidor perseguido: testimonios de un abogado...
Villegas Oropeza, Miguel.	Tapando agujeritos de la historia de la Revolución.
Zepeda, Eraclio.	Eraclio Zepeda.

1986
Aguilar, Enrique.	Elías Nandino. Una vida no/velada.
Agustín, José.	El Rock de la cárcel.
Ballentine, George.	Autobiography of an English Soldier in the...
Bassols, Narciso.	Cartas.
Blanco Moheno, Roberto.	Ya con ésta me despido: mi vida, pero las de los demás.
Beloff, Angelina.	Memorias.
Bulfill, José Angel.	Los amigos cubanos de Alfonso Reyes...
Buñuel, Luis.	Luis Buñuel, prohibido asomarse al interior.
Chacón, Rafael.	Legacy of Honor: The Life of Rafael Chacón.
Contreras, Tino.	Mi amor, el jazz.
Dimitroff, Stephen Pope.	Apprentice to Diego Rivera in Detroit.
Echeverría, Alicia.	De burguesa a guerrillera.
Flores, Edmundo.	Historias de Edmundo Flores: autobiografía...
Flores, Edmundo.	Historias de Edmundo Flores: autobiografía...
Fuentes Mares, José.	Intravagario.
Gallo, Delfino.	Las huellas de mi caminar (Perfil de una época).
García Carrera, Juan.	La otra vida de María Sabina.
García G., Rodolfo.	Entre dos estaciones.
González Rodríguez, Raúl.	Así gané: mi espíritu de lucha...
Guerrero, Euquerio.	Imágenes de mi vida.
Harkort, Eduard.	In Mexican Prisons: The Journal of Eduard Harkort...
Ibacache, María Luisa.	Gabriela Mistral y Alfonso Reyes vistos...
Lamarque, Libertad.	Libertad Lamarque.
Loustaunau, Adolfo C.	Los dos mundos de Fitin: relato auto-biográfico.
Macedo López, Juan.	Viaje alrededor de la nostalgia.
Maldonado Sánchez, B.	Braulio.
Martínez, Adrian.	Adrian: An Autobiography.
Martínez Martínez, Jorge.	Memorias y reflexiones de un obispo.
Mendoza Guerrero, T.	Los maestros y la cultura nacional...
Monroy Rivera, Oscar.	Sueños sin retorno: autobiográfico II.
Neri Vela, Rodolfo.	El planeta azul: misión 61-B.
Palacios, Adela.	Los palacios de Adela: apuntes autobiográficas.
Ramos Romo, Jesús.	Relatos de don Jesús Ramos Romo: narración...
Robson, Bobby.	Bobby Robson's World Cup Diary, 1982–1986.
Romo de Alba, Manuel.	El gobernador de las estrellas: autorretrato.
Sarmiento, J. Esteban.	Un sacerdote en la URSS y otros viajes.
Treviño, Tomas D.	Relatos de cacería en México.
Val G. E. Franz.	Conversaciones con María Sabina y tres curanderos...
Valadés, José C.	Memorias de un joven rebelde.

1987
| Alemán Valdés, Miguel. | Remembranzas y testimonios. |
| Almaguer, Gilberto. | Maestro rural en la década de los años 30... |

	Escudero Luján, Carolina.	Carolina Escudero Luján: una mujer…
	Farías, Ixca.	Casos y cosas de mis tiempos.
	Farías y Alvarez, Luis M.	Así lo recuerdo: testimonios políticos.
	García Narro, Anita.	Anita la corredora.
	Garibay, Ricardo.	Cómo se gana la vida.
	Garrido, Felipe.	La musa y el garabato.
	Garro, Elena.	Memorias de España 1937.
	Hernández E., Agustín.	Remembranzas de mi vida: testimonio de un lerdense.
	Lazcano Ochoa, Manuel.	Una vida en la vida sinaloense.
	Leñero, Vicente.	De cuerpo entero.
	López, Arcadia H.	Barrio Teacher.
	Martínez, Zarela.	Food from My Heart: Cuisines of Mexico…
	Millán Peraza, Miguel A.	¡A Tijuana! (nosotras las gringas).
	Modotti, Tina.	Una mujer sin país: las cartas a Edward Weston…
	Muñiz, Marco Antonio.	¡Soy un escándalo—dicen!
	Nava González, R. M.	Caminos de ayer.
	Nissan, Rosa.	Novia que te vea.
	Obeso Rivera, Sergio.	Sergio, arzobispo de Xalapa: su vida…
	Palacios Mendoza, E.	Cien leguas de tierra caliente…
	Palma, Erasmo.	Donde cantan los pájaros chuyacos.
	Payno, Manuel.	Un viaje a Veracruz en el invierno de 1843…
	Paz, Octavio.	One Word to the Other.
	Peña, Margarita.	Desde Bloomington.
	Pérez Olivares, Porfirio.	Memorias: un dirigente agrario.
	Portilla, Jorge.	De cuerpo entero.
	Prieto, Guillermo.	Una excursión a Xalapa en 1875.
	Quintero Rodríguez, Luis.	Doce sueños de un cardiólogo.
	Reyes, Alfonso.	Con leal franqueza: correspondencia…
	Rodriguez, Richard.	Days of Obligation.
	Rojo de Santos, Anita.	Madre e hijo luchan contra la leucemia…
	Ruy Sánchez, Alberto.	De cuerpo entero.
	Salado Alvarez, Victoriano.	Correspondencia de don Victoriano Salado Alvarez.
	Salazar, Diana Martha.	Aquel Saltillo de ayer (trocitos de la vida…).
	Salinas Rocha, Irma.	Mi padre.
	Sandoval Avila, Alejandro.	De cuerpo entero.
	Suárez, Fernández, Luis.	Alejo Peralta, un patrón sin patrones.
	Tablada, José Juan.	Obras IV. Diario (1900–1944).
	Taibo, Paco Ignacio II.	De cuerpo entero: Paco Ignacio Taibo II.
	Torrescano, María del C.	Mi vida.
	Treviño, Luis Carlos.	Luis Carlos Treviño: la vida de un hombre…
	Wauer, Roland H.	Naturalist's México.
	Zapata Vela, Carlos.	Conversaciones con Heriberto Jara.
1993	Alatorre, Antonio.	Antonio Alatorre.
	Allende, Fernando.	Mis memorias hasta hoy.
	Badú, Antonio.	Sortilegio de vivir: la vida de Antonio Badú…
	Behar, Ruth.	Translated Woman: Crossing the Border…
	Buñuel, Luis.	Mi último suspiro.
	Carballo, Isaías.	Gay.
	Chávez, César.	César Chávez: una entrevista.
	Conde, Teresa del.	Cartas absurdas: correspondencia entre…
	Félix, María.	Todas mis guerras.
	Ferrer Rodríguez, Eulalio.	Del diario de un publicista.
	Figueroa, Gabriel.	Conversaciones con Gabriel Figueroa.
	Figueroa, Gabriel.	La mirada en el centro.
	García Ruiz, Ramón.	Mis ochenta años: memorias.
	Goeritz, Mathias.	Conversaciones with Mathias Goeritz.
	González, Hugo Pedro.	Un mucho de mi vida y un poco de la política.
	González, Luis.	Luis González: minuta de viaje redondo.
	González-Crussi, Frank.	Day of the Dead and Other Mortal Reflections.
	González Parrodi, Carlos.	Memorias y olvidos de un diplomático.
	Gorostiza, José.	José Gorostiza y Carlos Pellicer.
	Guzmán-C, S.	Vagabond in México.
	Henestrosa, Andrés.	Entonces vivía yo en Ixhuatán…
	Icaza, Claudia de.	Gloria y Jorge: cartas de amor y conflicto.

	Jones Garay, Lupita.	Palabras de reina.
	León-Portilla, Miguel.	Miguel León-Portilla.
	Lucas, María Elena.	Forged under the Sun: The Life of María Elena Lucas.
	Mendoza, Lydia.	Lydia Mendoza: A Family Autobiography.
	Montes Zamora, Benjamín.	Auto-novela en refranes.
	Moraga, Cherrie.	Last Generation: Prose and Poetry.
	Muñoz Cota, José.	El espectro de las horas muertas.
	Neuman, Alma.	Always Straight Ahead: A Memoir.
	Paz, Octavio.	Itinerario.
	Pitner, Ernst.	Maximilian's Lieutenant: A Personal History…
	Rangel Frías, Raúl.	Los hijos del desierto: conversaciones con don Raúl Rangel.
	Ronstadt, Federico.	Borderman: Memoirs of Federico José María Ronstadt.
	Sánchez S., Teodoro.	Alma del teatro Guiñol Petul.
	Schueler, Donald G.	Temple of the Jaguar.
	Sheldon, Chalres.	Wilderness of the Southwest…
	Sierra Méndez, Justo.	Epistolario con Porfirio Díaz.
	Tablada, José Juan.	Las sombras largas.
	Torres Vda. de Morales, E.	¿Aparte las mujeres?
	Urrea, Luis Alberto.	Across the Wire. Life and Hard Times…
	Velázquez, Carolina.	¿A dónde desea hablar?
1994	Aguilar Castro, Salvador.	Veinte años de medicina rural.
	Alvarez, Augusto H.	Historia oral de la Ciudad de México…
	Arreola, Juan José.	Memoria y olvido: vida de Juan José Arreola, 1920–1947.
	Azpiri Pavón, Ramón.	Revelaciones de un…
	Blue, Paty.	La casa, la calle y otras debilidades.
	Bonifaz Caballero, Oscar.	Una lámpara llamada Rosario.
	Buitimea Romero, C.	Como una huella pintada: (testimonios).
	Carballo, Emmanuel.	Ya nada es igual: memorias, 1929–1953.
	Careaga Soriano, Teresa M.	Mi México de los veinte.
	Castellanos, Rosario.	Cartas a Ricardo.
	Cazals, Felipe.	Felipe Cazals habla de su cine.
	Covarrubias, Miguel.	Junto a una taza de café: (conversaciones).
	Cuevas, José Luis.	El gato macho.
	Curiel, Fernando.	Casi oficios: cartas cruzadas…
	Curtis, Samuel Ryan.	México under Fire: Being the Diary…
	Delgado de León, B.	Y dígalo que yo lo dije —: memorias…
	Domecq, Brianda.	Mujer que publica…
	Fuentes, Carlos.	Diana o la cazadora solitaria.
	García, Mario T.	Memories of Chicano History: The Life…
	García Ramos, Juan.	Paisajes en la senda de mi vida: memorias.
	González Chávez, Rafaela.	Testimonio zapopano. Rafaela González Chávez…
	Grosso de Espinoza, Anita.	Reflections by Mama Espinoza: An Autobiography.
	Guijosa, Marcela.	Altar de muertos: memorias de un mestizaje.
	Haro Oliva, Antonio.	Del brazo y por la vida: Nadia y Antonio.
	Imamura, Federico.	Casi un siglo de recuerdos: biografía de…
	Jacobs, Bárbara.	Vida con mi amigo.
	King, Carole Call.	A Good, Long Life: The Autobiography of Anson B. Call, Jr.
	Manzanero, Armando.	Con la música por dentro.
	Márquez Ocampos, Alfredo.	El soplo del viento.
	Martínez Portillo, Isabel Ma.	Dejando atrás Nentón: relato de vida de una mujer indígena.
	McKellar, Margaret Maud.	Life on a Mexican Ranche.
	Nieto de Leyva, Dalia.	Por qué me hice periodista.
	Palacios, Alfredo.	¡Este soy yo!
	Pillsworth, Elizabeth.	Interiors: An Exploration of Life and Death in…
	Revueltas, María.	Una familia chocarrosa.
	Rivera Marín, Guadalupe.	Frida's Fiestas: Recipes and Reminiscences…
	Shepherd, Grant.	Silver Magnet.
	Solórzano de Cárdenas, A.	Era otra cosa la vida.
	Taibo, Paco Ignacio II.	Cárdenas de cerca: una entrevista biográfica.
	Talamas Camandari, M.	Mi vida en mosaico: historia de una vocación.
	Veloz García, Rosa María.	Relatos de mi padre.
	Villanueva, René.	Cantares de la memoria: recuerdos de un folklorista.
	Villegas de Magnón, L.	Rebel.
	Vogt, Evon Z.	Fieldwork among the Maya…

Gerzso, Gunther. Conversaciones con José Antonio Aldrete-Haas.
González Crussí, Francisco. Partir es morir un poco.
Gutiérrez Herrera, Luis. Un son de recuerdos. [diarios sobre Tepeji...
Henestrosa, Andrés. Cartas sin sobre: confidencias y poemas al olvido.
Kahan, Ari. Wulf Kahan, My Father.
Kraig, Bruce. Cuisines of Hidden Mexico: A Culinary Journey...
López-Stafford, Gloria. A Place in El Paso: A Mexican American Childhood.
Madero, Francisco I. Madero y los sinaloenses.
Martínez de Oliveros, G. Tú escogiste a mí, para esta misión sublime.
Méndez M., Miguel. Entre letras y ladrillos: autobiografía novelada.
Morton, Lyman. Yucatán Cookbook: Recipes & Tales.
Nissán, Rosa. Hisho que te nazca.
Palafox García, Fidel. Memorias de un revolucionario.
Peralta, Braulio. El poeta en su tierra: diálogos con Octavio Paz.
Pitol, Sergio. El arte de la fuga.
Rangel Guerra, Alfonso. Ensayo de una vida: conversaciones con...
Robles Garnica, Héctor G. Guadalajara, la guerrilla olvidada: presos en...
Romero de Nohra, Flor. Gabriel Figueroa: hacedor de imágenes: conversaciones...
Rosado, Nidia Esther. Huellas en el umbral: autobiografía.
Sánchez, Mary. Vivir por un ideal: mis memorias.
Sedelmayr, Jacobo. Before Rebellion: Letters & Reports of Jacobo Sedelmayr...
Sierra, Justo. Correspondencia con José Yves Limantour (1885–1935).
Siqueiros, David Alfaro. Palabras de Siqueiros.
Sotelo Arévalo, Salvador. Historia de mi vida: autobiografía...
Toscano, Salvador. Correspondencia de Salvador Toscano, 1900–1911.
Urrea, Luis Alberto. By the Lake of Sleeping Children...
Veyre, Gabriel. Gabriel Veyre, representante de Lumiere...
Yetman, David. Sonora: An Intimate Geography.
Young, Biloine W. Mexican Odyssey: Our Search for the People's Art.
1997 Cárdenas, José Antonio. My Spanish Speaking Left Foot.
Cárdenas, Cuauhtémoc. Cuauhtémoc Cárdenas: un perfil humano.
Chávez, Ignacio. Epistolario selecto: 1929–1979.
Contreras, Gloria. Diario de una bailarina.
Cuevas, José Luis. José Luis Cuevas, el ojo perdido de Dios.
Edwards, R.M. "Down the ": Mexican War Reminiscences...
Elliott, Richard Smith. Mexican War Correspondence of Richard Smith Elliott.
Galicia Espinosa, Rutilo. Almacén de mis recuerdos.
Gómez Junco, Horacio. Desde adentro.
Gómez Ocón, Tegro. Mi viejo Mazatlán: memorias del Tegro.
Gutiérrez Elías, Humberto. Memorias de mis tiempos: la medicina en Chihuahua.
Hall, Arthur C. Those Wonderful Years in Mexico.
Herrera, Juan Felipe. Mayan Drifter: Chicano Poet...
Ibargüengoitia, Jorge. Misterios de la vida diaria.
Jaurrieta, José María. Con Villa (1916–1920), memorias de campaña.
Laidley, Theodore. Surrounded by Dangers of All Kinds...
Legorreta, Ricardo. Architecture of Ricardo Legorreta.
Longoria, Arturo. Adios to the Brushlands.
López Aranda, Susana. El cine de Ignacio López Tarso.
Manzanero, Armando. Relatos de mi infancia.
Martínez, Jorge. El Orozco de Jorge Martínez.
Morales, Dionicio. Dionicio Morales: A Life in Two Cultures.
Morton Morales, Alejandro. Memorias de un revolucionario.
Múgica Velázquez, F. Estos mis apuntes.
Pellicer, Carlos. Correspondencia 1925–1959.
Poniatowska, Elena. Me lo dijo Elena Poniatowska.
Prieto, Guillermo. Cartas públicas y privadas.
Nissán, Rosa. Las tierras prometidas: crónica de un viaje a Israel.
Ruiz Camarena, Merced. Tuyo o de nadie: cartas a Mercedes Martínez Carrillo.
Russek, Jorge. Una vida de película: autobiografía.
Sánchez Vázquez, Adolfo. Recuerdos y reflexiones del exilio.
Sierra Flores, José. De médico, poeta y...tampiqueño: relatos de un cirujano.
Soto Soria, Alfonso. Una vida, muchas vidas: memorias.
Tamayo, Rufino. Rufino.
Tausend, Marilyn. Cocina de la familia: More than 200 Authentic Recipes...

Appendix B: Selected Outstanding Autobiographies

Arenas Betancourt, Rodrigo. *Crónicas de la errancia del amor y de la muerte.* (Art)

Ballentine, George B. *Autobiography of an English Soldier....* (Mexican-American War)

Beteta, Ramón. *Jarano.* (Childhood, Revolution)

Blancornelas, Jesús. *Conversaciones privadas.* (Journalism, Politics)

Blasio, José Luis. *Maximiliano íntimo, el emperado Maximiliano y su corte.* (French Intervention)

Brondo Whitt, Encarnación. *La división del norte (1914)....* (Revolution, Medicine)

Bush, Ira Jefferson. *Gringo Doctor.* (Revolution, Medicine)

Calderón de la Barca, Madame. *Life in Mexico during a Residence....* (19th Century)

Carballo, Emmanuel. *Ya nada es igual memorias.* (Provinces, Literature)

Castellanos, Rosario. *Cartas a Ricardo.* (Women)

Contreras, Gloria. *Diario de una bailarina.* (Women, Music)

Díaz Covarrubias, Francisco. *Viaje de la Comisión Astronómica al Japón....* (Science)

Drees, Charles. *Thirteen Years in Mexico.* (Protestants)

Elliott, Richard Smith. *The Mexican War Correspondence of....* (Mexican-American War)

Flandrau, Charles M. *Viva Mexico.* (Porfiriato)

Flores Magón, Ricardo. *Epistolario revolucionario e íntimo.* (Revolution)

Frías, Heriberto. *Tomóchic.* (Porfiriato, Indians)

García Naranjo, Nemesio. *Panoramas de la infancia.* (Porfiriato, Provinces)

Gómez, Marte. *Vida política.* (Generalist)

Guiteras Holmes, Calixta. *Los peligros del alma.* (Indians)

Guzmán, Martín Luís. *El águila y la serpiente.* (Revolution)

Henríquez Ureña, Pedro. *Pedro Henríquez Ureña y Alfonso Reyes.* (Literature)

Holder, Maryse. *Give Sorrow Words: Maryse Holder's Letters from Mexico.* (Women)

Howard, Josefina. *Rosa Mexicano: a Culinary Autobiography with 60 Recipes.* (Food)

Juana Inés de la Cruz, Sister. *The Answer=La respuesta.* (Women)

Lombardo de Miramón, Concepción. *Memorias de....* (French Intervention)

Lombardo Toledano, Vicente. *Vicente Lombardo Toledano....* (Labor Leader)

López Díaz, Pedro. *Huellas de un destino: memorias.* (Medicine)

Marín, Rubén. *Los otros días: apuntes de un médico del pueblo.* (Medicine)

Martínez, Zarela. *Food from My Heart: Cuisines of Mexico....* (Food)

Mendoza Barragán, Ezequiel. *Testimonio cristero....* (Religion)

Morton, L.A. *Life and Adventures of Col. L.A. Norton.* (War with Mexico)

Novo, Salvador. *Continente vacío (viaje a Sudamérica).* (Travel)

O'Hea, Patrick A. *Reminiscences of the Mexican Revolution.* (Revolution)

Otalola, Simón. *La librería de Arana.* (Spanish Exiles)

Orozco, José Clemente. *El artista en Nueva York....* (Art)

Pollard, Hugh B.C. *A Busy Time in Mexico....* (Revolution)

Poniatowska, Elena. *Hasta no verte, Jesús mío.* (Women)

Prieto, Guillermo. *Mi guerra del 47.* (Mexican-American War)

Reed, John. *Insurgent Mexico.* (Revolution)

Rosales Alcaraz, José. *La huella de mis pasos.* (Family)

Salado Alvarez, Victoriano. *Memorias de Victoriano Salado Alvarez.* (Porfiriato, Education)

Santos, John Phillip. *Places Left Unfinished at the Time of Creation.* (Mexican–American)

Shepherd, Gary. *Mormon Passage: A Missionary Chronicle.* (Protestants)

Slocum, Marianna C. *The Good Seed.* (Protestants)

Spratling, William. *File on Spratling: An Autobiography.* (Art, Taxco)

Stevenson, Sara Yorke. *Maximilian in Mexico....* (French Intervention)

Tablada, José Juan. *En el país del sol.* (Travel)

Taracena, Alfonso. *Viajando con Vasconcelos.* (Politics)

Torres Bodet, Jaime. *Tiempo de arena.* (Childhood, Literature)

Vasconcelos, José. *Ulises criollo....* (Youth, Revolution)

Author Index

References are to entry numbers

Title Index

Numbers refer to entries, not pages.

293

Subject Index

References are to entry numbers

Academy de la Lengua 1601
Acapulco *see* Guerrero
Acevedo y de la Llata, Concepción *see* Madre Conchita
Actors and actresses: Aguascalientes (state) 277, 633; Arreola, Juan José 94; Blue Demon 200; Cachirulo 53; California 1186; Campeche (state) 633; Children 52; Conesa, María 52, 53; Durango (state) 277; Fábregas, Virginia 53; Families 607; Film *see* Films and directors, Actors and actresses; *Género chico* 1418; Iris, Esperanza 53; Kidnappings 1770; Mexican Americans 1435; Montoya, María Tereza 52, 53; Opera 1179; Paris 94; Querétaro 633; Radio 642; Sexual behavior 607; Sinaloa 277; Spanish 1198; Television 1770; Theater 812, 1186, 1199, 1418; United States 1435, 1569; Vaudeville 52; White slavery 1907; Women 952, 1199, 1363, 1907; Wrestlers 200; Yucatán 633; *Zarzuelas* 1418; *see also* Films and directors
Africa 256
Afro Americans 861, 1892
Agraz family 68
Agriculture and agriculturists: Chapingo 708, 1918; Chihuahua (state) 1454; Education 707, 1918; *Ejidos* 704; Guanajuato (state) 777; Laborers 704; Mexico (state) 1918; National School of Agriculture 707, 708, 1918; Revolution 707, 777, 778; Secretary of Agriculture 708; Sinaloa 704; Sunflowers 344; *see also* Land reform
Aguascalientes 8, 27, 34; *see also* Aguascalientes (state)
Aguascalientes (state) 8
AIDS 306, 569
Air pilots: Adventure 244; Africa 319; Air Academy 580; Air Force 580; Americans 244, 1673; Daniels, Josephus 244; Enríquez, Gerardo 1132; Hijacked 115; Mediterranean 319; Missions 318, 319; Oaxaca (state) 1132; Rescues 1132; Women 1139; World War II 319
Alamo 815, 1147, 1354, 1803; *see also* Texas
Alamos *see* Sonora
Alemán, Miguel 166, 1361
Allende, Salvador 116
Alvarez Bravo, Manuel 60
Ambassadors *see* Diplomats
Americans: Germans 1249; Mexico City 1249; Morelos 1249; *see also* Travel and travelers
Anarchy and anarchists: Baja California 592; Brousse Talavera, María 594; Delgado, Ramón 178; Flores Magón, Richard 178, 788; Liberal Party 591; Persecution 594; Porfiriato 591, 592; Prisons 591; "Regeneration" 591, 785; Rivera, Librado 178; United States 591, 592, 593, 594
Andrade, Sergio 44
Anecdotalists 1101
Anecdotes (genre) 534
Angeles, Felipe 74, 373, 543
Anglosajonismo 1835
Angostura 127
Anthropology and anthropologists: Aguirre, Beltrán, Gonzalo 26, 1412; Caso, Alfonso 40, 290, 892, 901; Chiapas 1870; Coras 1671; Harvard Research Ranch 1870; Herskovits, Melville J. 26; Huicoles 937, 1671; Mayas 1853; National Museum of Anthropology 1671; Nayarit 170; Otomies 1671; *La población negra de México* 26; Shamans 170, 937; *see also* Indians
Archaeology and archaeologists: French 988; Germans 420; Indians 1729; Mayas 92, 526; Yucatán 92, 386, 420, 526, 1729
Archbishops *see* Religious
Architects *see* Architecture and architects

Cuahtémoc Apartments 55
Cuba: Batista, Fulgencio 210;
Castro, Fidel 1524; Diplomats
210, 1112, 1481; Mexicans 268;
Revolution 210, 270; Travel
271
Cuernavaca *see* Morelos
Cuevas, José Luis 77
Culiacán 36; *see also* Los
Mochis

Dalevuelta, Jacobo 25
Daniels, Josephus 244
De la O, Genovevo 74
Decena trágica 55, 553, 1499,
1703, 1829, 1863; *see also* Revolution and revolutionaries
Delgado, Ramón 178
Denver *see* Colorado
Detectives: Criminals 1664;
Traven, B. 676; Trotsky,
Assassination of 676
Diaries: **1910–1919** 1703; **1920–
1929** 1206, 1849; **1930–1939**
1348, 1640, 1717, 1805; **1940–
1949** 1159, 1796; **1950–1959**
272; **1960–1969** 46, 1485;
1970–1979 753, 1714; **1980–
1989** 179, 1116, 1216, 1513, 1871;
1990–1999 233, 503, 775, 918,
1094, 1117, 1868, 1885; **2000–
2005** 99, 569, 1309, 1444
Díaz, Carmelita 38
Díaz, Porfirio 38, 166, 486, 553,
601, 622, 701, 878, 1297
Díaz del Castillo, Bernal 605
Díaz Ordaz, Gustavo 166
Diegueños *see* Indians
Diplomats: Aguascalientes
1009; Ambassadors 62, 189,
467; Americans 602;
Argentina 635, 745, 902,
1479, 1486, 1487, 1494, 1751;
Asamblea Internacional
Americana 715; Asia 1089;
Austria 709; Bolivia 715;
Brazil 635, 1486, 1494, 1828;
British 1296; Cárdenas,
Lázaro 717; Carranza, Venustiano 186; Childhood 186, 716,
717, 1009, 1052, 1323, 1478,
1484, 1645; Chile 1112; Con-
suls 1146; Correspondence
457, 571, 760, 1479, 1481,
1482, 1483, 1488, 1915; Cuba
210, 1112, 1481; Dominican
Republic 723; Economists
1644; Education 186, 717,
1323; England 745; Europe
363, 774, 1089, 1885; Families
716, 1002, 1009, 1645; Finland

210, 745; France 144, 210, 457,
709, 745, 841, 1323, 1494,
1531, 1751; Friends 365; General Claim Commission 1694;
Good Neighbor Policy 467;
Great Britain 144; Hague
Conference 1694; Honors
1480; International Court of
Justice 564; Italy 1485; Jalisco
1052; Latin America 1089;
Middle East 1885; Morrow,
Dwight 1212; Novelists 902;
Nuevo León 1478; Panama
745; Paris 1206; Petroleum
496; Poets 743; Poland 723,
745; Portugal 210, 715; Revolution 186, 1052; Rome 1206;
Russia 144; South America
774; Spain 189, 635, 715, 717,
718, 1322, 1485, 1486, 1494,
1751, 1867; Spanish Civil War
189, 715, 717, 718; Spouses
276, 1212, 1297, 1298; Sweden
210; UNESCO 1750, 1754;
United Nations 410; United
States 410, 635, 1485, 1640;
Uruguay 902; World War II
1751; Writers 1052
Directors *see* Films and directors
Divers: Quintana Roo 258; Red
Sea 218; Yucatán 258
Dr. Atl 100
Doctors *see* Medicine and doc-
tors
Domínguez, Belisario 61
Doniphan, Alexander *see*
Mexican-American War
Drugs: Abuse 31; Americans
1318, 1598; Dealers 1230;
Guerrero 922; Marijuana 922;
Music and musicians 1874;
Peyote 97, 1768; Politics and
politicians 1565; Prisons 1318,
1900; Tarahumaras 97; Travel
and travelers 849, 850; Writ-
ers 219; Yaquis 342
Durango (state): Agriculture
344; Americans 246; Child-
birth 345; Ciudad Lerdo 831;
Costumbrismo 831; Cristeros
1646; Education 629, 1646;
Families 629; Germans 209;
Laborers 831; Medicine and
doctors 345; Mining 246, 622;
Petroleum 246; Politics 510;
Protestants 851; Revolution
209, 510; Tepehuanes 246;
Theater 277; *see also* Travel
and travelers
Dwarfs 560

Echeverría Alvarez, Luis 432
Economia 36
Economists: Attolini, José 1218;
Chapingo 587; Education
587; *Sexenios* 588; Silva Her-
zog, Jesús 1218, 1644
Edinburg *see* Texas
Education and educators:
Administrators 713; Agricul-
ture 353, 707; Alba, Pedro de
873; *Ateneistas* 1760; Ateneo
Fuente 883; Baja California
288; Bellas Artes 391; Biographies 879, 1548; Blind 1819;
Brigadistas 1722; Cachuchas
750; California 1612;
Campeche (state) 578; Cárdenas, Lázaro 312; Casa de
España 432, 539; Caso, Antonio 56, 339, 375, 571; Chiapas
1050; Chihuahua (state) 84;
Childhood 876, 878; Classics
1753; Coahuila 50, 181, 883;
Cold War 1754; El Colegio de
México 539, 1490, 1496; Colima (state) 1056, 1504, 1846;
Colleges 181; Constitution
1917 396; Correspondence
1760, 1761, 1762; *Costumbrismo* 1056; Cristeros 833
1646; *Cuadernos Americanos*
1496; Curriculum 883, 1310;
Deaf 1612; Durango (state)
1646; Escuela de Verano 902;
Escuela Nacional de Agricultura de Chapingo 344; Examinations 1200; Families 874,
876; Federation of Teachers'
Unions 181; Guanajuato
(state) 1172; Guerrero 579;
Historians 665; Indians 711,
1050; Jalapa 103; Jalisco 75,
665, 762, 1114, 1200; Kikil 231;
Lancastrian system 726; Law
schools 42, 877; Literacy programs 1832; Medical schools
93; Mérida 231; Mexican
Americans 624; Mexico City
86; Mexico (state) 353, 726;
Michoacán 93, 825, 1670,
1820, 1847; Nayarit 1172,
1554; Nicaragua 1722; Nicolaita 224; Normal schools 1,
762, 1056, 1108, 1114, 1156,
1200, 1281, 1310, 1552; Normalistas 1753; Nuevo León
713, 1108, 1737; Oaxaca (state)
1449; Pedagogy 1200; Philolo-
gists 33; Photographers 259;
Politics and politicians 392,
665; Porfiriato 506, 707;

Agrarian reform 193; Americans 156, 157, 202, 905; Anecdotes 732; Baja California 151, 196, 291, 1167, 1252; Biographies 508; Books and reading 818, 820, 1152; *El buho* 109; Bullfights 202, 677, 678; Cárdenas, Lázaro 134, 1006; Carranza, Venustiano 299; Censorship 196; Chiapas 780; Chihuahua (state) 1822; Childhood 656, 780, 821, 1404; Colima (state) 368; Communism 193, 268; Correspondence 1004; *Costumbrismo* 1068; Creativity 1447; Cristeros 1100; Cuba 374; *El día* 1666; *Diario de Colima* 368; Drugs 196; Durango (state) 1822; *Economía* 36; Editors 456; Education 191, 656, 832, 970, 1501; Ejército Zapatista 535; England 482, 636; Escheverría Alvarez, Luis 1153; *Excelsior* 36, 109, 820, 868, 870, 1268; Exiles 36, 577, 656, 1693; Families 437, 655, 819, 820, 1012, 1031, 1844; *Fianzas* 36; Films 1359, 1827; France 487; Germany 1279; Guerrero 1031; *El Heraldo de Cuba* 1794; *El Heraldo de México* 1844; International 1142, 1452; Interviews 356; Islas Marías 696; *Jueves de Excelsior* 659; Kidnapping 299; Leftists 361, 677; León de Toral, Luis 9, 10, 157; *Letras de Baja California* 1167; *El Machete* 268; Madre Conchita 157; Malvinas 1710; Mella, Julio Antonio 157; *Mexican Herald* 1542; Mexico City 432, 612, 990, 1182, 1542; Michoacán 838, 1068, 1100; Movimiento de Liberación Nacional 354; Newspapers 202; Nicaragua 1538; *Novedades* 724, 1844; Nuevo León 916, 1501; Oaxaca (state) 821, 1065, 1120; Panistas 151; Paris 615, 677; Periodicals 1424; Politics and politicians 193, 678; Porfiriato 202, 970, 1068; Prisons and prisoners 157, 361, 535, 696; Querétaro (state) 1065; Radio 905, 1450; *La revista Mexicana* 656; *La revista moderna* 1822; *La revista moderna de México* 1822; Revolution 677, 678,

869, 970, 1175, 1716; Ruiz Cortines, Adolfo 192; San Luis Potosí (state) 1065; *El Siglo XIX* 456; Sinaloa 612, 614, 1012; Soap operas 1827; Sonora 1182; Spain 817, 1268, 1794; Storytellers 1925; Tabasco 1715, 1716; Tamaulipas 664; Television 577, 1450, 1844; Texas 683; Tlateloco 1399, 1404; Travel 818, 820, 868; Trotsky, Leon, assassination of 679; Ubico, Jorge 192; United States 990, 1450; *El Universal* 615; USSR 1154; Vasconcelistas 151, 1716; Vasconcelos, José 157, 1006; Vera Cruz (state) 191, 1065; *Visión* 659; Women 13, 201, 202, 437, 664, 990, 1120, 1152, 1153, 1154, 1252, 1399, 1404, 1538, 1710, 1827; World War I 487, 615; Youth 437; Yucatán 134; Zapata, Emiliano 1006
Journals (genre): **1900–1909** 635; **1910–1919** 635; **1920–1929** 635; **1960–1969** 1718; **1970–1979** 311, 1026; **1980–1989** 792; **1990–1999** 791
Juárez, Benito 602, 1585
Juaristas 46
Juvenile delinquents: Crimes 78, 204; Drugs 78, 1165; Gangs 78, 291; Language 78; Thefts 1165
Juventudes Socialistas Unificadas de México 146

Kahlo, Frida 60, 77, 516, 966, 1515
Kearny, Stephen W. 188, 695, 768, 1786
Kiddle, Lawrence B. 118
Kidnappings 299, 503, 947, 1770
Krutch, Joseph Wood 1932

Labor and laborers: Agriculture 704; Braceros 576, 1076, 1453; Carpenters 627; *El charrismo* 1739; Chiapas 1625; Childhood 1072; Coahuila 50, 1076; Communists 1011; *Costumbrismo* 1623; Durango (state) 831; Education 791; *Ejidos* 576, 704, 1625; Glass workers 686; Guanajuato 949; Guerrillas 1625; Hidalgo 791; Jalisco 1453; Leaders 704; Mexican Americans 390; Mexico City 1024; Miners

576; Morelos 897, 1625; Muleteers 1453; Nuevo León 369; Oaxaca (state) 1024; Organizers 897; Railroads 139, 286, 288, 369, 722, 829, 831, 969, 1149, 1623, 1739; San Luis Potosí 1149; Seamstresses 1453; Shoemakers 949; Sinaloa 704, 1756; Tamaulipas 1149; Telegraphers 1024; Unions 369, 390, 722, 829, 1739, 1756, 1897
Lacandones *see* Indians
Lagos de Moreno *see* Jalisco
Lake Chapala 162; *see also* Jalisco
Land reform 50, 708, 777, 778, 986, 1092, 1409
Law school 42
Lawrence, D.H. 226, 265, 1330
Lawrence, Freida 226, 265
Lawyers: Authors 252; Books 252; Childhood 1517; Communism 1839; Education and educators 334, 1093, 1517; Federal District 252; Foreigners 1093; Indians 1843; Jurists 1093; Morelos 1839; Prisons 1900
LEAR *see* Liga de Escritores y Artistas Revolucionarios
Lebanese: Families 1110; Hidalgo (state) 121; Immigrants 1231; Lebanon 1110; Mexico City 112, 1231; Puebla (state) 112; Yucatán 1231
Lecumberri 132, 315, 343, 1614, 1866, 1900; *see also* Prisons and prisoners
Lee, Robert E. 159
León *see* Guanajuato (state)
León de Toral, Luis 9, 10, 157, 1319, 1740
León Felipe 327; Literary periodicals 101; Spaniards 36, 327; Theater 101; Writers 101
Lesbians 991, 1537, 1825; *see also* Homosexuals
Letters: **1700–1709** 911; **1840–1849** 1273; **1920–1929** 593; **1930–1930** 653; **1940–1949** 1303, 1638, 1700; **1950–1959** 1193, 1247, 1831; **1960–1969** 118, 456, 564, 821, 1050, 1861; **1970–1979** 68, 312, 571, 594, 651, 709, 913, 967, 1287, 1476, 1486; **1980–1989** 106, 144, 175, 228, 388, 454, 477, 592, 787, 822, 867, 958, 1171, 1289, 1292, 1305, 1351, 1470, 1475, 1481, 1482, 1760, 1761, 1916,